ANATOMY
OF THE NEW
TESTAMENT

Robert A. Spivey

D. Moody Smith

ANATOMY OF THE NEW TESTAMENT

A Guide to Its Structure and Meaning

FIFTH EDITION

PRENTICE HALL
Englewood Cliffs, New Jersey 07632

Library of Congress Cataloging-in-Publication Data

Spivey, Robert A.
    Anatomy of the New Testament : a guide to its structure and
meaning / Robert Spivey, D. Moody Smith. — 5th ed.
      p.   cm.
    Includes bibliographical references and index.
    ISBN 0–02–415322–2 (pbk.)
    1. Bible. N.T.—Introductions. 2. Bible. N.T.—Criticism,
interpretation, etc. I. Smith, D. Moody (Dwight Moody) II. Title.
BS2330.2.S65   1995
225.6'1—dc20   93–46079
                                                CIP

Editorial/production supervision: Anthony VenGraitis/Virginia M. Livsey
Acquisitions editor: Maggie Barbieri / Ted Bolen
Editorial assistant: Meg McGuane
Text and cover design: Robert Freeze
Buyer: Peter Havens/Lynn Pearlman
Maps: Maryland Cartographics
Photo researcher: Eloise Marion

 1995, 1989, 1982, 1974, 1969 by Prentice-Hall, Inc.
A Simon & Schuster Company
Englewood Cliffs, New Jersey 07632

Printed in the United States of America
10 9 8 7 6 5 4 3 2 1

ISBN 0-02-415322-2

Prentice-Hall International (UK) Limited, *London*
Prentice-Hall of Australia Pty. Limited, *Sydney*
Prentice-Hall Canada Inc., *Toronto*
Prentice-Hall Hispanoamericana, S.A., *Mexico*
Prentice-Hall of India Private Limited, *New Delhi*
Prentice-Hall of Japan, Inc., *Tokyo*
Simon & Schuster Asia Pte. Ltd., *Singapore*
Editora Prentice-Hall do Brasil, Ltda., *Rio de Janeiro*

To Martha and Jane

Contents

Preface

*T*he appearance of *Anatomy of the New Testament* for the first time in soft cover affords us yet another opportunity to reconsider and revise the book. Several years ago, a comprehensive review article on recent New Testament textbooks excluded *Anatomy* on the grounds that, despite several revisions, it had maintained essentially the same character and content over the last couple of decades. Although we regretted that *Anatomy* was thereby excluded from consideration, we had to agree that its basic character has not changed. Possibly the discipline of New Testament criticism has itself changed more in the past quarter of a century than this book. We are glad that we conceived *Anatomy* as an introduction to the study of the New Testament, rather than New Testament criticism, and have tried to keep it free from domination by any single methodology. The focus of this book on the New Testament itself has met the needs of a number of instructors and many students, whose appreciation of its purpose has heartened and encouraged us through the years.

With each revision of *Anatomy,* both authors have gone over the text minutely and made innumerable additions, deletions, and alterations with a view to improving the book, keeping it current, and making it more accessible to the student. These changes are not always obvious but they have a great deal to do with the high level of acceptability that *Anatomy* enjoys among students who use it. We have also made more obvious changes in this edition. Most of the leading questions at the beginning of each section have been replaced or altered, making them correspond more closely to the discussion of the text. Throughout the book, we have used—and presumed— the New Revised Standard Version of the Bible, which has superseded the Revised Standard Version. This underscores our commitment to the use of inclusive language in accord with the intention of the New Testament writers themselves. Thus, when Paul writes *adelphoi* (brothers), he clearly means both men and women. Although the Greek word would have been understood to mean that (as indeed the English term "brethren" once did), contemporary usage and gender awareness compel us to abandon a language style that implies male superiority. Both Jesus' practice (Luke 8:1–3) and Paul's explicit formulations (Gal. 3:28; 1 Cor. 11:11–12) justify our changing the older usage. In cases in which the RSV's rendering still seems preferable, we have indicated this. Chapter 5, on the Gospel of John, has been extensively rewritten, with a number of additional pericopes treated. Perhaps the next most significant revisions are found in the chapter on Jesus (Chapter 6) and the concluding chapter on the early church (Chapter 12).

The authors were originally inspired by Northrop Frye's *Anatomy of Criticism* to break away from some of the patterns and preoccupations of biblical criticism. By more than a decade, this venture preceded the full scale advent of literary critical theory and practice in biblical interpretation; thus we were delighted when pioneering works, such as R. Alan Culpepper's *Anatomy of the Fourth Gospel* (1983), echoed our title while going far beyond our work in methodological self-consciousness and sophistication. In light of more recent developments, this approach may now seem tame to some. We obviously believe that the effort to understand the New Testament writings on their own terms is rewarding. Therefore, we affirm the necessity of viewing and seeking to understand those writings as products of an ancient religious community and its leaders. At the same time, we do not assume that the meaning of the New Testament is a repository of ancient lore or artifacts to be "mined out," after all these years, by the historical-critical method. Biblical interpretation is a dialogue or conversation with texts; in this case texts that are, to us, products of an unusual set of events and religious beliefs and claims. The methods and techniques of what has become known as biblical criticism are "servants" rather than "masters" in this task.

This late twentieth-century reading of the New Testament is, however, deeply affected by the historical-critical emphasis on the importance of hearing the ancient voices in and behind the text, and by modern efforts (largely exegetical) to do justice to the distinctive theological ideas and ethical interests of the earliest Christians. If readers are engaged by some of those ideas and interests, it should not be surprising. An important characteristic of the New Testament is that it takes such ideas and interests to be universally intelligible, whether or not they are accepted, and a major aspect of our purpose is to serve this intended intelligibility. Moreover, we are grateful that *Anatomy* has been used and found useful, not only by Christians of different church and theological commitments, but by teachers and students who stand outside the Christian community.

Anatomy intentionally emphasizes the content and interpretation of the New Testament, on the assumption that readers will want to know what the New Testament is about, and to understand the beliefs and purposes that informed the writing of the individual books. To help readers come to a more than superficial or secondhand understanding, we have dealt extensively with representative New Testament texts. (This characteristic feature is maintained and, hopefully, enhanced in the present edition.) Working outward from these texts, we then have endeavored to display and illumine the character and movement of the different writings. What has resulted is certainly no comprehensive or uniform coverage of the New Testament, but a series of "biopsies" designed to uncover the structure and meaning of the New Testament books, and of the collection as a whole—thus our title, *Anatomy of the New Testament: A Guide to Its Structure and Meaning*. Naturally, the discussions of New Testament texts represent the authors' interpretations. Although these often follow main lines, if not a consensus, of modern exegesis, other defensible interpretations are also possible. We seek not to stultify, but to encourage, students' independent efforts at understanding and interpretation.

The older, standard questions of introduction (authorship, date and place of composition, and so forth) have again been dealt with in summary fashion in the introductory notes at the beginnings of chapters, or at other appropriate places. If there is agreement on a problem, it is stated. If not, we give our position and reasons for holding it. In any event, such questions are of little concern to readers until they have some knowledge of, and involvement with, the content of the New Testament itself. Thus, the sooner they can get to the text, the better. Readers can return to these questions as they become aware of the relevance of such issues for the understanding of the text. Then they will be ready to consult more advanced and detailed works on the subject.

The views expressed or assumed in this book are genuinely, in a historical sense, well-considered and centrist. That is, they represent a tradition of scholarship. It is necessary and important to emphasize this fact, because the media's treatment of the history and other issues pertaining to the Bible and related literature often gives a misleading impression of what is possible or likely, and does not indicate adequately whether a consensus of scholarship exists or what that is. All things are possible, but by no means are all things equally likely. Journalists and media commentators are not in a position to make professionally competent judgments about what is a realistic or plausible proposal, and are often at the mercy of scholars, or other authors, who are advancing eccentric, if not outlandish, views.

We recommend the following procedure in the study of the New Testament with the help of *Anatomy*. After familiarizing oneself with the important issues concerning the origin of the book in question by reading the introductory notes, the reader should then look at the brief outline of the entire biblical document to gain some prior conception of what it is about. Then, the New Testament book should be read in its entirety, preferably in one sitting. Only then is one adequately prepared to dig into the representative texts with which the book mainly deals. In following this procedure, the reader should find the appropriate section of *Anatomy* both a guide and a help in understanding. Of course, these interpretative sections, which constitute the greater part of the book, will make little sense unless they are read with the New Testament in hand. The bibliographies at the end of each chapter, and at the end of the book, should provide guidance for further reflection and research.

The organization of *Anatomy* is simple and is related to the shape of the New Testament canon, the church's liturgical usage, and the history of early Christianity. Thus, after an introductory chapter that sets the historical stage, the book falls into two major parts entitled "The Gospels and Jesus" and "The Apostles and the Early Church." The focus of the entire New Testament message is on Jesus and what God did through him. The perspective throughout is that of the early church or churches, and of Christians who believed in him. This two-part structure does not mean that the Gospels and Jesus represent an earlier period of the New Testament, and the letters and other writings represent a later period, or that the Gospels have to do with Jesus, and the letters and other writings with the early church. The Gospels are products of the early church and reflect its faith and practice over a period of more than a half-century (approximately A.D. 30 to 100). The development of the church or churches can be studied by analyzing the Gospels. The other New Testament writings, while they speak more or less directly of the activities of Christians in the churches, nevertheless have to do with the gospel about Jesus Christ. Some (e.g., the genuine Pauline letters) are earlier than the Gospels; a few (e.g., 2 Peter) are almost certainly later. In studying the Gospels, we shall be asking what was said to the early church through the presentation of Jesus. In studying the other writings, we shall be asking what is said about the gospel of Jesus through their reflection and discussion of many matters and issues relating to the early church.

Although it is theoretically possible, and defensible, to reverse the order of Parts I and II, the present arrangement intentionally underscores the fact that Jesus of Nazareth is not only the central figure, but the historical beginning of Christianity and the New Testament. Thus, Part I concludes with a treatment of the "historical" Jesus of Nazareth. Naturally, it cannot be assumed that the historical information deduced in Chapter 6 was generally available to early Christians, although some of them undoubtably knew about matters that are now hidden from us. Nevertheless, an appreciation of Jesus' mission and message is illuminating and necessary for an understanding of the New Testament.

Acknowledgments

We again wish to acknowledge the source *New Testament Illustrations: The Cambridge Bible Commentary on the New English Bible*, edited by Clifford M. Jones (New York: Cambridge University Press, 1966), for the adaptation of the following figures: "Time Chart of the New Testament," "Diagram of the

Synoptic Problem," "Map of Galilee," "Diagram of the Temple," and "Diagram of Jerusalem." Adaptation of the "Diagram of the Formation of the Gospels" is courtesy of *Jesus in the Church's Gospels: Modern Scholarship and the Earliest Sources*, by John Reumann (Philadelphia: Fortress, 1968). Adaptation of the end map of the Mediterranean world is courtesy of *The Good News: The New Testament with over 500 Illustrations and Maps* (New York: American Bible Society, 1953). Adaptation of the end map of Palestine is courtesy of *The Westminster Historical Atlas to the Bible*, edited by George Ernest Wright and Floyd Vivan Filson, revised (copyright, 1945, by the Westminster Press; 1956, by W. L. Jenkins; adapted by permission). Several paragraphs from *Interpreting the Gospels for Preaching* by D. Moody Smith (Philadelphia: Fortress, 1980) have been used with the permission of the publisher.

We are grateful to teachers and colleagues, and especially to students we have taught at Florida State University, Randolph-Macon Woman's College, the University of Richmond, and Duke University for their stimulation and advice in the present undertaking, as well as to colleagues whose suggestions and criticisms have contributed to this edition. In particular, Richard Hays, Ed P. Sanders, Dan O. Via, and Franklin W. Young, all of whom are colleagues at Duke, have offered valuable advice on bibliography. Several former graduate students who have used *Anatomy* in teaching in college, university, or seminary and have made many helpful critical comments and suggestions: C. Clifton Black of Perkins School of Theology, Southern Methodist University; R. Alan Culpepper of Baylor University; Amy-Jill Levine of Swarthmore College; Clarice J. Martin of Colgate-Rochester Divinity School; James Mueller of the University of Florida; and Marianne Meye Thompson of Fuller Theological Seminary. Emerson Powery (presently a doctoral student in New Testament at Duke) has assisted in important ways in the perfecting of this manuscript and the production of the book. Needless to say, the authors assume all responsibility for the content of this and previous editions.

We thank Maggie Barbieri and Ted Bolen, our editors, and their predecessors, Helen McInnis, Kenneth J. Scott, Charles E. Smith, and John D. Moore, for their interest in this book. We are also grateful for the continued support of the administration and secretarial staff of the Divinity School of Duke University. Once again, Sarah Freedman has tirelessly typed and retyped our material on her word-processor. In countless ways, Martha Spivey and Jane Smith continue to encourage and support our commitment to this project, which has now extended over more than a quarter-century. The dedication of the book attests to our gratitude for their toleration and significant help.

R. A. S.
D. M. S

List of Illustrations, Maps, Charts, and Diagrams

List of Abbreviations

EH—*The Ecclesiastical History* of Eusebius.

IB—*The Interpreter's Bible*, eds. George A. Buttrick et al., 12 vols. (Nashville, Tenn.: Abingdon, 1952–1957).

IDB—*The Interpreter's Dictionary of the Bible*, eds. George A. Buttrick et al., 4 vols. (Nashville, Tenn.: Abingdon, 1962). Supplementary Volume (1976).

KJV—the King James Version of the Bible.

LXX—the Septuagint (see the Glossary).

NEB—*The New English Bible*.

NRSV—the New Revised Standard Version of the Bible

par., parr.—parallel or parallels (usually in the Gospels).

RSV—the Revised Standard Version of the Bible.

TDNT—*Theological Dictionary of the New Testament*, eds. G. Kittel et al. and trans. G. W. Bromiley, Vols. I-X (Grand Rapids, Mich.: Eerdmans, 1964–1976).

Significant Pre-New Testament Dates
336–323 B.C. Conquest and Rule of Alexander the Great
167–164 B.C. The Maccabean Revolt
63 B.C. Roman Rule of Palestine Begins

Date	Events	Herods	Governors of Judea	Roman Emperors	New Testament Writings
		Herod the Great (37–4 BC)			
10 BC					
	Birth of Jesus (before 4 BC)			Augustus (27 BC–AD 14)	
AD		Archelaus (4 BC–AD 6)			
10		Philip the Tetrarch (4 BC–AD 34)	Coponius (6–9) Marcus Ambivius (9–12) Annius Rufus (12–15)		
20		Herod Antipas (4 BC–AD 39)	Valerius Gratus (15–26)	Tiberius (14–37)	
30	Ministry of John the Baptist Ministry of Jesus Crucifixion of Jesus Paul's Conversion		Pontius Pilate (26–36)		
40		Herod Agrippa I (37–44)	Marcellus (36–37) Marullus (37–41)	Caligula (37–41)	
50	Paul's first missionary activity Council of Jerusalem Paul in Corinth Paul in Ephesus Paul's journey to Jerusalem and arrest		Cuspius Fadus (44–46) Tiberius Alexander (46–48) Cumanus (48–52) Felix (52–58)	Claudius (41–54)	1 & 2 Thessalonians Galatians 1 & 2 Corinthians Romans
60	Paul, prisoner to Rome Paul, prisoner in Rome Paul's martyrdom under Nero Jewish War (66–70)		Festus (58–62) Albinus (62–64) Gessius Florus (64–66)	Nero (54–68)	Philippians Philemon
70	Destruction of the Temple (70) Siege of Masada (72–73)	Herod Agrippa II (53–100)		Galba (68–69) Otho (69) Vitellius (69) Vespasian (69–79)	Mark Colossians Ephesians
80				Titus (79–81)	Hebrews Matthew 1 Peter Luke
90	Council of Jamnia Domitian Persecution			Domitian (81–96)	Acts Gospel of John Letters of John Revelation to John Pastorals' James
100				Nerva (96) Trajan (98–117)	Jude 2 Peter

*Chronology is only approximate, especially in regard to dating the books of the New Testament.

Significant Post-New Testament Dates:
Jewish revolt under Bar Kochba (132–135)
Fall of Jerusalem (135)
Pax Romana (27 B.C.– A.D. 180)
Constantine, emperor of Rome (306–337),
converted and made Christianity the
official religion of the Roman Empire.

ANATOMY
OF THE NEW
TESTAMENT

Prologue: The Nature of the New Testament

*T*he New Testament consists of twenty-seven early Christian writings that with the Old Testament, the Bible of Judaism, form the Christian Bible. Although the New Testament is thus comparable to the Old, there are significant differences. The Old Testament is more than three times the length of the New and the material in it was written down over a period of nearly a thousand years; the New Testament was written and composed in a fraction of that time, probably less than a century. The Old Testament was written in Hebrew, the language of ancient Israel; the New Testament in Greek, the language of the Hellenistic world.

The four Gospel narratives stand at the beginning of the New Testament. They are followed by another narrative, the Acts of the Apostles, a history of the earliest church. Then come the epistles, twenty-one of them. Finally, Revelation, a book of apocalyptic visions, stands at the end of the collection. The twenty-one books styled epistles or letters are themselves of different types. A number of them are real letters (e.g., the Corinthian letters of Paul). Yet quite possibly many are not; at least they may not have been originally composed as letters (e.g., Hebrews, James, 1 Peter, and 1 John). They have characteristics more appropriate to treatises, sermons, or tracts.

The story of how and why these books were written and at length gathered into the collection we now call the New Testament is a long and complicated one. Each book originated within a particular historical situation. The individual books were preserved, circulated among early Christians, and gradually brought together because they were deemed useful and authoritative in the church. By the beginning of the third century, the four Gospels, Acts, and the letters attributed to Paul were widely regarded as scripture. In fact, Paul's letters had been collected and were being read much earlier

2 Pet. 3:15–16; cf. Col. 4:16), and the Gospels were widely used by Christians in the course of the second century.

Not until the fourth century, however, did canonical lists appear containing exactly the twenty-seven books of our New Testament. Thus Christians and churches got along for centuries without the New Testament in exactly the form we have it, and for a century or more without anything approximating our complete collection of Gospels, Acts, Epistles, and Revelation. That they were able to do so is testimony to the fact that the vitality and strength of early Christianity lay in its enthusiastic faith and community life, two factors much in evidence in the writings of the New Testament themselves.

Further, the early Christians used as their Bible what they later came to regard as the Old Testament—the scriptures of Israel and contemporary Judaism. From the beginning, synagogue and church have appealed to the same scriptures, and at times they have heatedly debated their proper interpretation. Christian faith and church life have therefore never been without an authoritative book. The great fourth- and fifth-century manuscripts of the New Testament (Sinaiticus, Vaticanus, and Alexandrinus) are complete Bibles, containing the Old and New Testaments. Thus the scriptures of Christianity consist of both testaments; and the New Testament is, and always has been, not only incomplete but inconceivable apart from the Old.

The Transmission of the New Testament

How we got the New Testament is a long and fascinating story in itself, and one that consists essentially of two parts, called in scholarly circles *text* and *canon*. We have just touched upon the process of the selection of books, that is, the history of the development of the canon (Greek *kanōn,* rule; see also pp. 454–456). Matters pertaining to the preservation and transmission of the New Testament books as manuscripts (that is, before printing) are dealt with by the discipline known as textual criticism, a process that includes the study and cataloging of the manuscripts of the New Testament, as well as efforts to determine the original reading or wording of texts where there are differences in existing manuscripts.

There are far more ancient copies of the Greek New Testament than of any other writings or documents from antiquity. Over five thousand ancient manuscripts of some part of the New Testament are known to exist, together with several thousand copies of ancient translations into such languages as Latin, Coptic, and Syriac. The existence of this wealth of material is reassuring to the modern reader or scholar, but it also presents problems. Virtually no manuscripts are exactly the same; there are differences in wording, readings, or even content. For example, the most ancient manuscripts do not contain the so-called longer ending of Mark (16:9–20) found in the King James Version and long recognized as a part of the Christian scriptures. Rather, according to these manuscripts the Gospel of Mark ends abruptly

Codex Sinaiticus, one of the great fourth-century manuscripts of the New Testament, discovered by C. Tischendorf at the monastery of St. Catherine on Mt. Sinai in 1859. *(Courtesy of American Bible Society and British Museum.)*

with the reported fear of the women who had just found Jesus' tomb empty (16:8). Similarly, John 7:53–8:11, the story of the woman taken in adultery, was not part of the earliest known manuscripts of that Gospel. The question therefore arises: Which ancient authorities are to be followed? To side with the majority seems reasonable, but this solution presents problems, because most of the extant manuscripts are relatively late, dependent on the earlier ones, and less reliable. Generally speaking, the most ancient manuscripts are more trustworthy, although this may not always be the case. An early and possibly original reading may be found in later manuscripts. (Thus in 1 John 4:3 the reading "dissolves Jesus," rather than "does not confess Jesus," fits the context, and although not found in the oldest manuscripts has been taken by some modern commentators to be original.)

Textual critics attempt to assess the relative merits of manuscripts and readings and, among other things, to decide what stood in the most ancient or original text. Such work is demanding, sometimes tedious, and is often uncertain in its results. Nevertheless, the work of textual critics over the past two centuries has produced a text of the Greek New Testament that is certainly much closer to the original than that used by the translators of the famous King James Version published in the early seventeenth century. Since the invention of the printing press in the fifteenth century, manuscripts are no longer copied, so the production or reproduction of variant (i.e., differing) readings has ceased. But the task of refining the text goes on, and even in the twentieth century hitherto-unknown manuscripts have been found. For example, the Bodmer papyri (P^{66}, P^{75}) partially preserve texts of the Gospel of John dating from the beginning of the third century, and Rylands papyrus 457 (P^{52}), a fragment of John 18, dates from the first half of the second century.

The earliest manuscripts were written on papyrus, a product somewhat like paper that was made in sheets. They were bound in codices, which were the forerunners of modern books. Somewhat later the New Testament was copied onto more durable, and expensive, vellum (leather) sheets, and the earliest relatively complete copies from the fourth century survive in that form (e.g., Vaticanus at the Vatican Museum in Rome and Sinaiticus at the British Museum in London). That any manuscript discoveries will produce a radically different New Testament is highly unlikely. One can be confident that what we read in a good modern translation represents substantially what the ancient authors wrote.

Of the many English translations (or versions) of the New Testament, the King James, or Authorized, Version still stands as a monument of the English language, despite the fact that its Greek textual basis is known to be seriously flawed. Without doubt the Revised Standard Version (RSV), which preserved something of the cadence and style of the King James in modern dress, provided a good compromise between faithfulness to the original languages and syntax and the modern English idiom. The RSV was with good reason called the final revision of the King James, but it has now been revised as the New Revised Standard Version (NRSV). The NRSV incorporates inclusive language, as well as a number of other changes or improvements. For this reason we now follow the NRSV except where the authors find reason to disagree with the translation. There are other good translations, but some recent popular translations of the Bible are quite tendentious, theologically or in other ways. Students should consult their instructors before using other translations.[1]

---

1. A number of competent linguists and biblical scholars evaluate and criticize the most popular English translations in *The Word of God: A Guide to English Versions of the Bible,* ed. Lloyd Bailey (Atlanta: John Knox, 1982). Since the publication of this volume, however, several important new translations have appeared, including the New Revised Standard Version.

The task of translation is a demanding one, and must continually be re-done. Languages grow and change, so that certain words disappear or change their meanings. Thus in 1 Corinthians 13 in the KJV the Greek word *agapē* is translated "charity," but in modern versions it is quite properly rendered "love." "Charity" now means generosity or gifts to the poor. Words in one language do not necessarily have exact equivalents in another. For example, the Greek *logos,* translated "word" in the prologue of John's Gospel (1:1–18), has a much broader range of meanings in Greek, where under some cir-cumstances it means "statement," "discourse," "reason," or even "reckon-ing." Moreover, the punctuation of an English translation, or of modern Greek editions, has been introduced by modern editors to aid reading. An-cient manuscripts had little or no punctuation. Similarly, the chapter and verse divisions of the Bible are later, medieval additions. Chapter divisions often accord with sense or narrative divisions remarkably well. Yet the reader and interpreter must remember that they are later impositions upon the text; therefore, they may not accord with how the author, or earlier readers, in-tended or perceived the text to be divided.

Reading the New Testament

A major principle of biblical criticism and interpretation is that the Bible should be read like any other book. Of course, different books are appropriately read in different ways, and the Bible itself has been read quite differently by various people or groups. That the Bible should be read like any other book has usu-ally meant that the individual books of the Bible should be read with appreci-ation for who wrote them, under what circumstances, and for what purpose.

Many Christians, however, have read the Bible on the assumption that God is, in effect, its author, and that all the writings comprising it stand on the same level, or that they all say the same thing—at least they do not disagree. In a certain sense, such a reading assumes the standpoint of the finished, or collected, canon of scripture. Yet the individual authors of the several books or writings could not have known that their works would eventually com-pose something called holy scripture, in this case the New Testament.

Still, the overall purpose of the canon of scripture, to define Christian life and faith, is quite in accord with that of the major New Testament books. Thus, it is entirely proper to read them with a view to understanding what is being said about God and God's relationship to the human race and to individuals. This way of reading does not mean that one has to accept the New Testament's claims in order to understand it. Our approach to the New Testament, and that of modern exegesis or interpretation generally, is based on the premise that the reader can understand what the New Testament and its individual books are about and appreciate their claims upon human life and allegiances without a prior commitment to belief in them. At the same time, like all im-portant literature, this scripture rewards a serious and sympathetic reading.

We have already observed that since the New Testament was written in ancient, Hellenistic Greek, the English reader is dependent upon a translation, and that translations vary in quality and character. Nevertheless, the presumption that one can indeed understand the New Testament's content in translation is underscored by the hundreds of languages and dialects into which it has been translated, often for missionary purposes. Modern printing presses have made the wide dissemination of the New Testament possible, and organizations such as the Gideons have made such dissemination their special mission.

This situation is, however, much different from that in antiquity. Although the New Testament was copied frequently, as the thousands of surviving manuscripts attest, on the whole the copies were made for churches rather than individuals. Doubtless more Christians heard the New Testament read aloud than read it for themselves. The New Testament itself indicates that these writings were read in church. In 1 Thessalonians (5:27) Paul commands that his letters be read to the congregation. Similarly, in the letter to the Colossians the readers are told that when the letter has been read in their congregation, it should be read in the church of Laodiceans, and that the Laodicean letter should be read in Colossae (4:18). "The public reading of scripture" (1 Tim. 4:13) may imply that some Christian writings are so regarded, and in 2 Peter, probably written after A.D. 100, Paul's letters are lumped with "other scriptures" (3:16). Even in the Gospels there is a word directed to readers (Mark 13:14), probably those who would read the Gospel aloud in church. The author of the Book of Revelation clearly states that he expects his book of prophecy to be read aloud so that members of the church will hear it (Rev. 1:3). At mid-second century, Justin Martyr, who calls the Gospels "the memoirs of the apostles," speaks of their being read on Sunday during worship (*Apology* 67, 3), apparently an established practice and one that reflects a more primitive usage. Although the private reading of scripture as a devotional act is now common, quite possibly more Christians still hear the New Testament read in church than read it for themselves.

Students of the New Testament who are studying with the help of books such as *Anatomy of the New Testament* are in the nature of the case not reading for private devotion or public worship. It is indeed relevant for such study, however, to recognize that the major New Testament writings were originally written with a view to their being read before congregations, that is, in church. This situation is as true of the Gospels as of the epistles or the Book of Revelation. Thus, reading the New Testament intelligently requires an understanding that these books were originally read and heard within Christian churches. Although the New Testament does not have to be read for religious purposes and in a religious community, it needs to be read with an understanding and appreciation of those purposes and communities.

INTRODUCTION

*T*he first-century Mediterranean world was dominated by the Roman Empire and by Hellenism, that is, Greek language and culture. Rome ruled a world that had been conquered by Greece centuries before. Underneath the apparent unity and calm of a common language and a political hegemony, however, signs of forces that reflected widespread human longing and dissatisfaction were at work. Chapter 1 of this text focuses upon both the factors working for stability and those encouraging ferment. Out of this ambivalent environment, the Christian faith originated and in it the New Testament writings were conceived, read, and eventually regarded as sacred.

Because of their decisive roles in the development of the Christian faith, two crucial areas for study and reflection are (1) the religious and cultural heritage of the people of Israel, who chafed under Roman rule but who also expected that the God who had delivered them out of slavery in Egypt and exile in Babylon would not fail them, and (2) the intense religious crisis of the Hellenistic world under Roman rule, especially as seen in the dissolution of traditional Greek, Homeric religion and the rapid growth of mystery cults with their promise of meaningful life and individual immortality. This situation of change, frustration, fervor, and hope was the matrix for the emergence of a religious community centered around Jesus, a man of Israel; this community grew within two centuries into a religious movement of worldwide importance.

This scene from the Arch of Titus in the Roman Forum celebrates Titus' capture of Jerusalem in A.D. 70. The victorious Romans bear triumphantly the sacred objects of the Jerusalem temple, including the seven-branched lampstand symbolizing the presence of God.   *(Courtesy of Jewish Museum.)*

Chapter 1

The World of the New Testament

The Jewish World

Jesus was a Jew. So were his first disciples. *Jesus Christ* means Jesus the Messiah of Israel, the anointed king of Davidic lineage (cf. 2 Sam. 7:12–15 and Psalm 89:3–4). In fact, the earliest Christians did not think of themselves as members of a new religion separate from Judaism. Yet Jesus and his disciples represented something new within Judaism. This newness consisted not in original or unique ideas but in the aspects of ancient traditions and hopes that were taken up, reinterpreted, and emphasized.

No new movement can be understood, however, apart from its historical antecedents and the factors that helped to produce it. The primary background of Jesus, early Christianity, and the New Testament was first-century Judaism. A remarkable continuity or similarity exists between the Judaism of today and that of the first century, despite the changes that succeeding centuries have wrought. This continuity is in itself a clue to the character of that ancient faith.

Both Judaism and Christianity are historical religions, and it belongs to the nature of both to emphasize continuity. They share a faith in a God who deals with human beings, individually and collectively, in such a way that God's will can be discerned in history. Crucial to both religions is the idea that God *reveals* or has been *revealed* in history. The holy scriptures of both religions are largely narratives of the past: legends, sagas, and historical accounts. Broadly speaking, they are testimonies to God's historical revelations. The Hebrew Bible (Christian Old Testament) is a vast collection of legal, cultic, devotional, and narrative material set in a historical framework. It is the literary product of nearly a thousand years of Israel's history. Although the New Testament is much briefer and covers a much shorter period of time, it too tells of people and events in the conviction that God has wrought wondrous deeds in history that are of utmost importance for the future of humanity. Consciously and deliberately the New Testament writers take up the story of the Old Testament and bring it to a culmination.

The limits of the Hebrew Bible had not actually been officially defined in the time of Jesus and earliest Christianity. Yet, according to the New Testament, Jesus himself speaks of "the law and the prophets" (Matt. 5:17) and quotes from the Psalms (Mark 15:34; cf. Psalm 22:1). Thus he seems to have known the threefold division of sacred scripture—law, prophets, and writings (cf. Luke 24:44)—that is reflected generally in the New Testament. According to tradition, the Hebrew canon of the Hebrew Bible was fixed by the rabbis at the Council of Jamnia in about A.D. 90, although in fact the main lines had been established much earlier. This Hebrew, Jewish canon is accepted by most Protestant Christians. Other, Catholic Christians accept as canonical the apocryphal or deuterocanonical books contained in the Septuagint (see Glossary).

Judaism was a religion of revelation, history, and a book. As such, it was a religion steeped in tradition, but this tradition was not an end in itself. Rather it was a means by which Israel identified and understood itself as a distinct and chosen people, the people of the Lord. Moreover, much of the literature of the Old Testament and the oral and written traditions that developed from it were understood as divine directions intended to regulate Israel's response to the Lord's goodness. The most influential law code the Western world has known, the Ten Commandments, begins: "I am the Lord your God, who brought you out of the land of Egypt, out of the house of slavery. You shall have no other gods before me" (Exod. 20:2–3). The statement of what God has done leads to the statement of what the people ought to do in response,

A portion of the Isaiah Scroll of the Dead Sea Scrolls, housed in the Shrine of the Book in Jerusalem. This scroll is at least as old as the copies of the Old Testament books used by the earliest Christians.   *(Courtesy of Israel Information Services.)*

forming the basic structure of Old Testament law. The principal activity of many Jewish religious leaders in the time of Jesus was the interpretation and fulfillment of that law.

Revelation and history, tradition and law, although immensely important, were not the whole of Judaism. A part of obedience to the law was, in fact, the performance of worship worthy of God. The center of this worship was the temple in Jerusalem, and the heart of the temple was the sacrificial altar, where priests offered sacrifice to God. Until its destruction by the Romans in A.D. 70, the temple served as the focal point of Jewish worship. Its importance to the life of first-century Judaism can scarcely be overestimated. Not only was the temple regarded as the center of the universe and the place where the last days were to be consummated, it also served as a means for structuring time, both through the daily sacrifices and the seasonal festivals. Any violation of the temple by the Roman authorities or others was sufficient to cause a major Jewish revolt. Further, the Jewish sect of Qumran (see below, pp.23-27) originated in part as a reaction to the corruption of temple worship, and Jesus was accused of trying to destroy this sacred institution of Jewish piety (Mark 14:58 par.).

The other major Jewish religious institution was the synagogue. Although there was but one Jerusalem temple, there were many synagogues. Even in Palestine, but especially in the diaspora (see Glossary), the synagogue was for most the practical center of Jewish religious life. Although the origin of the synagogue is hidden in obscurity, by the first century it had become a central Jewish institution, a kind of community center for study of the Jewish law, the Torah, and a place for regular weekly worship, including reading and commentary on the Torah and prayers for the congregation. Unlike the temple that was presided over by the priests, the synagogue was a lay organization that allowed broader participation, such as Jesus' reading from the Torah in the synagogue (see Luke 4:16) and Paul's extensive use of synagogues in his missionary work (see Acts 18:4).

Another factor played a large role in first-century Judaism, namely, the land. The small piece of territory at the eastern end of the Mediterranean Sea, which is variously called the Holy Land, Palestine, or Israel, has been the occasion and cause of both hope and frustration for Jews for three thousand years. At least from the days of the Davidic monarchy the land was regarded as the promise and gift of God to his people. The promise reached back into the days of the patriarchs Abraham, Isaac, and Jacob, who dwelt in and around the land but did not possess it (cf. Gen. 12:1–3). Yet Israel believed that God had promised the land to her, and in this faith she occupied and defended it. Israel could never rest easy in the land, however, for, subject to frequent threat and attack, she was only secure when the more powerful surrounding nations were momentarily weak or looking in other directions. In the late eighth century B.C. the territories of all the Israelite tribes except Judah were overrun by the Assyrians, and less than a century and a half later the Babylonians invaded Judea, laid siege to Jerusalem, and overthrew it. The Davidic kingship came to an end, and many of the people were deported into Babylonian captivity.

The subsequent history of the land has been a troubled one. In fact, the modern state of Israel represents the first instance of Jewish control of the land since shortly before the time of Jesus, and that control is still not uncontested. Since the Babylonian exile the land of Israel has been ruled by other peoples, whether Persians, Romans, or British. The question of the possession and rulership of the land was quite as important in Jesus' day as it is today, for the land was then occupied by the Romans and ruled by puppet kings and imperial procurators. The hope for the restoration of Jewish dominion under Davidic kingship was an important aspect of the background of Jesus' ministry.

The Jordan River coils southward from the Sea of Galilee through harsh hills.   *(Courtesy of National Geographic Society.)*

A HISTORY OF TRAGEDY AND RENEWAL

What was the relationship of history, faith, and hope in Israel?[1]

From the Babylonian conquest of Judea in 587 B.C. to the time of Jesus' death, the Jews in Palestine lived mostly under foreign domination, relieved only by a century or so of relative independence under the Hasmonean dynasty just prior to the advent of the Romans in 63 B.C.[2] In the Babylonian conquest num-

1. The questions are meant to help the student read with interest and understanding. They are not meant to be exhaustive, but should rather stimulate reflection, enlarge perspectives, and sharpen focus on a major issue in the reading.
2. The concerns of postexilic Israel are reflected in the later Old Testament books and treated directly in Ezra and Nehemiah. The Maccabean period is dealt with in 1 and 2 Maccabees. The *Jewish Antiquities*, a continuous history of the Jews to the Roman War by the first-century Jewish historian Josephus, is doubtless the most valuable single non-Biblical source.

bers of Jews were taken east by their captors to Mesopotamia. Others fled south to Egypt. The so-called diaspora, or dispersion of the Jews, began. From this time onward, Jews in increasing numbers were to be found living outside their Palestinian homeland.

Shortly after the middle of the sixth century B.C. Babylonian overlordship was replaced by a Persian one. Jews were allowed to return to their homeland and to begin the restoration of the Jerusalem temple, which had been destroyed by the Babylonians. Although we have an incomplete picture of Jewish life under Persian rule, conditions were certainly much improved. More than two centuries of Persian domination came to an end late in the fourth century before Jesus, when Alexander of Macedon and his armies moved east, sweeping everything before them. Alexander overran the Jewish homeland, and over the years he and his successors attempted to introduce Greek culture and customs, as was their practice in all conquered territories. Alexander was as much a missionary of Greek culture as a conquering general. After his death in 323 B.C. his empire broke up as quickly as it had been formed. And although his successors could not preserve political unity, they were able to continue the process of Hellenization, that is, the spreading of Greek culture.

After the division of Alexander's empire, the Jews found themselves situated between two rival centers of power—the Seleucids, who controlled Mesopotamia and Syria, and the Ptolemies, who ruled Egypt. The geographical setting of Israel as a buffer zone between the two great powers of the Fertile Crescent made struggle over Palestine inevitable. By and large, Jewish Palestine during the third century was controlled by the Ptolemies with a minimum of interference in Jewish internal affairs. After they defeated the Ptolemies in 198 B.C., a similar policy at first characterized the Seleucids' rule. Following a period of changing rulers, however, Antiochus IV (called Epiphanes because he proclaimed himself to be "God manifest") ascended to the Syrian throne in 175 B.C., and the situation changed. Already there were Hellenizing Jews in Jerusalem and elsewhere who were all too eager to adopt Greek customs and dress, in part because of the economic and other advantages they thought assimilation would bring (1 Macc. 1:11–15). In due course, however, more pious Jews (*Hasidim*) strongly objected to such accommodation, and the seeds from which conflict would sprout were quickly sown as positions hardened on both sides. Because Antiochus probably saw in such Jewish resistance dangerous opposition to his own rule, he decided to suppress the Jewish religion. Heathen altars were erected in Jewish towns and abominations were sacrificed in the Jerusalem temple (2 Macc. 6:1–6). Resistance was likely to mean death.

In the face of such depredations and threats, Mattathias, the patriarch of the Hasmonean family, rose to the occasion when in 167 B.C. emissaries of Antiochus came to his town of Modein to enforce the command to perform pagan sacrifice (cf. 1 Macc. 2:15–28). Proclaiming that "even if all the nations that live under the rule of the king obey him, and have chosen to do his commandments . . . yet I and my sons and my brothers will continue to live by

Antiochus IV (Epiphanes—"[God] Manifest") on a Greek coin. The reverse side shows Apollo and bears the words: Basileōs Antiochou—"(coinage) of King Antiochus."   *(Courtesy of American Numismatic Society.)*

the covenant of our ancestors," he killed a Jew who had come forward to offer sacrifice, as well as one of the king's officers. Then he and his sons took to the hills in open rebellion. Said Mattathias: "Let everyone who is zealous for the law and supports the covenant come out with me!" (1 Macc. 2:27).

Mattathias died soon thereafter, and his son Judas, called Maccabeus, assumed command of the rebel force. (The family is often called Maccabean, after him.) Victorious in combat, in 165 B.C. Judas Maccabeus and his men seized the temple and reclaimed it for Judaism. This victory has ever since been celebrated in the feast of Hanukkah (dedication), even though it was not until 142 B.C. that the last remnants of the Syrian Hellenizers were driven from Jerusalem.

Although the Maccabean or Hasmonean dynasty was generally welcomed as a blessed relief and the fulfillment of long-frustrated expectations, its promise far outstripped its actuality. The propensity of the later Hasmoneans to style themselves as kings and high priests, as well as the internecine struggle among them, led to disillusionment. As kings they were not sons of David and as priests they were not descendants of Zadok, and thus they could be viewed as interlopers. When the Romans arrived on the scene about a century after the Maccabean Revolt, their general, Pompey, supported one Hasmonean claimant, Hyrcanus II, against the other, Aristobulus II. Although some supporters of Aristobulus offered fierce resistance, particularly at the temple, the Roman occupation of Palestine and the Holy City could scarcely have been regarded as a disaster by most Jews. For while Roman domination may have been inevitable, the conduct of the later Hasmoneans made it seem initially less distasteful to Jews than it might otherwise have been. The Romans allowed the weak Hasmonean Hyrcanus II to hold the office of high priest and ethnarch. But Palestine was now in fact Roman territory, and the power behind the throne was Antipater of Idumea, a master of political intrigue who had helped engineer the Roman coup in the first place.

Antipater brought his remarkable career to a culmination by having the Romans declare his son Herod king of the Jews. This Herod ruled effectively, if brutally, from 37 to 4 B.C. and figures prominently in Matthew's story of Jesus' infancy. He is commonly known as Herod the Great, in distinction from the lesser Herods who followed him. During his long and successful rule Herod accepted the necessity of appealing to Jewish religious sensibilities, at the same time devoting himself to the task of Hellenizing the culture and life of Palestine. He built cities according to the Hellenistic patterns, and he constructed stadiums, gymnasiums, and theaters. In non-Jewish areas (e.g., Sebaste, the ancient Samaria) he built pagan temples. Yet he also rebuilt the Jerusalem temple in a more magnificent style. Despite his efforts, the Jews did not love or trust Herod; nor did he trust them. He executed his Hasmonean wife Mariamne and eventually two of her sons, along with his ambitious and able son Antipater, who had married a Hasmonean princess. Obviously Herod feared that the memory of the Hasmoneans would inspire the Jews against him.

After the death of Herod, the kingdom was split into three parts and divided among three surviving sons. Philip became tetrarch of the region northeast of the Sea of Galilee, including Iturea and Trachonitis, and reigned over that largely Gentile area from 4 B.C. until A.D. 34. Herod Antipas became ruler of Galilee and Perea and ruled from 4 B.C. until A.D. 39. Archelaus became ruler of Samaria, Judea, and Idumea, but was deposed after a short reign. Following the deposition of Archelaus in A.D. 6, a Roman procurator was installed as ruler of Judea. The procuratorship remained in effect continuously until the brief reign of Agrippa (37–44) and was resumed thereafter. Pontius Pilate (26–36) was the fifth of these procurators, surely one of the worst from the Jewish point of view. He took money from the temple treasury, brought military insignia with the emperor's image into Jerusalem, and ruthlessly destroyed a group of Samaritans who were watching a prophet perform a miracle. It is an understatement to say that he was not overly sensitive to Jewish religious sensibilities.

Yet Roman rule was not unremittingly brutal or oppressive. The procurator of Judea lived not in Jerusalem but on the Mediterranean coast in Caesarea. Although he had final responsibility, much authority was granted to the Sanhedrin, a group of about seventy distinguished Jewish elders—priests, scribes, and laymen. The high priest was the official head of this group and was, as he had been since the Babylonian exile, the most important Jewish governmental figure. In the villages, synagogues served as law courts where scribes were the authorities for interpreting and applying the law, or Torah.

Jesus was born during the reign of Herod the Great, lived in Galilee under Herod Antipas, and died in Jerusalem during the procuratorship of Pilate and the high priesthood of Caiaphas. Although Jesus was doubtless influenced by the political conditions of the times, there is little evidence that he made

Aerial view of Masada, ancient Roman fortress occupied and defended by Jewish resistance fighters against a Roman legion led by Vespasian during the last months of the Roman War (A.D. 66–73). Rather than surrender, the surviving Jewish defenders committed suicide on the eve of the Roman soldiers' capture of the Jewish stronghold.   *(Courtesy of the Jewish Museum, New York City.)*

much impact upon them. On the one hand, Jesus and his followers would not have encouraged any who advocated armed resistance against Roman rule.[3] Although Jesus spoke frequently of the kingdom of God and aroused hopes that he himself would become king, he evidently did not intend to lead a rebellion (cf. Luke 4:5–8; Matt. 4:7–10; John 6:15). For example, he did not explicitly forbid the payment of taxes to Caesar (Mark 12:13–17 parr.). On the other hand, Jesus was executed as a messianic pretender, a claimant to the throne of Israel, and thus a political rebel.

3. Such resisters have been known as Zealots, although David M. Rhoads, *Israel in Revolution: 6–74 CE: A Political History Based on the Writings of Josephus* (Philadelphia: Fortress, 1976), pp. 52–59, points out that a party specifically called Zealot does not emerge before A.D. 66 (p. 53). It is usually inferred from Josephus that Judas the Galilean founded the sect in A.D. 6. Cf. E. M. Smallwood, *The Jews Under Roman Rule: From Pompey to Diocletian* (Leiden: Brill, 1976), p. 154. Nevertheless, Richard A. Horsley, *Jesus and the Spiral of Violence: Popular Jewish Resistance in Roman Palestine* (San Francisco: Harper & Row, 1987), argues that there was no organized party advocating armed revolution during the period with which we are concerned.

Gradually during the first century the tension between Roman and Jew heightened.[4] What the Romans regarded as Jewish provocations led to retaliation, which in turn increased the polarization of sentiment. More and more Jews became willing to fight and die, convinced that God would vindicate them in their righteous cause. Jewish Christians, among others, did not share the widespread enthusiasm for war, and when its outbreak seemed imminent those in Jerusalem fled for safety, according to tradition to Pella across the Jordan River.[5] In A.D. 66 war broke out. Although the Jews fought bravely and enjoyed some initial success, they had little chance against Roman power. In A.D. 70 the Romans took Jerusalem after a long and grueling siege and laid it waste, destroying the temple. A few years later the last Jewish resistance at the fortress of Masada was overwhelmed. Even then the Jewish will to resist was not broken. When word circulated that Emperor Hadrian intended to rebuild Jerusalem as Aelia Capitolina and to erect a temple to Jupiter on the ruins of the Jewish temple, the Jews rallied around a leader called Bar Kochba ("Son of the Star"), whom the renowned Rabbi Akiba hailed as the Messiah of Israel. Once more (A.D. 132–135) the Jews fought fiercely, but after a time were subdued. The Romans went ahead with their building plans and after the new city was complete forbade any Jew to enter it on pain of death. The trend of many centuries reached its logical end. Judaism had become a nation without a homeland over which the Jews themselves ruled.

Because the Jews believed that their land had been given them by the same God who had called them to be his chosen people, those who lived in Palestine chafed under foreign domination. Indeed, the character of Judaism during the time of Jesus and the early church was much affected by conditions in the Jewish homeland. Even though Jews generally looked for relief from foreign oppression and the restoration of the Davidic monarchy, many were content to wait upon God for the fulfillment of this hope, some thinking that it was near at hand. Certain other Jews had in effect already made their peace with Hellenistic culture and Roman rule and probably did not really yearn for their overthrow. Then, of course, there were large numbers of Jews living outside Palestine for whom political independence was not a burning issue. Indeed, rebellion in the homeland presented the grim and unwelcome possibility of retaliation against Jews elsewhere.

Moreover, it would be a mistake to view the Judaism of Jesus' time solely in terms of its reaction to an international, and domestic, political situation with unfortunate consequences for Jews. Many Jews continued to be primarily concerned with the right understanding of the law and the proper worship of God. The development of various schools of thought continued under Roman rule, and the Romans were willing to tolerate this so long as there was not overt

---

4. Smallwood, *The Jews Under Roman Rule,* pp. 256–272, points out that Judea suffered from uncharacteristically bad Roman government during the period leading up to the rebellion.
5. Eusebius, *EH,* III, v. 3.

Coin of the Simon Bar Kochba War (A.D. 132–135). On the first side is a temple with four columns, within which there are a shrine and two scrolls of the law; the inscription reads, "Simon." On the other side are the *lulab* (leafy branch) and *ethrog* (citron), sacred objects carrried in procession at the Feast of Booths. The inscription reads, "For the liberty of Jerusalem." *(Courtesy of American Numismatic Society.)*

dissension or violence. Postexilic developments had already led to the formation of several schools of religious opinion among the Jews, making for a rather complex situation in the time of Jesus. We must now examine that situation more closely to understand why differing positions and parties existed and how their presence shaped the setting in which Christianity appeared.

A PERSISTENT OBEDIENCE

What attitudes toward the law can be detected in Judaism?

If anything is central to Judaism, it is the law (Hebrew, *torah,* meaning "law" in the sense of "instruction"). Notwithstanding its human mediation through Moses, the Jew regarded the law as divine revelation. "The stability of the World rests on three things, on the Law, on worship, and on deeds of personal kindness" *(Pirke Aboth* 1, 2).[6] Of course, proper worship and the nature of deeds of kindness are defined by the law. Strictly speaking, the law consists of the five books of Moses—the Pentateuch—that stand at the beginning of the Bible. Obedience to the Torah is, and has been, the paramount obligation of the Jew; it is the way to true righteousness. Interpretation of the law was historically the province of priests and scribes. Ezra, the great fifth-century scribe and "scholar of the text of the commandments of the Lord and his statutes for Israel" (Ezra 7:11), was the descendant of an important

6. Cited by G. F. Moore, *Judaism in the First Centuries of the Christian Era, The Age of the Tannaim,* I (Cambridge, MA: Harvard University Press, 1927), p. 268.

priestly family (7:1–5).[7] Although most law-observant Jews were members of no sect or special group, the law was so central to Judaism that such groups can be categorized according to their attitude to it.

THE PHARISEES

The Pharisees . . . are considered the most accurate interpreters of the laws, and hold the position of the leading sect. [Josephus, *The Jewish War*, II, 162]

The scribes and Pharisees sit on Moses' seat; therefore, do whatever they teach you and follow it, but do not do as they do; for they do not practice what they teach. [Matt. 23:2 f.]

When Paul noticed that some were Sadducees and others were Pharisees, he called out in the council, "Brothers, I am a Pharisee, a son of Pharisees. I am on trial concerning the hope of the resurrection of the dead." [Acts 23:6]

Probably the single most influential and significant religious group within the Jewish community of New Testament times was the Pharisees. The Gospels make clear that they were important during the time of Jesus, and they became even more influential after the disastrous conclusion of the Jewish War (A.D. 70). After that war a rabbinic council assembled near the Mediterranean coast at Jamnia. The Council of Jamnia became a center for the study and interpretation of the law. Although its influence has sometimes been exaggerated, it played an important role in the dissemination of the Pharisaic point of view throughout Judaism. The Gospels' portrayal of the Pharisees is doubtless colored by the fact that they usually appear as opponents of Jesus. Yet the representation of them as staunch defenders of the law is surely accurate (cf. Mark 2:24; 10:2).

The history of the Pharisees and even the origin of their name is obscure. Very likely they stemmed from the Hasidim, or "pious ones," whose ferocious allegiance to the nation and the law gave impetus to the Maccabean revolt. The word *Pharisee* seems to be derived from a Hebrew verb meaning "to separate." If so, it would appropriately designate the Pharisees as those separated or chosen by God for full obedience to the law. Yet Pharisees did not withdraw from society. Pharisaism was fundamentally a lay movement and Pharisees emphasized the necessity of obeying the law in all areas or aspects of life. The Pharisees seem to have been the original custodians of the oral law, that is, the law revealed to Moses on Sinai but, unlike the scriptural Torah, not committed to writing. In the Gospels, the Pharisees accuse Jesus of not following the traditions of the elders (Mark 7:5), and Jesus in turn accuses them of preferring such human tradition to the commandment of God (7:8,13). Paul, himself a former Pharisee (Phil. 3:5), speaks of how far advanced he had become in the traditions of his forefathers (Gal. 1:14). These

7. E. P. Sanders, *Judaism: Practice and Belief 63 BCE–66 CE* (Philadelphia: Trinity Press International, 1992), pp. 170–173.

traditions of the oral law were eventually committed to writing in the Mishnah (see Glossary), though not until more than a century after the period of Christian and New Testament origin.[8] Because they had begun to understand Judaism primarily as interpretation of and obedience to the law, the Pharisees were well situated to reconstitute and redefine Judaism in the aftermath of the destruction of the temple in the Roman War. Although earlier Pharisees may well have shared traditional Jewish hopes for the reestablishment of God's rule over the land of Israel, the Mishnah does not discuss them, but concentrates on specific commands to which obedience is expected.

Two famous and important Pharisaic leaders were Hillel and Shammai, contemporaries and rivals who flourished in the latter part of the first century B.C. and the first decade of the following century. Around them gathered rival schools or houses of legal interpretation. Shammai's was known for its stricter, harsher interpretation of the law, whereas the interpretations of the house of Hillel were more liberal. Hillel's school eventually came to dominate. Some of the sayings attributed to Hillel closely parallel sayings ascribed to Jesus. Among these is the negative form of the Golden Rule (cf. Matt. 7:12; Luke 6:31): "What is hateful to yourself do not do to your neighbor. That is the entire Torah. All the rest is commentary. Now go forth and learn."[9]

In the New Testament the Pharisees are frequently spoken of together with the scribes, and the impression is created that they are closely allied if not identical groups. The impression is not false, although it must be clarified. The scribes were authoritative custodians and interpreters of the law before the appearance of a distinct group called Pharisees. Moreover, not all Pharisees were scribes. The historic task of the scribes was, however, largely taken up by the Pharisees, whose consuming interest was to interpret and apply the law to every sphere of life. They continued and expanded the traditional interpretations of the law, the fruition of which is to be found in the rabbinic literature, a large body of interpretative material from the earlier centuries of our era dealing with every phase of the law and with almost every aspect of religious and secular life.[10]

8. For an incisively stated interpretation of Pharisaic origins and the oral law, see Ellis Rivkin, *A Hidden Revolution* (Nashville, Tenn.: Abingdon, 1978).

9. Cited by Jacob Neusner, *From Politics to Piety: The Emergence of Pharisaic Judaism* (Englewood Cliffs, NJ: Prentice Hall, 1973), p. 13. It is found in the Babylonian Talmud (see note 10), Sabbat 31a. Versions of the Golden Rule are found also in various Jewish and other writings (e.g., the apocryphal Tobit 4:15 and Sirach 31:15).

10. The basic document of the rabbinic literature, dating from the early third century, is *The Mishnah*, of which the standard English translation is that of H. Danby (London: Oxford University Press, 1933). *The Babylonian Talmud*, trans. I. Epstein, 35 vols. (London: Soncino Press, 1935–52), includes, but is in the main a kind of learned commentary upon, the Mishnah. There is also a Palestinian Talmud. It is shorter than the Babylonian Talmud and dates from the early fifth century, whereas the latter dates from the late fifth century. A valuable introduction to the range of rabbinic literature is the work of C. G. Montefiore and H. Loewe, *A Rabbinic Anthology* (New York: Meridian, n.d.).

THE SADDUCEES

The Sadducees hold that the soul perishes along with the body. They own no
observance of any sort apart from the laws. . . . There are but few men to whom
this doctrine has been made known, but these are men of the highest standing.
[Josephus, *Jewish Antiquities,* XVIII, 16 f.].

Then the high priest took action; he and all who were with him (that is, the
sect of the Sadducees), being filled with jealousy arrested the apostles and put
them in the public prison. [Acts 5:17 f.]

A second major group within Judaism, also mentioned in the Gospels, is
the Sadducees. As in the case of the Pharisees, their history and the de-
rivation of their name are not entirely clear. Presumably the name is related
to the proper name of Zadok, a high priest appointed by Solomon. Whatever the history of the name and of the group, by New Testament times the
Sadducees were the priestly aristocracy. In Acts 5:17 the high priest and the
Sadducees are linked, and in 4:1 the priests, the captain of the temple, and
the Sadducees appear together. Pharisees and Sadducees were thus religious brotherhoods centering upon the authoritative interpretation of the
law and temple worship, respectively. As such they represented the chief
foci of Jewish faith as it existed prior to A.D. 70. Although the temple and its
service of worship had declined in practical importance as the majority of
Jews came to live outside the land of Israel, it was nevertheless the symbolic
center of Judaism. On the altar sacrifices were offered so that the people
might commune with God. Sins were dealt with and a right relationship between God and the people restored and maintained. Probably the most
graphic example of this priestly function was the yearly ritual of the Day of
Atonement, when the high priest alone entered the unapproachable Holy
of Holies in the temple and there, as the representative of the people, came
into the very presence of the Holy One. On this day his action signified
divine favor in that he entered, met, and was not destroyed by the God of
Israel.

As custodians of religious tradition and cultic ceremony the Sadducees
were somewhat more conservative than the Pharisees. The priests themselves held office by hereditary right. Moreover, the Sadducees represented
established wealth and position. With regard to obedience to the law, they
rejected the oral tradition and thus the effort of the Pharisees to extend the
law's application to every situation in life in a binding way. They accepted
only the word of scripture as authoritative. Politically, they were quietists
who generally cooperated with the Romans. As members of the establishment it was in their interest to do so. They would have nothing to do with
the relatively late doctrine of the resurrection of the dead, but rather adhered to the older and more typically Biblical (Old Testament) view that
death is simply the end of significant conscious life. In this they differed
from the Pharisees, as well as from Jesus and the early Christians.

Jerusalem and the temple area. The domed building is a Muslim shrine, the Dome of the Rock, which stands near the place where the ancient Jerusalem temple was located.   *(Courtesy of Israel Government Tourist Office.)*

THE ESSENES

The Essenes have a reputation for cultivating peculiar sanctity. Of Jewish birth, they show a greater attachment to each other than do the other sects. They shun pleasures as a vice and regard temperance and the control of the passions as a special virtue. [Josephus, *The Jewish War*, II, 119 f.]

The Hebrew reads "to the house (or place) of trumpeting. . . ." The inscription comes from the Jerusalem temple of the time of Jesus (Second Temple), and is inscribed upon a stone from the southwest corner, where, according to Josephus (*The Jewish War*, IV, 582), a priest blew the trumpet to signal the onset and end of the Sabbath. (Courtesy of the Israel Antiquities Authority. Exhibited and photographed, Israel Museum).

In addition to the Pharisees and Sadducees there existed at the time of Jesus a group called Essenes, whose exact identity and extent are not entirely clear. Two important Jewish writers of the first century, the philosopher Philo and the historian Josephus, speak of them, although they are not mentioned by name in the New Testament. In recent decades, however, our knowledge of Essene or Essene-type groups has been immensely enlarged by the discovery of a monastery and an immense cache of documents at Qumran on the northwest shore of the Dead Sea.[11] Apparently an Essene community existed there at the time of Jesus.

The Qumran movement, which began sometime during the second or early first century B.C., was characterized by revulsion at the impropriety of the temple worship presided over by an illegitimate high priesthood of Hasmonean rather than Zadokite lineage and based upon an erroneous festival calendar. A figure called only the "teacher of righteousness" or the "righteous teacher" was apparently the founder of this group. Unlike the Pharisees

---

11. A handy collection of the important documents in translation has been made by
    G. Vermes, *The Dead Sea Scrolls in English,* 3rd. ed. (Baltimore: Penguin, 1987). For
    other works relevant to the scrolls, see the Suggestions for Further Reading at the end of
    this chapter.

Cave near Qumran where some of the Dead Sea Scrolls were found.   *(Courtesy of Israel Information Services.)*

and Sadducees, they withdrew from the mainstream of Jewish life, which they regarded as wholly corrupt, and often formed monastic communities. Yet this withdrawal had a positive as well as a negative side. It was a separation not only for the sake of the preservation of holiness but for a positive task and goal. First of all, the members of the community sought to carry out punctiliously the ritual and ethical requirements of the law and thus render a more acceptable obedience to God. This obedience was enforced under a strict discipline and severe punishment was meted out for even minor infractions:

> Whoever has gone naked before his companion, without having been obliged to do so, he shall do penance for six months.
> Whoever has spat in an Assembly of the Congregation shall do penance for thirty days.
> Whoever has been so poorly dressed that when drawing his hand from beneath his garment his nakedness has been seen, he shall do penance for thirty days.
> Whoever has guffawed foolishly shall do penance for thirty days.
> Whoever has drawn out his left hand to gesticulate with it shall do penance for ten days.[12]

---

12. From the Community Rule, Vermes, *The Dead Sea Scrolls in English,* p. 84.

In addition, they looked toward the future vindication of Israel, or at least of their own community as the remnant of the true Israel. This vindication was expected in the form of an apocalyptic drama, indeed, a conflict in which the forces of light would overwhelm those of darkness.[13] The victory would never be in doubt, because God was to fight on the side of his elect. Such terms as *light, darkness,* and *elect* highlight the basic character of Qumran thought. Almost everything was seen as a choice between good and evil, with no compromise allowed:

> He has created man to govern the world, and has appointed for him two spirits in which to walk until the time of His visitation: the spirits of truth and falsehood. Those born of truth spring from a fountain of light, but those born of falsehood spring from a source of darkness. All the children of righteousness are ruled by the Prince of Light and walk in the ways of light, but all the children of falsehood are ruled by the Angel of Darkness and walk in the ways of darkness.[14]

This way of perceiving the world, often called *dualism,* was reflected in the group's extremely rigid attitude toward the law, in its implacable hostility toward those regarded as enemies, and in its view of the coming culmination of history. The triumph of the good people over the bad would result in the elimination of evil from the world.

For the purpose of a historical understanding of Jesus, his disciples, and early Christianity, the Qumran documents are quite important. They reveal another Jewish sect of the same period that was engaged in alternately searching the scriptures and the heavens for signs of God's approaching kingdom. For the Christians these hopes and expectations found fulfillment, although not in the way anticipated. For the Qumran community and other Essenes there was apparently only disappointment in this world. The monastery was destroyed by the Romans in the war, and the inhabitants hid their sacred scrolls in nearby caves, where they were accidentally discovered nearly two thousand years later.

Because the history of this sect has to be reconstructed on the basis of references and allusions in its own writings and in those of ancient Jewish authors such as Philo and Josephus, its origins and relationships remain somewhat obscure. Recurrently, it is proposed that the Scrolls are actually Christian documents or that this and similar facts about them have been intentionally suppressed. Such proposals are baseless and often sensationalist. No specifically Christian documents have been found at Qumran, and the writings of the sect do not explicitly mention Jesus or other early Christian

---

13. Such an encounter is described in the community document designated the War Rule(cf. Vermes, *The Dead Sea Scrolls in English,* pp. 103-127).
14. From G. Vermes' translation of the Community Rule (or Manual of Discipline), in *The Dead Sea Scrolls in English*, pp. 64 f.

figures. Theories that the unnamed "teacher of righteousness" was Jesus, or some other Christian figure, require great leaps of the imagination.

THE FOLLOWERS OF JESUS

The Qumraners, or Essenes, as they may be called, were not purely passive in their hopes and expectations. Rather, they saw themselves, and particularly their separatist existence in the desert, as the fulfillment of the prophecy of Isaiah 40:3 (cf. Community Rule, 8). They were in the wilderness preparing the way of the Lord. In this respect there is a striking similarity between the Qumran community and the New Testament church. In the New Testament the same Old Testament passage is found on the lips of John the Baptist (John 1:23), who views his task in a similar way. Both the desert community and Jesus and his disciples lived in an atmosphere of apocalyptic or eschatological expectation. They looked forward to the coming of God. In fact, there were other similarities between the two groups. Both stood apart from prevailing forms of Jewish piety. Both looked to a central leader or founder, whether Jesus or the "teacher of righteousness"; in different ways both maintained a distinctive view of the law; both formed a community or sect of believers within Judaism. There has been a great deal of excitement over the Qumran discoveries; they have not only enlarged our view of ancient Judaism, but in several significant ways have brought us closer to the origins of Christianity.

Yet, there are also significant differences. Christians insisted upon what they regarded as the essential meaning of the law rather than the letter. Jesus was denounced as a wine bibber and a friend of tax collectors and other really disreputable people, and his disciples and the early Christians, men and women, continued to live among other folk. They did not withdraw to themselves. Instead of savoring in advance their own salvation at the expense of others, most Christians went out to preach their good news to humanity at large.

Strange as it may seem to characterize Christians as Jews for whom the law was a central concern, that is exactly what the earliest followers of Jesus were. Jesus himself simply assumed that the scriptures and law of Israel were authoritative, and his debates with opponents were based on that common ground. His brother James, the first leader of the church at Jerusalem, shared this assumption. If anything, he was more concerned than Jesus himself with the centrality of the law and its observance. The Apostle Paul, a former Pharisee, is generally credited with having struck down the requirements of the law as essential for Christians. There is some truth in this assessment of his work. Yet, as we shall see, the depth and extent of the controversy Paul launched within the Christian community is testimony to the importance of the law. Indeed, Paul himself never doubted that scriptural law contained God's commandments; he doubted only that people could gain God's approval through their unaided effort to obey the law.

AN ABIDING HOPE

What were the hopes and expectations of the Jewish people?

Judaism in New Testament times was characterized not only by a memorable past and earnest efforts to obey the law of God in the present but also by its attitude toward the future. The Qumran discoveries are important evidence of this hope. As we have already noted, most Jews had definite ideas about the future, which were usually tied to the national destiny.

At one end of the spectrum stood those like the men of Qumran who looked for the dramatic intervention of God in history to destroy the wicked and establish forever the righteous Israelites. At the other stood the Sadducees, whose position of relative security and comfort in relation to the Roman authorities made them little disposed either to sedition or to an apocalyptic outlook. The Sadducees looked for no cataclysmic end of history and no resurrection of the dead. In this respect they seem to have been in substantial agreement with the theology of preexilic Israel. From time to time some, like the Zealots, sought to realize their hope for the recovery of national autonomy through armed resistance, perhaps aided by an expected divine intervention. (Such an expectation seems to be reflected in the War Scroll of the Qumran community.) Apart from such extremes stood the Pharisees, who may have hoped for "the redemption of Israel" (Luke 24:21), but who did not expect to initiate it by violent revolution.[15] Although the Pharisees abjured the kind of active cooperation with Roman authority in which the Sadducees engaged, they served along with priests and Sadducees on the Sanhedrin, the highest Jewish court of appeal under Roman rule. Moreover, they had a history of political involvement during the Maccabean period. Unlike the Essenes, the Pharisees were not monastically inclined.

It is difficult to say with certainty how the Pharisees expected Israel's national destiny to be fulfilled. The rabbinic documents, which generally express a Pharisaic point of view, do not look forward to an *imminent* apocalyptic drama whereby God would bring ordinary history to an end and restore the fortunes of Israel. But the rabbinic literature is not necessarily an accurate guide to Pharisaic expectations during the period of Jesus and the writing of the New Testament books. It reflects the attitude of Judaism after the Roman War and the uprising of Bar Kochba, when disappointed Zealot and revolutionary hopes made apocalyptic and messianic speculations about such matters unattractive. Yet earlier the Pharisees, like the Essenes, probably cherished such apocalyptic and messianic hopes:

> See, Lord, and raise up for them their king, the son of David, to rule over your servant Israel in the time known to you, O God.

---

15. According to Josephus (*The Jewish War,* II, xvii, 3), Pharisees were among the prominent men who attempted to dissuade the revolutionaries who were in the process of launching the rebellion against Rome.

Undergird him with the strength to destroy the unrighteous rulers, to purge
Jerusalem from Gentiles who trample her to destruction. . . .
At his warning the nations will flee from his presence; and he will condemn
sinners by the thoughts of their hearts.[16]

In the intertestamental apocalyptic literature we find the expectation of a
decisive culmination of history. The hope was widely shared. This world or
this age was to come to a conclusion with the restoration of Israel's fortunes
and the resurrection of her righteous dead, marking the inauguration of the
messianic age. After a period of from several hundred to a thousand years,
the general resurrection (that is, of all the dead) would take place as a prelude to the final judgment of God. Then God would usher in the "age to
come," the consummation toward which all history was moving. It is too
much to speak of a single plan or scheme, but the existence of similar ideas
and expectations, if not in systematized form, in the New Testament shows
that they were common currency in the Judaism of Jesus' day.

Apocalyptic and similar ideas were not espoused solely out of patriotic interests and hopes. The doctrine of the resurrection of the dead provided a
lively individual hope and a means of justifying God's ways. If, as experience
dictated, the righteous servants of God's law suffer in this life, they may expect better things when the dead are raised. The doctrine of the resurrection became the hallmark of the Pharisees (cf. Acts 23:6), so that in time a
virtual anathema could be pronounced against those who disbelieved it. Belief in the resurrection appears rarely in the Old Testament, notably in Isaiah
26:19 and Daniel 12:2. Thus it is not surprising that the Sadducees did not
feel obliged to share it. Nevertheless, the New Testament reports that Jesus
(Mark 12:26 f.) as well as Paul (Acts 23:6) believed in the resurrection. In doing so they were following a Pharisaic Jewish tradition.

The whole complex of apocalyptic ideas, including the resurrection of the
dead, the dualism of good and evil, the distinction between this age and the
age to come, and the destruction of evil and the triumph of good in a cataclysmic cosmic upheaval and judgment, cannot be explained fully on the basis of the earlier, Old Testament tradition of Israel, whether historical,
prophetic, or cultic. The apocalyptic frame of mind has marked affinities with
Persian, particularly Zoroastrian, thought. This is especially true of the dualism, cosmic eschatology and the last judgment. To what extent they may reflect direct borrowing or even more subtle influences is debatable, although
such outside influences cannot simply be discounted, especially in view of
the exposure of many Jews to foreign influences in the exile and the diaspora
after the sixth century B.C. But the oppression and frustration of the Jews in
their homeland doubtless provided the necessary seedbed and impetus for

16. Psalm of Solomon 17, in the Pseudepigrapha, has been regarded as typical of Pharisaic
    messianic hope; vss. 23, 24, 27 are quoted. The passage is cited from R. B. Wright's
    translation in J. H. Charlesworth (ed.), *The Old Testament Pseudepigrapha* (Garden City,
    NY: Doubleday, 1985), II, p. 667.

such ideas to develop. In due course this same kind of thinking provided the fertile ground out of which Christianity emerged. For John the Baptist came proclaiming the imminent judgment; Jesus announced the inbreaking of the kingdom of God in power; and the early Christians proclaimed that Jesus had risen from the dead and would come again in glory to render judgment (cf. also Daniel 7). Although Jesus surely felt himself to be a son of Abraham, as did the early Christians generally (cf. Gal. 3:29), and consciously stood in the tradition of the law and the prophets, he was the heir of ideas and perspectives that were unknown to the patriarchs, Moses, or Amos. Some of these were perhaps "foreign" in the sense of being non-Israelite. Yet the substance and framework of Jesus' message had deep roots in his people's history and faith. Apart from the glory and the agony of that history Jesus can scarcely be fully understood. In his insistence on obedience to God's will in the present as the key to the future, Jesus exemplifies Israelite faith. Jesus proposed a reinterpretation of both obedience and hope, but in the indissoluble linking of the two he was a true son of Abraham.

Judaism is history, law, tradition, worship, and the land. But perhaps more than anything else, Judaism is and always has been a people of the covenant—a people with a unique sense of identity and purpose, a chosen people, with all the distinctiveness as well as the dangers that such a concept implies. Our discussion of Judaism has naturally and perhaps inevitably focused upon the major religious groupings of the first century. But, as we have noted, most Jews were probably members of no definable religious group. To the majority of these people, or at least to the less conscientiously pious among them, the term *people of the land (am ha-aretz)* was applied. They were often looked down upon by those who were more scrupulous observers. Quite possibly Jesus himself was numbered among these humble folk (cf. John 7:15); certainly many of his followers were. In the Gospel of John they are described as ignorant of the law and accursed (7:49). But although frequently disparaged and even ridiculed, such folk were not necessarily unaware of their heritage and identity. This sense of belonging, together with resistance toward the claims of the religious establishment, is reflected in the attitude of Jesus himself. He was clearly aware of his identity as an Israelite, a Jew, yet he reacted sharply against claims of religious superiority. Like Jesus, the earliest Christians were Jews, and only gradually began to think of themselves in any other way.

JESUS WITHIN JUDAISM

How did Jesus and his disciples relate to Jewish history, tradition, and hopes?

Taking for granted that Jesus was a Jew, we must ask how he appeared to his contemporaries in early first-century Judaism. In doing so, we are asking a historical question that is in many respects difficult to answer. Chapter 6 deals with aspects of this question in some detail, but it is useful to make some observations at this point.

Of course, *Jesus Christ* means Jesus the Messiah, for *Christ* is simply the Greek form of the Hebrew (or Aramaic) word *Messiah,* meaning anointed. For nearly two thousand years Christians have understood Jesus to be the Christ, but Jews by definition have rejected that claim. Christians have characteristically assumed that first-century Jews were eagerly awaiting the appearance of the Messiah; however, when Jesus appeared claiming to be that Messiah, these same Jews summarily rejected him. This simple picture, which fits with parts of the New Testament, nevertheless does justice neither to the complexities of the actual situation within Judaism nor to the difficulties in understanding what Jesus, his disciples, and their Jewish contemporaries thought.

In the first place, the modern discovery of ancient Jewish documents such as the Qumran Scrolls and the publication of other ancient Jewish writings of the Pseudepigrapha reveal that there was no single messianic hope to which Jesus' appearance would have corresponded. The Essenes of Qumran apparently expected two Messiahs, a royal and a priestly one. Their future hopes, and the hopes of many other Jews, did not center upon the appearance of a single royal Messiah of Davidic lineage. To speak of *the* messianic hope is to impose Christian categories upon a Judaism that in the first century was more complex. Nevertheless, the affirmation that Jesus was the Messiah would not have been strange to Jewish ears. It belongs in that, and in no other, religious, ethnic, and cultural setting. That is, the Christian affirmation that Jesus was the Christ or Messiah shows that the movement had its origin in Judaism, because in no other setting would such a term or title have been used.

Beyond this, the common Christian belief that Jesus himself claimed to be the Messiah must also be subjected to careful scrutiny (see pp. 237–245). The general assumption that he did is based largely on his statements in the Gospel of John, where Jesus speaks frequently about himself, his messianic (or divine) prerogatives, and his unique role. The Synoptics, however, present a different picture, for in these Gospels Jesus' own proclamation or teaching centers upon the inbreaking kingdom of God, and he speaks relatively rarely of himself. Although in the Synoptics Jesus is an authoritative figure who believes that God has sent him on a mission of crucial and epoch-making significance, he is at the same time remarkably terse at the point of defining his own function or role. In the Gospel of Mark (8:27–30) he comes close to rejecting the title Messiah (cf. also Matt. 26:64; Luke 22:70). Naturally, Christians, who by definition believed Jesus was the Messiah, would attribute that belief to him, and we see this happening in the New Testament itself. Still, as in the case of the messianic hope, when we look more closely we find that the situation is less simple than it at first appears. Even if we find that Jesus believed himself to be the Messiah, it is necessary to ask what he would have understood that title to mean for his conduct and ministry.

In Chapter 6 Jesus is presented as one who healed, taught, suffered, and died. Such activities and such a fate do not correspond well with Jewish messianic hopes as we know them. Nevertheless, each of those aspects of his career is intelligible within the setting of early first-century Palestinian Judaism; moreover, there is little reason to doubt that the traditions pertaining to these activities are rooted in the ministry of Jesus himself, whatever his self-perception or messianic consciousness may have been.

As a healer, Jesus falls into a category of persons well known in antiquity. Their existence in Palestinian Judaism at the time of Jesus is attested in ancient sources.[17] Whatever one makes of the means and effects such persons used and achieved, large numbers of people were impressed. Indeed, contemporary religion has its share of faith healers and faith healing, and the number of people who believe that such healings take place can be numbered in the millions. This observation is not meant to pass judgment on Jesus' healings or to lump him with other practitioners, whether ancient or modern, but to point out that in this respect Jesus belongs within a broad category of persons to whom others have ascribed powers of healing. It is beyond question that Jesus was so regarded by his contemporaries, even by those who opposed him, and in all probability, his miraculous healing powers first attracted attention to him, as the Gospels indicate (Mark 1:45).

Perhaps most modern Christians and others who revere Jesus, when they think of his activities, regard him first of all as a teacher or preacher. The Gospel of Mark presents him as beginning his ministry preaching (1:14) and teaching (1:21), and the other Gospels follow suit (Matt. 4:23; Luke 4:14; cf. John 3:2). The image of Jesus as a teacher is historically accurate, but to understand his teaching we must see him against his contemporary Jewish background. What would he have assumed that everyone knew and believed? Certainly the authority of the law as the scriptural expression of God's will was of central importance. What would other Jews and Jewish groups or parties have thought of him and his teaching? Jesus is frequently portrayed as arguing with other Jews, especially Pharisees and scribes, and their disputes concern matters of obedience to God's will. Hence they debate questions of law, that is, basically questions of scriptural interpretation, inasmuch as the ancient Jews regarded scripture as the source of God's word and law. The questions concerned what it meant and how it was to be applied. In the Gospels Jesus sharply disputes traditional modes of understanding and interpretation (see Mark 2:23–28; 10:2–9; John 7:19–24). But such highly charged discussions do not put Jesus outside Judaism; rather, they confirm that he belongs within a Jewish context, where such disputation about the meaning and application of God's law was characteristic and common.

The distinctive feature of Jesus' teaching was his proclamation about the kingdom of God (see pp. 224–233). In some important sense Jesus looked for the manifestation or coming of God's kingly rule on earth, although his statements about the kingdom's appearance present a variety of perspectives that

---

17. See Geza Vermes, *Jesus the Jew: A Historian's Reading of the Gospels* (London: Collins, 1973), pp. 58–82.

are not easy to hold together. Nevertheless, Jesus' proclamation of the kingdom is most important for understanding him. It lends to his mission and message a center and sense of urgency that we perceive as characteristic of him. Mark aptly writes that Jesus began his ministry announcing that the kingdom of God was at hand (1:15).

That Jesus suffered and died was a central affirmation of the earliest Christian belief and preaching (1 Cor. 15:3). It is also a historical fact, and one that brings Jesus into closest relation with the Roman authorities who ruled Palestine at the time, as well as his fellow Jews. Pontius Pilate, the Roman governor, earned for himself a place in history (and infamy) by presiding over the execution of the world's most famous victim of capital punishment. Exactly what forces led to Jesus' execution is an important question, one that historians debate. Historically, most Christians have believed that Jesus was rejected by the Jews, who took offense at his messianic claims and his radical views of the law, turning him over to the Romans for execution. If Pilate is regarded as the unwitting tool of Jesus' Jewish opponents, that representation owes something to the Gospels themselves. In all probability, the historical facts, as far as they can be recovered, present a much less clear, more ambiguous picture. Certainly not all Jews in Jerusalem, much less the entire Jewish nation, were involved in the trial, condemnation, and execution of Jesus. Quite possibly the Jewish temple authorities, who exercised considerable power delegated to them by Rome, opposed Jesus as a dangerous threat to the status quo, and hence to their status (cf. John 11:47–50). Moreover, if Jesus could be presented to the Romans as one who had claimed messianic, i.e., kingly, authority, the Romans would have been all too glad to put him out of the way.

Jesus lived and died a Jew. In a real sense his death was the consequence of his unswerving allegiance to the God of Israel at a time when his people lived under foreign, and sometimes oppressive, dominion. His disciples were, of course, Jews, and, as far as we can tell, they continued to regard themselves as such. His own brother James became an important figure in the early church (Acts 15; Gal. 2) and apparently represented and led that wing of the new community that strongly affirmed its Jewishness. But the early Christian movement spread across the Mediterranean world, making most of its converts among people who never had been, and would not become, Jews. The story of Jesus and of his first followers is, however, inextricably tied, to and rooted in, the Judaism of the land of Israel.

The Greco-Roman World

Judaism provided the ingredients from which the new faith took shape. The pilgrimage and travail of Israel, its scriptures and its expectations, furnished the essential frame of reference for Jesus and his earliest followers. Yet Christianity soon broke away from Judaism and spread rapidly among Gentiles

Ancient Roman theater capable of seating more than three thousand people. It stands in Amman, Jordan, on the site of the ancient (63 B.C.) Decapolis city of Philadelphia. *(Courtesy of Pan American Airways.)*

throughout the Mediterranean world. In a sense, it became a universal form of Judaism. But how and why did this happen to the sect of Jesus' followers in particular? The answer to this question remains in part a mystery. Nevertheless, some valid reasons can be discerned by observing the conditions of the world into which Christianity spread.

LANGUAGE AND CULTURE

What was the lasting importance of Alexander the Great?

Several hundred years before the beginning of the Christian era, in about the third century B.C., the Hebrew scriptures were translated into Greek. This important version is known as the Septuagint. According to an ancient legend found in the Epistle of Aristeas (see the Glossary), the translation was made by seventy-two Jewish elders, working in Egypt for the royal library, because of scholarly appreciation for the importance of the books. In all probability, however, the translation was made on the initiative and for the benefit of the Jews themselves, most of whom could by then read and understand Greek better than their ancestral Hebrew tongue.

ALEXANDER THE GREAT

The Jews had become widely scattered in Egypt and other places as a result of the Exile. They spoke Greek largely because of the remarkable influence of one man, Alexander of Macedon. Few individuals have had a greater impact upon the history, culture, and religion of the world than Alexander. Born in 356 B.C., he succeeded to the throne of his father, Philip of Macedon, in 334. Two years later he set out from his home in Macedonia to begin the conquest of the Persian Empire, which for years had menaced and invaded Greece. In eight years, he and his army swept as far south as Egypt and as far east as the Indus River at the westernmost reaches of India, where only logistics and the homesickness of his soldiers halted his advance. Although the Persian Empire and army proved ineffective against the more homogeneous and better disciplined army of Alexander, his military accomplishment cannot be minimized. Courageous, capable of brutality, but at times humanely sensitive, he ranks as one of the great military leaders of all time.

Of greater importance than military feats, however, was the cultural revolution that he accomplished. Alexander was not only a soldier but also a man of letters and a student of Aristotle. He intended to establish Greek culture and language in the areas that he conquered, and his success in this respect was remarkable. Alexander's conquests created genuine cultural mixtures throughout the ancient world, with the Hellenic (Greek) element as the common factor everywhere. This achievement was exemplified in the fact that he and his soldiers took women of the East as wives. Following his conquest he seemed content to remain there, and apparently regarded Babylon as his capital. But after a short stay, quite unexpectedly, he died of a fever in 323 B.C. at the age of thirty-three, leaving no legal heir capable of succeeding him. His lieutenants struggled for control of his empire and soon managed to pull it apart. Thus the fruit of his military conquest, although immense, proved ephemeral, for his empire dissolved almost as quickly as it had emerged.

Although Alexander did not succeed in establishing a Macedonian empire that would survive his death, his efforts to spread Greek language and culture and to embed them in the life of the East proved highly successful, especially in the cities. As his heritage he left a string of Greek cities across the area of his conquest, outposts of Greek civilization. Probably the largest and most successful of these was the great Egyptian center of Alexandria, which appropriately bore his name. Here a large colony of Jews settled, and the first and most important translation of the Hebrew scriptures into Greek was made.

Alexander created for the first time one far-flung cultural world, and momentarily a political world as well. His conquests made it possible to conceive of humanity as a unity, and perhaps Alexander himself viewed the world and its people in that way. His view of himself and his mission can only be inferred from his deeds. He sought out divine oracles in that connection and gladly received divine honors. Such honors were reserved only for gods in Greece, but in the East were often accorded powerful rulers. It is tempting to see in Alexander one who thought of himself as a son of God destined to unify humanity. Possibly he did, although we cannot safely draw such a conclusion from the evidence. In any event, Alexander's role as well as his accomplishments sowed seeds that later came to fruition in the worldwide Christian movement.

THE GREEK LANGUAGE

Alexander gave a particular form and character to the world into which Christianity was born. Nothing is more important for history and culture than language, and nothing promotes communication and understanding like a common language. Among other things, Alexander bequeathed to the Mediterranean world a common language, Greek. It was not the Greek of Plato or Sophocles, but another newer and somewhat simpler dialect known as *koine,* or common, Greek. This Greek became the *lingua franca* of the ancient world three hundred years before the time of Christ.

People from widely separated areas and with vastly different backgrounds could talk to each other in Greek. Perhaps they could not construct complex Greek sentences with perfect syntax and inflection, but they could make themselves understood. Needless to say, this gift of common speech was of considerable importance in encouraging commerce and various sorts of interchange throughout the Alexandrian world. Indeed, in the centers of Greek culture established by Alexander, conscious attempts were made to promote and spread the manners and customs of Hellenic civilization, especially the athletic games. The world that Alexander left was one world in a sense that it had never been before. Previously there had been great overarching empires such as the Assyrian, the Persian, and the Egyptian, and certainly different peoples and cultures had interacted; yet never before had there been such an attempt to create a common world civilization as was actually and purposefully brought about by Alexander and his successors. This mixture of Hellenic (Greek) and Oriental elements is called Hellenistic civilization.

The importance of this universal Mediterranean civilization for Judaism and its offspring Christianity can scarcely be overestimated. For Judaism it was at once a challenge and a benefit—a challenge in that it threatened just those distinguishing features of life that characterized the Jewish community as such, but a benefit in that it made possible greater extension of the scope and influence of Judaism, especially Greek-speaking Judaism. For Christianity it was an immense boon. Without Alexander the rapid spread of Christianity throughout the Greco-Roman world might never have taken place. Certainly the Christian message had a power of its own, and its impact can-

The magnificent ruins of a temple to Olympian Zeus in Athens.   *(Courtesy of Greek Press and Information Service.)*

not be attributed to favorable cultural factors alone. Nevertheless, it is a striking fact that the spread of Christianity in the first centuries occurred principally in those areas that fell under the sway of Alexander's, or at least of Greek, influence.

The New Testament itself was composed entirely in Hellenistic Greek, although the Gospels are in part based on earlier Aramaic sources, either written or oral. Except in Palestine and Syria, and perhaps to some extent even there, the preaching of the gospel was in Greek. In most places of any importance Greek was the language that was spoken and understood by both preacher and hearer. Even in Rome, to which Christianity spread at a very early time and which we generally associate with the Latin language, Greek was generally spoken and understood by cultured people. Yet despite the important role that Greek language and culture played in its spread, it would be incorrect to call Christianity simply a Greek religion. Viewed from the standpoint of its origin and original constituents, it is also Oriental and especially Jewish. It is not, therefore, the purely Greek element, but precisely this combination of Greek and Jewish, West and East, that was characteristic of Christianity in the Hellenistic world.

GOVERNMENT

How did the Roman Empire enable Christianity to spread so rapidly?

Alexander created a world but did not live to govern it. That task was ultimately performed by Rome. It is, of course, true that the limits of Alexander's conquests and those of the Roman Empire at its height were not the same. Alexander's conquests extended farther to the east, whereas the Roman Empire's orbit stretched far beyond Italy to the north and west. Yet in a sense the worlds of Alexandrian Hellenism and of Rome were one world.[18] Through conquest of Greece and wholesale appropriation of Greek culture in the second century B.C., Rome fell heir to the legacy of Greece just when the empire was emerging as the dominant military force and political power of the Western world. For a half-century before Christ and nearly half a millennium after, the Roman Empire gave to the Mediterranean world a political unity and stability. That unity, though not unbroken, was as continuous and dependable as any so large and varied a segment of the world has known before or since. The marvel is not that the Roman Empire fell—crumbled is the better word—but that it stood so long. At the time of its greatest extent and vitality—that is, during the New Testament period—the Roman Empire stretched from Syria and Palestine to the British Isles. Of western Europe, only Germany and the Scandinavian countries remained outside the Roman orbit, and only Scandinavia completely outside. The southern and westernmost parts of Germany came under Roman domination, as did Austria as far north as the Danube.

The birth and development of Christianity as a world religion came about during the two centuries when Rome was at the zenith of its power (i.e., from 27 B.C., the accession date of Augustus Caesar, to A.D. 180, the year of the death of Marcus Aurelius, the philosopher emperor). This period, often referred to as the *pax romana* (Roman peace), was a favorable time for the origin of a movement like Christianity. There was enforced peace and internal order. Our present Western systems of law owe more directly to the Romans than to the Hebrews, and the *pax romana* was a time of lawfulness as well as peace. The Romans administered the empire with firmness, occasionally with brutality, but with a certain sensitivity for the varieties of people and customs within their bounds. Local law enforcement and administration were left in the hands of local officials. Where local administration or law enforcement broke down, as in the case of Judea at the time of Jesus, the Romans intervened to make sure that anarchy did not result. Roman officials were not universally good, as we have already noted. Pontius Pilate, for example, left a great deal to be desired. Yet the Romans themselves

---

18. The great classical historian M. Rostovtzeff regarded the culture of the Roman Empire as basically Greek: see *A History of the Ancient World,* I: *The Orient and Greece,* trans. J. D.Duff (Oxford: Clarendon, n.d.), pp. 281 f.

removed Pilate from power. Although it is true that Jesus died on a Roman cross and that Christians were persecuted by Romans, it is equally true, and probably just as important, that early Christianity benefited considerably from the relatively peaceful and lawful conditions of Roman rule that accompanied its beginnings.

Early Christianity profited also from the network of roads and sea transportation that the Romans had developed and maintained, largely for military purposes. Again, policing of the roads was left to the various provinces and localities as long as they could do the job, but when and where conditions demanded, the Roman military intervened to keep roads open for travel and free of bandits and other potential harassments. It would certainly be wrong to imagine that travel in ancient times was as easy as it is today. Yet travel between virtually all parts of the empire was possible, and it was easier to go from Jerusalem to Rome in Paul's day than it was to travel from the East Coast to California in this country 150 years ago.

Thus favorable conditions of language and culture as well as an orderly government and a workable transportation system favored the spread of the Christian gospel in the Greco-Roman world. They help to explain the rapid growth of the church and the ways in which the gospel found expression—not the least of which is the New Testament itself, a collection of books written in Greek, and in many cases written from one Christian or group of Christians to or for another. These documents attest not only a lively faith but also a sense of tangible relationship between one Christian church and another, which was made possible by the conditions of the time. Moreover, they display a concrete sense of mission to the inhabited world (Greek, *oikoumēne*), a concept not previously unknown but given particular point and form by the vision and work of Alexander the Great and the political reality of the Roman Empire.

Although the classical age of the Greek city-state preceded the time of Alexander and the establishment of his empire, the form of the Hellenistic city persisted into the time of the rise of Christianity and beyond. This urban atmosphere that featured local political control, temples to the various gods, citizens' assemblies for discussion and debate, the gymnasium for instruction of the young, and stadiums for athletic games provided the matrix for the rise of the Christian faith. The missionary endeavors of Paul and others within this religious, social, and political synthesis were made possible by common language, political stability, and the accessibility of these cities—some of which had been newly created. At the same time, the spiritual ferment of the times provided an openness to religious messages from a variety of sources, including the early Christians. Consequently, early Christians declared their message in this urban setting, even though the origins of Jesus and the first disciples were much less cosmopolitan.

Within the Hellenistic city the house or household played a central role. It was much larger than the modern nuclear family—perhaps more like the extended family of several generations ago, consisting of more than one or two generations of kinspeople. Moreover, it also included household employees and slaves. The head of the household was of necessity a relatively affluent and influential person. The household provided not only a residence but also an important mode of social identity, and even a livelihood for a number of persons who would have otherwise lacked such essentials of everyday life.

The conversion of the head of a household was a major coup for the early Christians. For one thing it would enormously increase the likelihood of the conversion of other members of the household. Religion was less a matter of individual, personal choice in the ancient world than it is in contemporary society. Nevertheless, Christianity by its very nature introduced an element of individual decision. One had to confess faith (Rom. 10:10; 1 Cor. 12:3) and be baptized (Acts 8:36). Even if one's householder or master were converted, one might remain an unbeliever. This seems to have been the case with Onesimus, whom Paul later converted and sent back a Christian to his master Philemon (Philem. 15–17).

Moreover, the conversion of the head of a household meant that the church acquired a place of worship. Paul speaks of several such householders who were hosts to the churches he founded or knew (Rom. 16:3–5, 23). We tend to think of a church primarily as a building. But there were no such buildings available for the earliest Christians. Upon reaching a new city, Paul may have preached initially in synagogues, as Acts portrays him, and perhaps he occasionally even hired a public hall (cf. Acts 19:9); but the principal meeting place of Christian cells or churches was the private home. Thus the householder, who could provide such a place of meeting, was a most important convert for the Christian community.

RELIGION

How did Christianity differ from other religions in the Greco-Roman world?

According to the book of Acts, the apostle Paul began his famous speech to the Athenians by saying, "Athenians, I see how extremely religious you are in every way" (17:22). Indeed, the world of New Testament times was a religious world; thus Christianity did not originate in a time of religious decline. Whatever may have been the general state of culture in the first century, religion did not lack vitality and vigorous manifestations.

A striking characteristic of the religious situation was its variety. This too is represented in Paul's speech, for he mentions the objects of their worship, among which is an altar inscribed to an unknown god, as if the Athenians were taking no chances on omitting, and therefore offending, any deity. People participated in various rites and ceremonies according to law, taste, or desire. The period was also marked by syncretism: various religious traditions merged together or were interpreted in terms of one another.

Such toleration did not mean that people by and large did not take religion seriously. If anything, just the opposite was the case. Only from the Christian or Jewish point of view would this toleration of, and participation in, a multiplicity of religious cults be taken as idolatry. The exclusivism of Judaism and Christianity was itself regarded as odd and even impious in ancient times, and the refusal of Christians and Jews to worship any god other than their own led their neighbors to brand them as atheists. This persistence in worshiping only one God was perhaps the factor that most clearly distinguished Christians and Jews in the ancient world, and it may have had something to do with the fact that of the religions of that civilization, only Christianity and Judaism survive today. Yet elements of these other religions have survived in Judaism and particularly in Christianity. For example, the date of Jesus' birth is unknown; Christmas is the Christianized version of an ancient Roman rite celebrating the winter solstice and return of the sun. Easter is a distinctly Christian holiday, but rabbits and eggs are pagan intrusions.

The specific manifestations of piety in the Greco-Roman world are far too numerous to discuss here fully. Nevertheless, it is helpful to notice several basic types of religion that were popular and significant. These include the traditional and official religions of the Greco-Roman pantheon (a Greek word meaning a temple dedicated to "all the gods"), the state-inspired worship of the ruler, the more individualistic mystery religions, as well as Gnosticism, and Hellenistic Judaism. Within and against this background, early Christianity emerged.

TRADITIONAL AND OFFICIAL RELIGION

At the time of the emergence of Christianity and the writing of the New Testament books, the traditional religion of the Roman Empire was a complex and somewhat amorphous combination of both Greek and Roman elements. Prior to the Christian era there had been a distinctly Roman religious cult involving especially the gods of the hearth and the family, of which the public religion was an extension and enlargement. This state or city cult was presided over first by the king, and later by a pontifical college made up of several prominent men of the realm. Ancient Greek religion of the pre-Christian period seems to have consisted originally of a variety of local deities, each with a holy place. These were later submerged under, or incorporated into, the pantheon of very human gods known to us from Homer, who is the fountainhead of classical mythology. By the beginning of the Christian period an amalgamation of Greek and Roman deities had taken place. It was taken for granted that the Greek and Roman gods were for the most part actually the same gods, even if they had different names, and an equation of the various gods of the Homeric pantheon with Roman gods had been worked out. For example, the three prominent Greek gods, Zeus, Hera, and Athena, were identified with the Roman Jupiter, Juno, and Minerva, respectively. Moreover, the purely Greek god Apollo was worshiped on the Palatine Hill in Rome.

By the beginning of the Christian era the traditional piety of Greece and Rome was facing competition from newer religions, especially those of Oriental origin, which were gaining enthusiastic adherents. Moreover, people

of some education and intelligence had difficulty taking the myths and stories that were told about the gods seriously, at least insofar as they were understood as literal accounts of what actually took place or of the nature of
divine reality. Folk of a philosophical bent, especially the Stoics, had been interpreting the myths in an allegorical way for some time. That is, they took
them to be narrative representations of philosophical truths, which really had
nothing to do with the stories per se and could stand independently of them.
Thus the old gods got a new lease on life. For example, Zeus, the head of the
Homeric pantheon, could be identified with "the general law, which is right
reason, pervading everything . . . the Supreme Head of the universe" (Zeno,
Fragments, 162, 152).[19] The Stoic monism, according to which God or the
logos (Greek for *word* or *reason*) pervades the universe much as the soul or
animation pervades the body and gives it unity and purpose, was thereby reconciled with a mythology that had quite a different origin and meaning. Especially those stories of the gods consorting and cavorting with each other
in ways that sober people came to regard as shameful were allegorized away,
making room for the Stoic ethic, which centered in willing conformity with
that reason or logos that governs the universe and the individual. The Stoics themselves, however, were not coldly rationalistic. Philosophy was for
them a vital piety, as it was for many literate Greeks. Although such piety
might be grounded in a philosophical pantheism, its expression often took
the form of hymns and prayers to a personal God, as can be seen from a portion of Cleanthes' famous *Hymn to Zeus:*

> Thou, O Zeus, art praised above all gods; many are thy names and thine is all
>   power for ever.
> The beginning of the world was from thee; and with law thou rulest over all
>   things.
> Unto thee may all flesh speak; for we are thy offspring.
> Therefore will I raise a hymn unto thee: and will ever sing of thy power.
> The whole order of the heavens obeyeth thy word: as it moveth around the
>   earth:
> With little and great lights mixed together: how great art thou, King above all for
>   ever![20]

The ancient Greco-Roman religion survived not merely in Stoic reinterpretation but also in more naive popular worship. As such, it remained the
traditional public religion of the Roman Empire, just as its predecessors had
been the official cults of old Rome and of the Greek city-states. We find some
indication of its survival in the New Testament. According to Acts the people
of Lystra, in what is now Asia Minor, hailed Paul and Barnabas as Hermes and
Zeus, respectively, upon their performance of a miracle. Moreover, a temple
of Zeus was located near that city (Acts 14:12 f.). There was in the city of Eph-

19. Cited from C. K. Barrett, *The New Testament Background: Selected Documents,* rev. ed.
    (San Francisco: Harper & Row, 1989), p. 67.
20. Ibid., p. 67.

Head of Augustus (Gaius Julius Caesar Octavianus), first Roman emperor (27 B.C.–A.D. 14).   *(Courtesy of Metropolitan Museum of Art, Rogers Fund, 1908.)*

esus a great temple of Artemis (cf. Acts 19:23 ff.), the ruins of which have been unearthed in modern times by archaeologists, as have many other temples to the Greco-Roman deities. In addition, the Roman emperor Augustus, who was ruling at the time Jesus was born, made a serious effort to promote the traditional public cult, especially the ancient Roman practices and ceremonies. Upon the death of the high priest, he went so far as to assume that office himself, reviving a custom long fallen into disuse, according to which the kingship and high priesthood were united in one man.

There was an increasing tendency to regard the emperor as a divine figure and to place him among the pantheon of gods to whom worship was due. Although Augustus coyly spurned divine honors during his lifetime, they were accorded him upon his death. By the end of the first century, it was no longer a question of ascribing divine honors and worship to deceased emperors. Now such veneration was required for the living emperor as well. Not surprisingly, this led in due course to a confrontation between the young

Christian church and Rome, for Rome insisted upon emperor worship as a pledge of allegiance—or devotion—to the emperor and thus to the empire. As Pliny, governor of Bithynia in the early second century, writes to the emperor Trajan, "All who denied that they were or had been Christians I considered should be discharged, because they called upon the gods at my dictation and did reverence, with incense and wine, to your image which I had ordered to be brought forward for this purpose. . . ."[21] It was, in fact, a sort of loyalty oath, one that many Christians could not conscientiously take. When emperor worship is seen against the background of the many gods and many lords of the ancient world (cf. 1 Cor. 8:5), however, and when the benefits accruing to humankind from the emperor's rule are recalled, we can understand why the authorities did not regard divine homage as too much to ask of any subject. Moreover, worship of the supreme ruler was not unknown in earlier times.

Even though Hebrew religious tradition clearly separated the king from the divine, the amalgam of Mediterranean culture and religion included an Egyptian religious tradition in which the Pharaoh appeared as divine and immortal. Indeed, Alexander's unification of the Mediterranean world opened the way to a synthesis in which the king could be titled savior, lord, god. Roman emperors were actually slow to press claims of divinity, until under Domitian (81–96) emperor worship was made a test of loyalty to Rome. Then Christians who understood Jesus as the true bearer of such divine titles began to be persecuted for failure to honor the emperor and the empire. The Romans were perplexed to find peoples who stubbornly refused to participate in emperor worship—the people of Israel who declared their allegiance to the one God of Abraham, Isaac, and Jacob and the people of the new covenant who declared themselves a messianic community.

POPULAR RELIGION

Although the official religious rites of Greece and Rome were by no means dead at the beginning of the Christian era, they did not represent the principal form of personal piety. Their continued existence, and whatever vitality they had, was probably due largely to the role they played in expressing the political and cultural solidarity of the Roman Empire and the Greco-Roman world. No sustained and systematic attempt was made to establish public religion to the exclusion of private practices and societies, however, and it is in the latter that the burgeoning variety and strength of religion in later antiquity can be most clearly seen.

Unfortunately, our knowledge of these practices and societies is quite limited, owing in no small measure to the aura of secrecy that surrounded many of them. This is especially true of the *mystery religions,* which were gaining in prominence and popularity at the beginning of the Christian era. The vows

---

21. From Henry Bettenson (ed.), *Documents of the Christian Church,* 2nd ed. (New York: Oxford University Press, 1963), p. 3.

of secrecy taken by the followers of these religions were meticulously observed. Much of the ancient material on the mysteries comes to us second-hand through Christian and Jewish sources. Consequently, we do not know in detail, or with a high degree of assurance, what they were like.

The most closely guarded secrets of the mystery religions were their rites of initiation, through which the novitiate first received the benefits that the cult deity bestowed. Apparently the candidate somehow reenacted or saw reenacted the cult myth—that is, the story about the god or gods on which the cult was based. Through participation in the cult ritual the candidate received the salvation that was the very reason for the cult's being.

Perhaps the best account of the mystery ritual is found in Apuleius, *The Golden Ass* (xi, 22–26), from which the following, deliberately vague description of an Isis initiation is taken:

> Then behold the day approached when as the sacrifice of dedication should be done; and when the sun declined and evening came, there arrived on every coast a great multitude of priests, who according to their ancient order offered me many presents and gifts. Then was all the laity and profane people commanded to depart, and when they had put on my back a new linen robe, the priest took my hand and brought me to the most secret and sacred place of the temple. . . . Thou shalt understand that I approached near unto hell, even to the gates of Proserpine, and after that I was ravished throughout all the elements, I returned to my proper place: about midnight I saw the sun brightly shine, I saw likewise the gods celestial and the gods infernal, before whom I presented myself and worshipped them. Behold now have I told thee, which although thou hast heard, yet it is necessary that thou conceal it; wherefore this only will I tell, which may be declared without offence for the understanding of the profane.[22]

The myth of the cult naturally varied with the different mystery religions. Among others, there were the Eleusinian mysteries of Greece; the cult of Attis and Cybele, originating in Asia Minor; as well as that of Isis and Osiris, which had its origin in Egypt. Most of the cults were based originally upon fertility rites celebrating the return of the growing season. In time, however, the meaning of the cult myth was seen against the background of human life and death, so that through initiation into the mysteries one could assure oneself of a happy destiny beyond death. Scholars once confidently asserted that the common factor in the cult myths was the death and resurrection of a deity, in which the initiate participated vicariously through the rites and thus rose from the dead with the god (cf. Rom. 6:1–11). This interpretation has been subject to dispute, but it is probably not completely misleading. Even though early Christian belief in the death and resurrection of Jesus was not based on the cult myths of the mystery religions, it found a kind of parallel there. Thus people could recognize in Christianity, as in the mysteries, an important dimension of personal salvation.

22. Cited from Barrett, *The New Testament Background,* pp. 127 f.

The god Mithras is kneeling on a prostrate bull, drawing back its head and stabbing it behind the shoulder with a short sword. A dog and a snake are springing up to drink the blood of the victim. A scorpion seizes the scrotum with its claws. Mithras was the Persian solar deity, whose worship became popular at the close of the Roman Republic. Many similar groups, all probably of the Roman period, have been found in different parts of the Roman Empire. 2nd Cent. A.D. (?). *(Courtesy of the British Museum.)*

The traditional religions of Greece and Rome, like the religion of Israel, had focused primarily upon the ordering of life in this world, and did not promise the adherent a glorious life after death. The mysteries, however, appealed to human hopes and fears in the face of death and offered to those who became initiates the promise of eternal life. Membership in them presumed a belief in their efficacy and required a conscious act of the will, a decision. Thus the mystery religions had a character decidedly different from the traditional official religions and in some respects not unlike Christianity. That is, they were private, they were oriented around hope and assurance for the future, and they were voluntary. To some outsiders, early Christianity may have seemed to be a mystery cult. Unlike Judaism and Christianity, however, the mysteries did not claim the exclusive loyalty of their adherents. A person might worship Zeus and the emperor and at the same time be an initiate of one or more mysteries. In fact, the official religions and the mysteries were complementary; they applied to different spheres of life, the one to public order and morality, the other to the need for emotional satisfaction and the assurance of present and ultimate security of one's personal being and destiny. Thus several Roman emperors, including Augustus, were initiated into the Eleusinian mysteries.

At some time after the mystery religions moved into the center of the stage, there appeared another important spiritual phenomenon that was in some ways like them. We say "phenomenon" for it is not quite certain that *Gnosticism* should be called a religion. It was found in various places and in various forms. Until fairly recently most of our knowledge of Gnosticism came from Christian writers of the late second, third, and later centuries, all of whom portray Gnosticism as a Christian heresy in which a special knowledge (Greek *gnōsis*—hence the name Gnosticism) is made the key to salvation. Such a description is not entirely inaccurate. The process of salvation in Gnosticism involves, first of all, a knowledge or sense of one's profound alienation from the world. Thus one must find a way out of imprisonment in this world and into the world above. This release can be accomplished only by a special dispensation of knowledge by which the secrets of the way back to one's heavenly home are divulged. In Christian Gnostic systems Jesus is the heavenly revealer who awakens the adherents from their stupor in this world, reminds them of their heavenly home, reveals the secrets of the way, and also leads them back. The way back was often conceived as a rather long road, a tortuous climb back through the seven or more heavens, in each of which the Gnostics shed another part of the veil of flesh until the divine essence— the very quintessence of their being—arrived safely home.

Gnosticism was once regarded as the acute Hellenization of Christianity, a distorted translation of the Christian message into Greek ways of thinking and speaking. Yet recent research and discoveries have shown that Gnosticism is not simply derived from Christianity, and that it owes more to the East, to Syria, Persia, and Babylonia, and perhaps even to Judaism, than to classical Greek culture. (In this respect it is not unlike the mystery religions, many of which came from the Orient.) The exact nature and origin of Gnosticism are still obscure, however, and remain matters of controversy among historians of religion.

We can, nevertheless, get a fairly clear grasp of the thrust and meaning of Gnosticism. Wherever it appears, in whatever form, it is characterized by an extreme dualism of God and the world. In contrast to the Stoic monism, in which God and the world are essentially related and, indeed, indwell one another, Gnosticism takes God and the world to be separate and incompatible. Far from being the creation of the one God, as in orthodox Jewish and Christian thought, this world is at best an excrescence from the divine world, at worst the creation of an antigod. Its very existence is the antithesis of God's salvation. The mystery religions were primarily motivated by a desire to secure human existence in the face of death. Gnosticism also had this goal in view, but combined with it an abhorrence of evil, which was in general identified with this world and its history.

According to Gnosticism, people live in the world, but at least some of them are not of it. For while human bodies are made of the same substance as the world, there is, or may be, hidden within each one a spark of the divine life. Salvation is then the rescuing of the divine spark from its imprisonment in the material world, and specifically in the flesh. The first and essential step is the recognition that one is not at home in this world, that one's essential being is related to the divine world and can find its way home.[23]

> Therefore if one has knowledge he is from above. If he is called, he hears, he answers, and he turns to him who is calling him, and ascends to him. And he knows in what manner he is called. Having knowledge, he does the will of the one who called him, he wishes to be pleasing to him, he receives rest. Each one's name comes to him. He who is to have knowledge in this manner knows where he comes from and where he is going. He knows as one who having become drunk has turned away from his drunkenness, [and] having returned to himself, has set right what are his own.[24]

This concept of salvation had its practical effects upon the life of the Gnostics, who felt themselves to be alien, and, in a sense, already withdrawn from the concerns of ordinary human life. This estrangement sometimes expressed itself in radical withdrawal from the world and its life, that is, asceticism. But it could also result in a free indulgence in sensual pleasure; because the flesh and the physical world had no significance, what one did with them was of no importance. Whichever course was followed, the Gnostic refused any positive, constructive participation in this human life, which was regarded so highly by the deluded non-Gnostic.

Early Christianity was deeply engaged with the Gnostic problem throughout the second century, and probably even earlier. In the Gospel of John Jesus says, "Those who love their life lose it, and those who hate their life in this world will keep it for eternal life" (12:25; cf. Mark 8:35), certainly a gnosticizing statement about the nature and sphere of salvation. Compared with Jewish hopes of the restoration of Davidic kingship, important aspects of early Christian hope seem closer to Gnosticism. Thus we see traces of the contact and conflict with Gnosticism not only in the Gospel of John but in

23. A similar point of view is found in a set of documents known as the Hermetic literature, or Hermetica. In their present form, these documents date from about the third century. They are not Christian, although they may have been influenced by Judaism. Whether they ought to be called Gnostic is a debated point. See Barrett, *The New Testament Background,* pp. 93–103, for examples from the Hermetica.

24. Gospel of Truth, 22:3–20; from George MacRae's translation in *The Nag Hammadi Library in English,* J. M. Robinson (ed.), 3rd rev. ed. (San Francisco: Harper & Row, 1988), p. 42.

the Johannine letters, Colossians, and the Pastoral Epistles, as well as the extensive anti-Gnostic literature that appears from the time of Justin Martyr in the middle of the second century. In addition, a large collection of Gnostic literature going back to the second century (although the actual manuscripts are somewhat later) has in this century been uncovered in Nag Hammadi in southern Egypt. It was obviously used by people who considered themselves Christians. Some of the books, such as the Gospel of Truth and the Gospel of Thomas, are apparently Gnostic interpretations of Christianity. Others have little explicit connection with anything we can identify with Christianity, except that they were apparently used by this Gnostic Christian church.

The discussion of Gnosticism raises the question of what influence it had on the formation of New Testament Christianity. It has been argued that Gnosticism came into being before the Christian faith arose and that when it came into contact with Christianity its doctrine already involved a myth about a redeemer who visited human beings in order to give them the knowledge of life. Some such doctrine is indeed found in the literature of Manichaeism (named for its third-century founder Mani). Mani was obviously influenced by Christianity and Jesus figured in his teaching. It also appears in Mandaeism, the religion of a small Iranian sect that still exists and whose origin and antiquity is a matter of keen dispute. The sharpness and vigor of the modern debate are probably not unrelated to the fact that the Mandaean "redeemer myth" has real similarities to the Christian doctrine of Jesus as the Son of God whom the Father sent into the world, especially as it is set forth in the Gospel of John. Yet the existence of such a myth cannot be documented in sources that clearly antedate Christianity. Nevertheless, the Gnostic perspective or attitude infiltrated Christianity at a very early time, as the New Testament itself shows.

Among the other major religious forces of the first-century Mediterranean world were the philosophical sects, including Pythagoreans, Epicureans, Cynics, and the already mentioned Stoics. The latter two, in addition to advocating reorientation of the moral and spiritual life according to special philosophical–religious tenets, were noted for their itinerant preachers who sought disciples and converts as they traveled from city to city discussing and debating the nature of the good life. Such teachers, who were quite often accompanied by disciples, sought to convince listeners of the evil of this world and to persuade potential converts of the truth of the contemplative, ascetic life. These wandering moralists established a precedent and provided a pattern for early Christian preachers, though the literature of the New Testament attests to the special care with which Christian missionaries sought to distinguish themselves from abuses attributed to such peripatetic philosophers (cf. 1 Thess. 2:9; 1 Cor. 9:4–12; 3 John 6–8). If to some Christianity seemed to be another mystery religion, to others it may have appeared to be another school of popular philosophy (cf. Acts 17:16–21).

There were, of course, other manifestations of belief and what we might call superstition and magic. These we can only note in passing. Many people in the ancient world were fascinated or oppressed by Fate (Greek, *heimarmenē*) or Fortune (Greek, *tyche*). Fortune came to be personalized and venerated as a goddess. The stars were thought to determine the course of people's lives, their fate. As a result, astrology, the "science" dealing with the influence of the stars on life, gained considerable popularity as the key to the secrets of human existence.[25] At the same time, some people relied on magic, invoking on occasion even the names of Yahweh and Jesus. There were also hero cults dedicated to those who had been elevated to the status of gods or demigods. Among these were the healing cult of Asclepius, who claimed many shrines and spas and thousands of devotees who attributed to him miraculous cures no less amazing than those attributed to Jesus in the Gospels. Although early Christians rejected magic (cf. Acts 8:9–24; 19:19), some educated people dismissed the new faith as exactly that—magic and superstition.

DIASPORA JUDAISM

In the complex religious picture of the Greco-Roman world, Judaism was a significant factor. Most Jews did not live in Palestine, but in other parts of that world. As noted previously, this diaspora or dispersion of Jews to the far corners of the world began as early as 587 B.C. with the conquest of Judah and the destruction of Jerusalem by the Babylonians. As conditions within the homeland became more difficult during the later postexilic period and the number of Jews increased, the prospects of living outside Palestine became increasingly attractive.

It is customary and useful to distinguish between the Judaism of the land of Israel and that of the diaspora. Both shared in most of the basic elements of Judaism mentioned at the beginning of this chapter, yet outside Palestine significant change had taken place, much of which resulted from Hellenization. Hellenization, or accommodation to Greek culture, also took place within Palestine, as recent research has made clear.[26] Outside Palestine, however, Judaism of necessity began to take on some of the characteristics of a religion as distinguished from a nation. Nevertheless, the Jewish people succeeded in maintaining their ethnic identity and a certain separateness in their ways and places of living. Yet Jews mingled to some extent with Gentiles, were inevitably influenced by them, and vice versa. Adjustments to life in a predominantly Gentile world became necessary.

As has already been indicated, one of the most important adjustments was in language. Judaism in the Greco-Roman world was largely Greek speaking. The fact that the Hebrew scriptures had been translated into Greek and were read and interpreted in that language doubtless influenced the way in which

---

25. See M. Hengel, *Judaism and Hellenism: Studies in Their Encounter in Palestine during the Hellenistic Period,* trans. J. Bowden (Philadelphia: Fortress, 1974), I, 238–241, who shows Jewish involvement in astrological speculation.
26. Ibid., esp. I, 103–106.

they were understood. Philo of Alexandria, a contemporary of Jesus and Paul, affords a notable, if perhaps extreme, example of the kinds of changes that could take place. A Jew who never once thought of surrendering that hallmark of Judaism, the law, Philo nevertheless interpreted the Hebrew scriptures in terms of Hellenistic philosophy and piety by using the well-established Greek method of allegorizing (see *Allegory* in the Glossary). Thus he could wring meanings from Biblical texts of which the original authors would never have dreamed. Hellenistic Judaism had already produced religious books containing ideas that were more Greek than Jewish. For example, one reads in Wisdom of Solomon 3:1–9 of the immortality of the souls of the righteous dead, a fundamentally Greek idea, quite foreign to the Hebrew scriptures, which has since become rather common in Christian thought.

Another adjustment forced on the Jews by the dispersion involved their public worship. Up until the destruction of the temple of Solomon at Jerusalem, the principal form of worship was sacrificial, officially performed at the Jerusalem temple, though sometimes actually carried out elsewhere, much to the disgust of some prophets and other purists. After the fall of Jerusalem, the destruction of the temple, the deportations, and the flight of refugees, another form of worship began to gain preeminence, that of the synagogue, or individual congregation. In New Testament times synagogues were sprinkled around the Mediterranean world, as well as in Palestine. The Acts of the Apostles portrays Paul (and by implication other Christian missionaries) preaching the gospel in the local synagogue whenever he entered a new town.

The synagogues of the dispersion thus provided a ready-made platform for the early Christians, who, without necessarily ceasing to regard themselves as Jews, brought the good news of God's new salvation in Jesus the Messiah to their fellow Jews and any others who might by chance listen. Inasmuch as new ideas and terms had already crept into the Hellenistic synagogue from the surrounding pagan culture, it need not surprise us to see these also in the New Testament. The New Testament writings, at least in their present form, were addressed to a church that had grown up in the midst of the Hellenistic culture of the Roman Empire. The importance of the Greek-speaking Judaism of the dispersion for early Christianity is epitomized in the fact that the New Testament is written in Greek. Moreover, the Old Testament, which is so frequently cited in the New, is as a rule quoted from the Greek version.

Diaspora Judaism also prepared the way for the universal emphasis and success of the Christian gospel. The Hellenistic synagogue itself did not disdain the missionary enterprise. There is some evidence of a sustained and serious effort to convert Gentiles to Judaism (cf. Matt. 23:15), although Judaism was not focused upon mission and conversion to the extent early Christianity was.[27] And not a few Gentiles were attracted by the antiquity and

27. But see Dieter Georgi, *The Opponents of Paul in Second Corinthians: Religious Propaganda in Late Antiquity* (Philadelphia: Fortress, 1986), esp. pp. 83–151.

moral seriousness of the Jewish religion. The technical term for the conversion of Gentiles was *proselytism* and converts were called *proselytes*. Even where proselytism was not actively pursued, the situation of the Jews in the midst of an alien and potentially hostile culture required that they look outward and have a decent respect for public opinion. One sees such an outward-looking perspective in Philo, and perhaps even more noticeably in the great first-century Jewish historian Josephus. His extensive *Jewish Antiquities* is an elaborate exposition and explanation of the entire history and faith of his people for a literate Gentile audience. It is at once our best single historical source for the so-called intertestamental period and a monumental effort to make Jewish history intelligible to the wider world.

First-century diaspora Judaism was an important movement in and of itself, and it is of an extraordinary significance for the Christianity of New Testament times. For the modern student it illumines the path that Christianity traversed from its beginnings as a sect of Palestinian Judaism to the status of a world religion.

THE EARLY CHRISTIANS

The people by and for whom the New Testament writings were composed were members neither of a Palestinian Jewish sect nor of a world religion. They belonged to a new religious movement that was conscious of its Jewish origins, that took the scriptures of Judaism to be authoritative, and that was often confused with its parent in the variegated religious scene of the first-century Mediterranean world. Remarkably, this confusion benefited the new movement when its preachers were able to use to their advantage the platform provided by the synagogue.

Those who were Jews, whether from Palestine (Peter, James the brother of Jesus) or the Jewish diaspora (the apostle Paul), would continue to think of themselves as such as long as they lived (Gal. 2:15). But they nevertheless became conscious of the fact that most of their fellow believers were Gentiles and that most Jews had not believed that Jesus was the Messiah (Rom. 9:1–5). How matters would resolve themselves, that is, how the division between Jewish believers and the majority would be resolved, was a matter they were willing to leave to the providence of God as they carried forward their mission to the broader, mostly Gentile world (Rom. 11:25–32).

The urgency of that mission was at first motivated by the belief, rooted in Jesus' own proclamation of the kingdom of God, that a decisive turning point in history was just ahead. Jesus would return soon to effect salvation and judgment (1 Thes. 4:13–18; Matt. 25:31–46). This vibrant hope and eager anticipation did not lead to a relaxation of missionary zeal or effort. If anything, the reverse was true. Doubtless the early preachers of the gospel saw in their own success signs of God's favor and evidence of the fulfillment of scriptural prophecy and Jesus' own prophetic words.

The Jesus movement in its inception was both Jewish and Palestinian, and Jesus' own disciples did not organize themselves into a sect or exclusive communities, although they certainly met together (cf. Acts 2:43–47). They were not, properly speaking, a separatist movement. Thus Jesus and his first disciples stood in some contrast to the Essenes or Qumraners who withdrew from other Jews to live in the desert. That this engagement with the world continued to be the case after Jesus' departure may perhaps be inferred from the narratives of the early chapters of the Book of Acts. There the disciples are portrayed as living in Jerusalem, virtually in the shadow of the temple, mingling freely with other Jews as they testify to Jesus. Even when Paul returns to Jerusalem from his missionary work in the Gentile world, the Jerusalem Christian leaders express to him their pride that the many Jewish believers ("how many thousands . . .") are faithful to the law. They are concerned, moreover, about his own reputation for having abandoned it (Acts 21:20–21). Moreover, Acts fails to report that any Jerusalem believers interceded for Paul after his arrest by the Roman authorities; perhaps they regarded his presence as a threat to their solidarity with Israel. Later Christian tradition speaks of James the Just (Jesus' brother) and of the high regard in which he was held by his fellow Jews in Jerusalem, at least until he was murdered in the turbulent years just preceding the outbreak of the Jewish–Roman War (Eusebius, *EH,* II, 23).

Even the apostle Paul never calls the earliest believers *Christians.* Acts reports they were first so called in Antioch (11:26), after they had received Gentiles into their community. Clearly in such Gentile cities the Christians first became aware of their identity as such, and in these environs they found it necessary to organize themselves into separate and distinct associations. Under such circumstances distinctly Christian communities—churches—came into being. It may well be that this happened only, or first, outside the boundaries of historic Israel under circumstances in which Christians wanted a community and an identity distinct from that of the surrounding culture. Acts represents Paul as having preached first in synagogues as he carried the gospel to the cities of the eastern Mediterranean. If so, however, his followers did not remain within the synagogue, that is, within Judaism, but quickly broke away and organized as distinctly Christian churches. This state of affairs may have to do with the fact that Paul's converts were predominantly Gentiles; for Paul thinks of himself as apostle to the Gentiles (Gal. 2:9) and addresses his constituents as if they were, at least for the most part, Gentiles. Even though it has been suggested that the Acts accounts of Paul's going first to synagogues in a new city may not be historically accurate, Paul could have first done that, as Acts says, only to find that his greatest appeal lay outside the synagogue, with Gentile hearers. Moreover, non-Jews, "God-fearers," did attend Jewish synagogues.

Certainly Paul had to face the question of whether Jewish dietary restrictions and other marks of Jewish identity, especially circumcision, were applicable to Gentile converts (Gal. 2:11–16; 5:1–3). As we shall see (pp. 268, 311–314), he emphatically denied that they were. Paul then represents a form of the Christian movement that was in tangible ways breaking away from Judaism. No wonder his missionary work and its effects were regarded with some alarm by more conservative believers in Jerusalem and Judea. Acts quite credibly portrays their fear that Paul's practice would undercut their own acceptance among their fellow Jews (21:20–22; cf. Rom. 15:30–32).

With the exception of Judaism, the religious cults and movements of antiquity are seldom mentioned in the New Testament writings. As one might expect, such specific references as occur are found mostly in the Book of Acts, which recounts Christianity's advance from Jerusalem to Rome by way of Asia Minor (Turkey), the Aegean, and Greece. In Lystra (a city in present-day Turkey) Barnabas and Paul are mistaken for Zeus and Hermes (Acts 14:12). The pagan piety of ancient Athens, with its many objects of worship, is noted by Paul in his address on the Areopagus of that city (17:22–23). The worship of the goddess Artemis, whose great temple stood in Ephesus, becomes a major factor in the opposition Paul encountered there (19:23–41). When the apostles Peter and John visit new converts in Samaria, they encounter the recently baptized Simon, a magician who had already attracted great attention to himself and hoped to increase his powers with the endowment of the Holy Spirit (Acts 8:9–24). The apostles reject him, and it becomes clear that his motives and practice are to be regarded as suspect (8:20–23). Later Christian authors routinely denounce Simon Magus, as they call him, portraying him as the founder and fountainhead of all heresy, especially Gnosticism (see pp. 47–49). To what extent these allegations are based on fact is debatable, for although Acts certainly puts Simon in a bad light, it does not portray him as espousing the typically Gnostic themes and attitudes that appear in later sources.

In the New Testament, pagan piety is characterized in general, if derogatory, ways. The Thessalonians are said to have turned from idols to serve a living and true God (1 Thess. 1:9). The Corinthians are told that when they were heathen (or Gentiles), they were led astray to dumb idols (1 Cor. 12:2). The Galatians' preconversion state is described by Paul as slavery to the elemental spirits *(stoicheia)* of the universe (Gal. 4:3, 9). In 1 Timothy (6:20) believers are warned away from "what is falsely called knowledge" *(gnōsis)* in what may be the earliest specific reference to Gnosticism in Christian sources.

One reads such New Testament references to pagan religions in light of the fact that they have long since passed from the scene and scarcely notes how striking it is that the early Christian writers seemed so confident that would be their fate. Such confidence looks less remarkable now than it must have been then, for at that time the religious life of pagan antiquity still seemed vital and robust. Nevertheless, within a couple of centuries pagan worship was clearly on the wane in the face of the rapid advance of Christianity. When in the early fourth century the Roman emperor Constantine converted to Christianity, the die was cast for the foreseeable future.

With Judaism the situation was notably different. The unbelieving Jew is the source of continual preoccupation in the New Testament, most clearly in such major books as John, Acts, and Romans. It is as if the writers realize that Judaism will remain a factor for Christians to contend with, and vice versa. They deplore the fact that Jews have not believed in Jesus, the one predicted in scriptural prophecy, but do not deny the status accorded them by the reception of scriptural revelation in the first place. Tellingly, when Paul refers to the Corinthians' preconversion state (1 Cor. 12:2) he says they were Gentiles (NRSV: "pagans"), using the Jewish term to describe the uncircumcised. Are they now Jews? Not exactly, but Paul, perhaps unconsciously, assumes that the baptized believers stand with Jews over against the pagan or heathen world.

The fact that the Jesus movement developed in the direction of a distinct religious community organized into churches is important for our approach to the New Testament. The individual writings, Gospels as well as letters, were composed in and for churches that understood themselves to be set apart from the synagogue as well as the broader pagan world. They were all written in Greek, the most widely used and understood language of the Mediterranean world, not in Aramaic, the language of Palestine, or in (closely related) Hebrew, the holy language of the Bible (Old Testament) and Jewish scholarship (e.g., the Mishnah). As we shall see, it is impossible to determine where most of these ancient books were written, although in some cases we can know with certainty (e.g., 1 Cor. 16:9). Nevertheless, it is a safe assumption that the New Testament books were written in and for the churches of the Greek-speaking, mostly Gentile, Mediterranean world. That is, they are products of a Christian church or churches. They represent a new religious community we now call Christianity in its crucially important initial and formative stage.

As one reads and studies the New Testament writings, it is important to bear in mind that they stand between the world of Judaism and the broader, predominantly Gentile world of Greco-Roman antiquity. The importance of the Jewish world is evident in the frequent references to scripture and to biblical figures such as Abraham, Moses, and David. The Gentile world is evident in the Book of Acts and the many New Testament letters, most of which are addressed to churches composed largely of Gentile converts. These two worlds together constitute the world of the New Testament. Without doubt the structure and meaning of the New Testament, its *anatomy,* have become evident to readers and to believers who stand outside that world. Yet by placing the New Testament writings within that world, their purpose and character become more sharply evident to the modern reader.

Suggestions for Further Reading

Throughout the bibliographies, series titles have usually been omitted to conserve space. Some works mentioned in notes are not repeated in the bibliographies.

PRIMARY SOURCES

The Old and New Testaments are cited according to the New Revised Standard Version, as is the Apocrypha of the Old Testament, which is now bound with some editions of the NRSV and other modern translations. Josephus' *Jewish Antiquities* and *Jewish War* are conveniently available in original Greek and translated in the Loeb Classical Library (Cambridge, MA: Harvard University Press), as are the works of Philo, Eusebius' *Ecclesiastical History,* and the writings of the Apostolic Fathers. Most of these writings are also available in other translations in paperback.

For Jewish pseudepigraphical writings (writings circulated under the names of ancient personages, but not accepted as scripture by Christianity or Judaism), see the translations and commentary in J. H. Charlesworth (ed.), *The Old Testament Pseudepigrapha,* 2 vols. (Garden City, NY: Doubleday, 1983 and 1985). A briefer selection and discussion of representative intertestamental texts is G. W. E. Nickelsburg and M. E. Stone, *Faith and Piety in Early Judaism: Texts and Documents* (Philadelphia: Fortress, 1983). Apocryphal and pseudepigraphal writings are treated by Nickelsburg, *Jewish Literature Between the Bible and the Mishnah: A Historical and Literary Introduction* (Philadelphia: Fortress, 1981). A somewhat more technical introduction is M. E. Stone (ed.), *Jewish Writings of the Second Temple Period: Apocrypha, Pseudepigrapha, Qumran Sectarian Writings, Philo, Josephus* (Philadelphia: Fortress, 1984), in the Compendia Rerum Iudaicarum ad Novum Testamentum series (see below).

The *Mishnah,* which is the basic collection of material stemming from the earlier rabbis, has been translated and published by H. Danby (London: Oxford University Press, 1933). H. Maccoby, *Early Rabbinic Writings* (in the Cambridge Commentaries series cited below), is a compact introduction and anthology of ancient sources. A reliable translation of the Qumran scrolls is G. Vermes, *The Dead Sea Scrolls in English,* 3rd ed. (Baltimore: Penguin, 1987), and the same author's *The Dead Sea Scrolls: Qumran in Perspective* (Philadelphia: Fortress, 1981) has served as a general introduction to the literature and issues. More recently, there is the comparable volume by M. A. Knibb, *The Qumran Community,* in the Cambridge series cited below. A comprehensive collection of the Qumran documents and fragments, together with concordances, is being published by Westminster/John Knox in North America and J. C. B. Mohr in Germany under the general title of *The Dead Sea Scrolls,* J. H. Charlesworth (ed.). J. A. Fitzmyer, *The Dead Sea Scrolls: Major Publications and Tools for Study,* rev. ed. (Atlanta: Scholars, 1990) remains valuable for bibliography. F. C. Grant (ed.) *Hellenistic Religions: The Age of Syncretism* (New York: Bobbs-Merrill, 1953), is a convenient collection of sources. For Gnostic writings see Bentley Layton (ed.), *The Gnostic Scriptures: A New Translation with Annotations and Introductions* (Garden City, NY: Doubleday, 1987), as well as J. M. Robinson (ed.), *The Nag Hammadi Library in English,* 3rd rev. ed. (San Francisco: Harper & Row, 1988). An excellent and compact anthology of sources relevant to the background of the New Testament is C. K. Barrett (ed.), *The New Testament Background: Selected Documents,* rev. ed. (San Francisco: Harper, 1987).

A valuable new selection of sources and commentary is the series Cambridge Commentaries on Writings of the Jewish and Christian World: 200 B.C. to A.D. 200 (New York: Cambridge University Press, 1984–). Currently available or announced are volumes on *Jews in the Hellenistic World* by J. R. Bartlett (1985); *The Qumran Community* by M. A. Knibb, *Early Rabbinic Writings* by H. Maccoby, *Outside the Old Testament* by M. de Jonge (1985), *Outside the New Testament* by G. N. Stanton, *Jews and Christians: Graeco-Roman Views* by M. Whittaker (1984), and a general volume, *The Jewish and Christian World 200 B.C. to A.D. 200* by A. R. C. Leancy (1984).

MODERN WORKS

B. Reicke, *The New Testament Era: The World of the Bible from 500 B.C. to A.D. 100,* trans. D. E. Green (Philadelphia: Fortress, 1968), is still a useful survey, but the most up-to-date handbook is E. Ferguson, *Backgrounds of Early Christianity,* rev. ed. (Grand Rapids, MI: Eerdmans, 1993). On Judaism, G. F. Moore, *Judaism in the First Centuries of the Christian Era,* 3 vols. (Cambridge, MA: Harvard University Press, 1927–1930), was long a standard work. One should now consult E. P. Sanders, *Judaism: Practice and Belief 63 BCE.–66 CE* (Philadelphia: Trinity Press International, 1992). E. Schürer, *The History of the Jewish People in the Age of Jesus Christ (175 B.C.E–A.D. 135),* rev. and ed. G. Vermes, F. Millar, M. Black, and M. Goodman, 3 vols. (Edinburgh: Clark, 1973–1987), has been brought up to date. The first volume is particularly valuable for its historical overview; the third is an introduction to the literature. See also: F. F. Bruce, *Israel and the Nations: From the Exodus to the Fall of the Second Temple* (Grand Rapids, MI: Eerdmans, 1963); S. J. D. Cohen, *From the Maccabees to the Mishnah* (Philadelphia: Westminster/John Knox, 1987). The history and institutions of Judaism are treated in the first two volumes of the Compendia Rerum Iudaicarum ad Novum Testamentum: S. Safrai, M. Stern, et al. (eds.), *The Jewish People in the First Century: Historical Geography, Political History, Social, Cultural and Religious Life and Institutions* (Philadelphia: Fortress, 1974 and 1976). The second volume (1976) is particularly useful for aspects and institutions of Jewish life important for understanding the beginning of Christianity. In addition, M. Hengel, *Judaism and Hellenism: Studies in Their Encounter in Palestine during the Hellenistic Period,* trans. J. Bowden, 2 vols. (Philadelphia: Fortress, 1974), must be taken into account. An introduction to important issues regarding the nexus of Judaism and Christianity in Palestine is found in E. M. Meyers and J. F. Strange, *Archaeology, Rabbis, and Early Christianity* (Nashville: Abingdon, 1981). For political conditions during the life of Jesus and the first generation of Christianity, see D. M. Rhoads, *Israel in Revolution: 6–74 CE.* (Philadelphia: Fortress, 1976); also D. Mendels, *The Rise and Fall of Jewish Nationalism* (New York: Doubleday, 1992), and M. Goodman, *The Ruling Class of Judaea: The Origins of the Jewish Revolt Against Rome A.D. 66–70* (Cambridge: Cambridge University Press, 1987). Pharisaic Judaism before and during the period of Christian origins is treated by J. Neusner, *From Politics to Piety: The Emergence of Pharisaic Judaism* (Englewood Cliffs, NJ: Prentice-Hall, 1973), a statement of that scholar's perspective and a summary of aspects of his compendious work. His more recent *Judaism in the Beginnings of Christianity* (Philadelphia: Fortress, 1984) incorporates and refocuses some earlier material in light of this important issue. For an alternative viewpoint, see E. P. Sanders, *Jewish Law from Jesus to the Mishnah: Five Studies* (Philadelphia: Trinity Press International, 1990). J. H. Charlesworth (ed.), *The Messiah: Developments in Earliest Christianity and Judaism* (Minneapolis: Fortress, 1992), contains a remarkable collection of essays on various aspects of messianism and christology by notable Jewish and Christian scholars.

On Judaism in the wider ancient Mediterranean world, see V. Tcherikover, *Hellenistic Civilization and the Jews,* trans. S. Applebaum (Philadelphia: Jewish Publication Society, 1959); also E. M. Smallwood, *The Jews Under Roman Rule* (Leiden: Brill, 1976). J. J. Collins, *Between Athens and Jerusalem: Jewish Identity in the Hel-*

lenistic Diaspora (New York: Crossroad, 1983), is a wide-ranging canvassing of the sources for Hellenistic Judaism aside from Philo and Josephus with a view to sketching its religious and theological profile. Ancient attitudes toward Judaism are dealt with by J. G. Gager, *The Origins of Anti-Semitism: Attitudes Toward Judaism in Pagan and Christian Antiquity* (New York: Oxford, 1983). A. F. Segal, *Rebecca's Children: Judaism and Christianity in the Roman World* (Cambridge, MA: Harvard, 1986), treats both religions as divergent heirs of ancient Israelite tradition and faith. R. A. Kraft and Nickelsburg have edited a collection of valuable essays on *Early Judaism and Its Modern Interpreters* (Philadelphia and Atlanta: Fortress and Scholars, 1986).

For the broader Hellenistic world, including its religion, as it impinges on early Christianity and the New Testament a definitive handbook is H. Koester, *Introduction to the New Testament, Volume One: History, Culture and Religion of the Hellenistic Age* (Philadelphia: Fortress, 1982). An excellent brief survey is C. J. Roetzel, *The World that Shaped the New Testament* (Atlanta: John Knox, 1985). Traditional Greek and Roman religion is treated by H. R. Rose, *Religion in Greece and Rome* (New York: Harper & Row, 1959). W. Burkert, *Greek Religion,* trans. J. Raffan (Cambridge, MA: Harvard, 1985) is an excellent and recent comprehensive treatment. Burkert has also written *Ancient Mystery Cults* (Cambridge, MA: Harvard University Press, 1987). The popular religious life against which Christianity competed and eventually triumphed is evoked by R. Mac-Mullen, *Paganism in the Roman Empire* (New Haven: Yale, 1981). For Gnosticism see H. Jonas, *The Gnostic Religion,* rev. ed. (Boston: Beacon, 1963), as well as K. Rudolph, *Gnosis: The Nature and History of Gnosticism,* trans. R. M. Wilson (San Francisco: Harper & Row, 1983). E. M. Yamauchi, *Pre-Christian Gnosticism: A Survey of the Proposed Evidences* (Grand Rapids, MI: Eerdmans, 1973), denies that Gnosticism antedated Christianity. On the broader historical background, see W. W. Tarn, *Hellenistic Civilization,* 3rd ed. rev. with G. T. Griffith (London: Arnold, 1952; paperback, Meridian), and F. E. Peters, *The Harvest of Hellenism: A History of the Near East from Alexander the Great to the Triumph of Christianity* (New York: Simon & Schuster, 1970), the latter notable for the effort to incorporate the religious and philosophical dimensions of history. Also quite useful for reference is N. G. L. Hammond and H. H. Scullard (eds.), *The Oxford Classical Dictionary,* 2nd ed. (Oxford: Clarendon Press, 1970).

For other relevant readings on early Christianity and its environment, see Suggestions for Further Reading at the end of Chapter 12.

PART ONE

THE GOSPELS
AND JESUS

*T*he Christian faith began with the mission of Jesus of Nazareth, an event that could be understood only in the context of the history of Israel and communicated only by means of the literary and thought patterns of the first-century Mediterranean world. The new religious faith was thus grounded in the story of a particular person, who lived and died in the land of Israel. Our study of the New Testament therefore focuses in Part I upon the story of Jesus, first as portrayed in the Gospels (Chapters 2, 3, 4, 5) and then as portrayed by means of historical criticism (Chapter 6). Although the earliest New Testament documents are the letters of Paul, the prior position of the Gospels in the New Testament collection accurately reflects the conviction of the early Christian community that the story of Jesus was the beginning of the faith.

In the Gospel stories matters of life and death, both for individual Christians and for the churches, were filtered through the narration of Jesus' actions and words. From without, the Christians faced problems connected with Jewish leaders in Israel, the Roman government in the empire, and a Hellenistic culture that pervaded everyday Mediterranean life. From within, the churches struggled with the relation of the old and the new Israel, the nature of discipleship, the extent of the Christian mission, the place of miracles, the nature of power, order, and authority in the community, the relation between faith and ethics, and the delay of the end time. In speaking to these questions the early Christians acknowledged the authority of Jesus, while at the same time assuming the freedom to retell his story in the light of their changed situations.

Plaque from a tenth-century German or north Italian book cover. Agnus Dei (lamb of God) displayed on a cross between emblems of the four evangelists—Matthew, the man; Mark, the lion; Luke, the ox; and John, the eagle. *(Courtesy of Metropolitan Museum of Art. Gift of J. Pierpont Morgan, 1917.)*

Chapter 2

Mark: The Gospel
of Suffering

Notes on the Nature of the Gospels, Gospel Criticism, and the Origin of Mark

THE NATURE OF THE GOSPELS

*B*efore turning to Mark's Gospel, we need to have in view the nature of the Gospels. The Greek word for gospel, *euangelion,* means "good news." This word had acquired religious significance in the Roman Empire, chiefly in the cult of the emperor, in which the appearance of the Roman emperor, his accession to the throne, and his decrees were known as glad tidings or gospels. Perhaps the New Testament usage was partly derived from the "good tidings" of freedom from bondage which Isaiah proclaimed to the people of Israel emerging from the Babylonian exile (see Isa. 40:9; 52:7; 61:1). In the New Testament itself, *euangelion* also signifies good news of salvation (see for example, Matt. 11:5; Rom. 1:1; 1 Cor. 15:1; Mark 1:1). Early usage of *euangelion* implied the oral nature of such news (cf. Gal. 1:6–12). Not until years after they were written were New Testament writings called Gospels, but with the appearance of Mark, Matthew, Luke, John, and the apocryphal Gospels, the Gospel became a distinctive literary category or type.[1] This literary type can be defined negatively. The Gospels are not biographies of Jesus in the modern sense, for they lack the usual interest in personal character and in chronological order. Neither are they myths, tales of the gods, because Jesus of Nazareth, the central figure of the Gospels, was a historical person. Yet elements of both biography (a story of a particular historical person) and myth (a tale of divine action) are present in the Gospels. Basically the Gospels are religious proclamations based upon historical event.

The writing of the first Gospel was no casual, accidental affair. Until the time of Mark (or some unknown predecessor), the oral tradition about Jesus and the Hebrew scrip-

---

1. To distinguish between Gospel as a book (e.g., Mark) and gospel as the Christian message, we shall capitalize the former but not the latter. On the use of the term "Gospel" for written documents, see Helmut Koester, *Ancient Christian Gospels: Their History and Development* (Philadelphia: Trinity Press International, 1990), pp. 24–31.

tures were authoritative for the early church. Although Papias, a second-century Christian bishop, knew of written Gospels, he still preferred the living tradition of the Lord to "the content of books" (Eusebius, *EH*, III, 39, 3 ff.). In early Christianity the Lord's authority did not stop with his life and death. He was a living Lord; consequently, the tradition was living and developing. When some Christians took the step of writing down, and hence partially fixing, this tradition, it was only because of pressing needs of the church.

One obvious reason for writing Gospels was the death of the apostles, those who had been with Jesus. The church could ill afford to lose the tradition of Jesus. Mark probably originated in the mid-sixties when, according to tradition, Paul and Peter, the two great apostles, were martyred.[2]

Other motives were also at work in the writing of the Gospels. A church facing persecution needed to know the way in which Jesus himself had faced persecution. The early church, furthermore, struggled to understand itself apart from the law, organization, rites, and customs of Judaism. As the Christian mission expanded into the Gentile world, a further crisis was posed by the problem of how a religion basically Jewish in origin could appeal to the Hellenistic world without losing its identity and distinctiveness. The church also had to speak to the problem posed by the delay of the expected parousia (second coming of Jesus) and the end of the world. These, and more specific needs, were at work in the writing of Gospels.

Seemingly these problems could have been handled without resorting to the narrative form of literature. It was because the early church looked for its basic direction and guidance to the events of Jesus' life, death, and resurrection that the Gospel became a most appropriate vehicle for the Christian message. Indeed, our first known Gospel (Mark) probably originated under the threat of persecution, just as Jesus' ministry had taken shape under the threat of danger and death.

GOSPEL CRITICISM

The Gospel According to Mark is attributed by tradition to the John Mark who was a companion of Paul and an associate of the other apostles (Acts 12:12, 25; 15:37, 39). Tradition connects him with Peter as well, but the reliability of this tradition is questionable.[3] Possibly all four canonical Gospels were first read by early Christian communities as anonymous writings. Their present titles were attached to them when they were later incorporated into the four-Gospel canon. (Of course, there may have already been traditions associating them with apostolic or other early figures.) For the sake of convenience, we shall continue to use the customary names to identify the respective Gospels, and their authors.

Mark is generally thought to be the earliest Gospel. This view is based upon a com-

---

2. The martyrdoms of Paul and Peter are not recounted in the New Testament (but cf. John 21:18–19 on Peter and Acts 20:25, 38 on Paul), and are first mentioned in 1 Clement (5:3–7), one of the writings of the Apostolic Fathers. (1 Clement is usually dated in the last decade of the first century.)

3. See the report by the Christian bishop and historian Eusebius (ca. A.D. 260–340) concerning the earlier tradition from another bishop, Papias (ca. A.D. 150), in *The Ecclesiastical History*, III, 39, 14: "Mark became Peter's interpreter and wrote accurately all that he remembered, not, indeed, in order of the things said or done by the Lord." On the figure of Mark the definitive work is now C. Clifton Black, *Mark: Images of An Apostolic Interpreter* (Columbia, SC: University of South Carolina Press, 1994).

parison with the other two Gospels that are quite similar, Matthew and Luke. These three Gospels are known as the Synoptic Gospels. (*Synoptic* means that they see together; that is, they present a common view of Jesus' ministry.) One can evaluate this evidence with the help of a synopsis of the Gospels, a volume in which the Gospels are arranged in parallel columns for easy comparison. Two striking facts emerge from such a study:

1. The order of events in the narratives of Matthew, Mark, and Luke is frequently the same. Where it is not, Matthew and Luke almost never agree with each other against Mark, although each alone may, and frequently does, agree with Mark against the other.

2. A similar observation can be made about the wording of the text in the parallel portions (where all three have basically the same material). Sometimes it is identical in all three, but where it is not, Matthew and Luke only infrequently have the same wording in disagreement with Mark.

Thus in both cases, order of events and wording, one sees Mark and Matthew agreeing against Luke or one sees Mark and Luke agreeing against Matthew rather frequently; the rarity of agreement by Matthew and Luke against Mark in parallel passages is striking.

If, then, Mark is the common factor, or middle term, without which Matthew and Luke rarely agree, then Mark must be the source of the other two, if it is not the result of the conflation (i e , putting together) of those documents. In the late eighteenth century J. J. Griesbach argued that Matthew wrote first and was followed by Luke, who knew his work. Mark then followed, drawing upon both of his predecessors. The Griesbach hypothesis was superior to the then-traditional view that the Gospels were written in the canonical order, for it explained why Mark is the middle term between Matthew and Luke. It also had the advantage of explaining the relationship on the basis of the Gospels themselves, without recourse to hypothetical documents or sources that no longer exist, such as Q, M, and L. But most scholars find it difficult, if not impossible, to understand Mark as the combination of Matthew and Luke.

Several considerations make it difficult to believe that Mark is such a conflation. Mark is shorter, stylistically cruder, and more difficult to understand than is Matthew or Luke. It used to be thought that Mark had condensed the Gospel of Matthew, but Mark contains little of the teachings of Jesus found in Matthew. Would a condenser have omitted the most striking part of Matthew? Where Mark and Matthew report the same incidents, Mark's account is often actually longer and more detailed. Would a condenser have lengthened individual stories by adding various details? Such considerations support the view that Mark is our earliest Gospel, not a later condensation.[4]

There are many cases, however, in which Matthew and Luke have similar or identical sayings of Jesus completely lacking in Mark. The different use and arrangement of

---

4. For a fuller discussion see W. G. Kümmel, *Introduction to the New Testament,* trans. H. C. Kee, rev. ed. (Nashville: Abingdon, 1975), pp. 33–60. A different solution, the priority of Matthew, is proposed by W. R. Farmer, *The Synoptic Problem: A Critical Analysis* (New York: Macmillan, 1964), who represents Griesbach's position. C. M. Tuckett (ed.), *Synoptic Studies: The Ampleford Conferences of 1982 and 1983* (Sheffield: JSOT, 1984), is representative of the continuing discussion. The fundamental essay of Griesbach has been translated by Bernard Orchard in *J. J. Griesbach: Synoptic and Text-critical Studies 1776–1976,* ed. Orchard and Thomas R. W. Longstaff (Cambridge: Cambridge University

The Synoptic Tradition

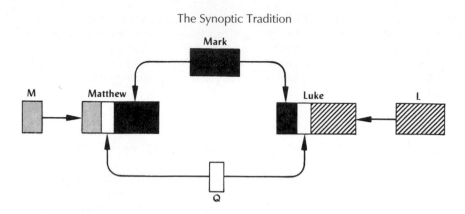

this material in Matthew and Luke would seem to indicate that neither copied the other. If not, Matthew and Luke have most probably drawn upon a common source other than Mark. This source no longer exists independently, and is usually called Q (German *Quelle,* meaning "source"). The twentieth-century discovery of the Gospel of Thomas among the Nag Hammadi Gnostic documents has provided a parallel to the hypothetical Q, for Thomas is a collection of Jesus' sayings without narrrative framework. In addition to Mark and Q, both Matthew and Luke had access to special traditions either oral or written: these materials, distinctive to each, are sometimes referred to as M and L. This most widely accepted solution of the synoptic problem is called the two-document (Mark and Q) or four-document (Mark, Q, M, and L) hypothesis.

The insights of *source criticism* just described have been augmented by the results of *form criticism,* a discipline that goes behind the written sources to investigate the period of the oral tradition about Jesus. Form criticism as a discipline or method of biblical scholarship was developed in Germany, where it is known as *Formgeschichte* (form history). That name is more adequate than its customary English counterpart, for it makes clear that more is at stake than literary or traditional form. Form criticism, based on the insight that the Gospels are composed of discrete units of tradition, studies these units—sayings, stories, parables, apocalyptic discourses—with a view to understanding how their form is related to their function and history in the primitive church. Form critics think that most of the tradition originally existed as individual units or pericopes and that there was a stage at which these units of tradition, stories and sayings, were told and retold by word of mouth (cf. 1 Cor. 11:23); with good reason they assume that such traditional units were preserved and transmitted because they served the needs and purposes of the church.

These separate units of tradition can be classified according to type, because oral tradition tends to operate in certain general, fixed ways. For example, there are parables, aphorisms, clusters of sayings, anecdotes, wonder stories, and narratives dominated by a saying. The identification of such primitive forms helps to distinguish earlier tradition from later editing, and thus to locate the earliest material. One major goal of form criticism is the reconstruction of the life situation out of which the pericope arose

Press, 1978). The most recent thorough study of the synoptic problem is E. P. Sanders and Margaret Davies, *Studying the Synoptic Gospels* (Philadelphia: Trinity Press International, 1989), in which neither Griesbach nor the commonly accepted two-document (Mark and Q) theory is embraced, although the authors accept the priority of Mark.

and to which it is addressed. Although reconstructions in most cases remain hypothetical, the form-critical attempt to postulate settings, functions, and histories for units of tradition sheds light upon their meaning and interpretation. Finally, these self-contained units, "pearls" of tradition, were strung together in a connected narrative, probably first by Mark. According to the earlier form critics, Mark was not so much an author as a redactor, a compiler of the tradition.

Redaction criticism, the analysis of the editorial work of the writers in relation to their sources, established that the writers used the tradition available to them in creative, constructive, and different ways. The basic insight of redaction criticism is that the evangelists were authors and theologians painting their own portraits of Jesus and addressing themselves to important theological, ethical, and practical issues in the church of the first century.

Redaction critics may have relatively high, or relatively low, estimates of the historical trustworthiness of the material conveyed in the Gospels. They bracket out the historical question, however, in order to understand the apparent intention of the evangelists in their use of tradition.

Redaction criticism takes it as fundamental that the Gospels, especially the Synoptics, are based upon, or arise out of, three settings in life. First, there is the setting of Jesus' actual historical ministry. This setting was real, and its importance is not to be dismissed. In the case of most stories and sayings of Jesus, however, that setting is impossible to reconstruct except in a general way. Second, there is the setting in the life of the early church that preserved the Gospel tradition. Without doubt, tradition was preserved and transmitted because it performed a valued function in the religious community. This is the insight of form criticism, which deals with this period of oral, or informal, transmission. Third, there is the situation of the evangelists themselves. These situations gave rise to the Gospels. The Gospels are not to be viewed as the products of these settings pure and simple; they are more than the last stage in the development of the tradition of Jesus in the church. The evangelists sought to speak with relevance and power to their own situations, while being faithful to Jesus. The resulting portraits reflected in their respective writings are the subject of this and the following three chapters.

The rise of form and redaction criticism went hand in hand with a recognition of the deeply religious and theological character of the Gospels, as well as the traditions out of which they were formed. It was commonly said that the Gospels were proclamation or witness rather than biography or history. Because of the Gospels' (especially Mark's) emphasis upon the death and resurrection of Jesus, his fulfillment of scripture, and the role of John the Baptist in introducing him, it was also thought that they developed out of the early Christian preaching. In such preaching, as attested in Paul (1 Cor. 15:3–8) and Acts (10:34–43; 13:23–31), these elements, particularly Jesus' death and resurrection, play a predominant role. In the Acts speeches there is also reference to Jesus' ministry, especially his healings, which do not figure in Paul's account of his own preaching (cf. also 1 Cor. 1:17; 2:1–2). The formal similarity to Mark, especially in emphasizing Jesus' death, is hardly insignificant.

That the Gospels reflect emphases of early preaching is undoubtedly true, but whether or how they developed directly from that preaching is much more difficult to know. In any event, the assertion that the Gospels were more akin to preaching than to biography makes a valid point. Their purpose was quite similar to that of preaching or religious instruction: the evangelization of converts, the confirmation of believers in their faith, and the nurturing of members of the churches in the way of true discipleship. Thus the Gospels were not written primarily to record history or to present a biography of Jesus.

The Formation of the Gospels

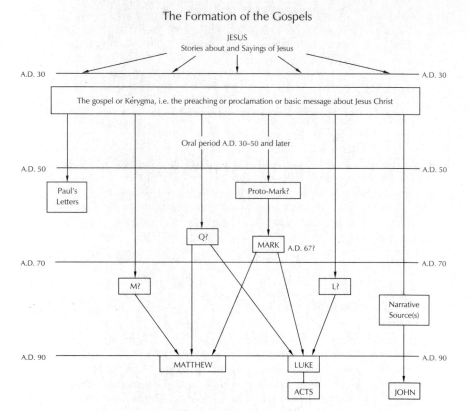

The formation of the Gospels, according to the most widely accepted theory of synoptic relationships.

The Gospels show little, if any, interest in Jesus' background, education, appearance, personal development, and associations (other than with his disciples). They are unlike current biographies and do not reflect what we regard as typical biographical interests.

The fact that the Gospels are unlike modern history or biography does not mean, however, that they are in no sense historical or biographical. The proper comparison is with ancient histories and biographies. When such comparisons are made, it is clear that the Gospels as a group are, indeed, quite different from Tacitus' *Histories,* Josephus' *Jewish Antiquities,* or even the narrative of King David in 1–2 Samuel. Still, in antiquity biography was distinguished from history, and comparisons with ancient biographies, especially popular biographical literature, are somewhat more profitable. The role played by Socrates in the ancient biographical tradition is not unlike that played by Jesus. Although Plato's *Apology* and other dialogues are works of greater literary and philosophical sophistication than the Gospels, the portrayal of Socrates, the good and wise man who sacrifices his life for moral principle when he could compromise with evil and live, is not unlike the story of Jesus in the Gospels. Plato had moral and broadly philosophical–religious reasons for presenting Socrates in the way he did, and these reasons were similar to the motivations of the evangelists. Xenophon's *Memorabilia* was a more popular presentation of Socrates, and in that sense more like the Gospels. The portrayal of the popular first-century philosopher Apollonius of Tyana, written several centuries later by Philostratus, is like the Gospels in that it presents a religious and philosophical thinker who both teaches and works miracles. Neither Socrates nor Apollonius affords close parallels to Jesus in every aspect, but their respective biographical treatments show much closer affinities with the Gospels than do modern biographies. Thus ancient readers of the Gospels, whether Christians or others, would have recognized these presentations of Jesus as biographies of a genre familiar in the popular literature of antiquity.

Utilizing the insights of modern criticism, our method for determining the message of each Gospel consists of four steps: (1) *Outlining the structure:* By determining the anatomy or basic outline (for example, its beginning, climax, and end), we can begin to discern the intention and meaning of the Gospel. A detailed outline, not always possible, would involve ordering the separate sayings or episodes, known as pericopes, into the overall structure. (2) *Identifying emphases:* Emphases that are obvious because of frequency become evident in the reading of each Gospel; other emphases become evident in examining the order and structure of the Gospel. The identification of such emphases is not only informed by the structure but also serves to test any theory of the structure. Any overall interpretation of a writing must take into account dominant emphases. (3) *Distinguishing tradition from redaction:* By seeing which earlier material is selected and how it has been shaped, we can arrive at probable conclusions about the intention of the author. This technique of criticism is more difficult to employ in the case of the Gospel of Mark because we do not have the sources of tradition that Mark used. Yet by isolating traditional forms, form criticism helps in discerning that Gospel's traditional basis. (4) *Imagining the historical context:* Some historical situation or combination of situations provided the impetus for the writing of each Gospel. On the basis of our knowledge of the history of early Christianity and the culture in which it lived, we imagine an occasion that most likely fits the origin of the Gospel in question. Obviously such historical judgments must correspond to the life of the ancient rather than the contemporary church.

Of course, all four methodological steps mutually inform and correct each other. No neat, simple procedure removes the necessity for common sense and historical imagination as primary ingredients for understanding.

THE ORIGIN OF MARK

The date and place of origin of any of the four Gospels, including Mark, are difficult to determine, because the internal evidence is indirect and the external evidence is meager. The key passage for dating Mark is the apocalyptic discourse, particularly 13:2 and 13:14, which points to the imminent destruction of Jerusalem, thus reflecting the period of the Jewish resistance to Rome, the fall of Jerusalem, and the leveling of the temple (A.D. 66–70). Whether Mark was written just before or just after that disaster is a matter of debate. According to the earliest testimony, the Gospel of Mark originated in Rome, where Peter was preaching, and where Mark recorded what the apostle had spoken about Jesus (see Eusebius, *EH*, VI, 14, 6).

Against the Roman origin of Mark various other suggestions have been offered: Galilee, because of Mark's emphasis on that region (see especially Mark 14:28 and 16:7); or the rural, small-town area of southern Syria (see, e.g., 1:38; 7:24; 8:27), because of Mark's accurate knowledge of the first-century agriculture of Syria–Palestine. Nevertheless, there are still important reasons for taking seriously the traditional Roman provenance of the Gospel of Mark. In 15:21 Mark identifies Simon of Cyrene as the father of Alexander and Rufus, as if the latter would be known to the readers, and

Nero, emperor of Rome (A.D. 54–68), on a Roman coin. *(Courtesy of American Numismatic Society.)*

in Romans 16:13 Paul sends greetings to a Rufus who is an eminent member of the Roman church. Apparently Mark was written to an audience that included Gentile Christians (see Mark 10:12—divorce by women was not possible in Jewish Palestine—and 5:41; 7:3 f., 11, 34; 15:22, where ignorance of Jewish practices is assumed).

Further, events in Rome during the mid-sixties admirably fit Mark's emphasis upon persecution. The suffering of Jesus (8:31; 9:31; 10:33 f.), the centrality of the cross (chaps. 14 and 15), and the necessity for a suffering and serving discipleship (8:34–38; 9:33–50; 10:38–45; 13:9–13) seem to reflect an urgent message to a persecuted community. Tacitus, the first-century Roman historian, describes persecution of Roman Christians in the mid-sixties by the emperor Nero, who evidently, in order to enlarge his palace complex, started a great fire that burned much of Rome:

> Therefore, to scotch the rumour, Nero substituted as culprits, and punished with the utmost refinements of cruelty, a class of men, loathed for their vices, whom the crowd styled Christians. . . . First, then, the confessed members of the sect were arrested; next, on their disclosures, vast numbers were convicted, not so much on the count of arson as for hatred of the human race. And derision accompanied their end: they were covered with wild beasts' skins and torn to death by dogs; or they were fastened on crosses, and, when daylight failed were burned to serve as lamps by night. [*Annals*, XV, 44]

Mark's Gospel fits such a situation of persecution in Rome. It was likely written there shortly before the destruction of Jerusalem by Titus in A.D. 70.

Certainty in such matters is unattainable, but this view accommodates both the internal evidence (of the Gospel itself) and the earliest testimony. It also explains why Mark should have been adopted and used as the principal narrative source independently by Matthew and Luke. The church at Rome was already influential (cf. Rom. 1:8), and its Gospel would have been regarded as authoritative by other Christian writers.

Fuller interpretation of Mark awaits the exegetical sections in this chapter, but a few general guidelines will aid in reading. Mark is not simply biography or objective history, but rather religious proclamation with historical foundations. The Markan Gospel developed from traditions about Jesus that circulated in the Christian community prior to the writing of the Gospel; Mark did not create this story afresh. At the same time this Gospel aimed to strengthen first-century Christians in the face of persecution.

OUTLINE OF MARK

Prologue: The Spirit and Jesus in the World (1:1–15)
The Gospel of Power: Jesus Opposes His Enemies (1:16–8:21)
    Encounter with Demons and Sickness (1:21–45)
    Debate with the Pharisees (2:1–3:6)
The Power of Suffering: Jesus Wins His Disciples (8:22–15:47)
    Two Stages of Discipleship (8:22–9:9)
    Faith to Produce Healing (9:14–32)
    Jesus Approaches His Death (10:1–14:72)
    The Cross of Jesus (15:33–47)
Epilogue: The Future Victory (16:1–8)

Prologue: The Spirit and Jesus in the World (1:1–15)

Why does Mark's Gospel begin with Jesus' baptism by John?

Mark's opening hardly sounds like an objective biography of Jesus of Nazareth. Neither an apology (as in Luke 1:1–4) nor a genealogy of Jesus (as in Matt. 1:1–17), the opening of Mark could scarcely attain a higher note of faith. Jesus Christ is named as though Christ were his last name. His name, however, was Jesus, and Christ is a bestowed title of honor, meaning "anointed one" or "messiah." Any lingering expectation of a neutral history is dispelled by the final title, "Son of God." The significance of this designation for Mark becomes clearer at the climactic point of the opening story when Jesus is told by a voice from heaven that he is "my Son, the Beloved" (vs. 11). The key introductory phrase of the opening verse, however, is probably "the beginning of the good news." By the prologue's end (vs. 14) this phrase has become "proclaiming the good news of God." Something has enabled "the beginning of the good news" to become "proclaiming the good news." (NRSV now properly uses "good news" to translate *euangelion,* "gospel.")

Mark starts, strangely, not at the beginning but in the middle of things. Mark begins with the baptism when Jesus was already an adult, instead of with Jesus' birth or childhood. Mark did know something about Jesus' earlier life, for later we are informed about Jesus' occupation and family (Mark 6:3). In Mark's view the baptism of Jesus is the crucial initiatory event for Jesus.

The Old Testament prophecy (1:2–3) points forward toward some kind of fulfillment. (Although Mark declares that the prophet Isaiah spoke these words, they are actually a combination of Malachi 3:1, Exodus 23:20, and Isaiah 40:3.) Something will happen. In fact, by the end of the prologue, the verb tense has shifted to the Greek perfect, "The time is *fulfilled,* and the kingdom of God *"has come near"* (1:15). Again, we apparently have an indication of the crucial importance of Jesus' baptism by John.

John the baptizer stands at the center of the next section (1:2–8). John is a wild man; he is in the wilderness, a preacher of judgment and repentance. He wears clothes of the wilderness, camel's hair and a leather girdle (cf. the description of Elijah in 2 Kings 1:8); he eats food of the wilderness, locusts and wild honey. As John speaks of the one who comes after him (vs. 7), he clearly stands at the beginning of the gospel (cf. Acts 1:22; 10:37), as different as he may be from Jesus.

A striking feature of this section is its remarkable emphasis upon repentance for all the people of Judea and Jerusalem, as if a full-scale national repentance were taking place. Mark probably views this repentance as an anticipation of the coming Messiah. John's decisive act is to baptize the people in the river Jordan. Through this rite of baptism, a cleansing or preparation takes place. Moreover, John declares that this baptism with water would be completed later by one who would baptize with the Spirit. Earlier we read a prophecy about John the baptizer (vss. 2, 3); now John himself prophesies (vss. 7, 8). Just this fact of his prophesying indicates that the Spirit is appearing. In first-century Judaism the Spirit, often the enabler of biblical prophecy (cf. Isa. 61:1–2; Ezek. 2:2; 11:5; Hos. 9:7), was thought by many to have departed Israel with the last prophets (Haggai, Zechariah, and Malachi) and was expected only in the last days.[5] As John clearly points to the approach of another, Jesus, he also foreshadows an irruption of the end time, the time of the active Spirit.

A different mood pervades the next section (vss. 9–13). Whereas previously we had John the baptizer, the crowds, and baptism in the river, now Jesus alone appears. The heavens open, the Spirit descends, and a voice from heaven speaks; Mark has shifted to "cosmic language."[6] At his baptism, the Spirit descends upon Jesus and a voice says, "You are my Son, the Beloved; with you I am well pleased." This utterance combines portions of Psalm 2:7 and Isaiah 42:1. Thus Mark proclaims the occurrence of a cosmic event in which the Son of God is designated. Does this mean that Jesus did not become Son of God until his baptism? Mark offers no opinion; the text asserts simply that at this baptism God's Spirit rested upon Jesus, who was declared Son of God.

The title *Son* was used commonly as a designation for Israel in the Hebrew Scriptures (Exod. 4:22; cf. Jer. 31:9 and Hos. 11:1) and for those who especially represented the people of Israel, such as the king or high priest. Most likely sonship did not mean biological descent from God but signified spe-

---

5. See the coming of the Spirit in Acts 2:17–22, especially the prophecy from Joel 2:28–32.
6. J. M. Robinson, *The Problem of History in Mark and other Marcan Studies* (Philadelphia: Fortress, 1982), pp. 74–76. Cf. U. W. Mauser, *Christ in the Wilderness* (Naperville, IL: Allenson, 1963), pp. 77 ff.

cial selection by God for a task. The appropriate response of sonship, therefore, is obedience to the task. This Hebraic understanding of sonship suggests that the voice from heaven revealed to Jesus that God had chosen him for a task. In fact, the unexpected climax of Mark's introduction occurs when the Spirit drives Jesus into the wilderness where he is tempted by Satan (vs. 12). The Spirit did not offer Jesus triumph and resolution; instead the Spirit brought conflict with the power of evil, with Satan.

The importance of the Spirit's driving Jesus into the wilderness is underscored by the fact that Jesus was already in the wilderness at his baptism. Why then does Mark emphasize the wilderness motif? Both Moses (Exod. 34:28) and Elijah (1 Kings 19:8) spent forty days on Mount Sinai; moreover, the people of Israel wandered forty years in the wilderness before they could enter the Promised Land. Jesus' sojourn in the wilderness may then anticipate the founding of a new Israel, a new religious community.

The most striking feature of the Markan temptation story, especially in comparison with the temptation stories in Matthew (4:1–11) and Luke (4:1–13), is its lack of narrative detail. In this Markan episode, Jesus' activity is overshadowed by the supernatural conflict between the Spirit and Satan. The outcome of this conflict, however, has already been anticipated in Jesus' baptism. By Jesus' act of submission to John's baptism the Spirit has come and with this coming Satan already is being defeated (see 3:23–29; cf. 10:38).

In these successive sections of Mark's introduction, the Spirit is the decisive factor. The Spirit is promised by John the Baptist and is already emerging in his prophecy (1:2–8). During Jesus' baptism (1:9–11) the Spirit descends upon him. In the temptation (1:12–13) the Spirit drives Jesus into conflict and victory over Satan. A likely clue to the meaning of Mark's introduction appears in the answer Jesus later gives to the accusation that he is in league with Satan: "But no one can enter a strong man's house and plunder his property without first tying up the strong man; then indeed the house can be plundered" (Mark 3:27). Jesus' baptism and temptation manifest an initial conquest of Satan by the Spirit. Therefore, the way is cleared for Jesus' later conflicts with the demons, his religious opponents, and even his disciples. After Jesus' obedient submission to baptism, the Spirit drives him into a conflict that eventually will result in final victory.

The note of future victory resounds in the conclusion of Mark's introduction (vss. 14–15), where instead of "the beginning of the good news" we now hear of "preaching the good news of God."[7] After Jesus' baptism and temptation, the preaching of the good news of God can take place, because the Spirit has become active in Jesus' obedience. The crucial phrase, "the kingdom of God has come near" (vs. 15), means neither that victory has fully arrived nor that triumph remains entirely future; Mark proclaims that God's ruling presence is now nearer than it was before. This message, this gospel,

---

7. For other Markan uses of *euangelion,* "good news" or "gospel," see 1:1, 15; 8:35; 10:29; 13:10; 14:9. (Only in 8:35 does NRSV translate "gospel.")

rather than Jesus himself, is the object of belief (vs. 15). Therefore Mark concludes his introduction with Jesus' preaching the good news of God that demands repentance and belief. The introduction has suggested to the reader that the gospel concerns a victory (the Spirit over Satan) to be won only through conflict (the wilderness) and obedience (the baptism of Jesus). The rest of Mark's Gospel narrates Jesus' present triumph in conflict through his exorcisms, debates, and suffering, in order to effect the future triumph of the disciples, if they will repent and believe.

The Gospel of Power: Jesus Opposes His Enemies (1:16–8:21)

Now that the Spirit has met Satan in the temptation of Jesus, the public action of Jesus can begin. Jesus came preaching that the kingdom of God is drawing near, and this kingdom proclamation by its very nature aroused opposition. Forces are at work against the emergence of the kingdom, for the old order does not easily yield. So Jesus calls and commissions disciples to be with him and to share his work (1:16–20; 3:13–19).

In the first half of the Gospel of Mark (1:16–8:21), opposition to Jesus comes in the main from two camps—the demons and the Pharisees. Jesus opposes the demons with exorcism and the Pharisees with debate. Consequently, the first half of Mark centers upon Jesus' miracles and teachings. Indeed, as we shall see, miracles and teachings are mingled within individual units of tradition because both are means for opposing his enemies. The two opposing forces differ in that the demons recognize Jesus and do battle against him, whereas the Pharisees, though also antagonistic to Jesus, do not recognize his true identity.

In the second half of Mark (8:22–15:47), the major opposition to Jesus is not that of enemies but rather of friends, his disciples. To be sure, the disciples did not put Jesus to death; the chief priests and scribes, along with the Roman authorities, were responsible for his crucifixion. Still, the disciples did oppose Jesus because they failed to understand why he had to suffer and die. Unless we keep in mind the disciples' misunderstanding opposition, the full meaning of Jesus' actions and teachings against the demons and the Pharisees will be missed. The Gospel of Mark depicts an opposition of enemies met by direct action through exorcisms and debates; however, the opposition of friends is met by indirect persuasion, even apparent defeat in death.

This preference for persuading rather than compelling the disciples relates to a major problem in the first half of Mark. After several disclosures of divine healing power, Jesus curiously commands keeping these miracles secret (1:43 f.; 3:12; 5:43). This is an aspect of what is called the messianic secret in Mark. In effect, the Jesus of Mark avoids the making of disciples by powerful deeds. When demons had been exorcised (and opponents silenced in debate) the task of making true disciples still remained.

In this first half of Mark, miracles dominate. There are nature miracles, such as stilling the storm (4:35–41; 6:45–52) and feeding the multitudes (6:30–44; 8:1–10); there are healing miracles, such as the healing of the leper (1:40–45) and the raising of the dead girl (5:35–43); and there are miracles of exorcism, the driving out of demons (1:21–28; 5:1–13; see also 1:34; 3:22). The exorcisms likely provide the key to understanding the miracles in this Gospel. Mark summarizes the activity of Jesus in Galilee as that of preaching and casting out demons (1:39), and Jesus appoints the Twelve to the same tasks (3:14, 15; cf. 6:13). Evidently, for Mark, miracles are essentially the same as exorcisms and thus do not constitute a separate class of acts or events. All Jesus' actions represent his overcoming the power of evil.

Thus a crucial question related to these mighty acts is whether Jesus performs such acts with the power of Satan or of God (3:20–30). For Mark, Jesus performs exorcisms with the help of God; anyone who denies this source of Jesus' power (cf. 3:30) must be on the side of Satan. Now that the strong man, Satan, has been bound by the Spirit, Jesus is to plunder the house, to rid the world of demons (3:27). In demon exorcism we are to recognize a transcendent battle taking place in the life of Jesus and his contemporaries. Demons inhabit human beings; they are part of human history. Yet their power comes from beyond, from Satan. Similarly, Jesus exorcises demons, but he claims a power from beyond; for in Mark he is the Son of God, the one upon whom the Spirit descended in the baptism.

ENCOUNTER WITH DEMONS AND SICKNESS (1:21–45)

Are Jesus' miracles in Mark signs of his compassion or something more?

The first exorcism in Mark (1:21–28) follows the calling of disciples and is set within the context of Jesus' teaching in the synagogue on the Sabbath. Opposition between the teaching of the scribes and the authority of Jesus characterizes this scene. At first no one truly recognizes Jesus except the demon, who cries out, "I know who you are, the Holy One of God" (1:24; cf. 3:11; 5:7). Perhaps the demon used this exalted title of Jesus to gain power over him. In the ancient world, knowledge and use of the name gave the speaker magic power.[8] More obviously, the demon's recognition of Jesus involves immediate opposition . . . an enemy has appeared ("Have you come to destroy us?"). The result of Jesus' appearance is heightened activity by the demon,

---

8. See C. K. Barrett, *The New Testament Background: Selected Documents,* rev. ed. (San Francisco: Harper & Row, 1989), pp. 34 ff. Two memorable scriptural attempts to gain control through knowledge of the name are Jacob's wrestling with the angel (Gen. 32:29) and Moses at the burning bush (Exod. 3:13).

resulting in the man's convulsing and crying out. Jesus and the demon have absolutely nothing in common, only antagonism.

This exorcism implies a "before and after" motif, which occurs explicitly in other Markan accounts of Jesus' miracles (see 6:45–52). Before the exorcism there is opposition, violence, crying out; afterward there is silence, victory, and the spread of Jesus' fame. Yet this particular exorcism does not end with a neat resolution of all difficulties. We are perplexed because the bystanders label the exorcism "a new teaching," instead of "a mighty deed." This response makes the encounter something more than an exorcism of an unclean spirit, for the question of Jesus' authority is thus brought to the fore (see 1:22, 27). Clearly for Mark, Jesus' action and teaching are not finally separable. Moreover, the inconclusive result (". . . and they kept on asking one another") suggests that the exorcism had produced no final resolution. Jesus still had to debate with the Pharisees. This episode ends, perhaps ironically, on the note of the spread of Jesus' fame, a fame that will lead not to apparent success but to death.

A brief healing episode (1:29–31) and two summary sections (1:32–34; 1:35–39) separate Jesus' first exorcism from the next major healing event (1:40–45). The healing of the disciple Simon's mother-in-law focuses attention upon the disciples who cannot heal. The disciples are impotent, even though the ill woman is one of their relatives. Jesus' healing enables her to serve. As we learn later, the disciples also have to become servants, though in a different way (see 9:35; 10:35–45; 12:1–11). Therefore, even this brief episode may point beyond itself to the necessity for service by the disciples, something that becomes possible only after they allow themselves to be served by Jesus' death (10:45). A summary section of healing and exorcism follows (1:32–34). The people flock to a healer, the healings take place publicly; curiously, Jesus "would not permit the demons to speak, because they knew him."

In the following section (1:35–39) Jesus retires to a lonely place to pray. In response to the disciples' demands Jesus acknowledges only that he will go to preach in the next towns. The narrative also mentions that he continued "casting out demons" (vs. 39). Evidently Jesus' primary mission is preaching (1:14) and even the casting out of demons is secondary to it. This section (beginning with 1:21) concludes a connected series of episodes taking us through a day to the evening (1:32–34) and the following morning (1:35–39). Perhaps Mark places this series here because it presents typical acts of Jesus.

A key action of Jesus throughout the Gospel is praying. On three other occasions in Mark, Jesus prays. Each time, the motif of faithful discipleship is the common thread of the diverse incidents. After the feeding of the five thousand, Jesus prays (6:46); the immediate consequence is his calming appearance to the disciples terrified by the storm. At the healing of the epileptic boy Jesus tells the disciples that they are unable to heal because they have not prayed (9:29). In the Garden of Gethsemane Jesus also prays for strength to accept his impending death, while the disciples sleep (14:32–42). To become disciples, they will have to "keep awake and pray" (14:38). For Mark

Jesus' primary mission is neither healing nor exorcising demons; Jesus brings near the kingdom of God to effect *discipleship.*

The subsequent episode tells of Jesus' healing of a leper (1:40–45). No demon appears in this healing miracle; the conversation takes place between Jesus and a man. Here for the first time Jesus is moved with pity, and when the man speaks to Jesus, there seems to be something like the element of faith: "If you choose, you can make me clean." In distinction from the exorcism, this healing shows Jesus in touch with the person to be healed, moving more closely within the human realm and eliciting the response of faith. As in the case of the exorcism, the meeting with Jesus produces results; the victim is made well of leprosy and made fit for communion with others. Once again Jesus enjoins silence (cf. vs. 34), but this time he is not obeyed. Although this scene depicts Jesus as acting out of compassion and the man's incipient faith, somehow things are still not right. Because the healed man goes "to spread the word," Jesus can no longer move about openly. Instead of righting everything, the healing seems to deter Jesus from his mission— that of preaching the good news of God and making true disciples—that is, believers in the good news (1:15).

In summary, the Markan exorcisms and healing depict one phase of the struggle that erupts with the mission of Jesus. The purely transcendent struggle between the Spirit and Satan foreshadowed in the temptation (1:12–13) now takes place at the transcendent–historical level of the "Holy One of God" versus the demons (1:24). As we see later, the conflict moves farther within history in the opposition between Jesus and the Pharisees and finally between the suffering Son of Man and his disciples. Although the miracles, the most public deeds of Jesus, inspire an impressive reception (1:28), they also produce inconclusive results, especially with the disciples.

In these passages Jesus' demand for silence about his miracles is critical for understanding how Mark used the stories of Jesus' miracles. We have in Mark an apparent contradiction: the healing tradition does not convey the crucial aspect of Jesus' ministry, yet much of Mark's Gospel, especially the first half, consists of miracle stories. Why then does Mark combine this miracle tradition with injunctions to be silent about the miracles (the so-called messianic secret)? For Mark the heart and center of Jesus' ministry is his suffering and death on the cross. Moreover, the winning of true disciples can take place only through the suffering death of Jesus. Belief in Jesus' power to effect miraculous healings was a given in Mark's church. Mark neither doubts nor disdains the miracle tradition of Jesus; however, he sets that tradition within the special perspective of Jesus' death. Therefore, according to Mark, Jesus does not want people to extol his miraculous deeds; rather he characteristically enjoins silence about them.

Mark's Christian contemporaries knew of divinely empowered miracle workers; moreover, apocryphal stories of Jesus also emphasized his magical powers. In the Infancy Gospel of Thomas the child Jesus is pictured as a great miracle worker: He makes sparrows of clay; he kills a lad who disturbs a pool he made; he destroys a child who strikes his arm; he stretches a short beam into a longer one to aid Joseph, his carpenter father. Such a popular, one-sided emphasis on Jesus as a divine miracle worker is rejected in the Gospel of Mark, not by ignoring that role but by placing it within the context of Jesus' passion. Thus Mark suggests that the fundamental miracle of discipleship, that is, of believing, comes not through Jesus' miracle powers but rather through his death.

Miraculous signs, though not denied, are insufficient to turn followers of Jesus into genuine disciples. Later in Mark, Jesus replies to the Pharisees who come seeking a sign from heaven, "Why does this generation ask for a sign? Truly, I tell you, no sign will be given to this generation" (8:12). According to Mark, public signs of power are not the basis of faith.

DEBATE WITH THE PHARISEES (2:1–3:6)

How are the debates like the miracles?

Communication takes place in many ways. Debate persuades by allowing the listener to hear both sides. Debate, therefore, communicates in conflict, and the Gospel of Mark is an example of such communication by conflict. In Mark, Jesus' teaching takes place primarily in debate, with the Pharisees, with his enemies, or with the disciples, his friends. The debates with the Pharisees and the scribes have parallels with debates in the writings of the rabbis; however, the key for understanding the Markan debates is the exorcisms. Earlier we were puzzled by the people's astonishment at Jesus' *teaching* (1:22) when the story related the driving out of an unclean spirit. Mark seems deliberately to commingle healing action and teaching authority so that Jesus' conflicts (with demons, Pharisees, and disciples) are all of a piece. The healing of the paralytic (2:1–12) demonstrates that healing action ("Stand up and take your mat and walk") and authoritative teaching ("Your sins are forgiven") are inextricably interwoven and suggests implicitly that Jesus has to wrestle with the stubbornness of the Pharisees as well as crippling disease. Indeed, the community of Markan Christianity, as represented in the disciples, is both to perform works of power (6:13) and to practice forgiveness (11:25).

The prelude for this section is once again the calling of disciples, in this case a tax collector named Levi (2:13 f.; cf. 1:16–20).[9] The closely related following episode shows Jesus eating at table with sinners and tax collectors (2:15–17). Sinners presumably had in some obvious way broken the Mosaic law (cf. Luke 7:36–50). Tax collectors were hired by those agents who purchased the right to collect taxes for the Roman government and in turn were allowed to extract heavy taxes from the Jewish people. Evidently the two groups were social outcasts, yet Jesus and his disciples ate at table with them. The scribes and the Pharisees object to the disciples about Jesus' conduct,

9. Levi does not appear in the later Markan list of the twelve disciples (3:16–19); but cf. Matt. 9:9, where the Levi of this Markan story has become Matthew, who is named as one of the Twelve.

though not to Jesus himself. (Perhaps the involvement of the disciples at this point indicates that the issue was still a live one in the early church.) Even though not addressed directly, Jesus replies with an answer that silences everyone. He comes to the sick; that is the physician's duty. Jesus' opponents fail to grasp that a new society of disciples, those who follow Jesus, is being formed. The ancient rigid distinctions of clean and unclean, especially the procedure for forgiveness (see vs. 7), are being swept away in the new community that Jesus inaugurates.

The following section (2:18–22) concerning fasting probes this new society further. This time Mark distinguishes not only between Jesus and the Pharisees but also between Jesus' disciples and those of John the Baptist. Both the Pharisees and the disciples of John fast. But Jesus, as the bringer of good news, asserts the absurdity of fasting, for his disciples now experience a new reality ("the bridegroom").

The statement (vs. 20) implying that they will fast after Jesus' death may in the Markan context refer to the suffering and persecution that the disciples will have to endure. In the second half of Mark, Jesus speaks unequivocally about the necessity of suffering. Indeed, Jesus' words (especially vs. 20) do not allow the reader to forget the impending death. The final words of the episode (2:21 f.) mark an end to the debate and an answer to the conflict over fasting. Everything stresses newness—the bridegroom is present, new cloth and new wine are available; fresh skins are needed, for the old cannot determine the new. The old order must make way for the new; real disciples know and act upon this "newness."

The first two episodes of this section stressed the breaking forth of a new society in connection with Jesus; the following two episodes focus on unorthodox Sabbath activity. Even though it is the disciples who have violated the Sabbath (2:23–28), the Pharisees now debate directly with Jesus. Jesus answers their charge by quoting scripture, citing the example of David (see 1 Sam. 21:1–6).[10] The criterion, suggested by the David episode, is apparently that need takes precedence over law. Moreover, the first half of Jesus' final word ("The sabbath was made for humankind, not humankind for the sabbath"—vs. 27) also bears out this view, which in isolation sounds quite modern—that is, human considerations take precedence over legalistic ritual. Yet the final clause ("so the Son of Man is lord even of the sabbath") indicates that we have in Jesus' saying something more than a general humanitarian principle. The appearance of the Son of Man signifies the beginning of the end time, the irruption of a new age (see p. 227 f.; cf. Dan. 7:13 and Mark 13:26). Jesus' disciples can now violate the Sabbath, because they are beginning to live out of the new time being ushered in with Jesus: the time for joy (vs. 19), the time for wine (vs. 22), and the time for forgiveness of sinners (vs. 17; cf. vs. 10).

---

10. Mark seems to have erred in that Ahimelech, not Abiathar, was high priest at the time of this incident (1 Sam. 21:2).

The next episode places the debate with the Pharisees in the context of healing (3:1–6). In the synagogue, the stronghold of the Pharisees, Jesus is being watched—the Pharisees are not at first named. The atmosphere is that of a test of Jesus (cf. also 8:11; 10:2; 12:13, 15), similar to his time of testing in the wilderness. A comparison of this episode with the previous exorcism of the unclean spirit (1:21–28) illuminates how debate conflict is both similar to and yet also different from demon conflict. Jesus commanded the demon to be silent (1:25). Now, before the healing is performed, his opponents are silent before his question, "Is it lawful to do good or to do harm on the sabbath, to save life or to kill?" (3:4). After the exorcism, even though there was questioning of his authority, Jesus' fame spread (1:27 f.). Now, after Jesus' Sabbath healing, his enemies plot to destroy him (3.6).

These enemies are labeled as Pharisees and Herodians. The Herodians may have been followers of Herod Antipas, tetrarch of Galilee and Perea (4 B.C.–A.D. 39) during the life of Jesus. Possibly they were royalists who hoped for restoration of a united monarchy, as in the time of Herod the Great (37–34 B.C.). However the Herodians are identified, their presence at this point hints at Jesus' impending suffering and death. The only action specifically attributed to Herod Antipas in Mark is the beheading of John the Baptist (6:14–29; note vs. 29). Every Markan reference to the Herodians or to Herod explicitly points to a conflict ending in the death of Jesus (cf. 8:15 and 12:13; also 3:6 and 6:14 ff.). The new is upsetting to the old; the Pharisees, the champions of Sabbath observance, cannot tolerate the presence of the Son of Man, who is lord even of the Sabbath, so with the Herodians they plot Jesus' death.

The remainder of the first half of Mark may be characterized as a development of what is already implied in the opening scenes of the Gospel. The old order's resistance to Jesus' message and action frees the good news to appeal to new multitudes, even those from Tyre and Sidon lying beyond Palestine (3:7–12). When rejected by the established religious authorities, Jesus forms the new Israel, founded upon the twelve disciples (3:13–19a). Whoever doubts the authenticity of this new community fails to see the clear manifestations of God's work through Jesus' casting out demons (3:28–30). Moreover, no one can rely upon a guaranteed privilege that reckoned physical descent as assurance of God's favor (3:31–35).

Nothing avails to eliminate the opposition to Jesus by the Jewish leaders. His parables about the breaking in of God's word are closed ciphers to all except the joyful few who really hear Jesus' word about a new society (4:1–20, esp. vss. 8 f. and vs. 20).

Even those who hear must receive further private instruction (see 4:33 f.), because Mark has in view the necessity for perseverance to the end (cf. 13:9–13). The hope for such endurance rests in the amazing power that accompanies Jesus ("Who then is this, that even wind and sea obey him?"—4:41). This power protects the disciples from the violent sea (4:35–41) and casts the fearsome unclean spirit Legion into the sea (5:1–13). Oddly, the people beg Jesus to leave their neighborhood because of his demon exorcism (vs. 7).

Galilee, Samaria, Syro-Phoenicia, and Syria.

Moreover, instead of the usual command to silence, Jesus urges the restored demoniac to tell his friends about the mercy God has shown (5:19–20).

This injunction to speak about God's action contrasts all the more with the ending of the next episode (5:21–43), which explicitly enjoins silence. The preceding episode of the demon Legion (5:1–20) emphasizes, however, the destruction of the old and the people's fearful response to that loss. In the present double episode of the raising of Jairus' daughter and the healing of the woman, we have the typically Markan technique of intercalation, inserting one story or comment into another, presumably in order to interpret the one by the other (see, e.g., 2:1–12 and 9:14–32). Thereby two central themes of the second half of Mark, the necessity for faith (vs. 34) and the resurrection from the dead (vs. 41), are highlighted and connected. The command to silence is appropriate to these themes. Although the people still figure in this narrative as they did in the exorcism, the center of attention is beginning to shift more clearly to the response of disciples (see vss. 31, 37, 40). The importance of the disciples becomes more evident in the following stories: Jesus is rejected by his own people (6:1–6); he appoints the twelve disciples for a mission of healing and exorcism (6:7–13); John the baptizer is beheaded by Herod and his body is given to his disciples (6:14–29), perhaps in anticipation of the role for which Jesus is beginning to prepare his disciples. The disciples' return from the mission and the miraculous feeding of the multitudes (6:30–44) are to be viewed as a foreshadowing of the Lord's Supper and the death and resurrection of Jesus.

Conflict with the religious leaders becomes most acute in the following chapter where the Markan Jesus abolishes the crucial distinctions of purity embedded in the cultic law of Judaism (see 7:11–23). Moreover, the extension of Jesus' powers in exorcising the demon from the daughter of the Gentile Syrophoenician woman (7:24–30) foreshadows an extension of the new religious community beyond the borders of Israel.

In summary, this brief journey through some of the remaining portions of the first half of Mark (up to 8:21) suggests that the debates with the Pharisees are matters of life and death (2:15–3:6). For Mark the new reality, especially the new society that will emerge in Jesus' disciples, represents a freedom toward the law that could not be tolerated within Pharisaism. Consequently, the religious leaders resist; they plan Jesus' death. In a certain sense Jesus opposed the demons more successfully and more easily than he did the Pharisees. Ironically, the reaction of the Pharisees and other authorities to Jesus, their rejection and the plotting of his death, becomes the means for the accomplishment of Jesus' victory in making disciples (8:31; cf. 8:34). For even though the disciples remained close to Jesus throughout the first half of Mark, they had yet to learn the secret of Jesus' power. That realization came only with Jesus' death and resurrection.

The Power of Suffering: Jesus Wins His Disciples (8:22–15:47)

The second half of the Gospel of Mark centers upon the passion of Jesus. The passion story includes Jesus' decision to go to Jerusalem (10:32–34), the events of the last days in Jerusalem (11:1–14:72), and finally his death on the cross (15:1–47). Jesus' predictions of the passion begin in Chapter 8. When we observe that the passion of Jesus thus embraces almost one-half of the Gospel, the characterization of Mark as a passion story with an extended introduction seems particularly apt. In the first half of Mark, Jesus has dealt with his opponents, the demons and the Pharisees. In the second half, the human opponents will deal with Jesus. They put him to death by the Roman form of capital punishment—crucifixion. Yet these last chapters do not dwell on the opponents of Jesus. Instead, the disciples and their understanding of Jesus become central.

At three crucial moments Jesus predicts the suffering he must undergo: "Then he began to teach them that the Son of Man must undergo great suffering, and be rejected by the elders, the chief priests, and the scribes, and be killed, and after three days rise again" (8:31; cf. 9:31; 10:33 f.). The disciples' continued misunderstanding or inability to accept this prediction becomes clear in the Garden of Gethsemane just before the arrest, trial, and crucifixion. They could not watch and pray while Jesus was going through temptation (14:38–41). The terse, seemingly final, verdict on the disciples is pronounced immediately after Jesus' arrest, "All of them deserted him and fled" (14:50). Indeed, even the closest disciple, Peter, denied Jesus not once but three times (14:66–72).

The disciples' denial and flight occur because of their inability or unwillingness to acknowledge that their own discipleship must share the same quality as Jesus' suffering. Mark's Gospel speaks not only about the nature of Jesus' messiahship but also about the nature of discipleship; the second half of Mark implies that there is no victory except through suffering and conflict.

Structural considerations show that Mark 8:22–10:52 is the central, pivotal part of the Gospel, introducing its second half. This long section begins with the story of the blind man who at first sees men like trees walking. It ends with the gift of sight to blind Bartimaeus, who then chooses to follow Jesus. Before this point in the Gospel is reached, Jesus' miracles are recounted in much detail. His teaching is frequently mentioned but not extensively described, except in scenes of controversy such as Mark 7:1–23, when Jesus denounces the Pharisees and the tradition of the elders. Mark contains a number of controversy scenes and stories. We have noted how these are related to the exorcisms, which are characterized by struggle between the demons and Jesus. With the first story of Jesus' bestowing sight (8:22–26), decisive new factors enter the picture. First, in response to Jesus' question Peter confesses Jesus as Messiah (8:27–30). Then Jesus repeatedly predicts his approaching suffering and death as the Son of Man. Jesus appears transfigured before his disciples (9:2–8), a foretaste of his resurrection, but they are far from understanding the meaning of this and other things that are transpiring.

Indeed, the whole section mirrors and emphasizes the disciples' lack of understanding, both of Jesus and of themselves. This is nowhere more evident than when Jesus instructs them in the meaning of discipleship (8:31–38; 9:33–37; 10:35–45). Whenever the disciples, or James and John, seek prefer-

Statue of Jesus carrying the cross by Justin Accrombessi, contemporary artist from Ghana.   *(Courtesy of Spartaco Appetiti.)*

ment, Jesus admonishes them by his own example: "Whoever wishes to be great among you must be your servant, and whoever wishes to be first among you must be slave of all. For the Son of man came not to be served but to serve, and to give his life a ransom for many" (10:43–45).

Immediately afterward Jesus enters Jerusalem (11:1–11) and the passion week is already beginning. This section is clearly a new phase of the Gospel. The structure, the arrangement of the material, and the emphases that emerge in the narrative show that a distinctive teaching about messiahship and discipleship is being set forth and emphasized in Mark 8:22–10:52. The theme of the true character of Jesus' messiahship leads to the reiterated and heavily emphasized teaching about discipleship. This section is a fitting introduction to the second half of the Gospel, which presents Jesus' death. The reader is learning what that death implies for Jesus' messiahship and for true discipleship.

Two Stages of Discipleship (8:22–9:9)

Why does Jesus respond as he does to Peter's confession?

The point of transition from the first portion of Mark to the second can be located in the incident at Caesarea Philippi, where Peter confesses Jesus as the Christ (the Messiah) and Jesus answers by declaring that his mission is one of suffering (8:27–33). The preceding episode, the healing of the blind man at Bethsaida (8:22–26), dramatically symbolizes what follows. This story stands out as the only two-stage healing in the Gospels. When Jesus first heals, the man sees only dimly and men look like trees walking; then Jesus heals again and the blind man sees everything clearly. The unique manner of this healing seems to prefigure the "seeing" of the disciple Peter in the next episode. Peter sees that Jesus is the Christ; however, he does not yet understand the suffering nature of Jesus' messiahship (vs. 32). Peter, like the other disciples, must go through a second stage of "healing" before he can become a true disciple (cf. 8:34 ff.).

Peter's confession occurs on the way to the villages of Caesarea Philippi, located at the far northern end of Palestine where Hellenistic influence was prevalent. The location suggests that underneath Jesus' query about his identity may lie the question of whether his ministry should extend beyond the borders of Israel. After his death it will. At any rate, the answers of others (John the Baptist, Elijah, a prophet) are inadequate (cf. 6:14 f.). When Jesus turns the question to the disciples, Peter, speaking for them, answers, "You are the Messiah." Jesus then charges them not to tell anyone who he is (8:30). Previous commands of silence concerned his exorcisms and healings; now Jesus commands silence about his identity.

This passage serves as the focal point for what has become known in New Testament research as the problem of the "messianic secret," a term that includes Jesus' commands to keep silent about his miracles (1:34, 44; 3:12; 5:43; 7:36) and his identity (8:27–30; 9:9), his private instruction to the disciples (7:17 f.; 9:39 f.; 10:10), and his private interpretation of parables (4:10 ff., 33 f.).[11] The two most frequent proposals for understanding the "messianic secret" are (1) that Jesus commanded silence to keep the uninstructed multitudes from learning about and perverting his nonpolitical messiahship into a political one or (2) that Jesus actually did not understand himself to be the Messiah; the secrecy motif is an attempt to explain, from the standpoint of the early church's faith that Jesus was the Messiah, why Jesus was not publicly recognized as such and why the Jesus tradition was relatively devoid of messianic claims. The first explanation depends entirely on the argument from silence, for there is nothing about such a motivation in the text. In the second case, there is, of course, a tension between Jesus' relative silence about his own role and the evangelists' (and church's) faith in him as the Christ. But both these solutions betray a modern preoccupation with the question of whether, or in what sense, Jesus thought that he was the Messiah. Moreover, they fail to take account of the several types of material grouped under the "messianic secret" motif. In Mark the question is not whether Jesus was Messiah, but why he was the kind of Messiah he was.

Within the Gospel itself the "messianic secret" focuses the reader's attention on the question of the nature of Jesus' messiahship and consequently upon the nature of Christian discipleship. The disciples, including Peter, misunderstood the role of Jesus as the Christ. As the Son of Man (the apocalyptic, heavenly figure?) Jesus must suffer many things and be killed, and after three days rise (8:31). Peter's rebuke of Jesus leads to Jesus' rebuke of Peter (vss. 32 f.). The disciples' expectation of a miracle-working Messiah who delivers his followers from all unpleasantness into great reward (cf. 10:32–45) is rejected. The "messianic secret" restrains and tones down the miracle tradition of Jesus precisely because the reader is being forced to acknowledge and accept Jesus' suffering. In fact, the community of Christians (followers of Jesus) is for Mark not possible until after Jesus' death and resurrection.

The subsequent section on discipleship (8:34–9:1), spoken not only to the disciples but also to the multitudes, characterizes following Jesus as fellowship in service and suffering. Thus the character of Jesus' messiahship determines what discipleship must be. The disciples, in becoming followers of Jesus, have taken the first step; however, they have not yet realized the full implications of discipleship. Victory can be realized only in conflict. Just as the Spirit fought Satan, and just as Jesus opposed demons and Pharisees, so too the disciples must continue to struggle until the end. That, according to Mark, cannot be far off: "There are some standing here who will not taste death until they see that the kingdom of God has come with power" (9:1; cf. Mark 13:24–37). Nowhere, however, does Jesus himself connect the coming

---

11. The classic treatment is still that of William Wrede, *The Messianic Secret,* trans. by J. C. G. Greig (Cambridge: Clark, 1971). See C. M. Tuckett (ed.), *The Messianic Secret* (Philadelphia: Fortress, 1983), which contains a number of recent and important essays on the subject.

kingdom with his title, Christ. In Mark at least, Jesus is not to be understood primarily as the political messiah, the expected restorer of Israel.[12] The most frequent Markan designation for Jesus is the Son of Man. As Son of Man he exercises freedom over the law (2:10, 28), goes to his suffering and death (8:31 and passim), and will come again as eschatological judge (8:38; 13:26; 14:62). Thus the community Mark envisions is one that awaits the end time.

Jesus' teaching after Peter's confession (8:34–9:1) focuses upon the nature of discipleship rather than on the identity of the one whom the disciples follow. Not until the following episode, the transfiguration scene (9:2–9), does Mark return to the question of Jesus' identity. There Jesus, with three disciples, climbs a high mountain where he is transfigured. His clothes become glistening white, like those of the angels; moreover, even Moses and Elijah appear to speak with him. According to Israel's tradition, Moses gave the law from a mountain (Exod. 19:16 ff.) and Elijah prophesied from a mountain (1 Kings 19:9 ff). Thus Jesus converses with the two men representing Israel's heritage of the law and the prophets. Again the disciples misunderstand (vs. 6), not realizing that the coming of Jesus in some way fulfills the law and the prophets, for Jesus alone remains (vs. 8).

The climactic statement of the transfiguration scene, by the voice from the cloud ("This is my Son, the Beloved; listen to him!"—vs. 7), alludes to the kingly tradition of Israel (cf. Psalm 2:7). If any other Old Testament figure was worthy of this distinguished company on the mountain, it would be David, the king of ancient Israel (cf. 2:25; 10:47 f.; 12:35 ff.). Possibly his exclusion prevents any political misunderstanding about the role of Jesus. At any rate, the voice announces to the disciples that Jesus is the eschatological king of Israel, the true final king. Jesus is Son of God with kingly power. At another crucial revelation of Jesus' identity in Mark, similar words have been spoken (1:11). Indeed, Mark's opening, "The beginning of the good news of Jesus Christ, the *Son of God*" (1:1), has already coupled this designation with Jesus. Such kingly power has to be viewed, however, in the context of the injunction "listen to him" (vs. 7). In the following teaching (9:9–13), Jesus not only charges the disciples to be silent but explicitly links his power with both John's suffering ("Elijah has come"—vs. 13) and his own (vs. 12). The final Markan designation of Jesus as Son of God occurs at the cross (15:39). Jesus' kingly power fulfills the law and the prophets by enduring suffering (see 14:21, 27).

A definite scheme thus appears: at the baptism, Jesus is declared Son of God by a voice from heaven. At the transfiguration, Jesus is announced as Son of God by a voice from the cloud to the three major disciples. At the cross, Jesus is proclaimed Son of God by a Gentile centurion. By implication, the kingdom comes with power (9:1) when the Son of God's suffering is accomplished and is both affirmed and imitated by the inclusive community that exists after Jesus' death and resurrection.

---

12. See 8:29; 13:21 f.; 14:61; 15:32. Mark of course does not deny the appropriateness of this title when properly used (cf. 1:1; 9:41; 12:35–37).

FAITH TO PRODUCE HEALING (9:14–32)

Why is the father's attitude superior to that of the disciples?

From this point to the end of the Gospel, the disciples are often in the foreground (see esp. 9:33–41; 10:23–31; 13:1 ff.) and always in the background. In 9:14–32, the healing of an epileptic boy, Mark combines two stories, the one showing how a father's faith enables his son to be healed and the other drawing a contrast between the master's ability and the disciples' inability to heal, in order to present an example of genuine faith for the disciples. They are unable to heal because they do not yet understand the nature of true belief (cf. 9:32).

The argumentative disciples form a contrast with the beseeching father. He cries out, "I believe; help my unbelief!" (vs. 24), thereby demonstrating that all things are possible to the believer (vs. 23). Of course, this prayer for healing originates from the crisis of the father's desperate need. The disciples cannot heal because they do not pray (vs. 29). Prayer is characteristic of Jesus (1:35; 6:46). Later the ability to pray seems almost equivalent to the act of faith: "So I tell you whatever you ask for in prayer, believe that you have received it, and it will be yours" (11:24; cf. 11:22–26). The necessity for prayer becomes evident in the major Markan prayer episode, Jesus in the Garden of Gethsemane (14:32–42). The disciples are to wait while Jesus prays (vs. 32), but they are also warned to pray (vs. 38). Jesus asks that suffering (the cup) might pass from him; however, he prays that God's will, not his own, be done. The disciples cannot heal, because they neither pray nor believe; they do not experience the suffering of Jesus. The necessity for such suffering is made explicit at the close of this healing episode (9:30–32). Again, Jesus predicts further conflict, but the disciples "did not understand what he was saying, and were afraid to ask him" (vs. 32).

In fact, fear dominates the disciples (cf. 4:40; 5:15; 9:6, 32; 10:32; 16:8). Probably such fear underscores the condition of the community to which the Gospel is addressed. Mark's Gospel was likely written to a church undergoing persecution (cf. pp.67–68 above). According to Mark, this fear can be overcome by faith (vs. 23). The worst the disciples had to fear from persecution was death. In the healing of the epileptic boy, however, even the verdict, "He is dead" (vs. 26), proves false, because of the father's faith. Moreover, although Jesus, as the Son of Man, will be killed, after three days "he will rise" (vs. 31). If the disciples truly follow Jesus, then they too will go through persecution into victory. Indeed, the end time will be one of vindication (see 13:20 f.) if they continue and endure.

For the time being, however, the disciples are afraid. Out of their fear and lack of faith they dispute about greatness (9:34), are not open to lowly children (10:13), and deter nondisciples from casting out demons (9:38). They have still to understand that Jesus' messiahship demands discipleship of service (vs. 41) to one another (vs. 50).

JESUS APPROACHES HIS DEATH (10:1–14:72)

What theological belief holds the themes of the narrative together?

As Jesus goes into Judea (10:1) and enters Jerusalem (11:1), he moves inevitably toward his suffering and death. The narrative of the events leading up to and including Jesus' crucifixion is in Mark dominated by four separate but interrelated themes: fulfillment of the old, desertion by the disciples, victory through failure, and the necessity of Jesus' death. While they are characteristic of Mark, each is also traditional in the sense that it was shared by other Christians. This section of the Gospel sums up the Markan themes we have seen emerging from the beginning.

FULFILLMENT OF THE OLD

The Pharisees try to trap Jesus by raising the question of divorce (10:2–12), but Jesus declares that the will of God is communicated through the scripture rather than being identical with the scripture. (Jesus is not a literalist; some aspects of scripture are more important than others.) A man who obeys the law goes away sorrowful because his allegiance is finally to himself rather than to God (10:17–22). Jesus triumphantly enters Jerusalem, the holy city of Israel, but only to cleanse the holy temple (11:1–19). Indeed, Jesus cannot accept the crowd's accolades ("Blessed is the coming kingdom of our ancestor David!"—11:9) because Christ is not the Son of David (12:35–37) in a political sense. The kingdom that Jesus announces brings the end of history (chap. 13) rather than the restoration of Israel's kingdom. The religious leaders of Israel reject this leader and the new society created by him (12:1–12) because they quibble about taxes (12:13–17) and resurrection (12:18–27) and ignore God's coming near. In the narration of the passion itself, there are many allusions to the Old Testament. Scripture is fulfilled, but in ways that could hardly have been anticipated.

DESERTION BY THE DISCIPLES

The disciples continue to follow Jesus; however, they question his "hard" sayings (10:23–31) and they follow only in fear (10:32). Just before Jesus' trial they all flee (14:50). Moreover, Mark underscores that fact with the little tale of the young follower of Jesus who flees away naked (14:51–52). The most crushing rejection of Jesus occurs in Peter's denial (14:53–72), especially tragic when viewed against Jesus' prediction and Peter's protest (14:26–31). Even as Jesus is put on trial before the Council, Peter is tried and found wanting.

VICTORY THROUGH FAILURE

The disciples are, however, the closest followers of Jesus, and in spite of their desertion, Jesus will still come to them in Galilee after his death. In fact, the Last Supper anticipates such a reunion (14:12–28). The disciples may confidently look forward to it. Their confidence has several grounds: Jesus shows mercy, even to little children (10:13–16); the God who can do all things is at work (10:23–31); the only requirements are a recognition of need (10:46–52; cf. 9:23), the practice of forgiveness (11:25), and a letting go of self (12:41–44)—that is, a response of faith (11:20–26). Indeed, the transfiguration scene (9:2–13) probably represents a proleptic glory that both Jesus and the true disciples will share.

NECESSITY OF JESUS' DEATH

The disciples' paralyzing fear in the face of persecution (see 13:9, 19) cannot be taken as final, for Jesus' death by crucifixion is the way in which God's victory will be achieved for them (10:32–45). This death is not only predicted by Jesus but is also prepared for by the anointing with costly ointment (14:1–9) and celebrated in the Last Supper (14:12–25). It occurs at the instigation of one of the disciples (14:10 f.). Although Jesus himself prays that his death may be avoided, he accepts the cross as God's will (14:32–42). In the scenes immediately before and during the crucifixion, Jesus' innocence is apparent (14:53–65; 15:1–15) and his behavior is exemplary (15:16–32). Thereby Mark shows the injustice of the human agents in Jesus' death and the perfect submission of Jesus to a death that ultimately triumphs through God's will.

Significantly, the context in which the reader of Mark views Jesus' suffering in his trial and death (chaps. 14–15) is the prediction of the suffering and future triumph of the church of Jesus (chap. 13). This address by Jesus, known as the "little apocalypse," maintains a tension between the imminence of the end (vss. 14, 26, 29, 30, 35) and the recognition that the time of its coming is unknown. Not even Jesus knows exactly when it will come (vss. 7, 21, 32). Mark's apocalyptic look into the future is an explicit warning to the church against understanding Christian existence as present power, even in miraculous acts (see vss. 6–8, 21–27). The present consists of suffering that, because it is acknowledged, accepted, and not avoided, will eventually lead to triumph. The Markan community that faces persecution is bolstered by its belief in the imminent end of history and the final triumph with Jesus in the fulfilled kingdom of God.

THE CROSS OF JESUS (15:33–47)

What is the meaning of Jesus' last words?

The Markan account of the crucifixion seemingly depicts an action accomplished by Jesus' opponents. Jesus remains passive. Pilate's question as to whether he is the king of the Jews is answered enigmatically (15:1–5). Jesus makes no plea for his life before the crowd when Barabbas is released (15:6–15). He does not protest the scourging (15:16–20). Someone else carries his cross. Furthermore, he does not even acknowledge those who mock his helplessness on the cross (15:21–32). The one action of Jesus upon which

Mark centers is the loud cry from the cross: "My God, my God, why have you forsaken me?" (15:34; cf. Psalm 22:1). Mark underscores the cry's importance by first giving it in Jesus' native Aramaic and then translating it into Greek. The meaning of this cry can only be understood from the context. The setting for Jesus' death is somber. At noon darkness comes over the whole land for three hours before he dies (vs. 33). Although generally it took at least twelve hours for someone to die by crucifixion, Jesus died after only six. At the critical moment, Jesus shouts this cry of apparent despair. Someone rushes to give him vinegar while others mockingly ask whether Elijah will come to help. Then he "gave a loud cry and breathed his last" (vs. 37). In reading the text, we observe that Jesus gave two loud cries just before his death. Possibly "My God, why have you forsaken me?" was a later addition spelling out what the "loud cry" was. If so, then Mark, or the tradition lying behind Mark, added these words for a specific reason. Whatever the answer to the question of the cry's origin, clearly this shout is the Markan key to Jesus' death.

Traditionally these words (vs. 34) have been considered the "cry of dereliction," the cry of despair at abandonment by God. Yet these words may be a cry of victory, for they are the opening words of Psalm 22, which begins in despair but ends on a note of triumph: "All the ends of the earth shall remember and turn to the Lord; and all the families of the nations shall worship before him. For dominion belongs to the Lord, and he rules over the nations" (Psalm 22:27 f.). Perhaps so, but the theological truth of such reasoning should not remove the element of despair and real suffering. Clearly the Psalmist suffers, and Jesus suffers; Mark intends for the reader to perceive Jesus' sense of despair, even to the point of apparently being abandoned by God. Thus Jesus' last fearful word in Mark maintains tension to the very end. No premature miracle rescues Jesus from this final struggle with God himself (cf. 14:36).

The preceding scene at the cross (15:29–32) stresses the Markan perception of the necessity for suffering. Here Jesus is mocked because he cannot save himself, although he has claimed to save others. The mockers ironically make Mark's point. Suffering cannot be avoided for Jesus, the disciples, and Mark's persecuted church, because thereby others can be saved.

Yet Mark claims for Jesus and the church victory in suffering. The mockery over his boast of destroying and rebuilding the temple in three days (15:29 f.) is answered by the tearing apart of the temple curtain at Jesus' death (vs. 38), for that death extends God's revelation and relation with Israel to all people. Fittingly, the Gentile centurion confesses Jesus as "Son of God" (vs. 39). The extension of God's salvation to everyone answers the mocking of those waiting for Elijah to take Jesus down. God has come down to open the temple. The principal actor in the passion is neither Jesus nor the people and officials, but God. In Jesus' suffering, God is acting to effect triumph. We might have anticipated this conclusion. Even when Jesus cried out in despair (vs. 34), his cry was addressed to God; he was praying. In Mark, prayer or faith makes all things possible, even victory in the face of apparent defeat (cf. 14:34 f.; 9:29; 11:24).

Part of the Via Dolorosa, the traditional way through which Jesus carried his cross to Golgotha.   *(Courtesy of Israel Government Tourist Office.)*

Mark in effect depicts three responses to Jesus' death: those of the centurion (vs. 39), the women (vss. 40 f.), and Joseph of Arimathea (vss. 42–47). The most important of these is that of the centurion (cf. 1:1, 11; 9:7). Unlike the disciples, who were earlier afraid (4:40; 6:50; 10:32), the centurion boldly confesses Jesus as the Son of God. This affirmation occurs directly after Jesus' death. Possibly the centurion was impressed with the manner in which Jesus died, but the Markan text mentions no such impression. Conceivably the centurion spoke in derision or contempt. We cannot know. What we do

Jesus' crucifixion by a contemporary African sculptor, E. G. Isacco.   *(Courtesy of Spartaco Appetiti.)*

know, however, is that "Son of God" is a key Markan designation of Jesus (1:1). At the baptism such sonship meant obedience to God (1:11); at the transfiguration such sonship announced the kingly power of Jesus (9:7); and now at the crucifixion the centurion proclaims Jesus as God's Son precisely at his death (cf. also 3:11; 5:17). Thereby Mark manifests Jesus' suffering messiahship as the key to discipleship.

The women confirm that Jesus is dead, for the disciples have all fled and they are the only ones left. Moreover, the Galilean women make peculiarly good and apt Markan witnesses of Jesus' death. We are told that they "used to follow him and provided for him" (vs. 41). Of course, "following" is another way of expressing discipleship (cf. esp. 1:17), and their "providing" picks up Jesus' emphasis upon "service" (the same Greek word, *diakonein* or *diako-*

nia, is used for both): "For the Son of man also came not to be *served* but to *serve,* and to give his life as a ransom for many" (10:45). Furthermore, Jesus charged his disciples, "Whoever wants to be first must be last of all and *servant* of all" (9:35). These women are the first followers of Jesus to see his death, witness his burial, and hear the resurrection report. They were apparently also the first followers to accept Jesus' way of service. Possibly the Markan church was noteworthy for the prominent role of women. The way of discipleship receives further explication in the action of Joseph of Arimathea, a respected member of the Jewish council (vs. 43). In contrast to the chosen disciples, he has courage (cf. 14:50). Furthermore, he seeks the kingdom of God, whereas the disciples appear to be seeking their own welfare (cf. 10:35–45).

The passion story ends with conclusive evidence of the death of Jesus. Pilate learns from the centurion that Jesus has died quickly (15:44). The body is laid and sealed in the tomb. Yet already in the centurion, the women, and Joseph of Arimathea, something new is being born.

Epilogue: The Future Victory (16:1–8)

Why do the women respond in fear?

After Jesus' death the Christian reader expects a happy ending: resurrection and glorious triumph. The note of victory is in fact present in Mark's epilogue, but it is restrained. Among the Gospels, only Mark fails to record an appearance of Jesus to the women or disciples.[13] The Gospel ends with verse 8 rather than the spurious ending, verses 9–20. The only evidence contradicting the natural assumption that the death is final is the empty tomb story, which in itself is ambiguous. The absence of Jesus' body does not necessarily prove his resurrection (cf. Matt. 28:13–15).

The opening verses (1–4) set the atmosphere for the incident. The women are going to perform a pious deed, to anoint the body of Jesus. Evidently burial was hasty and they could not anoint the body on the holy Sabbath. At the first opportunity ("very early") they go to the tomb. They have come to honor the dead Jesus, but their plans are upset. Mark portrays a young man sitting in the open tomb, who, from his apparel, must be an angel, a messenger from God. Naturally the women are quite amazed, but the angel chides them for their perplexity (vs. 6a). Earlier encounters with Jesus evoked similar awe and amazement from the crowds (1:27; 9:15), the Pharisees (12:17), and the disciples (10:24). This response, however, falls short of the required act of faith. Amazement and awe at Jesus' numinous,

---

13. Our interpretation of Mark's ending omits Mark 16:9–20 because this passage is doubtless a later addition to the text. See Taylor, *The Gospel According to St. Mark* (New York: Macmillan, 1955), p. 610.

divine quality are not enough. Neither is the reaction of fear (16:8) an adequate response to Jesus, whether on the part of Jesus' opponents (11:18) or his disciples (4:40; 9:6, 32). Amazement and fear are already linked at the first explicit reference to Jesus' unalterable movement toward Jerusalem (10:32). True discipleship consists of more than awe at the numinous or fear at the realities of human finitude. Something more, a response of faith, a victory through suffering, is required according to Mark (cf. 4:40; 10:52; 11:22).

The women, disciples, and Peter are promised that something more will occur. Jesus will go before them into Galilee (16:7). Of course, they have no guarantee other than the angel's word (cf. 14:28) that he will appear in Galilee. The precise reason for the choice of Galilee is not certain. Perhaps the disciples are to meet Jesus in Galilee, rather than Jerusalem, to gather forces for the Gentile mission. The precise meaning of the promise that they will see Jesus is also unclear. Perhaps the disciples are to await the second coming of Christ, the parousia, when God's kingdom will fully come (cf. chap. 13). More likely, they will await a resurrection appearance of Jesus ("there you will see him"; cf. 14:28). Indeed, the first resurrection appearances to the disciples were likely in Galilee (Matt. 28:16; cf. John 21:1). Whatever the exact meaning, the promise stresses the future. Everything has not yet happened; a future victory awaits. The Markan story of Jesus does not promise to deliver the church from persecution, even though in Jesus' life and death a first victory has been won. Satan was bound, demons were exorcised, opponents were defeated in debate, disciples were gathered. Moreover, the future promises a second, complete victory. But the future can still only be assured through faith. In the present the church faces strife and persecution (see 13:19).

Mark's concluding words ("for they were afraid") corroborate this interpretation. Some scholars challenge this ending, even though manuscript evidence decisively supports it, because it sounds like a half sentence.[14] Nevertheless, the present ending of Mark fits the Gospel. The women are left with fear, the normal and ever-present fear of a church undergoing persecution in the mid-sixties, probably at Rome. Of course, Mark wishes to encourage endurance, faith, and prayer in spite of fear, but the Gospel does not command faith only at its end. Instead, Mark's whole Gospel implies the need for faith in a final victory, because an initial triumph through suffering has occurred in Jesus. Mark is realistic enough to acknowledge fear and hopeful enough to proclaim the breaking of fear's power through faith in that future final victory promised by the suffering and resurrected Jesus.

---

14. In addition, the end of a manuscript, especially a papyrus scroll, could easily be lost. Although inferior manuscripts provide what was deemed a more satisfying ending to Mark (cf. 16:9–20), Matthew and Luke appear to know only our version, which ends at 16:8. Their respective resurrection appearance stories do not parallel Mark's longer ending (16:9–20). Cf. note 13.

Conclusion

A summary of our interpretation of the Gospel of Mark can best be made by reviewing the results of our four-step methodology:

In *structure* this Gospel presents a series of conflicts between Jesus, allied with God's Spirit (1:1–15), and opponents at various levels: Satan, demons, Pharisees, and finally disciples. The major Markan watershed is Peter's confession at Caesarea Philippi (8:22 ff.); from this point attention shifts to Jesus' relationship with his disciples. The first half of Mark shows Jesus' movement toward apparent success both in miracle and debate, whereas in the second half he moves toward apparent failure in death, as the disciples misunderstand.

We have found at least five themes or *emphases* in Mark: (1) the miracles of Jesus; (2) his passion; (3) the messianic secret; (4) the call to a discipleship of suffering and service; (5) the confession of Jesus as Son of God. Our interpretation reconciles the apparent contradiction of the first two emphases (the "strong Jesus" of miracles versus the "weak Jesus" of death) through the third emphasis, the secrecy motif, which suggests Jesus' use of persuasion rather than dramatic demonstration in making true disciples (the fourth emphasis). Mark took over the miracle tradition of Jesus but set it within the perspective of Jesus' passion, thus implying that the creation of the disciples' faith could occur only if Jesus abandoned miracles and accepted suffering as God's will. The fifth emphasis, Jesus as Son of God, gathers up all the others, and they in turn define Jesus' sonship.

The "messianic secret" motif occurs precisely at those points where the tradition was most likely to be understood to represent Jesus as a divine man with power to avoid any difficulty. In effect, Mark opposed such an attitude about Jesus and the life of discipleship. The declaration of Jesus' sonship at the baptism and at the transfiguration is affirmed only at Jesus' death.[15] Jesus is Son of God in suffering and death. Consequently, for Mark the nature of discipleship and of the Christian community is marked by faith that believes in spite of unbelief (9:24; cf. 5:34–36; 11:23 f.), and by a faithful remnant who suffer in the watchful, prayerful expectation of the final coming of the kingdom of God (13:33 ff.; 14:38).

Although we do not have the Markan sources of tradition from which to study his *redaction* of that material, we can see that such motifs as the "messianic secret" and the predictions of Jesus' suffering, death, and resurrection either occur in Mark's transitional sections or otherwise give evidence of the evangelist's hand. Moreover, we may safely assume that Mark selected and arranged the tradition in order to accomplish his purposes. Thus there is the dominance of miracle tradition in the first half and of the passion story in the second.

---

15. Note how the occurrences of "Son of God" confirm the Markan structure: 1:1, 11; 9:7; and 15:39.

Whether or not the Gospel was written at Rome, Mark reflects the *historical setting* of a church undergoing persecution. This crisis and time of apocalyptic expectation required a steadfast community of faithful and watchful disciples. Jesus Christ, the Son of God, had himself gone through persecution and no escape had been offered him. Jesus triumphed through his suffering, and the same victory is promised to the faithful disciple: "For whoever would save his life will lose it; and whoever loses his life for my sake and the gospel's will save it" (8:35).

Suggestions for Further Reading

THE SYNOPTIC GOSPELS

A classic work on the problem of Synoptic relations and sources is B. H. Streeter, *The Four Gospels: A Study of Origins,* rev. ed. (London: Macmillan, 1930). The arguments for the priority of Mark, its use by Matthew and Luke, their use of a common sayings source, Q, and their use of distinctive sources M and L are all stated here. The composition and nature of the hypothetical Q document is discussed by J. S. Kloppenborg, *The Formation of Q: Trajectories in Ancient Wisdom Collections* (Philadelphia: Fortress, 1987). The two major pioneering studies in form criticism are available in English: Bultmann, *History of the Synoptic Tradition,* trans. J. Marsh (New York: Harper & Row, 1968), and M. Dibelius, *From Tradition to Gospel,* trans. B. L. Woolf (New York: Scribner, 1934). A recent application of form–critical insights and perspectives may be found in G. Theissen, *The Gospels in Context: Social and Political History in the Synoptic Tradition,* trans. L. M. Maloney (Minneapolis: Fortress, 1991). K. F. Nickle, *The Synoptic Gospels: Conflict and Consensus* (Atlanta: John Knox, 1980), aptly summarizes a modern perspective on these Gospels. E. P. Sanders and M. Davies, *Studying the Synoptic Gospels* (Philadelphia: Trinity Press International, 1989), offers an inductive approach to the synoptic problem, together with discussions of form and redaction criticism, structuralist and rhetorical criticism, and the question of Gospel genre. To aid in the comparison of the Synoptic Gospels, Sanders and Davies provide a number of common pericopes in parallel columns. For the entire Gospels, see the NRSV *Gospel Parallels, A Comparison of the Synoptic Gospels,* ed. B. H. Throckmorton, 5th ed. (Nashville: Thomas Nelson, 1992). The RSV is the basis for *Synopses of the Four Gospels: English Edition,* ed. Kurt Aland (United Bible Societies, 1982), which also includes the Gospel of John. More complex than Throckmorton or Aland, but also illuminating, is R. W. Funk (ed.), *New Gospel Parallels,* 2 vols. (Philadelphia: Fortress, 1985), which includes the Gospel of John as well as apocryphal Gospels. For texts of the apocryphal Gospels, with introductions, the standard work (in two volumes) is W. Schneemelcher (ed.), *The New Testament Apocrypha,* trans. R. McL. Wilson (Louisville, KY: Westminster/John Knox, 1991–1992). Canonical and apocryphal Gospels are treated on the same level by H. Koester, *Ancient Christian Gospels: Their History and Development* (Philadelphia: Trinity Press International, 1990). On ancient parallels to the Gospels and Gospel tradition, see R. A. Burridge, *What Are the Gospels? A Comparison with Graeco-Roman Biography* (Cambridge: Cambridge University Press, 1992); and F. Martin (ed.), *Narrative Parallels to the New Testament* (Atlanta: Scholars, 1988).

THE GOSPEL ACCORDING TO MARK

Commentaries in series named in the General Bibliography, II, are not all mentioned individually at the ends of chapters. As a rule, commentaries on the Greek text are not listed.

Among the more helpful commentaries are E. Schweizer, *The Good News According to Mark,* trans. D. H. Madvig (Richmond, VA: John Knox, 1970); H. Anderson, *The Gospel of Mark* (London: Oliphants, 1976); and, most recently, M. D. Hooker, *The Gospel According to Saint Mark* (Peabody, MA: Hendrickson, 1991). An extensive and responsible commentary written from a somewhat more conservative viewpoint is W. L. Lane, *The Gospel According to Mark* (Grand Rapids, MI: Eerdmans, 1974).

W. Marxsen, *Mark the Evangelist: Studies on the Redaction History of the Gospel,* trans. R. A. Harrisville, et al. (Nashville: Abingdon, 1969) is fundamental for its redaction–critical approach, although some of its insights have been superseded. Moreover, C. C. Black, *The Disciples According to Mark: Markan Redaction in Current Debate* (Sheffield, England: JSOT Press, 1989), shows that over time redaction–critical interpretations of Mark have diverged widely. The influential work of W. Wrede (first published in Germany in 1901) is a groundbreaking attempt to understand Mark on its own terms: *The Messianic Secret,* trans. J. C. G. Greig (Cambridge: Clarke, 1971). Recent works represent different, and to some extent mutually exclusive, trends in Markan interpretation. H. C. Kee, *Community of the New Age: Studies in Mark's Gospel* (Philadelphia: Westminster, 1977), seeks the social, community setting as a key to understanding Mark as an apocalyptic writing. In *Mark as Story: An Introduction to the Narrative of a Gospel* (Philadelphia: Fortress, 1982), D. Rhoads and D. Michie treat Mark from the standpoint of modern literary criticism. Along similar lines, J. C. Anderson and S. D. Moore have edited a helpful collection of essays, *Mark and Method: New Approaches in Biblical Studies* (Minneapolis: Fortress, 1992); E. S. Malbon's essay, "Narrative Criticism: How Does the Story Mean?" is a clear and lucid contribution, a good beginning point. M. A. Tolbert, *Sowing the Gospel: Mark's World in Literary–Historical Perspective* (Minneapolis: Fortress, 1989), seeks the ancient literary genre to which Mark belongs and interprets the Gospel from the standpoint of the parable of the sower (Mark 4:3–9). The central theme of Christology is treated by J. D. Kingsbury, *The Christology of Mark's Gospel* (Philadelphia: Fortress, 1983). D. O. Via, Jr., *The Ethics of Mark's Gospel—In the Middle of Time* (Philadelphia: Fortress, 1985), speaks to literary and hermeneutical, as well as ethical, issues. Without denying the theological interests and accomplishments of Mark, M. Hengel, *Studies in the Gospel of Mark,* trans. J. Bowden (Philadelphia: Fortress, 1985), pursues longstanding questions of authorship and origin. Joel Marcus, *The Way of the Lord: Christological Exegesis of the Old Testament in the Gospel of Mark* (Louisville, KY: Westminster/John Knox, 1992), uncovers the scriptural foundations of the Gospel. B. L. Mack, *A Myth of Innocence: Mark and Christian Origins* (Philadelphia: Fortress, 1988), presents a brilliantly iconoclastic view of Christian origins that ultimately casts Mark in the role of villain. For a more orthodox approach to Mark, see A. Y. Collins, *The Beginning of the Gospel: Probings of Mark in Context* (Minneapolis: Fortress, 1992). For a convenient summary of recent research, see Frank J. Matera, *What Are They Saying About Mark?* (New York: Paulist, 1987).

Chapter 3

Matthew: The Gospel of Obedience

Notes on the Gospel of Matthew

*L*ike the Gospel of Mark, Matthew contains no direct reference to its author and place of origin. The earliest apparent reference to the Gospel of Matthew is a report from Papias (ca. A.D. 130):

> Matthew collected the oracles in the Hebrew language, and each one interpreted them as best he could (Eusebius, *EH,* III, 39, 16).[1]

This information is, however, unclear and of uncertain value. In fact, it does not seem to be a reference to our Matthew, which was written in Greek. Because our Gospel is based upon the Greek text of Mark and the Q sayings source, it is unlikely that it was written by Matthew, an Aramaic-speaking disciple and eyewitness (cf. Mark 3:18 parr.). Possibly Papias means that Matthew collected Jesus' sayings, which is what the Greek word (*logia*), translated "oracles," means.

The Gospel was probably at first anonymous, inasmuch as the present titles were only added as the Gospels were incorporated into a fourfold canon. Authorship may have been attributed to Matthew, one of the twelve disciples, because only this Gospel distinguishes Matthew as a tax collector (10:3; cf. Mark 3:18), making the incident of the calling of a tax collector (who is Levi in Mark 2:14) a story about Matthew (Matt. 9:9). We do not know the reason for this other than to give some prominence to Matthew.

The author was familiar with Jewish Christianity and wrote to a Greek-speaking audience. Possibly he was a Christian scribe, similar to the Jewish scribes of the law (see 13:52). He took over and expanded the Markan framework by adding two types of material: sayings common also to Luke (Q source) and his own special Matthean tradition, which came from oral tradition or from a written source or sources. As a result, the narrative portion is equaled, if not exceeded, by the sayings material. The Jesus of

1. See W. G. Kümmel, *Introduction to the New Testament,* rev. ed., trans. H. C. Kee (Nashville: Abingdon, 1975), pp. 53–55. Eusebius also wrote, "Matthew, had first preached to Hebrews, and when he was on the point of going to others, he transmitted in writing in his native language the Gospel according to himself" (EH, III, 24, 6).

Matthew is at least as much a teacher as an actor. Our five-part outline of Matthew (excluding the Introduction, 1:1–2:23, and Conclusion, 26:2–28:20) apparently reflects the evangelist's own design. The end of each major discourse section is clearly marked by an editorial conclusion (see 7:28 f.; 11:1; 13:53; 19:1 f.; 26:1 f.) Although much of the material found in the five discourse sections is paralleled in Luke, the organization into discrete discourses belongs to Matthew alone. For example, although Luke contains most of the sayings of Jesus found in Matthew's Sermon on the Mount (chaps. 5–7), only a part of them appears in Luke's shorter Sermon on the Plain. The Sermon on the Mount per se is known only from Matthew.

Matthew, like Luke, begins his narrative with an account of Jesus' birth, but the nativity stories of the two Gospels are quite different. Only Matthew informs us of the embarrassment of Joseph at the prospect of the birth of Jesus before his marriage with Mary is consummated (1:18–25), the visit of the wise men (Magi) from the East (2:1–12), or the departure of the Holy Family to Egypt (2:13–15). Such famous sayings as Jesus' pronouncement of comfort to the weary and heavy-laden are found only in Matthew (11:28–30), together with a number of parables (13:24–30, 36–43, 44, 45–46, 47–50, 51–52; 18:23–35; 20:1–16; also 25:31–46, if it is to be considered a parable). Among the Gospels only Matthew tells us, in connection with Jesus' death, of the fate of Judas (27:3–10, cf. Acts 1:18–20), Pilate's washing his hands of Jesus' blood (27:24), the placing of guards at Jesus' tomb (27:62–66), and the subsequent bribing of them (28:11–15). Finally the charge of the risen Jesus to his disciples from the mountain in Galilee is found in Matthew alone (28:16–20). There are other distinctively Matthean materials, but these are typical.

The place of origin of Matthew's Gospel is generally thought to be Syria, probably the city of Antioch. The oldest witness to the use of this Gospel may be Ignatius, bishop of Antioch. Although he does not cite it by name, his letters (A.D. 110–115) contain bits of distinctively Matthean material. In all probability, Matthew was written after A.D. 70, for its addition to the parable of the marriage feast ("The king was angry, and he sent his troops and destroyed those murderers and burned their city"—22:7; cf. Luke 14:21) apparently refers to the destruction of Jerusalem in that year. Because Mark was probably composed shortly before Jerusalem's fall, some time would likely have elapsed before Mark's authority became sufficient for the anonymous author of Matthew to use it as a primary source. Consequently, a date of about A.D. 80–90 seems likely. Indeed, the obvious tension between the Christianity of Matthew and the Judaism of the Pharisees (cf. Matt. 23) also suggests a date after the Roman destruction of the temple in A.D. 70. At this time Judaism retrenched in the face of the threat of possible extinction and began to develop toward a rabbinic, Pharisaic uniformity. Sectarian movements within Judaism, such as Jewish Christianity, became suspect and eventually may have been read out of the developing normative Judaism.[2]

Clearly this Gospel is more systematically and intricately organized than Mark. Matthew emphasizes fulfillment of prophecy, Jesus as teacher, and the place of the law and final judgment within the Christian congregation. These broad interests suggest a churchly Gospel written to give direction to the community in a time of transition as it faced problems pertaining to organization, separation from Judaism, and disappointed eschatological hopes. Matthew serves the church, and probably for that

2. W. D. Davies, *The Sermon on the Mount* (New York: Cambridge University Press, 1966), pp. 83–90; cf. G. D. Kilpatrick, *The Origins of the Gospel According to St. Matthew* (Oxford: Clarendon, 1946), p. 109.

reason the church placed it first in the New Testament canon. Because it is written to give guidance to the church, Matthew may be compared with a roughly contemporary document, the Community Rule of the Qumran community. The method of Old Testament interpretation in Matthew also bears some resemblance to that found at Qumran, particularly in the Habakkuk Commentary.[3]

OUTLINE OF MATTHEW

Introduction: The New Obedience (1:1–2:23)
The Higher Righteousness (3:1–7:29)
    Fulfilling Righteousness (3:13–17)
    Teaching Righteousness (5:17–20)
True Discipleship (8:1–11:1)
The Kingdom of Heaven (11:2–13:52)
The Forgiving Church (13:53–19:2)
    Peter as the Rock (16:13–23)
    Discipline in Community (18:15–22)
Judgment: Doing God's Will (19:3–26:1)
    Believing Doers of the Law (21:28–46)
    Doing Mercy without Calculation (25:31–46)
Conclusion: Obedience and Resurrection (26:2–28:20)
    The Great Commission (28:16–20)

Introduction: The New Obedience (1:1–2:23)

Matthew's Gospel begins with his special tradition. The tradition appears to be largely legendary: a genealogical list of Jesus' ancestors; a story of Jesus' birth; exotic wise men from the East, their encounter with Herod and worship of the baby Jesus; the flight to Egypt; the slaying of the innocent children; and the return to Nazareth. These matters may seem preliminary to the real work of Jesus, which for Mark began at Jesus' baptism and ended at the crucifixion. But these "Christmas stories" bear the heart of Matthew's message, his good news.

The genealogy (1:1 ff.) helps in understanding the birth story (1:18–25). At first glance, this list of Jesus' ancestors looks rather unpromising for determining Matthew's intent and purpose. We notice that the genealogy is said to be divided into three sets of generations of fourteen each—from Abraham to David, from David to the Babylonian deportation, and from Babylon to the Christ (vs. 17—unaccountably, the last set contains only thirteen generations). Abraham is the father of the Jewish people, for Israel's God is the God of Abraham, Isaac, and Jacob (see Gen. 12:1–3; cf. Matt. 3:9; 22:32). The Christ who climaxes this genealogy fulfills the hope of Israel; therefore, the age of fulfillment is dawning with the birth of the expected Messiah. This Christ is also descended from David, the great king in Israel's history. Indeed, the Lord

---

3. See Krister Stendahl, *The School of St. Matthew and Its Use of the Old Testament* (Philadelphia: Fortress, 1968), pp. 183 ff.

promised through the prophet Nathan that David's offspring would be established in a kingdom forever (2 Sam. 7:12–17). Thus Jesus Christ will fulfill Israel's hopes prefigured in Abraham and David (see 1:1). Yet the Babylonian exile, the next major division in the genealogy, meant disaster for Israel's hope of establishing a political kingdom in which God's rule would triumph. Perhaps for Matthew the deportation raises the question of whether fulfillment of Israel's hopes will take a form other than that of a Davidic political kingdom.[4]

The inclusion of women in the genealogy suggests a possibility of the unexpected; the Christ who comes may not correspond to the image of the Messiah for whom Israel was waiting. In the ancient world, descent was traced through the male; yet four women aside from Mary (vs. 16) appear in the genealogy: Tamar (vs. 3), Rahab and Ruth (vs. 5), and the wife of Uriah (vs. 6). Moreover, these are quite unusual women. Tamar disguised herself as a harlot to seduce her father-in-law Judah so that she could bear children, Perez and Zerah (Gen. 38). Rahab, the prostitute of Jericho, saved Joshua's two spies and consequently preserved her own life when the walls of Jericho fell (Josh. 2, 6). Ruth, the Moabite woman who was loyal to her Hebrew mother-in-law, gained her future husband Boaz one night during the grain festival (Ruth 3). And the wife of Uriah is none other than Bathsheba who bathed in the right place during "the spring of the year" and thus became the wife of David (2 Sam. 11–12). Possibly each of these women, or at least Rahab and Ruth, would be perceived as foreigners. In spite of their origins and questionable moral actions, God acted through each.

Within this setting, Matthew's story of Jesus' birth takes place. The genealogy indicates that Jesus' significant ancestry includes not only the men (especially Abraham and David) but also the women, Tamar, Rahab, Ruth, Bathsheba, and finally Mary. Moreover, there are Jews *and* Gentiles in this lineage.

The birth story itself (vss. 18–25) centers on Joseph's response to the pregnancy of his betrothed Mary. Although Matthew explicitly talks about a virgin birth (vss. 18, 20, 23, 25), the story focuses not upon wonder at the virgin Mary but, rather, on how Joseph will react to the dilemma posed by the question of whether she is pregnant from unfaithfulness or the power of God. Not only is the question posed within the birth story itself but also by the preceding section. Inclusion of the women in Matthew's genealogy raises the question

---

4. One might suppose Matthew's genealogy serves to prove that Jesus was the Messiah because he was descended from Abraham and especially David. Yet Joseph does not, according to the following verses, father Jesus, even though the genealogy would have to be traced through him to function as proof of Davidic lineage. This tradition might have originally (apart from 1:18–25) proved the Davidic descent of Jesus and therefore his messiahship, but in the Matthean context, biological descent from David through Joseph cannot be maintained. (Cf. Luke 3:23, where the problem of descent through Joseph has been seen.) Probably Joseph's legal status as the father of Jesus is what counts with Matthew.

The flight into Egypt of Joseph and Mary with the baby Jesus as portrayed by a contemporary Chinese artist, Hua Hsiao Kuan.   *(Courtesy of Spartaco Appetiti.)*

of how God works to achieve his purposes, and at the culmination of the birth story Joseph must decide whether Mary's pregnancy is God's action.

Joseph at first thinks that he has been wronged by Mary. "Being a righteous man," he decides to divorce her quietly (vs. 19). According to Jewish law, engagement, like marriage, could only be severed by divorce (cf. Deut. 24:1–4). A man could do one of two things: he could bring his betrothed to public trial, where conviction of infidelity might carry the penalty of death by stoning, or he could divorce his betrothed privately. Joseph generously opts for the latter course. At this moment, however, the angel intrudes and through a dream Joseph learns about a higher righteousness (see, for example, 3:15; 5:20; 5:33). He hears that this conception is from the Holy Spirit, the agent of God's activity on earth; furthermore, this son of Mary is to be named Jesus, whose name implies one who will "save his people from their sins" (vs. 21).

Matthew then continues with a reference to the fulfillment of Hebrew prophecy (vss. 22–23). These opening two chapters, which narrate Jesus' birth, are characterized by Matthew's use of a formula for Old Testament scripture citation (see also 2:6, 15, 18, 23; in addition, 4:15–16; 8:17; 12:18–21; 13:35; 21:5; 26:56; 27:9–10). These formula or fulfillment quotations are applied by Matthew to the story of Jesus in order to link his mission and message with the story of Israel. Thus the theme of Jesus as the savior of his people is developed in the quotation from Isaiah 7:14 (vss. 22 f.). The birth of Jesus fulfills the Old Testament and signifies Emmanuel ("God is with us"). This linking of Jesus as savior from sins and Jesus as a sign of God's presence also occurs near the opening of the Matthean miracle section (8:1 ff.). There another quotation from the prophet Isaiah ("He took our infirmities and bore our diseases"—53:4; Matt. 8:17) affirms that Jesus is the bringer of God's forgiveness (cf. Matt. 9:1–7). Still another, subsequent statement by Jesus sounds like a promise of Emmanuel: "For where two or three are gathered in my name, I am there among them" (18:20). This too is immediately followed by Jesus' declaration of the necessity for limitless forgiveness (18:21 f.).

This good news of forgiveness does not imply, however, that Matthew understands the Christian gospel to be devoid of human responsibility, for the heart of this story is Joseph's response. Joseph responds to the presence of God as experienced in a dream. Matthew states simply that when he "awoke from sleep, he did as the angel of the Lord commanded him; he took her as his wife" (vs. 24). Joseph obeyed; he practiced a higher righteousness. Throughout Matthew, beginning in this opening scene and ending with the last words of Jesus to the disciples (28:20), the themes of obedience and righteousness recur (see 5:17–20; 7:15–27; 21:28–32; 28:20).

The first half of chapter 2 (vss. 1–18) is dominated by the "wise men from the East," and the entire chapter is organized around a series of geographical places: the East, Jerusalem, Bethlehem, Egypt, and finally Nazareth. The wise men come to pay homage to the newly born king of the Jews. Perhaps they are Zoroastrian priests or Babylonian astrologers; without doubt they are Gentiles. Whereas Joseph showed the reaction of a loyal, just Jew to the birth of Jesus, now we see the response of wise Gentiles (see 28:19). They have come to worship him as they would a king or a god (2:2, 8, 11; cf. 14:33; 28:17). Their reaction to Jesus' birth contrasts with that of Herod, the political king, who can think of Jesus only as a threat to his rule. And with some reason, for the unusual star's appearance serves as a sign of a crucial event: the old age, typified by Herod's kingdom, yields to the new, manifested in the birth of Jesus. The midpoint of this chapter, a turning point of the narrative (vss. 13–15), discloses Matthew's intent. After the wise men have left, an angel of the Lord again appears to Joseph. This time Joseph is told to flee to Egypt, and again he obeys (vs. 14). By his response to the revelatory dreams the story moves forward in fulfillment of the scripture (vs. 15).

All this occurred in order "to fulfill what had been spoken by the Lord through the prophet, 'Out of Egypt I have called my son'" (vs. 15: cf. Hosea 11:1). Originally this verse recalled Israel's being brought out of Egypt. Now "my son" refers not to Israel, but to Jesus. Chapter 2, furthermore, suggests that Jesus is to be understood as a new Moses. Moses lived in Egypt before leading the people to the promised land; Jesus also fled to Egypt before coming to Nazareth. The Hebrew male children were killed at the birth of Moses; the Bethlehem male children were killed at the birth of Jesus (2:16–19; cf. Exod. 1:15–2:10). Yet the text seems to imply something more than a Moses–Jesus typology. Jesus is not a new Moses, but a new Israel. The Old Testament equated God's Son with the people, not Moses (Exod. 4:22). The Moses analogy is present within Matthew;[5] however, the text primarily proclaims the formation of a new Israel. Whereas in Judaism Moses was honored and respected, in the new community Jesus is worshiped (2:11; 28:17).

In his own demonic way Herod recognizes the breaking in of a new era. He tries without success to kill the new Davidic king (vss. 16 ff.). Fittingly, the chapter ends with Jesus in Nazareth (vs. 23). From this point, the focus of the narrative narrows, and a particular history replaces the prophetic, eschatological overview of the introduction. Whether the first two Matthean chapters contain history in the sense of observed and reported events is debatable. A comparison with the Lukan infancy narratives discloses agreement on certain points, such as the virginity of Mary, but otherwise there are wide-ranging divergencies and differences that are hard to reconcile. Be that as it may, the narrative does proclaim Matthew's understanding of the new Christian way. This way of radical obedience becomes possible with the appearance of Jesus, who both is and brings into existence the new Israel.

5. The "forty days and nights" of fasting in the wilderness temptation (4:2) picks up the "forty days and nights" Moses also fasted when he wrote the commandments from God (Exod. 34:28). In the antitheses (5:21–48) Jesus elaborates commandments of Moses; indeed, the entire Sermon is from the Mount (cf. Exod. 19:2 f.). Finally, the five-part structure of Matthew (see the initial outline) parallels the Pentateuch, the five books of Moses. See B. W. Bacon, *Studies in Matthew* (New York: Holt, 1930). On the other hand, it should be noted that in the first two chapters the Exodus texts dealing with the birth and childhood of Moses are not cited.

The Higher Righteousness (3:1–7:29)

Like the four other major Matthean sections, this one consists of both narrative and discourse. The narrative includes the baptism, temptation, preaching, and calling of disciples by Jesus (3:1–4:25). The discourse is the Sermon on the Mount (5:1–7:29). By this arrangement, Matthew uses the discourse of Jesus to interpret the narrative, which he has basically taken over from Mark. Our interpretation of this overall section, as a depiction of "higher righteousness," is borne out by a comparison of Matthew's treatment of John the Baptist with Luke's.

Both Matthew and Luke report John the Baptist's reaction to some people who come out to be baptized by him (3:7–10; cf. Luke 3:7–9—Q source). According to Luke, John's scathing attack is directed against the multitudes because they are not bearing fruit that befits repentance. Matthew characteristically has John the Baptist assault the Pharisees and Sadducees, who in the time of Jesus were distinct and important groups. Thus through his presentation of the incident, Matthew stresses that even the leaders are not bearing good fruit. Therefore, they are liable to judgment, and their claim to descent from Abraham will be of no avail against final judgment (vss. 9 f.). A higher righteousness is demanded.

This discussion of the necessity of bearing fruit receives further elaboration in the discourse of the Sermon on the Mount: "Every good tree bears good fruit, but the bad tree bears bad fruit" (7:17; cf. 7:18–20). Matthew prefaces this statement with an attack upon false prophets who appear in sheep's clothing, pretending to be righteous (7:15 f.). These false prophets rely upon their record of prophesying and casting out demons in the face of God's judgment (7:21–23). But their activity is of no avail unless they produce fruits—that is, deeds of righteousness, such as loving the enemy (5:44), not being angry with one's brother (5:22), praying without hypocrisy (6:5), not judging (7:1), and so on. Although the Matthean words of Jesus clearly define the higher righteousness (5:20) that Jesus demands, hearing is not enough; doing is indispensable (7:24). Therefore, Matthew moves from an emphasis on redefining righteousness to the necessity of practicing it. Higher righteousness is more than knowledge; it consists also of doing.

FULFILLING RIGHTEOUSNESS (3:13–17)

Why does Jesus seek baptism by John the Baptist?

Jesus' first act in the Gospel of Matthew occurs in connection with his baptism. In Mark, Jesus did not really act at the baptism; rather, he was acted upon by John the Baptist. Matthew, by way of contrast, shows Jesus acting during this baptism by John. In comparing this baptism story (Matt. 3:13–17) with that of Mark (Mark 1:9–11), we note four distinct Matthean characteristics: (1) the preaching of John the Baptist and Jesus are identical; (2) Jesus

The Baptism of Jesus

Matt. 3.13–17	Mark 1.9–11	Luke 3.21–22	John 1.29–34
[13]Then Jesus came from Galilee to the Jordan to John, to be baptized by him. [14]John would have prevented him, saying "I need to be baptized by you, and do you come to me?" [15]But Jesus answered him, "Let it be so now; for thus it is fitting for us to fulfil all righteousness." Then he consented. [16]And when Jesus was baptized, he went up immediately from the water, and behold, the heavens were opened and he saw the Spirit of God descending like a dove and alighting on him; [17]and lo, a voice from heaven, saying,	[9]In those days Jesus came from Nazareth of Galilee and was baptized by John in the Jordan. [10]And when he came up out of the water, immediately he saw the heavens opened and the Spirit descended upon him like a dove; [11]and a voice came from heaven,	[21]Now when all the people were baptized, and when Jesus also had been baptized and was praying, the heaven was opened, [22]and the Holy Spirit descended upon him in bodily form, as a dove, and a voice came from heaven,	[29]The next day he saw Jesus coming toward him, and said, "Behold, the Lamb of God, who takes away the sin of the world! [30]This is he of whom I said, 'After me comes a man who ranks before me, for he was before me.' [31]I myself did not know him; but for this I came baptizing with water, that he might be revealed to Israel." [32]And John bore witness, "I saw the Spirit descend as a dove from heaven, and it remained on him. [33]I myself did not know him; but he who sent me to baptize with water said to me, 'He on whom you see the Spirit descend and remain, this is he who baptizes with the Holy Spirit.' [34]And I have seen and have borne witness that this is the Son of God."
"This is my beloved Son, with whom I am well pleased."	"Thou art my beloved Son; with thee I am well pleased."	"Thou art my beloved Son; with thee I am well pleased."	

The story of the Baptism of Jesus nicely illustrates the similarities and differences among the Gospels as well as Matthew's distinct material and emphasis (3:14–15). The Johannine account actually contains material found in the broader synoptic setting and is not as distinctive as at first may appear.

(Adapted from B. H. Throckmorton, Jr., (ed.), *Gospel Parallels*, 4th ed. [Nashville: Abingdon, 1979].)

explicitly decides to be baptized; (3) his baptism fulfills all righteousness; and (4) the voice from heaven does not speak to Jesus but apparently to John the Baptist.

According to Matthew, both John the Baptist and Jesus proclaim "Repent, for the kingdom of heaven has come near" (3:2; 4:17).[6] Such identical messages show clearly that Matthew presumes a close relationship between John and Jesus. Yet Matthew also makes clear that John the Baptist's message is prophecy, "Prepare the way of the Lord, make his paths straight" (3:3; Isa. 40:3), whereas Jesus' coming is fulfillment, "The people who sat in darkness have seen a great light, and for those who sat in the region and shadow of death light has dawned" (4:16; Isa. 9:1 f.). Nevertheless, John the Baptist's injunction to bear good fruit (3:10) is supported and elaborated by Jesus at the close of the Sermon on the Mount (7:16). Moreover, Matthew's Jesus, unlike Mark's, decides to leave Galilee to be baptized by John (vs. 13). What happened without explanation in Mark (1:9) occurs in Matthew because of Jesus' conscious decision and action (cf. vs. 14).

In Matthew, John's protest about the inappropriateness of his baptizing Jesus is answered by the first words of Jesus, "Let it be so now; for it is proper for us in this way to fulfill all righteousness" (vs. 15). This answer, appearing only in Matthew, explains why the presumably sinless Jesus needed a baptism for repentance. Such an apologetic motif occurs in accounts of Jesus' baptism in noncanonical Gospels.[7] Jesus' reply may also be understood as his acceptance of a requirement for the whole nation, to establish an identity between himself and his people. Both explanations seem to make Jesus' baptism a routine of going through the motions. But in Matthew Jesus himself initiates the action and says that this baptism is "to fulfill all righteousness" (cf. 5:17), a central Matthean theme. Consequently, we need to look more carefully into Jesus' reply.

In Matthew *"righteousness"* means that conduct which is in agreement with God's will and well pleasing to him. It is rightness of life before God. Matthew does not speak about righteousness merely as a preliminary step toward the kingdom of heaven, but rather as the very substance of this kingdom (see 5:6, 10, 20; 6:33). The fulfilling of all righteousness should be understood in the context of the preceding verses (3:11 f.), where John declared that he himself only baptized with water for repentance, but that after him would come one who would baptize with "the Holy Spirit and fire." The Holy

---

6. Matthew's preference for "kingdom of heaven" rather than "kingdom of God" probably reflects his characteristically Jewish reserve about using the name of God.

7. In the Gospel of the Ebionites, John asked Jesus to baptize him *after* the voice spoke from heaven. The Gospel According to the Nazaraeans reports the following dialogue: "Behold, the mother of the Lord and his brethren said to him: 'John the Baptist baptizes unto the remission of sins, let us go and be baptized by him.' But he [Jesus] said to them: 'Wherein have I sinned that I should go and be baptized by him? Unless what I have said is ignorance (a sin of ignorance)." Hennecke, *New Testament Apocrypha,* I, 169 and 160 resp.

Spirit, of course, signifies the presence of God (see 1:18), and fire depicts judgment, as the context implies ("unquenchable fire"). The coming of Jesus, then, is the sign of both God's presence (cf. 1:23) and his judgment. The relationship between the two was already anticipated in John the Baptist's previous speech (3:7–10). Judgment comes to whoever does not bear fruit. But, as this passage makes clear (3:13–17), God's presence now makes it possible to bear fruit, because the Holy Spirit has come with Jesus. Jesus willingly undergoes baptism, for because of the Spirit's presence he can now be obedient (bear fruit) and fulfill all righteousness, being well pleasing to God (vs. 17).

The unexpected plural in Jesus' answer to John, "it is proper for *us* in this way to fulfill all righteousness," must in this context refer to Jesus and John the Baptist. John the Baptist also is obedient ("he consented"—vs. 15). Jesus obeyed in his decision to come from Galilee to be baptized, and John the Baptist acted to complete Jesus' obedience. With their fulfillment of all righteousness, the Spirit of God appears visually to Jesus and aurally to John the Baptist (in Mark 1:11 the voice spoke to Jesus).

This interpretation of the story of Jesus' baptism is supported by the following temptation story (4:1–11). The beloved Son of God, announced in the baptism, now acts as the Son in response to each temptation. "If you are the Son of God" (vss. 3, 6) does not really imply that Jesus might not be the Son of God. The baptism (3:17) left no doubt that Jesus was the Son of God. The only doubt concerns the nature of the sonship, whether Jesus will act in obedience to God or on his own authority. Just as obedience characterized his baptism, so the temptations show the Son of God acting in accordance with the will of God (vss. 4, 7, 10).

After the temptation, Jesus first goes to territory close to the Gentiles (4:12–16), where he begins to preach (vs. 17) and immediately calls disciples (vss. 18–22). These disciples respond by following him (vss. 20, 22). A brief summary section of healings (vss. 23–25; cf. Mark 1:21–3:11) shows how he attracts crowds from everywhere and leads into the first discourse, the Sermon on the Mount.

TEACHING RIGHTEOUSNESS (5:17–20)

In what respect does the righteousness of Jesus' disciples exceed that of the scribes and Pharisees?

The Sermon on the Mount (chaps. 5–7) has been acclaimed as the heart and center of Christian faith. This section contains the first and most important discourse of the Gospel. In all probability, the Sermon was not spoken by Jesus on one occasion, for much of the same material is scattered throughout the Gospel of Luke (see, for example, the Sermon on the Plain, Luke 6:17–49, but also 12:22–34). Hence the arrangement of the tradition probably reflects Matthean interests and concerns.

"The Baptism of Christ" by Nicolas Poussin (1594-1665) (Courtesy of National Gallery of Art, Washington, D.C.)

The significance of the Sermon on the Mount for Matthew is illustrated by the fact that Matthew's passion story picks up motifs already prepared for in the Sermon. For example, in Gethsemane Jesus prays word for word the third petition of the Lord's Prayer: "Your will be done" (26:42; cf. 6:10). Jesus also advocates peace in the confrontation at his arrest (26:52; cf. 5:39). Moreover, Jesus never relaxes the commandments; he is innocent and righteous (27:4, 19, 24; cf. 5:19). Further, Jesus refuses to reply to the high priests' request for an oath (26:63; cf. 5:34). All these instances are Matthean additions not found in the Markan text.

Two aspects of the staging characterize this discourse. First, Jesus appears as a rabbi, a teacher (5:2). This initial depiction of Jesus contrasts with that of Mark, where Jesus initially appeared as a miracle worker and healer (Mark 1:21 ff.). Second, the Sermon is delivered from the Mount. Two other crucial events, the transfiguration scene (17:1 ff.; similarly, Mark 9:2 ff.) and the final word to the disciples (28:16 ff.; only in Matthew), occur on a mountain in the Gospel of Matthew. The delivery of the Sermon from the mountain is reminiscent of Moses' receiving the law on the mountain in the wilderness (Exod. 19). According to Matthew, a new teaching comes from the mountain—a righteousness higher than that delivered by Moses.

In addition, two observations about the content of the Sermon show its character and meaning. First, it begins with a series of nine beatitudes or blessings (5:3–12). Of these, the first three describe the condition of those for whom Jesus' message is good news: "the poor in spirit," "those who mourn," and "the meek" (5:3–5). These conditions should not be understood as requirements for blessing. Rather, Matthew declares the unmerited grace or blessing of God, and future participation in the kingdom of heaven is promised simply to those who have need. Even the last six beatitudes (5:6–12), which might be taken as ethical requirements, are still within the setting of unconditional blessing. Any merit is ascribed to the astonishing generosity of God. Thus the opening of the Sermon on the Mount stresses God's favor rather than his demand. Second, the Sermon on the Mount ends with a clear call to obedience (7:15–29): "You will know them by their fruits" (7:16). Entrance into the kingdom of heaven will reward whoever "does the will of my Father in heaven" (7:21); the wise man hears Jesus' words and does them (7:24). Hence the grace of God does not make obedience unnecessary.

We now turn to the word of Jesus about the law and prophets (5:17–20), which appears only in Matthew. In the first three verses Jesus declares his complete acceptance of the law and the prophets. Nothing will pass away from the law until all is accomplished. No one may relax one of these commandments or teach anyone else to do so. This complete acceptance of the law is difficult to understand in view of later criticism of the law. The final verse demanding a "higher righteousness" (vs. 20) already hints at criticism, but other passages are more explicit. John the Baptist is identified with the law and the prophets, yet he who is least in the kingdom of heaven is greater than he (11:11–15). Matthew follows Mark in Jesus' criticism of the law's distinction between clean and unclean: "Listen and understand: it is not what goes into the mouth that defiles a person, but it is what comes out of the mouth, that defiles" (15:10; cf. Mark 7:14 f.; though Matthew does omit Mark's statement that Jesus declared all foods clean—Mark 7:19). Nevertheless, Jesus' words (vss. 17–19) make clear that he expects nothing less than fulfillment of the law. Although Matthew does contain a torrid diatribe against the scribes and Pharisees (chap. 23), this criticism is directed toward their failure to practice and observe the law (23:3) and their hypocrisy (23:13, 23, 25).

In another passage, however (22:34–40; cf. Mark 12:28–34), Jesus discusses the nature of the law and the prophets and says that the first and great commandment is love of God, and the second love of neighbor. *All* the law and the prophets depend on these commandments (vs. 40). This conclusion, which appears only in Matthew, suggests that the "higher righteousness" that Jesus teaches consists of a primary relation with God and a secondary relation with other people. This view of higher righteousness helps to explain the castigation of the scribes and Pharisees that follows (chap. 23). As we noted, they are chastised because they do not observe the law and are hypocrites. Yet by any "normal" measure the scribes and Pharisees were the most observant group within Israel, during both the time of Jesus and that of Matthew. Only by the extraordinary norm of the love of God and the love of neighbor, which nevertheless is derived from the law and the prophets, could they be denounced. Of course, in Jesus' call for a higher righteousness this high standard is set for his own disciples.

We have already encountered the verb *to fulfill* in Matthew. At the baptism Jesus and John the Baptist fulfilled all righteousness (3:15), primarily by their respective acts of obedience. Here in the Sermon, "whoever does them and teaches them will be called great in the kingdom of heaven" (vs. 19b). Jesus fulfills the law and the prophets not only in deed but also in teaching. Matthew understands the congregation of followers of Christ as founded not only upon Jesus' action but also upon his teaching. Jesus' closing words in the Gospel reiterate this theme: "Go therefore and make disciples of all nations . . . teaching them to obey everything that I have commanded you" (28:19 f.).

The key to Jesus' teaching about fulfillment of the law and the prophets lies, of course, in the enigmatic last verse of this passage (5:20), where Jesus calls for more righteousness than that of the scribes and Pharisees. The rest of the Sermon seeks to teach this higher righteousness, which becomes explicit in the antitheses of the Sermon on the Mount.

The six antitheses (5:21–48; only in Matthew) are so designated because of the antithetical form in which they are cast, "You have heard that it was said. . . . But I say to you. . . ." These antitheses indicate that Jesus pays attention to a person's intention as well as to the actual deed. His words would therefore advise the hearer to root out evil thoughts so that evil actions will not follow. One might observe that such good advice is easier to give than to heed. It is sometimes difficult to refrain from killing, committing adultery, and hating one's neighbor; it is almost impossible to keep from anger, lust, and hate of one's enemy. These words are not, however, a counsel of despair, for the extremely radical nature of their demand elicits from the hearer the recognition that these are more than human commands. In a sense, the antitheses set forth both the will and the presence of God. The commandments are transparent so that God shines through them. Indeed the Sermon's opening beatitudes already indicated the present blessings of God. Moreover, Jesus' following teaching emphasizes the availability of God in prayer (6:5–15) and everyday life (6:25–34). Therefore, the final, seemingly impossible requirement, "Be perfect, therefore, as your heavenly Father is perfect" (5:48), is Jesus' call to align oneself with the perfection or righteousness of God, which God not only requires but also manifests. With the demand for the higher righteousness comes the gift of God's presence. In Matthew's presentation Jesus does not introduce a new teaching so much as draw out the radical implications of the old.

Matthew develops the entire Sermon under the implied rubrics of love of God and love of neighbor as the fulfillment of the law and the prophets (cf. 7:11 f.). The antitheses call for an unlimited concern for the neighbor (vss. 21–48; see also 7:1–5), whereas the remaining sections of the Sermon point to the one gracious source of life. What is impossible apart from God becomes a fulfillable promise in his presence (6:33). The Sermon on the Mount begins with the promise of blessings (5:1–12) and ends with the demand for obedience (7:24–27). This tension characterizes the Jewish Christianity of Matthew and is actually typical of the New Testament as a whole. God's grace does not nullify human responsibility; it enables people to obey. Jesus does not set aside the commandments of God but points the way to their fulfillment.

True Discipleship (8:1–11:1)

In the first major section of the Gospel, Jesus appeared as Messiah of the word (chaps. 3–7), but in the second he appears as Messiah of the deed. Matthew has brought together ten miracle narratives (chaps. 8–9), accounts of Jesus' actions, which lead naturally into the missionary discourse (chap. 10) describing the deeds required in discipleship (10:42).

This movement from Jesus' miracles to the disciples' working is reflected in Matthew's threefold division of the miracle section. The first part (8:2–17) portrays Jesus as bearing the infirmities and diseases of all people—the leper, the centurion's servant, the disciple's mother-in-law. By his healings Jesus fulfills the prophet Isaiah's word, "He took our infirmities and bore our diseases" (8:17; cf. Isa. 53:4). The middle and dominant division (8:18–9:17) places the disciples at the center of action. The initial episode (8:18–22) concerns "following," that is, discipleship. Next Jesus responds to the plight of the perishing and faithless disciples (8:23–27). Then his power is manifest in the exorcism of the two demoniacs (8:28–34) and the healing and forgiveness of the paralytic (9:1–8). After these miracles Jesus immediately calls the disciple Matthew, who is a tax collector and thus socially unacceptable; indeed, Jesus has come not to call the righteous, but sinners (9:9–13). Therefore, Jesus' disciples rejoice rather than fast as John's disciples do (9:14–17). In distinction from the previous division's emphasis on the disciples, the third and final part of the miracle section (9:18–23; cf. Mark 5:21–43) concerns faith. Indeed, Matthew has reduced the narration about the raising of the daughter and the healing of the woman with the hemorrhage (9:18–26) to a bare minimum to emphasize the essential point of the father's faith. The same is true of Matthew's treatment of the healing of the two blind men (9:27–31; cf. Mark 10:46–52); moreover, faith is implicitly the subject of the final healing of the dumb demoniac (9:32–34). Without faith there is no miracle.

Matthew's miracle stories here portray a compassionate healer, drawing out disciples who believe in working with God rather than the prince of demons (9:34). Thus Jesus calls out faithful disciples who will continue his own work. In other words, he calls for faithful disciples to join him in the labor of sharing the suffering of people. The view that Matthew seeks to define discipleship within this section (chaps. 8–10) is confirmed by the opening, transitional verse: "When Jesus had come down from the mountain, great crowds *followed* him" (8:1; cf. Mark 1:39 f.). "Following"—that is, discipleship—then becomes the theme of the succeeding Matthean miracle section (chaps. 8 and 9).

The missionary discourse (chap. 10), which immediately follows the miracles, links the twelve *disciples* directly with the acts that Jesus has just performed: "Then Jesus summoned his twelve disciples and gave them authority over unclean spirits, to cast them out, and to cure every disease and every sickness" (10:1; 8:16–17). Finally, the closing transitional sentence of this section reads, "Now when Jesus had finished instructing his *twelve disciples,* he went on from there to teach and proclaim his message in their cities" (11:1; only in Matthew). The Twelve are to carry on the ministry of Jesus.

The composition and character of Matthew's missionary discourse (chap. 10) suggest that this tradition does more than simply report Jesus' instructions to his twelve disciples. This discourse concerning the nature of true discipleship is intended also for the disciples in the congregation of Matthew's time. This is evident in the changes Matthew has made in the Markan tradition (cf. Mark 6:7–13). First, Matthew has no report of the disciples' actually carrying out the mission that he gave them. Although his Markan source contained the statement that "they went out and proclaimed that all should repent . . .," Matthew lacks even that (Mark 6:12 f.; cf. Matt. 10:14 f.). For Matthew, this missionary task was delivered to the church that came into existence with the death and resurrection of Jesus (28:19 f.). Second, Matthew inserts a passage from Jesus' apocalyptic discourse concerning the future end of the world (Mark 13:9–13) into the missionary discourse (Matt. 10:17–25) as instruction for the church in its present situation. In Matthew these words are spoken by Jesus to the church for application to the time between Jesus' resurrection and his parousia; thus Matthew changes an apocalyptic warning into churchly instructions.

Perhaps the most puzzling of Jesus' sayings within this discourse is the injunction to the disciples, "Go nowhere among the Gentiles, and enter no town of the Samaritans, but go rather to the lost sheep of the house of Israel" (10:5–6, only in Matthew; see also 15:24), for this imperative contrasts sharply with the concluding words from the risen Jesus at the close of Matthew, "Go therefore and make disciples of all nations . . ." (28:19). Although the restriction of Jesus' mission, and that of the disciples, to the confines of Israel may simply reflect an earlier stage of the tradition that Matthew retains without agreement, another suggestion for Matthew's intent seems more plausible. Within the discourse itself Jesus also predicts that the disciples "will be dragged before governors and kings because of me, as a testimony to them *and the Gentiles*" (10:18; cf. Mark 13:9 f.). This narrative, in the future tense, makes sense if Matthew conceives of Jesus' ministry as basically directed toward the people of Israel, but the ministry of the disciples and the early church as directed to both the people of Israel and the Gentiles. (See 1:1–25 with its emphasis on the heritage of Israel—the descent from Abraham; and 2:1–23 with its emphasis on the extension to Gentiles—the worship of the wise men.) This interpretation also helps account for the omission by Matthew of Mark's report of the disciples' actually going on the missionary journey. For Matthew that mission, in its full significance, occurs only after Jesus' death and resurrection.

In this treatment of discipleship Matthew has shown Jesus as the Messiah in deed, whose miracles alleviate the suffering of humanity (8:16 f.). In turn, the disciples are to respond with obedient deeds. They realize true discipleship insofar as they acknowledge Jesus' lordship and follow him, performing acts of mercy toward others (10:42; cf. Mark 9:41).

The Kingdom of Heaven (11:2–13:52)

Were Matthew presenting a historical narrative in the usual sense, we might next expect information about what happened to the disciples after they responded to Jesus' missionary imperative (chap. 10). Instead, we read of the further activity of Jesus and the reactions, both positive and negative, that he elicits: first, the relationship of John the Baptist and Jesus (11:2–19); next, chastisement of the cities that rejected Jesus (11:20–24); then, pronouncements of blessing upon those who accept the yoke of Jesus (11:25–30); next, controversy with the Pharisees involving a series of miracles (chap. 12); and, finally, a series of parables initially addressed to the crowds, but adapted by Matthew for the disciples (chap. 13).

The key to this section lies not so much in the order of events as in the way in which Matthew has brought his own special interests to them. Four emphases stand out:

1. The section is devoted overall to the question of the nature of the kingdom of heaven. The opening incident raises the Christological question, "Are

you the one who is to come, or are we to wait for another?" (11:3). However, Jesus' answer and the ensuing discussion transform that question into one about the nature of the kingdom of heaven. Although John the Baptist is greater than anybody else born of woman, "yet the least in the kingdom of heaven is greater than he" (11:11). Moreover, in a later debate with the Pharisees about whether Jesus casts out demons by God or Beelzebub, the climactic answer again focuses on the kingdom: "But if it is by the Spirit of God that I cast out demons, then the kingdom of God has come upon you" (12:28). Finally, the discourse of this section unveils the "secrets of the kingdom of heaven" (13:11). The seven kingdom parables, with which this section ends, show that, for Matthew, understanding of Jesus as the Christ comes through understanding Jesus' proclamation about the kingdom of heaven.

2 . This kingdom of heaven is a kingdom of mercy. Jesus answers John the Baptist's disciples by enumerating his deeds of mercy (11:5; cf. Luke 7:22). Furthermore, Jesus' demand for discipleship is a yoke that is gentle and restful, because Jesus himself is gentle and lowly in heart (11:28–30; only in Matthew). Sabbath observance is understood within the context of mercy (12:7 f.; cf. 9:13 and Hos. 6:6). Indeed, Jesus' parable of the sower proclaims God's abundant mercy; the sower generously sows seed everywhere without distinction, and the seed on good soil bears grain prodigiously (13:3–8).

3 . The kingdom of heaven is, however, not mercy only; judgment also occurs. Chorazin, Bethsaida, and Capernaum will be brought down on the day of judgment because they rejected the words of mercy (11:20–24). Jesus' opponents, especially the Pharisees, will be brought to account on the day of judgment because they have not borne the good fruit—that is, acts of mercy (12:33–37). Indeed, this present generation is an evil one (12:45; only in Matthew). Finally, at the close of the age "all causes of sin and all evildoers" will be gathered out of the kingdom and thrown "into the furnace of fire, where there will be weeping and gnashing of teeth" (13:42; only in Matthew; cf. 8:12; 13:50; 22:13).

4 . Jesus' disciples are the ones who will realize the true nature of the kingdom of heaven. Those who have been gathered to Jesus learn that the kingdom is both mercy and judgment. They are the infants who learn that this yoke is easy (11:28–30; only in Matthew). They are the true family of Jesus. Matthew alone records Jesus' saying that the disciples are his mother and brothers (12:49; cf. Mark 3:34). Matthew also directs the final six kingdom parables to the disciples, for they are the ones who know the secrets of the kingdom (13:10–17). Indeed, Matthew omits Mark's castigation of the disciples, "Do you not understand this parable? Then how will you understand all the parables?" (Mark 4:13). In Matthew the opposite point is true—the disciples do understand; therefore, when Jesus asks them, "Have you understood all this?" the only possible answer is "Yes" (13:51). Matthew then concludes, "Therefore every scribe who has been trained for the kingdom of heaven is like the master of a household who brings out of his treasure what is new and what is old" (vs. 52; only in Matthew). The new refers to the king-

dom of mercy, new in comparison with Pharisaic insistence on strict Sabbath observance (cf. 12:12b); the old refers to the kingdom of judgment, the old expectation of judgment under the criterion of obedience to the will of God (cf. 12:50). Therefore, the scribe trains for the kingdom by accepting the new mercy and by carrying out the old obedience. Matthew speaks to the church in the time between resurrection and the parousia, a time of mercy and judgment. The disciples have no security other than the gracious presence of Christ (cf. 10:40; 28:20). They are to work between the times so that at the future judgment they will be found merciful. Matthew thus prepares for the subject matter of his next section, the church.

The Forgiving Church (13:53–19:2)

The kingdom of heaven has been characterized as an eschatological reality, already present in mercy and expected in judgment (11:2–13:52). Now, stress falls upon the church, the community of disciples existing between the resurrection and the parousia, those who are closely identified with the mercy motif of the kingdom of heaven.

Here as in every other section of Matthew narrative is informed by discourse. What Jesus teaches controls his own actions and those of his opponents and disciples. The concluding discourse (17:22–19:1) centers upon the nature and authority of the church. Fittingly, then, the climactic action of the narrative (13:53–17:21) is Jesus' establishment of Peter as the rock upon which the church is built (16:17–19). We receive clues as to the nature of this section simply by observing the heightened role of Peter. For example, Matthew takes over Mark's story of Jesus' walking on the water (14:22–33; Mark 6:45–52) and, instead of using it as an occasion to illustrate the disciples' misunderstanding (Mark 6:51 f.), shows Peter's amazing, albeit faltering, courage in trying to walk on the water. When he sinks from fear, Peter cries out with a Christological confession, "Lord, save me" (14:30). Partly because of Peter's action, at the end of the story the other disciples worship Jesus and confess, "Truly, you are the Son of God" (14:33). Matthew's stress on the Christological foundation of the church is evident in the exalted titles for Jesus in this part of the Gospel: "Lord" (15:22; 16:22; 17:4, 15), "Son of God" (14:33; 16:16), "Son of Man" (16:13, 27 f.), and "Son of David" (15:22). All are Matthew's distinctive additions to his inherited tradition.

The increased emphasis upon Peter is matched by a more prominent role for the disciples throughout this section. Perhaps the clearest evidence is Matthew's treatment of the two feedings of the multitudes. In the feeding of the five thousand (14:13–21; cf. Mark 6:30–44), Matthew omits the question in which the disciples misunderstand Jesus (Mark 6:37). In Matthew the disciples immediately understand, but they doubt their ability to supply bread for the multitudes: "We have nothing here but five loaves and two fish" (14:17). Moreover, in Matthew the disciples actually fetch the food (14:18).

Finally only Matthew depicts the disciples' duplication of Jesus' action in distributing the loaves to the crowds (vs. 19b; cf. Mark 6:41). Similarly, in the feeding of the four thousand (15:32–39; cf. Mark 8:1–10), the disciples again immediately understand their task; they are concerned only about their ability to accomplish it (vs. 33; cf. Mark 8:4). Once more the disciples actually give the bread to the people in imitation of Jesus (vs. 36; cf. Mark 8:6). Matthew also omits distribution of the fish to the crowds (Mark 8:7), thereby bringing his account closer to the actual celebration of the Lord's Supper in the church's life. By implication, the disciples are ministers of the church. Through Matthew's use of the tradition, these events in the life of Jesus are in the process of becoming events in the life of the church.

By using the framework of Mark (Mark 6:14–9:32), by abbreviating and adding other material, especially that not found in other Gospels, Matthew has turned this section into a discussion about the church. On the surface we have here a series of incidents: the death of John the Baptist, the two feedings, the healing of the Canaanite woman, controversy with the Pharisees and the Sadducees, the confession by Peter, the transfiguration, and an extended teaching section. Such a surface view, however, does not do justice to the careful way in which Matthew illuminates the nature of the community brought into being by the life, death, and resurrection of Jesus and charged to act with disciplined forgiveness until his coming again.

PETER AS THE ROCK (16:13–23)

How and why does Matthew's account of Peter's confession differ from Mark's?

Only in Matthew does Jesus explicitly accept Peter's confession at Caesarea Philippi (cf. Mark 8:27–33; see pp. 83ff.). Indeed the source of Peter's insight is said by Jesus to be none other than "my Father in heaven" (16:17). Furthermore, Peter has the keys to the kingdom: whatever he binds and looses (that is, his solemn decisions in matters of discipline) will be upheld on the judgment day (vs. 19; cf. 18:18).[8]

In spite of this praise of Peter for his recognition of the Messiah, after Jesus' announcement that he must suffer (vs. 21), the two engage in controversy (vss. 22 f.). Although Matthew may seem to be simply following Mark, so that Peter's difficulty with Jesus should be overlooked, this explanation is not sustained by closer scrutiny of the text. Matthew could have omitted the rebuke by Peter and the retort of Jesus, as Luke did (Luke 9:18–22). Moreover, Matthew not only includes the rebuke by Peter, but he increases

---

8. Our interpretation of this celebrated passage stresses the founding of the church through Peter rather than the founding of the episcopacy through Peter. Without going into the much-debated question of the authenticity of 16:17–19, we contend that Matthew speaks here not so much of the primacy of Peter as of the primacy of the church (cf. esp. 18:17–18). Peter represents the disciples and the disciples in turn represent the church. See Raymond E. Brown, Karl P. Donfried, John Reumann, et al., *Peter in the New*

Peter's opposition to Jesus' suffering by adding Peter's words, "God forbid it, Lord! This must never happen to you" (vs. 22). At one moment in Matthew Peter is literally praised to the heavens and at the next moment he is thrust into the company of Satan (vs. 23).

Matthew's tension between praise and blame for Peter is deliberate. It means that although the church has accepted Jesus as the Lord and the Son of the living God and has thus been granted the authority to bind and loose on earth, individual Christians, like the disciple Peter, have to accept Jesus' suffering. Even the disciple Peter is not spared suffering. Christians must imitate Christ. Even though the church has the authority to bind and to loose, disciples cannot avoid Christ's way. Thus Matthew's earlier identification of Christ with the role of the suffering servant (12:18–21) takes on new meaning, for the disciples must also become suffering servants (cf. 5:10–12).

The inescapability of suffering as a disciple is now depicted in Jesus' definition of discipleship as taking up one's cross and following him (16:24–28). To his Markan source (cf. Mark 8:34–9:1) Matthew adds that, when the Son of Man comes in glory, "he will repay everyone for what has been done" (vs. 27). Matthew's emphasis on obedience implies that although the church exists between the resurrection and the second coming, with great power to bind and to loose, every disciple is still accountable to the Judge for what he has done. Peter is pronounced blessed, but his blessedness, along with that of all disciples, will have to endure and be judged.

To sum up this episode, confession of Christ leads to the founding of a church whose authority is binding. The disciples, however, must be neither complacent nor self-righteous; they must do the will of God to prepare for the future judgment. The nature of the church that has been founded becomes transparent in the following discourse.

DISCIPLINE IN COMMUNITY (18:15–22)

How does discipline make community life possible?

Just as Peter's confession of the Christ was not simply an occasion for praise and rejoicing, so too Matthew's depiction of the disciples' liberation from the Pharisaic interpretation of the law (15:1–20) does not mean the creation of a community without discipline. Matthew's concluding discourse for the church (17:22–19:2) asserts that the Christian disciple comes under discipline of the churchly community. The incident of the temple tax (17:24–27), which serves as a transition to the discourse, illustrates the point. In this distinctively Matthean scene that follows a prediction of suffering (17:22), Je-

Testament: A Collaborative Assessment by Protestant and Roman Catholic Scholars (Minneapolis and New York: Augsburg and Paulist Press, 1973), for a discussion of Peter as an object of exegetical investigation and theological reflection. For a fresh historical treatment of Peter, see Pheme Perkins, *Peter: Apostle For the Whole Church* (Columbia, SC: University of South Carolina Press, 1994)

sus and Simon Peter discuss whether the temple tax should be paid. Although "the children are free" (17:26), Jesus orders the paying of the tax in order not to give offense (17:24–27). The members of the church possess freedom, yet freedom is restricted by the necessities of a community (cf. 1 Cor. 10:23 f.).

Our present passage (18:15–22), in agreement with what precedes, indicates that it may be necessary for the church to exclude people in exercising its authority to bind on earth (18:18). Of course, this power of excommunication does not exist for the purpose of condemning people, for the church acts under rules (vss. 15 f.) and always in forgiveness (vss. 21 f.). This concern for the individual Christian is indicated by the talk about "children" (18:3) and "little ones" (18:5, 10, 14). These "little ones" are to be received, not because they are actual children but rather because they are the disciples, the members of the congregation, who journey from the privilege of forgiveness (18:10–14) to deeds of obedience (18:5–9). Indeed, these same little ones are blessed in the beatitudes. They are poor in spirit; they are mourning and meek (5:3–5); they yearn after righteousness, mercy, purity in heart, peace, knowing that they are blessed (5:6–12). Matthew sets the discipline of the church in the context of God's grace. Even the community that exercises discipline consists of "little ones" who are in constant need of mercy (18:14).

Therefore, the passage containing the most rigorous word of discipline in Matthew ("Let such a one be to you as a Gentile and a tax collector"—vs. 17b) closes with the most definite promise of Christ's presence ("For where two or three are gathered in my name, I am there among them"—vs. 20). The church exists, then, not only with authority to bind and to loose, but also in the authority of the gracious presence of Christ. Consequently the church's most characteristic activity is that of worship (2:2, 8, 11; 8:2; 9:18; 14:33; 20:20; 28:9, 17). Such worship, adoration of the Lord, allows the church to bind or loose by offering forgiveness on the authority of Jesus. Therefore, Matthew concludes his exhortation for discipline in the church community with a word of Jesus about the radical necessity to forgive (18:21 f.) and with a long parable (only in Matthew) about the punishment of the wicked servant who does not forgive (18:23–35).

The church community is founded upon the confession of Jesus as the Christ. In its exercise of authority for judgment and discipline the constant limiting factor is Jesus' demand for forgiveness (cf. 6:14 f.). Matthew's congregation of believers is the forgiving church.

Judgment: Doing God's Will (19:3–26:1)

Matthew's discussion of the church as the forgiving community leads into a final major section: the church facing the last judgment. The judgment theme is found in Jesus' apocalyptic pronouncement (chap. 24), especially in the command of watchfulness for the coming end (24:36–51), and in the parables of the wise and foolish bridesmaids (or virgins), the talents, and the great judgment (chap. 25). The church, which exists in the blessedness of forgiveness, also has to live under the threat of judgment. In the light of this judgment, the disciples are called to do God's will.

Although again Matthew is dependent upon Mark's framework (Mark 10–13), his use of Q and his special M tradition and his shaping of all the material have made this section a manual on how the church meets judgment by doing the will of God. For example, the opening unit of tradition, the debate with the Pharisees about divorce (19:3–12; cf. Mark 10:1–12), places a discussion about doing the will of God in the proper Jewish–Christian context of the law. Several other episodes also concern interpretation of the law: the rich young man (19:16–30), paying taxes to Caesar (22:15–22), the resurrection question (22:23–33), the great commandment question (22:34–40), and the "woes" against the scribes and Pharisees (chap. 23, esp. 23:23 f.).

To do the will of God, one must properly understand the nature of the law. Matthew is concerned about discerning the will of God in the law and, most important, obeying it. In discussion with the Pharisees, Matthew has apparently softened Jesus' radical prohibition against divorce (cf. Mark 10:10–12) by allowing it on the grounds of unchastity (19:9; cf. 5:32). Yet in the very next episode Matthew shows a demand for obedience to the law more stringent than that of his Markan source, for the young man must be perfect (19:21; cf. Mark 10:21). The will of God cannot be equated with either a stricter or more lenient interpretation of the Jewish law. The one thing necessary for the doing of God's will is the presence and empowerment of God: "For mortals it is impossible, but *for God* all things are possible" (19:26).

Matthew's concept of reward for doing God's will is different from the idea of reward as so much accumulated merit. Instead, Matthew proclaims that there are no degrees of reward; the only and final reward (25:41–46) is God's presence, already anticipated in the doing of God's will. For example, Jesus answers the disciples' question about reward (19:27–30) with the parable of the laborers in the vineyard (20:1–16; only in Matthew), which teaches that no one grumbles in the joy of God's generosity (see vs. 15). Moreover, those who reject Jesus' authority, notably the Pharisees (see esp. chaps. 21 and 22), do not bear fruit (21:19), or, if they do, they keep it for themselves (21:33–44); therefore, they cannot escape judgment. The narrative portion of this entire section (19:3–23:39) then ends with the chastisement of the scribes and Pharisees. Their discernment of the law and their obedience were for their own justification instead of the doing of God's will. Thus at the judgment they will be condemned, even though their understanding of God's will may not be wrong (23:3).

A final indication of preoccupation with judgment in this section of the Gospel is the narrative setting in the territory of Judea and the city of Jerusalem (see 19:1; 21:1, 10; 24:1). At Jerusalem the condemnation of Jesus takes place, but that judgment ultimately turns against Jesus' enemies and in favor of his disciples if they continue to do God's will. Jesus' second coming as the Son of Man will determine whether disciples are sheep or goats, accepted or rejected (25:31 ff.). The test for discipleship is the same one Jesus had to pass: the doing of God's will, not one's own (26:39). The passages selected for further examination confirm this understanding of Matthew's view of judgment.

BELIEVING DOERS OF THE LAW (21:28–46)

Is promising to do the law enough?

The parable of the two sons (21:28–32; only in Matthew) has to do with the authority of Jesus and, in the last analysis, the authority of the church. The preceding incident (21:23–27) closed with Jesus' saying that he would not tell the chief priests and elders by what authority he was acting. Note how this parable is related to the previous episode by the reintroduction of John the Baptist (vs. 32; cf. vs. 25).

In the parable itself the son who first said he would not go, but then went, actually did the will of the father. This means that mere words claiming obedience (cf. vs. 30) are without value. Jesus' authority can only be understood in terms of whether association with him produces actual obedience. Furthermore, Jesus' opponents, the chief priests and elders (21:23), who turn out to be Pharisees (cf. 21:45), are condemned because even though they saw John's righteousness they did not believe him (vs. 32). (Clearly for Matthew the Pharisees are becoming surrogates for Jesus' opponents.) This

The last judgment with Christ separating the sheep from the goats. Part of an early fourth-century Christian sarcophagus.   *(Courtesy of Metropolitan Museum of Art. Rogers Fund, 1924.)*

"higher righteousness" requires both an actual obedience and belief. The nature of such belief becomes clearer in the following parable.

In the parable of the wicked tenants (21:33–46; cf. Mark 12:1–12), the owner sends his servants and his son "to collect his produce" (vs. 34), all to no avail, because the tenants kill the emissaries from the owner. The climax of the parable is reached when the owner returns, puts the tenants to death, and delivers the vineyard to other tenants "who will give him the produce at the harvest time" (vs. 41; cf. Mark 12:9). Matthew's conclusion to the parable, which is not in his Markan source, states that the kingdom "will be taken away from you and given to a people that produces the fruits of the kingdom" (vs. 43; cf. Mark 12:11). The trouble with the wicked tenants was not their failure to produce fruit (cf. 21:19) but their refusal to acknowledge the rightful owner of the fruit. The Pharisees do not believe; they try to justify themselves by their obedience rather than acknowledging the gracious God. According to Matthew, the Pharisees recognize that this parable is directed against them (see 21:45 f.). We note that Matthew underscores the necessity for obedience, but additionally asserts the need for belief in the giver of all obedience—God through Christ (cf. 21:42). Only thereby will the church be delivered from self-righteous, possessive obedience.

DOING MERCY WITHOUT CALCULATION (25:31–46)

Why are both the sheep and goats surprised?

Matthew's understanding of judgment and the end time is contained in the final discourse (chap. 25), which comments upon the apocalyptic disclosures that precede (chap. 24; cf. Mark 13). The parable of the ten bridesmaids (25:1–13; only in Matthew) and the parable of the talents (25:14–30; cf. Luke 19:12–27) give a framework for viewing judgment. The prospect of judgment may be wrongly met in one of two ways—either in relaxed carelessness about the future, as seen in the five foolish bridesmaids (or virgins), or in paralysis caused by anxiety over the severity of the judge, as seen in the wicked and slothful servant.

The judgment itself is depicted in the final parable (25:31–46; only in Matthew), which tells about the shepherd who will separate the sheep from the goats. The standard of separation is simply whether the one judged has performed acts of mercy for a fellow human being (25:35 f.). The element of surprise in this parable is that neither the righteous nor the unrighteous realized that their deeds of mercy were acts performed (or not performed) for the Lord (vss. 37 ff.). The climactic word of Jesus, "Truly, I tell you, just as you did it to one of the least of these who are members of my family, you did it to me" (vs. 40), alludes to the fact that mercy for the neighbor, and service to others, is service to Christ (cf. 7:21–23). Therefore, the true disciple shows mercy to others without calculation, without thinking such deeds will somehow cause God's judgment to be more favorable. Such noncalculation grows out of a relation with Christ in which anxiety is diminished and the disciple responds to whatever human need is at hand, especially to the neighbor (10:40–42).

Those who show mercy act without calculation, without thought that thereby they will ensure their future blessedness. They are merciful because they have been shown mercy; moreover, their deeds for the neighbor are deeds for Christ, who is present in the least of the brethren. Thus Matthew pictures the church in the time between the first and second comings. The church's role of obedience in that time has been most clearly anticipated in the death and resurrection of Jesus, Lord of the congregation, who serves as the paradigm for the Christian life.

Conclusion: Obedience and Resurrection (26:2–28:20)

At the outset of this concluding section Matthew gives clear indication that Jesus' passion occurs at the bidding of God. The passive voice ("will be handed over to be crucified," 26:2; see also 26:18) suggests divine causation. The action of both Jesus and the other characters is determined by a power not their own. For example, the woman who anoints Jesus' head with the expensive ointment (26:6–13) prepares his body for burial even though her action might ordinarily be understood as the expression of a mere sentiment or as an anointing of kingship (see 27:11, 29, 37, 42). Ironically, however, her anointing for death is also an anointing of the future Lord of the congregation. Moreover, Matthew hints at the victory of the resurrection by reminding the reader that Jesus is the Son of God (27:40, 43; only in Matthew). The power of resurrection over death is also evident in the supernatural events surrounding Jesus' death: the earth shook, rocks were split, saints were raised from the dead and appeared to many in the holy city (27:51–54; cf. Mark 15:38 f.).

Matthew subtly transforms the Markan passion story so that the element of Jesus' suffering, which cannot be removed completely, is modified by Jesus' obedience, which in turn becomes a paradigm for disciples. Insofar as Jesus acts or speaks in the passion, he voluntarily accepts his death; he obeys God's will. He could have called legions of angels, but "how then would the scriptures be fulfilled?" (26:54, 56; cf. Mark 14:48–50). Matthew adds to Mark's account of Jesus' accepting the cross ("yet not what I want but what you want"—26:39; cf. Mark 14:36) a reinforcing word of obedience, "My Father, if this cannot pass unless I drink it, your will be done" (26:42). Thereby, Matthew shows that in his passion Jesus fulfills the "higher righteousness" he set forth in the Sermon on the Mount (6:20; cf. 7:24); Jesus acts as the one who fulfills "all righteousness" (3:15). The Jesus of Matthew not only demands obedience, he also enacts obedience. His resurrection and establishment as Lord of the congregation are based upon faithful obedience to God.

THE GREAT COMMISSION (28:16–20)

How do Jesus' final words convey the message of the Gospel of Matthew?

In the final words of Matthew (28:16–20) the resurrected Jesus charges the disciples—that is, the Christian congregation—with the task of teaching all nations to observe what he has commanded (28:20). Such observance is now possible because Jesus has obeyed: at death the bruised reed did not break; he brought judgment to victory (12:20; only in Matthew).

Matthew follows Mark in depicting the burial of Jesus and the subsequent discovery of the empty tomb by the women. To this he adds the appearance of Jesus to the women (28:9 f.) and an account of the efforts of the Jewish leaders to make it appear that the body was stolen (28:11–15; cf. 27:62–66). The second and final appearance of the risen Jesus is obviously of greatest importance for Matthew. It occurs in Galilee (26:32; 28:7) at a mountain (5:1; 15:29; 17:1). The disciples' reaction to this climactic moment is described briefly: "They worshiped him" (see 2:2; 18:26; 28:9); "but some doubted" (vs. 17). The report of doubt strikes the reader as inappropriate, since the disciples have just worshiped Jesus. In other resurrection appearances doubt also occurs, but in those instances some further action of Jesus overcomes the doubt (Luke 24:41; Mark 16:14; John 20:25). Here the expression of doubt is simply followed by the word of Jesus. As the disciples make no further response, we can only conclude that Jesus' word overcomes the doubt. We shall discover in looking more closely at this passage that doubt is finally to be vanquished in the disciples' obedience to Jesus' subsequent command.

Before exhorting the disciples to action, the resurrected Jesus declares, "All authority in heaven and on earth has been given to me" (vs. 18). Jesus' authoritative announcement has an implicit reference to the cosmic enthronement of the apocalyptic Son of Man depicted in Daniel: "And to him was given dominion and glory and kingship, that all peoples, nations and languages should serve him; his dominion is an everlasting dominion that shall not pass away, and his kingship is one that shall not be destroyed" (7:14). The combination of authority, dominion, and extension to all nations makes this passage relevant to Jesus' word. Jesus' authority in heaven and on earth exists until "the end of the age," that is, while the church exists. Previously, Matthew dealt with the subject of authority as an aspect of Jesus' earthly activity: he taught with authority (7:28 f.), he healed with authority (8:9), he forgave with authority (9:6, 8). Now the authority of the resurrected Jesus is expressed precisely through the disciples' earthly task of making obedient disciples. The new thing about this authority is that with Jesus' resurrection it is extended to include all the nations.

The resurrected Jesus' word to the disciples—"teaching them to obey everything that I *have commanded you*" (vs. 20a; cf. 24:34 f.)—refers them to his previous teaching. The resurrected Lord's words are rooted not in heavenly visions or revelations but in words already spoken by the earthly Jesus. Yet Matthew does not allow the authority of the resurrected Jesus to rest simply with Jesus' activity on earth. Accordingly, the disciples, in the presence of the Resurrected One, will extend his authority to all nations. Consequently, the church's mission extends beyond those who claim election simply because of membership in the chosen people Israel (3:9; 21:33–43; cf. 2 Cor. 11:15–29).

Matthew's distillation of the resurrected Jesus' authority to the simple command to make disciples, baptize, and teach obedience (28:19, 20a) may contain another subtle warning. In the spurious ending of Mark's resurrection account (16:9–20), Jesus gives a commission to his disciples that includes preaching, baptizing, and performing charismatic acts of healing, exorcism, and speaking in tongues.[9] On the surface, these phenomena seem much more impressive as evidence for the authority of Jesus and his disciples than Matthew's simple obedience. However, Matthew has already prepared the reader for this more austere concept of authority, for he has denied that such manifestations were proof of faith and obedience (7:21–23). True discipleship will be demonstrated not in ecstatic, marvelous activity but rather in obedience. More than ever the disciples themselves are called to obey the words Jesus commanded. What at first appeared to be simply a call to missionary endeavor on closer inspection turns out to be a call for discipleship that embraces obedience.

Looking now more directly at the imperative from the resurrected Jesus (vss. 19, 20a), we find that the task is divided into three stages: making disciples, baptizing them, and teaching them to observe all that Jesus has commanded. Matthew definitely emphasizes the first and the third stages, for he sees the church as the community of discipleship (13:52; 16:13–20; 27:57), which consists of lowliness, readiness for suffering, and above all obedience (10:40–42; 16:24–27; 18:1–6; 22:11–14). The esteem in which Matthew holds discipleship is illustrated by the fact that he recognizes only one level of church membership. In first-century Judaism the ambitious disciple hoped one day to become the teacher or rabbi. But in Matthew, Jesus says to his disciples, "But you are not to be called rabbi, for you have one teacher, and you are all students" (23:8; only in Matthew). Doubtless Matthew understood Jesus' warning to apply also to matters of rank and office in the church. Although Matthew never has the disciples address Jesus with the title teacher or rabbi (instead their more customary form of address is "Lord"), there can be little doubt that the final words to the disciples establish once and for all

---

9. Although Mark 16:9–20 is a spurious ending (see p. 93), it may well represent tendencies at work in the early tradition of the church.

that the Lord of the congregation is, in the last analysis, the only Rabbi or Teacher.

The Gospel According to Matthew has thus come full circle. The initial emphasis on the radical obedience of Joseph (1:24) has now been expanded through the body of the Gospel to spell out the way of righteousness (3:15; 5:6, 20; 6:33) that is fulfilled in obedience (7:21; 21:28–32; 25:31–46). The disciples are to observe all that Jesus has commanded. Yet this radical demand becomes possible because in Jesus, his mission and message, God has come near (1:23; 18:20). Above all, the way of righteousness was fulfilled by the action of Jesus, particularly his obedient submission to death (20:26–28). Therefore, the final word of the resurrected Jesus assures the disciples that the Lord of the congregation both is and will be with them until the close of the age. The continuing presence of Jesus with the congregation means that these final words are not a farewell from Jesus. As long as the congregation continues, the resurrected Jesus lives and abides in the obedience of his disciples to his teaching.

Conclusion

In summary, our investigations show that the Gospel of Matthew is an interpretation of the tradition of Jesus based upon Mark's Gospel, the Q collection of sayings, and other traditions. Matthew's interpretive procedure does not, however, mean that he did not stand in the service of the tradition of Jesus that he received. He clearly intends to remain faithful to it. Both Matthew and Luke combine the predominantly narrative Gospel of Mark with the predominantly discourse collection of Jesus' sayings known as Q. Thereby these Gospels serve as a check against any inclination within the early Hellenistic Christian community toward making the Christian faith into a kind of mystery religion dominated by the pattern of a dying and rising god. In effect, Matthew and Luke are saying that Christian faith involves a particular teaching.

Matthew's stress on the words that Jesus spoke binds the Christian revelation to the historical Jesus, one whose past words and actions demand and promise obedience. The Christian congregation, therefore, knows its unity and origin in the historical Jesus. Even though Matthew may contain words of Jesus that were never spoken by him during his ministry, in bringing together the narrative and the discourse traditions it limits in principle the revelation of Christian faith to Jesus of Nazareth. Matthew and the other canonical Gospels thereby preserve the distinctive character of Christian faith, the so-called scandal of particularity: a particular person at a particular time and place is claimed as the relevation of the creating and judging God of the universe.

We can now review generally our use of four approaches in understanding Matthew's Gospel:

View of present-day Jerusalem.   *(Courtesy of Israel Government Tourist Office.)*

The *structure* of Matthew is clear-cut. The Introduction (1:1–2:23; see the outline at the beginning of the chapter) sets the tone for the rest of the Gospel. The coming of Jesus establishes a new and more radical obedience (Joseph); moreover, this obedience takes place within a new Israel, where Jew and Gentile (wise men) worship together. Matthew then sets forth the Gospel in five major sections, each consisting of narrative–discourse and reminiscent of the five authoritative books of Moses. Book 1 (3:1–7:29) depicts the "higher righteousness" both effected (the baptism) and demanded (Sermon on the Mount) by Jesus. Book 2 (8:1–11:1) previews the life of discipleship by showing that the miraculous deeds of Jesus call for deeds of love and service in the mission of the disciples. Book 3 (11:2–13:52) puts earthly activity into the perspective of the kingdom of heaven. Present mercy stands within the context of future judgment; the followers of Jesus are to train for this future event. Book 4 (13:53–19:2) sets this present mercy into the context of the forgiving church, where the basis for discipline and exclusion becomes the unwillingness to practice forgiveness. Book 5 (19:3–26:1) appropriately concludes with the expectation of future judgment on the basis of deeds, not beliefs. Furthermore, the doers of mercy are those who live in faith without thought of reward. The Conclusion (26:2–28:20) reports Jesus' obedient submission to death and God's response, which is the resurrection. Finally, the risen Jesus commissions the disciples to obey and to teach obedience, knowing that he abides with them until the close of the age.

Matthew's carefully worked out structure already indicates this Gospel's *major emphases*. We may now bring them together under three headings: the new obedience, its source, and its community. Matthew advocates a higher righteousness, which is a new obedience. The higher righteousness enables and requires radical obedience, and the spelling out of this obedience becomes clearer in Matthew's treatment of the law. Nowhere does he claim that the law has been abolished; on the contrary, the law is affirmed. Without deeds, professions of loyalty to Jesus are empty (7:21). Yet Matthew emphasizes the love of God and the love of all peoples, which must not be neglected through preoccupation with carrying out details of the law. Thereby Matthew seeks to make the will of God present and alive.

The second major emphasis is upon the source of higher righteousness, the Lord Jesus. In one sense the Jesus of Matthew is a more majestic figure than is the Jesus of Mark. Matthew tends to abbreviate Mark's miracle stories and consequently to make them even more inexplicable as human events. Yet this abbreviation is a primary means for emphasizing the importance of Jesus' teaching. Even in the miraculous acts, Jesus is a teacher, an extraordinary first-century rabbi. This teaching makes Jesus an authoritative, majestic figure. The Jesus of Matthew, however, is also lowly and obedient. He fulfills the scripture by becoming the suffering servant who not only teaches obedience to disciples but actually performs it. The mighty Lord goes to his death in obedient lowliness, thereby fulfilling the way of higher righteousness.

The third and final emphasis follows from the preceding ones: the higher righteousness fulfilled in Jesus Christ must be realized in the congregation or community. This community of the followers of Jesus learns that the present is determined by the mercy of God's presence, even for the sinner. The beatitudes proclaim God's love for the poor in spirit, the meek. The congregation knows itself as the "little ones," who obediently await the final judgment in the presence of Jesus.

Our total interpretation has depended upon observation of Matthew's *redaction* of the tradition. Among other things, redaction criticism shows that Matthew's treatment of the disciples is significantly less harsh than is that of his predecessor Mark. Yet our study suggests that Matthew has a more realistic view of the disciples' actual behavior than has Mark. Matthew recognizes that the disciples do "understand" Jesus; after all, they followed him. Nevertheless, they were still of "little faith" (see 8:23–27; 14:31; 16:8; 17:20) because they had not yet acted in obedience. According to Matthew, they could not obey until Jesus completed his own obedience through death and resurrection.

The general *situation* that produced the Gospel of Matthew is implicit in the document itself. Matthew's Gospel arises out of Judaism and yet Matthew insists that Jesus' message differs from the Judaism of the Pharisees. This insight explains the tension between the Gospel's emphasis on the law and the role of Israel on the one hand (e.g., 5:18 f.; 10:6), and its espousal of a higher righteousness and universal mission on the other (5:20; 28:16 ff.). Matthew calls for a higher level of obedience to the law than that required by those noted for their observance, that is, the Pharisees. Only against a Jewish background can the origin of Matthew's position be understood.

Although Jewish, the eschatology of Matthew cannot be classified as apocalyptic in the usual sense. Matthew's church did not cherish the belief that the end of the world was just around the corner and that people should gird themselves by extreme piety and ethical effort for the imminent encounter with God. True, Matthew emphasized the coming of the final day (chap. 24; cf. also 4:17; 26:28), yet he also spoke about a time of waiting for the church. For Matthew the church's time was truly significant (see 24:6, 36 ff., 42 ff.). Indeed, the close of Matthew (28:16–20) would make no sense if the evangelist expected the end immediately.

Matthew strikes out in more than one direction. On the one hand, as we have seen, he attacked Pharisaic Judaism's interpretation of the law. On the other, Matthew would have rejected a Christianity developing without regard for its roots in Israel and the Old Testament into an unrestrained and undisciplined spiritualism. Such a Christianity developed later, and Matthew may have already sensed its danger. At any rate, Matthew understood Christian faith to be firmly rooted in the historical Jesus. While rejecting Pharisaism, he used the teaching of Jesus to oppose any lack of moral responsibility. Matthew called his congregation to the obedience that Jesus had both commanded in his teaching and fulfilled in his passion.

It is evident from Matthew that this church is a community with Jewish roots. Standing within this community, Matthew maintains the Jewish themes of righteousness and obedience to the law; but he sets them within the context of faith in Jesus Christ, in whom they are fulfilled. Because of God's action through Christ and his continuing presence with the congregation, the end of Christian faith is not at all unlike the way. Thus, the kingdom of heaven is both present and future. Therefore, Matthew's Gospel mirrors not only the life of Christ but also Matthew's view of the life of the Christian community.

Suggestions for Further Reading

E. Schweizer, *The Good News According to Matthew,* trans. D. E. Green (Richmond, VA: John Knox, 1975), is a solid commentary, accessible to the general reader. More recently, there is D. J. Harrington, *The Gospel of Matthew* (Collegeville, MN: Liturgical, 1991), as well as the first volume of U. Luz's work, *Matthew 1–7: A Commentary* (Minneapolis: Augsburg, 1989). For the advanced student who can use Greek, the three-volume commentary of W. D. Davies and D. C. Allison, *A Critical and Exegetical Commentary on the Gospel According to Saint Matthew* (Edinburgh: T. & T. Clark, 1988 ff.), will be a rich source of exegetical insight and information.

G. Bornkamm, G. Barth, and H. J. Held, *Tradition and Interpretation in Matthew,* trans. P. Scott (Philadelphia: Westminster, 1963) is a classic work of redaction criticism still worth reading. W. D. Davies, *The Setting of the Sermon on the Mount* (New York: Cambridge, 1964), also remains a significant work. Important studies of the Sermon on the Mount include R. A. Guelich, *The Sermon on the Mount: A Foundation for Understanding* (Waco, TX: Word Books, 1982), and H. D. Betz, *Essays on the Sermon on the Mount* (Philadelphia: Fortress, 1985). J. D. Kingsbury, *Matthew: Structure, Christology, Kingdom,* rev. ed. (Minneapolis: Fortress, 1989), emphasizes literary and theological aspects of Matthew. Much recent research attempts to locate the Gospel of Matthew historically, ethnically (Jewish or Gentile Christian), and sociologically. Typical of such interests in different ways are A.-J. Levine, *The Social and Ethnic Dimensions of Matthean Salvation History: "Go nowhere among the Gentiles . . ." (Matt. 10:5b)* (Lewiston, NY: Mellen, 1988); J. A. Overman, *Matthew's Gospel and Formative Judaism: The Social World of the Matthean Community* (Minneapolis: Fortress, 1990); D. L. Balch (ed.), *Social History of the Matthean Community: Cross Disciplinary Approaches* (Minneapolis: Fortress, 1991). Kingsbury's *Matthew,* rev. ed. (Philadelphia: Fortress, 1986), is a valuable survey of the interpretation of Matthew, as is D. Senior, *What Are They Saying About Matthew?* (New York: Paulist, 1983). Important twentieth-century essays on Matthew have been collected by G. Stanton (ed.), *The Interpretation of Matthew* (Philadelphia: Fortress, 1983). J. P. Meier, *The Vision of Matthew: Christ, Church, and Morality in the First Gospel* (New York: Paulist, 1979), remains a good general treatment of Matthew for the serious reader. See also G. N. Stanton, *A Gospel for a New People: Studies in Matthew* (Edinburgh: Clark, 1992).

Chapter 4

Luke: The Gospel of Witnessing

Notes on the Gospel of Luke

*A*n early tradition about the Gospel of Luke, from the Muratorian Canon,[1] states that both the Gospel According to Luke and the Acts of the Apostles were written by the same author. This view is supported by the opening verses of each book, which in both cases contain dedications to a certain Theophilus, and by Acts' reference to a "first book" (1:1). The two books definitely display a kinship in style and emphasis. Yet neither Luke nor Acts makes a direct claim about the author's identity. Luke–Acts is an anonymous two-volume work. Presumably they were composed to be read together, although in the canonical arrangement their original close connection is interrupted by the Fourth Gospel. Together Luke–Acts comprises approximately one-fourth of the New Testament.

To be accepted by the church at the end of the second century, a Gospel needed a claim to apostolic authority. According to tradition, Mark rests upon the authority of one great apostle, Peter; similarly, Luke rests upon the authority of another, Paul. In his letters, Paul mentions as a companion, "Luke, the beloved physician" (Col. 4:14; Philemon. 24; 2 Tim. 4:11). This Luke may have accompanied Paul on some of his missionary journeys. The occasional use of "we" in Acts (e.g., 16:10 ff.) suggests the author is a participant in the events, although this is not certain.

If some doubt attaches to the relationship with Paul, a few things may be said with certainty about the author of the Gospel According to Luke. He was more self-consciously an author than were the writers of either Mark or Matthew. The preface (1:1–4) makes explicit the literary aim of the Gospel: it is dedicated to Theophilus and speaks knowingly of previous works on the same subject. Probably the author of Luke was a Gentile Christian. He spoke Greek as his native tongue and knew something of Hellenistic literary convention.

---

1. A catalogue of New Testament writings originating in Rome about A.D. 200. For the text see Edgar Hennecke, *New Testament Apocrypha,* I, ed. W. Schneemelcher and trans. R. McL. Wilson, rev. ed. (Philadelphia: Westminster/John Knox, 1991), pp. 34–36.

On the other hand, Luke seems to know little about Palestinian geography. He apparently conceives of Samaria as lying north of Galilee or, alternatively, of the two provinces as lying side by side on an east–west axis with a corridor between them. In 17:11, there is a statement most easily translated: "And it happened that in going to Jerusalem he passed through the middle of Samaria and Galilee." This is, of course, the wrong order on a journey from north to south. Both RSV and NRSV have Jesus passing between Samaria and Galilee, a possible translation, but one that still does not convey a sense of knowledge of the region's geography.

Although Luke used the Gospel of Mark, as did Matthew, he used this source more critically. Whereas Matthew took over practically all of Mark, Luke used about half. Like Matthew, Luke used the sayings source Q. In addition, there is a considerable body of tradition found only in Luke.

The material found only in Luke (usually designated L; see pp. 63–64), beginning with the preface (1:1–4), is typical of that Gospel. A birth narrative, parallel with Matthew's but significantly different, follows (1:5–2:40; see below, pp. 136–139). Only Luke gives us a story of Jesus' childhood, as he describes the boy Jesus in the temple (2:41–52). Several of the best-known parables of Jesus are found only in Luke: the good Samaritan (10:29–37); the prodigal son (15:11–32); the rich man and Lazarus (16:19–31); and the Pharisee and the publican (18:9–14), among others. Only Luke mentions Zacchaeus, short of stature and sinfully rich, who climbed a tree to catch sight of Jesus (19:1–10). Several of these parables and stories emphasize God's love and the importance of repentance. In the passion and resurrection narratives, only Luke mentions Jesus' going before Herod (Antipas) in Jerusalem (23:6–12), as well as the dramatic resurrection appearance to two disciples on the Emmaus road (24:13–35).

A number of Lukan stories have affinities with the Gospel of John. The parable of Lazarus recalls Jesus' raising Lazarus from the dead (John 11:1–44). Only Luke and John mention the sisters Mary and Martha (Luke 10:38–42; John 11:1–44). Luke's story of the miraculous catch of fish (5:1–11) is echoed in John's account of the risen Jesus' appearing to disciples beside the sea (21:1–14). Only Luke (24:36–49) and John (20:19–29) recount appearances of Jesus to the Twelve in Jerusalem; only they deal with the ascension of Jesus (Luke 24:50–51; Acts 1:1–11; John 20:17, cf. vs. 27). Finally, these evangelists in particular emphasize that women were among Jesus' earliest followers (Luke 8:1–3; John 19:25–27; 20:11–18; cf. 4:7–42). Strangely, John reflects knowledge of much of the narrative and historical data otherwise distinctive of Luke, but little if any of the considerable amount of teaching material (characteristic of L) found only in the Third Gospel.

As in the case of the other Synoptic Gospels, the exact dating of Luke is difficult. Like Matthew, Luke seems to know about the actual destruction of Jerusalem (cf. Luke 21:20 and 19:43 f.). The earliest date for Luke would therefore be sometime after Jerusalem's fall in A.D. 70. Because the introduction of Acts alludes to the Gospel (1:1), Luke was presumably written before the final version of Acts. The letters of Paul were written in the middle of the first century but were not assembled before the end of the century. It is unlikely that the author of Luke–Acts knew the Pauline letters. At least he does not mention them. Nor does what he writes indicate knowledge of events of the second century. Therefore, a date sometime before the end of the first century is probable. According to the preface (1:1–4), Luke apparently belongs to the third stage of the Christian tradition; he speaks of eyewitnesses, collectors ("ministers of the word"), and his own composition. If so, then a date only shortly before the turn of the century would be appropriate. Luke–Acts was likely written sometime between A.D. 80 and 100. Little can be said about the geographical origin of Luke other than that it probably did not originate in Palestine. Although the occasion of the writing of Luke is unknown, the evangelist's general purpose may be inferred from the fact that this is the only Gospel with a sequel, an Acts of the Apostles. The rest of this chapter and Chapter 7 examine this purpose more closely. We may, however, anticipate our study by suggesting that Luke presents a view of the history of salvation extending from the time of Israel through the life of Jesus and continuing in the history of the church. The good news for Israel is extended through Jesus and the apostles to all people.

The outline or structure of the two-volume work Luke–Acts depicts this history of salvation in an explicit manner, for the Gospel can be characterized as a movement from Galilee to Jerusalem:

Introduction:	Birth of John and Jesus in Jerusalem	1:1–2:52
Part One:	Gathering Witnesses in Galilee	3:1–9:50
Part Two:	Journey to Jerusalem	9:51–19:27
Part Three:	Jesus' Triumph in Jerusalem	19:28–24:53

And the Acts of the Apostles as a movement from Jerusalem to Rome (see pp. 292–293):

Introduction:	Birth of Church in Jerusalem	1:1–2:47
Part One:	Witnesses within Israel	3:1–12:25
Part Two:	Journey to the Gentiles	13:1–21:14
Part Three:	Paul's Triumph in Rome	21:15–28:31

Thus the author of Luke–Acts uses geography as a key for communicating the story of the triumphal march of the new religious movement from the obscurity of Galilee through the capital city of ancient Israel to the very center of the Roman Empire. Indeed, the journey theme, occurring as it does in the middle sections of both Luke and Acts, reflects the evangelist's intention of writing a narrative to depict the sweep of God's victorious action, primarily through Jesus and Paul. Luke has expanded the Markan story of Jesus' journey to Jerusalem (Mark 8:27–10:52) into a dominating motif and metaphor for Jesus and the early church (Luke 9:51–19:27).

OUTLINE OF LUKE

Preface: A Time for True Remembering (1:1–4)
Introduction: A Universal Story (1:5–2:52)
    Twofold Witness to Jesus (2:22–40)
    Initial Victory in the Temple (2:41–52)
Gathering Witnesses in Galilee (3:1–9:50)
    The Offense of Jesus' Preaching (4:16–30)
    Sure Witness to the Word (8:1–21)
Witness to the Word on the Journey to Jerusalem (9:51–19:27)
    Jesus' Word about the Present (15:1–32)
    Jesus' Word about the Future (19:11–27)
The True Israel through the Passion and Resurrection (19:28–24:53)
    The True Inheritors (20:9–19)
    Fulfilling the Scripture (24:13–35)

Preface: A Time for True Remembering (1:1–4)

In what sense did Luke intend to write history or biography?

With a preface of a sort not found in the other Gospels, yet common in the writings of antiquity, Luke makes the reader conscious of his predecessors and purpose (1:1–4). That the preface was a literary convention can be seen from a comparison of the opening sentences of Luke and Acts with prefaces of the first-century Jewish historian Josephus. His *Against Apion,* Book I, opens with the following statement:

> In my history of our Antiquities, most excellent Epaphroditus, I have, I think, made sufficiently clear to any who may peruse that work the extreme antiquity of our Jewish race, the purity of the original stock and the manner in which it established itself in the country which we occupy today. . . . Since, however, I observe that a considerable number of persons . . . discredit the statements in my history concerning our antiquity, . . . I consider it my duty to devote a brief treatise to all these points, in order at once to convict our detractors of malignity and deliberate falsehood, to correct the ignorance of others, and to instruct all who desire to know the truth concerning the antiquity of our race.

Book II begins:

> In the first volume of this work, my most esteemed Epaphroditus, I demonstrated the antiquity of our race, corroborating my statements by the writings of the Phoenicians, Chaldeans, and Egyptians. . . . I also challenged the statements of Manetho, Chaeremon, and some others. I shall now proceed to refute the rest of the authors who have attacked us.[2]

Not only the Gospel of Luke but the Acts of the Apostles begins with such a preface. Thus the parallel with Josephus is even more impressive. The very fact that Luke followed the prevailing literary fashion of his day indicates part of his purpose—to make his Gospel acceptable to the literate individual. Still, the preface has a more definite purpose.

With the statement that many others have undertaken to compile a narrative about the things that he will relate, Luke forgoes any claim to originality. Indeed, originality is not the point. Nor does he claim a divine revelation superseding all other previous accounts. Yet the opening verses give the unmistakable impression that he means to write a Gospel superior to its predecessors. Although there have been other compilers, as well as eyewitnesses and ministers of the word, Luke purposes to write an account more adequate than anything yet presented. Among Luke's many sources were most likely Mark, the Q source, and special Lukan tradition.

---

2. Cited according to H. St. J. Thackeray's translation, *Josephus,* Vol. 1 (Cambridge, MA: Harvard University Press, *The Loeb Classical Library,* 1926), pp. 163–165, 293.

Luke's historical situation can be inferred from the statement concerning his predecessors (vs. 2). In all, there are three stages of the gospel tradition. The first stage of eyewitnesses consists of those who have been with Jesus most intimately, for example, the twelve apostles (6:12 f.; cf. Mark 3:13 f.). Later we learn that apostles are those eyewitnesses who were with Jesus from the baptism to the ascension (cf. Acts 1:21–26). The second group, ministers or servants of the word, pass on the eyewitness tradition by preaching. Although in Acts ministers of the word are first of all the apostles themselves, there are other ministers, such as Stephen and Philip, who preach the word. The final stage, in which Luke himself stands, is that of the compilers of the tradition. With the advantage of hindsight the compiler is able to see what is most important and worthy of being preserved. Although Luke stands within that third phase, he intends to surpass all the rest. By "following all things closely" (vs. 3), he expects to give both an orderly and truthful account of the life, death, and resurrection of Jesus (vs. 4). Not only does Luke consider this compilation of the tradition more adequate than that of its predecessors, but he also considers this third stage the most advantageous perspective. In some ways it offers a more comprehensive and truer perspective than that even of eyewitnesses, although the latter are certainly indispensable.

Luke stresses that he is going to write an "orderly account" (vs. 3). This cannot mean that he is going to arrange his account differently, for Luke generally follows Mark's order. Probably Luke refers to his general scheme for placing Jesus within the history of salvation so that Jesus fulfills the story of Israel and initiates the story of the church. Perhaps the "Theophilus" to whom he addresses this work (vs. 3) is an actual person: an esteemed or eminent citizen, perhaps Luke's patron; or conceivably the name "friend of God" (which is what *Theophilus* means) stands for the religious reader who as a "God fearer" is interested in Christianity.[3] Whoever Theophilus may have been, he was certainly someone who had a preliminary knowledge of the Christian faith and was willing to read both the story of Jesus and that of the early church. He represents all who wished to know the truth about these things (literally, "words"—vs. 4). The implied reader is an interested inquirer, if not a new convert.

Luke's preface suggests his purpose. He seeks to write a Gospel of Jesus that will serve as the foundation for belief. Luke understands himself as living at a time in which true remembering needs to take place; he wishes to recover and reformulate roots so that the certainty and continuity of Christian faith from the beginning up to the present can be established: from Israel through Jesus to the church. The reader must hear the full Christian story.

---

3. See Acts 10:2, where Cornelius, the first named Gentile convert, is said to "fear God" (p. 282 below). The technical term "God fearers" (Greek *sebomenoi*) was applied to Gentile associates of the synagogue who apparently accepted Jewish monotheism without submitting to the whole law or, in the case of males, circumcision.

"The Holy Family" by El Greco (1541–1614).   *(Courtesy of National Gallery of Art, Washington, D.C. Samuel H. Kress Collection.)*

Introduction: A Universal Story (1:5–2:52)

The first two chapters of the Gospel According to Luke are concerned primarily with the birth stories of John the Baptist and Jesus of Nazareth. This tradition is not contained in the other Synoptic Gospels, even though another infancy narrative is, of course, found in Matthew. The persons and incidents in these chapters for the most part disappear in the rest of the Gospel. Nevertheless, these opening episodes set the tone for what follows and suggest who Jesus really is.

This Gospel opens with a priest named Zechariah, who will be father of the Baptist, in the temple at Jerusalem (1:5 ff.), a city important to Luke. Like none of the other Gospels, Luke begins in Jerusalem. In the central journey section Jerusalem is the destination (9:51). There in his last days Jesus takes over the temple (19:47; 21:37 f.; 24:53; only in Luke). Jesus' resurrection appearances occur in Jerusalem and its vicinity rather than in Galilee as Matthew states (24:6; cf. 24:13, 18, 33) and Mark clearly implies (14:28; 16:7; cf. John 21:1). Finally, the disciples wait in Jerusalem until the Holy Spirit manifests itself so that they may witness to the rest of the world (see Acts 1:4, 8).

"The Adoration of the Shepherds" by Giorgione (1477–1510). *(Courtesy of National Gallery of Art, Washington, D.C. Samuel H. Kress Collection.)*

A prominent characteristic of Luke's opening chapter is the twofold nature of figures and events. The birth of Jesus is coupled with the birth of John. A revelation occurs to Mary, the mother of Jesus; a revelation is also given to Zechariah, husband of Elizabeth, mother of John the Baptist. John is the forerunner, Jesus is the fulfillment (1:45). The babe in Elizabeth's womb leaps at the meeting with Mary, mother of Jesus (1:39–45). John is the "prophet of the Most High" (1:76); Jesus is the "Son of the Most High" (1:32). The two are not, however, set against one another but are in continuity. John the Baptist serves as a witness and a prophet to Jesus (cf. 1:80 with 2:40, 52; also see 3:4 ff.). In addition, both Simeon (2:22 ff.) and the prophetess Anna (2:36 ff.) testify to Jesus.

Luke also sets the story within the context of world history: "In the days of Herod" (1:5), "In the sixth month" (1:26), "In those days a decree went out from Caesar Augustus" (2:1; cf. 3:1). At the same time Luke emphasizes the role of women and the humble: Elizabeth and Mary are in the foreground; the shepherds come and worship Jesus (2:8 ff.; cf. 1:53; 6:20; 7:22). A romantic, idyllic quality pervades this section where salvation emerges among humble folk, women exult in childbirth, and shepherds come to worship a baby in a manger.

TWOFOLD WITNESS TO JESUS (2:22–40)

What do Simeon and Anna, who receive Jesus in the temple, represent or embody?

The Simeon episode (2:22–35) shows that Jesus' parents were law-abiding adherents of the Jewish faith (cf. 2:39). After Jesus' circumcision on the eighth day (2:21), attention turns to the purification of the mother of a son, which according to Jewish law took place on the thirty-third day after circumcision or the fortieth day after birth (see Lev. 12:2–8). Although purification actually is for the mother, not the child, this story depicts the parents as bringing the child Jesus "to do for him according to the custom of the law" (vs. 27). Perhaps Luke is unfamiliar with Jewish practices, or perhaps this manner of narration enables Luke to keep Jesus the center of attention even when the mother's purification would be taking place.

As the scene begins it presents a contrast between the old man Simeon, who has been patiently waiting for the consolation of Israel, and the child Jesus. Upon seeing Jesus, he exclaims, "Lord, now lettest thou thy servant depart in peace" (2:29–32). The astonishment of Jesus' father and mother at Simeon's words (2:33) is itself surprising, for they already knew that Jesus was to be a messianic figure (cf. 1:32 ff.; 2:13 ff.). Further, Simeon's speech contains a new item, for Jesus' coming is "a light for revelation to the Gentiles" (vs. 32). Jewish parents would understandably be surprised, especially since the news comes from a devout fellow Israelite (cf. vss. 34 f.). Even this point is not entirely novel, however, for Simeon's speech goes back to Isaiah, who made similar prophecies (cf. 52:10; 42:6; 49:6). The principal point of this episode, and of the entire introduction, is that Jesus will bring salvation for all people, even Gentiles. He is meant for old and young, for women like Mary and Elizabeth, and for priests and shepherds.

In the final part of this episode the old prophetess Anna appears (2:36–38). She is exemplary for her chaste widowhood as well as for her great piety. Again we have Luke's twofold witness: An old man and an old woman praise Jesus. Her actions are similar to those of the early Christians who also went to the temple in order to worship and pray (cf. Acts 2:46–3:1). Furthermore, what she anticipates—"the redemption of Jerusalem" (vs. 38)—is effected in the early church by the life of Jesus (cf. 19:28–24:53, esp. 24:21). Antiquity, represented by the old woman and the old man, foresees the new salvation and calls attention to that redemption's ancient roots in Israel. It is noteworthy that Luke chooses a woman, as well as a man, to prophesy redemption, for he has already emphasized the role of women throughout the infancy narrative.

INITIAL VICTORY IN THE TEMPLE (2:41–52)

What impression is conveyed by Jesus' first action in Luke?

The one boyhood story of Jesus contained in any of the canonical Gospels places Jesus in the temple.[4] This Lukan emphasis upon the temple was already apparent in the initial scene with Zechariah and the preceding encounters with Simeon and Anna. After Jesus' first action, a triumphant demonstration before the rabbis in the temple, his parents question him because his unexplained absence has caused them great anxiety. He replies, "Did you not know that I must be in my Father's house?" (2:49). The temple is Jesus' inheritance because he fulfills the hope of Israel.

Strikingly, the question is posed by Jesus' mother (2:48) rather than his father. Throughout the introduction, Mary rather than Joseph has the lead. In the purification episode, Simeon speaks to Mary (2:34). In fact, Mary is mentioned twelve times in the opening two chapters. And, finally, "his mother kept all these things in her heart" (2:51). Yet in the rest of the Gospel she is not particularly important and is even rebuked (8:19 ff.). The fact that her womb bore Jesus and that her breasts were sucked by him is declared insignificant in comparison with those "who hear the word of God and keep it" (11:27 f.; only in Luke). Luke's emphasis upon Mary does not stress the virgin birth; the narrative concentrates on a series of wonders rather than one particular miracle. The consistent flow of marvels underlines the fact that "with God, nothing will be impossible" (1:37).

---

4. The apocryphal Gospels contain numerous stories of the infancy of Jesus, sometimes grotesque and occasionally distasteful; see Hennecke-Schneemelcher, *New Testament Apocrypha*, I, 414–469.

The essential point of the birth stories, around which Luke's introduction is built, is the overwhelming power of God. Luke uses the miraculous birth of Jesus (Luke 1–2) to introduce Jesus' life in the same way as he uses the miraculous birth of the church (Acts 1–2) to introduce the church's mission. The outpouring of the Spirit upon various people at Jesus' birth is matched in Acts by the Spirit's descending upon apostles and disciples. The close of the introduction anticipates further developments (2:52). This verse echoes an earlier one (2:40). Further manifestations of God through the Spirit are thereby foreshadowed, for what was begun by the Spirit (cf. 1:15, 35, 41, 67; 2:25, 26) is now to be accomplished in the ministry of Jesus. The characters passively receive the Spirit; God's power acts in Jesus' birth. Only with the final episode, Jesus in the temple, does someone act with authority. And Jesus' action paves the way for Luke's first major section, in which Jesus gathers witnesses in Galilee for the journey to Jerusalem and the temple.

Although Luke's infancy narratives diverge sharply from Matthew's, there are important points of contact or similarity. Most striking is their agreement on the conception of Jesus through the Holy Spirit (Matt. 1:18; Luke 1:34–35) and without human paternity, the virgin birth. This aspect of Jesus' birth is emphasized even more strongly in Matthew (1:18–23) than in Luke. In both Gospels Jesus' advent is announced by an angel; in both it takes place in Bethlehem (Matt. 2:1; Luke 2:4–5); in both Jesus is of the lineage of King David, but through his nominal father Joseph (Matt. 1:20; Luke 1:27). In both, although in quite distinct ways, Jesus is presented as the fulfillment of Israelite hope and prophecy. Despite such similarities, the stories are for the most part different. The familiar manger scene with shepherds in attendance is found only in Luke. The wise men from the East appear only in Matthew. Difficult historical and literary questions are raised. Aside from the fact that the Matthean and Lukan stories do not agree, the birth of Jesus is not narrated, and scarcely even mentioned (cf. Gal. 4:4), elsewhere in the New Testament. Yet the agreements between Matthew and Luke in the midst of divergences suggest that there was an earlier tradition of Jesus' birth upon which both drew. Paul and Mark at least know Jesus was of the line of David (Rom. 1:3; Mark 1:47–48), and John may also be aware of this feature (7:42). The differences between Matthew and Luke would seem to preclude either writer's having known the other, although Luke's knowledge of Matthew has been suggested. If Luke knew Matthew (or vice versa), he shows a remarkable disregard for the other's narrative. The problems involved in trying to explain one narrative in light of the other justify our interpreting each narrative on its own terms.[5]

---

5. For a comprehensive treatment of the historical and theological issues surrounding the birth narratives, the standard work is still Raymond E. Brown, *The Birth of the Messiah*, Rev. ed. (New York: Doubleday, 1993)

Gathering Witnesses in Galilee (3:1–9:50)

Thus far any source of Luke's narrative has been his special tradition, but at this point (3:1) the major source becomes the Gospel of Mark. A part of this segment of Luke (comprising most of 6:17–7:35), found also in Matthew but not in Mark, is probably derived from the Q source. We would be on relatively uncertain ground in trying to deduce the aims and purposes of Luke from his use of this source, simply because we do not possess Q. We shall therefore largely confine our distinguishing of tradition from redaction to Luke's use of the Markan source. In addition, we continue to assume that the special Lukan material reveals something of the purpose of this Gospel.

Luke locates the beginning of Jesus' ministry in two spheres, that of world history (3:1; see also 2:1) and that of God's word. This word is first preached by John, the son of Zechariah (Luke 3:2 ff.). Luke's account of the Baptist's activity is similar to Matthew's, but with some remarkable differences. For example, whereas Matthew carefully showed that Jesus was baptized by John to fulfill righteousness (Matt. 3:13 ff.), Luke minimizes the fact that Jesus was baptized by John (cf. 3:20 f.). At the same time, John the Baptist preaches exactly the same message of repentance and forgiveness (3:3), which becomes the heart of Jesus' own proclamation (see Luke 15; 24:47 and pp. 148ff.). As the opening birth stories already indicate, this Gospel shows a high regard for John (cf. 7:28). Yet the Baptist still belongs to the old Israel (16:16), for he is the one who points ahead to the new time of Jesus (3:16).

Characteristic Lukan emphases abound in this section. Jesus is a universal savior: the genealogy goes from Jesus back to Adam, the first man (3:38), not to Abraham (Matt. 1:1 f.). Jesus is an example of piety: whenever a crisis arises, he is at prayer (5:16; 6:12; 9:18, 28 f.). Moreover, the Spirit descends upon

Caesar Augustus (27 B.C.–A.D. 14) and Tiberius Caesar (A.D. 14–37) on Roman coins.   *(Courtesy of American Numismatic Society.)*

Jesus while he is praying almost as if the Spirit were summoned by prayer rather than by the baptism (3:21; cf. Mark 1:9 f.). The Gospel of Luke apparently seeks to establish the practice of prayer as a basis for the continuing life of the church (see Acts 1:14; 2:42). Emphasis upon the church's contemporary situation may be reflected in Luke's omission of Mark's summary of Jesus' preaching, "The time is fulfilled, and the kingdom of God has come near; repent, and believe in the good news" (Mark 1:15). Although Luke also mentions the kingdom in this section, in Luke Jesus rarely preaches about the kingdom as if it were imminent (see 4:43 and 8:1; cf. 9:27). This loss of a sense for the imminent coming of the kingdom is related to Luke's greater emphasis on the church, and on salvation history.

Jesus' gathering of disciples in Galilee is a focal point of this section of the narrative. Many people flock to him (4:15, 42; 5:1, 15); some are in opposition (5:30; 6:2) and remain only in the crowd (6:17; 7:11), but he gathers the disciples (5:1–11). Indeed, from the disciples, he calls the twelve together whom he "named apostles" (6:13; cf. Mark 3:14). Here in his own territory Jesus gathers those who will be witnesses to carry on his work after his death. (At Jesus' ascension, two men address the disciples as "men of Galilee"—Acts 1:11.) The continuing importance of women is shown by their inclusion alongside the Twelve as part of Jesus' retinue (8:2 f.). Later, they too, along with the Twelve, will be witnesses: "The women who had come with him *from Galilee* followed, and saw the tomb, and how his body was laid; then they returned, and prepared spices and ointments" (23:55 f.; see 23:49). Luke seeks to establish certainty of witness (cf. 1:4): there are people who had accompanied Jesus all the time, from his baptism until the day when he was taken up (see Acts 1:21 f.).

THE OFFENSE OF JESUS' PREACHING (4:16–30)

What reason do the people of Nazareth have to become angry with Jesus?

In Mark, Jesus' first public act is to exorcise a demon (1:21–28); in Matthew it is to deliver the Sermon on the Mount (chaps. 5–7); in Luke it is to preach in his home synagogue at Nazareth. The special importance of this episode is indicated by its position at the beginning of Jesus' public ministry. Moreover, Luke departs uncharacteristically from the Markan order as he moves forward and expands Mark's simpler narrative (Mark 6:1–6).

Jesus appears as a pious Jew: "He went to the synagogue, as his custom was, on the sabbath day" (vs. 16). He there reads from the prophet Isaiah, whose message from the Old Testament (Isaiah. 61:1–2; 58:6) proclaims the end time; the Spirit acts, good news is preached to the poor, and a new age has dawned. After finishing, Jesus says, "Today, this scripture has been fulfilled in your hearing" (vs. 21; only in Luke). In other words, salvation has appeared with Jesus, who comes to preach good news to the poor, release the captive, and proclaim the arrival of deliverance. The kingdom is not merely

View of present-day Nazareth. A small and prosperous city today, Nazareth was an insignificant village in Jesus' time, not mentioned in the Old Testament or in other ancient sources. *(Courtesy of Israel Government Tourist Office.)*

imminent; it has in some sense already arrived. That the kingdom is good news for the poor, for the depressed and deprived, is an emphasis that recurs elsewhere in the Gospel (e.g., 1:52–55; 6:20–21, 24–25; 14:13, 21). It is characteristic of Luke's Jesus.

The reception accorded Jesus by the people of Nazareth is indeed startling. They at first accept him as the one who brings salvation (vs. 22). In Luke's source (Mark 6:1–6), the people immediately took offense at Jesus' claim to authority. In Luke, "Is not this Joseph's son?" (vs. 22), seems at first to proceed rather from surprise than anger (cf. Mark 6:3). Nevertheless, in Luke too Jesus is eventually rejected, not because he claims authority but because he extends salvation to the wrong people, to outsiders.

Clearly, Jesus thinks he will be expected to perform miracles as he has in Capernaum (vs. 23; although Luke has not yet reported any miracles). Jesus rejects any such request, declares that a prophet is not acceptable in his own country, and then speaks of the miracles in the Old Testament that the prophets Elijah and Elisha performed, not for the people of Israel, but for foreigners. Immediately, the audience's anger is aroused. Jesus' proclamation extends deliverance beyond Israel to the Gentiles. They drive him out

Ruins of ancient synagogue at Capernaum, built in the second or third century on the site of one Jesus visited.   *(Courtesy of National Geographic Society.)*

of the city and almost kill him, but he escapes (vss. 29 f.). We might now expect Jesus to leave Palestine to preach to Gentiles, but Luke, like the other canonical Gospels, reports no major mission outside Israel. For Luke the matter is resolved: Jesus' saying finds fulfillment in the church's mission; Acts makes clear that the Gentiles hear the word (cf. Acts 11:18; 13:46; 22:21; 28:28).

The incidents that follow this opening scene further reveal Luke's program. What Jesus has done in Nazareth, he now proceeds to do in Capernaum (4:31 ff.). He refused to perform a miracle at Nazareth, but in this synagogue and on this Sabbath, he heals. Jesus heals now because he is on his way toward his goal. When the people try to hold him, he says, "I must preach the good news of the kingdom of God to the other cities also; for I was sent for this purpose" (4:43). Precisely because this preaching to other cities cannot be done by Jesus alone, the necessary conclusion of the opening Nazareth scene is the calling of disciples. When Jesus' ministry has concluded, these disciples will be the instruments for spreading the message beyond Israel to the cities of the Gentiles.

A comparison between the calling of disciples in Luke (5:1–11) and in Mark (1:16–20) shows that the stories are quite different (cf. also John 21:1–14). Luke alone includes a miracle, that of the great catch of fish. Stress is laid, however, upon the consequence of the miracle, Simon Peter's confession of sin: "Depart from me, for I am a sinful man, O Lord" (vs. 8). After this repentance, Simon Peter and those with him become fishers of men or true disciples. But the Pharisees and their scribes upbraid them for eating with "tax collectors and sinners" (5:30). Jesus defends his disciples' behavior, however: "I have not come to call the righteous, but sinners to repentance" (5:32). The opposition to Jesus and his purpose is here graphically portrayed.

Another example of Luke's repentance motif is the story of the woman "who was a sinner" (7:36–50). Although this story has some affinities with Mark (14:3–9; cf. John 12:1–8), its present form has a distinctly Lukan cast. In Luke, the sinful woman who shows great love to Jesus serves as the occasion for a parable of Jesus that stresses that someone who has been forgiven then loves (7:43). Yet the actual incident first mentions the woman's love, then Jesus' forgiveness (cf. 7:47 f.). That her love is an expression of repentance is clear from the story: she is a sinner, she weeps, she kisses the feet of Jesus. Her repentance and love and Jesus' forgiveness contrast with the moralism of Simon the Pharisee, their perplexed host.

Jesus' presence elicits two kinds of response, either rejection by those who cling to a narrow view of righteousness or repentance by those who accept his promise of salvation. Those who repent become witnessing disciples to the forgiveness that Jesus brings.

SURE WITNESS TO THE WORD (8:1–21)

In what sense is the parable of the sower really about the work of the church?

In the introduction of this passage, a number of witnesses are gathered around Jesus: the Twelve and the women who not only follow Jesus but also support him from their own financial resources (8:1–3). At its close, the mother and brothers of Jesus, who come to see him, are told, "My mother and my brothers are those who hear the word of God and do it" (8:21). This sequence is designed by Luke to demonstrate that true disciples not only hear Jesus' word but also go out to become preachers of this word (cf. 8:15; see 1:2; Acts 6:1–7).

In comparing this section with its parallels in Mark (4:1–34; 3:31–35), a major difference becomes evident: Luke shifts the position of the discussion about the true mother and brothers of Jesus hearing God's word (8:19–21) so that it now follows, rather than precedes, the parable of the sower. The change reflects Luke's concentration upon the theme of the word of God. For example, in Luke's interpretation of the parable of the sower Jesus says more directly than in Mark, "Now the parable is this: The seed is the word of God" (8:11; cf. Mark 4:13 f.). Mark says only that the sower sows the word.

"The Repentant Magdalene" by Georges du Mesnil de la Tour (1593–1652).
(Courtesy of National Gallery of Art, Washington, D.C. Ailsa Mellon Bruce Fund.)

Luke's version of the parable of the sower (8:4–8) unfolds much as in Mark (4:1–9) except that Mark emphasizes response to Jesus' teaching in parables, whereas Luke stresses response to Jesus' message of the word of God. By a series of slight changes Luke transforms the passage into an exhortation for careful and sure witness to the word of the gospel. Such phrases as "the seed is the word of God" (8:11; cf. Mark 4:13), "then the devil comes and takes away the word from their hearts that they may not believe and be saved" (8:12b; cf. Mark 4:15), and "they are those who, hearing the word, hold it fast in an honest and good heart, and bring forth fruit with patience" (8:15; cf. Mark 4:20) show Luke's intention to emphasize the importance of hearing and holding to the word of God. By slight alterations Luke makes his point. By the same token, the saying about not hiding the lamp (8:16) refers in Luke to those who hear the word and patiently bring forth fruitful witness (8:15; cf. Mark 4:20). Gathering sure disciples in Galilee assures the faithful continuation of the word of God in the witness of the church.

The next episodes in Luke, basically following the order of Mark, are a series of miracles: the miracle of calming the waves (8:22–25); the driving out of the demons at Gerasa (8:26–39); the healing of the woman with the flow of blood (8:43–48); and the raising of the dead daughter (8:40–42, 49–56). This series culminates when Jesus "called the twelve together and gave them power and authority over all demons and to cure diseases, and he sent them out to proclaim the kingdom of God and to heal" (9:1–2). The witnesses are gathered, are convinced, and even Herod begins to wonder (9:7–9). The crowds are filled, for after the feeding of the five thousand "twelve baskets of broken pieces" are left over (9:10–17). Only then are the disciples asked to affirm that Jesus is the Christ of God (9:18–20).

The conclusion of the first part of Luke, "the gathering of witnesses in Galilee," begins a discussion of Jesus' identity, especially the necessity of his suffering (9:21–27, 43b–45). At the close of this first major section, instead of Mark's "whoever is not against *us* is for *us*" (Mark 9:40), Luke's Jesus says, "whoever is not against *you* is for *you*" (9:50). These are clearly instructions for the early church. Luke anticipates the separation of Jesus from his disciples in the postresurrection period after Jesus has ascended into heaven (cf. Acts 1:9–11).

Witness to the Word on the Journey to Jerusalem (9:51–19:27)

The Galilean witnesses gathered by Jesus must journey with him to Jerusalem. Luke's second major section, which narrates the journey, seems much longer than the short distance (about sixty miles) and the brief time (about three days) that it would take to travel by foot from Galilee to Jerusalem. Although Jesus is on the way to Jerusalem all this time, he seems to make little physical progress (see 9:51; 10:1, 38; 13:22, 33; 17:11; 19:11).

Luke's reason for such an extensive account of the journey is not simply an interest in geographical matters, for it is difficult to answer questions about Jesus' itinerary from Galilee to Jerusalem on the basis of the information in the text. For example, despite Luke's interest in Samaritans (10:29–37), we are left uncertain as to how Jesus went through Samaria, which lies on the most direct route from Galilee to Jerusalem (cf. 9:52–53; 17:11; see above, p. 131). Luke does make clear, however, as the journey progresses, that certain people are present with Jesus throughout the trip. Continuity in witness to the work and word of Jesus is thereby assured (cf. 23:49).

The opening verse is a key to this section: "When the days drew near for him to be taken up, he set his face to go to Jerusalem" (9:51; only in Luke). Jesus goes to Jerusalem because "today, tomorrow, and the next day I must be on my way; because it is impossible for a prophet to be killed outside of Jerusalem" (13:33; only in Luke). As prophet to Israel, Jesus goes to die at

Jerusalem, the capital of Israel.[6] The journey turns out to consist largely of instruction in the purpose and meaning of Jesus' mission and death.

A comparison of the structure of Luke's Gospel with that of the Acts of the Apostles reveals a striking similarity that helps to illuminate the reason for the journey. In Acts the order is as follows: first, the Spirit's appearance and the gathering of witnesses in Jerusalem; second, journeys of missionaries, especially Paul; third, Paul's arrest and trial ending in Rome. In Luke the order is similar: first, gathering of witnesses in Galilee; second, the journey to Jerusalem accompanied by preaching the word; third, Jesus' arrest, trial, crucifixion, and resurrection in Jerusalem. Luke–Acts shows a continuity of witness stretching from Galilee to Rome; the journey motif emphasizes an orderly, gradual spread of the new faith.

Luke throughout this section stresses the theme of witness, in two senses: (1) a witness *observes* something; (2) a witness *testifies* to something. These senses correspond to his distinction between "eyewitnesses and ministers of the word" (1:2). The first two episodes (9:51–56 and 9:57–62; mainly special Lukan material) indicate the necessity of following Jesus closely—that is, of *observing*. The mission of the seventy (10:1–17) implies that the Twelve remained with Jesus even during the sending out of the seventy (10:1; note "others"); moreover, the disciples are singled out: "Then turning to the disciples Jesus said privately, 'Blessed are the eyes that see what you see!'" (10:23; cf. Matt. 13:16). Other passages point out that disciples are always with Jesus so that his journey has been faithfully observed (11:1; 12:1, 22, 41; 16:1; 17:1, 5, 22; 19:28–40). By and large, these passages belong to the editorial work of Luke. By the end of this section the emphasis includes not only faithful observation but also faithful testifying to what has been observed (cf. 19:11–27).

This entire section (9:51–19:27) is a depiction of Jesus' telling the disciples about the word of God. They are shown that women matter (10:38–42). Luke's interest in women's relationships with Jesus doubtless reflects Jesus' own practice, as well as that of the earliest church. Prayer is also part of Jesus' life and that of those with him (11:1 ff.). The kingdom of God becomes present whenever Jesus casts out demons (11:20). Physical closeness to Jesus guarantees nothing by itself; the blessed are "those who hear the word of God and obey it" (11:27 f.). True disciples cannot be satisfied with the old rules of piety (11:37–12:3). Riches are clearly a barrier to hearing the word that Jesus proclaims (12:13–34; cf. 14:33; 16:11, 14, 19–31; 18:22–30; 19:1–10). Watchfulness and faithfulness are demanded over a long period of time (12:41–49), and repentance is necessary now (13:1–9). Jesus' ministry must continue for a considerable time (13:10–35); furthermore, the end of the world is not in sight (17:20 ff.). The messianic banquet with Jesus will include great multitudes, the unexpected (14:13), the Gentiles (14:23; cf. 17:18 and 10:33); but not all will enter (14:25–35). The following special Lukan ma-

---

6. Luke undoubtedly views Jesus as Messiah, but as such also the true prophet (see 1:76; 4:24; 24:19; Acts 3:22; cf. Deuteronomy 18:15–22).

terial from the journey gives the heart of Jesus' instructions, especially concerning repentance and forgiveness.[7]

JESUS' WORD ABOUT THE PRESENT (15:1–32)

What is the common theme of these three parables?

After Jesus says "Let anyone with ears to hear listen!" (14:35), we learn that "all the tax collectors and sinners were coming near to listen to him" (15:1). Into the center of the journey section, Luke inserts three parables, of which only the parable of the lost sheep is found in any other Gospel (cf. Matt. 18:12–14). These parables clarify and extend Jesus' word, which the disciples are to transmit to others. The Pharisees and the scribes have been irritated by Jesus' association with sinners (vs. 2). In contrast, the parables emphasize joy and openness to all (cf. 15:7, 10, 32), a prominent motif within Luke (cf., for example, 1:14, 44; 2:10; 6:23).

The first two parables pose an interesting problem of interpretation, for the general conclusion of each speaks of a sinner's repenting (15:7, 10), yet such repentance is hardly exemplified in the parables themselves. A lost sheep or a lost coin does not repent. The usual explanation is that the general conclusions anticipate and more properly belong to the third parable, that of the prodigal son. Moreover, this last parable contains the key passage concerning repentance, for the prodigal son repented— "when he came to himself . . ." (15:17).

An opposite conclusion could, however, be drawn: Luke's very purpose in using the two introductory parables was to *prevent* an incorrect reading of the parable of the prodigal son in terms that make repentance primary. The first two parables unmistakably emphasize the initiative of the one who seeks out the lost. Whether this is Jesus or God is not crucial (probably both are intended), for the decisive announcement is that salvation is present (see 4:21; 10:9, 11; 11:20; 17:20; 18:30; 19:9; 23:43). Luke is addressing the charge made against Jesus that he eats with sinners (vs. 2), and he claims that precisely the avowed sinner recognizes what is happening and, unlike the Pharisees and scribes, receives the forgiveness of God.

A more appropriate title for the familiar parable of the prodigal son might be the parable of the prodigal father. The parable runs smoothly and understandably through the son's realization that he would be better off as one of his father's hired servants (vss. 17 f.), at which point he returns home confessing himself a sinner. The surprise of the story is the way in which the father receives him. Instead of greeting him self-righteously ("I told you so") with a demand that he demonstrate his repentance, the father runs out to embrace him and gives orders to bring the best robe, the ring, shoes, and

---

7. Further elaboration of the repentance–forgiveness motif is given in these distinctively Lukan sayings: the word from the cross (23:34), the word to the criminal on the cross (23:39–43), and the charge to resurrection witnesses (24:47).

"The Return of the Prodigal Son" by Murillo (1617–1682).   *(Courtesy of National Gallery of Art, Washington, D.C. Avalan Foundation.)*

the fatted calf. He will have a feast for his son. There is joy and merriment for one who was lost and is now found (vs. 24).

To prevent our missing the point, the elder son is then introduced (vs. 25). He is angry; he cannot understand his father's joyful reception, much as the Pharisees and scribes cannot understand Jesus' association with sinners. But the father exclaims, "Son, you are always with me, and all that is mine is yours. It was fitting to make merry and be glad, for this your brother was dead, and is alive; he was lost, and is found" (vs. 32). The elder brother fails to recognize the joy and salvation that is already present. Thus he now needs to repent and to accept the good news of God's forgiveness (15:7, 10, 25–32). Only then is God's word truly heard.

These same themes of forgiveness and repentance recur in the remaining portions of the journey. The rich man tries too late to repent (16:19 ff.), and the poor man Lazarus cannot help him. Unexpectedly, some do repent because the kingdom is in their midst (17:11–21). He who hears Jesus' word is one who impetuously keeps knocking at the door (18:1 ff.) and admits that he is a sinner in need of God's mercy (18:9 ff.). Things turn out unhappily for those who are self-satisfied (18:18–23), yet whoever calls on the mercy of Jesus will receive sight (18:35–43). Even a rich chief tax collector will be saved if he sees himself as a sinner (19:1–10). The word Jesus proclaims during this journey effects salvation. Those who are close to him will testify to what they have heard and seen: "Today salvation has come to this house, because he too is a son of Abraham" (19:9).

At times, Luke seems to be saying that salvation has already fully arrived. But Luke knows that there is more to come; the history of the church will be unfolded by those acting under the Spirit of God. Although Jesus' final days in Jerusalem are coming, Luke does not think that nothing else remains to be done. Hence he closes this journey section with the parable of the pounds.

JESUS' WORD ABOUT THE FUTURE (19:11–27)

In what sense does the nobleman of this parable represent Jesus?

In Jesus salvation is present (see 10:18; 11:20; 17:20). Yet how does the presence of salvation in him relate to the coming kingdom of God? The opening of the parable of the pounds does not suggest the expectation of an imminent kingdom (19:11; cf. 21:8 and Acts 1:6 ff.). Seemingly, present salvation and future kingdom are distinguished in the thought of Luke, and the kingdom is in the indefinite future.

In the parable of the pounds, the nobleman goes into a *far country* to receive kingly power, a hint that in Luke's eschatology the king will return again only after a long journey. Before leaving he gives ten pounds to ten slaves, one pound each, with explicit instructions to trade with the money.[8] The citizens of his country do not want him to be their king; they resist by sending an embassy after him to oppose him. The parable is relatively complex (cf. the much simpler parallel in Matt. 25:14–30), for the unhappy citizens appear only at the beginning and the end of the parable and the relation between the citizens and the slaves is unclear. The point of the parable at first seems to be that when he returns, the king condemns the slave who in fear of him as a severe judge had simply hidden the gift away. But concentration upon future severity misses the point. Although the king does at the end deal severely with this slave and with his enemies (vs. 27), the one who waits and makes use of the gift of salvation (that is, who continues his witness to a forgiving God) over a long period of time need not fear.

Throughout this section Jesus' word brings forgiveness for whoever will receive it—sinners, people in the highways and hedges, a prodigal son, or foreigners. But if they do not see and testify to this word, then judgment will come. A joyful present and a threatening future have been proclaimed as they journeyed to Jerusalem. Now Luke brings Jesus into the city where he must die and be resurrected.

---

8. As the NRSV note points out, the pound was a relatively large sum, equivalent to three months' wages for a day laborer.

The True Israel Through the Passion and Resurrection (19:28–24:53)

In the third and final section of the Gospel of Luke, two distinctive motifs emerge: first, Jesus' triumph in the temple; second, Jesus' innocence. The temple motif is not new in Luke.[9] Now, however, he reiterates his emphasis more insistently. Jesus is teaching daily in the temple (19:47; 20:1; 21:37 ff.; 22:53); even after the resurrection the disciples return to the temple to bless God continually (24:53). Moreover, the apocalyptic discourse takes place in the temple rather than on the Mount of Olives as in Mark and Matthew (21:5–28; cf. Mark 13:1 ff. and Matt. 24:1 ff.). In Luke Jesus does not move from the temple. Why then does Luke so emphasize Jesus' frequenting the temple?

In the Acts of the Apostles the earliest church is also centered in the temple (cf. Acts 2:46; 3:1 ff.; 5:20). Apparently Jesus establishes himself in the temple in order that the early church may also operate from this base. Luke thereby also shows that the new faith in Jesus represents the true Israel and is the authentic extension and continuation of the dominant religious institution of Israel. (The temple had probably been laid waste at least a decade before he wrote.) Luke consequently assures both Jewish and Gentile believers of the antiquity and continuity of the new faith. The disciples, who return to the temple immediately after the resurrection appearances to bless God and to await the power of the Spirit (24:53), are neither a band of fanatics expecting the end of the world nor political revolutionaries against the Roman Empire. This latter emphasis becomes more explicit in the book of Acts (see pp. 293, 296), but is present already in the Gospel.

The second major motif of this passion and resurrection section, the trial and death of the *innocent* Jesus, fits the above view. A special Lukan detail illustrates this emphasis on Jesus' innocence. At Jesus' trial before Pilate, the elders of the people accuse Jesus of having forbidden the giving of tribute to Caesar (23:1–5; cf. Mark 15:1–5), but an earlier debate established the falsity of this charge (20:19–26). In Mark, Pilate, the Roman procurator, finds Jesus not guilty on one occasion (15:14), but in Luke this verdict of innocence occurs three times (cf. 23:4, 14–16, 22). Furthermore, in Luke the centurion at the cross says, "Certainly, this man was innocent" (23:47); whereas in Mark he says, "Truly this man was the Son of God" (15:39; cf. Matt. 27:54). The subtle way in which Luke opposes Jesus to Barabbas suggests that Jesus was not an insurrectionist like Barabbas (cf. Luke 23:19, 25 with Mark 15:7). Jesus' climactic word from the cross establishes his innocence: "Father, forgive them;

---

9. See the introductory section, especially 2:41–52. The order of temptations in the Gospel of Luke may reflect Luke's temple emphasis. In Luke 4:1–13, Jesus' temptation to throw himself off the temple's pinnacle is the last temptation (unlike the parallel in Matthew 4:1–11), perhaps to signal the temple scene as the climactic one.

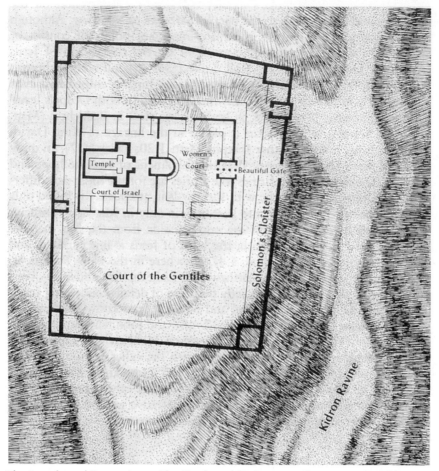

The temple and its precincts. The Garden of Gethsemane lies across the Kidron Valley at the foot of the Mount of Olives.

for they do not know what they are doing" (23:34; only in Luke). Luke further underlines Jesus' innocence as one of the thieves from the cross says, "We are getting what we deserve for our deeds, but this man has done nothing wrong" (23:41; only in Luke). This major theme receives further, unqualified substantiation in Acts: "This man . . . you crucified and killed by the hands of those outside the law" (Acts 2:23; cf. Acts 8:32 ff. and 17:30).

The innocent Jesus is falsely accused, tried, and executed. Instead of concentrating upon the guilt of those responsible for this miscarriage of justice, Luke focuses upon Jesus' triumph even under adversity. At the cross Jesus' general word of forgiveness (23:34) and his forgiveness of the repentant thief (23:39–43) show that guilt need not be overwhelming. Moreover, this Lukan passion story is the working out of God's plan for the true Israel. ("This Jesus, delivered up according to the definite plan and foreknowledge of God"—Acts 2:23; cf. 3:18 and Luke 22:22.) Jesus dies a martyr's death, prefiguring the martyrdom of others in the early church, especially Stephen and James (cf. Acts 7:54–8:3; 9:1; 12:1 ff.). But through all these events God's word of "repentance and forgiveness of sins" is being preached to all nations (24:47), and God's plan is thus fulfilled.

THE TRUE INHERITORS (20:9–19)

Who are the inheritors to whom the vineyard will be given?

In focusing intently upon the passion events up to and including Jesus' death and resurrection, Luke is obviously in company with the other Synoptic Gospels. In the parable of the wicked tenants Luke shows his understanding of the reason for Jesus' death and resurrection.

In the preceding passage (19:47–20:8), Jesus' authority for teaching daily in the temple has been challenged by the chief priests and the scribes. Comparing the opening of the parable with its Markan source (Luke 20:9; cf. Mark 12:1; Matt. 21:33), we are struck by Luke's distinction between the people *to* whom this parable is spoken and the chief priests and the scribes *against* whom it is spoken (cf. 20:19). In Mark's version (12:1 12), the parable is clearly a polemic against the chief priests, scribes, and elders because they have rejected God's servants, the prophets and even the "beloved son" (Mark 12:6; see pp. 70 f.). The identity of the Markan "others" who will receive the vineyard is indefinite, although the reader may surmise that they are the Gentiles (Mark 13:10; cf. also Matt. 21:43).

In Luke, however, this parable is addressed not to Jesus' opponents but to the people (vs. 9), who "were spellbound by what they heard" (19:48). Furthermore, the people protest strongly the destruction of the former tenants and the giving of the vineyard to others: "When they heard this, they said, 'Heaven forbid!'" (20:16b; only in Luke). This protest serves, however, to allow Jesus to restate his conclusion (vss. 17 f.) and to imply that the people finally accept Jesus' word, for the leaders acknowledge that the people are on Jesus' side (vs. 19) although they themselves are not.

Throughout this section Luke consistently portrays the people as being sympathetic to Jesus. They are the ones who praise God (18:43); they listen in the temple (19:48; 21:38); they observe Jesus' defeat of the authorities (20:26). They stand by watching at the crucifixion; it is the rulers who scoff (23:35). Within biblical and Jewish tradition, reference to "the people" carries with it the connotation of God's chosen people, the people of Israel.[10] Consequently the alignment of the people with Jesus implies that Jesus' word is finally accepted by Israel.

---

10. See "*laos*" in Kittel, *TDNT,* IV, 29–57, and especially Luke 2:32 and Acts 26:17, 23. Cf. Acts 4:10; 28:26 f.

In the Book of Acts, Luke clarifies the identity of the "others" (Luke 20:16). They are the true inheritors, for they are the "Israelites" and the Gentiles who hear the preaching (cf. Acts 2:22; 3:12; 13:16, 46–48). The last speech of Paul, at the conclusion of Acts, confirms that the Gentiles have become the true people of God because the old Israel has rejected the preaching (Acts 28:26–28). Yet Luke clearly shows by this parable that the people are on Jesus' side, so that "others," the inheritors, include both Jews and Gentiles. In Luke, a parable concerning the rejection of Jesus becomes also a parable stressing the true inheritors, those who *hear*.

Luke nonetheless emphasizes rejection in this parable, and in his own special way. Omitting the last lines of Mark's quotation (12:10; cf. Psalm 118:22) and adding an allusion to Isaiah (8:14–15), Luke thereby underscores the judgment that occurs for those who do not truly understand or interpret the scripture. They cannot tell the true Israel from the false. This necessity for rightly interpreting the scripture is the subject of our final Lukan passage.

FULFILLING THE SCRIPTURE (24:13–35)

Why is the risen Jesus not recognized immediately?

Before turning to the climactic "on the road to Emmaus" story, we need to observe the way in which Luke prepares for this scene. Throughout the passion, especially after the parable of the wicked tenants, two themes mutually reinforce each other: (1) these events necessarily happened; (2) they were closely and surely witnessed.

Definite things must happen before the end can come (Luke 21:12) to fulfill scripture (21:22; 22:37; esp. 24:25–27, 32). These things are done at the bidding of God, who alone is in command of the situation (see 21:18, a Lukan addition picking up 12:7). God's direction of the events is implicitly claimed by the assurance that these things happen to fulfill scripture: "Was it not necessary that the Messiah should suffer these things and then enter into his glory?" (24:26; cf. 22:15 f.).

Not only must these things happen, but they also have to be observed by the disciples, that is, the apostles. For after Jesus is gone, they will have opportunity to bear testimony (21:13; cf. Mark 13:10; see esp. Luke 24:48). To ensure this witness the apostles and women of Galilee are constant companions of Jesus. For Luke it is especially important for the apostles to be with Jesus (22:14; cf. Mark 14:17). We learn in Acts that an apostle is one who "beginning from the baptism of John until the day when he was taken up from us" was constantly with Jesus (Acts 1:21–26). The apostles continue with Jesus in his trials (22:28); they follow Jesus to the Mount of Olives (22:39; cf. Mark 14:26), and even when they fall asleep, it is "for sorrow" (22:45; cf. Mark 14:37). Luke omits Mark's statement "And they all forsook him and fled" (14:50). At the crucifixion, "all his acquaintances and the women who had followed him from Galilee stood at a distance and saw these things" (23:49;

cf. Mark 15:40 f.). Luke insists that ministers of the word based their testimony on eyewitness reports. They observed in order that the truth about these things might be known (see Luke 1:1–4).

The story of the empty tomb, which precedes the road to Emmaus story, bears out these preliminary observations (24:1–12; cf. Mark 16:1–8). Two men greet the women instead of a single young man (cf. Mark 16:5). This twofold witness guarantees authenticity (see pp. 137 ff.). Luke also subtly changes what had been a prediction of Jesus' future appearances in Galilee into a statement about what Jesus said while he was in Galilee (24:6; cf. Mark 16:7). This change brings his text into harmony with Luke's view that the resurrection appearances took place in Jerusalem (cf. Matt. 28:16). Luke's Gospel shows a clear, straightforward development: beginning in Galilee, extending to Jerusalem, and from there to the rest of the world (24:47). Moreover, Luke's story of the empty tomb points ahead to the confirmatory appearances to the disciples, for when the apostles first hear the report from the women, "these words seemed to them an idle tale, and they did not believe them" (24:11). Luke's stress upon both continuity and certainty required more than an account by fearful women.[11] Full recognition of the resurrected Jesus occurs only when his followers meet him on the road to Emmaus (24:13 ff.). That this meeting takes place "on the road" is in keeping with the journey motif of Luke. Furthermore, we hear twice in this episode about "the things that have happened" (24:14, 18); indeed, Jesus asks, testing them, "What things?" (24:19). These lines recall the Gospel's introduction, for this was to be a narrative about "the things which have been accomplished among us" (1:1; cf. 1:4).

The puzzle of this story is the initial nonrecognition of Jesus by the men. Perhaps they were kept from recognizing him because God willed it thus (vs. 16). Yet why should God want to keep them from recognizing Jesus? Probably they failed to recognize him because of their preoccupation with the tragic events of the preceding days (vss. 19–21). Jesus proceeds to interpret the scriptures to show that the Christ did have to suffer to enter into his glory (vss. 26 f.). Jesus' role in God's plan was that of a suffering servant (see 22:37; Isa. 53:12). Even this disclosure, however, does not enable them to recognize Jesus, although later they recall, "Were not our hearts burning within us while he was talking to us on the road, while he was opening the scriptures to us?" (vs. 32).

The crucial moment of recognition comes only during the meal: "Their eyes were opened, and they recognized him; and he vanished from their sight" (vs. 31). Later their report confirms that the decisive act was "the breaking of the bread" (vs. 35). There are at least two immediate possibilities for understanding the significance of the "breaking of the bread": (1) Jesus performed a familiar act that they had often observed; therefore, they recognized

---

11. Luke (24:22, and 24:12, if authentic) reports a visit by apostles to the tomb, which nevertheless proves inconclusive (cf. John 20:2–10).

"Supper at Emmaus" by Rembrandt (1606–1669).   *(Courtesy of Alinari Art Reference Bureau.)*

him; and (2) the "breaking of the bread" was a sacramental communal act of worship in the early church (Acts 2:42, 46), and Luke thereby implies that the believer knows the resurrected Jesus primarily in the sacrament of the Lord's Supper. Neither view is wholly satisfying, for neither is explicit in the text.

A somewhat different interpretation takes its cue from the act of eating. In the following story (24:36–43), even though Jesus appears directly to the disciples and tells them to look at his hands and feet, they still "disbelieved for joy" (vs. 41). Only after he has eaten does he pronounce his farewell address (vss. 44–49). Again, eating seems to be crucial for full recognition. During the Last Supper with the apostles (22:14–19) Jesus said, "I have earnestly desired to eat this passover with you before I suffer; for I tell you I shall not eat it until it is fulfilled in the kingdom of God" (vss. 15 f.; only in Luke). Evidently, Jesus would not eat until suffering was accomplished. That he now eats with the disciples implies that his suffering has been completed and that he is now raised to glory. Therefore, in Luke the scripture interpretation emphasizes the necessity for suffering (24:26 f.), and the eating with the disciples (24:30, 35, 42 f.) emphasizes that the suffering is accomplished and the glory of Jesus has begun. Now they can recognize him. With that sure foundation, the church can now receive its charge from the risen Christ.

Jesus' final words to the disciples suggest the plausibility of this interpretation (24:44–49). The redemption of Israel is effected by Jesus' suffering, which fulfills scripture (vss. 45 f.). Repentance and forgiveness of sins are to be preached beginning from Jerusalem and extending to all the world (vs. 47). The witnesses who have observed and who will now testify await only the coming of the Spirit (vss. 48 f.; cf. Acts 1:8). Because Jesus' word and deed are now accomplished and because his followers can continue the witness, the new Israel returns to the temple with joy and with Jesus' blessing (24:50–53).

Conclusion

Of all the Gospel writers Luke is the most interested in preserving the truth about the life of Jesus. But for him, as for most historians in the first century, truth is not simply equated with historical data. The purpose of the Gospel of Luke, like that of Mark and Matthew, is religious proclamation and reflection, not simply historical reporting. Luke wrote so that careful observation and a comprehensive and true outlook would be available to the church of his day.

The *structure* of Luke is distinctive. Only Luke follows his Gospel about Jesus with a second volume on the early church. In itself this structure indicates Luke's interest not only in Jesus but also in the church that he originated. A long-range perspective on the life of Jesus is also suggested by the preface, where Luke writes of three stages of the tradition: eyewitnesses, ministers of the word, and the writing of the Gospel.

In Luke's introduction Simeon, a man of Israel who has long awaited salvation, is finally rewarded by Jesus' appearance to him in the temple. Toward the close of Luke's story, Jesus frequents the temple and, in effect, triumphs in this central religious institution of Israel. After Jesus' death and resurrection the disciples return to the temple to wait for the coming of the Spirit, which will empower their preaching of repentance and forgiveness to all people. Their testimony to Jesus' message is certain because they have observed its beginning and end, from Galilee to Jerusalem.

This overall view of Luke is confirmed by the threefold division of the Gospel itself: gathering witnesses in Galilee (3:1–9:50), witness to the word on the journey to Jerusalem (9:51–19:27), and the establishment of the true Israel through the passion and resurrection (19:28–24:53). These main divisions show how the old is incorporated into the new. Israel is on a journey through the Old Testament culminating in the life of Jesus and moving into the early church.

The frequent *emphases* of Luke also support our proposed structure for the Gospel. These include the new faith as the true Israel, the history of salvation's expansion to include world history, and the necessity for accurate and continuous witness.

Luke affirms that the new religion is the true Israel. What happened to Jesus occurred according to the word of God, known through scripture. Thus Jesus' first public act was to preach fulfillment of the prophet Isaiah in the synagogue at Nazareth (4:16 ff.). Moreover, at the resurrection appearances Jesus interpreted his suffering as a fulfillment of scriptures (24:27, 44). These things are presented as sure because all were predicted and foretold. The witness of Jesus began and ended with correct interpretation of the scripture. A further emphasis supporting the theme of the true Israel is the centrality accorded the temple and Jerusalem. The Gospel opens with Zechariah in the temple in Jerusalem; at the introduction's close, Jesus is also in Jerusalem and in the temple (2:41–52). The journey section of the Gospel moves toward Jerusalem: "he set his face to go to Jerusalem" (9:51; cf. 13:33). The passion narrative centers on Jesus' teaching in the temple (19:47 f.). In addition, the Gospel closes with the disciples' return to the temple in Jerusalem (24:52 f.). This elaborate picture of Jesus in the temple and in Jerusalem implies that Jesus embodies the true Israel and that his followers are the authentic people of God.

The character of this New Israel as the nonsubversive, legitimate extension of the old receives confirmation in the elaborate detail showing Jesus' innocence of any wrongdoing. Jesus did not forbid the paying of tribute to Rome (20:19–26). Indeed, Rome, in the persons of both Pilate and the centurion, proclaimed the innocence of Jesus (23:4, 14 ff., 22, 47); moreover, the repentant thief declared Jesus free of any wrongdoing (23:41). This theme of innocence is extended and enlarged in Acts, particularly in Luke's portrayal of the favorable disposition of Rome to the new religious movement. Paul is declared thoroughly and completely innocent (Acts 25:25; 26:31 f.), even as Jesus was (Luke 23:47). Certainly any educated Roman reader would conclude that Christianity and Rome were not at cross-purposes.

The second major emphasis of Luke is that the true Israel aims to embrace the whole world. For Luke, the world outside Israel is not an adversary, but a mission field: Luke–Acts progresses from Galilee to Jerusalem and on to Rome. Furthermore, Luke records traces of world history (2:1; 3:1; also Acts 24:27) to keep this final goal in view. Involvement with the world occurs by God's acting in the Spirit through the person of Jesus (Luke) and through eyewitnesses and ministers of the word (Acts) to bring the gospel to all people (Luke 24:47 and Acts 2:38 f.). Luke's Christianity is universalistic: Simeon speaks about salvation "to the Gentiles" (2:32); Jesus' genealogy goes back to Adam (3:38); and in his opening sermon Jesus speaks favorably of Gentiles (4:24–29). Of course, the second volume shows the extension of the new religion beyond the confines of Israel to the known world (Acts 10:1–11:18).

The final major Lukan emphasis is witness (1:2), which consists of accurate observation (eyewitnesses) and truthful testifying (ministers of the word). Apostles, disciples, and women accompanied Jesus throughout his ministry; they in turn became, or were followed by, preachers who declared Jesus' own themes of repentance and forgiveness (Luke 15; 24:47; Acts 2:38). Forgiveness begins with the divine initiative, irrespective of human action; Jesus' actions embody this forgiveness in the present (7:48). Yet forgiveness elicits a human response of repentance. Whoever receives the forgiveness or mercy of God acts without anxiety for the future coming of God's judgment (cf. 19:1–10). In Jesus salvation becomes available (4:21; cf. 23:43); therefore, the ministers and preachers of the early church testify to what God has done and continues to do in Jesus. As witnesses they preach the good news (2:10; 3:18; 4:18; 7:22; 16:16) of forgiveness and repentance.

Luke's *redaction* of the tradition has been used as a key in the establishment of Luke's emphases. Luke's shaping of Mark—for example, in the parables of the sower (8:4–21) and the wicked tenants (20:9–18)—disclosed his emphasis on the word of God (8:11) and the true Israel (20:9). Especially noteworthy are the special Lukan additions, already noted, which serve to emphasize Jesus' innocence and his proclivity to forgiveness.

There have been many attempts to identify precisely the *historical situation* of Luke; none of them is conclusive. Our interpretation, instead of precisely locating the historical situation in which Luke was written, views the Gospel in the context of early Christianity generally. It was not designed primarily to convert the unbeliever, but speaks principally to Christians and "almost" Christians, showing the continuity and certainty of the Christian faith. According to Luke, the journey of Christian faith is made in joy and victory. The life and work of the church of Luke's time is authentic, according to the scriptures, because the true Israel is emerging and because the world is slowly and surely being Christianized. The forgiving Jesus is presented as both the fulfillment of the old and the originator of the new. The witnesses have not been arbitrarily chosen; they were prepared for their task, and their present successes show the sweep and power of the new way.

Luke's Gospel has something of the romance about it. There are women as well as men, some of questionable repute; there are journeys and quests; there are successful adventures. At the end of the Gospel the disciples are in the temple blessing God and waiting for the Spirit's coming with power for the mission. At the end of Acts of the Apostles, Paul is preaching in Rome and things will turn out well. Luke idealizes the story, no doubt, but he thereby testifies to the faith and history of Jesus and the early church. What was founded by Jesus, observed by the apostles, and proclaimed by them will continue without faltering until all have come into the kingdom of God and the fellowship of the Lord Jesus Christ "quite openly and unhindered" (Acts 28:31).

IMPORTANT NON-MARKAN PARALLELS IN LUKE AND MATTHEW

Such parallels are the basis of the Q-source hypothesis. Luke is given first because in order and form it often seems to represent an earlier or less developed version. Luke also follows Mark's order, where he uses Mark, more closely than does Matthew.

John Preaches Repentance	Luke 3:7–9, 11 // Matt. 3:7–10
John Announces the Messiah	Luke 3:16–17 // Matt. 3:11–12
Satan Tempts Jesus	Luke 4:2–12 // Matt. 4:2–11
Jesus Blesses Poor, Hungry, Persecuted	Luke 6:20–23 // Matt. 5:3, 4, 6, 11, 12
Discipleship Is Love for Enemies	Luke 6:27–36 // Matt. 5:39–42, 44–48
The Pitfalls of Judging	Luke 6:37–42 // Matt. 7:1–5
A Tree Is Known by Its Fruit	Luke 6:43–46 // Matt. 7:16–21; 12:33–35
Hearers and Doers of the Word	Luke 6:47–49 // Matt. 7:24–27
Jesus Heals a Centurion's Servant	Luke 7:1–10 // Matt. 8:5–13
John Questions Jesus	Luke 7:18–23 // Matt. 11:2–6
John, the Preparer for Jesus	Luke 7:24–35 // Matt. 11:7–19
Discipleship Is Leaving Everything	Luke 9:57–60 // Matt. 8:19–22
Discipleship Is Extending Jesus' Work	Luke 10:2–12 // Matt. 9:37–38; 10:7–16
Jesus Pronounces Doom on Unrepentant Cities	Luke 10:13–15 // Matt. 11:21–23
Discipleship Is Sharing Jesus' Rejection	Luke 10:16 // Matt. 10:40
Jesus Thanks the Father for the Gift of Wisdom	Luke 10:21–22 // Matt. 11:25–27
Discipleship Is Sharing in the Gift of Wisdom	Luke 10:23–24 // Matt. 13:16–17
Jesus Teaches How to Pray	Luke 11:2–4 // Matt. 6:9–13
The Father Will Answer His Children's Prayer	Luke 11:9–13 // Matt. 7:7–11
Jesus' Exorcisms Show God's Kingdom Is Present	Luke 11:14–23 // Matt. 12:22–30
The Danger of the Return of the Unclean Spirit	Luke 11:24–26 // Matt. 12:43–45
The Sign of Jonah and the Wisdom of Solomon	Luke 11:29–32 // Matt. 12:38–42
Sayings about Light and Darkness	Luke 11:33–36 //Matt. 5:15; 6:22–23
Jesus Pronounces Doom on the Pharisees	Luke 11:39–44 // Matt. 23:25–26, 23, 6–7, 27
Jesus Pronounces Doom on the Lawyers	Luke 11:46–52 // Matt. 23:4, 29–31, 34–36, 13
Discipleship Is Fearless Confession of Jesus	Luke 12:2–12 // Matt. 10:26–33; 12:32; 10:19–20

Discipleship Is Trusting God, Not Possessions	Luke 12:22–34 // Matt. 6:25–33, 19–21
The Unexpected Return of a Householder	Luke 12:39–46 // Matt. 24:43–51
Jesus Brings Division, Not Peace	Luke 12:51–53 // Matt. 10:34–36
Signs of the Times	Luke 12:54–56 // Matt. 16:2–3
The Kingdom of God Is Like Leaven in Bread	Luke 13:20–21 // Matt. 13:33
Entry into the Kingdom of God Is Difficult	Luke 13:25–29 // Matt. 7:13–14; 25:10–12; 7:22–23; 8:11
Jesus Laments over Jerusalem	Luke 13:34–35 // Matt. 23:37–39
The Banquet in the Kingdom of God	Luke 14:16–23 // Matt. 22:2–10
Discipleship Is Hating Family, Bearing a Cross	Luke 14:26–27 // Matt. 10:37–38
The Joyful Shepherd	Luke 15:4–7 // Matt. 18:12–14
God or Mammon?	Luke 16:3 // Matt. 6:24
The Violence of the Kingdom of God	Luke 16:16 // Matt. 11:12–13
The Permanence of the Law	Luke 16:17 // Matt. 5:18
Discipleship Means Unlimited Forgiving	Luke 17:3–4 // Matt. 18:15, 21–22
The Power of Even a Little Faith	Luke 17:5–6 // Matt. 17:20
The Surprise of the Day of the Son of Man	Luke 17:23–37 // Matt. 24:26–27, 37–41; 10:39; 24:40, 28
The Fate of a Nobleman's Servants	Luke 19:12–26 // Matt. 25:14–29
Jesus' Followers Will Share His Kingdom	Luke 22:28–30 // Matt. 19:28

Suggestions for Further Reading

E. Schweizer, *The Good News According to Luke,* trans. D. E. Green (Atlanta: John Knox, 1984) is a very useful commentary. More technical, but also excellent, is J. A. Fitzmyer, *The Gospel According to Luke,* 2 vols. (Garden City, NY: Doubleday, 1981, 1985), perhaps the standard commentary. In addition, there are now the worthwhile commentaries of D. L. Tiede, *Luke* (Minneapolis: Augsburg, 1988), and L. T. Johnson, *The Gospel of Luke* (Collegeville, MN: Liturgical, 1991), as well as C. F. Evans, *Saint Luke* (Philadelphia: Trinity Press International, 1990).

The basic study of the theology of Luke–Acts is H. Conzelmann, *The Theology of St. Luke,* trans. G. Buswell (London: Faber & Faber, 1960). Conzelmann's view that Luke divides history into three periods centering on Jesus has been attacked and qualified, but not overthrown. Still an important collection of articles on Luke is L. E. Keck and J. L. Martyn (eds.), *Studies in Luke–Acts,* rev. ed. (Philadelphia: Fortress, 1980). A significant general study is R. Maddox, *The Purpose of Luke–Acts* (Göttingen: Vandenhoeck & Ruprecht, 1982). For a close comparison of the many correspondences between Luke and Acts see C. H. Talbert, *Literary Patterns, Theological Themes, and the Genre of Luke–Acts* (Missoula, MT: Scholars, 1974). Another important literary study is R. C. Tannehill, *The Narrative Unity of Luke–Acts,* Vol. 1: *The Gospel According to Luke* (Philadelphia: Fortress, 1986), as well as J. D. Kingsbury, *Conflict in Luke: Jesus, Authorities, Disciples* (Minneapolis: Fortress, 1991). A social science perspective is represented by P. F. Esler, *Community and Gospel in Luke–Acts: The Social and Political Motivations of Lucan Theology* (New York: Cambridge University Press, 1987), who vigorously pursues the question of the specific Christian community for which Luke–Acts was written. J. A. Fitzmyer pursues his study beyond the commentary (above) in *Luke the Theologian: Aspects of His Teaching* (New York: Paulist, 1989). M. D. Goulder's two-volume work, *Luke: A New Paradigm* (Sheffield, England: JSOT, 1989), interprets Luke without recourse to the hypothetical Q and L traditions; apart from Mark, Luke relied mainly on Matthew. For a recent survey of scholarship on the Gospel of Luke, see M. A. Powell, *What Are They Saying About Luke?* (New York: Paulist, 1989). See also Suggestions for Further Reading at the end of Chapter 7.

Chapter 5

John: The Gospel of Jesus' Glory

Notes on the Gospel of John

*T*he Gospel of John differs widely from the other, Synoptic Gospels in a number of ways. In John the geographical locus of Jesus' ministry is mainly Judea rather than Galilee; Jesus travels to Jerusalem more frequently; his ministry takes place over a period of two or three years instead of one; there are fewer, but more impressive, miracle stories; and Jesus speaks in long discourses about himself and his mission. In addition, characteristic features and accounts of the Synoptics are missing from John; for example: Jesus' temptation, his parables, the Lord's Prayer, his epigrammatic teaching generally, the institution of the Lord's Supper, and the agony in Gethsemane. Conversely, many of the episodes found in John do not appear in the other Gospels; for example: the wine miracle at Cana, the woman of Samaria, the long controversies with the Jews, the raising of Lazarus, the washing of the disciples' feet, and the extended farewell discourse and prayer with the disciples.

In reading John after having studied the Synoptics, one can quickly grasp the extent and nature of these differences and discover others. How are they to be explained? Did John know the other Gospels and attempt to supplement, correct, or replace them with his own? Or did he not know them, either because he lived in a remote place or because he wrote before the other evangelists—at least before he was able to digest their works?

It was once assumed that the author of John, traditionally considered the latest of the Gospels, must have known the Synoptics and in some way have been influenced by them. It is possible, however, that both their differences and their similarities result from John's use of other related sources or traditions. Complex reconstructions of John's sources have been advanced by modern scholars, but these theories must in the nature of the case be hypothetical, for they lack support external to the Gospel itself. Probably the author knew a passion narrative other than Mark and drew upon a miracle tradition (perhaps a written source) with content different from, although related to, that found in the Synoptics. Whether he possessed a primitive gospel source that included not only Jesus' acts but also his passion is still a much-debated question.[1] But sources can scarcely account for all John's differences from the Synoptics. For example, his language, style, and theology are much closer to the three Johannine Epistles (cf. pp. 417–422) than to the other Gospels, and this similarity suggests that these writings may be the product of a common author or school.

According to the ancient tradition of the church, the Fourth Gospel, as well as the Johannine Epistles and Revelation, are the work of the apostle John (presumably the son of Zebedee, although this is not always clearly stated in the early sources), who lived to a ripe old age in the city of Ephesus and composed the Gospel while residing there.[2] But there are reasons for skepticism about this tradition, and even in antiquity the Johannine authorship of Revelation was subject to doubt. Our earliest sources are silent about any Ephesian residence of the apostle John. In writing to the Ephesians at the beginning of the second century, Ignatius makes a great deal of Paul's connection with Ephesus, but says nothing about John's having lived there. Yet if the tradition is right, John lived in Ephesus much longer and later than did Paul, and the memory of him should have been much fresher. Moreover, John is not widely quoted by orthodox Christian writers until the end of the second century. This fact suggests that the acceptance of John's Gospel as scripture on a par with the other Gospels was not immediate. In fact, there is reason to think that the Fourth Gospel was rejected in some quarters of the church. There are also traces of evidence suggesting that John the son of Zebedee may have been martyred early, perhaps at the same time as his brother James (Acts 12:2; cf. Mark 10:39). If so, the tradition that his Gospel was the last written is untenable. In fact, the Gospel of John itself does not name the son of Zebedee as its author. It is often assumed that the Gospel points unerringly in this direction. If, however, the ancient tradition of the church did not name John as the author, it is uncertain whether one would think of him in connection with this Gospel. According to tradition, John presents himself under the guise of the Beloved Disciple, but nowhere in the Gospel is the Beloved Disciple identified with John, not even in 21:24, where he is named the author of the Gospel, or at least the one who has caused it to be written. Significantly, none of the synoptic episodes in which John the son of Zebedee figures, or is named, is found in the Fourth Gospel (cf. Mark 1:16–20; 1:29–31; 3:13–19; 5:35–43; 9:2–8; 13:3–36).

Over and above the other reasons for questioning the traditional view of Johannine authorship, there is the character of the Gospel itself, especially the question of whether it represents an eyewitness report of Jesus' ministry. If we take the Synoptic Gospels, especially the synoptic tradition of Jesus' preaching, as a reliable guide to the way in which Jesus spoke and taught, then it is difficult to accept the Johannine pic-

---

1. The case for a primitive Gospel has been carefully and forcefully argued by R. T. Fortna, *The Fourth Gospel and its Predecessors: From Narrative Source to Present Gospel* (Philadelphia: Fortress, 1988), and earlier, *The Gospel of Signs: A Reconstruction of the Narrative Source Underlying the Fourth Gospel* (New York: Cambridge University Press, 1970). See also Urban C. von Wahlde, *The Earliest Version of John's Gospel: Recovering the Gospel of Signs* (Wilmington, DE: Michael Glazier, 1989).

2. For a discussion of these matters and a presentation of the relevant evidence, see C. K. Barrett, *The Gospel According to St. John: An Introduction with Commentary and Notes on the Greek Text,* 2nd ed. (Philadelphia: Westminster, 1978), pp. 100–134; also Raymond E. Brown, *The Gospel According to John (I–XII): Introduction, Translation, and Notes,* The Anchor Bible, 29 (Garden City, NY: Doubleday, 1966), pp. lxxxvii–civ. The fullest treatment is now R. Alan Culpepper, *John the Son of Zebedee: The Life of a Legend* (Columbia, SC: University of South Carolina Press, 1994).

ture of Jesus as historical in the strict sense. The words of John's Jesus have a different aura about them. The Johannine Jesus speaks frequently of his divine sonship; the synoptic Jesus does not, although all the evangelists believe that he is God's Son. Thus even those who defend Johannine authorship usually acknowledge that John has by no means presented a verbatim account of Jesus' words and deeds, but has exercised a free hand in reinterpreting what Jesus actually said and did.

The date and place of composition remain uncertain, but we are not completely at a loss in fixing the origin of the Gospel. The earliest certain evidence of its use (that is, commentaries, papyrus fragments, and the like) stems from Egypt. One tiny manuscript fragment of the Gospel (designated P[52]) dates from the early second century, proving that it could not have been written much later than A.D. 100. Possibly John was actually composed in Egypt. In that dry climate however, such physical evidence had the best chance to survive. So the Gospel could have been written elsewhere and brought to Egypt after a few years. Those who do not accept the traditional locus of Ephesus tend to favor a Near Eastern, especially Syrian, rather than an Egyptian origin. Possibly the Johannine tradition originated in Palestine or Syria, but the Gospel itself was published in Ephesus, as tradition holds. Although it can no longer be assumed that the Fourth Gospel is dependent on one or all of the other three, and is thus necessarily later, the situation of the church and the development of Christian thought that it reflects suggest a date no earlier than about the last decade of the first century.[3]

At several points in the Gospel there are references to those who believe in Jesus being put out of the synogogue (9:22; 12:42; 16:2). Such a threat is not found in the Synoptics and has been widely thought to be a key to John's setting and date, as has the fact that Jesus' opponents are called "the Jews." Of course, Jesus himself was a Jew (4:9, 22), as were his disciples. In what setting would such a designation of Jesus' opponents and such a threat occur? After the Roman war (A.D. 66–70) and the further loss of political power, it was necessary for Judaism to take stock of itself and of its defining characteristics. Only then did a clear distinction between what we now call Christianity and Judaism take place. (Indeed, for decades and even centuries some Christians, called Ebionites, still considered themselves Jews.) Among the Eighteen Benedictions of the ancient synagogue service, a reason of one, the Twelfth, anathematizes the Nazarenes and the heretics, presumably Jewish Christians. It has been dated traditionally in the ninth decade of the first century. Possibly it evidences, from the Jewish side, the expulsion of Christ-confessors from the synagogue.[4] Yet the Twelfth Benediction does not expressly mention expulsion from synagogue but being blotted out of the book of life, and its date as well as its function has been questioned. If it could be dated in the eighties, the Twelfth Benediction would be important evidence for the date as well as the setting of the Fourth Gospel. In any event, a date of composition during the last decade of the first century for the Gospel of John is likely on other grounds and a setting within, or at the boundary with, Judaism seems called for by the content of the Gospel.

If the Gospel stems from such a setting within Judaism, a Palestinian background or milieu becomes a distinct possibility, although there were, of course, large Jewish com-

---

3. Brown, *The Gospel According to John,* pp. lxxx–lxxxvi, especially lxxxv. Cf. Barrett, *The Gospel According to St. John,* pp. 127–128.

4. J. Louis Martyn, *History and Theology in the Fourth Gospel,* rev. ed. (Nashville: Abingdon, 1979) made this seminal proposal already in the first edition of his work (1968) and, with qualification, has stuck by it.

munities elsewhere. The many differences from the Synoptics and the apparently Hellenistic language and thought of the Fourth Gospel (e.g., the presentation of Jesus as
word *[logos]* and truth) once made a Palestinian origin appear impossible. The discovery of the Dead Sea Scrolls, however, changed all that. The language and dualism
of the community's *Community Rule,* at points remarkably similar to that of the Gospel
of John, showed that Palestinian Judaism of the first century took several forms and
was not simply the prototype of rabbinic Judaism. A Palestinian origin of the Johannine tradition no longer appears out of the question. Although the problem of the origin and background of the Fourth Gospel is vigorously debated, there is increasingly
a tendency to see it against a Jewish background, for reasons that will become evident
in the treatment of the Gospel itself.

It is uncertain whether the canonical text of John has been partially rearranged and
edited after having left the hand of the original author. Probably at least chapter 21 is
a later addition (cf. 20:30–31). It may well be that chapters 5 and 6 once stood in opposite order, for reversing them eliminates a strange and unexplained alteration of Jesus' locale from Galilee (4:43 ff.) to Jerusalem (chap. 5) and back to Galilee (chap. 6).
Moreover, 6:1 presupposes that Jesus has been in Galilee just previously. John 14:31
sets the stage for the arrest of Jesus, which does not actually occur until chapter 18.
Was the intervening material inserted later? Be that as it may, we shall take as a start-
ing point the Gospel in the form in which it lies before us in all extant Greek manuscripts and versions. The basic organization is rather simple:

OUTLINE OF JOHN

Introduction (1:1–51)
    The Prologue: Jesus Christ as the Word (1:1–18)
    The Witness of John the Baptist (1:19–51)
        John's Witness Against Himself (1:19–28)
        John's Witness to Jesus (1:29–34)
        Jesus Gathers Disciples (1:35–51)
The Revelation of Jesus' Glory before the World (2:1–12:50)
    Nicodemus (3:1–21)
    The Healing on the Sabbath at the Sheep Gate Pool (5:1–47)
    The Healing of the Man Born Blind (9:1–41)
The Revelation of Jesus' Glory before the Community (13:1–21:25)
    The Last Supper (13:1–38)
    The Promise of the Paraclete (14:15–17, 26; and 16:12–14)
    Jesus' Last Will: The Prayer of Consecration (17:1–26)

Introduction (1:1–51)

The Gospel of John falls into several rather well-defined parts. The first chapter stands apart from the body of the Gospel as a kind of introduction. It in
turn falls into two major parts: the prologue and the witness of the Baptist to
Jesus. Jesus receives his first disciples from John, who directs them to him,
telling them that Jesus is the lamb of God who takes away the sin of the world

(1:29; cf. vs. 34). The chapter ends on a note of expectation: the revelation of God will take place in Jesus' ministry (1:51). The prologue sets the stage for it.

THE PROLOGUE: JESUS CHRIST AS THE WORD (1:1–18)

Why is Jesus called "the Word"?

The prologue has a rhythmic, almost poetic character. Moreover, there is a peculiar chainlike progression in the repetition of key words in verses 1–5 and 9–12. A modern translation admirably preserves both the strophic form and this chainlike sequence(vss 1-5):

> In the beginning was the *Word;*
> *the Word* was in God's presence, and the *Word* was *God.*
> He was present with *God* in the beginning.
> Through him all things *came into being,*
>   and apart from him not a thing *came to be.*
> That which had *come to be* in him was *life,*
>   and this *life* was the *light* of men.
> The *light* shines on in the *darkness,*
>   for the *darkness* did not overcome it.[5]

The poetic mood of the prologue is, however, broken by 1:6–8 and 15 (set off in NRSV by a separate paragraph in the one case and by parentheses in the other), which refer not to the Word, the subject of the rest of the prologue, but to John the Baptist. Quite possibly we are here dealing with an early Christian hymn that the evangelist has annotated with references to the Baptist and incorporated into the Gospel. (Cf. Phil. 2:6–11; Col. 1:15–20; and 1 Tim. 3:16 for other such hymns.) Its language, style, and theology are "Johannine"; that is, the basic hymn and the Gospel appear to share a common perspective and vocabulary. The prologue falls into distinct sections that correspond roughly to its thematic divisions. In verses 1–5 the theme is God, creation, and the Word; in verses 6–8, John the Baptist; in verses 9–13, the Word in the world; and in verses 14–18, the community's confession of the Word.

Given this structure, the meaning of the prologue hinges on an understanding of its key term *Word* (Greek, *logos*) and its relation to the rest of the Gospel. Who or what is the Word? In the first place, the Word is Jesus Christ. When this is said, however, several related questions are cast into sharp relief. In verses 1–5 does the author intend to speak of the man Jesus of Nazareth? He can hardly mean that Jesus of Nazareth was with God before all creation and that he was the mediator of all creation. Where, moreover, does this concept of the Word originate? It is perhaps to be understood against the background of Greek philosophy, in which the term and concept of *logos* were quite important. Or it might be seen against the background

---

5. Brown, *The Gospel According to John,* p. 3.

of the Old Testament and Jewish concept of the word of the Lord. It is clear that the Word *denotes* Jesus Christ; what more remains to be determined.

The Greek philosophical meaning of *logos* is not related directly to John's use of the term. The Stoic understanding of *logos* as the world principle has little to do with the Word that is Jesus Christ. Nevertheless, the fact that the Greek term *logos* comprehends such varied meanings as explanation, argument, principle, thought or reason, language, speech, and divine utterance is relevant. So is the use of the term in late Jewish and other religious texts to designate God's agent in creation and world government; moreover, in the Hellenistic–Jewish Wisdom of Solomon (9:1–2) *word (logos)* as God's agent in creation is identified with *wisdom (sophia)*. It is clear enough that the *logos* of John is God's speech, his self-disclosure to the world, and, as the text makes plain, the means through which God creates. This range of meaning is the background of the author's usage.

The most obvious and immediate reference point of the concept of God's Word is the creation story of Genesis 1, which also opens with the phrase "in the beginning." Like Genesis, John speaks of the creation. Although Genesis does not say that God created all things by the Word, it does portray each stage of creation as resulting from God's speaking. "Then God said, 'Let there be light'; and there was light" (Gen. 1:3). The fact that in Genesis God first creates light is paralleled by John's emphasis on light throughout the prologue. Moreover, the motifs of darkness and light appear together in both places. In Genesis God speaks and there is light where darkness had heretofore prevailed—God separates the light from the darkness (1:3–5). This then leads to an account of the beginning of night and day. In John's prologue, however, the opposition between light and darkness develops into a sharply defined dualism, which is characteristic of the Gospel as a whole—distinctions are drawn between the forces of light and darkness, truth and falsehood, God and Satan, and so on. Such dualism was common not only to Zoroastrianism, Gnosticism, and late Platonism, but also to certain forms of Judaism. That a similar dualistic world view could arise even within first-century Palestinian Judaism has been shown by the discovery of the Qumran scrolls, in which a view of the world, human beings, and events very similar to that of the Gospel of John is presented. The affinity between John and Genesis reveals the common ground on which they stand. But the striking dualism of John is equally significant, for it shows that John belongs in a first-century religious world.

Nevertheless, it would be wrong to leave the impression that understanding the prologue first requires understanding the Greek use of *logos,* the Old Testament creation story, or first-century sectarian Judaism. All these are helpful, but John speaks clearly and directly apart from those contexts. John has always been a popular Gospel for Christians, most of whom have not had the faintest conception of its historical background. The text as it stands is richly suggestive and evocative. Any Christian reader would know that the Word was Jesus Christ before he read further in the Gospel, even though the name of Jesus is not called until the prologue has moved from the cosmic or the metaphysical plane to the historical.

The movement from the rather abstract, if dramatic and impressive, talk about the *logos* to the level of historical events takes place by stages. Verses 1 and 2 deal with the relation of the Word to God, which is defined in the closest possible terms without John's quite saying that *logos* and God are simply equivalents. The statement that "the Word was God" is immediately qualified by "He was in the beginning with God." The Word participates in God without exhausting God's being.[6] Still, in verses 3 and 4 the most exalted status and functions are attributed to the Word, God's agent in creation, and at the end of the Gospel Jesus is worshiped as Lord and God (20:29).

Through the Word, the God who creates will now save the world from its evil and folly. God's action in creation and redemption is one. Over against any purely otherworldly theology or spirituality, John affirms that the Word by which God creates the world is the same Word by which he redeems it. This Word can be identified with a special historical person and event, Jesus, whom John will name before the prologue is complete. The God who creates through the Word thus reveals and saves through the same Word. Since the coming of Jesus Christ, this Word cannot be conceived apart from him.

John's affirmation that the light shines in darkness (vs. 5) is the first hint of the advent of Jesus into the world. (Jesus himself will not be named until vs. 17; rather the subject is "the Word.") The ensuing description of the mission of John the Baptist (vss. 6–8), who heralded his coming, confirms this. It is followed by a more explicit reference to Jesus' appearance (vs. 9): "The true . . . light was coming into the world." The following paragraph (vss. 10–13) succinctly summarizes the world's and his own people's rejection of Jesus. Yet there are some who believe (vss. 12–13), whose happy destiny is to become children of God.

John the Baptist (called only "John" in the Fourth Gospel) is important both positively and negatively, so to speak. Positively, John is the primary witness to Jesus, "a man sent from God." Moreover, "everything that John said about this man was true" (10:41). John's place as the forerunner of Jesus was established in the Synoptic tradition. The Fourth Gospel goes beyond the Synoptics to see in John the witness of Israel's true tradition and heritage to Jesus. Still, there is also a negative aspect of the Gospel's portrayal of John. That is, the evangelist goes out of his way to make sure the reader understands that John was not the light (vs. 8), and John himself will deny that he is the Christ (vs. 20). Such demurrals are found only in the Gospel of John. Quite possibly the evangelist, or the Johannine community, confronted other Jews who believed that the Baptist was the Messiah, or Elijah, or the prophet (vs. 21). Some

---

6. The key phrase is translated variously: "the Word was God" (Douay, Jerusalem, KJV, RSV, NRSV); "what God was, the Word was" (NEB); "the Logos was divine" (Moffatt); and "the Word was divine" (Goodspeed).

such group is in fact mentioned in the Book of Acts (18:25; 19:3–5) in Ephesus of all places, the traditional site of the composition of the Fourth Gospel.

The very brief description of the mission of the Word in the world (vss. 9–13) takes on a richness of color and specificity in light of the Gospel's narration of Jesus' ministry, conflicts, and death and resurrection. Apart from that narrative these few lines remain bland or opaque. Read with that story in view they are poignant and touching. Particularly moving is the simple assertion: "He came unto his own, and his own received him not" (vs. 11 KJV). The public ministry of Jesus, as well as his passion, is the evangelist's spelling out of his tragic destiny. The dualism of the Gospel, its sharp distinction between light and darkness, truth and falsehood, is epitomized in the distance between the people who rejected him (vss. 10–11) and those who received him (vss. 12–13).

The final paragraph of the prologue (vss. 14–18) is introduced by the most important theological statement of the Gospel, and one of the crucial affirmations of the New Testament: "And the Word became flesh and lived among us" (vs. 14). John still does not mention Jesus by name, although the knowledgeable reader will know. Modern interpreters have debated whether John intended emphasis to fall upon the Incarnation, the Word's becoming human flesh, or upon the manifestation of divine glory, which occupies the latter part of the verse. The Gospel is actually ambiguous at this point, although 1 John makes clear that the real humanity of Jesus, his fleshliness, is of crucial importance (1 John 1:1–3; 4:1–3). In affirming that Jesus is full of grace and truth, John combines a typical Pauline term (*grace*; Greek, *charis*) with his own favorite designation of Jesus, *truth* (cf. 14:6).

At this point a Christological motif that will recur in the Gospel makes its first appearance. Neither "lived among us" (NRSV) nor "dwelt among us" (RSV, KJV) quite catches what is implied by John's language. He uses a verb (*skēnoun*) that could well be translated "tented" or "tabernacled" among us, evoking the whole tradition of the tabernacle or tent, and later the temple in which the glory of Israel's God was believed to dwell (Exodus 40:35; Numbers 14:10; 1 Kings 8:11; cf. Isaiah 6:1–3; Ezekiel 1–3, esp. 1:28; 2:12; 3:23). John does not quote Ezekiel, who in chapters 1–3 describes the departure of the glory or presence of the Lord from the temple in Jerusalem at the exile, but he seems to presuppose something like it. In any event, John repeatedly suggests that as the glory of God once tabernacled in a tent or building, now it dwells in Jesus. He reveals that Jesus himself spoke of the temple of his body (2:21), when his hearers naturally thought he was speaking of the Jerusalem temple. When the Samaritan woman asks Jesus where one ought to worship, whether on "this mountain" (Gerizim, the site of the ruins of the Samaritan temple) or in Jerusalem, Jesus answers, in effect, neither (4:20–23). True worshipers will worship in spirit and truth, says Jesus, subtly pointing ahead to the time when his followers will pray in his name (14:13–14).

In the concluding lines of the prologue, the Baptist reiterates his witness (vs. 15), and John testifies about the grace received from Jesus (vs. 16; cf. vs.

"Christ in Glory," a tapestry in the Coventry Cathedral, England, designed by Graham Sutherland. It is 78 feet long, 38 feet wide, and weighs nearly a ton. The figures on each corner symbolize the four Gospels.   *(Courtesy of Thompson Art Reference Bureau.)*

12–13). Then Jesus is compared and contrasted with Moses (vs. 17), the new with the old. The reader is left to puzzle about the status of the law given through Moses. On the one hand, it seems to pale before the grace and truth embodied in Jesus Christ (vs. 17; cf. vs. 14), now mentioned by name for the first time. Jesus will speak of it as "your law" (8:17; i.e., the law of the Jews). Yet he continues to assume its validity (7:19–24; 10:34–36), at least for Jews.

John's fundamental belief, however, is that the law, or scripture, when rightly read, points ahead to Jesus (5:39, 45–47). The final statement sets out John's distinctive theological point: Jesus, the only Son, and he alone, has seen and revealed God (vs. 18). Uncertainty as to whether John wrote "only(-begotten) Son" or "only-begotten God" does not obscure this point. Text-critical criteria actually favor the latter reading. Manuscript attestation for it is strong, and to call Jesus *theos* (God) completes the circle begun in verse 1, where the *logos* (Word) is called God. Moreover, at the end of the scenes in which the risen Jesus appears to the disciples as a group, Thomas, who has at first doubted, confesses Jesus as "my Lord and my God!" (20:28). Even though there is an epilogue to the Gospel (chap. 21), this verse looks very much like its original conclusion.

THE WITNESS OF JOHN THE BAPTIST (1:19–51)

JOHN'S WITNESS AGAINST HIMSELF (1:19–28)

Why does the Gospel not mention that Jesus was baptized by John?

After the prologue there is a long scene (vss. 19–51), composed of a series of episodes, in which John the Baptist (called only "John") appears and bears further testimony to Jesus. This testimony is first of all against himself, in the sense that under questioning from priests and Levites from Jerusalem, who are sent by the Pharisees (vss. 19, 24), John denies that he is the Messiah (v. 20), Elijah, or the prophet (vs. 22). The priests and Levites fade from the picture, but the Pharisees become Jesus' chief antagonists in the course of the Gospel. That John cannot be the Messiah is obvious enough, although the point of his denial that he is Elijah or the prophet is less clear. Both the presence of the Pharisees and John's denials require some further discussion.

The Pharisees appear also in the Synoptic Gospels, where Jesus frequently comes into conflict with them (cf. Mark 2:13–3:6), but in John they play a special role. Often they seem to be identical with "the Jews," who are also portrayed as Jesus' constant opponents (cf. chap. 9). Jesus and his disciples, as well as John the Baptist, although Jewish, are never referred to as "Jews." "The Jews," as well as the Pharisees, are Jesus' opponents. The mention of the Pharisees, who now only stand in the background (vs. 24), foreshadows their increasing opposition to Jesus.

The roles of Elijah and the prophet will have some significance in the Fourth Gospel. In some contrast to the Synoptics, where John the Baptist is said to be Elijah (e.g., Matt. 17:9–13), he here denies such a role. The ancient Elijah was an Israelite prophet whose activity is described in 1 and 2 Kings, but whose return was expected in some strands of biblical, Jewish, and early Christian thought (cf. Malachi 4:5; Mark 6:15; 8:28). Perhaps Jesus fulfills aspects of this expectation in the Fourth Gospel. The prophet is not just any prophet (cf. Mark 8:28), but a specific individual (cf. John 6:14). In Deuteronomy Moses promises that in the future "The Lord your God will raise up for you a prophet like me" (18:15). Jesus is repeatedly compared or contrasted with Moses in John (e.g., 1:17; 6:32–34), and Moses is said to have written about Jesus (1:45; 5:46). Even as Moses performed signs and wonders before Pharaoh and the Egyptians (Exod. 4:8, 9, 17, etc.) to authenticate himself as an emissary of God, in John Jesus performs signs to demonstrate that God has sent him. In the Fourth Gospel, then, Jesus is the prophet like Moses, but greater than Moses.

John answers the questions of why he is baptizing (inasmuch as he is not the Messiah, Elijah, or the prophet) in words partly familiar from the synoptic reports of Jesus' encounter with the Baptist (cf. Mark 1:7–8). John continues to employ this familiar language in the succeeding episode (1:29–34), evoking the synoptic scene in which Jesus is baptized by John. Yet the Fourth Gospel never mentions Jesus' being baptized. Perhaps the evangelist is so much concerned that the reader should understand Jesus' superiority to John (cf. 1:15, 30) that he does not narrate an event that would suggest the opposite.

JOHN'S WITNESS TO JESUS (1:29–34)

How does John's account differ from the Synoptics?

John's designation of Jesus as the Lamb of God (vs. 29) is without precedent or parallel in the other Gospels. Exactly what the term means has been disputed by interpreters, although it almost certainly has to do with the saving work that Jesus is to accomplish through his death. At the very earliest stages of the preaching of the gospel, Jesus' death was interpreted as a cultic, sacrificial offering for sin (1 Cor. 15:3). Subsequently, the account again reflects language familiar to most readers from the synoptic narrations of Jesus' baptism (vss. 31–34). The fact that this central event of baptism is not explicitly mentioned easily escapes notice. In distinction from the Synoptics, the entire episode is here narrated by the Baptist, in retrospect, so to speak.

The problem of the relationship of John and the Synoptic Gospels is epitomized in this scene. The reader who knows the other Gospels naturally assumes Jesus' baptism by John. But does John presume knowledge of this baptism as the basis of his account? It makes a certain sense to assume it, but perhaps it is precisely John's point not to mention the baptism because it implies Jesus' inferiority to, or dependence upon, John. The evangelist almost certainly knew that Jesus had been baptized by John, for that fact holds these traditions together. In light of the baptism they make sense. Moreover, the fact that the Baptist reflects on what he had seen and heard earlier implies that the reader will have prior knowledge as well. John's narrative is understandable as a retrospective narration of what is otherwise known from other Gospels (or perhaps from a pre-Gospel tradition). The point of the Fourth Gospel's account is no longer, as in the Synoptics, the role of John as fore-

"The Calling of the Apostles Peter and Andrew" by Duccio di Buoninsegna
(1228–1319). *(Courtesy of National Gallery of Art, Washington, D.C. Samuel H. Kress Collection.)*

runner of Jesus, but the witness of John to the saving work of Jesus. In fact, John's role as forerunner is explicitly played down (vss. 15, 30).

JESUS GATHERS DISCIPLES (1:35–51)

Why are the traditional messianic titles important?

With the same designation of Jesus as the Lamb of God (vs. 36), John sends two of his own disciples to follow Jesus. There issues a conversation between Jesus and his new disciples that is deliberately vague and suggestive of a future relationship. That one of the disciples is Andrew prepares the way for the introduction of Simon Peter, his brother (vs. 40), a disciple who will play a large role in John, as well as in the Synoptics and Acts, not to mention Paul (esp. Gal. 1:18–2:21). Andrew immediately reveals to his brother that he and his colleague have found the Messiah (vs. 4). (Only in John's Gospel does *messias,* the Greek transliteration of the Hebrew word for "anointed" appear;

elsewhere one finds only the Greek *Christos* or Christ, although the NRSV sometimes translates it "Messiah," particularly in the Gospels.) At just that point Jesus gives him the nickname Cephas (Aramaic for "rock"), or Peter.

There are here some surprising contacts with the Synoptics, especially Matthew (cf. Matt. 16:17, 19 and John 1:42 and 20:23). In the Synoptics it is Peter who first identifies Jesus as the Messiah or Christ (NRSV: "Messiah," although the Greek is *Christos*), after a public ministry in which his true identity has been something of a mystery. Typically, in John Jesus is identified as the Messiah even before his ministry begins, as he is calling his disciples. There is no messianic secret in John. This distinctly Markan motif was already fading in Matthew and Luke; now in John it seems to have disappeared. Jesus is known to his disciples for who he is from the very beginning, and his role and relation to God will be debated openly by his opponents. Yet there is a curious sense in which the messianic secret overshadows John as well. Although everyone seems to know that Jesus is the Messiah of Israel, or claims to be, no one, including his own disciples, really understands him until after he is glorified, that is, until after his crucifixion and resurrection.

As Messiah, Jesus is the one described in the law and the prophets (vs. 45), that is, in scripture. But Nathanael marvels that such a figure could emanate from the humble village of Nazareth (1:46). When, however, Jesus manifests his uncommon knowledge of Nathanael, the latter addresses this rabbi (i.e., teacher; vs. 38) as *Son of God* and *King of Israel*. The Messiah is the anointed King of Israel. Already in scripture the king is called God's son (Psalm 2:7), and *Son of God* will become the correlate of *Messiah* in early Christianity and the New Testament. Yet both titles will come to have new and somewhat different meanings in their Christian context. Nowhere can this growth and differentiation of meaning be seen more clearly than in the Gospel of John.

The effect of this long scene following the prologue is to show how the role and mission of Jesus is rooted in the traditions and hopes of Israel. Jesus transcends those traditions and hopes, yet cannot be comprehended apart from them. Jesus is defined in terms of his scriptural and traditional origins. The Fourth Gospel will then portray his ministry as a confrontation with other representatives of the same religious traditions, "the Jews." As Jesus claims those traditions and at the same time reinterprets them with reference to himself, he arouses intense opposition among other Jews. They do not believe that he is sent from, and speaks for, God. But just such a claim is set forth in the symbolic, highly pictoral language of Jesus at the end of this scene: "You will see greater things than these" (1:51).

John's story of the gathering of Jesus' first disciples comes at approximately the same place, at the beginning of the narrative, as do the synoptic call stories. Yet it is a very different story. The Synoptics depict Jesus calling disciples from their jobs as fishermen on the Sea of Galilee. Even within the Synoptics, moreover, there are wide differences between the accounts of Mark (1:16–20) and Matthew (4:18–22), on the one hand, and Luke (5:1–11) on the other. Mark and Matthew tell the familiar story of Jesus passing by the sea and calling two pairs of brothers—Peter and Andrew, and James and John the sons of Zebedee—away from their work as fishermen. Luke's story centers about Jesus' directing Peter and other disciples, including James and John, so that they make a large catch of fish. This story is more like John's final resurrection appearance story (21:1–14) than the other, synoptic stories of the calling of the disciples. John's account, as we have just seen, says nothing about boats, the sea, and the disciples' being fishermen, a fact that is mentioned only at the end of his account (21:3), and features the role of John the Baptist in sending his own disciples to Jesus. (That some of Jesus' disciples, like Jesus himself, had been adherents of John is not at all improbable.) Simon Peter and Andrew appear in John's account, as they do in Mark's, but efforts to see in the unnamed disciple accompanying Andrew (1:35, 40) John the son of Zebedee run afoul of the Gospel's silence on the matter. It is hard to imagine how the fourth evangelist would have understood his account in relation to the Synoptics. Apparently he was ignorant of them or deliberately ignored them for reasons best known to himself.

The Revelation of Jesus' Glory before the World (2:1–12:50)

The public ministry of Jesus in the Fourth Gospel is characterized by miracles and controversy, both of which are found in the other Gospels. But in contrast to the Synoptic Gospels, where Jesus takes a dim view of the desire for signs, in John the miracles are just such revelatory signs. Parables and other forms of public teaching, familiar from the Synoptics, are notable for their absence from John. Jesus does not teach a hostile world, but confronts it with his astonishing deeds and lofty claims. Thus heated controversy arises over who Jesus is, and such controversy is distinctive of the Fourth Gospel.

Before the controversy begins, however, there are two quite different, but related, episodes that open Jesus' public ministry. In one Jesus seemingly saves a host embarrassment by changing water into wine (2:1–11). In the other he drives vendors and money changers out of the Jerusalem temple (2:13–22). The former has no parallel outside the Gospel of John; the latter is found also in the Synoptic Gospels, but not until the end of Jesus' ministry. Indeed, the difference may have something to do with the fact that while John has Jesus go to Jerusalem for the annual Passover or Feast of Unleavened Bread three times, the Synoptics depict the ministry in a year or less, and Jesus goes up to Jerusalem for Passover only once, at the end. (The tradition that Jesus' ministry lasted three years is solely a product of the Gospel of John.)

The very different stories have in common one major motif: they show Jesus confronting and transforming the institutions of Judaism. The water he transforms into wine was kept in "six stone water jars for the Jewish rites of purification" (2:6). The wine produced is obviously the best of all; contrary to common practice, the best is kept until last (vs. 10). Probably the incident symbolizes the salvation or life that Jesus brings (cf. 15:1–11, where Jesus is portrayed as the vine). The temple that will be destroyed and raised up in three days is actually the temple of his risen body, although not even the disciples will understand until after his resurrection (vss. 19–22). These stories are epiphany stories, episodes in which Jesus manifests himself before his people, in the one case at a celebration of one of the most important events of human life, in the other at the center of Judaism, the headquarters of the people called "the Jews," who will oppose Jesus and his claims. Yet at this

"Christ and Nicodemus" by P. G. Master (active c. 1550).   *(Courtesy of National Gallery of Art, Washington, D.C. Samuel H. Kress Collection.)*

point in the narrative there is little of the heated controversy and hostility on both sides that will appear later.

NICODEMUS (3:1–21)

Why does Jesus seem rude to Nicodemus?

Jesus' encounter with his own people, culture, and religious tradition is most graphically represented in the story of the conversation with Nicodemus, who is described as a Pharisee and a leader (or ruler) of the Jews (3:1).

The most striking aspect of the beginning of this episode is that Nicodemus' apparent openness or friendliness to Jesus (vs. 2) is met by Jesus' abrupt retorts. Jesus, far from responding in a polite way, rejects Nicodemus' kind approach (vs. 3) and seemingly refuses to answer his questions in terms Nicodemus can comprehend (vss. 4–8). Nicodemus' puzzled question, "How can these things be?" (vs. 9), is really not hard to understand. Furthermore, Jesus' subsequent retort (vs. 10) is either incredulous or sarcastic, or both. From that point on Jesus goes into a kind of monologue (vss. 11–21), and, in fact, it is difficult to discern where Jesus stops talking and the evangelist takes up. With the veiled prediction of his ascension (vss. 13–14), Jesus speaks of himself in the third person. It is as if the evangelist were describing Jesus' life-giving work from a later perspective. Indeed, Jesus had already switched from the singular "I" to the plural "we" (vs. 11), as if he were speaking with, or on behalf of, the community of his followers.

The Nicodemus episode is typical of a literary technique that appears frequently in the Fourth Gospel and characterizes its understanding of revelation. Nicodemus *misunderstands* Jesus. Already the steward did not know the origin of the good wine (2:9). Nor did the Jews understand Jesus' word about the destruction of the temple (2:20). Apparently neither did the disciples understand until after Jesus was raised from the dead (vs. 22). Now, the impressively credentialed Nicodemus is equally in the dark (cf. 3:1: "He came to Jesus by night.") Later on, the woman of Samaria will think that Jesus is offering her a new water-delivery system rather than supernatural, life-giving water (4:15).

This technique of misunderstanding says something important about revelation in the Fourth Gospel. Old assumptions, standards, or traditions cannot comprehend Jesus, or the revelation of God in Jesus, even when applied in a positive way. Therefore, although Nicodemus is prepared to credit Jesus as a teacher sent from God on the basis of his signs (vs. 3), Jesus rejects this kind of acceptance. No one can see the kingdom of God unless he is born from above. In John Jesus uses an ambiguous Greek word (*anōthen*) that can mean either "again" (or "anew," RSV) or "from above" (NRSV). Obviously birth from above is a new birth, but the point is its source or origin. Nicodemus misunderstands Jesus, and takes the point to be mere repetition (vs. 4). He misunderstands the heavenly, so to speak, because he interprets it solely in terms of the very earthly reality of physical birth. A characteristic feature of Johannine misunderstanding is that Jesus' interlocutors misunderstand him because they try to interpret the new in terms of the old and the otherworldly in terms of the this-worldly. Jesus can only be understood on his own terms. He is self-authenticating. One believes his claims or one does not. He fulfills ancient expectations, but at the same time transcends them. Thus Jesus speaks of the necessity of being born of water and the Spirit, meaning in all probability the water of baptism as well as the accompanying gift of the Holy Spirit. By mentioning the Spirit, Jesus invokes divine causality. Coming to believe in Jesus, conversion, is finally the work of the Spirit, that is, of God.

As Nicodemus quietly departs from the scene, the evangelist speaks directly about the revelatory event of God's sending his Son in order that those who believe may have eternal life (3:16). After this thematic statement, which encapsulates the theology (or soteriology, i.e., doctrine of salvation) of John, the evangelist reflects upon the meaning of the sending of the Son, God's purpose in sending him and its actual results (vss. 17–21). Doubtless the author now interprets the effect of Jesus' appearance against the background of his own knowledge and experience of who has accepted him and who has not. Moreover, John here insists that the purpose of God's sending Jesus was salvation, not condemnation or judgment. Yet some people reject the light (vs. 19; cf. 1:5, 9) and incur judgment for themselves. In doing so, or by accepting the light, people reveal who they really are (vss. 19–21).

John's statements can be oversimplified and taken to mean that the people who were already good accepted Jesus, and the people who were bad rejected him. If that were the case, however, Jesus' coming would have changed nothing. Doubtless the meaning is that a person's true being—being in the light or being in darkness—is revealed only in how one responds when the light (i.e., Jesus) comes. Otherwise, who or what that person is cannot be known. Thus Jesus not only reveals himself and reveals God, but reveals the true character of every person he encounters (cf. 4:16–19, 29). His coming brings life, salvation, or judgment. Thus Jesus' coming is already the eschatological (i.e., final) event in the history of every person.

We now seemingly know the meaning of Jesus' coming into the world as expressed in his encounter with Nicodemus. Nicodemus did not understand, and presumably perished. Yet later this same Nicodemus returns to defend Jesus' right to a fair hearing (7:50–52) and finally (in John only) helps bury him (19:39–40). The coming of the Light and Word into the world is misunderstood and creates division. It seems a simple, black-or-white affair. Yet John understands that with people things are not always so straightforward, at least not immediately so. So Thomas, one of the twelve disciples, will have great difficulty understanding and believing Jesus, but will ultimately trust him (20:28). People may initially believe, but time and further events must unfold before they come to adequate faith. John has now given the reader a basis for understanding the issues involved and appreciating the complex unfolding of controversy and conflict that will surround Jesus' public ministry and lead eventually to his death.

THE HEALING ON THE SABBATH AT THE SHEEP GATE POOL (5:1–47)

Why is this episode crucial to the development of the plot of the Gospel?

The miracle stories of the Fourth Gospel are distinctive. They are significantly fewer than in the Synoptic Gospels but perhaps even more important, for they are signs manifesting Jesus' glory. John develops each story more fully by showing Jesus talking with bystanders and opponents about the implications of the miracle. This Johannine emphasis upon the explanatory discourses of Jesus reflects his concentration on the miracles as "signs" pointing to the nature and mission of Jesus (see 12:37 and cf. 20:30–31).

The Fourth Gospel employs some miracle stories otherwise unknown. The transformation of water into wine at Cana (2:1–12) has no parallel in the Synoptics; nor do the stories of the Samaritan woman (chap. 4—Jesus' knowledge of her past is miraculous), the man at the Sheep Gate pool (chap. 5), the man born blind (chap. 9), and the raising of Lazarus (chap. 11). Jesus' foreknowledge of Nathanael (1:45–51) may also be miraculous; in any case it also has no parallel. On the other hand, the bread miracle (6:1–14), the walking on the water (6:16–21), and the healing of the ruler's son (4:46–54) have definite synoptic parallels (cf. Mark 6:32–44; 6:45–51 parr.; and Matt. 8:5–10/Luke 7:1–10, respectively). Other incidents, including the passion (18:1–19:42), have clear synoptic parallels but are not miraculous (cf. 2:13–22; 12:1–11, 12–19; 13:21–30). Of the miracle stories found only in John, those of chapters 5 and 9 are similar to several synoptic stories. The changing of water into wine (2:1–11), however, is a feat unparalleled in the Synoptics, where Jesus' miracles are characteristically healings or demon exorcisms. Of the latter there is not one in John. Although Jesus raises the dead in the Synoptics, there is nothing like the elaborate story of the raising of Lazarus (John 11:1–44) anywhere else in the New Testament.

John's arrangement of the miracle stories is significant. Although there is no systematic progression from one to another, most are especially suited for their positions in the Gospel. The miracle of the new wine symbolically introduces Jesus' public ministry. The story of Jesus' revelation to the Samaritan woman (chap. 4) stands directly over against the inability of Nicodemus, the teacher of Israel, to grasp his meaning (chap. 3). The miracles of chapters 5 and 6 are integrally related to the long dialogues that follow them, which reveal who Jesus is and what he does for humankind. The most artfully constructed and theologically pregnant of the miracle stories (chaps. 9 and 11) appear last. In the one, Jesus bestows the gift of sight (light), and in the other, life. The raising of Lazarus from the dead gives concreteness to Jesus' claim that "just as the Father raises the dead and gives them life, so also the Son gives life to whomever he will" (5:21). Thus this miracle graphically portrays the character of his mission and work. Moreover, it leads directly to Jesus' own death, which, paradoxically, is the source of life to all who believe.

This Sabbath healing of chapter 5 is the first miracle story to be followed by a long discourse. Such a discussion, centering on the question of who Jesus is, is typical of the Fourth Gospel. We focus here on the healing itself and upon Jesus' opponents' initial reaction and response, without attempting to deal with every aspect of the chapter in detail. Yet the discussion of the entire chapter can be seen to hinge upon Jesus' pivotal statement (vs. 17) and the opponents' hostile response (vs. 18).

The scene is laid at the Sheep Gate of the city. The time is "a festival of the Jews," which is not further specified. Because of the festival Jesus had gone up to Jerusalem. At the beginning of the next episode we learn that Passover is near (6:4). Many critics have suggested that the order of these two chapters has somehow been reversed, for if chapter 6 preceded chapter 5, Jesus simply remains in Galilee, as he was at the end of chapter 4. If chapter 5 then followed chapter 6, the sequence would be much improved on several counts. To begin with, 6:1 has Jesus going to the other side of the Sea of Galilee, as if he had been in Galilee all along, which of course would be the case if chapter 6 preceded chapter 5. Jesus would remain in Galilee until just before Passover (6:4), and then would go up to Jerusalem, where at the time of the festival (5:1), obviously now Passover or the Feast of Unleavened Bread, he would perform this healing. Then would follow the disputes and the attempt to arrest Jesus recounted in chapter 7. Moreover, Jesus there refers to an attempt to kill him (7:19), and apparently has 5:18 in view, which would be perfectly normal if chapter 7 followed immediately upon chapter 5.[7]

Possibly the order of chapters 5 and 6 has been set deliberately, however, in order to make a theological point more forcefully. The dispute of the Jews with Jesus, particularly over his relationship to God the Father, would then precede, and provide the basis for, the discussions between them in the bread discourse (6:25–59). Also after the heated dispute with the Jews in chapter 5, it is perhaps less surprising that many of Jesus' own disciples turn back from following him.

In any event, in its present position, after the two opening epiphany stories (chapter 2), the Nicodemus discourse (chapter 3), the encounter with the Samaritan woman (4:1–42), and the healing of an official's son in Cana of Galilee (4:46–54), none of which have evoked great hostility against Jesus, the healing of the invalid at the pool and its ensuing dispute sets the tone for the remainder of the Gospel. Now the tension between Jesus and "the Jews" will be unremitting, and this has to do with the claims Jesus makes for himself, which are the claims the Johannine community makes for him.

7. See the discussion of Rudolf Bultmann, *The Gospel of John: A Commentary,* trans. G. R. Beasley-Murray, R. W.N. Hoare and J. K. Riches (Philadelphia: Westminster, 1971), pp. 209–210, 237.

The story of the healing is told with economy of style and speed. The man in question has been ill for thirty-eight years. Why it was necessary for the invalid to enter the pool while its water was stirred up (vs. 7) is unclear, though a later addition to the text (vs. 4b) attempts to explain this detail. In a fashion that might be considered Johannine, Jesus himself takes the initiative in the healing (vs. 6), since he knew the man had been lying by the pool for a long time. It is quite possible that the pool was some sort of spa where the lame and paralyzed (vs. 3) found relief and perhaps in some cases were healed. Probably the pool in question is the one discovered and excavated in this century not far from St. Anne's church in Jerusalem. That Jesus asks the man whether he wishes to be made well is a feature unique to this miracle story (vs. 6). The man does not answer directly, but his explanation (vs. 7) implies that he does indeed seek healing. Quite abruptly Jesus commands him to stand, take up his mat, and walk, and the man does so (vss. 8–9). Jesus' command parallels almost exactly his word to the paralytic lowered to him through the roof of a house in Mark (cf. Mark 2:9, 11). Moreover, the suggestion that the healed man had sinned appears in both accounts, although at different points and in different ways (John 5:14; cf. Mark 2:9–10). Otherwise, the stories are rather different, except for the fact that Jesus heals an ill person, perhaps a paralytic in both cases, in the face of opposition, real or potential. Earlier exegesis derived the Johannine story from the Markan, but to do so is quite a stretch.

For our purposes the origin of John's story is less important than its function in the Fourth Gospel. The opposition in John, in contrast to Mark, is not present when Jesus performs the healing, but appears subsequently and confronts not Jesus but the cured man who is unlawfully carrying his mat on the Sabbath (5:9–10). The man in effect shifts the blame to Jesus, who had commanded him to carry it (vs. 11). "The Jews," as they are called here and elsewhere, now attempt to pursue Jesus through the man whom he has healed, but cannot, because the man does not know where Jesus is (vss. 12–13). At this point Jesus accosts him and warns him against sinning any more (vs. 14), but the man responds by, in effect, turning Jesus in to the Jewish opponents (vss. 15–16). One is tempted to see in the cured man who betrays Jesus a recalcitrant member of the Johannine community who has, so to speak, defected. This possibility becomes more likely in view of Jesus' statement (vs. 17) and the Jews' interpretation of it, which leads them to seek his life (vs. 18). The motif of Sabbath breaking, well known from the Synoptics (e.g., Mark 2:23–28; 3:1–6), now disappears, as if Jesus' accusers had forgotten it in view of his greater blasphemy. Jesus' response to the accusation that he breaks the Sabbath is the seemingly innocuous statement, "My Father is still working, and I also am working" (vs. 17). The use of "Father" for God was not unknown in ancient Judaism and was characteristic of Jesus' speech in the Synoptic Gospels, as the "Our Father" in the Lord's Prayer shows. This usage was not blasphemous or offensive to Jewish sensibilities.

Jesus' calling God his Father evokes such vehement opposition, however, because it is said to be tantamount to "calling himself equal to God" (vs. 18). Certainly this interpretation would not have been the case in Judaism or in the Synoptic tradition. That is, calling God "Father" would not imply a claim to equality with God. Yet although Jesus does not immediately affirm this interpretation of his words, neither does he deny it. In the course of his subsequent discourse, he gives ample grounds for acknowledging that the accusation is true, as he describes the Son's work of giving life and holding judgment (vss. 19–20). The very point of Jesus' assertions seems to be that as the Son he assumes the work and prerogatives of God the Father: "Anyone who does not honor the Son does not honor the Father who sent him" (vs. 23). Yet at the same time: "The Son can do nothing on his own, but only what he sees the Father doing" (vs. 19). Paradoxically, Jesus' equality with God is contingent upon his utter obedience to the Father's will. If Jesus says that he and the Father are one (cf. 10:30), he affirms at the same time his own submission to God's will for his life and mission.

Still, this claim is too much for his fellow Jews, who with some reason see it as a challenge to their monotheistic faith. Although Jesus readily grants that he does nothing on his own and that he does not seek his own will, but the will of God who sent him (5:30), he cannot avoid the suspicion that he as a human being is infringing upon the divine majesty and blasphemously making himself God (10:33).

Put in other terms, according to John Jesus claims the status of God's final and definitive revelation. It is Jesus who makes God finally and fully known to human beings under the conditions and limitations of human life and death. Jesus is not to be judged by previous revelations, even those to Israel that have been recorded in scripture and hallowed by sacred tradition. Rather, they are to be judged by him. Therefore, his claim to reveal God cannot in principle be validated by appeal to other authorities.

Yet there are valid witnesses to him and to his claim, and these are spoken of in the final part of this chapter (5:31–47): John the Baptist (vss. 32–35); Jesus' own works (vs. 36); and the Father himself (vss. 37–38), but God's testimony to Jesus can only be heard and seen through Jesus (cf. 5:37 and 1:18). Nevertheless, scripture, when read aright, also testifies to Jesus (vss. 39–47). Moses wrote about Jesus (vs. 46), yet one would not have known this apart from the appearance and testimony of Jesus. John the Baptist is the single other human being who stands as a witness over against Jesus, before and during his ministry, and bears absolutely true testimony to Jesus (1:6–8; cf. 10:41).

Even Jesus' own works, though they testify about him to eyes of faith, may be rejected or inadequately interpreted (2:23–25). In chapter 9 we see an outstanding example of how Jesus' works are not so much a proof as a watershed. Everything depends on whether one acknowledges them to be real and valid. The final test of Jesus' work for the man born blind is that now he sees (9:25). One who sees cannot deny sight any more than he can deny his previous blindness.

THE HEALING OF THE MAN BORN BLIND (9:1–41)

How do these miracle stories present the message of the Fourth Gospel?

Between the healing of the invalid at the pool (chap. 5) and the present episode, the hostility against Jesus (5:18) has continued to mount. During the bread discourse, Jesus' conversation partners seem more perplexed than hostile, but by the end even some of his disciples are turning away from him (6:66). At the subsequent Festival of Booths (chap. 7) the authorities make an attempt to arrest Jesus, who is now aware that his life is in danger (7:19), but are unsuccessful. Chapter 7 is a rather tightly woven story, which is tied in with what preceded (7:1), has a clear narrative framework, and a conclusion that relates to what has occurred earlier in the account (7:45; cf. vs. 32). Chapter 8 is a much more loosely connected series of arguments and counterarguments between Jesus and the Jews, or the Jews who had believed in him (vs. 31). Its continuity derives largely from the bitterness of the exchanges and the fact that Jesus is still in the temple. There is no explicit connection between this chapter and the previous one, and no new incident or episode begins the discussion. The break and the need for some fresh opening narrative are so obvious that some ancient scribe inserted at the beginning the now famous story of the woman taken in adultery (7:53–8:11), which is missing in the oldest and most reliable manuscripts. Similarly, the chapter ends abruptly with "the Jews" unsuccessfully attempting to stone Jesus (8:59), who hides and leaves the temple. There is then no explicit connection with what follows; thus the story of the healing of the blind man (chap. 9) begins with Jesus simply walking along. We can later infer the locus of the narrative from the fact that Jesus tells the man to wash in the pool of Siloam, in Jerusalem and south of the temple mount (9:7, 11).

The healing itself (9:1–7) is in many respects similar to the synoptic miracle stories. The story is introduced with only the vaguest kind of connection with the preceding scene. Such a brief introduction is common in the Synoptics. The idea that sickness or deformity is punishment for sin (vss. 2 f.; cf. vs. 34) is an ancient one, and dies hard (cf. Luke 13:1–5; Exod. 20:5). Although Jesus rejects this belief (vs. 3), his own interpretation of the man's blindness is scarcely more acceptable to modern sensibilities. Here we have one of two remarkable parallels to the Lazarus story (see chap. 11), where the sickness of Lazarus is said to be for the glory of God and of the Son (11:4). The point, however, is not that God deforms people to show his own power, but that in and through such misfortune the power of God manifests itself (cf. Gen. 50:20). The second parallel (vss. 4 f. corresponds to 11:9 f.) consists of a subtle allusion to the coming death of Jesus. Already its inevitability has been indicated by passing references of the evangelist (2:22; 7:39) and by the attitude of the Jews in controversy with Jesus (5:18; 8:37, 40, 59). Now as the public ministry draws toward its close, Jesus' last acts of healing are placed under the shadow of the cross.

That Jesus says "I am the light of the world" (vs. 5, cf. 1:5, 9; 8:12) shows the close connection between the prologue and the Gospel proper. This statement of Jesus belongs to a group of "I am" sayings that are distinctive of the Fourth Gospel (e.g., 6:35; 10:11; 11:25; 14:6; 15:1) and reflect the Johannine view that Jesus proclaims himself and his dignity. By contrast, in the Synoptics Jesus proclaims not himself but the kingdom of God, and such "I am" statements are not found. Obviously, the theme of light is closely related to Jesus' gift of sight.

The miracle itself is described briefly and with restraint (vss. 6 f.). In Mark also Jesus is said to heal with spittle (8:23); once in Luke the healing likewise takes place after Jesus has sent the persons involved away (17:12–15). The pool of Siloam, where Jesus sent the man, was obviously nearby. For the evangelist, however, the significance of the pool was the Hebrew meaning of its name, "Sent." In the Gospel of John Jesus is frequently described as the one sent by God (e.g., 3:17). The man's obedience to Jesus and the results are described as succinctly as possible. In fact, the basic miracle story is much less elaborate and detailed than are many similar stories in the Synoptic tradition. This brevity may indicate that John possessed a primitive miracle story in simple form.

After the brief account of the miracle, there follows a longer dialogue concerned with questions fundamental to Johannine theology. At most, the Synoptic miracle stories concisely report the reaction to Jesus' miracles. By contrast, John develops the theological issues that arise as a consequence of the miracle. This emphasis is reflected in the literary form; a traditional story forms the basis of, and affords the springboard for, a developed dialogue. The dialogue, unlike anything in the Synoptics, is quite typical of John. Much the same pattern of events plus interpretation has already been observed in chapter 5. Indeed, it is characteristic of the style of the Gospel.

There are several interrogations of the blind man (9:8–12, 13–17, 18–23, 24–34). First the man's neighbors question him (vss. 8 ff.), then the Pharisees (vss. 13–17). Then the man's parents are questioned by the Jews (vss. 18–23). Finally, the Jews return to question the man himself a second time (vss. 24–34). Probably no distinction is to be drawn between Pharisees and Jews in this instance. John's characteristic designation of those who oppose Jesus and his work is simply "the Jews." When he does mention a particular sect of Judaism, it is the Pharisees. John tends to equate Jews and Pharisees, though the reason for this is not obvious.

If, however, John was written after the Roman war (A.D. 70), the main Jewish opponents of Christianity would have been Pharisees. The other principal sects, Sadducees, Zealots, and Essenes, had been either dissolved or sharply reduced in size and influence as a result of that conflict. Therefore, John's reference to the Pharisees is probably an indication that they were the

The same pool of Siloam used in Jesus' time still exists in Jerusalem today.
(Courtesy of Arab Information Center.)

group most actively competing with or opposing Christianity at the end of the first century. We shall see some indication that this is the case before the end of this chapter. By contrast, the synoptic material still views Jesus' ministry from the standpoint of Palestinian Judaism before the destruction of the temple, although the evangelists themselves do reflect a later time and distinctively Christian interests.

A brief narrative (vss. 8–12) reports more of the healed man's background and conveys the astonishment and even disbelief of his neighbors (vss. 8 f.). The man calmly and certainly identifies himself as the blind beggar whom they have known, and describes how and by whom he has been healed. When brought before the Pharisees (vss. 13–17), his assurance and simplicity are impressive (vs. 15). For the first time we learn that the healing had been performed on the Sabbath (vs. 14), a common feature of the Synoptic tradition, where Jesus is more than once accused of illegally performing healings—and therefore working—on the Sabbath (cf. also John 5). The division among the Pharisees (vs. 16) is typical of the division that Jesus causes. Some people reject him out of hand, because he violates their preconceptions of what a holy or righteous man must be: "He does not observe the sabbath." Others are at least open to the testimony of his works, to see them as "signs," signifying who Jesus is. The question is then put to the blind man (vs. 17): "What do you say about him? It was your eyes he opened." Earlier the man has simply spoken of "the man called Jesus." Now he says that Jesus is a prophet. The term *prophet* serves to indicate that Jesus is not a sinner, as his detractors contend, but a man sent from God.

The mounting opposition to Jesus next takes the form of the Jews' refusal to believe that the man had actually been born blind (vs. 18), so his parents are called to testify (vss. 18–23). The parents are obviously not anxious to involve themselves, but they do give a minimally truthful testimony. The man who claims to have been healed by Jesus the prophet is, in fact, their son who was born blind (vs. 20). For all questions about how or by whom he was healed, however, the parents refer the questioners back to their son (vs. 21).

The evangelist now interjects an explanation of the reticence of the parents (vss. 22 f.) that does not really fit the time of Jesus, but rather the end of the first Christian century. Only after the destruction of Jerusalem and the formation of the rabbinic Council of Jamnia might people have actually been forced to leave the synagogue for professing Jesus to be the Messiah or Christ.[8] The theme of being cast out of the synagogue occurs more than once in John (12:42; 16:2; cf. Luke 6:22) and is probably a reflection of that situation. Despite the parents' timidity, the attempt to discredit the claims of the man, and indirectly to discredit Jesus, comes to grief on the hard fact that a change has occurred in him. He was born blind, but is so no longer.

The same hearing continues and the man is called a second time (vss. 24 ff.). Despite the lack of conclusive evidence against Jesus, the opposition to him has now hardened (vs. 24). The serenity of the man healed contrasts with the obviously hostile jury. Rather than debating his questioners, he simply recites what he knows on the basis of what he has experienced. He was blind, but now he sees (vs. 25). No one can deny to him the truth of his tes-

---

8. See above, p. 165, and J. L. Martyn, *History and Theology in the Fourth Gospel,* rev. ed. (Nashville: Abingdon, 1979), esp. pp. 24–62. Cf. Brown, *The Gospel According to John,* pp. lxxxv, 374, 379 f.

timony! This most effective and infuriating response (especially in view of the failure to show that the man was not blind in the first place) drives the questioners now to take a new tack (vs. 26). Perhaps they suspect that Jesus has used spittle in the act of healing and is therefore guilty of adopting the tricks of an illegal sorcerer. At this point the man shows the first signs of irritation (vs. 27). His reply is intentionally cutting and draws a bitter retort (vss. 28 f.). Of course, the Jews' claim to be the true disciples of Moses would not have been accepted by the evangelist (cf. 5:45–47). That the man is Jesus' disciple has not heretofore been suggested. Nevertheless, it will turn out to be true.

In John's view, rejection of Jesus (vs. 29) is based upon a religious certainty that refuses to question itself, a harking back to an earlier revelation that is viewed as immutable, admitting of no further clarification, alteration, or argument. But, as we have seen, Jesus cannot be judged by earlier revelation and tradition. That Jesus' opponents do not know the origin of Jesus is altogether typical of John's thought. To know Jesus' true origin is to know that he is sent by God. The Jews ironically do not know the tragic truth of their observation that they are ignorant of Jesus' origin.[9] The man's response to the statement of the Jews, who have set themselves up as religious authorities (vs. 30), is a classic reflection upon the capacity of the self-styled judges to judge Jesus. His further clarification (vss. 31–33) strikes home, because it is based on presuppositions that the questioners-turned-accusers also share. The response of the man healed is so devastating that the Jews can only lash out in frustrated anger and vent their rage upon him. They cast him out— possibly out of the hearing room, but more probably out of the synagogue or the Jewish community (cf. vss. 22 f.). The latter interpretation is in accord with what follows (vss. 35 ff.). After the man healed has been ejected because of his refusal to repudiate Jesus, Jesus himself returns to him.

At this point the man still has no special theological knowledge about Jesus. In Jesus' question (vs. 35) we find one of the fairly numerous instances of the term *Son of Man* in John's Gospel. As in the Synoptics it appears on the lips of Jesus himself, presumably as a self-designation. The man's answer to Jesus' question is typically guileless (vs. 36). Only now does Jesus reveal his full and true identity (vs. 37). The man's response (vs. 38) indicates that he understands *Son of Man* to be a messianic title. "Lord, I believe" is a Christological confession, as is made plain by the statement that at this point the man worshiped Jesus. The final words of Jesus (vss. 39–41), now addressed not so much to the man as to the total situation, are a commentary on his whole mission.

What are we to make of the strange statement that Jesus has come in order that those who do not see may see and in order that those who see may become blind (vs. 39)? The traces of Jewish–Christian polemic in the latter part of the first century already noted in this chapter lead us to the conclusion that the same situation is in view here. Those who do not see are not

---

9. On the motif of Jesus' origin and background in the Fourth Gospel, note several earlier passages: 1:46; 3:31 ff.; 6:42; 7:15, 27, 41 f., 52; 8:23, 41 f., 57 f.

the physically blind, for in that case the import of Jesus' statement would be the absurd notion that as he goes about giving sight to the blind, so he also puts out the eyes of those who see. Obviously the blindness and sight referred to here are of a different order. At the beginning of this story (vs. 5) Jesus declared that he is the light of the world. He gives sight to those in darkness, but those who try to walk by their own light are blinded. To receive sight, to see the true light, one must recognize one's condition of blindness. Those who insist upon their prior revelatory knowledge ("we see") and their right to judge Jesus become blind because of this pretension. Their rejection of Jesus proves their blindness, whereas their insistence that they see confirms their guilt (9:41). From here it is only a step—perhaps the evangelist has already taken that step, but at least he lays the basis for it—to the application of this principle to humankind at large. The pretension that one already sees prevents the self-knowledge and recognition of one's true condition that is the first step to genuine sight. So the effect of Jesus' appearance is to blind such people (vs. 39), at least until they are ready to recognize their actual state.

We are now in a position to make some generalizations about this chapter and its relation to the Gospel as a whole. The chapter is a paradigm of Jesus' public ministry, portraying in dramatic form the statement of the prologue (vs. 5) that the light shines in darkness and the darkness has not overcome or comprehended it. Moreover, verses 9–13 of the prologue take on concreteness in the light of this story. At the same time it represents a movement or progression in Jesus' ministry. The hostility that has become evident already (cf. chaps. 7 and 8) could not be made plainer than it is here. Also, this portrayal of Jesus as the giver of sight and, by implication, of light, prepares the way for the final manifestation of Jesus as the giver of life (chap. 11). The principal point of the story does not lie in its contribution to historical knowledge of Jesus' ministry. The questions addressed arise not out of Jesus' own time but out of encounters between Christianity and Judaism or between Christianity and the unbelieving world generally. This point is clear from the concluding word of Jesus (vss. 39–41); in the terms of the narrative he succinctly characterizes his whole mission as one of judgment.

There is an apparent anomaly in this statement of Jesus. For elsewhere it is explicitly said that he does not come in order to judge (see 3:17 f., where the word *condemn* translates the same word, Greek *krinein*, "to judge"; also 12:47). From 5:22 onward, however, it is clear that the Son does judge. The difficulty is resolved if we recognize that the ultimate purpose of Jesus' coming is not judgment but salvation (3:16 ff.). Yet from this, judgment inevitably results—because some reject with great hostility the salvation that is offered and persist in evil (3:19 ff.). This negative statement of Jesus' purpose is doubtless influenced by the context, as it follows a narrative in which hostility toward Jesus and his work has been vigorously expressed.

In the background of this chapter and episode stands John's distinctive view of Jesus as the light and life of the world. The miracle itself is indispensable in that it manifests the fact that Jesus really changes people. The stubborn insistence of the healed man upon the fact of his healing bears eloquent testimony to this conviction. He grounds his relation to Jesus on what has actually happened to him, even though he cannot give this experience adequate expression until Jesus reveals himself to him; only then does he acknowledge and worship the Christ whose reality and activity on his behalf he has already confessed. Although the Johannine Christology is here in evidence, it is more or less in the background. In the foreground is soteriology (the concept of salvation and its effect)—not so much who Jesus is, but what he does. In fact, who he is becomes known through, and is grounded upon, what he does. As Jesus here manifests himself as the light of the world by giving sight to the blind, so later on (chap. 11) he appears as the resurrection and the life by raising the dead.

Interestingly, Jesus himself remains somewhat in the background, and there is a sense in which the real hero of the story is the nameless man who is healed. This is true of this particular miracle story as of no other in John. Neither the restored man of chapter 5 nor even Lazarus in chapter 11 emerges as a hero. The ruler of 4:46–54 comes off well, as in the synoptic parallels, but his character is not displayed and developed in the same way. However, if Jesus did not reappear at the end of chapter 9 to confirm the man in his newly found faith and to pronounce a final interpretative word over the whole affair, we would have to think that after the brief account of the miracle Jesus simply fades out of the picture, except as he is present in his embryonic disciple. This Jew who comes to belief in Jesus is truly an Israelite (cf. 1:47). That is, he comes to Jesus, the Messiah of Israel, in faith.

Although there is no exact parallel to this particular feature in any other Johannine miracle story, the account does bring to light an important Johannine characteristic—namely, the author's interest in the various types of people who confront Jesus. Clearly many of the characters who encounter Jesus are typical and perhaps symbolic. There is Nathanael, the true Israelite in whom there is no guile (1:47 ff.). There is Nicodemus, the teacher of Israel, who at first cannot comprehend Jesus and yet later defends him and finally returns to help bury him (3:1 ff.; 7:50; 19:39). In some contrast to Nicodemus stands the nameless Samaritan woman, the representative of a heterodox Judaism (4:7 ff.), whose dim perception of Jesus is nevertheless superior to that of Nicodemus.

Yet if the characters are symbolic, they are also lifelike. In chapter 11 Mary and Martha, along with the wily Caiaphas, stand out as real people. And even Pontius Pilate shows a touch of humanity in the passion narrative (18:28 ff.). Although the disciples do not appear in the farewell discourse except to ask questions, their questions are understandable in view of the total picture that John has painted. Thus Thomas' question (14:5; cf. 20:25) contributes to the traditional portrayal of him as "doubting Thomas." With the exception of Peter, and perhaps James and John, the other disciples are shadowy characters in the Synoptics. By contrast, in John some of these other disciples play significant roles (for example, Philip, Thomas, Lazarus, and Nathanael), but James and John are not mentioned by name.

The Johannine portrait of Jesus lacks the humanity of the other characters. This is all the more surprising in view of the intensely human—if authoritative—Jesus who emerges at many points in the Synoptic account. The Johannine Jesus, however, behaves strangely by human standards (see 2:4; 7:2–10; 11:6). John's portrayal of Jesus is not designed to represent his humanity for the benefit of the readers' curiosity and to make him personally more familiar. Although John does not deny that Jesus was really human, his primary interest and emphasis are focused by his conviction that through him God is speaking to the world. The single-mindedness of this theological concept is etched sharply against the background of John's perceptive presentation of humanity in all its color and concreteness. At this he is a master, and that is nowhere more apparent than in the story of the man blind from birth.

The Revelation of Jesus' Glory before the Community (13:1–21:25)

Jesus' glory is revealed throughout his public ministry, but the world cannot perceive this glory for what it is. The disciples see and believe, but their understanding before Jesus' death and resurrection is necessarily limited. During the final period of his ministry Jesus reveals himself directly and explicitly to his disciples.[10] Even then their perception is still limited, but ultimately they witness the risen Jesus and come to fully adequate faith.

After bestowing sight upon the blind man, Jesus describes himself as the gate and shepherd of his sheep (his followers) and consequently falls once again into furious debate with the Jews, after which he withdraws across the Jordan to escape their wrath (10:40–42). When, however, he learns of the mortal illness of his friend Lazarus, he returns to the Jerusalem area, to Bethany, where his friend lives. Meanwhile, Lazarus has died, as Jesus knew he must (11:11–15).

The raising of Lazarus from the dead (11:1–44) leads directly to the authorities' plotting Jesus' death (11:45–53). No longer does Jesus move freely in Judea, but now retreats to a town called Ephraim (11:54), near the wilderness. As Passover draws near (12:1: "Six days before Passover . . ."), Jesus goes to Bethany again, where he is entertained in the home of Lazarus by Lazarus' sisters Martha and Mary. Mary anoints the feet of Jesus, over the protest of

---

10. The disciples have usually been taken to mean the Twelve, although this is nowhere made explicit in the text. In 6:66 ff. all the disciples except the Twelve seem to be drawing back from Jesus. Yet immediately thereafter (7:3) it appears that Jesus has disciples other than the Twelve. Therefore one ought not to assume that "disciples" (after 6:66) always means the Twelve.

Judas (12:1–8). Subsequently Jesus enters Jerusalem in a procession, the so-called triumphal entry, recounted also in the Synoptic Gospels (12:12–19).

At this point in John's narrative there is an interlude in which Jesus appears among the festival crowd and makes mysterious pronouncements about his coming death that are scarcely understood by the onlookers (12:20–36a). Then the evangelist declares Jesus' public ministry to be at an end; despite all the signs he did, the result is unbelief (12:37), as the prophet Isaiah had predicted (12:38–40). Jesus then cries aloud, in effect summarizing his ministry or the saving purpose of God in that ministry (12:44–50). He announces once again that he has come as a light into the world (vs. 46), not to judge it (or condemn it), but to save it. His mission, he once again reiterates, has been to deliver the message that God has given him. From now on Jesus is with his own disciples only, except for the inevitable confrontation with the Jewish religious authorities and with Pontius Pilate, the Roman governor.

THE LAST SUPPER (13:1–38)

What is the relationship between the foot washing and the Lord's Supper?

Jesus withdraws with his disciples to the Last Supper, even as he does in the Synoptics. If we know those Gospels, we know that the end of his ministry is now near. Otherwise, we are nevertheless aware of the imminence of the end, for John says as much at the very outset (13:1). Judas is now primed to betray Jesus (vs. 2), and Jesus himself is confident in the full knowledge of his divine commission and destiny. The Johannine account of the Supper is remarkably parallel to the Synoptic, but with some significant differences. In fact, as the events of Jesus' ministry close in upon his imminent death, John and the Synoptics move closer together in their narratives. Yet in the Synoptic Gospels the Last Supper is a Passover meal, introduced by a brief narrative about the preparation for it (Mark 14:12–25 parr.); in John the meal occurs on the evening before the Passover was to be eaten (13:1–29; 19:31).

The most astonishing difference in the Johannine account, however, appears at the outset, where, instead of instituting the Lord's Supper with words familiar from the Synoptics (Mark 14:22–25 parr.) and Paul (1 Cor. 11:23–26), Jesus washes his disciples' feet (13:4–11). Only in John does Jesus perform this act (but cf. Luke 12:37). While John's reasons for seemingly substituting the foot washing for the institution of the Lord's Supper are not clear, stimulating imaginative interpretations, the meaning of the act itself is plain enough.

As Jesus comes to Simon Peter (vs. 6), that disciple protests having his feet washed by his master. ("Lord," may mean only "Sir," but it could have other connotations, since the Greek *Kyrios* is a widely used Christological title.) When Jesus tells Peter that he does not understand now but will later, this remark is apparently a veiled reference to Jesus' crucifixion and resurrection, after which the disciples will indeed understand (cf. 2:22). Yet Peter is still in the dark, so to speak, and continues to protest that Jesus will not wash his feet (vs. 8), at which point Jesus makes clear to him that the act that he intends to perform is necessary if they are to have a continuing relationship. Even in acceding to Jesus (vs. 9), Simon reveals that his understanding is scarcely better than that of Nicodemus or the woman of Samaria. Jesus does reassure him (vs. 10), but this reassurance likely falls on deaf ears, at least for the moment, as Simon Peter cannot yet understand the depths of what Jesus is saying. At least he does not demonstrate that he understands the hidden meaning of Jesus' deed.

The washing of the disciples' feet, the humble, slave's service that Jesus performs upon his disciples, symbolizes the service he performs in his death. Only after he has done it, however, will the disciples understand its meaning (vs. 7). Peter's revulsion at the prospect of Jesus' washing his feet is reminiscent of his similar reaction when in Mark's Gospel Jesus informs Peter that the Son of Man must suffer humiliation and death (Mark 8:31). Immediately afterward Peter rebukes Jesus. But then Jesus rebukes Peter in turn: "Get behind me, Satan! . . ." (vs. 33). The scene in John differs, but the dynamics, and the relationship of Jesus and Peter, are quite similar. In neither case can Peter understand. (The noting of the exception to Jesus' dictum that all the disciples are clean—vss. 10–11—is typical of the Fourth Gospel, where Jesus is betrayed by Judas, but only with Jesus' prior knowledge and at his behest.)

After first presenting the foot washing as a preenactment of his own suffering service for the disciples, Jesus then interprets his deed from yet another angle of vision (vss. 12–17). As Teacher and Lord he declares that the foot washing is for the disciples an example of how they should serve one another (vs. 15). One might say that there is first a theological (or soteriological) interpretation and then an ethical one; at any rate, the two are very closely tied together. As Jesus has served the disciples, the disciples must serve one another. This principle is reiterated time and again in the Gospel as well as in the First Epistle of John (13:34; 15:12–14; 1 John 3:16). (Whether Jesus instituted a rite of foot washing is debatable, but the broader, theological and ethical implications of his act are clear enough.)

Then comes the prediction of Jesus' betrayal by Judas (13:18–20), followed immediately by the story of Jesus' identification of Judas as the betrayer (vs. 21–30). The parallel accounts in the Synoptics (Mark 14:18–19 parr.) differ in detail but are recognizably similar. In fact, the Johannine version of the episode is more elaborate. Jesus puts the finger on Judas specifically, which is not at all the case in Mark. Further, Jesus actually reveals his identity only to the Beloved Disciple ("the one whom Jesus loved"—vs. 23), as it becomes evident that the other disciples present do not share this information (vs. 28–29).

The Beloved Disciple, found only in the Fourth Gospel, will reappear repeatedly in the narrative from this point on: perhaps at the door of the high priest's house (18:15–16); at the foot of the cross (19:25–27); at the empty tomb (20:2–10); at the appearance of the risen Christ by the sea (21:7); and finally with Peter and the risen Jesus at the very end of the Gospel (21:20–24).

It is as if everywhere Peter goes, the Beloved Disciple goes; moreover, every-thing Peter can do, the Beloved Disciple can do better. Even though the Beloved Disciple constantly outdoes Peter, however, Peter is not denigrated or played down. It is just that the Beloved Disciple has a special place. Tra-dition has identified him with John the son of Zebedee, but that identifica-tion is never explicitly made in the Gospel itself. Whether the Beloved Disciple was a real person is sometimes asked. Perhaps he is an ideal or sym-bolic figure. Certainly he is that, in the sense that he is the ideal disciple. Yet he seems also to be the special link between the Johannine Christian com-munity and Jesus (cf. 19:35). The fact that it was rumored that he would not die, yet he apparently had died (21:21–22), speaks on the side of his having been a historical figure. The Johannine community would scarcely have in-vented someone whose death then had to be explained.

After the identification of the betrayer to the Beloved Disciple—and to the reader—Jesus announces his glorification (13:31–33). His glory is revealed only in his death and resurrection; that is, these events are the revelation of Jesus' glory. In fact, Jesus is here announcing his impending death. To the outsider such talk is mysterious and enigmatic. The informed (i.e., believing) reader, however, knows its meaning. Just at this point Jesus issues the new commandment to his disciples, which echoes the command to love else-where in the New Testament, outside the Johannine literature (cf. Gal. 5:14; Rom. 13:9; Mark 12:33 parr.; Matt. 5:44). But in John the command is directed particularly to the circle of Jesus' own disciples. Their love for each other is a witness to the world of who, and whose, they are (13:35). Only in the Gospel of John does Jesus issue the love commandment at this point in the narra-tive. Jesus has manifested his own self-giving love, symbolized in the foot washing, and now he commands his disciples to show that same love to each other (vs. 34: "as I have loved you"). The Johannine version of the Lord's Sup-per begins and ends on the theme of love; indeed, only in the Fourth Gospel is the narrative of the Last Supper framed by the theme of love in such an ex-plicit way.

Almost as an afterthought Jesus predicts Peter's denial (13:36–38), as he does in all the Gospels. Although this prediction takes place after Jesus and the disciples have retired from the meal and the upper room in the Synop-tics, in John they still seem to be at the supper. (Luke, not uncharacteristi-cally, agrees with John in that the prediction of the denial comes before they have departed the meal.) In fact, it is not obvious that Jesus and his disciples have left the supper until the arrest scene (18:1), after the farewell discourses (chaps. 14–16) and Jesus' final prayer (chap. 17).

John's emphasis on the love of Jesus for the disciples and the importance of their love for one another dominates his account of the Last Supper and perhaps explains why the traditional narrative of the institution of the Lord's Supper is omitted, seemingly in favor of the foot washing. In the words of in-stitution Jesus indicates that he gives his body and blood for his followers (cf. Mark 14:22, 24; 1 Cor. 11:24–25). But in the foot washing, Jesus' self-

"The Last Supper" by William Blake (1799). *(Courtesy of National Gallery of Art, Washington, D.C. Rosenwald Collection.)*

giving service, which is motivated by his love for his disciples (13:1), is made even more explicit. Obviously John knows the tradition of the Eucharist; otherwise the words in which Jesus' disciples are commanded to eat his flesh and drink his blood (6:52–58) are scarcely intelligible. In the narrative of the Last Supper, however, John calls attention to the meaning of the Eucharist precisely by omitting it and offering a story that dramatizes both Jesus' saving work and the obligation of mutual love that Jesus places upon his followers.[11]

THE PROMISE OF THE PARACLETE (14:15–17, 26 AND 16:12–14)

Is the Paraclete identical with Jesus?

The farewell discourses (14:1-16:33)speak to the disciples' basic problem: How they can maintain their union or fellowship with Jesus in light of the loss of his physical presence and their continued existence in a hostile world. At the beginning Jesus assures them that ultimately they shall be with him (14:1–4), and at the end he tells them that he has overcome the world (16:33). Afterward, his prayer concludes with the petition that his followers may be with him in his eschatological glory (17:25). In the meantime, how-

11. Conceivably, John here assumes knowledge of Mark, or the synoptic accounts generally. Yet Paul, who is unaware of the Gospel narratives, knows that the Lord's Supper was instituted on the night Jesus was betrayed (1 Cor. 11:23), so it is equally possible that John was familiar with a similar tradition current in his own community.

ever, the disciples are not bereft of his presence. Jesus will send the Paraclete, the Spirit of truth (14:16 f.) or Holy Spirit (14:26), to be with them.

"Paraclete" simply transliterates the Greek term found in the gospel: *paraklētos,* which means literally "one called to the side of." English translators have rendered the word "Comforter" (KJV), "Counselor" (RSV), or "Advocate" (NRSV). In terms of ancient usage "advocate," which stands closest to the literal meaning of the word, seems most appropriate. In 1 John 2:1, Jesus is called our "advocate with the Father," and in that context this translation seems exactly right. When the Paraclete is first mentioned in the Gospel, he is called "another Paraclete" (14:16), as if, indeed, Jesus were the first. Thus the NRSV translates "another Advocate."

Yet the function of the Paraclete, according to Jesus, is not so much to plead a case before God as to remind, to teach, to comfort, or to counsel the disciples. Thus the translators of the KJV and the RSV with some reason chose the English term "comforter" or "counselor." The Paraclete performs those functions as he, in effect, continues the ministry and revelation of Jesus himself. "I will not leave you orphaned," says Jesus, "I am coming to you" (14:18). This statement immediately follows Jesus' pledging that he will ask the Father, who will send another Paraclete to be with them forever (14:16). In the farewell discourses Jesus speaks repeatedly of his own departure and his coming again to the disciples (14:2–4, 18; 16:7, 16). In doing so he apparently evokes the tradition of his exaltation and future return known to us from the New Testament's apocalyptic texts (e.g., Mark 13:26–27; 1 Thess. 4:13–18; Rev. 22:20). Such hopes were maintained also in the Johannine community, even apart from the Book of Revelation (John 21:22–23; 1 John 2:28; 3:2). John now reinterprets those hopes. The coming of Jesus is essentially a spiritual coming, his reappearance under the form of the Paraclete or the Holy Spirit.

Thus when Jesus says that the Paraclete will teach the disciples everything and remind them of what he has said (14:26) or that the Paraclete will guide them into such truth as they cannot yet bear (or understand, 16:12), in effect he makes the Paraclete the continuation or extension of his own revelation and presence. Jesus' continuing ministry through the Spirit or Paraclete is not only important but absolutely essential to the community of his disciples, that is, the church. Thus the Fourth Gospel stresses the importance of union with Jesus (17:20–23, cf. 10:16).

The Spirit's coming is also contingent on Jesus' physical departure in death (16:7). Only after his death will the disciples, or the church, be empowered. Only after his death will they truly understand what has taken place in his ministry. All along, the evangelist has informed the reader that the disciples would only understand what was happening later, in retrospect (2:17–22; 12:16; 13:7; cf. 14:29), after the coming of the Spirit (7:39). John takes full cognizance of what was surely the fact that Jesus' ministry, in its full theological significance and meaning, could not be comprehended at the time by eyewitnesses or even disciples. The same perception is expressed in the Markan idea of the messianic secret. In Mark, Jesus' true identity as Messiah is not known until Peter's confession (8:27–30), but even after it is known it is not understood. In John, Jesus' messianic role is announced and apparently understood by the disciples, who believe in him (2:11); yet they remain strangely uncomprehending, even through the farewell discourses. At their conclusion Jesus responds to the disciples' affirmation of him by predicting their desertion (16:32); still he goes on to suggest that they will ultimately represent him in the world (vs. 33).

As transmitted to us in the Fourth Gospel, the farewell discourses may contain earlier collections of material. In fact, we may find here two versions that have been joined together. In 14:31 Jesus says, "Rise, let us be on our way," seemingly indicating that the discourse has ended, apparently also implying that he and the disciples have been seated, or reclining, at table. (A similar command appears at Mark 14:42, however, at the conclusion of the Gethsemane scene.) In any event, 14:31 seems to be a major seam in the narrative that implies more than one version of the discourse existed. Similarly, there seem to be two final chapters of the Gospel, that is, two separate sets of resurrection scenes that do not really fit together in succession (chaps. 20 and 21). We have already noticed the difficulty in the narrative's progression created by the fact that chapter 6 now follows chapter 5, as well as the very loose connection of chapter 8 with its present context in the Gospel. All these literary problems imply that this Gospel, although extremely well crafted in many of its parts, is rather loosely put together. In that sense, the whole is somewhat less than the sum of its parts.

Yet the farewell discourses and the following prayer of Jesus are extremely important for understanding the Fourth Gospel. In a sense, they displace the apocalyptic discourse of the Synoptic Gospels (Mark 13 parr.) and give a rather different outlook on the future. The community of Jesus' followers is to look not to the imminent future for God's apocalyptically conceived interventions in history; rather it is to look immediately inward to the present manifestation of the Father and the Son in the church through the Spirit (cf. 14:22–23). What is revealed through the Spirit–Paraclete is the further relevance of Jesus, especially what Jesus continues to say to the church. The Gospel itself may then be viewed as a part of this ongoing revelation. It presents not so much the historical Jesus as the risen and exalted Jesus as he continues to commune and communicate with his disciples. Still, this Jesus stands in continuity with the earthly Jesus of Nazareth (cf. 20:31 and 1 John 1:1–3; 4:1–3).

JESUS' LAST WILL: THE PRAYER OF CONSECRATION (17:1–26)

Why is Jesus' final utterance cast in the form of a prayer?

Jesus' last prayer in John is a carefully wrought exposition of his legacy to his disciples.[12] His own death is mentioned, but in its peculiarly Johannine sig-

---

12. The title of this section is based upon that of Ernst Käsemann's famous monograph on chapter 17 and Johannine theology, *Jesu letzter Wille nach Johannes 17,* translated into

nificance as the glorification and consecration of the Son of God. In the Synoptics only Jesus prays in Gethsemane, "Abba, Father, for you all things are possible; remove this cup from me; yet not what I want, but what you want" (Mark 14:36; cf. John 12:27 f.). Although the synoptic accounts probably reflect the actual, human historical situation of Jesus, the Johannine prayer vividly illumines the message of the Fourth Gospel.

With the announcement that the hour has come (17:1; cf. 12:23; 13:31–32), Jesus signals, in a typically Johannine way, the imminence of the crucifixion as also the hour of his glorification. The glorifying of the Son is now to take place in his death and exaltation to heaven. In John, crucifixion, resurrection, and exaltation are tied closely together. God glorifies Jesus by turning his death into victory, and the glory that Jesus thereby shares is nothing less than God's imposing power as he makes it known to all people. Already the Word's becoming flesh and dwelling among humankind has been subtly compared with God's glory dwelling in the temple (1:14; cf. 2:19 ff. and 4:20 ff.). Now the close connection between the Father and Jesus allows the evangelist to assert that Jesus shares in the Father's eternal glory (cf. esp. vs. 5).

The definition of eternal life (vs. 3) shows the distance between John and any apocalyptic world view. Eternal life is an eschatological concept, and in chapter 3 it appears in conjunction with the term *kingdom of God,* so familiar from the Synoptic Gospels. The phrase *eternal life* also occurs in the Synoptics themselves (cf. Mark 10:17: "Good Teacher, what must I do to inherit eternal life?"). There it is understood to refer to the life of the age to come (Mark 10:30). Although in John eternal life is not robbed of its future dimension (14:1–7; 17:24), the evangelist emphasizes its present reality as knowledge of the only true God and Jesus Christ (vs. 3).

The Son glorifies the Father—that is, renders the praise and service due him—by obediently doing his work (vs. 4). Now he prays, "Father, glorify me" (vs. 5; cf. vs. 1). The new element in this petition is the reference to Christ's preexistence, his being with the Father before creation. There is thus a close connection between this passage and the prologue (1:1; see pp. 167 ff.). The meaning of the glorification of Jesus is that God fully affirms and accepts Jesus' work.

Because verse 5 harks back to verse 1 and brings to a conclusion the theme of the glory of Christ, we may regard verses 1–5 as the introduction of the prayer. The remainder and greater part of the chapter (vss. 6–26) contains Jesus' petition for the church, although the term *church* itself is never used. There is some justification for viewing verses 6–8 as the continuation of the first part, or as a transitional section, because in these verses (as perhaps in vss. 12 and 14) the ministry of the earthly Jesus as it touches upon the disciples is still in view. One might suggest that verse 4 refers to Jesus' ministry

English by Gerhard Krodel as *The Testament of Jesus: A Study of the Gospel of John in the Light of Chapter 17* (Philadelphia: Fortress, 1968).

before the world (chaps. 2–12), whereas verses 6–8 (cf. vss. 12, 14) focus upon his special work among his disciples.

It may seem strange that Jesus speaks of himself in the third person (vss. 1–5) and even refers to himself as "Jesus Christ" (vs. 3), a name that never appears on his lips in the Synoptic Gospels. In fact, through verse 8 the prayer contains no genuine petitions. Instead, Jesus tells the Father what he has done (vs. 4), what authority he has (vs. 2), and the nature of eternal life (vs. 3). The author of the Gospel uses the opening statement to provide the proper setting and orientation for the reader by having Jesus expound the character and meaning of his ministry. As the hour tolls and he goes to the cross (vs. 1), he does so in the full knowledge that in both life and death he glorifies God by accomplishing his work. The success of that work can be seen in the faithful disciples, whom he has called out of the world and instructed in the most intimate communion with himself (chaps. 13–16). The prayer occurs only after the Last Supper and Jesus' extensive discourses and conversations with the disciples; thereby the groundwork is laid for such statements about the disciples as we find in this prayer. Having now secured the disciples to himself, Jesus turns with them to God.

Throughout the farewell discourses the disciples remain full of misunderstandings and uncertainties. Jesus' own piercing retort (16:31 f.) reveals the inadequacy of their final solemn affirmation (16:29 f.). The evangelist knows well that the disciples will desert Jesus, and that their awareness of Jesus' significance and his work must remain incomplete until after his death (cf. 2:22; 7:39; 12:16; 13:7; 16:7–15; 16:31 f.). In the discourses Jesus tells his disciples things they cannot fully understand until he has departed from them. In the prayer, on the other hand, Jesus views his disciples as if they had already moved into this deeper understanding. The postresurrection church now comes into view, and the statements of Jesus about his disciples are now made not on the basis of their behavior during his earthly ministry but on their postresurrection faith, which is about to become a reality.

The petitions Jesus offers for his disciples are also well suited to reassure them (vss. 9–19). Significantly, Jesus prays only for his disciples and not for the world (vs. 9). The Johannine dualism between God, Jesus, and the disciples on the one hand and the world on the other, already visible (see vs. 6), is underscored. Still Jesus does not pray for the disciples to be taken out of the world, but to be kept unstained by its evil (vs. 15). They are not of the world, even as Jesus is not (vs. 16). As Jesus was sent by God to save the world rather than condemn it, so also the disciples are sent (vs. 18; cf. 20:21).

The kind of thoroughgoing dualism that divides humanity into the saved and the damned, though sometimes suggested in John, is not rigidly adhered to. The world is a hateful place, in that it hates Jesus and his followers (15:18), but Jesus nowhere encourages his disciples, or the church, to respond by hating the world. Jesus and his disciples are sanctified, made holy, in the truth that the world by definition does not know (vss. 17, 19). Thus Pilate will ask, whether naively or cynically (18:38), "What is truth?" Yet both Jesus and the disciples are holy for the sake of the world, that the world may know (vs. 23). Thus truth, the truth of God, sets Jesus and the disciples apart from the world.

As Jesus looks toward future believers (vss. 20–23), he reiterates the need for unity, what will subsequently be called the unity of the church. Remarkably, precisely this unity is for the sake of the world's believing (vs. 21) and knowing (vs. 23) the truth in which Jesus and the disciples have been sanctified. The Johannine church looks inward in love and faith to assure itself of its basis and ground, but then looks outward to the world, as Jesus himself was sent into the world.

It is characteristic of John and of the Jesus of John to hold the future church in view (17:20; cf. 10:16; 20:29). This church is grounded not only in the Jesus whose historic ministry is fundamental to its existence but in the future, and not just its earthly future. Finally, Jesus prays that the union of the disciples with him will be eternal, that they will share the eschatological, and primordial, glory (vs. 24). The sharp distinction between the church and the world is reiterated at the end (vs. 25), but the prayer concludes with Jesus' promise that he will continue to make God's name—his truth and reality— known, for the sake of his love. That love was manifest for and in Jesus (vs. 25). It extends now to the believers, but through them also to the world (3:16). When the author of 1 John wrote that God is love (4:8; cf. vs. 12), he did not misunderstand the Gospel.

The death that the reader has been prepared to witness and to understand must now take place. So Jesus moves into the garden, where Judas betrays him, and thence to the court of the high priest, to Pilate's judgment seat, and to Golgotha. Even the Johannine Jesus dies a real death and is buried, and, according to John's firm conviction, is really raised from the dead.

Yet the risen Christ does not add anything essentially new to the historical Jesus as John portrayed him in the Gospel. For in a sense the Johannine Jesus already is the risen Christ, the exalted one. Until his hour arrives, however, he cannot be recognized as such. Not even his disciples, who believe in him, can comprehend the full import of his mission and message. Only in the light of his death and exaltation does his true nature become manifest to his own disciples, who are then able to see the real meaning and import of his earthly ministry. Whoever the author of the Gospel may have been, he was certainly such a disciple, and his portrayal of Jesus takes into account the fuller knowledge of him that is only possible after his death.

Conclusion

As we observed earlier, recent scholarship has tended to place the *historical origin* of the Fourth Gospel in Jewish–Christian circles. The Qumran Scrolls offer many affinities with John, which indicates something about its provenance. Even though the Scrolls do not prove that the Gospel in its present form is Palestinian, a Palestinian origin of the Johannine tradition seems more likely now than a generation ago. Certain of the Scrolls manifest a dualistic way of thinking that is strongly reminiscent of John. Although it is too much to argue on the basis of the Scrolls that the Fourth Gospel is relatively early (before A.D. 70 or the end of the Jewish–Roman war), the Johannine tradition may well reach back to a much earlier period than the Gospel itself. The development of Christian thought and the sharp hostility to Judaism (or between Jews who confess Jesus to be the Messiah and those who reject him) manifested in the Gospel make a date toward the end of the first century probable.

The question of the authorship of the Fourth Gospel was much debated in an earlier day of critical scholarship, but the results of that debate do not help much in understanding its circumstances of origin. Although tradition equates the Johannine Beloved Disciple with John the son of Zebedee, one of the Twelve, that identification does not occur in the Gospel itself. The Gospel of John does, however, assert that the Beloved Disciple is the witness who stands behind the Gospel and caused it to be written (21:24). It is notable that this disciple first appears only when Jesus has reached Jerusalem for his final visit (13:23). Wherever he is found (cf. also 18:15–16; 19:26–27; 20:2–10), except at the foot of the cross, he is accompanied by Peter. It has been inferred from these facts that (1) the Beloved Disciple was a Jerusalem follower of Jesus, which would accord with the emphasis on Jesus' Jerusalem activity in John, and (2) that the Beloved Disciple was seen as somehow a rival to Peter in authority. There is probably some truth in both these inferences. The Gospel of John likely represents a Jerusalem or Judean tradition, and the Beloved Disciple may be the source and authority of the Johannine Gospel and tradition. Obviously, the Fourth Gospel wishes to be understood as a narrative based on an eyewitness, or on eyewitness testimony.

Distinguishing *tradition* from *redaction* is much more difficult in John than in the Synoptics. As we have seen, even in Mark the separation of tradition from redaction is often possible. Moreover, we know that Matthew and Luke relied on Mark, and the so-called Q source may be inferred from their common, non-Markan material. Thus the identification of the editorial and compositional work of Matthew or Luke is a feasible task.

As far as John is concerned, the prior question is whether the fourth evangelist knew or used any of the Synoptic Gospels. Are they to be presupposed in reading the Gospel of John? Correspondingly, did the evangelist write with one or more of them in view? Where John runs parallel to the other Gospels, comparisons with them are necessary and useful, as we have seen. There are obvious points of contact with them, whether mediated by direct, literary relationships or through common sources or oral tradition.

The passion narrative provides the longest and largest field for comparison, but offers no easy resolution. The general course of the narrative and the individual episodes are for the most part the same. Yet many of the differences are hard to explain as deliberate changes, assuming John knew the other Gospels. For example, John would then have omitted the account of the nocturnal trial before the Sanhedrin (Mark 14:55–65), although the condemnation of Jesus for blasphemy fits John's view of how the Jewish authorities regarded Jesus. On a smaller scale, John would not have reported the rending of the veil of the temple (Mark 15:38), although it seemingly supports John's view that Jesus displaces the temple (John 2:21; cf. 1:14). While John's account must be viewed in light of the Synoptics, it is difficult to understand as derivative from one or all of them.

Alternatively, John is often thought to have used other narrative sources, no longer extant. Indeed, in chapters 5 and 9 the Gospel's accounts seem to be based on earlier narratives, similar to the Synoptics, but not identical with them. In fact, the relationship of the Johannine and synoptic passion narratives may be explained in a similar way. Whatever his sources, John has obviously presented his narratives and materials in a distinctive form.

This observation leads to the question of the Fourth Gospel's *structure*. The fourth evangelist recounts Jesus' ministry, and although his version is quite different from the Synoptics it is recognizably the same story. After the prologue there follows an account of the Baptist and of the calling of Jesus' disciples. This in turn is followed by a narrative of Jesus' public ministry, at least part of which is in Galilee. Finally, Jesus enters Jerusalem to face his opponents and his ultimate fate. After having instructed his disciples and eaten a last meal with them, he is arrested, put on trial, and executed. The broad outline of the Gospel is thus similar to that of the Synoptics, especially the two-part structure of Mark.

Nevertheless, there are peculiarly Johannine features. Jesus' public ministry is even more sharply distinguished from his last days in Jerusalem than in the Synoptics. After the conclusion of the public ministry (chap. 12), Jesus has nothing more to do with the Jews or this world. To be sure, he goes to his death at their hands, but they are only agents of the divine plan, of which he seems to be fully aware. This sharp division in the structure of the Fourth Gospel corresponds to the Johannine dualism, in which the forces aligned with evil are drawn up against those aligned with Christ. Indeed, the division is reflected in the prologue's statements regarding the reception of Jesus' mission (1:10–12). As in the other Gospels, Jesus' crucifixion is a public event, but its real significance is only understood by the faithful, who now view it in the light of his glorification.

Of course, the time span, character, and locale of Jesus' public ministry differ markedly from the Synoptics, in which the setting is Galilee. In John, Jesus goes repeatedly to Jerusalem, and most of the action takes place there. He appears at Jewish festivals, including three Passovers. There he can be contrasted with the sources of revelation in the old Israel, and he engages the Jewish authorities in debate about himself and his role. Moreover, the patterns of his speech and action differ in ways we have already noted.

The *emphases* of the evangelist are mirrored in the structure of his Gospel. Jesus reveals himself, and God, to the world through signs and words (chaps. 2–12), after which he reveals himself fully to his disciples in a most intimate interchange in seclusion from that world (chaps. 13–17). The Fourth Gospel speaks frequently of Jesus' revealing his glory, which is not a personal quality, but Jesus' transparency to the will and work of God. Jesus glorifies God in that he lets God's glory shine through him by doing the work of God— that is, carrying out the mission that God has given him (John 5:36; 9:4; 17:4). God glorifies Jesus by revealing himself as God in and through his works. God's glory is already seen in Jesus' public ministry in a preliminary way. His miracles are signs of the glory. But finally and most importantly, the glory is seen in the crucifixion (12:23), which is the culmination and completion of the manifestation of the glory. According to John, the last word of Jesus is, "It is finished" (19:30). His work of glorifying God has been accomplished. The resurrection for John can then only be the divine *Yes* to what is already present in Jesus' life and death. Jesus performs preliminary signs indicating who he is, but in his self-giving death he becomes a model or symbol of God's self-giving love (13:34 f.; 15:12; cf. 1 John 4:9–12). That Jesus manifests God's glory precisely in his death epitomizes the paradox of the Incarnation, the Word's becoming flesh, i.e., really human.

Quite obviously John's emphasis falls heavily upon the questions of who Jesus is and what his appearance means, not only in the signs and passion narratives but in the words of Jesus himself. Only in the Fourth Gospel does Jesus talk at length about himself and his mission. For John it was imperative that this Christology be put on Jesus' own lips, for he maintains that the Christian affirmations about Jesus of Nazareth are inseparable from the historical figure. Moreover, such affirmations are the only adequate explanations of who he really was and is. John doubtless wrote to serve the needs of the church of his own day, but what he wrote was just as surely, in his own view, revealed truth.

John wrote not a church history, not a manual of discipline, not an apocalypse, not a treatise, but a Gospel narrative. Thus, with considerable literary skill and theological acumen he reminded his readers that faith is knowing Jesus and being sustained by the food and drink that he gives to those who hunger and thirst. It is walking by the light of Christ, and walking the way he walked (1 John 2:6). It is dependence on the source of life, the only true God and Jesus Christ whom he has sent. According to John, the fundamental question to which faith must answer is the question posed by Jesus Christ: who is he? The measure of John's importance is that he identified this question and out of his own conviction gave a decisive theological answer. He embraced and focused the emphases of earlier witnesses and tradition and helped determine the direction and shape of Christian thought for the centuries to come. It is not coincidental that Christians have tended to read the other Gospels, indeed the whole New Testament, in light of John's theologically freighted presentation.

"Crucifixion" by the German painter M. Grünewald (completed 1511), a panel of the Isenheim Altarpiece, represents the Johannine account of Jesus' death. The figures, other than Jesus, are Mary, the disciple John, Mary Magdalene, and John the Baptist. The latter repeats John 3:30; the letters INRI above the cross are the initial Latin letters of the inscription, "Jesus of Nazareth, King of the Jews." *(Courtesy of Marburg Art Reference Bureau.)*

Suggestions for Further Reading

Commentaries on John are quite numerous. The work of R. E. Brown, *The Gospel According to John,* 2 vols. (Garden City, NY: Doubleday, 1966, 1970), is still the standard commentary for the student who does not use Greek. (Inability to read Greek will inhibit the use of Rudolf Bultmann's famous commentary, as well as those of C. K. Barrett and Rudolf Schnackenburg.) B. Lindars, *The Gospel of John* (Grand Rapids, MI: Eerdmans, 1972), is quite a useful commentary of reasonable scope, as is R. Kysar, *John* (Minneapolis: Augsburg, 1986).

There are several noteworthy works on John by renowned scholars: C. H. Dodd, *Historical Tradition in the Fourth Gospel* (New York: Cambridge University Press, 1963); E. Käsemann, *The Testament of Jesus: A Study of the Gospel in the Light of Chapter 17,* trans. G. Krodel (Philadelphia: Fortress, 1968); O. Cullmann, *The Johannine*

Circle, trans. J. Bowden (Philadelphia: Westminster, 1976); M. Hengel, *The Johannine Question,* trans. J. Bowden (Philadelphia: Trinity Press International, 1989). J. L. Martyn, *History and Theology in the Fourth Gospel,* rev. ed. (Nashville: Abingdon, 1979), is extremely important for the historical setting and purpose of the Gospel, as is R. E. Brown, *The Community of the Beloved Disciple* (New York: Paulist Press, 1979). R. A. Culpepper, *Anatomy of the Fourth Gospel: A Study in Literary Design* (Philadelphia: Fortress, 1983), breaks fresh ground, applying the newer literary criticism to the Fourth Gospel. Similar interests are pursued in different ways by F. F. Segovia, *The Farewell of the Word: The Johannine Call to Abide* (Minneapolis: Fortress, 1991).

J. H. Neyrey, *An Ideology of Revolt: John's Christology in Social Science Perspective* (Philadelphia: Fortress, 1988), moves in another new direction methodologically. David Rensberger, *Johannine Faith and Liberating Community* (Philadelphia: Westminster, 1988), puts the insights of Martin, Brown, and Wayne Meeks into the service of an exegetically based liberation theology. A now older, source-critical method is pursued by R. T. Fortna, *The Fourth Gospel and Its Predecessors: From Narrative Source to Present Gospel* (Philadelphia: Fortress, 1988). J. Ashton, *Understanding the Fourth Gospel* (Oxford: Clarendon, 1991), utilizes the insights of Martyn and others in offering a comprehensive interpretation of the Gospel, as does J. Painter, *The Quest of the Messiah: The History, Literature, and Theology of the Johannine Community,* 2nd ed. (Nashville: Abingdon, 1993). M. M. Thompson, *The Humanity of Jesus in the Fourth Gospel* (Philadelphia: Fortress, 1988), raises a centrally important theological issue.

D. M. Smith, *Johannine Christianity: Essays on Its Setting, Sources, and Theology* (Columbia, SC: University of South Carolina, 1984), is representative of scholarly interests up to about 1980. The same author's *John Among the Gospels: The Relationship in Twentieth-Century Research* (Minneapolis: Fortress, 1992), charts the course of the discussion of this modern, and very ancient, problem. G. S. Sloyan, *What Are They Saying About John?* (New York: Paulist, 1991), admirably reports on the most important recent research on the Fourth Gospel. See the end of Chapter 11 for bibliography on the Epistles of John and Revelation.

Chapter 6

Jesus the Messiah

Introduction: The Tradition About Jesus

To write a life of Jesus is impossible, for we cannot reconstruct the course of Jesus' ministry in any detail or understand his psychological development. Moreover, we have no specific information about his appearance, home, environment, or education. The nature of the Gospel sources does not permit this kind of historical endeavor. Sources for the historical Jesus outside the Gospels, both canonical and extracanonical, are meager.

We learn little about Jesus from contemporary secular and Jewish sources. Perhaps the most important attestation of Christianity, and therefore of Jesus, in Roman historical writings is found in the *Annals* of Tacitus (early second century), who reports the false accusation by Nero that Christians were responsible for the disastrous fire in Rome (A.D. 64). The first-century Jewish historian Josephus recounted Jewish history during the period of Jesus' life, and although he described the Essenes and John the Baptist in some detail, he barely mentioned Jesus. When the likely Christian embellishments of his writings are discounted, it is certain only that Josephus refers to "James, the brother of Jesus who was called the Christ" (*Jewish Antiquities,* XX, 200).[1] Polemical references in the Jewish Talmud contain little independent tradition about Jesus.[2] Although no early non-Christian source questions the historical existence of Jesus, at the same time the literature takes little notice of him.

The apocryphal Gospels appear at first glance to provide extensive sources for the historical Jesus.[3] These Gospels, which did not become part of the Christian New Testament canon, can be divided into three basic types: (1) Later, popular Gospels that contain imaginative stories about Jesus, including his hidden childhood. (Much of this material, like the Infancy Gospel of Thomas, served to satisfy pious curiosity and probably even to entertain the faithful.) (2) Gnostic Gospels, like the Gospel of Philip and the Nag Hammadi Gospel of Thomas, which present a secret teaching of Jesus that elaborates a way of salvation higher than that given in the common Gospel tradition (The Gospel of Thomas does contain a number of sayings of Jesus that are probably authentic, but many are found also in the canonical Gospels in somewhat different form.) (3) A few Gospels such as the Gospel of the Hebrews and the Gospel of Peter, which are possibly early or embody early traditions, but are known only through surviving fragments (Peter) or brief quotations in other sources (Hebrews). Although the apocryphal Gospels

1. For a listing and discussion of these references, see Maurice Goguel, *Jesus and the Origins of Christianity,* I, trans. Olive Wyon (New York: Harper & Row, 1960), pp. 70–104, and Joseph Klausner, *Jesus of Nazareth,* trans. Herbert Danby (New York: Macmillan, 1926), pp. 17–62. Note also Morris Goldstein, *Jesus in the Jewish Tradition* (New York: Macmillan, 1950). Samuel Sandmel, *Judaism and Christian Beginnings* (New York: Oxford University Press, 1978), p. 397, has summed up the situation aptly: "Accordingly, though Jesus was a Jew, there are no Jewish sources of any value about him."
2. There is an earlier, fuller reference to Jesus in the *Antiquities* (XVIII, 63–64) that is at least in part the product of Christian editing, for it has Josephus affirm that Jesus was the Christ and that he rose from the dead.
3. For appreciative treatments of the apocryphal Gospels, see Helmut Koester, *Ancient Christian Gospels: Their History and Development* (Philadelphia: Trinity Press International, 1990), and John Dominic Crossan, *Four Other Gospels: Shadows on the Contours of the Canon* (Minneapolis: Seabury/Winston, 1985).

seem to offer much additional teaching and narrative material, with the exception of the Gospel of Thomas they are of little help in reconstructing the historical Jesus.[4]

Other sources for the historical Jesus are sayings attributed to him and preserved outside the Gospels (canonical or apocryphal)—for example, the word of Jesus handed down by Acts, "It is more blessed to give than to receive" (20:35).[5] Although some of these sayings may be authentic, they are relatively few and do not greatly affect understanding of him.

In fact, little tradition about Jesus is found in the literature of the New Testament apart from the Gospels. On several occasions Paul refers to the tradition of the Lord that he had received (1 Cor. 11:23–26; 15:3 f.; cf. 7:10, 12, 25). Probably Paul knew more Jesus tradition than at first appears.[6] Nevertheless, the rarity of Paul's citation of Jesus' words or deeds proves the rule: little tradition of Jesus can be identified with certainty in the latter half of the New Testament.

Thus the principal sources for knowing the historical Jesus are the canonical Gospels, but they do not include the information necessary for what we think of as a biography. In previous chapters we have learned that the Gospels are dominated by their religious and theological perspectives, and serve chronological, psychological, or factual interests in limited ways, if at all. With the exception of the infancy narratives of Matthew and Luke, which differ widely, they tell us nothing of Jesus' life before the beginning of his brief ministry. Yet these Gospels proclaim the good news in the form of the story of Jesus.

Among the canonical Gospels, the Gospel of John, of course, stands out as obviously different. Not only does it recount a two- or three-year ministry, as against only one year or less in the Synoptics, but—as we have seen—its portrayal of Jesus is unique. The Johannine Jesus speaks mostly of himself, whether addressing disciples or others, and his themes are Christological; that is, he discusses his dignity and role as Messiah and Son of God. This portrayal of Jesus is undoubtedly more the product of early Christian faith and reflection than of history or historical tradition. With the exception of the

---

4. For texts and discussions of apocryphal Gospels, see E. Hennecke, *New Testament Apocrypha,* I, ed. W. Schneemelcher and trans. R. McL. Wilson, rev. ed. (Philadelphia: Westminster/John Knox, 1991). For a complete translation of the Nag Hammadi corpus, including Gnostic Gospels and many other writings, see James M. Robinson (ed.), *The Nag Hammadi Library in English,* 3rd rev. ed. (San Francisco: Harper & Row, 1988). David R. Cartlidge and David L. Dungan, *Documents for the Study of the Gospels* (Philadelphia: Fortress, 1980), provide a valuable collection of material from the apocryphal Gospels and other writings relevant to an understanding of the New Testament Gospels.
5. See Joachim Jeremias, *The Unknown Sayings of Jesus,* trans. R. H. Fuller (London: SPCK, 1957).
6. On Paul's knowledge and use of such tradition, see Dale C. Allison, Jr., "The Pauline Epistles and the Synoptic Gospels: The Pattern of the Parallels," *New Testament Studies* 28 (1982), 1–32.

"The Alba Madonna" by Raphael (1483–1520).   *(Courtesy of National Gallery of Art, Washington, D.C. Andrew W. Mellon Collection.)*

passion narrative, most of the content of John is not paralleled in the other Gospels and vice versa (see pp. 163–166).

Nevertheless, the Gospel of John may provide us with some data that are historically correct, even where it contradicts the Synoptics. (For example, Jesus probably visited Jerusalem more than once in his career.) Of course, among the Synoptics, Matthew and Luke appear to rely upon Mark for the framework, outline, or order of Jesus' ministry. Where they depart from Mark in this respect, they differ also from each other. They are not therefore independent sources for the course of Jesus' ministry. It is a measure of John's independence of the others that its framework differs widely from that of Mark.

In this chapter we attempt to reconstruct a single portrait of Jesus of Nazareth that emerges out of the Gospel portraits. Our justification for this procedure lies not only in contemporary historical interest in Jesus but also in the fact that the four Gospel portraits stand at the beginning of the New

Testament. In ancient Gospel manuscripts there is one general heading, "The Gospel," followed by "According to Matthew," etc. Although their portraits are obviously different, the Gospels invite an encounter once again with the same Jesus of Nazareth, a distinct and real historical figure. Although there are four Gospels, the New Testament suggests that there is but one gospel message and one Jesus.

KERYGMA, GOSPELS, AND JESUS OF NAZARETH

New Testament Christianity was founded upon belief in the resurrection of the crucified Jesus; his apparently ignominious death was seen as the decisive act of God for the salvation of humankind (1 Cor. 15:3). This faith was at first held in anticipation of his imminent return in glory to judge and to rule. From the beginning Christians felt impelled to announce to others the good news (gospel) of what God had done in Jesus. This proclamation or *kērygma* (see the Glossary) was based upon what God had done through Jesus rather than on what Jesus himself had done. Its power did not rest in new knowledge or wisdom but rather in an event—the death and resurrection of Jesus.

That event is the seed from which the Gospels ultimately grew. The Gospels presuppose, and to a remarkable extent are based upon, early Christian faith and preaching. The words with which the Fourth Gospel closes are also applicable to the others: "These [things] are written so that you may come to believe that Jesus is the Messiah, the Son of God, and that through believing you may have life in his name" (John 20:31). This also was the purpose of the proclamation of the gospel generally. Even the traditions of Jesus that came to the Gospel writers from oral tradition and written sources were already, down to individual units, shaped by the interests of the church. (This is the lasting contribution of form criticism; see pp. 64–65 above.) In fact, early Christians remembered the tradition of Jesus only because they were convinced that God had acted for them in this man, especially in his death and resurrection.

In studying the Gospels, it is important to keep in mind the history of Christian faith and experience that they presuppose. In earlier generations Christian readers have more or less shared this faith. They have thus read the Gospels with the proper major premise in view. Yet preconceptions and prejudices have often distorted such reading. Whether or not modern readers share the faith of those early Christians, they are in a position to understand what it was and how it influenced the telling of the story. One must bear in mind also that the Gospels in their present form are not, for the most part, the product of the earliest witnesses, but that they appeared only as, or after, these witnesses passed from the scene (John 21:20–24; Luke 1:2). They are the legacy of those primal witnesses as it was bequeathed to the church.

THE BASIC TRADITION OF JESUS

Unless one is determined to regard everything in the Gospels as historical (and that can be accomplished only by dogmatic desire, not by critical judgment), some means for identifying the materials that stem from Jesus himself must be established. Several criteria or guidelines will prove useful.

1 . The oldest material will usually be found in the *cores* of stories, parables, or sayings proper, as distinguished from introductions, endings, and transitions, which are often the work of later editors or authors. (This criterion will prove more useful in the Synoptics than in John, where narrative and discourse are often more smoothly woven together.) For example, in Mark 4 the introduction (vss. 1–2) is likely editorial. The general statement about parables (vss. 10–12) together with the interpretation (vss. 13–20) is probably a later development of the tradition. The one explains the mystery of unbelief, the other interprets the parable so that it explains the success or failure of the church's later preaching of the gospel. The parable itself (vss. 3–9), however, is in all probability the kernel that originates from Jesus. (This parable, without the introduction or the following interpretation, is found in the Gospel of Thomas, 9.)

2 . An important criterion is *cultural, religious, and linguistic appropriateness* or intelligibility. In other words, is what is attributed to Jesus intelligible in a first-century Palestinian Jewish environment in which Aramaic was the commonly spoken language? In general, Jesus' debates about the meaning of the law are intelligible in that context. Also the term *Son of Man*, apparently Jesus' favorite self-designation, is a known idiom in Aramaic (or Hebrew), but not in Greek. Likewise, *kingdom of God,* an important theme of Jesus' preaching, is a biblical concept. On the other hand, the saying of Jesus in the Gospel of Thomas (37) encouraging nudity can scarcely be ascribed to the historical Jesus, for it flies in the face of Jewish custom and does not cohere with his other teaching (see 5 below). Moreover, any quotation of scripture that follows the Septuagint (Greek translation) too closely becomes at least suspect (cf. Matt. 13:14–15), since Jesus would have cited the targums (Aramaic translation), if not the original Hebrew.

3 . The criterion of *dissimilarity* accords a high probability of authenticity to sayings of Jesus or similar materials that are not likely to have been derived from contemporary Judaism and that are not easily ascribed to the early church—although something unheard of or unthinkable in a Jewish milieu would hardly be authentic. Again, the terms *kingdom of God* and *Son of Man* are easily ascribed to the historical Jesus as authentic. Although both can be found in the Judaism of the first century or earlier, neither occupies as important a place as it does in the teachings of Jesus. At the same time, neither term has anything like the importance in the teaching of the early church (as attested in New Testament writings outside the Gospels) that it has in the

Gospels and especially in the sayings of Jesus. This criterion is useful if used with care and discrimination.

4. The criterion of *multiple attestation* means the occurrence of sayings, concepts, narratives, or other materials in more than one stream of tradition (as distinguished from where Matthew or Luke is simply following Mark). Again, *Son of Man* and *kingdom of God* appear not only in all the Gospels but also in their underlying sources, that is, in Mark (used by Matthew and Luke), Q (used by Matthew and Luke), M (distinctively Matthean material), L (distinctively Lukan material), as well as the relatively independent Gospel of John and even the Gospel of Thomas (86). Something similar could be said of Jesus' miracles, his teaching about obedience to God, and his crucifixion: they also appear in the different streams of tradition. Even though the specific healing miracles of John are found in none of the other Gospels, they too strongly attest the fact that Jesus was known as a healer.

5. Any reconstruction of Jesus' career or of his teaching must finally, and most importantly, take account of the principle of *coherence*. It is important that any given saying or fact about Jesus should cohere with an emerging picture of him. For example, the portrayal of Jesus as one accused of breaking the Sabbath coheres with the instances in which on other grounds he clashes with the authority of scribes, tradition, or even scripture. Thus, we seek to portray with even greater detail the one coherent, historical figure who stimulated the varied tradition.

The birth narratives are not really exceptions to the rule that we know very few personal details of Jesus' life. They are not intended to answer such human interests, but rather to convey certain important theological ideas.[7] Basically, they show that Jesus' coming is the result of God's purpose rather than human intention. According to both Matthew and Luke, Jesus was conceived of the Holy Spirit, born of the Virgin Mary, and yet descended from David through Joseph. In neither Matthew nor Luke is there any hint or indication that knowledge of this miraculous birth played a role in Jesus' ministry. Nor is it mentioned elsewhere in the New Testament.

We possess in considerable quantity traditional materials, basic to the Synoptic Gospels, that have to do with the *miracles* of Jesus, his *teaching,* and his *death*. The existence of these three separate strands of the fundamental tradition raises the question of their interrelationship. A coherent picture of Jesus must somehow show how the three major tradition areas unite in one historical figure. How, for example, does the powerful Jesus who performs miracles relate to the Jesus who is powerless to prevent his own death? This particular problem is already seen and dealt with by the authors of the Gospels.

---

7. Cf. Raymond E. Brown, *The Birth of the Messiah: A Commentary on the Infancy Narratives in Matthew and Luke,* rev. ed. (New York: Doubleday, 1993), p. 8: "It is the central contention of this volume that the infancy narratives are worthy vehicles of the Gospel message; indeed, each is the essential Gospel story in miniature."

The basic tradition of Jesus includes not only facts but meaning. The early Christians did not feel free to read any meaning into Jesus. They saw his deeds, words, and death in the light of the commonly held conviction that he was the Messiah. Therefore, in our presentation we speak of the healing Messiah, the teaching Messiah, and the suffering Messiah. All the Gospels unanimously and unequivocally see all three main aspects of Jesus' mission and message as messianic, and our reconstruction takes this viewpoint into account. The reconstruction of such a portrait does not, however, prove that Jesus claimed to be the Messiah (much less that Jesus *was* the Messiah); it only makes this messianic claim comprehensible in terms of tradition.

In an important sense this claim or belief that Jesus is the Messiah represents the conviction that he is the Christian Messiah. That is, Jesus himself, his fate, and belief in and about him, colored decisively the conception of messiahship held by Christians and attributed to Jesus. At the same time, early Christians never ceased believing that he was also the Messiah of Jewish and biblical expectation, and in this conviction they constantly appealed to scripture to prove their point.

In this chapter we must depend upon the portraits of Jesus that appear in the Gospels. In the belief of the church that produced the New Testament, they complement rather than contradict one another: each evangelist looked at the same Jesus from a different perspective. They were concerned less about exactness in detail than about being true to their basic conceptions of Jesus. Something of the same freedom and loyalty should accompany our study of the tradition of Jesus.

The Healing Messiah

The reader of the Gospels quickly learns that Jesus was a miracle worker. This impression is particularly strong in Mark, where miracle working seems to be his chief activity prior to the final week in Jerusalem, and in John, where the stupendous character of the miracles and their faith- (or opposition-) evoking quality are evident. Yet when one reads some of the apocryphal Gospels (e.g., the Gospel of Peter or the Infancy Gospel of Thomas), one is struck by the relative restraint of the canonical narratives.

Whatever one thinks of the possibility of miracles in the modern world, the tradition of Jesus as miracle worker is in all probability rooted in his own activity (see Acts 2:22; 10:38). Moreover, there were circles within early Christianity in which the working of miracles was held in very high esteem (1 Cor. 12:29; 2 Cor. 12:12).

In all likelihood individual miracle stories of the Gospels, most of which are self-contained units, were collected or grouped together before their incorporation into our canonical Gospels. By this means Jesus could have been presented as a man endowed by God with special powers, a type familiar to the Hellenistic world and not unprecedented in Judaism. This presentation of Jesus implies not only an interest in miracles but a correspondence between his activity and that of his followers. That is, there were miracle working and miracle workers in the church (see, e.g., Acts 3:1–16; 1 Cor. 12:10, 28). Yet such a presentation, although it had some popular acceptance, could not and did not survive in independent form, for it lacked any distinctively Christian element and substituted wonder for faith. Moreover, taken alone it did not deal with the central scandal of Jesus' life, the fact of his crucifixion, which was well known among Gentiles and Jews. Nevertheless, the presentation of Jesus as miracle worker had some historical, factual basis and did attest the Christian conviction that God was at work in him. Interestingly enough, although Paul does not speak of Jesus' own miracles, he does mention those attributed to apostles and others as well as his own (1 Cor. 12:9 f.; 2 Cor. 12:12).

Although understanding the relation of Jesus to early Christianity remains the central problem of Christian origins, the reality of that relation is hardly a matter of doubt. Early Christianity stemmed from Jesus. Its literature reflects a constant harking back to him as the basis of its faith. The preservation of so many miracle stories testifies to this fact. At the same time Christianity quickly became a religion about Jesus rather than a movement of which Jesus was personally the leader and founder. The gospel of Jesus was preached to Jews and then to Gentiles with a view to gaining their allegiance to Jesus or, more properly, eliciting their faith in Jesus as Lord, Christ, or Son of God. Probably the miracle stories were preserved in such numbers because they called attention to the extraordinary nature of Jesus and could be used to commend him as a person of divine origin and mission.

The most characteristic miracles in the Synoptics are Jesus' healings, especially the exorcism of demons (noticeable for their absence in John), which Mark emphasizes. Miracle stories comprise a large part of each of the Gospels. Nearly one-third of the Gospel of Mark is devoted to them. Matthew and Luke report practically all the Markan miracles and add several more; the Gospel of John contains yet other miracles (signs). In Peter's first speech to the Gentiles, no mention is made of Jesus' teaching, but the good news includes "how God anointed Jesus of Nazareth with the Holy Spirit and with power; how he went about doing good and healing all that were oppressed by the devil" (Acts 10:38). Even the Talmud (see the Glossary) acknowledges that Jesus healed, but dismisses his work as that of a sorcerer.[8] Clearly demon exorcism and healing were among Jesus' principal activities.

Yet there has always been a certain ambiguity about miracles. When after many healings the crowds gathered around Jesus, his family "went out to restrain him, for people were saying, 'He has gone out of his mind.' And the scribes who came down from Jerusalem said, 'He has Beelzebub, and by the

---

8. See Klausner, *Jesus of Nazareth,* pp. 27 f. In the most famous talmudic statement about Jesus (Babylonian Talmud, Sanhedrin 43a), he is said to have been hanged for sorcery and leading Israel astray. Klausner comments that the authorities of the Talmud "do not deny that Jesus worked signs and wonders, but they look upon them as acts of sorcery."

ruler of the demons he casts out demons'" (Mark 3:21 f.). Thus healing miracles could be the work of God or the devil; they do not prove messiahship. Indeed, according to one major New Testament emphasis, Jesus' power is not in mighty works, but in his crucifixion and death. Christ crucified is "to those who are called, both Jews and Greeks . . . the *power* of God and the wisdom of God" (1 Cor. 1:24). Moreover, to desire miracles as proof of Jesus' messiahship would be to seek after signs (cf. 1 Cor. 1:22). When the Pharisees come to Jesus asking for a sign, he replies, "An evil and adulterous generation asks for a sign; but no sign will be given to it except the sign of the prophet Jonah" (Matt. 12:39; see Mark 8:12). Despite such reservations about signs in the Synoptics and Paul, miracles do function as signs of who Jesus is in the Gospel of John. This is only one of the many differences between the Fourth Gospel and the others. In all probability the Synoptics are closer to Jesus' own view, whereas in John later controversy about Jesus' identity has led to the use of the miracle tradition in a different way.

Before looking more closely at miracles in the Gospels, we need to understand the first century's view of miracles so that the miracle tradition is set within its environment. This, in turn, will set the stage for our final section when we look at miracles from a modern perspective.

MIRACLES IN THE FIRST CENTURY

Why were miracles more common in the ancient world than they are today?

In the first century, indeed in the New Testament itself, Jesus is not the only miracle worker. For example, in the Acts of the Apostles Simon the Magician is said to have done great wonders and to have amazed people by his magic. Moreover, he tried to buy the Spirit from the apostles and was refused because according to Peter the gift of God could not be obtained with money (Acts 8:9–24). Simon desired the Spirit because the disciples performed signs and great miracles (Acts 5:12). The apostle Paul himself performed wonders (2 Cor. 12:12). Even some rabbis, who were known primarily as teachers, performed miracles. Onias, the Circlemaker, a rabbi in the first century B.C., is reported to have made it rain for Israel neither too fiercely nor too gently, but in moderation.[9] A famous miracle worker in Hellenistic literature was Apollonius of Tyana, a Pythagorean philosopher who lived during the first Christian century.[10] He is reported to have miraculously exorcised a demon from a young man who later became a philosopher and a miracle worker himself. Of course, in the Bible itself (i.e., the Old Testament) healings and

---

9. C. K. Barrett, *The New Testament Background: Selected Documents* (San Francisco: Harper & Row, 1989), pp. 191–192.

10. Ibid., pp. 82–85. See Cartlidge and Dungan, *Documents for the Study of the Gospels,* pp. 205–242, where extensive portions of Philostratus' *Life of Apollonios of Tyana* are reproduced.

other miracles are reported. Especially significant are those of Elijah (e.g., 1 Kings 17:17–24) and Elisha (2 Kings 4:18–37), which are not unlike those of Jesus.

Within this context the miracles of Jesus are not quite so unusual. In fact, some early Christians felt constrained to enlarge the miracle activity of Jesus beyond what is reported in the Gospels. Consequently, in the apocryphal Gospels bigger and better miracles are attributed to Jesus. According to the Infancy Gospel of Thomas, Jesus fetches water for his mother with a garment instead of a pitcher. When the carpenter Joseph discovers that one of the boards for a bed is too short, his son Jesus corrects the situation by stretching the board to the proper length. In the same Gospel, Jesus makes twelve clay birds that become real birds after he claps his hands. When a young boy disturbs a pool of water in which Jesus is playing, Jesus withers him as if he were a tree.[11] Under the influence of popular piety Jesus became a real magician. Probably miracle stories served both to entertain the pious and to support their belief that Jesus was the Christ, the Son of God.

It is understandable, therefore, that Jesus should have been portrayed as a miracle worker in the Gospels, especially in view of the fact he had been known as a healer during his lifetime. Very likely his healings and exorcisms first attracted attention to him. The tendency to enlarge upon the miracles of Jesus, which we observe in the apocryphal Gospels, may have already been at work in the earliest tradition. Whether the Gospels have furthered or checked this tendency is a good question. John obviously highlights Jesus' miracle-working power. Matthew, on the other hand, reduces the dimensions of the miraculous by abbreviating Mark's miracle stories.

MIRACLES IN THE SYNOPTIC GOSPELS

Must the miracles reported in the Gospels be accepted or rejected as a group?

Miracle in modern usage is an occurrence contrary to known scientific laws. Because the evangelists wrote at a time in which there was no commonly accepted concept of "known scientific laws," they understood miracles as powers, wonders, mighty works, signs. These strange, remarkable happenings caused people to be amazed and terrified, and to wonder whether these occurrences were manifestations of the power of God (the good) or of Satan (the evil). Remembering this background, we may nevertheless, for convenience's sake, speak about miracles in the Gospels, for the term corresponds roughly to the reported events.

To understand miracles in Jesus' ministry, we must first take account of the view of the world and history in which they are set, then attempt to classify the miracles according to type, and finally explore the relation of mira-

---

11. See Hennecke, *New Testament Apocrypha,* I, 444–449.

cles to faith. We deal primarily with the Synoptics rather than with John, because in all probability they are closer to Jesus' own position in their estimate of miracles.

THE ESCHATOLOGICAL CONTEXT

The proclamation of the kingdom of God was central to the preaching and teaching of Jesus (cf. Mark 1:14). Jesus himself appears to have linked his mighty works to the appearance of the kingdom: "But if it is by the finger of God that I cast out the demons, then the kingdom of God has come to you" (Luke 11:20; cf. Matt. 12:28). His work is at the same time a manifestation of his having overcome the powers of Satan, i.e., evil: "When a strong man, fully armed, guards his castle, his property is safe. But when one stronger than he attacks him and overpowers him, he takes away his armor in which he trusted, and divides his plunder" (Luke 11:21–22; cf. Mark 3:27). When Jesus is asked on behalf of John the Baptist whether he is the coming one, that is, the Messiah or charismatic leader who would inaugurate the rule of God, he responds: "Go and tell John what you have seen and heard: the blind receive their sight, the lame walk, lepers are cleansed, the deaf hear, the dead are raised, the poor have good news brought to them" (Luke 7:22; cf. Matt 11:4–5). He instructs his disciples that in healing the sick they should say to them, "The kingdom of God has come near to you" (Luke 10:9). In Jesus' own view, then, his miracles are signs of the breaking in of the eschatological kingdom.

The breaking in of the kingdom of God in the miracle activity of Jesus is not, however, the kingdom's final realization. The miracles signify an inaugurated kingdom, not a completed one. This setting of Jesus' miracles within the context of such an "inaugurated eschatology" means that the miracles point to the working of God rather than to the status of Jesus. God's kingdom, not the rule of Jesus, is inaugurated. Moreover, from the standpoint of Jesus' opponents these miracles or wonders are ambiguous and could be viewed as the work of Satan as well as of God. Jesus refuses to use the miracles as signs to validate himself (Mark 8:11 f.; Matt. 12:39). Similarly, the temptation stories show Jesus declining to elicit support by the performance of miracles or spectacular feats (Matt. 4:1–11; Luke 4:1–13). The healings bear witness to the kingdom's appearance; this extraordinary presence of God is consistently and continually proclaimed in Jesus' message.

TYPES OF MIRACLES

Now that we have discerned the framework of the proclamation of the kingdom in which the miracles occur, we turn for a closer look at the actual miracle stories themselves. The Synoptic Gospels contain basically four types: exorcisms, healings, resuscitations, and nature miracles. All except exorcism are found also in John. The first three have to do with human subjects; the fourth involves inanimate matter. Generally speaking, the exorcisms pertain to what we would call mental disorders and the healings to physical diseases; for our purposes they both can be treated under one heading—healings.

In the Gospel of Mark *exorcisms* (1:21–28; cf. 32–34) and *healings* (1:29–31, 40–45; cf. 32–34) are narrated in rapid succession; it becomes clear that these acts are closely related and that both belong to the essence of Jesus' saving, or healing, work. In the exorcism of the demon at the synagogue of Capernaum and the cleansing of the leper, similar elements characterize each narrative. There is a forceful approach to Jesus (vss. 23–24; cf. vs. 40); Jesus responds vigorously or compassionately (vs. 25; cf. vss. 41, 43); the evil spirit or force departs (vs. 26; cf. vs. 42). Although in the one case there is an immediate crowd reaction (vs. 27) and in the other none is reported, in both stories Jesus' fame is said to spread throughout the area (vss. 28, 45). In both Jesus is portrayed as responding immediately to a dire situation or need, albeit one that has presumably existed for some time prior to the encounter with him. In both Jesus acts, and speaks, decisively so as to overcome the evil spirit or disease.

Even though Jesus in both stories acts as an authoritative, charismatic figure, in neither case does the question of his messiahship arise. Whether the command to silence (vs. 44; cf. vss. 25, 34) originates with Mark or Jesus himself, its effect is to subordinate the role of Jesus' healing to his primary proclamation of the nearness of the kingdom of God. As best we can tell, this order of priorities goes back to Jesus himself.

The question of whether the miracle described in Mark 1:40–45 actually happened should be considered in light of the fact that the "leprosy" spoken of need not have been the incurable disease called by that name today. Moreover, in antiquity similar miracles have been attributed to others.[12] Nevertheless, such considerations are not decisive in determining what may have occurred. There is an overall impression of authenticity that stems from the fact that the miracle is narrated with restraint and does not call attention to itself. It is pointless to offer scientific or psychological explanations of what happened; although these cannot be ruled out in principle, they are purely speculation in light of the silence of the text about most matters of detail.

An example of *resuscitations* is the story of the raising of Jairus' daughter (Mark 5:21–43; cf. Matt. 9:18–26 and Luke 8:40–56).[13] It is strangely interrupted by an account of the healing of the woman with the hemorrhage (Mark 5:25–34 parr.). Yet this break in the story of the resuscitation is not accidental, for the interlude illustrates the power of believing (cf. 5:36). The woman, who is ritually unclean (Lev. 15:25), approaches Jesus from behind. Strikingly, the healing of the woman with the hemorrhage occurs without Jesus' being aware of her presence. Consequently, Jesus did not intend the miracle (see 5:28–30). If the miracle happens without Jesus' intent, then in a

---

12. See R. Bultmann, *History of the Synoptic Tradition,* trans. J. Marsh (New York: Harper & Row, 1968), pp. 218–244. Also F. W. Beare, *The Earliest Records of Jesus* (Nashville: Abingdon, 1972), pp. 72–74.

13. Only two other resuscitations are reported by the Gospels: the raising of the widow of Nain's son (Luke 7:11–17) and of Lazarus (John 11:1–44). For parallels, see Bultmann, *History of the Synoptic Tradition,* pp. 233 f.

sense the miracle happened to Jesus as well as to the woman. This healing of the woman makes the implicit point that belief in Jesus is actually faith in the power that works through Jesus rather than in Jesus himself (5:30, 34).

The role of belief or faith is then taken up in the raising of Jairus' daughter (5:36). Jesus' raising of the dead girl may rest upon an actual incident in which he aroused a girl who was in a coma (cf. vss. 35 f., 39), although it is now impossible to be certain. As it stands, however, it raises the question of whether belief in God goes so far as to affirm the victory of Jesus over death. Thus the story of Jesus' raising of Jairus' daughter possibly uses an actual incident of healing to affirm a central matter of faith, God's power to raise the dead. Such faith becomes the center of attention in the Fourth Gospel. There Jesus first claims the God-given power to raise the dead (5:25–29), then most dramatically exercises that power as he restores Lazarus to life, calling him forth from the grave (11:43).

Two examples of *nature miracles* are the feeding of the five thousand (Mark 6:30–44; cf. Matt. 14:13–21; Luke 9:10–17 and John 6:1–14) and the stilling of the storm (Mark 4:35–41; cf. Matt. 8:18–27 and Luke 8:22–25). In the Gospels' accounts of the feeding of the five thousand, the evangelists have exercised freedom in detail regarding the occasion of the miracle. They agree, however, that Jesus is surrounded by hungry throngs at a place where food is not accessible. We cannot isolate an earlier, nonmiraculous version of the story; the central point is that of a miraculous feeding, possibly with

The Jordan River flowing into the Sea of Galilee, from the north.   *(Courtesy of Israel Government Tourist Office.)*

eucharistic overtones. It is beside the point to explain this story as some kind of picnic in which Jesus and his disciples encouraged the people to generosity. Jesus may have taken part in such meals with the disciples and a large multitude. Yet the question of whether such an incredible miracle took place remains still unanswered. The form of this story clearly reflects the eucharistic practice of the early church (see Mark 6:41). Therefore, the miracle may be a postresurrection story, based upon the Christians' experience in the Lord's Supper that the living Christ feeds the hungry multitudes (cf. John 21:9–14; Luke 24:28–35). Such a conjecture is supported by the fact that this nature miracle concentrates more upon the person and action of Jesus than do most other miracle stories. This kind of emphasis on Jesus may reflect a concern of the early church more than the attitude of the historical Jesus and is characteristic of the Fourth Gospel (see 6:15 ff.). But again, the compassion upon the multitudes is what we would expect of Jesus of Nazareth. The essence of the story agrees with our evolving picture of the historical Jesus. The form, however, reflects the interests of the early church. In this case, as in others, one can well imagine that some actual event has been elaborated in a miraculous mode, but we can scarcely get beyond conjecture. It is worth noting, moreover, that a similar amazing feeding was attributed to the prophet Elisha (2 Kings 4:42–44). Conceivably, the biblical story has been transferred to Jesus, although the details differ. More likely, the telling of the Jesus story has been influenced by the Elisha account (cf. the barley loaves in 2 Kings 4:42 and John 6:9).

The stilling of the storm on the Sea of Galilee also belongs in the category of nature miracles (Mark 4:35–41 parr.). Its present form may obscure an earlier story about the exorcism of a storm demon. Jesus silences the storm as he silenced the demon (4:39; cf. 1:25). As it now reads, however, it demonstrates Jesus' authority over nature and challenges the disciples' lack of faith (4:40 f.). Moreover, this action by Jesus seems to embody that salvation ascribed to God in the Old Testament: "You silence the roaring of the seas, the roaring of their waves, the tumult of the peoples" (Psalm 65:7; cf. 89:9). The entire miracle story makes Jesus the object of religious awe. Probably we have here a Christological confession, occasioned not so much by a single incident out of Jesus' life as by the total impact of Jesus, particularly his death and resurrection. Again this conclusion does not mean that no actual historical event lies at the root of this story. Doubtless Jesus was frequently in a boat on the Sea of Galilee with his disciples. But again any specific event that may have formed the basis of this story is no longer accessible to us.

MIRACLES AND FAITH

A consistent theme of all three types of miracle story is the response of faith. But what is the relation between faith and miracles? In many instances faith seems to be the triggering mechanism that produces miracles. God is always ready to perform miracles; consequently, if a person has faith, miracles occur. Support from the Gospels for this understanding is found especially in such statements as, "And he [Jesus] could do no deed of power there, except that he laid his hands on a few sick people and cured them. And he was amazed at their unbelief" (Mark 6:5 f.; cf. Matt. 13:58). Furthermore, Jesus replies to the woman with the hemorrhage, "Daughter, your faith has made you well; go in peace and be healed of your disease" (Mark 5:34 parr.). The disciples' astonishment at the withered fig tree prompts Jesus to say, "Have faith in God. Truly I tell you, if you say to this mountain, 'Be taken up and thrown into the sea,' and if you do not doubt in your heart, but believe that what you say will come to pass, it will be done for you" (Mark 11:22 f. and Matt. 21:21; cf. 1 Cor. 13:2). In John, of course, it is the other way around. Miracles as signs lead to faith, although they sometimes meet resistance (John 9; cf. 2:23–25). But traces of the other view of the relation of miracles and faith appear even there (4:48–50; 5:6; cf. 14:13 f.).

Yet before we conclude that according to Jesus faith produces miracles or whatever the believer wishes, we should remember that in the Gospels even Jesus did not have his own way. The temptation stories set the tempo for Jesus' entire life in that he refuses to assert his own power. Moreover, in Gethsemane Jesus prays, "Abba, Father, for you all things are possible; remove this cup from me; yet not what I want, but what you want" (Mark 14:36 parr.). Because the cup was not removed, we can only conclude that faith is not presented as an automatic device for accomplishing the will of Jesus or of the believer. Faith's ultimate object is God and his will. In the Gospels, faith means that one trusts, accepts, and responds affirmatively to the coming of God. If in some instances faith appears as the condition for a miracle, or vice versa, the reader ought not to conclude that this represents the fundamental understanding of faith in the Gospels or in the ministry of Jesus. The faith that Jesus demands is belief in the good news of his announcement of the coming of God and the kingdom. Everything else depends on such faith (Mark 1:15; 8:34–38; Matt. 12:28; and so on). After his departure from them, the believers' faith was directed to Jesus himself, or to what God was accomplishing through him.

Undoubtedly Jesus did perform miracles: demons were cast out, the sick were healed, the people were amazed at his actions (see Mark 1:27; 2:12; 9:15). Yet these extraordinary acts were ambiguous and did not prove that Jesus was the Messiah. Some people saw them as the work of the devil; others saw and did not believe (cf. Mark 3:22). These events, like many at that time and many since, aroused temporary wonder, amazement, and faith. But in themselves, the miracles did not produce the faith that changed sinners into persons who obeyed and trusted God instead of themselves, forgave their enemies, and lived out of the assurance of God's favor.

MIRACLES IN A MODERN PERSPECTIVE

Most people regard a miracle as a breach of scientific, natural law. Taken literally, however, such language can be misleading, because scientific laws are statements about cause and effect based upon empirical observation. Out of observation and experiment a law is formed, then with more testing it is found to be inadequate, so the law is reformulated; then it is again found to be inadequate, reformulated again, and so forth. We need to keep in mind that scientists themselves realize that the models or laws that the scientific process constructs are only aids toward understanding reality. These laws are impersonal oversimplifications that are useful in a pragmatic way but are not determinative of reality. To mistake these scientific, natural laws for reality itself pushes the observer into a flat scientific (actually unscientific) view of the world in which all complexity and mystery are abolished for the sake of clarity and certainty.

Miracle stories convey mystery; they speak about extraordinary events, situations in which things are more than they seem. Miracle stories claim that a power is at work which is personal concern—understood in the New Testament as the will of God. The point of miracle stories is not scientific explanation; their point is beyond all such explanation. Thus we do the miracle stories no service if we "explain" them so as to remove their miraculous, mysterious character.

One viewpoint seeks to reconcile biblical miracles with a modern view of the world by assigning them to those areas of experience that have not yet been explored or explained by science. Thus all conflict with the sciences is avoided. But the increase of scientific knowledge threatens radically to reduce such areas, and thus the scope of the miraculous activity of God. Conversely, it is possible to regard all events as miraculous because they stem from God. This notion is usually associated with pantheism (from the Greek words *pan,* "all," and *theos,* "God"; God is all). The first option views a miracle as an event contrary to known natural law and reduces God's activity to peripheral, occasional interventions. The second option, pantheism, asserts God's activity in every event and hence renders human activity insignificant. Yet neither of these viewpoints corresponds with the biblical perspective, and each threatens to dissolve miracles either into remote and barely conceivable possibilities or into everyday occurrences.

According to the Gospels, Jesus' miracles were real, specific, and discernible events. Yet they occurred in an atmosphere of eschatological expectation and faith. When wrenched from this context, they look like the works of a magician or a sorcerer. In his own time and in the earliest church the question of miracle could not be separated from faith in Jesus' preaching and power, both of which had to do with the dawning kingdom of God. Faith could not, and cannot, prove the miracles happened; faith in God's rule provides the context in which their meaning can be discussed. Apart from this eschatological context, Jesus' miracles, if they are not rejected outright, must be viewed as occult phenomena with certain parallels in ancient and modern times. If, however, one believes that the new age was really dawning in Jesus, a basis is provided for understanding the miracles. Early Christians believed this was happening. In their time and subsequently, such faith has lent reality and meaning to accounts of the miraculous.

The Teaching Messiah

The earliest extant documents of Christianity, Paul's letters, contain surprisingly little teaching that Paul attributes to Jesus himself. From this it might be inferred that Paul worked at a time, or in places, where no extensive tradition or body of Jesus' sayings was known or used. Yet Paul does on occasion cite a word of Jesus' (1 Cor. 7:10; 9:14; 11:23–26), so the practice of preserving and referring to Jesus' own words cannot have been unknown to him (cf. Rom. 12:14–21; 13:8–10). He may have known more of the Jesus tradition than he reveals. Still, the focus of Paul's preaching and teaching is elsewhere, preeminently upon the meaning of the crucifixion and resurrection.

Aside from Paul's own occasional example, there are stronger indications that Jesus' sayings, his teachings, were preserved and transmitted among his followers. All the Gospels, including John, portray Jesus as a teacher and contain evidence of the existence of the teaching material in earlier, pre-Gospel forms. The Gospel of Matthew's famous Sermon on the Mount (chaps. 5–7) is paralleled in Luke by a Sermon on the Plain (6:20–49), which, although much shorter, is obviously an alternative, probably earlier, recension of much of the same material. Therefore, the Sermon on the Mount seems to be neither a single utterance of Jesus nor a composition of Matthew. Rather, it is based upon a traditional collection of Jesus' sayings, which Matthew has doubtless augmented. Traces of similar sayings of Jesus may be found, for example, in the letter of James. But the most impressive evidence for collections of Jesus' sayings is the parallel materials of Matthew and Luke, of which the Sermon on the Mount (or Plain) is only a part. This parallel material was scarcely copied from one Gospel by the author of the other, but was drawn by both from the same or a similar source, which was in all likelihood a collection of Jesus' sayings that lacked narrative structure or framework, called by scholars the Q source (see pp. 62–64). A similar collection of Jesus' sayings, the apocryphal Gospel of Thomas, has now been found among the Coptic Gnostic manuscripts uncovered at Nag Hammadi in upper Egypt.

Moreover, the shape of certain narratives in the Gospels suggests that they functioned primarily to preserve a saying of Jesus. Also, smaller complexes (groups) of sayings in the Gospels may have once circulated as separate units before having been incorporated into the Gospel. Probably some ancient and genuine materials found their way into Gospels, such as the Gospel of the Hebrews or the Gospel of the Egyptians, which are known to us from early Christian writers but that are otherwise lost. Perhaps eventually copies of some of these long-lost Gospels will, like the Gospel of Thomas, become known again.

The evidence of the collection, preservation, and transmission of Jesus' sayings, whether in oral or written form, shows that some early Christians regarded Jesus as a rabbi, a teacher (cf. John 1:38)—whatever else he may have been. The anonymous and now unknown Christians to whose interest and care we owe the preservation of sayings of Jesus probably distinguished themselves by this very interest and activity. Our debt to them is immeasurable. It is surprising and scarcely a matter of chance that outside the Gospels, into which such material has been taken up, we rarely find sayings of Jesus in the New Testament, although they begin to appear more frequently in the early second-century Christian writings known as the Apostolic Fathers.

For some, Jesus has always been the supreme teacher. Thus before the Gospels were even written there were collections of Jesus' sayings, his teachings. Our portrait of the healing Messiah already suggested the urgency with which Jesus spoke, preached, and taught, as he proclaimed the nearness of the kingdom of God. Therefore, any attempt to understand his teaching that does not take account of the centrality of the kingdom, as well as the air of expectation it engendered, is fundamentally flawed. Certainly in the Synoptic Gospels Jesus' kingdom proclamation is set in the context of apocalyptic eschatology, that is, the view that God will soon intervene in human affairs in some decisive way, to change their course and character, and to establish his rule.[14]

THE PROCLAMATION OF THE KINGDOM OF GOD

Did Jesus' proclamation of God's kingdom imply the imminent end of the world?

In the Synoptic Gospels the message of Jesus centers upon the kingdom of God. "Now after John was arrested, Jesus came into Galilee, proclaiming the good news of God, and saying, 'The time is fulfilled, and the kingdom of God has drawn near; repent, and believe in the good news'" (Mark 1:14 f.; the formulation may be Mark's, but it accurately summarizes Jesus' message). After the scribe applauds Jesus' summary of the law in the twin commandments of love of God and neighbors, Jesus says to him, "You are not far from the kingdom of God" (Mark 12:34). In the beatitudes Jesus says, "Blessed are you who are poor, for yours is the kingdom of God" (Luke 6:20; Matt. 5:3). Concerning John the Baptist, Jesus says, "Truly, I tell you, among those born of women no one has risen greater than John the Baptist; yet the least in the

14. Albert Schweitzer, *The Quest of the Historical Jesus,* trans. W. Montgomery (New York: Macmillan, 1968), strongly insisted on this interpretation of Jesus' kingdom proclamation. His book, published in German in 1906 and translated into English in 1910, has deeply influenced Jesus research in this century. Marcus Borg, *Conflict, Holiness, and Politics in the Teaching of Jesus* (New York: Edwin Mellen, 1984), represents a challenge, in quite recent research centered in the North American Jesus Seminar, to the equation of the kingdom of God with the end of history. Whether apocalyptic eschatology should be translated into modern idiom as the end of history is, indeed, a valid question.

kingdom of heaven is greater than he" (Matt. 11:11; Luke 7:28). In one peti-tion of the Lord's Prayer Jesus prays, "Your kingdom come. Your will be done, on earth as it is in heaven" (Matt. 6:10; cf. Luke 11:2). Jesus' exorcisms sug-gest the coming of the kingdom: "But if it is by the finger of God that I cast out demons, then the kingdom of God has come to you" (Luke 11:20; Matt. 12:28). Obviously, Jesus' proclamation is pregnant with the kingdom of God. Yet the meaning of Jesus' kingdom proclamation is debatable. (We should keep in mind that *kingdom* also means kingship, rule, or reign, and the Greek term *basileia* could be translated accordingly; the emphasis is upon God's ruling rather than upon a territory or people ruled.)

Two major questions concerning Jesus' concept of the kingdom must be dealt with head on. First, did Jesus announce the kingdom as present or fu-ture, or some combination of the two? Second, was the kingdom primarily an ethical goal, to be attained by human decision and effort, or an apocalyp-tic event to be brought about on God's initiative only?

Both questions were put forward most clearly and most relentlessly by Al-bert Schweitzer, the great biblical scholar and humanitarian, who argued per-suasively that nineteenth-century historians and theologians had interpreted the Gospels in light of their own presuppositions, which were read into the text, and had produced a Jesus who was the projection of modern ethical ideals. Moreover, he insisted that the kingdom of God in Jesus' view was a future, cataclysmic, apocalyptic event, which God himself would inaugurate in order to end all worldly history and conditions. Interpreting the Gospel accounts from the standpoint of their many apocalyptic passages (e.g., Mark 13; 8:38; cf. also 1:14), which he read in the light of ancient Jewish apoca-lyptic texts, he sharply rejected the notion that the kingdom of God was ei-ther a fully present reality or an ethical goal. Moreover, Jesus' ethic, according to Schweitzer, was an ethic of the brief interim before the kingdom's advent. Only under such emergency conditions could one think of turning the other cheek (Matt. 5:39) or of giving up one's coat and cloak (Matt. 5:40).

Although the questions of the time and manner of the kingdom's coming and its ethical implications are closely related, we shall reserve the latter for treatment under Jesus' radical demand. In considering the former question, we shall group the varied sayings according to present or future orientation to reach tentative conclusions about Jesus' temporal emphasis. As a check upon our findings, we briefly investigate seven kingdom parables (Matt. 13). Then we shall be able to say more precisely how Jesus' kingdom proclama-tion is oriented to the present and future.

THE KINGDOM AS PRESENT AND FUTURE

Altogether the three Synoptic Gospels contain well over a hundred refer-ences to the kingdom of God. This contrasts with fewer than forty references in the rest of the New Testament, including the Gospel of John, where the kingdom is not a prominent element of Jesus' teaching. As we would expect, the Gospels of Matthew and Luke, which embody the bulk of Jesus' teachings, contain more references than does Mark (54 in Matthew, 41 in Luke, 19 in Mark).

Despite numerous sayings about its future coming, the kingdom of God is occasionally said to be somehow present in Jesus' mission and message. Several passages refer to Jesus' activity as indicative of the kingdom's presence. Jesus says that his exorcisms by the finger or Spirit of God show that "the kingdom of God has come upon you" (Luke 11:20; cf. Matt. 12:28). As we can be reasonably certain that Jesus did perform exorcisms (see pp. 217 f.), it is probable that he himself was responsible for relating the exorcisms to the kingdom's presence. On another occasion when Jesus was asked by Pharisees when the kingdom was coming, he is said to have replied, "The kingdom of God is not coming with things that can be observed; nor will they say, 'Look, here it is!' or 'There it is!' for in fact, the kingdom of God is among you" (Luke 17:20 f.; cf. Thomas 3 and 22).[15] Evidently the present already contains what the Pharisees seek in the future. After the seventy go out upon their mission and find that they also can conquer demons, Jesus says to them, "I watched Satan fall from heaven like a flash of lightning from heaven" (Luke 10:18). Satan's defeat marks the beginning of the end time (cf. Mark 3:27; Rev. 20:1–3). In some sense the kingdom is present. This point is confirmed by the parables (see pp. 228 ff.).

The kingdom of God in the message of Jesus is nevertheless also future; further, the evidence for this futuristic emphasis is quite clear. In addition to the passages cited above (p. 224), after the confession of Peter at Caesarea Philippi, Jesus instructs the disciples, "Truly, I tell you, there are some standing here who will not taste death until they see that the kingdom of God has come with power" (Mark 9:1; Matt. 16:28; Luke 9:27). At the Last Supper, Jesus says to the disciples, "Truly, I say to you, I shall not drink again of the fruit of the vine until that day when I drink it new in the kingdom of God" (Mark 14:25; Matt. 26:29; Luke 22:18). Jesus speaks frequently about entering and receiving the kingdom of God. Such sayings also fit the concept of a future or coming kingdom (Matt. 5:20; 7:21; 18:3; 19:23; 25:34; Mark 9:47; 10:15; 15:43; Luke 9:62; 12:32; 18:17).

If we can associate with the kingdom other references to the coming of the end time, such as the coming of the Son of Man, the tribulations of the last day, the coming of the judgment, then we have an abundance of indirect evidence that Jesus understood the kingdom as future. The apocalyptic discourse (Mark 13; cf. Matt. 24 and Luke 21) speaks again and again of the impending future tribulation that ushers in the rule of God. Although it contains much material that did not originate with Jesus, it would scarcely have obtained its present form had he not proclaimed the future, coming kingdom of God. One surprising thing about the apocalyptic discourse, however, is the near absence of the term *kingdom* itself (but cf. Luke 21:31).

---

15. The final phrase, "among you," may be translated "within you," but such a translation does not fit the rest of Jesus' kingdom teaching.

Nevertheless we can only conclude on the basis of individual sayings and related apocalyptic references in the teaching of Jesus that he himself proclaimed the kingdom as coming. But this conclusion has to be coupled with Jesus' message of the kingdom as also present. There is a tension between present and future in the Gospels that presumably goes back to Jesus himself.

JESUS AND APOCALYPTICISM

In the tradition of the Synoptic Gospels Jesus proclaims the kingdom as both present and future. If Jesus is understood against the background of Jewish apocalyptic thought, he was no ordinary apocalyptic thinker. Two traits characterize apocalyptic teaching, but only the first of them is fully shared by Jesus. First, apocalypticism looks toward a future consummation of history that God will command. But second, this event is set in a dualistic framework and occurs as the final climax of an overall "plan" for history. Jewish apocalyptic literature, which developed during the period between the Maccabean uprising and the final destruction of Jerusalem after the Bar Kochba rebellion (167 B.C.–A.D. 135), embodied the fundamental hope that "the succession of world powers, Babylonian, Median, Persian, Seleucid Greek, [and Roman] would be brought to an end by an act of God in history whereby God himself will take the dominion into his own hands."[16] This view reflects pessimism about any possibility of humans' extricating themselves from the present evil situation. The powers of Satan, represented by the foreign powers dominating the Jewish people, had won the upper hand. The only hope was the advent of God's new age, in which the old powers would be annihilated and his reign established. This world view deals in dualistic contrasts: good and bad, new and old, God and Satan. In its perspective on history and God's plan it presumes that the world has become progressively more evil, descending from an initial paradise to the present hell on earth. This evil, instigated by humankind and God's adversary Satan, is especially rampant against God's elect in the last days. But God's plan, visible only to the discerning elect, calls for a final intervention in which everything will be reversed, so that the oppressed will triumph and the rulers will be destroyed.[17] Therefore, apocalypticism calls for repentance in the face of the terrible judgment of the imminent end.

Jesus' expectation is related to this apocalyptic world view, but apart from the apocalyptic discourse (Mark 13 parr.) he does not lay out a scenario. John the Baptist, the angry preacher of judgment (see Matt. 3:1–12), deserves the title of apocalyptist more than Jesus, and the Book of Revelation with its graphic and detailed description of the end time has quite appropriately been

16. Norman Perrin, *The Kingdom of God in the Teaching of Jesus* (Philadelphia: Westminster, 1963), p. 53, is presenting the view of F. C. Burkitt. The early stages of such apocalyptic thought can be seen in the Book of Daniel (chaps. 7–12); its further development is found in the apocryphal 4 Ezra and in the War Scroll of the Qumran community.

17. See Daniel 7:2–8, the Book of Revelation, and the Qumran War Rule (War of the Children of Light Against the Children of Darkness), which depicts the final eschatological battle.

called the Apocalypse (see Rev. 21:1–8). Jesus is an eschatological teacher who proclaims the imminent kingdom (Mark 1:15 par.; Matt. 8:11 f. par.). Yet Jesus proclaims neither knowledge of the plan of God nor a pessimistic, dualistic rejection of this world.[18] Jesus rejects the apocalyptic penchant for looking for signs and speculating about the exact time for the end (Mark 8:12; cf. Matt. 16:1; Luke 11:29; 17:20 f.). Even in the so-called apocalyptic discourse, which is largely the product of a later time, Jesus refuses to speculate (Mark 13:32). When the Pharisees ask Jesus about the time of the kingdom's coming, Jesus replies that the kingdom is not coming "with things that can be observed," for it is already in their midst (Luke 17:20 f.). John the Baptist's disciples inquire whether Jesus is the sign that the apocalyptic end time has arrived (Matt. 11:2–6; Luke 7:18–23). Jesus' only answer is to describe what he is doing. Because his acts of preaching and healing are good news, they are hardly the dreadful, cataclysmic signs of the end of the world.

Jesus strongly implies that the kingdom is inaugurated in his ministry. It is in the process of being realized, but it has not yet fully come, for its completion is still future. Such was the secret of Jesus' message about the kingdom; moreover, his parables bear this viewpoint out.

THE KINGDOM AND THE PARABLES

In our discussion of Jesus' proclamation of the kingdom we have thus far deliberately ignored the numerous kingdom parables. It is not too much to say that if Jesus taught anything, he proclaimed the kingdom of God and that if he taught in any specific form, he spoke in parables.

Before looking at a representative group of kingdom parables in Matthew 13, we need to understand something of the nature of the parable. Jesus spoke parables to drive home one point by way of an analogy drawn from the everyday world. The parables are not stories told to illustrate general truths; they are sharp words with implied directives for concrete situations. Our use of religious language to interpret the parables must not lose sight of the fact that parables seldom mention God or use religious language. In the parables Jesus talks about eschatology and God in everyday language, implying that the meeting with the unexpected, with God, occurs within the world.

The parables of Jesus accumulated redactional additions during the course of their oral and written transmission. This material was added to make them meaningful to later situations. One way in which the early church made Jesus' parables applicable was by allegorizing them, giving them new meaning by making each point of the parable refer to some Christian truth. In Matthew the interpretations of the parables of the sower (13:18–23) and of the weeds in the field (13:36–43) are examples of such allegorization; however, this sort of interpretation may not be true to the original intent of the parables.

---

18. Schweitzer, *The Quest of the Historical Jesus,* placed Jesus within such a dualistic background, but in doing so ignored much of his teaching.

In Jesus' parables, attention is focused not upon the particulars but upon the total impact of the story. By contrast, allegory allows the particulars to dominate by referring each element to some previously known framework of meaning. If, however, the many elements of the parable are viewed as a whole, it is impossible to translate the parable into other terms; any generalization about a parable is always secondary. Consequently in our interpretation of certain parables we need to keep in mind that genuine understanding occurs simply in reading and hearing the parables. The directive, the stimulus to action or to repentance, that they imply is clear enough in most parables. We need here ask only about the view of the kingdom that they imply or assume.

Chapter 13 of Matthew serves our purpose well, for the evangelist has gathered there a collection of Jesus' kingdom parables. Although Matthew uses Mark as his source, he includes material not found in Mark. The parables in the latter category (as distinguished from their interpretation) probably also originated with Jesus. Interestingly, Matthew's redaction of Mark 4:10–12, by making the parables a means of clarifying Jesus' message rather than ob-

A farmer plowing in Galilee, in a scene not unlike that in the time of Jesus. Modern technology has only recently replaced this ancient mode of agriculture. *(Courtesy of Israel Government Tourist Office.)*

scuring it (Matt. 13:13; cf. vss. 34–35), doubtless comes closer to the actual purpose of Jesus than does Mark.

The parable of the sower (Matt. 13:3–8; cf. Mark 4:3–8; Luke 8:5–8; Thomas 9) requires some knowledge of Jesus' time and place to be understood. First, the harvest image was already connected with the eschatological notion of the culmination of world history, for the end time was viewed as the harvest time (cf. Isa. 9:1–7; Psalm 126). Second, the yield of grain (13:8) was excessively large; a tenfold yield would have been a good harvest, and a yield of seven and a half an average one.[19]

Assuming that this parable was spoken by Jesus, we may dispense with the interpretation (13:18–23), for it is quite difficult to imagine that this allegory tells what the parable meant to the first hearers. For example, the identification of the birds with "the evil one" is artificial and would have been unlikely to occur to Jesus' listeners. The parable points quite simply to activity taking place in the present: seed being sown, but much seed being lost. Jesus speaks this parable about the sower not to encourage endurance from people already committed to him (cf. vs. 21) but to declare what is happening in their midst. The unexpected element of the parable is the size of the harvest—vs. 8. Since a good yield would be tenfold, these results are incredible. Even now the sowing is taking place; moreover, the future harvest will be beyond imagination. Evidently the parable's movement portrays in everyday, yet unexpected, language Jesus' proclamation of the kingdom. The present is for Jesus the time of the hidden coming of the kingdom; the future will witness an unbelievable consummation of that kingdom. Deliverance is not only future but already present in a hidden way.

The parable of the weeds in the field (Matt. 13:24–30; cf. Thomas 57) also has an allegorical interpretation that is clearly secondary—it is actually separated from the parable itself—and does not belong to Jesus' message (13:36–43). According to the interpretation, Jesus warns against false security by depicting vividly the punishment and reward of the last judgment. But this interpretation obscures the surprising point of the story. Again we have a parable of the harvest. This time, instead of announcing a magnificent future yield and thereby claiming hidden significance for the present sowing, the parable depicts the future as a time of judgment, a process of separation (vs. 30). But the present is a time when judgment cannot be exercised (vs. 29). Actually the weight of the parable falls on the latter point. Final judgment belongs to God, not to human beings (cf. Matt. 7:1 and Luke 15). Any attempt to bring judgment into the present misses the point of Jesus' proclaiming the kingdom as inaugurated (cf. Matt. 13:44 ff. and Mark 2:18 ff.), even though not realized.

The following twin parables, the parable of the mustard seed (Matt. 13:31 f.; cf. Mark 4:30–32; Luke 13:18 f.; Thomas 20) and the parable of the leaven

---

19. See J. Jeremias, *The Parables of Jesus,* rev. ed., trans. S. H. Hooke (New York: Scribners, 1963), p. 150.

(Matt. 13:33; cf. Luke 13:20 f. and Thomas 96), also speak about present and future. Exaggeration has occurred in the Matthean and Lukan accounts, for in actuality the mustard seed only becomes a large shrub about nine feet in height rather than a tree.[20] Also the specified measure of meal is a huge quantity of flour for a housewife, approximately fifty pounds (cf. Gen. 18:6). Many modern interpreters have viewed these parables as depicting the growth of the kingdom of God, which starts small but through the course of years grows through human effort until it encompasses the whole world. But this interpretation misses both the eschatological urgency of Jesus' message and the thrust of the images themselves. Jesus uses the tiny and insignificant mustard seed and leaven to surprise the hearer with the tremendous results: the tree that shelters the birds and enough dough to feed a host of people. These are parables not of growth but of contrast. Jesus contrasts the small, present beginning with the great result to come in the future. The process of growth is nowhere mentioned, so that the "how" of this great result remains a mystery.

The twin parables of the treasure (Matt. 13:44; cf. Thomas 109) and the pearl (Matt. 13:45 f.; cf. Thomas 76) further elaborate the theme of present response to the kingdom. No calculation is involved; the finder of the treasure and the finder of the pearl have in common the knowledge that the find overshadows everything else. The finders do not understand themselves as surrendering everything but as gaining the one essential thing, the treasure or the pearl. In one instance, the treasure is found accidentally by a laborer in the field; in the other, the merchant finds the pearl after a great search. But in both cases, everything is forgotten in the joy of finding the treasure and the pearl.

These two parables, which deal with present response to the kingdom, are followed by the parable of the net and the fish, a parable relating to the future (Matt. 13:47–50; cf. Thomas 8). Jesus' original parable probably consisted simply of the image of throwing the net and gathering and sorting the good and bad fish (vss. 47–48), but Matthew's redactional addition (vss. 49–50; cf. Matt. 8:12; 13:42; 22:13) correctly interprets this parable in light of the final judgment. The future orientation becomes evident when this parable is seen together with the parable of the weeds and the wheat (13:24–30), for the latter's secondary point was that judgment could and would take place in the future.

In summary, Jesus' parables, like his kingdom message, stress both the present and the future: a small beginning now is to be consummated fully in the future. This present beginning is a time for great joy. Whoever seeks to control the future by immediate judgment loses the future reward. Whoever discerns the present activity of God will be astonished at the final results.

---

20. Jeremias, *The Parables of Jesus,* p. 31, suggests that the tree imagery heightens the eschatological flavor of the parable and reflects Daniel 4:17.

We may now draw certain conclusions about the kingdom of God in the proclamation of Jesus. First, God's rule, not human effort, was foremost in his conception of the coming kingdom. Jesus never viewed the kingdom of God as a slowly evolving movement within history that could be brought about by humankind's adhering to the principles of his own ethics. When in John's Gospel Jesus says that his kingdom is not of this world (18:36), the synoptic teaching is transposed to a Johannine key, but is not falsified. The kingdom was both present and future, yet its nature was not described in apocalyptic imagery any more than its presence was conceived as a purely inner or spiritual reality. The kingdom involved both the action of God and the response of the people. The present hidden reality of the kingdom challenged disciples to accept it now, and thus enabled them joyfully to anticipate the future. God was the primary actor; somehow in the words and deeds of Jesus God was at work to effect a magnificent future consummation. Jesus' eschatological message proclaimed an "already" and a "not yet." Already in Jesus' activity the kingdom is inaugurated, but it has not yet fully come.[21]

THE EXPECTATION OF JESUS' RETURN

Both Paul (e.g., 1 Cor. 15) and the Synoptic Gospels (e.g., Mark 13), as well as the Book of Revelation, reveal the early Christians' expectation that the risen Jesus would soon return in glory to reveal his true identity, hold judgment, and inaugurate the kingdom of God. This return is often spoken of as the *parousia* (Greek for "appearance"). Understandably, therefore, many Christians regarded the present as only an interim, a time of waiting or preparation for the consummation. This expectation is expressed in the phrase, apparently common in early Christian worship, "Our Lord, come!" (1 Cor. 16:22; cf. Rev. 22:20).

Although this apocalyptic expectation was clearly important to many, if not most, of the first generation of Christians, remarkably it did not become a part of the earliest Christian confessions, as far as can be judged from the New Testament.[22] Still, apocalyptic traditions began to grow, perhaps as soon as it was apparent that the end was somewhat delayed in coming, and perhaps in part to explain the delay. Embryonic forms of such traditions are found in 1 Thessalonians 4:15–18, 1 Corinthians 15:23 ff., and 2 Thessalonians 2:3–12. A more developed example is Mark 13, called the Little Apoca-

---

21. The Jesus Seminar, chaired by Robert W. Funk, constitutes a body of scholarly opinion that on the whole rejects the ascription of apocalyptic, futuristic eschatology to Jesus. This view is represented in the works of Borg, Crossan, and Funk and R. W. Hoover cited at the end of this chapter, as well as in the book of Burton Mack noted in the Suggestions for Further Reading of chapter 2. In our view they correctly react against Albert Schweitzer's portrayal of Jesus as a single-minded apocalyptic prophet, but on inadequate grounds eliminate the strong future dimension and orientation from Jesus' proclamation.

22. H. Conzelmann, "On the Analysis of the Confessional Formula in 1 Corinthians 15:3–5," *Interpretation,* 20 (1966), 23, states flatly, "No old confessional formula speaks of the parousia."

lypse because of its similarity to the Apocalypse of John (Revelation), and the parallel material in Matthew and Luke.

As we have seen, Jesus himself spoke of impending eschatological events, particularly the coming of the kingdom, but the growth of apocalyptic tradition in early Christianity was largely the work of Christian prophets or seers. Paul speaks of prophets and ranks them second only to apostles (1 Cor. 12:28). The best-known Christian prophet is John of Patmos, the author of the Book of Revelation. It is noteworthy that he sometimes speaks in the name of Jesus himself (esp. in chaps. 1–3). Probably prophets regularly spoke in the name of Jesus, *ex ore Christi* ("out of the mouth of Christ"). The synoptic apocalypses, although they are based upon some genuine words of Jesus, are largely the work of such prophets, and the warnings against false prophets in these very discourses (Mark 13:22; Matt. 24:11) attest their origin among the "true" prophets. The necessity for criteria to test early Christian prophets is recognized in 1 John 4:1–3, as well as in the writings of the Apostolic Fathers (see the Didache xi, 7–xiii, 7). The work of Christian prophets was not limited to apocalyptic utterances, but they originated and thrived in the atmosphere of eager expectancy that pervaded early Christianity.

That Paul also expected the consummation of history in the near future can scarcely be doubted in view of his apocalyptic statements and the way he takes up such materials or traditions. Moreover, scattered throughout the Gospels are sayings of Jesus that anticipate the end, including a distinct group in which he speaks of the coming of the Son of Man (e.g., Mark 8:38), by which Christians have assumed he meant his own return. To what extent the latter sayings express Jesus' own viewpoint is, as we have seen, debatable. It is clear, however, that they would never have been preserved (or formulated) by Christians had they not themselves lived in a state of eschatological expectation. More likely than not this expectancy was rooted in Jesus' own anticipation of God's rule.

The antiquity of the apocalyptic, eschatological material is confirmed by the fact that it is to a considerable extent preserved in the Gospels, documents for which the expectation of the imminent return of Jesus had already become a problem. Luke thinks of the ministry of Jesus as the center of time and presents his own era as the period of the church's life and mission, analogous to that of Israel. Obviously, Luke has expanded the short interval before the Lord's anticipated return in view of the continuation of the normal course of history. The Gospel of John shows that the whole eschatological question was being reconsidered in some Christian circles (see John 11:23–26; 14:22–24). Perhaps the death of the aged Beloved Disciple (21:20–23) provided the catalyst for this process. That there was a problem, or perplexity, among many Christians because Jesus had not returned is evident from the explanation given in 2 Peter (3:4–9). Mark, the earliest Gospel, clearly manifests a lively hope and expectation (1:15; 8:38–9:1), although there are signs already of an awareness of some delay (13:32, 37).

THE RADICAL DEMAND OF THE KINGDOM

In what way is Jesus' kingdom proclamation related to his demand for obedience to God?

As we have seen, the heart of Jesus' message was proclamation of a kingdom *both* present *and* future. It included God's action and the necessity for human response. Yet how does the good news of the inauguration of God's kingdom relate to the ethical demand of Jesus? Is the urgency of the demand undercut by the proclamation of God's presence? We now deal directly with these important questions.

THE SERMON ON THE MOUNT

The most concentrated expression of Jesus' radical statement of the will of God occurs in the Sermon on the Mount (Matt. 5–7). The higher righteousness (5:20) is defined by prohibitions against anger (5:22), the lustful look (5:28), divorce (5:32), and swearing (5:34). Jesus also commands nonresistance to evil (5:39) and love for one's enemies (5:44). All this reaches a stunning climax: "You, therefore, must be perfect, as your heavenly Father is perfect" (5:48).

Such words of Jesus (5:21–48), called the *antitheses* because they are set over against the law of Moses or its common interpretation, are so radical that they would hardly have originated in the early church. Further words, such as the prohibitions against anxiety (6:35), the command not to judge (7:1), and the injunction to do the will of the Father (7:21), strike the reader as extraordinarily demanding. Basically, they must be from Jesus, despite the fact that they appear only in Matthew. Their radical character can hardly be ascribed to Matthew or to the transmission of his tradition, because this Gospel and its tradition show a more conservative treatment of the matter: Jesus fulfills the law and the prophets (5:17).

Is Jesus' radical demand a call for righteousness *for* the kingdom or *of* the kingdom? Does this call for obedience to the will of God lay down conditions *for* entrance into the kingdom, or does it show those deeds that signify the presence *of* the kingdom? If the former, then the kingdom truly is future; if the latter, then the kingdom may be both present and future.

Our basic understanding of the Sermon has already been set forth in the treatment of Matthew (see pp. 107–111). Although some material in Matthew 5–7 may come from the evangelist or his tradition, rather than from Jesus, the Sermon taken as a whole does not misrepresent Jesus. Two conclusions are unavoidable. On the one hand, no hint at all is given in the Sermon that anything less than obedience to the demands of Jesus is required. On the other hand, we do not read that this obedience is to take place through the unaided effort of the hearer of Jesus' words. The validity of these observations may be elaborated from several perspectives. First, the opening Beatitudes proclaim that God loves those who eagerly receive what is graciously occurring in the present. The blessing of God, as present action, works to effect higher righteousness, greater obedience. Second, although this new reality means a deeper regard for the life of one person with another (Matt. 5:21–48), still this new life, according to Jesus, is built on the relationship that the Father has already established with his people (5:48). Third, barriers to the relationship with God—hypocrisy, prayer for show, anxiety about one's own destiny—have to be eradicated (see Matt. 6). Seeking first the kingdom and righteousness of the Father enables one to find freedom and enjoyment in the present. Fourth, the future belongs to God (7:1; cf. 7:7). God's grace accompanies Jesus' command, yet whoever encounters the grace of God must still bear good fruit (7:19) and face God in the future judgment (7:24–27).

Reward is not just some future prize for good deeds accomplished in the present; reward belongs already to the right relationship with God. Present blessings and obedience simply become expanded and enlarged in the future. Jesus' proclamation of the kingdom seeks to bring a response from his hearers, a response defined as doing the will of God. Thus the righteousness that Jesus demands is not righteousness *for* the kingdom, not even the proper attitude with which to unlock the kingdom. Instead Jesus demands the righteousness *of* the kingdom. To be sure, this kingdom is only partially present, inaugurated, but the power of the kingdom is already at work. The Sermon reveals that Jesus speaks as one convinced that the kingdom is breaking into the present and will be consummated in the future both as the act of God and the response of obedient people.

JESUS AND THE LAW

Indirect support for the unity of Jesus' kingdom preaching and ethical teaching may be seen in the fact that Jesus' words, especially in the Sermon on the Mount, express an attitude toward the law only possible for one convinced that the eschatological time was beginning. In the antitheses Jesus opposes his understanding of the law to that of Moses, even though no ordinary rabbi would dare assume that kind of authority. His "but *I* say to you" implies that for him the present is a time of radical reinterpretation of the law. This reinterpretation, characterized by the command to love one's enemies and by prohibitions against lust, anger, and swearing, is rooted in the dawning of the kingdom of God. Nowhere does Jesus' daring become more evident than in his apparent abolition of the law's crucial distinction between clean and unclean: "Listen to me, all of you, and understand: there is nothing outside a person that by going in can defile, but the things that come out are what defile" (Mark 7:14 f.; cf. Matt. 15:1–20). With God's coming near, distinctions of the sacred and the profane, the clean and the unclean, are no longer valid. Jesus' message urges his hearers to seek and to do the will of God in the law in view of the coming kingdom.

The rejection of the distinction between clean and unclean represents the most extreme position taken by Jesus over against the law. Such a re-

The late Roman synagogue at Khirbet Shema in Galilee. Note the *Bema* (podium) facing Jerusalem in far wall and the *Beth Ha-Midrash* (House of Study) in upper right.   *(Courtesy of Eric M. Meyers.)*

jection did not immediately take hold throughout the early church. The apostle Paul apparently embraced it (cf. Gal. 2:10–14), but does not cite Jesus' word in support of his position. It is the exception rather than the rule, however, when Paul quotes a word of Jesus. Moreover, this sweeping overhaul of the understanding of the law agrees in tenor not only with the antitheses of the Sermon on the Mount but also with such radical injunctions as the command to let the dead bury their dead (Luke 9:59–60; cf. Matt. 8:21–22). This last exhortation is a sharp departure from ancient Jewish custom and piety.

The solution, therefore, to the problem of eschatology and ethics in Jesus' message entails a recognition that the kingdom is both present and future. The kingdom is present in blessing; therefore, no one can afford to spend time in calculating the end of time. God is present; therefore, people have to respond, to hear, and to obey today. Yet the kingdom is also future. Final judgment can be exercised by no one other than God. The urgency of Jesus' demand derives not primarily from the ancient law (although the law is not rejected in principle) but from the onset of the kingdom or rule of God, a prospect that dominates the future.

THE RELATIONSHIP OF JESUS TO HIS MESSAGE

If Jesus thought of himself as Messiah, what would that have meant to him and his contemporaries?

The center of Jesus' message is the proclamation of the inaugurated kingdom of God. The person of Jesus does not stand at the center of his message. Jesus points to God, not himself, for he speaks not about his own person, but about God's rule. The Synoptic Gospels show little interest in Jesus' personality or self-consciousness, for they are concerned with his mission and message. Yet it would be a mistake to infer that the question of Jesus' identity is of little or no importance. The relationship of Jesus to his proclamation of the kingdom is an important question raised by the tradition itself. The evangelists, the Gospels, have an answer to that question: he was the Messiah or Christ.

The New Testament unequivocally maintains that the identity of Jesus is related to his work. In other words, the question "Who was he?" cannot be separated from the question "What did he do?" At least in the Synoptics, eschatology and ethics, rather than Christology per se, are the center of Jesus' proclamation. In his message Jesus proclaims God's kingdom and calls people to obey God, whereas in his deeds he manifests the kingdom's power. Thus Jesus presents himself as the crucial figure in the history of God's dealing with Israel and with humanity.

THE QUESTION OF JESUS' MESSIANIC CONSCIOUSNESS

A logical beginning place for understanding Jesus' view of himself is the various Christological titles used by either Jesus or his contemporaries. The major titles are Son of God, Savior, Lord, Messiah or Christ, Son of Man, and prophet. Of these the first three appear only rarely, if at all, in the Synoptic Gospels. Son, in the sense of Son of God, is common in the Fourth Gospel although Savior and Lord are not. Of course, the Johannine Jesus proclaims himself, his messianic dignity and sonship, whereas in the other Gospels he does not. But John's presentation can no longer be taken at its face value as historical. For had Jesus actually spoken in the terms he employs in the Fourth Gospel, it is impossible to understand why the other Gospels and traditions should so little reflect this fact, inasmuch as the faith they too affirm is enunciated by the Johannine Jesus. Therefore, our study of Jesus' self-consciousness must begin with the Synoptics, and the last three titles, Messiah or Christ, Son of Man, and prophet, are the most important ones for this investigation.

Messiah (Christ). The basic messianic hope of first-century Israel was the hope for a national Messiah, usually expected to be an heir of King David, and perhaps Son of God (see Psalm 2:7). We recall that Messiah means simply "anointed." Although others in Israel were anointed, in this case the term refers particularly to the anointing of the Davidic king. He was to overthrow the political enemies of Israel, establish the chosen people in a new and perfect reign of David, and inaugurate the kingdom of God. (Not all hopes for the restoration of Israel were, however, tied to the figure of the Messiah. See above, p. 31.) Of Jesus' actions the entry into Jerusalem (Mark 11:1–10 parr.) and the subsequent overthrow of the money changers in the temple (Mark 11:11–19 parr.) are most susceptible to such political interpretation. The most significant evidence for the political character of Jesus' messiahship, however, is the fact that he was executed as a messianic pretender, a political threat to the Roman government and the status quo (John 11:47–50). At the trial Pilate asks him, "Are you the King of the Jews?" (Mark 15:2), and the inscription over the cross describing the charge against him read "King of the Jews" (Mark 15:26; cf. 15:18, 32). Nevertheless, the total impression of the tradition works against viewing Jesus as a messianic political figure. At the temptation the devil is rebuked when he offers Jesus political power (Matt. 4:8–10 par.); moreover, Jesus denies that he is seeking to establish an earthly kingdom (Mark 10:42–44; cf. John 18:36). Despite the one blow struck in his defense, Jesus himself offers no resistance at his arrest, trial, and death (Mark 14:47–49; cf. Matt. 26:52). If Jesus was arrested and executed as a politically subversive messianic pretender, this fact only shows how thoroughly his opponents misunderstood or misused him.

From New Testament times onward Christians and others have assumed that Jesus claimed to be the Messiah of Jewish expectation. But this assumption is questionable on two grounds. First, Jewish future expectations, and specifically messianic expectations, were likely much more complex than the New Testament testimony would lead us to believe. To what expectation, if any, did the career and claim of Jesus correspond? The probable answer is that the messianic script was rewritten in light of Jesus' actual career. Second, the Fourth Gospel aside, the New Testament evidence that Jesus claimed messiahship is not as overwhelming as one might suppose.

Although at least three incidents recounted in the Synoptics apparently indicate that Jesus espoused a messianic claim—the confession of Peter at Caesarea Philippi, John the Baptist's question to Jesus, and Jesus' answer to the high priest at the trial—in the case of each, close examination shows that matters are not so simple as may at first appear. In the earliest, Markan account of the confession at Caesarea Philippi (8:27–33), Peter says that Jesus is the Messiah; Jesus does not, however, accept the title without qualification. When John the Baptist sends emissaries to Jesus to determine whether he is the one to come, the Messiah, Jesus does not give a direct answer. Although Jesus' response is usually taken as affirmative, he points only to his activity and does not claim or accept any title (Luke 7:18–23; Matt. 11:2–6). In the trial scene Jesus answers the high priest's question about messiahship positively (Mark 14:62), but the historicity of this exchange is at least questionable. Moreover, the Matthean and Lukan versions of the incident do not contain this clear, affirmative answer (Matt. 26:64 and Luke 22:67), and it is possible that their text of Mark did not. In view of the unanimous testimony of the New Testament writers that Jesus was the Christ, it is quite striking that the Synoptic writers so seldom portray him as making, or even accepting, messianic claims. Whether Jesus thought of himself in explicitly messianic terms or when he began to think in such terms is a question difficult to decide. It is clear enough, however, that he did not measure the response to his message and action by the titles that hearers might confer upon him.

Son of Man. At first the situation seems quite different with the Son of Man title, which appears frequently in Jesus' speech as a self-designation. As a rule, no one else used this title as a designation for Jesus. In fact, it is rarely used by anyone else in the entire New Testament. Consequently, *Son of Man* appears to be the title by which Jesus designated and understood himself. Yet this seemingly obvious conclusion requires further scrutiny in the light of the background of the term and its varied uses in the synoptic tradition.

The term *Son of Man* (Aramaic, *bar nasha*) was apparently not uncommon in the Aramaic speech of Jesus' time, although it is an oddity in Greek. It seems to have served as an indefinite pronoun meaning "anyone" or "a man." Perhaps it could also stand as the personal pronoun "I," although this is still disputed among experts in the Aramaic language. In any event, this term clearly could have been used by Aramaic-speaking contemporaries of Jesus, and thus by Jesus himself. Because the term is so frequently used of Jesus in the Gospels and only rarely by anyone other than himself, the assumption that it was used by Jesus and that it appears in the Gospels because it was used by Jesus seems a valid one. Beyond that, it is impossible to say anything with certainty, for there is no consensus about the matter in modern Gospel and Jesus research. Interestingly enough, aside from the use of the term in Daniel 7:13 (cited in Mark 14:62 parr.), in the Book of Ezekiel God frequently addresses the prophet as "Son of Man." Unfortunately, however, in both Daniel and Ezekiel the NRSV obscures the potentially important Christological reference by translating the term "mortal" or "human being."

In order to grasp the varied functions of the title, it is useful to classify Son of Man sayings in the Gospels according to three basic types, although these do not quite comprehend all the various usages: (1) sayings that speak of a future, glorious Son of Man; (2) those that speak of the present, suffering Son of Man; and (3) those that speak of an authoritative earthly Son of Man. By and large, the usages do not overlap; that is, they occur in separate sayings or traditions.

1. Mark records that after Peter's confession at Caesarea Philippi, Jesus says, "Those who are ashamed of me and of my words in this adulterous and sinful generation, of them the Son of Man will also be ashamed, when he comes in the glory of his Father with the holy angels" (8:38; cf. Luke 9:26 and Matt. 16:27). Here is the *future, glorious Son of Man*. The apocalyptic discourse of Mark 13 (parr. in Matt. and Luke) brings out details of the Son of

Man's coming—how he will "send out the angels, and gather his elect from the four winds, from the ends of the earth to the ends of heaven" (Mark 13:26 parr.).[23] The nature of the relationship between Jesus and this Son of Man remains unclear, although the fact of a relationship is clearly asserted: "And I tell you, every one who acknowledges me before others, the Son of Man also will acknowledge before the angels of God" (Luke 12:8 f; cf. Matt. 10:32 f.). In the apocalyptic Son of Man sayings Jesus never explicitly says that he is the Son of Man, nor is that a necessary inference, although most readers, as well as the evangelists, assume that identification. In fact, Jesus seems to speak of the Son of Man as someone other than himself.

2. The sayings concerning the *present, suffering Son of Man* are more stereotyped and less varied than are those in the first category. They teach "that the Son of Man must undergo great suffering, and be rejected by the elders, the chief priests, and the scribes, and be killed, and after three days rise again" (Mark 8:31 parr.; 9:31 parr.; 10:33–34 parr.).[24] After the final saying of this type Jesus speaks explicitly of his redemptive mission, "For the Son of Man came not to be served but to serve, and to give his life a ransom for many" (Mark 10:45 par.; cf. Luke 22:27). The Son of Man here is clearly Jesus.

3. A less clearly defined type deals with the *earthly activity of Jesus as Son of Man,* apart from his suffering. In this role Jesus has authority to forgive sins (Mark 2:10 parr.) and is lord of the Sabbath (Mark 2:27 f. parr.). Also, the earthly Son of Man is accused of being a glutton, a drunkard, a friend of tax collectors and sinners (Matt. 11:18 f.; Luke 7:33 f.); moreover, as Son of Man, Jesus has nowhere to lay his head (Matt. 8:20; Luke 9:58).[25]

How we are to understand the Son of Man sayings and the relationship among the three types? Are they all authentic words of Jesus? Did one group of sayings or the other originate in the early church? How is it possible to relate the suffering Son of Man and the future glorious Son of Man, especially when Jesus talks of the latter as if he were someone other than himself?

Because references to the *apocalyptic Son of Man* appear in all strata of the Synoptic tradition (Mark, Q, and the material distinctive to Matthew and Luke) as well as in John (5:27), the case for the authenticity of these sayings appears to be strong. Yet this conclusion has been seriously challenged on the basis of the fact that *Son of Man* does not appear in the tradition alongside, or in association with, sayings about the kingdom of God. This has to be regarded as a striking and potentially significant fact.

Moreover, the once generally held view that there existed a pre-Christian Son of Man Messiah, or messianic expectation, in the Old Testament or an-

---

23. For other apocalyptic Son of Man sayings, cf. Luke 12:40; 17:22–30; 18:8; 21:36; Matt. 13:41–43; 19:28; 24:29–44; 25:31 ff.
24. See also Mark 9:9 par.; Mark 9:31; cf. Matt. 17:22 f. and Luke 9:44; Mark 10:33 f. parr.; Mark 14:21 par.; Mark 14:41; cf. Matt. 26:45 and Luke 22:48.
25. Cf. also Luke 11:20 f. (Matt. 12:40); Matt. 13.36 ff. and Luke 19:10.

cient Judaism, has been increasingly questioned. The figure of the Son of Man in Daniel (7:13 14), a heavenly apparition, is in that book explicitly identified with "the holy ones of the Most High" (7:18), the righteous remnant of Israel. In certain Jewish apocalypses such as 1 Enoch (48:2 ff.) and 4 Ezra (chap. 13), a messianic figure is called "Son of Man," or simply "Man" (4 Ezra), but the question is whether the use of the phrase indicates the existence of an established messianic category. Even when viewed over against the numerous references to the coming, or apocalyptic, Son of Man in the Gospels, the relatively few instances of the term in earlier or contemporary Jewish sources do not constitute a strong case for it as a Jewish messianic category. Thus it is not clear from Jewish sources that "Son of Man" was already a title for the Messiah.

If one assumes that this coming Son of Man is simply Jesus, who will return after his death, it is not necessary to think that the title represents a Jewish apocalyptic, messianic idea. Then Jesus was in those instances where he speaks of a coming Son of Man simply referring to himself. And thus Jesus anticipated and foresaw not only his earthly fate but also his future resurrection and ultimate return. That is the traditional Christian view.

If, however, one questions whether Jesus would have foreseen so explicitly his own fate after death and doubts the authenticity of many of the other Son of Man sayings, especially those predicting his suffering (as modern criticism has), the traditional view presents problems. Under those circumstances it is no longer clear that in the apocalyptic Son of Man sayings Jesus referred to himself. (When these sayings stand by themselves, they do not obviously designate Jesus.) But if he did not refer to himself, it is necessary to suppose that there was a category of expectation, that of the heavenly, coming Son of Man, which he assumed that his readers would know and understand. Yet, as we have just observed, the evidence for such a category in Judaism outside the New Testament is not altogether clear. Alternatively, it has been suggested that Jesus never used the title or term for himself at all; rather, it came into being as a Christological title in a branch of the early church and was placed upon his lips. Yet if that were the case, it is strange that "Son of Man" appears now as a title only in the Gospels, not elsewhere in the New Testament, and only on Jesus' lips. One would think it would have survived elsewhere.

Most modern critical scholars agree that the *suffering Son of Man sayings* in their present form are stereotypical; they clearly project Jesus' fate as the Gospels recount it and as faith believed in it, and are likely the product of the later, postresurrection church, if not of Mark himself (upon whom Matthew and Luke rely). This does not necessarily mean that Jesus took no thought of the future, or specifically of the prospect of his own fate. In a number of synoptic passages occurring before and during the passion week, Jesus seems to contemplate or anticipate his death (e.g., Luke 13:31–35; Mark 14:22–25, 36). In such passages, moreover, Jesus does not characteristically refer to himself as the Son of Man. In fact, in one such case he evidently calls himself a prophet and links himself with the prophets of old (Luke 13:33–34).

Not surprisingly, the Son of Man sayings that represent Jesus as acting with *authority,* and some of those in which he refers to himself as Son of Man in an almost offhand way (e.g., Matt. 8:20; Luke 9:58), are once again becoming the center of attention. It may be that sayings such as Mark 2:10 and 2:27–28 agree with the later church's understanding of Jesus' authority, as many modern interpreters have thought. But they may also reflect Jesus' own speech, or at least his authoritative self-understanding. Because there are real difficulties in accepting the suffering Son of Man sayings as authentic, and because it is difficult to suppose that Jesus either spoke of his own return from heaven (the traditional view) or that he used "Son of Man" to refer to a mythical, apocalyptic figure other than himself, the origin of these Son of Man categories in Jesus' own speech becomes doubtful. Yet it is difficult to conceive of how this language could have arisen in the early church apart from Jesus, especially when only Jesus uses the term. Consequently, these less easily categorized sayings may well hold the key to Jesus' view of himself as an authoritative messenger of the kingdom of God. Just as Jesus spoke of the kingdom of God as something his hearers would know about, but without defining it, so he may have spoken of himself as Son of Man, allowing his followers to discern in his word and works its true significance. Thus the title itself does not evoke messianic traditions that would detract from, or misinterpret, his kingdom proclamation. Understandably, early Christians would then have subsequently used the term in sayings about Jesus' death and second coming.

Prophet. There remains the possibility that Jesus thought of himself also as a prophet. As has already been observed, Ezekiel is addressed by God as "Son of Man" precisely in his prophetic role (Ezekiel 2:1; 3:4, 17). *Prophet* is not usually taken to be a messianic title but rather a role or function. One thinks first of all of the prophets of Israel, whose words and deeds are recorded in the Old Testament. They pronounced warnings and judgments against injustice and inequity, and foretold the intervention of God in human affairs for weal or woe. Certainly Jesus' conduct closely paralleled that of Old Testament prophets in certain respects, as some of his contemporaries recognized (Mark 6:15 parr.). Furthermore, Jesus almost certainly referred to himself as a prophet (Mark 6:4 parr.; cf. Luke 13:33), and one of his disciples is portrayed as describing him as "a prophet mighty in deed and word before God and all the people" (Luke 24:19).

In important respects Jesus is aptly characterized as a prophet, particularly a prophet of the kingdom of God. In the view of some modern scholars he was an apocalyptic prophet, although we have noticed that *apocalyptic* can be applied to him only with significant qualifications. It should be noted that the prophetic role coincides with an ancient expectation of the appearance of a prophet like Moses (Deut. 18:15–22). Such a prophet came to be associated with Jewish eschatological hopes for the intervention of God in history, and the expectation was taken up by early Christians (cf. Acts 3:22).

Some Christians, as well as others, have been glad to recognize Jesus as a prophet, if not *the* prophet of Deuteronomy. But in the confession of Peter (cf. Mark 8:27–30) the prophetic title seems to be rejected in favor of the designation of Jesus as Christ (Messiah); thus, most Christians have regarded as inadequate the view that Jesus was a prophet. In doing so, however, they tend to attach to his messianic dignity associations that derive more from Christian confession and worship than from the historic, Jewish background of the concept. In any event, whatever else Jesus may have been, his career recalls the role of the prophet in the great Israelite tradition.

Jesus emphasized obedience to God and his rule, and did not expound upon his own titles or dignity. Yet he must have reflected upon his own role in the mission upon which he embarked. The crucial aspect of Jesus' self-concept becomes clear in his reply to the inquiry of John the Baptist's disciples, "And blessed is anyone who takes no offense at me" (Matt. 11:6; Luke 7:23). In context, Jesus says that he asks nothing more than acknowledgment of the miracles that are occurring and the good news that is being proclaimed. In other words, the center of Jesus' message is the eschatological salvation being offered the hearer. Although Jesus did not announce himself or proclaim his own messianic dignity, his message and actions were based upon convictions about his unique mission and calling. Thus, to question Jesus' so-called messianic self-consciousness is not necessarily to take the position that his identity, role, and importance in the history of God's dealing with his people were matters unimportant to him. The following observations speak to the character and strength of Jesus' purpose and self-consciousness.

JESUS' CALL TO DISCIPLESHIP

Jesus' authoritative self-consciousness is implicit in his call to discipleship. Jesus gathered disciples (Mark 1:16–20), crying out, "Follow *me* and *I* will make you fish for people" (Mark 1:17; Matt. 4:19; cf. Luke 5:10). He summoned Levi, the tax collector, with a curt, "Follow me" (Mark 2:14; Luke 5:27 f.; cf. Matt. 9:9). Jesus speaks; people drop what they are doing and follow then or not at all (cf. Luke 9:59–62). The Gospels report that the Pharisees had disciples (Matt. 22:16), as did the later rabbis and John the Baptist (cf. Mark 2:18 parr. and John 1:35). Yet despite certain analogies with other leaders and teachers, Jesus stands out as one who called disciples with an unprecedented authority.

Jesus called disciples to a close, personal relationship with himself (Mark 1:17; 2:14). The source of that authoritative action lay in his proclamation of the dawning of the kingdom (Mark 1:15), for this sense of God's immediate presence gave impetus to the call. Henceforth, the disciples had a new allegiance: the old had to be left behind, whether vocation (fishing, tax collecting), possessions (Mark 10:17–31 parr.), or sacred obligations (Matt. 8:22 par.). Discipleship promised no easy way. The disciples were called to proclaim the kingdom and heal the sick (Mark 6:7–13; cf. Matt. 10:1–11:1; Luke

9:1–6; 10:1–12) and to follow Jesus in service and suffering (Mark 10:32–45 parr.). Nevertheless, the relation to Jesus promised a blessed future for whoever, without shame, remained close to him (Mark 8:38; cf. Matt. 16:27 and Luke 9:26).

THE AUTHORITY OF JESUS

For the sake of clarity, further evidence for Jesus' implicit authority may be divided into four groupings:

1. That Jesus *acted* with authority in the exorcisms and healings as well as in the calling of disciples has already become apparent. Of first importance is the fact that these acts were all the more authoritative by virtue of their having been done in the context of Jesus' proclamation about the dawning kingdom of God.

2. Jesus indirectly *claimed* an unprecedented immediate relationship with God. An indication of this close relationship was Jesus' use of *abba,* the child's intimate, everyday word for father, to address God. This way of speaking to God was so unusual that the Synoptics record only one instance of it, in the Garden of Gethsemane, where Jesus prayed, "Abba, Father, for you all things are possible; remove this cup from me; yet not what I want, but what you want" (Mark 14:36; cf. Rom. 8:15; Gal. 4:6, where Paul's use of the term may go back to Jesus). Moreover, since Jesus refers to God as Father rather frequently, it is probable that he often used this intimate form of address in prayer. Ultimately, Christian trinitarian language about God (Father, Son, and Holy Spirit) is rooted in this relationship and mode of speech. (Of course, Christian trinitarian doctrine developed over several centuries after the Gospels were written.) A second indication of such an intimate relationship was Jesus' remarkable use of *amen* to introduce a pronouncement (see for example Matt. 5:18, 26). Ordinarily *amen,* meaning "so be it," was a liturgical response. In Jesus' usage, however, it is a solemn assurance, like the swearing of an oath. Thus even Jesus' style of teaching claimed an unprecedented authority.

3. Jesus authoritatively grants *forgiveness* to all sorts of people. The forgiveness of God was, of course, nothing new to Judaism, but Jesus proclaimed a more radical forgiveness. Without hesitation he admitted sinners into his fellowship (Mark 2:13–15; Luke 15:2). For him all people were basically in need of forgiveness because no one could merit God's favor (Mark 2:17; Luke 18:9–14). But beyond this, Jesus is reported to have himself spoken a word of forgiveness over sinners, even the unrepentant (Mark 2:5; Luke 23:34). In so doing, he assumed a unique position of authority (Mark 2:7). Although proclaiming the kingdom of God, both in terms of judgment and forgiveness, Jesus spoke primarily in terms of the latter: "I have come to call not the righteous but sinners" (Mark 2:17 parr.; cf. Luke 7:36–50).

4. The final evidence for Jesus' assumption of authority is his *radical interpretation of the law.* Jesus was and remained a Jew in his obedience to

the law, as the Gospel tradition attests. Yet Jesus radically interpreted the law in at least three particular respects: first, he denied that impurity could invade an individual from external sources (Mark 7:1–23 par.). Such an extreme qualification of the ancient world's distinction between clean and unclean constituted an attack upon the law's cultic dimension, whether or not Jesus acknowledged it. Second, Jesus set his own authority over against that of Moses, especially in the antitheses of the Sermon on the Mount (Matt. 5:21–48; cf. Mark 10:2–9). Jesus does not, however, contradict Moses so much as he goes beyond him in the radical nature of his demand. Third, Jesus set scripture over against scripture and by so doing assumed authority over the written word of scripture (Mark 10:2–12; cf. Matt. 19:3–12). Jesus' authoritative actions and attributes should, however, be viewed within the context of ancient Judaism. The impression that he stood outside Judaism is a reasonable inference from the Gospel of John, but not from the synoptic tradition.

How could Jesus assume such authority? The probable explanation is rooted in and proceeds from the central proclamation of Jesus concerning the irruption of the kingdom of God. This emergent rule of God rendered all other authority provisional and transitory. The preaching of the inaugurated kingdom gave to Jesus' message a fresh, revolutionary quality that inevitably offended those who respected traditional authority.

Healings were occurring; disciples were being called; forgiveness was being offered; a new community of "forgiven sinners" was being formed; and the law was being radically reinterpreted. Something new was appearing in many forms. Jesus' treatment of the law typified his opposition to the status quo, which was the primary source of opposition to him. Jesus touched a nerve in first-century Judaism. Eventually the separation of his followers ("Christians") from the old religious community resulted. Understandably, certain Jewish leaders rejected Jesus and his authority; opposition led ultimately to his being handed over to be crucified by the Roman government as a politically dangerous revolutionary. To this last dramatic chapter of Jesus' ministry we now turn.

The Suffering Messiah

Our efforts to reconstruct the historical Jesus have been guided by the principle of coherence. According to the tradition, Jesus of Nazareth was a man who healed, taught, and suffered a criminal's death. Our portrait of him must include these three elements in a coherent, understandable way or else historical criticism is unable to make sense of the tradition. The necessity for coherence becomes a problem when we now turn to the final element in the historical Jesus tradition, the death of Jesus. Why was Jesus crucified? Was his death simply the tragic end of a man who had gone about doing good, both in deed and word? How was it possible that one who had performed miracles could die in such weakness? How could one who evidently attracted such crowds of followers have been completely deserted at the last days? Such questions were potentially embarrassing. Yet rather than conceal Jesus' death, the early Christians proclaimed it.

Already some indications of answers to these questions have become apparent. The teaching Messiah turned out to be something more than an instructor in good works, piety, and universal kindness. At the center of Jesus' teaching was the kingdom proclamation. As herald of the kingdom, Jesus claimed an authority that startled and astounded some and threatened others. The challenge of Jesus' authoritative message and activity met resistance that finally culminated in his death.

We have already observed that the healing Messiah possessed authority. But without faith in the power or rule of God, healing did not take place. Jesus' healings were an expression of the power of the inbreaking rule or kingdom of God. Nevertheless, the healings that Jesus effected demonstrated not only his rulership but his service to God and others. The Gospel of Matthew aptly and succinctly characterizes the miraculous healing power of Jesus with the passage from Isaiah, "He took our infirmities and bore our diseases" (Matt. 8:17). Surprisingly, just that passage could be applied to the death of Jesus (Matt. 26:28; cf. Rom. 5:8 and John 3:16). Perhaps the powerful miracle-working Jesus and the crucified Jesus complement, rather than contradict, each other.

We have also come to recognize Jesus' limited use of power by the way in which the miracle tradition is treated in both Mark and Matthew. The heightened miracle tradition in the first half of Mark did not succeed in producing true discipleship. The disciples became truly faithful only after Jesus' death and resurrection. In Matthew, condensation of the Markan miracle tradition focused attention upon the word of Jesus rather than upon his miracle power. Each Gospel affirms that Jesus worked miracles, yet each Gospel sets the miraculous within the framework of a ministry that concludes with Jesus' crucifixion. Jesus' power did not deliver him from that apparently ignominious end. Jesus' words and works led unerringly to his death. In this sense it is correct to say that the Gospels are passion narratives (stories of Jesus' suffering and death) with extended introductions, as the nineteenth-century German theologian Martin Kähler observed.

Jesus was executed by the Romans during or just before the annual Jewish Passover feast. The exact date is uncertain, although it was probably A.D. 30, give or take a year or two.[26] Jewish authorities played a role in the arrest

---

26. The actual dates of the life of Jesus do not correspond exactly to the B.C.–A.D. (or B.C.–B.C.E.) scheme of dating that we commonly use. This scheme, according to which our era begins with the year of Jesus' birth, was only introduced in the sixth century. Unfortunately, the date of Jesus' birth was incorrectly calculated, if, as both Matthew (2:1) and

and trial of Jesus, as the Gospels allege, although the Christian sources show a tendency (which must be viewed critically) to shift responsibility from the Romans to the Jews. Even though the Gospels state that Jesus had fore-knowledge of his impending death and Christian belief takes it for granted that he willingly consented to die, the execution of their leader obviously took his disciples by surprise and left them in disarray (Mark 14:27). The famed inscription on the cross ("The King of the Jews," Mark 15:26) indicates that Jesus was condemned and died as a messianic pretender. Yet his fate contrasted sharply to normal expectations concerning a king (1 Cor. 1:23). Other messianic pretenders met similar fates (Acts 5:35–39; cf. 21:38) and did not gain the recognition to which they aspired. Why should Jesus differ from them? Why should his followers continue—or begin—to insist that he was the Messiah or Christ? The most obvious answer is that they believed him to have been raised by God from the dead and set at God's own right hand (Acts 2:24 ff.; 1 Cor. 15:4). Once this is granted, however, further problems arise. Why should belief in a resurrection mean that the resurrected one was the Messiah? The bestowal of that title would follow only if the claim had previously been made, or at least entertained by the disciples. Moreover, even a report of his resurrection, which certainly was not universally believed, did not fully explain the tragic fate of Jesus as the Messiah, the one destined to rule over an earthly kingdom of Israel.

For those followers who believed in Jesus' resurrection the tragic implications of the crucifixion were overcome. But there remained the task of convincing others that his ignominious death really did not contradict the traditions and expectations of Israel's Messiah. To accomplish this task, believers in Jesus turned to the scriptures. Thus the earliest references to Jesus' death were often accompanied not only by the proclamation of his resurrection but also by the assertion (1 Cor. 15:3) and a demonstration (Luke 24:25–27; Acts 2:24 ff.) that he had died "in accordance with the Scriptures." That is, his death was in accord with the will of God as revealed in the Bible. Thus the earliest Christians doubtless had to explain Jesus' crucifixion because it was a problem, a "stumbling block," as Paul says, to other Jews (1 Cor. 1:23). Even the proclamation of the resurrection could not be made credible until the stigma of the cross was removed or explained (Gal. 3:13; 2 Cor. 5:21). It is surely significant that the passion narratives of the Gospels are studded with Old Testament quotations and allusions. Their fundamental purpose was to expound, to whatever audience, the importance and necessity of Jesus' death as the accomplishment of God's will. Doubtless such references were found already in the preaching, teaching, and controversies of the primitive church.

Luke (1:5) indicate, Jesus was born before Herod's death (4 B.C.). The exact date of Jesus' birth, as well as his crucifixion, is not known. For a good discussion of the problem of the chronology of Jesus' ministry and death, see E. P. Sanders, *The Historical Figure of Jesus* (London: Penguin, 1993), pp. 282–290, who concludes: "Granting we cannot be certain, I shall accept 30 C.E. as being approximately the year of Jesus' death" (p. 290).

For the earliest believers, however, the cross was not just a liability to be explained. It was seen as the focal point of salvation, the event and means of God's redemption. This understanding of the cross as in some important way a redemptive event was a part of the confessional tradition that Paul had received ("He died for our sins in accordance with the scriptures," 1 Cor. 15:3; cf. Rom. 4:25 and Heb. 13:20), and it lies at the heart of the ancient words of institution of the Lord's Supper (1 Cor. 11:23–26; cf. Mark 14:22–25). From the beginning, or very near it, Jesus' death on the cross has been an important element of Christian preaching and liturgy, as, for example, in Paul's view of baptism (Rom. 6:3–11) and the Lord's Supper (1 Cor. 11:17–34). It is therefore a recurring motif in the New Testament, in the Pauline letters particularly, but also in the Gospels, where the relative length of the narration of Jesus' final week in Jerusalem indicates its importance. For some time many New Testament scholars have regarded it as probable that the Gospels' passion narratives were based upon earlier narrative traditions or sources. The prominence of Jesus' death in early Christian preaching and liturgy (i.e., the Lord's Supper; cf. 1 Cor. 11:23), apparent from other sources, suggests that some recitation of the narrative of Jesus' death became fixed in the tradition long before the evangelists wrote. If so, this would explain the existence of two parallel narratives of the passion in Mark and John, which often differ unaccountably, as well as other independent passion traditions in Matthew and especially Luke.

THE PASSION AND DEATH OF JESUS

Why did Jesus risk his life by going to Jerusalem?

Although the Fourth Gospel records several trips to Jerusalem, perhaps correctly, the Synoptic Gospels give the impression that Jesus journeyed from Galilee to Jerusalem only at the close of his ministry. This journey occupies a central place in these Gospels. As we discovered, Luke made that journey the crucial middle section of his Gospel (Luke 9:51–19:29). Mark's tradition describes the journey to Jerusalem as a decisive and awesome step: "They were on the road, going up to Jerusalem, and Jesus was walking ahead of them; and they were amazed, and those who followed were afraid" (Mark 10:32; cf. Matt. 20:17 and Luke 18:31).

Why did Jesus make this final visit to Jerusalem? Some New Testament interpreters take at face value the Markan view that Jesus went to Jerusalem to die. For example, it is maintained that the conviction dawned upon Jesus at Caesarea Philippi that he must go to Jerusalem and die in order to bring in the kingdom of God.[27] This view takes Mark (8:31) at face value, but so far as we can tell from the Synoptic Gospels themselves, Jesus did not act in Jerusalem as if he were carrying out a preconceived plan to die. The hypothesis rests in part upon the view that Jesus took upon himself the role of

27. Schweitzer, *The Quest of the Historical Jesus,* pp. 386 f.

the suffering servant of Isaiah 53: "For the Son of Man came not to be served but to serve, and to give his life a ransom for many" (Mark 10:45). It is quite possible, however, that this saying reflects the faith of the early church rather than the consciousness of Jesus. In that case, it is a statement in retrospect of what Jesus accomplished.

As an alternative hypothesis we suggest that Jesus went to Jerusalem to preach the coming kingdom of God, for no person who had a message for Israel would fail to take it to the capital city. His proclamation of the coming of God's rule was in effect a radical questioning of the prevailing religious, social, and political order. It was a challenge to the temple and its authorities, as well as to conventional interpretation of the law. In the carrying out of this mission Jesus could hardly have been blind to the possibility that his own death might result (cf. Luke 13:33). But Jesus' kingdom proclamation does not center upon his own role, and the traditions of the kingdom say nothing explicitly about his intention to die. The view that Jesus sought to bring in the kingdom through his suffering thus lacks the support of the Gospels themselves.

THE EVENTS OF JESUS' PASSION AND DEATH

Unlike other traditions in the Synoptics, the passion story, beginning with the entry into Jerusalem (Mark 11:1; Matt. 21:1; Luke 19:28), constitutes a full, detailed narrative covering a period of days. The narrative seems true to life. The opponents of Jesus have the upper hand, and Jesus dies. The impression of accuracy is heightened by the remarkable agreement of the Synoptic Gospels in sequence of events and in details, an agreement considerably greater than in earlier portions. This becomes even more pronounced with the arrest, trial, and crucifixion of Jesus. Moreover, the Fourth Gospel (John 18–19) agrees much more closely with the Synoptics here than at any other point.

The major episodes of the passion story in their general order are the triumphal entry into Jerusalem (Mark 11:1–10); the cleansing of the temple (Mark 11:15–19); the controversies about authority (Mark 11:27–33; 12:1–12, 13–17, 18–27, 28–34); the apocalyptic discourse (Mark 13); the anointing of Jesus (Mark 14:3–9); the Last Supper (Mark 14:12–25); Jesus in the Garden of Gethsemane (Mark 14:32–42); Jesus' arrest and trial (Mark 14:43–65); the release of Barabbas (Mark 15:6–15); and finally the crucifixion and burial of Jesus (Mark 15:16–47). The narrative follows a sequence that must be broadly historical. That is, the crucial events must have occurred in the order in which they are presented: entry into Jerusalem, temple cleansing, the subsequent question about authority, the Last Supper, Gethsemane, Jesus' arrest, the crucifixion, and burial. Thus we may proceed with some confidence to the following reconstruction of Jesus' activity and reception in Jerusalem.

Jesus' triumphal entry into Jerusalem was open to dangerous misinterpretation. The acclamation of the crowds, "Blessed is the coming kingdom of our ancestor David!" (Mark 11:10; cf. Matt. 21:9; Luke 19:38), suggests that

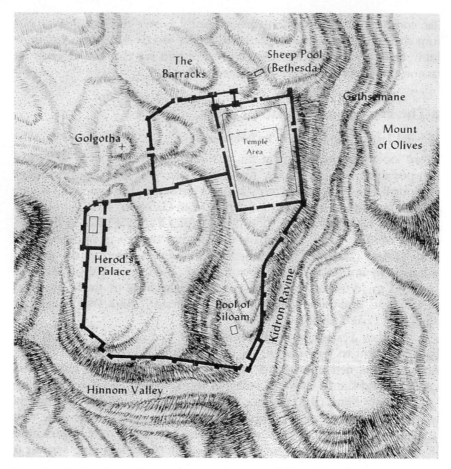

Jerusalem in the time of Jesus. The exact location of the walls is, however, a matter of some uncertainty, although it is generally agreed that Golgotha, the site of Jesus' execution (as commemorated by the Church of the Holy Sepulchre), was outside them, as this map shows.

Jesus was a political king who would restore the fortunes of Israel by leading a revolution to overthrow Roman domination. With respect to these hopes Jesus' first action upon entering Jerusalem was ambiguous; he went into the temple and drove out the traders and money changers (Mark 11:15–19). Ordinarily the Court of the Gentiles, where this event must have taken place, would have been well policed, with a Roman garrison stationed nearby. How Jesus was able to get away with such an act is a major and unresolved historical question. The question is particularly difficult if Jesus' act is viewed as an armed assault, but that is improbable. Aside from the fact that the whole Jesus tradition scarcely supports this interpretation, it is by no means clear what Jesus would have hoped to gain for an armed revolt by the expulsion

Entry of Jesus into Jerusalem. Sculpture from a lintel over a doorway near Massa
Carrara, Italy (*ca.* 1175).   *(Courtesy of Metropolitan Museum of Art. Purchase,
1962. The Cloisters Collection.)*

of money changers and vendors from the temple precincts. If, however, the
central focus of Jesus' mission and message was proclamation and inauguration of the kingdom of God, it is reasonable to suppose that he would have
gone to the Holy City, and to the holiest place in the city, to announce the
coming of that kingdom (Mal. 3:1: "See, I am sending my messenger to prepare the way before me, and the Lord whom you seek will suddenly come to
his temple.").

It is usually assumed that the temple's corruption provoked his hostility
against its custodians. But the selling of animals for sacrifice and the changing of money were a necessity for continued temple worship and, indeed, a
convenience for the many pilgrims at the feast. Further, it is often thought
that the vendors and money changers were overcharging or cheating the
people, even though this idea is nowhere explicitly stated. The more likely
implication of Jesus' act is that he was, for whatever reason, attacking the
whole temple cult and sacrificial system. Such an attack should not be understood as Jesus' advocacy of a higher form of religion, but as a manifestation of his belief that in view of the advent of God's kingly rule, present modes
of worship and obedience were being called into question. Radical opposition to the temple would then be a logical extension of Jesus' rejection of
cultic, particularly purity, laws.

Nor would such opposition have been unprecedented in the history of Israel. In Jeremiah 7 the prophet lashes out at those who find false security in
the temple, and in the synoptic version of the temple incident Jesus quotes
Jeremiah's words (Jer. 7:11). Jesus' acute consciousness of God as king defines
his ministry and links him to the prophetic tradition. For good reason people
took Jesus to be a prophet (Mark 6:15; 8:28; cf. Matt. 21:11; Luke 24:19), and
he gladly identified himself with that role (Mark 6:4 parr.; Luke 13:33–34). Understandably, the religious leaders reacted violently to his action (Mark 11:18);

at the trial they accused him of having come to destroy the temple (Mark 14:57 f.; cf. 13:2). Perhaps the charge was accurate (cf. Acts 6:14; John 2:19).

The events leading to Jesus' death center more upon the question of what authority Jesus possessed than upon the messianic question specifically (Mark 11:28). The opponents of Jesus tried to fit him into the category of a political revolutionary (cf. Mark 12:13–17) and to engage him in theological disputes (cf. the resurrection question in Mark 12:18–27 and the query about the First Commandment in Mark 12:28–34). But Jesus continued to threaten their security by proclaiming the immediacy of God's rule (cf. Mark 12:17, 27, 34), which demanded the response of the whole person (cf. the poor widow in Mark 12:41–44). Jesus preached the dawning kingdom of God rather than a political, spiritual, or moral ideology. That emphasis becomes most evident in the passion story's apocalyptic discourse, for the final days herald the triumphant coming of God's rule and the world's judgment (note especially Mark 13:24–26 and 32 f.). The apocalyptic discourse's position in the passion story elaborates authentically the eschatological aspect of his last message.

It is uncertain whether the Last Supper that Jesus shared with his disciples was a Passover meal. It is presented as such in the Synoptics but not in John, where it takes place the evening before Passover (John 13:1; 19:31; cf. Mark 14:2). In any event, the setting makes clear that the meal was eschatological: "Truly, I tell you, I will never again drink of the fruit of the vine until that day when I drink it new in the kingdom of God" (Mark 14:25). This word of Jesus indicates that by this time he knew that his death was imminent. His overwhelming conviction about the immediacy of the reign of God elicited followers but also aroused opponents who now sought his death. The proleptic anointing of Jesus' body for burial (Mark 14:3–9) and his betrayal by Judas (Mark 14:10–21) point to the impending fate. Not only had ordinary piety been offended, but Jesus' kingdom proclamation made him vulnerable to misunderstanding or misrepresentation as a political revolutionary. Ironically, it has often been thought that Judas' betrayal resulted from his disappointed realization that Jesus was not going to lead an armed revolt against Rome. But about Judas' motivation one can only speculate; the texts are silent except to imply he did it out of greed (esp. Matt. 26:14–16).

In the Garden of Gethsemane Jesus prayed that he might escape death if he would not thereby betray God's rule and will (Mark 14:36; cf. 8:35). Soon after Gethsemane Jesus was alone, deserted even by his closest disciples (Mark 14:37, 40; see esp. Peter's denial, 14:66–72). The Gethsemane story may not be the report of an eyewitness—who was there to witness Jesus' prayer?—yet it makes sense of the last hours of Jesus. In substance if not in detail, it must have a historical basis. It is hard to imagine that the intensely human portrayal of Jesus' feelings was simply invented. The church's Christology was moving in another direction. (Thus the Gospel of John has no narration of the Gethsemane scene.)

The dramatic scene of Jesus' arrest is told simply and starkly by Mark (14:43–50), followed closely by Matthew, who adds a memorable word of Je-

View of Jerusalem with the Garden of Gethsemane in the center and the Mount of Olives in the background.   *(Courtesy of Pan American Airways.)*

sus addressed to the would-be defender who has just struck off the ear of the high priest's slave: "Put your sword back into its place: for all who take the sword will perish by the sword" (Matt. 26:52). Luke's version seems to have Jesus stop Judas before he can kiss him (Luke 22:47–48), and John has no Judas kiss at all. Yet in John (18:1–11), as in the other Gospels, Judas takes the lead in Jesus' arrest. Not surprisingly, the Gethsemane scene, which is interrupted by the arresting party in the Synoptics, is missing from John, where Jesus seems to be in total control of events. At this point the remaining disciples desert Jesus (Mark 14:50: presumably Peter, James, and John, cf. vs. 33), although Peter follows the arresting party to the place where the council has gathered (14:53–54), but only to deny him (14:66–72). Like the Gethsemane scene, the betrayal of Jesus by one of his disciples and the denial by another would scarcely have been invented by the early church.

The Jewish trial scene (14:55–65) raises some difficult historical questions; our subsequent conclusions, therefore, must remain conjectural. Although

The inscription, found in Caesarea, the Roman occupation headquarters on the Mediterranean coast of Palestine, identifies Pontius Pilate as the Prefect of Judea. The name "Pilatus" is clearly visible on the second line, and the title is partially effaced on the third line. On the top line "Tiberieum" refers to the Roman Emperor Tiberius who reigned during the time of Jesus (cf. Luke 31–2) and in whose honor Pilate had evidently erected the building from which this stone comes.   *(Courtesy of the Israel Antiquities Authority. Exibited and Photographed, Israel Museum.)*

the authorities, including the high priest, condemned Jesus because he claimed to be the Messiah, no other record exists of any Jewish court ever condemning anyone as a messianic pretender. Jesus was executed not by the Jewish form of capital punishment, stoning (cf. Acts 5:26; 7:58; John 10:31), but by Roman crucifixion. Probably Jesus was only arraigned before Jewish authorities and then delivered to the Romans, who executed him as a messianic pretender (i.e., King of the Jews). The evening Sanhedrin trial in which Jesus was condemned to death (Mark 14:58–65) has obviously been elaborated in the tradition. John and Luke do not report it. Although Jesus' radical view of obedience and his seeming disregard for tradition doubtless aroused opposition among Pharisees, even as the Gospels report, the Markan account of the trial and death of Jesus—indeed, of the passion week—indi-

cates little or no opposition on their part. The chief priests now lead the opposition against Jesus.

The trial before Pilate (Mark 15:1–15 parr.) is marked by Jesus' seeming
unwillingness to speak, the mortal hostility of the chief priests, scribes, and
elders, and Pilate's ineffectual effort to give Jesus a fair hearing. That Jesus'
accusers prefer the rebel Barabbas to Jesus is telling. The crowd is manipu-
lated by the chief priests, who are the villains in the account, to ask for Barabbas' release and Jesus' crucifixion.

In Matthew Pilate protests his own innocence, and the people shout
(27:25): "His blood be on us and on our children," a statement that has sometimes been construed as the Jewish assumption of guilt for the death of Jesus. Actually, it is part of a trend in Matthew, and in the Gospels generally, to
shift blame for Jesus' death from Roman to Jewish authorities. In Matthew
"the people" are presumably the people of Jerusalem only, and the reference
to Jesus' blood upon their heads is probably an allusion to the coming destruction of Jerusalem by the Romans (A.D. 70), in which thousands of
Jerusalemites died. This is another indication that Matthew wrote after that
event (cf. 22:7).

After the rather summary trial, Jesus is routinely beaten (Mark 15:15),
mocked by the Roman soldiers (15:16–20), and led out to Golgotha, where
he is crucified (vss. 21–32) and is again mocked, this time by passersby (vs.
29). According to the Markan account Jesus died rather quickly (15:44) and
with a loud cry (15:37). At his death his body was requested by Joseph of Arimathea, whom Mark identifies as a member of the Sanhedrin (15:43). Pilate
granted his request and Jesus' body was taken down on the evening of the
crucifixion. Joseph then buried Jesus, according to Matthew (27:60) in his
own new tomb.

In all probability the story of the burial is based upon a kernel of historical
fact. It is simple, brief, and direct. The principal character, Joseph of Arimathea,
is mentioned in all the Gospel accounts, including John, where Nicodemus
joins him in burying Jesus (19:39). He is unknown from other sources, but just
this fact leads us to trust the reports. Otherwise it would be difficult to account
for the introduction of this person to perform the important task of burial.

The series of connected incidents in the passion tradition makes narrative
and even historical sense, and the events absorb our interest purely as story.
Yet the passion story cannot be read simply as a neutral detached account of
the last days of Jesus in Jerusalem. The faith of the church interprets the
meaning of Jesus' passion and death. The conviction that somehow God is
at work in the very death of Jesus governs the telling of the story.[28] The reader

---

28. The horror of death by crucifixion is presumed, but not dwelt upon, in the Gospel
    accounts. The Roman author Cicero had called it "that cruel and disgusting penalty"
    (*Against Verres*, V, 64, cited by Martin Hengel, *Crucifixion: In the Ancient World and the
    Folly of the Message of the Cross* [Philadelphia: Fortress, 1977], p. 8). Note especially pp.
    1–10, 22–38, for the utter horror of this form of execution. Cf. the further description
    quoted by Goguel in *Jesus and the Origins of Christianity*, II, pp. 534 f.

does not look away from the incidents to grasp this dimension and understand their meaning. Rather the events contain their own meaning, their own depth dimension, which is conveyed within the story but is not identical with it. Jesus really died and his death clarified for his disciples who he was.[29]

Probably Jesus did not enter Jerusalem with the express intention of dying, but rather to proclaim the coming kingdom of God. But if Jesus' death were not understandable as the outcome of his life, then there would be no reason why the Christian faith should be tied to this historical person's death. Why not *anyone's* death? Or, why any death at all?

In ascribing to Jesus predictions of his suffering and death (Mark 8:31; 9:31; 10:33), his followers in effect maintained that he willed his own death by his life. That is, Jesus' death climaxed and actualized his proclamation of the irruption of the kingdom of God. Jesus' radical sense of the nearness of God, his consequent break with the traditional standards of righteousness, his association with sinners, and his assault upon the temple aroused a reaction that eventuated in his death. To be sure, Jesus did not go about his mission in Jerusalem blindly. He knew that his message and action had set in motion forces that might cause his death, but he did not seek it.

Although we have so far concentrated upon his death, Jesus' full identity was only seen in the light of the resurrection. But our reading of the Gospels confirms that the resurrection cannot be separated from the death. For early Christian faith, the passion and resurrection were one story. Whether the early Christians were right, whether the story was true, still remains a matter of faith. Certainly Jesus died on a cross, that much is virtually indisputable. Yet whether that cross was really the salvation event depends upon whether the resurrection report is believed. Without the cross, the resurrection is meaningless, but without the resurrection the cross remains only a tragedy.

THE RESURRECTION OF JESUS OF NAZARETH

In what sense was the resurrection of Jesus an event? A belief? A hope?

According to the New Testament, the resurrection is central for faith: "If Christ has not been raised, then our proclamation has been in vain and your faith has been in vain" (1 Cor. 15:14; cf. 15:17). Without the resurrection there would have been no Gospels, no history of the apostles, no letters, no vision of the future, and no church. The origin of New Testament faith is the victory over death realized in Jesus of Nazareth.

Although the modern mind might find congenial the view that the resurrection stories are simply interpretations of Jesus' true identity as the one sent by God and have nothing to do with an actual event, the nature of the

---

29. This conviction finds expression in the belief that the events of the passion story took place in fulfillment of scripture. For example, verses 24, 29, and 32 in Mark 15 allude to Psalm 22, verses 18, 7, and 1, respectively. The Gospel of John is more explicit in the citation of the Psalm (John 19:24 quoting Psalm 22:18).

resurrection tradition resists such a conclusion. This tradition does not read like a mythological tale. Its realistic quality allows for and demands historical investigation. To maintain that the event of Jesus' resurrection is removed from historical investigation denies the factual claim of the early Christian faith. On the other hand, to maintain that historical investigation can decide about the resurrection denies the uniqueness and mystery of the event. Whether the resurrection of Jesus occurred is a question "for the answering of which evidence is relevant, but the evidence might all be believed without the question itself being answered in the affirmative."[30] Keeping in mind, then, the important—but not decisive—role of historical criticism in investigating the resurrection, we turn to the nature of the resurrection tradition and to the problem of the nature of the resurrection itself.

THE RESURRECTION TRADITION

The major New Testament sources of the resurrection tradition are 1 Corinthians 15:3–8, Mark 16:1–8, Matthew 28:1–20, Luke 24:1–53, and John 20:1–21:25. They present a bewildering array of material. The variety of the resurrection tradition itself poses a problem. Thus our first task is to understand the discrepancies and similarities within the resurrection tradition, and then to look at the two major types of resurrection tradition—the empty tomb reports and the accounts of resurrection appearances. Only then can we classify the traditions as to their various emphases and attempt a preliminary understanding of the nature of the resurrection.

Discrepancies within the New Testament resurrection traditions are obvious. According to Paul's tradition (1 Cor. 15:3–8) Jesus appeared first to Peter, then to the Twelve, and so on. In the Synoptic Gospels no appearance to Peter is directly reported (but cf. Luke 24:34 and John 21). In Mark and Matthew, only the women visit the tomb of Jesus. Luke adds that Peter then follows alone (24:12; cf. 24:24). In John's Gospel, Mary visits the tomb; then Peter and the Beloved Disciple follow. In Mark and Matthew, Jesus appears to the disciples in Galilee; in Luke and John he appears in Jerusalem. Paul's tradition reports resurrection appearances to the five hundred and to James; the Gospels make no mention of any such events. Mark and Matthew do not report Jesus' eating with his disciples; Luke and John do. According to Luke, Jesus vanishes from the sight of two disciples on the road to Emmaus. Both Luke and John hand on the tradition that Jesus passed through closed doors. Both Matthew and John report a first resurrection appearance to women outside the tomb. Such obvious discrepancies and variety raise questions about the nature of the resurrection tradition. Does a substantial historical core exist, or do these reports represent only the early Christians' imagination?

Paul's resurrection tradition (1 Cor. 15:3–8) lists a number of eyewitnesses to the appearances of the resurrected Christ. This tradition does not claim that the witnesses saw the resurrection itself—that is, the emergence of Je-

30. I. T. Ramsey, *Religious Language* (New York: Macmillan, 1957), p. 149.

sus from the tomb or his resuscitation—but rather that they saw the resurrected Christ. Paul, however, admits that he was untimely born (vs. 8); that is, his own resurrection appearance was unusually late. Paul's tradition places the initiative for the appearances not with those to whom the risen Christ appeared but with the Resurrected One himself. Moreover, the resurrection is said to have taken place "on the third day" (vs. 4). Although this time reference was probably not meant to be exact, it stresses that the resurrection occurred shortly after Jesus died. The phrase "in accordance with the scriptures" (vs. 3) declares that what happened in Jesus was not the death and resurrection of just any man but of one who fulfilled the promise of God to Israel. The tradition also makes it quite explicit that he who was raised and appeared to his followers and Paul is the same Jesus who died and was buried. The Christ of faith is linked by this resurrection tradition to the historical Jesus. Remarkably, Paul does not mention the empty tomb.

In Mark (16:1–8) no resurrection appearance is reported. Instead there is only the story of the empty tomb, in which the young man announces that Jesus has risen and will appear to the disciples in Galilee. Again, the initiative is with Jesus. This resurrection tradition is characterized by the women's awe at finding the tomb empty (vss. 5, 6, 8). They came piously to pay homage to the dead body, but the crucified Jesus departed ahead of them.

Matthew's tradition (28:1–20) enlarges that of Mark. His story of the empty tomb includes a resurrection appearance to the women (vss. 9–10; cf. John 20:14–18), which is followed by an appearance to the disciples in Galilee (vss. 16–20). Here the dominant mood is one of joy and worship. In contrast to this response, we read that the chief priests and elders have made elaborate precautions to prevent the theft of Jesus' body (27:62–66; 28:11–15). The resurrected Jesus speaks to his disciples about their future tasks and affirms his identity with the historical Jesus (". . . teaching them to obey everything that I have commanded you," vs. 20; see pp. 123–125).

Luke (24:1–53) contains the most elaborate tradition of the resurrection in the Synoptic Gospels. The empty tomb is subordinated to the resurrection appearances, for, as Luke puts it, "these words seemed to them an idle tale, and they did not believe them" (vs. 11). In the road to Emmaus story (vss. 13–35), the two disciples do not recognize Jesus by his physical appearance. They only know him when, taking the initiative, he explains the scriptural basis for his death and resurrection and performs the familiar act of blessing, breaking, and giving the bread (vss. 30–31, 35). Jesus then eats with his disciples to show that he is not a disembodied spirit (vss. 36–43), even though he has just been reported to have vanished and appeared again in the same context (cf. vss. 31 and 36). Like Matthew, Luke includes Jesus' final instruction to his disciples, which expresses his own understanding of the gospel message: "Repentance and forgiveness of sins is to be proclaimed in his name to all nations, beginning from Jerusalem" (vs. 47). Luke's resurrection account ends with Jesus' departure (vss. 50–53; cf. Acts 1:9–11). In Luke, as in the other accounts, something happens because of the resurrected Jesus' initiative. Furthermore, it is again made clear that the risen Jesus could not be known apart from his historical life and death. More elaborately than in Matthew, the task of the church is explained and handed over to the disciples.

In the Gospel of John's account (John 20:1–21:25) Mary Magdalene comes alone to the tomb; Peter and the other disciples follow later (20:1–10). Then Mary receives an appearance of the risen Christ whom she recognizes only after he speaks her name (vss. 11–18). Curiously, she is told not to hold him (vs. 17), for he has still to ascend to the Father. Before departing to the Father Jesus gives the disciples the Holy Spirit (20:22), after having demonstrated that he is the same Jesus who has been crucified. This point is underscored in the appearance to Thomas (20:26–29). The first Johannine resurrection appearances, like those of Luke, are reported to have occurred in Jerusalem. The appendix of John, however, contains an appearance in Galilee (chap. 21; cf. Matt. 28:16–20) in which Jesus directs his disciples so that they are able to make a catch of fish on the lake (21:1–14; cf. Luke 5:1–11). Then he eats with them in a scene that is faintly eucharistic. Finally, there follows an encounter in which the risen Jesus three times questions

"The Resurrection" by Giovanni diPaolo.   *(Courtesy of National Gallery of Art, Washington, D.C.)*

Peter about his love for him (21:15–23). The effect seems to be to restore the fallen Peter, who denied Jesus before his death.

The basic elements of the Gospel tradition are the empty tomb narratives and the appearance stories. The empty tomb story appears in all four Gospels, although it is not mentioned by Paul in the earliest report of the resurrection appearances. Quite possibly it circulated later than the reports of appearances. This conclusion rests in part upon evidence within the resurrection stories themselves that the tradition of the empty tomb was not initially known to the disciples (e.g., Luke 24:34; cf. John 21:3). Its inclusion in the Synoptic Gospels can be attributed to their dependence on Mark, although its appearance in John may be due to a separate tradition. There are also parallels to the empty tomb story in the history of religions.[31] Moreover, we need to keep in mind that the empty tomb was an ambiguous witness to the resurrection. It attests the absence of the body, but not necessarily the reality or presence of the risen Jesus. Matthew elaborates a defense against the rumor that the disciples stole the body of Jesus (28:11–15; cf. 27:62–66). Conceivably such a rumor circulated quite early as a response to Christian claims. On the other hand, the empty tomb story itself may reflect the deliberation of faith about what actually happened to Jesus' body, for according to the best New Testament evidence the early disciples were convinced of Jesus' resurrection, not by the empty tomb but by the appearances.[32] These appearances of the risen Christ attest most accurately the nature of the resurrection tradition. In effect the disciples exclaimed, "He appeared to me!" Their faith had been broken by Jesus' death and they had fled. Yet something had happened at the resurrection, and their faith was restored as belief that God had raised him from the dead.

The appearance traditions present a varied picture insofar as they portray the mode of Jesus' resurrection. Jesus ate with the disciples—they could see and touch the marks of the nails; but he could go through closed doors and vanish from their sight. It is a misnomer to speak of the "physical" resurrection. Paul claimed that the appearance to him was of the same nature as the appearances to Peter, the Twelve, and so on (see Acts 9:1–9; 22:4–11; 26:9–18), but how could that be a physical appearance? Indeed, in the same chapter of 1 Corinthians, he describes the resurrected body as a spiritual, not a physical, body and says that flesh and blood (that is, the physical body) cannot inherit the kingdom of God (1 Cor. 15:50; cf. 15:35–58). The decisive emphasis in all accounts is that the one who appeared was the same Jesus who had also died and been buried. Faith believed that the risen Jesus was no figment of the imagination; *Jesus* had been raised from the dead. Therefore,

---

31. See E. Bickermann, "Das leere Grab," *Zeitschrift für die Neutestamentliche Wissenschaft,* 23 (1924), 281–292.
32. For a positive evaluation of the historicity of the empty tomb, see H. von Campenhausen, "The Events of Easter and the Empty Tomb," *Tradition and Life in the Church,* trans. A. V. Littledale (London: Collins, 1968), pp. 42–89.

the disciples knew that death had been conquered. Exactly how remained a mystery, but that it was conquered Paul was as certain as the evangelists: "But thanks be to God, who gives us the victory through our Lord Jesus Christ" (1 Cor. 15:57).

In summary, the varied resurrection traditions point to some basic assumptions about the resurrection. The death of Jesus had left the disciples in confusion (Luke 24:4) or fear for their lives (Mark 14:50). At Jesus' death, he was completely alone, forsaken by all of them (cf. John 16:32). But at the resurrection, the disciples were changed and made new. This transformation is implicit in the various traditions. It was not of their own doing; they attributed it to the resurrected Jesus who had appeared to them, the same Jesus they had known in his life and death.

Conclusion

The fundamental working assumptions of this chapter have been two: (1) although the Gospels are religious, kerygmatic documents, they have not deliberately perverted or falsified the object of their attention, Jesus of Nazareth. (2) By working with three major areas of the tradition of Jesus—healing, teaching, and suffering—it is possible to understand the nature of each and their unity in the one historical figure Jesus. Thus the criterion of coherence was crucial for our portrait of Jesus. We have sought to represent the mystery of Jesus of Nazareth, a unique historical person. In the consequent portrait, we have consistently attempted to understand the connection between the mission and message of Jesus and the church's message about him.

Jesus performed miracles of healing, out of compassion rather than for power. Jesus proclaimed the irrupting rule of God, without claiming to know the future or making humankind's response insignificant. Jesus demanded forgiveness of enemies, fellowship with sinners, radical obedience to the heart of the law, and announced God's blessing to the poor, the repentant, the believing, and the merciful. Jesus called disciples and followers, without promise of immediate reward, but with a command to service. Jesus went to Jerusalem to proclaim the kingdom, and neither sought nor rejected the death that came. According to the faith of the first and subsequent generations of Christians, God raised him from the dead.

Suggestions for Further Reading

Many popular books about Jesus, especially lives of Jesus, are really historical novels that rely upon the imaginations—more or less disciplined—of the authors. Certainly the principal source of reliable information about Jesus is the canonical Gospels. The apocryphal Gospels, which are not found in the New Testament, may be consulted in *New Testament Apocrypha,* vol. 1: *Gospels and Related Writings,* ed. W. Schnee-melcher, trans. R. McL. Wilson, rev. ed. (Philadelphia: Westminster/John Knox, 1991). References to Jesus in ancient Jewish sources are collected and discussed by Morris Goldstein, *Jesus in the Jewish Tradition* (New York: Macmillan, 1950). A recent treatment of the question of extrabiblical versus canonical sources for Jesus is found in J. P. Meier, *A Marginal Jew: Rethinking the Historical Jesus,* vol. 1: *The Roots of the Problem and the Person* (New York: Doubleday, 1991), pp. 89–166. Meier lays an excellent groundwork for studying the question of the historical Jesus. Translations of the more important extrabiblical sources have been published by F. F. Bruce (ed.), *Jesus and Christian Origins Outside the New Testament* (Grand Rapids, MI: Eerdmans, 1974), in a volume of convenient size and scope. A definitive collection of texts and translations has been published by W. D. Stroker, *Extra-Canonical Sayings of Jesus* (Atlanta: Scholars, 1989), who groups the sayings according to R. Bultmann's form-critical categories.

The history of nineteenth-century attempts to write a life of Jesus is brilliantly recounted and criticized by Albert Schweitzer, *The Quest of the Historical Jesus,* trans. W. Montgomery with an introduction by J. M. Robinson (New York: Macmillan, 1968). Although he had predecessors, Schweitzer established the eschatological character of Jesus' kingdom teaching. A history of subsequent discussion of this problem is provided by N. Perrin, *The Kingdom of God in the Teaching of Jesus* (Philadelphia: Westminster, 1963). Bruce Chilton (ed.), *The Kingdom of God in the Teaching of Jesus* (Philadelphia: Fortress, 1984), has published a collection of important twentieth-century essays on the subject, including a valuable introductory chapter. W. B. Tatum, *In Quest of Jesus: A Guidebook* (Atlanta: John Knox, 1982), provides a helpful survey of major figures and important issues involved in research on Jesus.

Among the older modern works on Jesus, R. Bultmann, *Jesus and the Word,* trans. L. P. Smith and E. H. Lantero (New York: Scribner's, 1934), and G. Bornkamm, *Jesus of Nazareth,* trans. I. and F. McLuskey with J. M. Robinson (New York: Harper & Row, 1960), are still of historical importance. A number of the most important works on Jesus from the past two centuries (e.g., Reimarus, Schleiermacher, Strauss, Weiss) were edited and translated in a Lives of Jesus Series edited by L. E. Keck and published in the 1970s (Philadelphia: Fortress). Unfortunately, they have been allowed to go out of print.

G. Vermes, *Jesus the Jew* (Philadelphia: Fortress, 1973) and *Jesus and the World of Judaism* (Philadelphia: Fortress, 1984), attempts to see Jesus afresh against the background of Judaism, as do the more recent significant books on Jesus, for example, A. E. Harvey, *Jesus and the Constraints of History* (Philadelphia: Westminster, 1982), and E. P. Sanders, *Jesus and Judaism* (Philadelphia: Fortress, 1985). Obviously Meier, *A Marginal Jew* (above), falls into this category, as does J. D. Crossan, *The Historical Jesus: The Life of a Mediterranean Jewish Peasant* (San Francisco: Harper, 1991). It is characteristic of their differences that Meier is skeptical of the value of extrabiblical sources, while Crossan values some of the Apocryphal Gospels, particularly the Gospel of Thomas, quite highly. Important for general background are S. Freyne, *Galilee from Alexander the Great to Hadrian, 323 B.C.E. to 135 C.E.: A Study of Second Temple Judaism* (Wilmington, DE, and Notre Dame, IN: Michael Glazier and University of Notre Dame Press, 1980), and the same author's more recent *Galilee, Jesus and the Gospels: Literary Approaches and Historical Investigations* (Philadelphia: Fortress, 1988). See also works on Judaism mentioned at the end of Chapter 1.

Representative works on the parables of Jesus include: J. Jeremias, *The Parables of Jesus,* trans. S. H. Hooke, rev. ed. (New York: Scribner's, 1966), available also in a simplified version for students who do not use Greek in *Rediscovering the Parables* (New York: Scribner's, 1966); D. O. Via, *The Parables: Their Literary and Existential Dimension* (Philadelphia: Fortress, 1967); J. D. Crossan, *In Parables: The Challenge of the Historical Jesus* (New York: Harper, 1973); B. B. Scott, *Hear Then the Parable: A Commentary on the Parables of Jesus* (Minneapolis: Fortress, 1989). Most of the modern works on Jesus also deal seriously with the content and meaning of his sayings and teaching, as well as his understanding of his own role.

As to the latter question, whether or not Jesus presented himself as the Messiah is less hotly debated now that the complex character of Jewish messianic and eschatological thought has become more evident. In the last several decades, discussion has centered on the Son of Man concept or title, by which Jesus designates himself in the Gospels. In support of the view that Jesus spoke of the apocalyptic figure but did not actually identify himself explicitly as the Son of Man is H. Tödt, *The Son of Man in the Synoptic Tradition,* trans. D. M. Barton (Philadelphia: Westminster, 1965). There has been, moreover, doubt in some quarters that Jesus spoke of the appearance of the Son of Man at all; cf. Perrin, *Rediscovering the Teaching of Jesus* (New York: Harper & Row, 1967), p. 198. The most recent research, however, tends to confirm that at least on some occasions or for some purpose Jesus spoke of himself as "Son of Man" and to cast doubt on the originality of the apocalyptic dimensions of the title; cf., for example, B. Lindars, *Jesus Son of Man: A Fresh Examination of the Son of Man Sayings in the Gospels in Light of Recent Research* (Grand Rapids, MI: Eerdmans, 1983); also D. R. A. Hare, *The Son of Man Tradition* (Minneapolis: Fortress, 1989). On the discussion of the role of the Son of Man in the Fourth Gospel, see D. Burkett, *The Son of Man in the Gospel of John* (Sheffield, England: JSOT, 1991), pp. 11–50, esp. 16–37.

The miracles of Jesus were treated by R. H. Fuller, *Interpreting the Miracles* (Philadelphia: Westminster, 1963); and more recently by G. Theissen, *The Miracle Stories of the Early Christian Tradition,* trans. F. McDonagh (Philadelphia: Fortress, 1983). A broader study that sets miracles in their sociohistorical contexts is H. C. Kee, *Miracle in the Early Christian World: A Study in Socio-historical Method* (New Haven: Yale University Press, 1983). An older work, R. M. Grant, *Miracle and Natural Law in Greco-Roman and Early Christian Thought* (Amsterdam: North-Holland, 1952), investigates ancient perspectives and is still worth consulting.

The relationship of Jesus to political activity in Palestine is explored by M. Hengel in two small books: *Was Jesus a Revolutionist?,* trans. W. Klassen (Philadelphia: Fortress, 1971), and *Victory over Violence: Jesus and the Revolutionists,* trans. D. E. Green (Philadelphia: Fortress, 1973). Hengel resists earlier attempts to portray Jesus as a nationalist, political figure. But R. A. Horsley, *Jesus and the Spiral of Violence: Popular Resistance in Roman Palestine* (San Francisco: Harper & Row, 1987), sees in Jesus a more genuinely revolutionary figure, although not a national messiah. M. J. Borg, *Conflict, Holiness and Politics in the Teachings of Jesus* (New York: Edwin Mellen, 1984), portrays Jesus as a national leader, but one who senses the danger of a confrontation with Roman power. E. Bammel and C. F. D. Moule (eds.), *Jesus and the Politics of His Day* (New York: Cambridge University Press, 1984), is a rich mine of information on specific problems and issues. On the social context and consequences of Jesus' ministry, see the proposals of G. Theissen, *A Sociology of Early Palestinian Christianity,* trans. J. Bowden (Philadelphia: Fortress, 1978). In a more recent work, *The Gospel in Context: Social and Political History in the Synoptic Tradition,* trans. L. M. Mahoney (Minneapolis: Fortress, 1991), Theissen uses local color and recognizable historical references and allusions to trace the Gospel tradition into Jewish Palestine and toward the historical Jesus.

P. Winter, *On the Trial of Jesus*, T. A. Burkill and G. Vermes, (eds.), rev. ed.,(Berlin: Walter de Gruyter, 1973), emphasizes the literary and historical problems surrounding the trial and finds that the Gospels have overplayed the Jewish role. A similar view is taken by W. R. Wilson, *The Execution of Jesus: A Judicial, Literary and Historical Investigation* (New York: Scribner's, 1970). The Roman role is also emphasized by S. G. F. Brandon in *Jesus and the Zealots* (Manchester: Manchester University Press, 1967) and in *The Trial of Jesus* (London: Batsford, 1968). The basic correctness of the Gospel accounts of this matter is supported by J. Blinzler, *The Trial of Jesus,* trans. I. and F. McHugh (Westminster, MD: Newman, 1959). E. Bammel has edited a valuable collection of essays, *The Trial of Jesus: Cambridge Studies in Honour of C. F. D. Moule* (London: SCM, 1970), mostly in agreement with the viewpoint of Blinzler. D. R. Catchpole, *The Trial of Jesus: A Study in the Gospels and Jewish Historiography from 1770 to the Present Day* (Leiden: Brill, 1971), and G. S. Sloyan, *Jesus on Trial: The Development of the Passion Narratives and Their Historical and Ecumenical Implications* (Philadelphia: Fortress, 1973), provide rich bibliographical and other resources.

R. H. Fuller has made a study of the resurrection traditions, *The Formation of the Resurrection Narratives,* 2nd ed. (New York: Macmillan, 1980). There is a more recent comprehensive exegetical study by P. Perkins, *Resurrection: New Testament Witness and Contemporary Reflection* (Garden City, NY: Doubleday, 1984), and the more theologically oriented work of G. O'Collins, *Jesus Risen: An Historical, Fundamental, and Systematic Examination of Christ's Resurrection* (New York: Paulist Press, 1987), as well as a sympathic treatment by P. Lapide, *The Resurrection of Jesus: A Jewish Perspective,* trans. W. C. Linss (Minneapolis: Augsburg, 1983). On the birth narratives the commentary of R. E. Brown, *The Birth of the Messiah,* rev. ed. (New York: Doubleday, 1993), is the basic work. Brown has also issued a comprehensive, two-volume study, *The Death of the Messiah: From Gethsemane to the Grave: A Commentary on the Passion Narrative in the Four Gospels* (New York: Doubleday, 1994).

Four recent studies of Jesus perhaps typify the diverse present state of research: M. J. Borg, *Jesus: A New Vision* (San Francisco: Harper, 1987); G. N. Stanton, *The Gospels and Jesus* (Oxford: Oxford University Press, 1989); M. de Jonge, *Jesus, the Servant Messiah* (New Haven, CT: Yale University Press, 1991); E. P. Sanders, *The Historical Figure of Jesus* (London: Penguin, 1993). Borg portrays Jesus as a specific religious type, a holy man, and denies he expected the advent of the kingdom as the end of history. Stanton approaches Jesus through the Gospels' portrayal of him, following his earlier approach in *Jesus of Nazareth in New Testament Preaching* (Cambridge: Cambridge University Press, 1974). De Jonge develops his study out of a conversation with Schweitzer, Bultmann, their opponents, and the advocates of the so-called new quest of the historical Jesus. Sanders sets Jesus firmly in the context of first-century Judaism and its apocalyptic eschatology.

The conclusions of the North American Jesus Seminar are published in graphic, color-coded form by R. W. Funk and R. W. Hoover, *The Five Gospels: The Search for the Authentic Words of Jesus* (New York: Macmillan, 1993).

There is a recent full-scale treatment of John the Baptist, Jesus' precursor: R. L. Webb, *John the Baptizer and Prophet: A Socio-Historical Study* (Sheffield, England: JSOT, 1991).

PART TWO

THE APOSTLES AND THE EARLY CHURCH

*T*he critical question for the origin of Christian faith is "How did the proclaimer become the proclaimed?" That is, how did Jesus, who proclaimed the irrupting kingdom of God, become himself the subject of proclamation in the apostles' preaching? Of course, the death of Jesus and belief in his resurrection were critical factors. In studying the Acts of the Apostles (Chapter 7) and the Pauline letters (Chapters 8 and 9), we have an opportunity to reflect both about the historical development and the theological grounding of the Christian church upon Jesus who was proclaimed as Christ.

In one sense, the writing of Acts, and its subsequent acceptance into the Christian canon, represents a decisive step in the formation of the early church. Acts provides a continuing stress on history (as does the Gospel of Luke) and a new emphasis on the importance of the church alongside Jesus Christ. New Testament faith has both personal and corporate dimensions; it is concerned not only with the individual but also with the Christian community. We shall see how Acts wrestles with such questions as the scope of the Christian mission, the relation of the church to Judaism, the Christians' attitude toward the Roman Empire, and the connection between the power of the Spirit and the church's apostolic authority (Chapter 7). Then we shall observe how

Paul, the first great Christian theologian, develops such related questions as the human condition and the nature of sin, the work of Christ in bringing God and humanity together, the marks of Christian community, and the tension between present life in Christ and the future end of history (Chapters 8 and 9).

In studying the post-Pauline writings (Chapters 10 and 11), it becomes evident that the movement from the apostles to the later church is characterized by a concern for giving the community institutional form as Christians gird themselves for a long period of existence in the world. In these writings we see a tightening of discipline and doctrine, the development of orthodoxy over against heresy. The affirmation of the goodness of creation, the demand for action as well as belief, insistence upon the indispensability of the scriptures of Israel, the subordination of extreme religious behavior for the common good, the distinction between clergy and laity, the right ordering of family relations, the Christians' respect for and fear of the state, the inspiring figure of Jesus as suffering servant and as the one victoriously seated in the heavens, the call for brotherly love, and the dramatic call for faith in the final victory of God— all these reflect the range and depth of the coming of age of the church under the leadership of the apostles and their successors.

The Roman Forum with the Arch of Titus and the Colosseum in the background. Just to the left of this picture is the site of Mamertine Prison where according to tradition Paul and Peter were prisoners.   *(Courtesy of Robert Spivey.)*

Chapter 7

Acts: Mission and Witness

Notes on the Acts of the Apostles

Acts was written by Luke, the author of the Gospel, probably within the last two decades of the first century. The book ends with Paul's debating and preaching while under arrest in Rome. We are not told about his ultimate fate, but there are strong hints (cf. Acts 20:22–25, 38) that Luke actually knew of Paul's death, even though he did not report it. Paul arrived in Rome about A.D. 59 and, according to the last statement of Acts (28:30 f.), remained there two years. Presumably he died in the early sixties during the reign of the Emperor Nero nearly a decade before the quelling of the Jewish rebellion against Rome. Luke wrote his Gospel after that rebellion and the Book of Acts was composed subsequently (Acts 1:1). Luke used Mark as a source for his own Gospel and Mark itself was not composed until about A.D. 65 or later (see pp. 67–68 and 131f).

By his own account (1:1–3) Luke used sources in composing his narrative of the ministry of Jesus, and he may have had sources for the Book of Acts. The detailed account of Paul's journeys in chapters 13–28 is probably based on some record of Paul's travels. In addition to this itinerary, Luke knew traditional stories from the earliest days of the church (e.g., 3:1–10; 5:1–11). Whether he had any traditions of the speeches he records is another question, to be considered as we examine some of the speeches. Following the practice of ancient historians, he likely wrote these speeches with considerable freedom, impressing them with his own literary style and thought. Luke has skillfully tied the narrative together with summary statements (e.g., 2:43–47), in which he speaks in general terms of the activities of the early church.

Like the Gospels, Acts is a narrative, a story, and it may profitably be read as such. Yet Acts is more than just a story, even as the Gospels are. In and through the story the author's understanding of the meaning and truth of the subject matter can be perceived. Within a schematic presentation Luke gives us a great deal of information about the early church. A comparison with Paul reveals that, although Acts may contain some inaccuracies, it is in touch with actual historical events.[1] Still, Luke apparently did not know a great many things about the origin of Christianity that we may infer from other

---

1. That Acts has a solid historical foundation in the times that it portrays is shown by H. J. Cadbury, *The Book of Acts in History* (New York: Harper & Row, 1955). More recently, the same point has been made by M. Hengel, *Acts and the History of Earliest Christianity*, trans. J. Bowden (Philadelphia: Fortress, 1980).

documents, and he seems to have omitted deliberately some things that did not accord with his understanding of the essence of apostolic Christianity.

For example, Luke does not tell how Christianity reached Rome, although Christians are already there when Paul arrives (Acts 28:14 ff.). Paul's letter to the Romans also makes it clear that Christians were there before him. Presumably Christianity also reached Egypt at a rather early date, but we learn nothing about this development from Acts. Nor do we learn anything about any expansion of Christianity to the East. In fact, we are told nothing very specific about the founding of the church in Antioch (11:9), probably the most important early Christian center outside Jerusalem. After chapter 12 all activity is centered about Paul and those associated with him, for Luke uses Paul to personify the entire Gentile mission.

The prominence given Paul should be seen over against the fact that Acts relates little about the activities of the Twelve. With the exception of Peter they are all shadowy figures. True, John accompanies Peter in the early chapters, but he is at best a silent partner. The report about James in chapter 12 includes neither the reasons for his martyrdom nor the conditions under which it took place. There is, of course, a list of the eleven apostles (Acts 1:13), but little is said about what happened to the group individually or as a whole. Probably Luke concentrates on Paul at least partly because he has information about him and lacks reports about the Twelve; however, in certain cases other factors may have been at work in the selection of material.

Paul's letters indicate that there was considerable disagreement and even hostility toward his Gentile mission on the part of some of the more conservative members of the Jerusalem community, who believed that Judaism was, so to speak, the prerequisite for Christianity. Luke does not avoid reporting this dispute. As we have noticed, the question of the gospel and the Gentiles is raised throughout the Book of Acts, although the sharp edge of the controversy is consistently dulled. In every instance (cf. chaps. 11, 15, 21) the problem is amicably settled without harsh words or bitterness. Yet it keeps recurring. How much Luke knew of the extent of these controversies is hard to say. Surely he should have known a great deal had he been Paul's companion (see p. 130). In any case, he portrayed the life of the early church and the development of the Christian mission as more harmonious and free of disagreement and friction than they actually were. Doubtless for the sake of the gospel as he understood it, Luke exercised some selectivity in reporting events in the early church.

OUTLINE OF ACTS

Introduction: A New Beginning (1:1–2:47)
Jesus' Departure (1:1–11)
The Apostolic Witness (1:12–26)
Spirit, Gospel, and Church (2:1–47)
The Growth of the Church and Its Witness (3:1–12:25)
Stephen's Martyrdom (6:1–7:60)
Mission to the Gentiles (10:1–11:18)
Christianity's Triumphal March (13:1–21:14)
Paul's Speech at Pisidian Antioch (13:17–41)
Paul's Speech in Athens (17:16–34)
Jerusalem to Rome (21:15–28:31)

Introduction: A New Beginning (1:1–2:47)

The first two chapters of Acts lay out and define the themes and principal concerns that are fundamental to the rest of the book. For this reason they merit careful examination. Numerous issues may be raised as one studies these chapters, but our basic question concerns what Luke emphasizes and underscores in his narrative.

JESUS' DEPARTURE (1:1–11)

Why is the return of Jesus delayed?

The beginning of the Acts of the Apostles (1:1–2) harks back to Luke's earlier work, the Gospel, which is also addressed to Theophilus. The brief description, "all that Jesus did and taught, from the beginning until the day when he was taken up to heaven," corresponds to the content of the Gospel. The "many proofs" of the resurrected Christ (vs. 3) are found in the final chapter of Luke (24:36 ff.; perhaps in 24:44 ff.). Even without such clear indications, however, there would be strong reasons for supposing that the two books are by the same author, for they are written in the same style and from the same general point of view. The story that began with Jesus will now be continued; the Gospels seem to anticipate and presuppose a continuation of the story. The reader will now be told what form that continuation took.

Despite the obvious points of contact, there are apparent discrepancies and inconsistencies between the resurrection accounts of Luke 24 and the narrative of Acts 1. Nothing is said about forty days of resurrection appearances in the Gospel; nor is there any mention of the kingdom of God in all of Luke 24 (cf. Acts 1:3). The command to stay in Jerusalem (vs. 4) appears also in Luke 24:49, but the word of Jesus about the baptism of John and baptism by the Holy Spirit (vss. 4 f.) is not found in Luke 24 (but cf. Luke 3:16). Is Luke simply careless? Probably the explanation lies rather in a difference of emphasis and purpose.

Luke's interests come to light in the next section (vss. 6–11, esp. 6–8). The hope that the two disciples on the road to Emmaus had already voiced (Luke 24:21) is now put in the form of a question: "Lord, is this the time when you will restore the kingdom to Israel?" The disciples seem to be asking whether Jesus as Messiah will now fulfill the traditional hopes of the Jewish nation with the inauguration of the kingdom of God on earth. Jesus does not answer directly. Instead he replies that it is not for them to know the times and seasons that the Father has fixed by his own authority (cf. Mark 13:32). In other words, these matters must not be their primary concern. Such hopes as they have will be fulfilled in God's own way at the time of his choosing. Thus the disciples' expectations are effectively put off.

Crucifixion of Jesus as represented by a contemporary Brazilian sculptor,
A. Solimoes.   *(Courtesy of Spartaco Appetiti.)*

The reason for this delay is then given (vs. 8): "But you will receive power
when the Holy Spirit has come upon you; and you will be my witnesses in
Jerusalem, in all Judea and Samaria, and to the ends of the earth." The time
of the kingdom is not yet, because the gospel must first be preached throughout the world. The witnesses to Jesus have a mission to perform. The coming of the Spirit has already been mentioned (vs. 5); now its specifically
missionary function is spelled out. The Spirit empowers the disciples for their
mission, which is described in stages: Jerusalem, Judea, Samaria, and the
ends of the earth (vs. 8). These stages correspond to the plan of the Book of
Acts, in which the mission of the church unfolds by degrees: first in Jerusalem
and the environs, then Samaria, then Syria, Asia Minor, Greece, and finally
Rome. With Paul's preaching of the gospel in Rome the Book of Acts comes
to an end. This commissioning of the disciples for a worldwide mission is in
close agreement with Luke 24:47, where the risen Jesus tells them that repentance and forgiveness are to be preached in his name to all nations, beginning from Jerusalem.

Christ giving the law to the apostles. A relief marble fragment from the second half of the fourth century.   *(Courtesy of Metropolitan Museum of Art. Beata M. Brummer, 1948, in memory of Joseph Brummer.)*

Luke's description of the ascension of Jesus (vss. 9–11) has become the model for its conception and artistic representation in the church. But the ascension is portrayed in this way only in Acts. Even in the Gospel of Luke it is described much more enigmatically (24:51). Here Luke carefully reconstructs the scene to drive home a point. The ascension is now viewed not from the standpoint of Jesus but of the waiting disciples. Jesus indeed ascends to heaven and will return in like manner. The disciples ("men of Galilee"), however, are not to stand looking up into heaven in expectation of him, for they have already been given a task. They can perform it with the assurance that their ultimate hopes and expectations will not be disappointed, for Jesus will return in God's good time. Yet the interval gains importance as the period of the church and its mission. To that work the disciples' and the reader's attention is directed.

The Apostolic Witness (1:12–26)

What is the significance of the selection of a twelfth apostle to replace Judas?

The disciples returned from the Mount of Olives, where the ascension apparently took place,[2] and gathered in an upper room in Jerusalem (vss. 12–14). The list of disciples present agrees with that found in Luke 6:14–16 with one obvious exception—Judas Iscariot, the betrayer of Jesus (cf. vss.

2. According to Luke 24:50 f. the ascension took place at or near Bethany. This seeming disagreement suggests that Luke may have mistakenly taken Olivet and Bethany to be the same place. In any event Bethany is on the opposite, eastern slope of the same ridge as the Mount of Olives.

16–22).[3] It is somewhat strange that Peter describes in such detail the fate of Judas to his fellow disciples and companions. Presumably most of them were in as good a position as he to know what had occurred; moreover, they would have surely known who Judas was, so why was it necessary for Peter to identify him so thoroughly? Peter's apparent aside (vss. 18 and 19) underscores the difficulty, for here Peter seems to translate the Aramaic word *Hakeldama,* which would certainly not have been necessary for his Aramaic-speaking hearers, and refers to "their language," as if his hearers spoke a language different from that of the inhabitants of Jerusalem. This cannot have been the case. The whole aside has to be understood as a notation addressed to the reader, and for this reason verses 18 and 19 appear in parentheses and outside the quotation marks in the NRSV. In the Greek text, however, the words were not set apart; the author evidently felt no obligation to distinguish clearly between Peter's words to his hearers and his own message for his readers. Probably he would not have considered such a distinction nearly so important as we would. Thus, as we read Luke's account, we may well ask to whom the speeches of the chief characters are directed and to what extent they are means by which Luke sets before the *reader* the meaning of the events that are unfolding. To understand the speeches we must always ask what role they play in the unfolding of the Book of Acts.

The Old Testament quotations (vs. 20; cf. Psalms 69:25 and 109:8) form not only the culmination of the first half of Peter's speech but also the transition to the second part (vss. 21–22), in which he sets forth a course of action. A replacement for the disqualified and defunct Judas must be chosen: "Let another take his position of overseer." Furthermore, the replacement must have a specific qualification; he must have accompanied Jesus and his disciples during his ministry up to the time of his ascension. He may then become a witness, with the apostles, to the resurrection. In the selection of the new apostle (vss. 23–26), two candidates are put forward by the group, but the final choice is left for God (or Jesus, depending on who is here meant by "Lord"). The replacement will be no less an apostolic figure than the eleven original disciples.

Luke is careful to show that the number of the original twelve apostles was again filled out before the beginning of the church's missionary activity. (The word *apostle* comes from the Greek *apostolos,* which is in turn related to the verb *apostellein,* "to send out"; the apostles are literally "those sent out.") The concept of *twelve* apostles probably originates with the *twelve* tribes of Israel (cf. the saying of Jesus in Luke 22:30 and Matt. 19:28). Perhaps Luke was aware of this connection with the Old Testament and the

---

3. The Acts' description of Judas' death differs from that given in Matthew 27:3–10, except that in both cases the name of the place where he died or was buried is the Field of Blood. Perhaps the fact that Luke preserves the Aramaic name whereas Matthew's version appears to be based upon the Old Testament quotation indicates that Luke's version is the older. (Matthew purports to quote Jeremiah, but the exact passage cannot be found; cf. Zech. 11:12–13.)

Israelite nation, because for him the church, led by the apostles, was the new Israel. Yet Luke, like Paul, seems more interested in the close relation between apostleship and the resurrection of Jesus (Acts 1:22; cf. 1 Cor. 9:1: "Am I not an apostle? Have I not seen Jesus our Lord?"; also 15:8, where Paul explicitly relates the appearance of the risen Jesus and his apostleship). Unlike Luke, however, Paul did not believe that having been a disciple of Jesus was an indispensable qualification of an apostle. Paul himself had not been, and he distinguishes between the Twelve and the apostles in 1 Corinthians 15:5, 7. Although Paul evidently regarded the Twelve as apostles, he did not limit apostleship to them. Nevertheless, precisely this identification of apostles with the twelve disciples of Jesus has informed the Christian understanding of "apostle" and "apostleship" down through the centuries. The church has come to share Luke's view that there existed a complete and fully qualified group of twelve apostles identical with the inner circle of Jesus' disciples.

After Matthias is selected he plays no role in the story—nor do many of the Twelve. In fact, the Twelve were not the only early proclaimers of the gospel of Jesus Christ. Not even in Acts do they play the predominant role in preaching; only Peter appears as a real flesh-and-blood figure. Luke, who has written to Theophilus in the first place so that he may know the truth of the things of which he has been informed (Luke 1:4), uses the concept of the Twelve to assure the reader of the legitimacy, historical accuracy, and therefore the truth of the Christian message.

In chapter 1 Luke has done two principal things. First, he has explained the meaning of Jesus' departure and of the indefinite period before his return. Second, through his treatment of the reconstitution of the twelve apostles, he has shown that there is continuity between Jesus and his disciples on earth. The apostles guarantee this tradition, for they have firm connections with Jesus of Nazareth, of whose resurrection and life they are witnesses. Luke can now turn his attention to the description and exposition of the earliest missionary preaching of the Christian church. The messenger (Jesus) has become the message.

SPIRIT, GOSPEL, AND CHURCH (2:1–47)

How does the coming of the Spirit relate to Peter's proclamation?

Chapter 2 falls into two main parts, verses 1–13, a depiction of the descent of the Holy Spirit upon the disciples and the reaction of the bystanders, and verses 14–42, an account of the earliest missionary preaching by Peter. The remainder of the chapter (vss. 43–47) gives a brief general description of the life of the Jerusalem church. It is one of the author's typical summary reports.

The day of Pentecost, coming on the fiftieth day after the Sabbath of the Passover (according to the Jewish calendar), would be the forty-ninth day after the resurrection and, according to the Lukan chronology, a little over a

week after the ascension of Jesus.[4] (Jesus' resurrection appearances continued over a period of forty days.) In the Gospel of John, however, the Holy
Spirit comes, not at Pentecost and after the ascension of Jesus, but directly
from the risen Jesus himself on the Sunday following his crucifixion (John
20:19–23). Indeed, the ascension as such is not described in John (cf. 20:17).
Luke evidently separates into chronological sequence events or experiences
that were not so divided in the memories of other early Christians (i.e., the
resurrection of Jesus, the ascension, and the bestowal of the Holy Spirit).

Luke regarded the coming of the Holy Spirit (cf. vss. 1–4) as a miraculous
event. Yet we should not assume that Luke attached primary importance to
such signs as the wind and fire. For him the most marvelous thing was the
inspiration of the apostles and their speaking in tongues. Only highly unusual
accompanying circumstances could do justice to this remarkable event. The
rushing of the wind and the tongues "as of fire" are subordinate to the main
miracle of inspired speech.

In all probability Luke is describing a genuine experience of early Christianity. We learn also from Paul that the gift of the Spirit was associated with
speaking in tongues (1 Cor. 14). Be that as it may, Paul assumes that without
interpretation this speaking in tongues (glossolalia) is unintelligible to the
hearer, as indeed it generally is when practiced by pentecostal Christians today. In Luke's view, however, a miracle of translation has also occurred. Although no explicit connection is made, from ancient times commentators
have seen in the miracle of understanding at Pentecost the resolution of the
confusion of tongues at the Tower of Babel (Gen. 11:1–9).

The description of the circumstances under which the multitude came together and the course of events as a whole show Luke's own perspectives
and interests. When the disciples are gathered in one place, the Spirit descends and they immediately begin proclaiming "God's deeds of power" (vs.
11) in all the languages of those Jews who have come from far and wide to
dwell in Jerusalem, presumably for the feast of Pentecost. These people hear
the commotion and come together. Some inquire sincerely as to what all this
means (vs. 12). Others understandably attribute the uproar to new wine (vs.
13). Luke thus provides as auspicious an occasion and hearing as possible
for Peter's sermon or speech. Accordingly, the audience, although Jewish, is
thoroughly cosmopolitan and representative of the eastern half of the
Mediterranean world, the mission field of early Christianity (vss. 8–11). To
this great congregation Peter addresses himself, standing with the Eleven (vs.
14) to emphasize the authoritative character of his speech. The speech is not
only Spirit-inspired but also apostolic. Indeed, this speech of Peter (2:14–42)
is the first Christian missionary sermon.

---

4. According to Acts 1:3 Jesus continued to appear to his disciples for forty days after the
   resurrection. Note the close connection of the Christian celebrations of Good Friday,
   Easter, and Pentecost with the Jewish feasts of Passover and Pentecost or Weeks
   (*Shavuot*).

After Peter first explains that the Christians are not drunk (vss. 14–16), he declares that their speaking fulfills what was spoken by the Old Testament prophet Joel. There then follows the long quotation from the Book of Joel (2:28–32), which is a description and prediction of what will happen in the days when God restores the fortunes of Judah and Jerusalem (Joel 3:1). Not only will there be the standard apocalyptic signs (vss. 19–20) but also the pouring out of God's Spirit (vss. 17–18), which results in visions, dreams, and especially prophecy. Apparently Luke understands the speaking in tongues of the apostles and their companions as the prophecy of which Joel spoke.

This first Christian preaching begins with an appeal to the Old Testament, which is typical of the New Testament as a whole, for the Christian gospel is understood as the fulfillment of an ancient promise. Jesus Christ is the culmination of what God has been doing from creation on in the history of Israel. So even the gift of the Spirit and the speaking in tongues are set forth as fulfillment of Old Testament prophecy. The Christians, as this text states, believed themselves to be possessed of prophetic power and authority. Thus they were able to perceive and declare the fulfillment of the words that the prophets and writers of the Old Testament cast out ahead of them, so to speak. The early Christian preachers, therefore, implicitly claimed a better understanding of Old Testament texts than their human authors could have had.

The prophetic word (vss. 17–21) was doubtless understood to concern both the present manifestation of the Spirit and the forthcoming signs of the end, as well as the appeal of the Christian preaching for conversion in the light of these startling occurrences (vs. 21). Before this appeal could be made, however, its specifically Christian basis had to be set forth, for Peter has so far only said that the time for fulfillment of the Old Testament prophecies and of God's promises to his people has come. The distinctly Christian proclamation appears in verses 22–24. Most surprising is the brevity of the reference to Jesus' ministry (vs. 22). Jesus himself is not presented as the acting subject. Rather he is the means or agent through whom God acts, even in his miracles. The divine purpose at work in the crucifixion is made quite clear (vs. 23), and the same purpose is also discerned in the resurrection (vs. 24) as the Old Testament proof from prophecy (vss. 25–28) shows. The author recognizes that the words of the Psalm (16:8–11) were generally believed to have been spoken by David about himself, but he maintains (vss. 29–31) that they were actually meant to apply to Jesus.

Only after the Old Testament proof is the disciples' witness to the resurrection mentioned (vs. 32), though even then it is passed over rather briefly. Emphasis falls rather upon the ascension of Christ to heaven (vs. 33), again confirmed by the Old Testament (vss. 34 f.; from Psalm 110:1), and upon the gift of the Spirit. Apparently, Peter does not draw a sharp distinction between the raising of Jesus from the dead and his ascension (or exaltation) to heaven. In Luke's own mind, however, the distinction is very clear. Jesus is first raised from the dead; then after forty days he ascends into heaven. Luke's view probably represents a later development in relation to what is attributed to Peter.

The speech reaches its pinnacle and conclusion in verse 36. Once again God is the subject who acts upon Jesus. Jesus becomes, or at least is recognized as, "Lord and Messiah" only with the resurrection and exaltation. This point of view is rather uncommon in the New Testament, for Jesus is usually regarded as having been the Messiah during his earthly ministry. Yet just because this verse does not conform to that common conception, and because it would scarcely have been set forth at a time when that conception was widespread, it may well present a primitive point of view. Certainly the crucifixion and resurrection were pivotal points in primitive Christian experience and faith.

Peter's appeal for conversion and repentance follows naturally (vss. 37–42). As he has already indicated ("Therefore let the entire house of Israel know . . ."—vs. 36) and as the situation demands, it is still addressed to Jews. Yet there is already a hint that it will not be limited to them (see vs. 39). The hearers are called upon to repent and to be baptized, and the gift of the Spirit is promised. No explanation is given as to why believers had to be baptized. According to every indication, baptism was practiced from the very beginning, yet we do not know precisely why or how it became the ritual of initiation into the Christian community.[5]

Whereas the practice of baptism was universal, the call to repentance has a particularly Lukan ring. Of course, Luke was not the first to set forth a relation between baptism and repentance or to describe conversion in terms of repentance. The understanding of repentance as the essential element of Christian conversion is, however, quite characteristic of Luke (see pp. 148–150). Although repentance and forgiveness were already possible for the Jew (cf. Psalm 51), Luke believed that God's forgiveness and the possibility of repentance were made known in an unprecedented and universal way in the coming of Jesus. Baptism "in the name of Jesus Christ" (2:38) was the symbolic expression of repentance and the acceptance of God's forgiveness. The act itself implies a washing away of sin.

---

5. Paul, whose letters are the earliest New Testament writings, simply mentions baptism as a matter of course, as if it were a long-accepted practice. In Matthew 28:19 Jesus commands it. But Paul did not know Matthew, and that command very likely reflects early Christian practice. At best there is no explanation of why baptism should be commanded. Acts mentions some disciples, presumably Christians, who knew only the baptism of John the Baptist and had not received the Holy Spirit (19:1–7). In the Gospels and the missionary speeches of Acts, John's baptism marks the beginning of Jesus' own ministry, and John's baptism in water is contrasted with Christ's baptism in the Holy Spirit. All this suggests that Christian baptism is somehow rooted in the baptism of John. Yet baptism may have been practiced by Christians quite apart from the influence of John, inasmuch as the Jewish community may have baptized new converts, as well as circumcising males. The Qumran community also practiced baptism or lustrations (washings), but their rite was repeatable, whereas early Christian baptism—or at least the form with which we are familiar—was a once-for-all ceremony. But cf. M. Black, *The Scrolls and Christian Origins* (New York: T. Nelson, 1961), pp. 91 ff. On baptism see O. Cullmann, *Baptism in the New Testament,* trans. J. K. S. Reid (London: SCM, 1950), and G. R. Beasley-Murray, *Baptism in the New Testament* (New York: St. Martin's, 1962).

Peter's Pentecost sermon is the first of a number of speeches in the Book of Acts. Ancient historians sometimes used a speech by a leading figure as a literary device to convey something to their readers that they thought was important for an understanding of persons or situations (cf. p. 267 above). Such a procedure was understood by the reader and not considered dishonest or fraudulent. Luke's composition and use of speeches seems to follow this ancient practice, although he may have drawn upon earlier traditions or sources.[6]

At the end of Peter's speech and the account of the conversions, Luke presents a glimpse of the life of the early Jerusalem church. Such general summaries were probably composed by Luke. They recur frequently in Acts and usually reflect such knowledge of the early church as could be gathered by the author from the traditional stories that he narrates. For example, the reference to common ownership (vss. 44 f.) is probably a generalization based upon the stories of Barnabas and Ananias and Sapphira (4:36 f.; 5:1–6). The signs and wonders, as well as the "awe" (vs. 43), are exemplified in such miracle stories as 3:1–10, 9:32–35, and 9:36–43. The general favor that the Christians found among the people (2:47) is also mentioned in 4:21 and 5:33–39, quite possibly traditional material. Such matters as the great number of converts, the breaking of bread, and attendance in the temple are included in the summary without the direct support of traditional stories. This is not to say that Luke simply manufactured them, but he may have believed he had a right to describe these activities and attribute them to the early church on the basis of what he knew of Jesus and the disciples, and of what he knew of the church of his own day. Of course, we cannot be sure that Luke did not possess more detailed information from earlier days that did not come to him in the form of traditional narratives. In that case, his editorial summaries might contain historically valuable material. Yet we have already noted that Luke did not hesitate to set forth the ascension in distinct and different ways, in the Gospel and Acts, apparently supplying details as needed.

The immediate success of the Christian witness at the very heart of Judaism, the constant presence of Christians around the temple, and the table fellowship and piety of Christians all represent typical Lukan motifs. Especially significant is the emphasis on Christianity's acceptance and prominence in the Holy City of Judaism, for in Luke's view the church is the new, and true, Israel. Thus Luke's conception of the piety and life of the early Christian church appears in 2:42–47.

In the opening chapters of Acts Luke accounts for the departure of the risen Jesus from his disciples, the reason that he has not yet returned, the

---

6. Traditional materials and perspectives may be more prominent in some speeches than in others. R. F. Zehnle, *Peter's Pentecost Discourse: Tradition and Lukan Reinterpretation in Peter's Speeches of Acts 2 and 3* (Nashville: Abingdon, 1971), finds considerable evidence for tradition in Acts 3, whereas he maintains that the Pentecost speech of Acts 2 is mainly a Lukan composition.

existence and mission of the church, and the foundation of that church upon the apostolic witness. Then he proceeds to report the bestowal of the Spirit upon the disciples and to give an extended example of the preaching of the apostolic church, followed by a brief characterization of its life. This preaching (i.e., Peter's speech) contains the elements that became characteristic of Christian preaching in subsequent ages: the announcement and demonstration of the fulfillment of scripture, the centrality of the crucifixion and resurrection, a characterization of the historic ministry of Jesus, the announcement of the coming of the Spirit, and an appeal for repentance and conversion, which naturally includes the offer of forgiveness.

The Growth of the Church and Its Witness (3:1–12:25)

Our initial insights into the way the author of Acts works, as well as his interests and goals, must be tested for their adequacy in illuminating the rest of the book. The first major section (chaps. 3–12) depicts the gradual extension of the church beyond the confines of Judaism and Palestine.

STEPHEN'S MARTYRDOM (6:1–7:60)

What is the importance of Stephen and the Hellenists for the development of the narrative?

The power manifest in the preaching and healing activity of the apostles in Jerusalem is portrayed in chapters 3–5. The stories found there are not told simply for their own sake; they show important aspects of the church's life and mission about which Luke wants his readers to know. They depict the Christians' preaching and healing in Jerusalem, especially in the vicinity of the temple, the center of the Jewish religion. The location is significant, for Luke wants his reader to understand that Christianity emerged out of the very heart of Israel and that it is the true expression of the ancient faith. The refusal of the apostles to be silent, even when officials warned or punished them (4:19 and 5:29), shows how strong was the sense of mission in the very earliest Christian congregation. Yet in chapters 3–5 the mission is confined to Judaism and indeed to the city of Jerusalem.

In chapters 6–7, however, the basis is laid for the extension of the witness. Chapter 6 describes the "complaint" of the Hellenists against the Hebrews: their widows had been overlooked in the daily distribution, which must have been the church's way of looking out for its poor and disadvantaged (6:1). Who are these Hellenists and Hebrews? It is clear that they are Christians. Beyond that, absolute certainty is not possible. Probably by "Hebrews" is meant Aramaic-speaking Christians. In that case "Hellenists" means Greek-speaking Christians (note the Greek names, vs. 5), although, as soon becomes apparent, they are distinguished by factors other than language.

Apparently the seven Hellenists who were appointed to serve tables and to see that their widows were not slighted did not stick strictly to their jobs, as Luke's narrative makes clear.

Stephen first appears not as a waiter, or even an administrator, but as a wonder worker and especially a debater, incurring the hostility of the Jews (6:8–15). (Traditionally, the seven have been considered the first *deacons,* an office in the early church [Phil. 1:1; Rom. 16:1], for the same Greek word, *diakonos,* means "waiter" or "deacon.") The charges made against him (vss. 11, 13 f.) indicate a sharp break on the part of some Christians with the institutions of Judaism. The accusation about destroying the temple (vs. 14) has a familiar ring, for according to Mark 14:58 it was first leveled at Jesus himself (cf. Mark 13:2; 15:29; John 2:19). Insofar as Stephen is accused of questioning the validity of the law (6:13), he stands with the apostle Paul and later Hellenistic Christianity against Judaism and the Jewish or Judaizing Christians. Whatever Stephen's views, he held them with great tenacity. If anyone had hoped that Stephen's appearance before the council (the Jewish Sanhedrin) would exonerate him of the suspicions and charges against him, those hopes would certainly have been cruelly dashed by Stephen's speech.

The speech (7:1–53) is in its present form the composition of Luke himself. It does not answer the question of the high priest (7:1), and the council probably would not have endured such a long, and, from their point of view, largely superfluous and defamatory speech in answer to so simple a question. The speech contains an extensive statement of the theological position of Stephen, which is by implication that of the Hellenists. Although it does not deal with the charges made against him, it sheds some light on how such charges may have arisen, for Stephen denounces the past disobedience of the Israelite people, questions the necessity of the temple (vss. 47 ff.), and concludes with a strong denunciation of the betrayal and murder of Jesus. The final reference to the law (vs. 53) is almost an afterthought.

The reaction of Stephen's hearers to such a speech was predictable. The account of his subsequent death, traditionally the first Christian martyrdom, includes an additional bit of information about a young man named Saul, who held the coats of those who were stoning him (vss. 58 ff.). This Saul, under his Roman name Paul, became the great Christian apostle to the Gentiles. Around him the latter half of the Book of Acts revolves. We know from Paul's own letters (esp. Gal. 1:11–24) that he was a persecutor of the church before he himself became a Christian, and it is certainly not impossible that he was in Jerusalem and present on this occasion. If so, history has seldom witnessed stranger ironies. Stephen, the first Christian critic of Judaism, is martyred in the presence of the one who was to become the decisive figure in Christianity's separation from Judaism.

The bulk of chapter 8 describes the missionary harvest reaped as a result of the persecution that broke out on the heels of Stephen's martyrdom. Philip makes converts in Samaria (cf. Acts 1:8), and on the road south from Jerusalem to Gaza he converts an Ethiopian eunuch to Christianity and baptizes him on the spot. Others also went out from Jerusalem preaching the word, but Luke tells us only of the instances involving Philip. His statement (8:4; cf. 11:19–21) very likely conveys exactly what happened in this first demonstration of the maxim that the blood of the martyrs is the seed of the church.

Because, according to Luke's account, the gospel has now spread outside Jerusalem into the territories of ancient Israel (Judea, Samaria, and Galilee), we are prepared for the next step, the evangelization of the Gentiles. Now the apostle to the Gentiles must appear at the center of the stage. So we are next told of Paul's conversion (chap. 9). Aside from the crucifixion of Jesus, this is the best-attested event in the entire New Testament. There are no less than three accounts in the Book of Acts (cf. also chaps. 22 and 26). In addition, there is the account from Paul's own hand in Galatians (1:11–17), as well as other allusions to the event in his letters (e.g., 1 Cor. 9:1; 15:8).

With the appearance of Paul, we reach a point in the narrative at which it is possible to check the accuracy of the Acts account and also to learn something more about the methods and intentions of Luke as an author. The comparison of Acts with the evidence of Paul's letters is a complex and difficult task, and one that we shall not undertake in detail. Nevertheless, the consensus of scholarship allows us to adopt the general principle that, where Acts contradicts or cannot be made to fit what Paul says, the critical reader must prefer Paul. He provides firsthand information, whereas Acts is secondary.

Luke's primary purpose in writing, moreover, was not that of a contemporary historian or journalist. He was not much interested in the variety and complexity of events and phenomena that constituted early Christianity. Reporting accurately everything that happened would not have accomplished his purpose. He wished to tell the story of how Christianity spread in a way

"The Conversion of St. Paul" by Tintoretto (1518–1594).   *(Courtesy of National Gallery of Art, Washington, D.C. Samuel H. Kress Collection.)*

that would not only inform the reader but also edify the church and bring it to a better understanding of the ways in which God had accomplished his purpose in its history. Hence, in describing the expansion of Christianity, Luke concentrates on Paul, the imposing missionary figure of the previous generation about whom he has some information and concerning whom he can presuppose familiarity on the part of at least the Christian reader. Luke knows, however, that Paul did not found the Gentile mission.

MISSION TO THE GENTILES (10:1–11:18)

Why is Cornelius' conversion described at such length and with much repetition?

Peter is portrayed by Luke as the founder of the mission to the Gentiles and the representative of the "liberal" position that the gospel can be preached to those outside the bounds of organized Judaism, presumably without their first becoming members of the Jewish congregation. Thus, Peter's position is close to that of the apostle Paul, who struggled so valiantly for the principle that Peter seems to have established with relative ease. If Peter actually secured so large a victory at the outset, however, we might wonder why Paul had so much difficulty. In fact, Paul himself had something less than admiration for Peter, whose tolerant conduct among Gentiles was at first what we would expect on the basis of this Acts narrative, but who later seems to have reversed his field (cf. Gal. 2:11 ff.). In the light of Paul's struggle and his description of Peter's conduct in Galatians (pp. 312–313 below), we might ask whether Peter actually won a victory as a result of this incident, or whether he himself was as fully committed to the mission to the Gentiles as Acts would lead us to believe. Nevertheless, the Book of Acts indicates that the question about the status and obligations of Gentile converts did not die easily. It is the chief subject matter of chapter 15, and in chapter 21 Paul finally arrested in Jerusalem for the last time in an incident growing out of this question and controversy.

Acts gives a lengthy account of the conversion of Cornelius and the subsequent discussion of its meaning. The complexity of the narrative stems in some measure from the editorial work of Luke, who has woven together older traditional material. The long account can, of course, simply be read as an interesting story. One need not ask what purpose it serves at this point in the narrative. But such an approach would ignore the most important question. Furthermore, one should ask why so much of the story, especially the reports of visions, is repetitious.

The vision of Cornelius at Caesarea instructs him to summon Peter from Joppa (10:1–8). Even while his emissaries are on the way, Peter in turn has a vision (10:9–16). Cornelius' men then explain to Peter the purpose of their mission and bring him with them to Caesarea (10:17–19). After Cornelius has explained the details of his own vision (10:30–33), Peter delivers what amounts to a missionary sermon; the Holy Spirit descends upon those standing about, and Peter commands that they be baptized. When Peter returns to Jerusalem he is criticized by the circumcision party for going to uncircumcised men and eating with them. So Peter, to justify his actions, recounts the entire course of events (11:1–18). Upon hearing this, his critics have no further argument. Indeed, they glorify God and fall into line with the position that Peter has espoused.

Although Cornelius' vision (10:1–8) does not require detailed explanation, it is worth observing that he was a Roman officer and thus a representative of the power and prestige of the empire. He is also described as "a devout man who feared God" (vs. 2), which may mean that he was a Gentile associate of a Jewish synagogue who had not formally become a Jew. That he was still a Gentile is clear from the subsequent narrative and discussion of his conversion to Christianity.

Cornelius' approach to Peter is made at the direction of an angel. The angel comes at midafternoon (vs. 3) while Cornelius is at prayer, and Cornelius sees him clearly. There can be no mistaking the divine origin of the instruction to be delivered. Of the character or appearance of the angel we are told nothing; Luke is only interested in the origin and authority of the message, symbolized by the angel. In Acts several such messages are delivered in visions, also an indication of divine authorization. Thus, in the next stage of the narrative Peter sees another vision while standing on the housetop at midday, as the emissaries from Cornelius approach the city of Joppa.

The meaning of Peter's vision (10:9–16) is not so obvious as that of Cornelius. In fact, Peter is said to be puzzled about it (vs. 17). In itself the vision seems to indicate that all animals may be eaten without regard for Jewish custom and law. There is little reason for Peter to be perplexed about this, except in view of the approaching mission from Cornelius, about which, of course, he as yet knows nothing. Luke and the reader know about it, however. Therefore, the perplexity at this point is really more appropriate to the reader than to Peter, a sure sign that Luke has his reader in mind. Peter's perplexity disappears by the time he reaches Cornelius at Caesarea (vss. 28 f.). In the meantime the Spirit has instructed him to go with the three men who have come from Cornelius, for the Spirit has sent them. Peter goes with them to the house of Cornelius, who has already gathered his close friends and family for what he obviously expects will be an important occasion. This is underscored by the way in which he greets Peter (vs. 25). Peter's response is like that of Paul and Barnabas in a similar situation (14:15). Only at this point do we discover that Peter has now understood the meaning of this vision on the rooftop at Joppa: "God has shown me that I should not call anyone profane or unclean" (vs. 28). The vision evidently had to do primarily with the status of human beings rather than of animals. This interpretation of the vision becomes possible only in the light of the events that follow it. A new meaning is given to the vision different from the one that had seemed obvious, but that had left Peter "puzzled" (vs. 17). God shows no partiality. Yet the specific point about dietary laws may also be relevant, for the barrier to table fellowship between Jew and Gentile has been breached (cf. 15:23–29).

This point is not, however, immediately developed. Instead, we hear Cornelius describe his vision to Peter (10:30–33). So Peter first tells Cornelius his vision, or its meaning (vs. 28); then Cornelius tells Peter his. (Compare a similar repetitious recounting of dreams in Genesis 40 and 41.) Luke would not have recounted all this had it not served his purpose; for even if his report were strictly historical, there must have been some reason for him to give such an overly complete account. He could have simply reported that Cornelius recounted to Peter his vision and all that had happened in connection with it. Probably the clue to Luke's procedure is found in verse 33: "So now all of us are here in the presence of God, to listen to *all that the Lord has commanded you to say.*" Luke is concerned to show that the initiator of all these events is God. No one acts until moved to do so by the divine initiative, and Cornelius anticipates nothing else from Peter but what he has been commanded of God. The abundance of visions and reports of visions emphasizes that what is taking place is something other than the working out of a human scheme to evangelize the Gentiles. Thus the break with the past in the offering of the gospel to the Gentiles comes about by the will and action of God, who gives explicit guidance and direction to the major participants in this drama.

Now that all has been properly prepared, Peter delivers his sermon (10:34–43). It has a great deal in common with the other missionary speeches of Acts. The initial statement, however, applies specifically to the present unprecedented situation (vs. 34 f.), making clear that God is favorably disposed toward what is about to happen. In addition, the tenor of the speech sets it somewhat apart from similar pronouncements. Peter, after his opening remarks, introduces the main body of his speech, the Christian message, with the phrase "you know" (vs. 36), thus making his presentation of the gospel a kind of review of matters with which his audience is already familiar. Apparently they have not been converted up to this point because the time has not been right. In the latter part of the speech (vss. 39 ff.) emphasis falls on the crucifixion and resurrection of Jesus and on the authority of the witnesses and their obligation to proclaim the gospel of forgiveness of sins in Jesus' name to all (vs. 42). This statement implies that Peter's own proclamation to these Gentiles is fully justified.

Before Peter can make the characteristic appeal for repentance and conversion (cf. 2:37–42), the Holy Spirit descends upon his hearers (vs. 44), who promptly begin speaking in tongues (vs. 46). All this is witnessed by Jewish Christians (vs. 45), who are amazed that God should give the Spirit even to Gentiles. That these people, Gentile though they may be, should be baptized is now a foregone conclusion (vss. 47 f.). The Jewish Christians are in no position to object, inasmuch as they themselves have observed the manifestation of the Spirit. That the Spirit should be given before baptism could only be taken as an unmistakable sign of the will of God in the matter.

Peter now returns to Jerusalem, where he encounters the criticism of the circumcision party (11:1 ff.), those who assumed that all believers should be circumcised and otherwise qualify as Jews. In response to them he explains fully what happened. Again Luke is not content simply to say that Peter gave an explanation, but gives a full account of it. We now get the second rendition of Peter's vision (vss. 4–10) and the third of Cornelius' (vss. 13–15). Thus Luke drives home the significance of the events he is recounting. In fact, the whole point of Luke's narrative really comes to focus in Peter's somewhat repetitious response to his critics. Only here does the sense of the preceding narrative finally become entirely clear: God wills the conversion of worthy Gentiles to Christianity. Although it is not obvious from the question (vs. 3) that this is what the Jewish Christians are challenging, their final concession (vs. 18) indicates that for Luke precisely this question is settled by the conversion of Cornelius.

A closer examination of certain details of the text confirms this observation. In 11:14 Cornelius' account of his vision is expanded to include as its central point the expectation that Peter will preach the gospel to him and his household. This expectation was not expressed in the earlier accounts (cf. 10:33 and 10:3–6). In Peter's report of his own sermon (11:15), the Holy Spirit no longer falls upon the Gentiles toward the conclusion of his speech (cf. 10:49), but at the beginning, a further indication of the divine initiative. The descent of the Spirit is then likened to Pentecost (chap. 2). This is a new dispensation of the Spirit of God in fulfillment of Jesus' own promise (11:16; cf. 1:5), and Peter draws its full implications for the missionary practice of the church: "If then God gave them the same gift that he gave us when we believed in the Lord Jesus Christ, who was I that I could hinder God?" (vs. 17). Peter had no idea of preaching to Gentiles. Rather the Gentile mission originated in an epoch-making revelation by God of his purposes for the church and the gospel. Moreover, the vision follows the conversion of Paul (9:1–31, esp. vs. 15), the apostle to the Gentiles. This interpretation of the meaning and significance of the conversion of Cornelius and its aftermath is borne out in Luke's report of the Jerusalem Council, where Peter defends the Gentile mission on the basis of the Cornelius incident (see Acts 15:7–9).

Christianity's Triumphal March (13:1–21:14)

Luke now narrates the movement of Christianity from the East to the West, from Antioch in Syria to Greece, making the transition from Jerusalem to the West seem natural and normal. He skillfully dovetails these two major parts of his account so that the coming mission to the Gentiles is prefigured by the conversions of Cornelius and Paul and by the speech of Stephen. Already the Pentecost scene, with the descent of the Spirit and the preaching of Peter before the representatives of many lands, points ahead to the wider missionary effort. After the center of action shifts away from Jerusalem, we are kept aware of the authority and vitality of the Jerusalem church, and of the contact between it and the Gentile mission (15:1–35). The church's work and geographical distribution may become diverse, but its origin, loyalty, mission, and purpose are one. Luke shares this conviction with other New Testament writers, but he expresses it in a unique way.

This portion of the Gentile mission falls into several sections defined by Paul's various activities:

1. First missionary journey: Cyprus and Asia Minor (13:1–14:28)
2. Jerusalem Council (15:1–35)
3. Second missionary journey: entry into Greece (15:36–18:22)
4. Third missionary journey: Ephesus and Greece (18:23–21:14)

Note how this part of Acts shows the progress of gospel witness across the world. The concentration on Paul's missionary journeys in Acts typifies the perspective of the author. The gospel is on the move.

PAUL'S SPEECH AT PISIDIAN ANTIOCH (13:17–41)

How is Paul's turning to the Gentiles typical of the Book of Acts?

In chapters 13 and 14 we find the first description of missionary activity beyond Palestine and Syria. Paul and Barnabas are commissioned, not by the Jerusalem church, but by the church at Antioch (13:1–3), and sent off under its auspices. This church had been founded already by those fleeing Jerusalem during the persecution of the Hellenists (cf. 11:19–20). It is perhaps understandable that the Jerusalem church had some reservations about the activities of the Antioch church and that the Antiochene Christians harbored some resentment toward the mother church. After all, the Jewish Christians had been able to remain in Jerusalem after the founders of the Antioch church had been driven out, presumably because of their radical views about their ancestral traditions (see Acts 7).

The most important incident of chapter 13 is the sermon of Paul (13:17–41) in the synagogue at Pisidian Antioch. Throughout Acts and until the end of his missionary labors in Rome, Paul is portrayed as appealing first to the Jews in every city he visits. Although such a procedure fits almost too well with Luke's conviction about the relation of Christianity to Israel, the Hellenistic Jewish synagogue doubtless provided an almost indispensable foothold for the earliest Christian preaching. In keeping with the setting, Paul's sermon is an address by an Israelite to Israelites, although some God-fearers, Gentiles attracted to the synagogue, are also present (vs. 16). It is designed to portray Jesus, the son of David, as the culmination of their history of salvation, the One promised by God. In proof of this, Paul calls upon the Old Testament to show how the ancient prophecies are now fulfilled in him, especially in his resurrection. Many of the Jews believe (vs. 43), but some do not, and, characteristically, the nonbelievers work systematically to undermine him (vs. 45). This resistance moves Paul and Barnabas to condemn

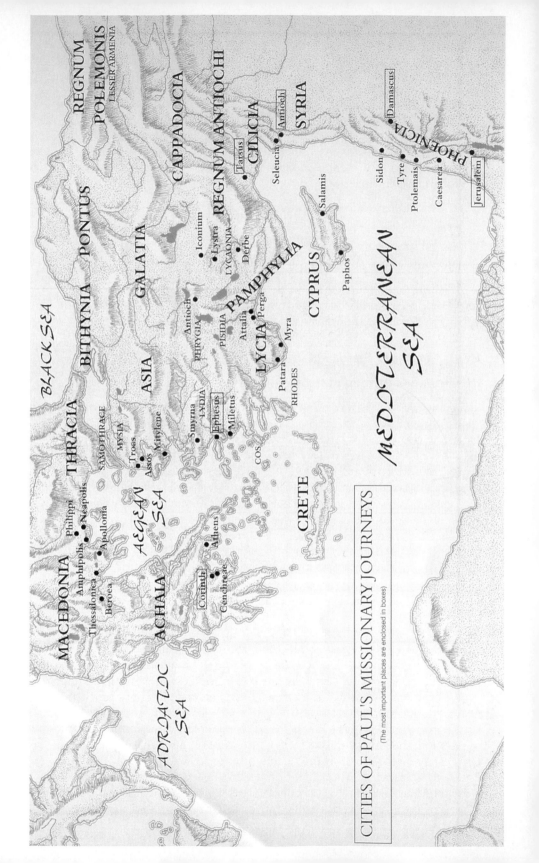

CITIES OF PAUL'S MISSIONARY JOURNEYS
(The most important places are enclosed in boxes)

these recalcitrant Jews and to turn forthwith to the Gentiles, still quoting the Old Testament (Isa. 49:6) to justify their action (13:44–47).

In 14:15–18 Paul and Barnabas are at Lystra making their first address to a purely pagan audience. This speech has less in common with the sermon of chapter 13 and the earlier missionary speeches than with Paul's address to the Athenians (see pp. 287). At the end of chapter 14 Paul and Barnabas return to Antioch. The question of whether non-Jewish converts to Christianity had to be circumcised in accordance with Jewish law was not raised in the Cornelius incident (10:1–11:18), although we were left with the impression that they were not. Now at the beginning of chapter 15 a group of Christians from Judea who insist upon circumcision arrives in Antioch. Their appearance provides the occasion for the resolution of this and related questions in favor of Paul and Barnabas at the Jerusalem Council. Circumcision is not required. Yet a similar or related question is again raised against Paul in chapter 21.

At the end of the Jerusalem Council (chap. 15) and after a sharp dispute over John Mark, Paul and Barnabas separate. Paul returns to the scene of their earlier missionary activity, taking Silas with him (15:36–41). Thence he heads west and, reaching Troas, sees the vision of the man from Macedonia (16:9) that leads him to extend his missionary effort to Europe. Macedonia and Greece henceforth become, with Ephesus, the main focus of his missionary activity until his imprisonment and subsequent journey to Rome. His chief missionary accomplishments were in the Greek cities of Philippi (chap. 16), Thessalonica (17:1–9), and Corinth (chap. 18) and in the Asian city of Ephesus (chap. 19). Luke, however, gives an extended account of the relatively brief visit of Paul to Athens.

PAUL'S SPEECH IN ATHENS (17:16–34)

How and why does Paul's preaching in Athens differ from other missionary sermons in Acts?

Obviously, Luke regards Paul's stay in Athens as an important event. As a mission field Athens is certainly not typical, for Paul's efforts there seem to have borne little fruit. However, Luke's account of his visit occupies a prominent place and includes the longest rendition in Acts of a sermon before an entirely Gentile audience.

Luke's brief description of the character of Athens and the Athenians shows that he has some awareness of the nature as well as of the importance of the city.[7] Yet he reports that Paul was not at all impressed by Athens and was shocked by the profusion of idols he found there (vs. 16). His displeasure led him to engage in debate, not only in the synagogue, as had previously been his custom, but even in the public marketplace (vs. 17). Although Luke does not say so explicitly, this area is presumably the same marketplace where centuries before Socrates engaged his fellow Athenians in discussions.

---

7. The Athens of Paul's time was not large even by ancient standards. E. Haenchen, *The Acts of the Apostles: A Commentary,* trans. H. Anderson et al. (Philadelphia: Westminster,

The Parthenon, celebrated temple of Athena, built in the fifth century B.C. on the Acropolis at Athens.   *(Courtesy of Greek Press and Information Service.)*

Perhaps Luke is aware of a certain parallel here, even though he does not mention Socrates' name, for we read that Paul is accused of being a preacher of "foreign divinities" (vs. 18). The Greek could as well be translated "strange demons" and thus corresponds closely to that *daimōn* that led Socrates to raise those simple, pointed, and troublesome questions that at length roused the ire of his fellow Athenians and led to his execution as an atheist.[8]

Paul's lack of appreciation of Athenian culture is no greater than the Athenians' misunderstanding of him, as his encounter with the Stoic and Epicurean philosophers shows (vs. 18). The epithet that some of them apply to him, "babbler," means literally "cock-sparrow." It was a term of derision for a person who, without real understanding, picks up ideas from here and there, as the sparrow picks up seed, and passes them off as his own. That this estimate of Paul is an offhand judgment based on no genuine understanding of him may be inferred from the fact that the philosophers seem to take Jesus and the resurrection to be two gods. (This is not quite as absurd

1971), p. 517, puts the total number of citizens (not total population) at about five thousand.

8. *Daimōn* has in this case the meaning "good spirit" rather than "demon" as the latter is usually understood. The accusation against Socrates was twofold: (1) corruption of the young and (2) neglect of the traditional gods and the recognition of new and strange deities (*daimonia*).

a misunderstanding as it may seem, for the Greek word *anastasis,* resurrection, is feminine in gender, and pagan gods frequently had goddesses as consorts.) In the light of this beginning, the Athenians' desire to hear Paul's teaching in greater detail is difficult to understand. Luke suggests that it only stems from their insatiable curiosity about anything new (vss. 20 f.).

Paul was taken to the Areopagus (vs. 19) by the Athenians, and there he made his speech. At the time of Paul a court was held on the Areopagus—the name means "hill of Ares" (the Greek god of war)—a small promontory west of the more famous Acropolis. Although it has sometimes been suggested that Paul was himself taken there to be tried, this is nowhere explicitly stated (although the verb *took hold of* in verse 19 could imply arrest). Moreover, the whole affair does not read like a legal proceeding. Rather, Paul is put on display, almost as if he were some kind of freak, by a crowd of intellectual dilettantes.

Paul's initial remark (vs. 22) is probably not to be taken in a negative or sarcastic sense. Rather, as the following verses show, it is the point of contact with the pagan audience that Paul hopes to follow up and develop in his delivery of the Christian message. This becomes clear when Paul concedes that the "unknown god" is worshiped in a valid, if inadequate, way by the Athenians (vs. 23). The time has now come, however, for the unknown God to be revealed in the Christian preaching. A right understanding of this God will mean the recognition of the erroneous character of the pagan worship that has heretofore been offered (vss. 24 f.). This point of view is not, of course, unique to Christianity. It is also Jewish, and this part of Paul's speech may owe something to earlier Jewish missionary propaganda. Furthermore, although the idolatry and polytheism described here may have been practiced and taken seriously by many people in the ancient world, the cultured Greek would have also shared something of Paul's attitude. In fact, verses 24 ff. may owe as much to Stoic philosophy as to Judaism and the Old Testament.

The concepts (vss. 26–29 esp.) actually fit better into the Stoic view of the cosmos (world) than into the biblical–Jewish conception of the history of salvation. For verse 26 has to do with the characteristic Stoic ideas of the providence of God and verses 27 and 28 with his immanence or presence in the world. Moreover, just at the point at which we might have expected a quotation from the Old Testament, Paul quotes the Greek poet Aratus (vs. 28).[9] Thus does Paul accommodate his message to what is familiar and acceptable to his Greek hearers. At the same time, he drives home the argument against idolatry (vs. 29). Although verses 26–28 are now frequently cited as biblical proof of the unity of all peoples under God, in this context they are probably not intended primarily to set forth that idea. Rather, they are an argument

9. *Phaenomena,* 5; cf. Cleanthes, *Hymn to Zeus,* 4. Only the last of the two quotations marked in the NRSV has been positively identified. "In him we live and move and have our being" has sometimes been attributed to an Epimenides, but it may not be a quotation at all.

from the evidence of the existence of God in human beings and nature to a conclusion concerning the nature of God and the proper knowledge and worship of him. God orders the world and humanity (vs. 26) in such a way that they should be disposed to seek him (vs. 27), and so indwells the creation that this seeking is by no means vain (vss. 27 f.). Indeed, as the quotation from Aratus shows, the idea of divine immanence is understood to imply that humankind already has a close relationship to God: "For we too are his offspring." Probably Luke takes this to mean that man is God's creature in line with the Old Testament and Hebraic point of view and not in the sense of kinship that the poet originally intended. Nevertheless, creaturehood here already implies the possibility of knowing and having access to God.

Only in verses 30 and 31 does Paul turn from these arguments about natural theology, which many Hellenistic Jews or even pagans might have found perfectly congenial, to the distinctly Christian message. The whole history of paganism down to the moment in which Paul speaks is described simply as "times of human ignorance" that God has overlooked (vs. 30). The pagan world will presumably incur no guilt as a result, provided that it now repents. No mention at all is made of the ministry and crucifixion of Jesus in this preaching of repentance; only the coming judgment is invoked, and only in connection with it is Jesus mentioned. Even then Paul only alludes to him as the man whom God has appointed to judge the world, giving assurance of this "to all by raising him from the dead." At the mention of the resurrection of the dead, Paul is interrupted; some hearers become contemptuous (the Jewish and Christian notion of resurrection is foreign to them) but others remain curious (vs. 32). Paul departs (vs. 33), and although we have the impression that his preaching to the Athenians was something less than a success, he does make a few converts (vs. 34).

The speech is notable on several counts. First, it differs from the missionary speeches of chapters 1–13 in its total lack of reference to the Old Testament and the history of Israel. Second, in important respects it is remarkably dissimilar to the thought of the genuine letters of Paul. Third, it has certain affinities with the speech ascribed to Paul and Barnabas in 14:15–18. In fact, this is one of the rare places in the New Testament in which a positive, though highly qualified, estimate of pagan piety and culture is expressed or implied and a natural theology is set forth. Each of these points deserves further comment.

We have already noticed that at just the point we would have expected Paul to refer to the Hebrew scriptures (Old Testament) he quotes a pagan poet. The Old Testament would have been of little use in confirming the truth of the Christian message before a non-Jewish audience who did not accept its authority in the first place. The appeal to this purely Gentile audience had to be made on the basis of arguments from Hellenistic natural theology and Greek literature. This shift does not mean that the use of scripture in Christian preaching was regarded either by Paul or Luke as a purely apologetic device. There is ample reason to suppose that both regarded it as revelation in and of itself. Yet the non-Jewish hearer could only be brought to assent on other grounds. Similarly, in the brief missionary sermon of Paul and Barnabas before a non-Jewish audience at Lystra (14:15–18), there is no reference or allusion to scripture or the narrative of salvation history. In recounting the speeches to Gentile audiences in this way Luke may be following a common procedure, or may be influenced by a common practice of the Hellenistic Christian mission in his own day. If his letters are any indication, Paul did not limit his use of the scriptures to situations in which he was addressing Christians of Jewish background only.

This observation leads directly to our second point. The first three chapters of the Epistle to the Romans suggest that Paul's attitude toward the pagan world was not that portrayed in the Areopagus speech. Whereas in this speech pagan piety and the possibility of a natural theology are the point of contact and, in fact, the basis of his preaching, in Romans practically the reverse is true (see pp. 340–343). In Romans, the knowledge of God is in principle possible because of creation and the natural order, but the possibility of such knowledge is not the basis of Christian preaching. Rather it is grounds for condemnation, because, although present, it does not lead to a proper acknowledgment of God (1:18–23). In Acts the hearers are credited with worshiping God without knowing him; in Romans the human race is charged with knowing God but not worshiping him. Whereas in Acts 17:30 the past prior to the preaching of the gospel is simply a period of ignorance for which no blame is placed, in Romans human history is the history of sin. Further, when the salvation event is announced in Acts 17:31, Paul speaks primarily of the coming judgment, with a backward look at the resurrection. In Romans 3:21 ff. the salvation event is described in terms of the cross.

Admittedly in Acts Paul's speech is interrupted, but we have the impression that with the mention of the resurrection and judgment he has said all he meant to say. Thus in many important respects Paul's Areopagus speech seems to be the antithesis of the theology of Paul in Romans. This observation naturally leads to the question of whether this speech is Paul's or whether Luke has put into Paul's mouth what he considers to be an appropriate and typical missionary sermon to Gentiles. In order to ascribe the speech to Paul, one may surmise that after this occasion Paul gave up this apologetic approach. Yet there is little indication in all the genuine Pauline letters that the apostle himself ever espoused such a theological position as we find in the Acts speech. It is much easier historically to understand the Areopagus speech as the composition of Luke. This, of course, does not mean that Paul did not visit Athens and preach there (cf. 1 Thess. 3:1).

Thus Luke seems to be presenting what he considers a typical missionary sermon to Gentiles. This observation can be supported further by our third point, namely, that the Areopagus speech has its closest affinities with the speech of Paul and Barnabas to a pagan audience at Lystra (14:15–18). The Lystra speech manifests certain specific points of agreement with the Areopagus address. Especially striking are the concept of divine creation (vs. 15), the notion that God has tolerated the idolatry of the Gentiles in times past (vss. 15 f.), and the belief that the beneficent natural processes attest a divine author (vs. 17). Except for the lack of direct reference to Christ, the Lystra speech is quite similar to the one at Athens. And like the latter, it is dissimilar to the speeches of chapters 1–13 and unlike the theology of the Pauline epistles.

Both the Athens speech and the Lystra speech are most unlike the Pauline theology and the rest of the New Testament in their ascription of a positive and significant role to a natural knowledge of God, a knowledge both possible and extant apart from the Jewish and Christian traditions. They are also unique in regarding the history of humanity prior to the coming of Christ and the preaching of the gospel as one of ignorance rather than sin. The revelation in Christ is not, first of all, the revelation of God's wrath (cf. Rom. 1:18) and of human sinfulness, but of a coming judgment and the necessity of repentance (Acts 17:30 f.) and forgiveness. Thus, for Luke the human predicament is not quite so desperate as for Paul, and pagan culture and piety are allowed to play a positive preparatory role for the appearance of the gospel.

The idea of a valid general revelation apart from Israel and the Old Testament, although rare in the New Testament, was taken up and developed by Christian apologists and theologians of the second and third centuries and has persisted among Christians down to the present. For Luke, the entire world and its history provide the scope for the Christian mission and message. Its roots are to be found not only in the history of Israel but also in general human history and culture. Luke's Gospel traces the genealogy of Christ back to Adam, and in Acts the necessary presuppositions of Christian preaching are found in a popular philosophic view of God and the world, as well as in the Old Testament.

Jerusalem to Rome (21:15–28:31)

What is the final outcome of Paul's arrest and trials?

This final major section of Acts is devoted entirely to the fortunes of Paul from his last visit to Jerusalem until his arrival as a prisoner in Rome. According to Luke, Paul was taken into custody by the Romans to save him from an angry Jerusalem mob. They accused him of "teaching everyone everywhere against our people, our law, and this place," as well as defiling the temple by bringing Greeks into it (21:28). From the point at which Paul is arrested near the temple in Jerusalem (21:33) to the end of the book, he is a Roman prisoner. (Probably he, like Jesus, died at the hands of the Romans, although Luke does not tell us.) Paul is at first held for a couple of days in Jerusalem. Then he is transferred to Caesarea, the site of the Roman governor's headquarters (chaps. 24–26), and finally, on the basis of his own appeal as a Roman citizen to trial by Caesar, he is sent to Rome (chaps. 27–28). At each stage Paul's innocence is affirmed (23:29; 25:25; 26:31 f.). There the story simply ends, with Paul a prisoner in Rome, albeit with certain freedoms and privileges. As we take leave of him he is still "proclaiming the kingdom of God and teaching about the Lord Jesus Christ with all boldness and without hindrance" (28:31).

The larger part of chapters 22–28, with the exception of the sea voyage to Rome (chap. 27), is devoted to extensive descriptions of Paul's defense of himself before the representatives of Judaism and Rome. It is as if the prophecy of 9:15 were being literally fulfilled: "He is an instrument whom I have chosen to bring my name before Gentiles and kings and before the people of Israel." Luke describes Paul's hearings and speeches in considerable detail. Paul's conversion, reported in full in chapter 9, is repeated with some variations in chapters 22 and 26. In the course of many scenes and speeches several themes are often reiterated. Paul has not betrayed Judaism; rather, he understands his whole mission to pertain directly to the fulfillment of the hope of Israel. Paul's mission to the Gentiles is not simply his own idea but the direct result of divine causation and directive. Thus Paul's conversion is always closely linked to his commission to preach to the Gentiles—as it is by Paul himself (Gal. 1:15 ff.). Paul's innocence of any crime is established with certainty. The various hints, statements, and indications tending to exonerate Paul are well summarized in the conversation between Agrippa and Festus (26:32), where Agrippa says that Paul could have been released had not he appealed to Caesar. Yet the fact that he must stand before the emperor (27:24) is not finally a tragedy, although it has tragic overtones (e.g., 20:22–25, 38), but the culmination of the triumphant spread of Christianity across the known world and the high point of Acts. Although Paul's imprisonment and journey to Rome might be regarded by some as the result of the work of evil men or the quirk of a cruel fate, for Luke they are the fulfillment of the will of God.

Conclusion

The *structure* of the Acts of the Apostles must be considered in conjunction with Luke's Gospel. At the same time the division between the Gospel and Acts is more than a convenient literary device. It marks a major division in Luke's theology and perception of history. Luke envisages a drama of three distinct phases: the period of Israel and her prophetic message; the fulfillment of this prophecy in the earthly mission of Jesus; and the mission of the church, likewise a fulfillment of ancient prophecy. His threefold division of the history of salvation can be discerned from the shape and structure of his writing. Scripture, the Old Testament (cf. Luke 1:5–2:51 esp.), constitutes the first part of a story of salvation that finds its culmination in the coming of Jesus as the Christ (Gospel). But this fulfillment was not limited to the historic appearance of Jesus of Nazareth; it embraced also the existence and mission of his church (Acts).

The basic structure of Acts itself is quite simple. After the ascension, the election of Matthias, and the inaugural preaching of the gospel by Peter,

The theater of Ephesus, where Paul was arraigned before an angry mob (Acts 19:28–41). It can seat over twenty thousand people.   *(Courtesy of D. Moody Smith.)*

which take place in or around Jerusalem, there are three principal divisions. The first deals with the establishment and growth of the church within Palestine (chaps. 3–12), the second with the expansion of the church to the Gentile world (chaps. 13–21), and the third with Paul's victory against opposition (chaps. 22–28). Even as the journey of Jesus to Jerusalem forms the central part of the Gospel, so the missionary journeys of Paul are the central portion of Acts. Just as the last part of the Gospel deals with the arrest, trial, and death of Jesus, so the last seven chapters of Acts narrate the arrest of Paul, his trials, and the eventual journey to Rome. The motifs of journeying and witnessing thus predominate in Acts as in Luke's Gospel.

The *emphases* of Acts are intricately bound to its structure, and are intimately related to those of the Gospel. In fact, the same emphases—Christianity as the new Israel, worldwide expansion, and the importance of witnessing—are developed somewhat further in Acts. In the Gospel, Luke is tied to the tradition of Jesus, which he cannot radically change, but in Acts he can with a relatively free hand tell the story of the church's advance so as to bring out its meaning and truth.

Luke was deeply convinced that Judaism should have become Christianity, and, as it had not, that the promises to Israel were being fulfilled through Christ in the church. Thus the new faith is the proper and genuine continuation and fulfillment of the old. The many quotations from, and allusions and references to, the Old Testament clearly convey this emphasis.

In fact, the culmination of Paul's ministry in Rome (recounted in chap. 28) is his application of the famous Isaiah 6:9–10 passage to those Jews who had not believed his preaching (vss. 25–28). The larger part of Israel has forfeited its inheritance to the Gentiles by rejecting the gospel, and the young Christian church has now become the true Israel.[10]

Acts is often called "the first church history," and in a sense it is. Yet insofar as it is a history at all, it is history of a very special kind. It has been written from a definite theological perspective with certain purposes in view. When all allowances are made for Luke's motivations and interests, however, it is apparent that a major part of Luke's purpose in Acts is to tell an interesting and, for the most part, happy story. He describes the establishment of Christianity and its progress across the Greco-Roman world during the apostolic age. The scope of the gospel is universal, and it will not be denied. Although we hear of persecutions and martyrdoms in the course of this story, the storyteller's attitude remains confident and optimistic throughout, and the narrative is brought to an end on a positive note (28:30 f.). The gospel knows no obstacle too great and no enemy too powerful to stand in the way of its successful march from Jerusalem to Rome. The universal emphasis, which is subtly conveyed in Luke's Gospel (cf. Luke 3:38; 4:24–30), becomes the principal subject matter of Acts.

The centrality of Luke's emphasis upon the universality of the Gospel implies an emphasis on witnessing. Again, what is handled somewhat indirectly in the Gospel becomes a major theme of Acts. In Acts 1 Luke's first concern was to show that in the apostolic group, the Twelve, a firm basis for the witness to Jesus had been established. Matthias, who was chosen by God to replace Judas, qualified for his role by virtue of intimate and long-time knowledge of Jesus. If Luke emphasizes the universality of the gospel, he does so by telling of the apostles and others witnessing. Their witnessing encounters persecution, as we had already been led to expect by the Gospel. Indeed, the witness (Greek, *martyrs,* gen. *martyros*) may even become a martyr, as in the case of Stephen, not to mention Peter, Paul, and others who are arrested and otherwise harassed.[11] Although Luke takes full account of such dangers,

10. This fact is also reflected in his Gospel, 4:16–30. Jesus begins his ministry with a clear indication that he is to be rejected by the Jews and accepted by Gentiles.

11. The tradition of Paul's martyrdom is found only in extracanonical documents: 1 Clement v, 7; Acts of Paul, x; Eusebius, *EH,* ii, 22. The supposed site of Paul's burial is commemorated by the ancient church St. Paul Outside the Walls in Rome. The present

he does not dwell upon them, for he is fully convinced that such opposition fails utterly to impede the spread of the gospel and the growth of the church.

The method of *redaction criticism,* which can be so profitably applied to the Gospel, yields less fruit in Acts. Although we can identify the major sources of the Gospel (Mark and Q) with some certainty, it is quite difficult to separate tradition from redaction in Acts. Nevertheless, the assumption that sources and traditions of some sort lie behind Acts is probably warranted, and evidence of the author's editing can surely be found in the summary reports and transitions and especially in the overall structure. It is also likely that the speeches in their present form are largely his composition. The material of Acts is permeated with Luke's own point of view, which can usually be identified with some confidence.

As to the *historical occasion* or *situation* of Acts, while the author probably writes for the general reader, the needs and purposes of the church are nevertheless in the forefront. No doubt he expected the work to be useful to the church for apologetic or missionary purposes. As an apologist, Luke wants to show that Christianity is not a subversive movement. In the Gospel he goes out of his way to prove that Jesus was innocent of any crime (Luke 23:47; see pp. 151–152). A similar motif appears in the statement about Paul that Agrippa made to Festus, the Roman procurator: "This man could have been set free if he had not appealed to Caesar" (26:32). Christians are arrested not because the authorities have seen them commit a crime but because of their involvement in some public incident, and often because of the accusations or actions of others, whether Jews or Gentiles. That Luke should have had some interest in showing Christians innocent of any crimes against the state is thoroughly understandable. After all, Jesus had been crucified by the Roman authorities, whatever role the Jewish leaders may have played, and this fact was apparently widely known. Thus, from the outset Christianity stood under the suspicion of being a subversive movement, and this suspicion could only have been heightened by the refusal of Christians to participate in the worship of the Roman emperor. Luke intends to show that the charge of subversion is groundless.

Luke's literary aspirations, reflected in the formal prefaces and in the style and tone of his work, make it very difficult to pin down a definite time and place of origin within early Christianity. Because of his apologetic concern to show Jesus and the church politically innocent in relation to the Roman Empire, a Roman origin has sometimes been suggested. This suggestion is plausible and possible, though not compelling. But the same widely shared literary style and historical interests that make Acts difficult to locate within the first century contribute to our understanding of its general situation. The character and quality of this book suggest a Christianity well on its way to be-

structure was rebuilt in modern times after fire destroyed the fourth-century building. That Peter should suffer martyrdom is suggested, but not reported, in the New Testament (John 21:18–19). According to tradition his remains lie under the altar of St. Peter's basilica in the Vatican.

coming an established world religion. Indeed, subsequent history confirmed the worldwide vision of Luke–Acts, for within less than three centuries the new faith would become the official religion of the Roman Empire.

Suggestions for Further Reading

The best commentary on Acts as a theological document is E. Haenchen, *The Acts of the Apostles: A Commentary,* trans. H. Anderson, R. McL. Wilson et al. (Philadelphia: Westminster, 1971). In response to Haenchen's historical disinterest, I. H. Marshall, *The Acts of the Apostles: An Introduction and Commentary* (Grand Rapids, MI: Eerdmans, 1980), takes a much more positive view of its historical value. The most recent technical commentary is H. Conzelmann, *Acts of the Apostles,* trans. J. Limburg, A. T. Kraabel, and D. H. Juel (Philadelphia: Fortress, 1987), in the Hermeneia Series. C. K. Barrett's commentary has been announced for the new International Critical Commentary series. Two excellent, if less technical, commentaries are G. A. Krodel, *Acts* (Minneapolis: Augsburg, 1986), and L. T. Johnson, *The Acts of the Apostles* (Collegeville, MN: Liturgical Press, 1992). R. C. Tannehill, *The Narrative Unity of Luke–Acts: A Literary Interpretation, Vol. 2: The Acts of the Apostles* (Minneapolis: Fortress, 1990), is actually a commentary on the narrative employing newer, literary-critical perspectives.

F. J. Foakes-Jackson and K. Lake (eds.), *The Beginnings of Christianity,* 5 vols. (London: Macmillan, 1920–1933), is a landmark of scholarship; the work has now been reissued (Grand Rapids, MI: Baker Book House). M. Dibelius, *Studies in the Acts of the Apostles,* ed. H. Greeven and trans. M. Ling (New York: Scribner's, 1956), is a collection of pioneering essays in the literary analysis and interpretation of Acts. On the historical basis of Acts, H. Cadbury, *The Book of Acts in History* (New York: Harper & Row, 1955), is still useful. M. Hengel, *Acts and the Earliest History of Christianity,* trans. J. Bowden (Philadelphia: Fortress, 1979), stresses the value of the Book of Acts for any reconstruction of earliest Christianity. A lack of scholarly consensus on the historical character of Acts is, however, reflected in quite recent publications: R. I. Pervo, *Profit with Delight: The Literary Genre of the Acts of the Apostles* (Philadelphia: Fortress, 1987), characterizes Acts as a historical novel intended as much to entertain as to edify. C. J. Hemer, on the other hand, launches a learned defense of the historicity of Acts in *The Book of Acts in the Setting of Hellenistic History* (Tübingen: Mohr, 1989). Perhaps ironically, both insist on setting Acts in its proper, contemporaneous literary context. Much less conservative than Hemer, but similarly interested in the historical basis of Acts, is G. Lüdemann, *Early Christianity According to the Traditions in Acts: A Commentary,* trans. J. Bowden (Minneapolis: Fortress, 1989), who analyzes the text by means of redaction criticism in order to lay bare historical traditions. On another important issue, J. Jervell, *The Unknown Paul: Essays on Luke–Acts and Early Christian History* (Minneapolis: Augsburg, 1984), emphasizes the Jewish–Christian character and interests of Luke, while at an opposite extreme, J. T. Sanders, *The Jews in Luke–Acts* (Philadelphia: Fortress, 1987), characterizes the author as anti-Jewish. The most extensive history of research, W. W. Gasque, *A History of the Criticism of the Acts of the Apostles* (Grand Rapids, MI: Eerdmans, 1975), is avowedly conservative in perspective. For a more recent, briefer survey, see M. A. Powell, *What Are They Saying About Acts?* (New York: Paulist, 1991). For works on the history of earliest Christianity, see the Suggestions for Further Reading, Chapter 11; for works on Luke–Acts, Chapter 4. (Books listed here deal primarily with Acts.)

Chapter 8

Paul: Apostle to the Gentiles

Notes on Paul's Career

*T*he Acts of the Apostles presents Paul as the Apostle to the Gentiles, a role that he ascribed to himself, or that was given to him by the Jerusalem apostles (Gal. 1:15–16; 2:7–9). Doubtless there were other important missionary preachers, for example, Barnabas, Apollos, Prisca (Priscilla), and Aquila, all of whom are mentioned by Paul and in Acts. Nevertheless, Paul stands out in Acts and in the New Testament generally as the leading figure in the earliest expansion of Christianity into the Greco-Roman world.

His importance was not lessened, but perhaps enhanced, by the fact that he was a center of controversy, as quickly becomes apparent from the reading of his letters, especially Galatians and 2 Corinthians. To some extent Paul's controversial character is subdued in Acts, but Luke nevertheless narrates an initial controversy that arose because of the preaching of the gospel to Gentiles (Acts 15) and later the arrest of Paul because of disturbances attending his final visit to Jerusalem (Acts 21).

To understand the importance of Paul's work, we need to think our way back to the very beginning of Christianity, when there was no consciousness of its being a new religion distinct from Judaism. Like Jesus and his Galilean disciples, Paul was a Jew; moreover, he was a Pharisee (Phil. 3:5). And, like Jesus, he did not set out to found or spread a new religion, but to announce what God was doing within the framework of the old. Thus neither Jesus nor Paul uses the terms *Christianity* or *Christian,* and Paul only rarely speaks of Judaism (Gal. 1:13) because he assumes it as his religious background. Both Jesus and Paul presuppose Israel and the history and tradition known from scripture as the basis or matrix of God's new revelation.

Whether Jesus anticipated the spreading of God's word to the Gentiles before the appearance of the kingdom in power is a debated question. Quite likely he did not (cf. Mark 9:1; Matt. 10:23). Paul, by contrast, was himself converted in Damascus, Syria, outside the Holy Land, and learned to be a Christian from people who were neither Jesus' disciples nor closely associated with them. (The version of the gospel that Paul first heard is summarized by him in 1 Cor. 15:3–7.) Paul's initial positive experience with Christianity seems to have taken place in the company of people who already represented the Gentile, or Hellenistic, missionary thrust of Christianity (cf. Acts 11:19–20). Paul quite naturally became involved in this missionary enterprise (Acts 11:21–26), for he himself was not a native of Palestine but of Tarsus, near the Mediterranean coast in present-day Turkey. His native language was Greek, in which all his letters are written and in which he was able to express himself fluently and in quite precise terms. Whether a significant part of his education took place in Jerusalem, as he claims in Acts (22:3), is debatable, but by his own testimony he was a serious student of Jewish traditions and law (Gal. 1:14; 2 Cor. 11:22; Phil. 3:4–6).

Precisely because of this dedication to his ancestral faith, Paul was at first a vehement and vigorous opponent of the followers of Jesus. In his own letters, as well as in Acts, Paul's role as persecutor of the early church is made unmistakably clear (Gal. 1:13; 1 Cor. 15:9; Acts 9:1–2; cf. 7:58; 8:1). Doubtless Paul saw the new religious movement as a renegade Jewish sect, a dire threat to the integrity of Judaism. The reasons for his view are not entirely clear. Acts does not tell us why precisely and neither does the Apostle. Christians are likely to assume that allegiance to the crucified Jesus as Messiah would have been grounds for Paul to persecute Christians, as such allegiance would entail a defection from Judaism in order to embrace Christianity. But such an assumption, though reasonable from a later perspective, does not fit the situation of the first generation of Christ confessors, who did not believe that by embracing Jesus they ceased to be Jews. Possibly some Jews would have believed Jesus' crucifixion rendered him accursed, and hence unfit to be Messiah (cf. Paul's quotation of Deut. 21:23 in Gal. 3:13); however, simply the belief that a certain person was the Messiah would not disqualify one as a Jew, even if that belief turned out to be false.

Perhaps Paul persecuted believers in Damascus because he opposed their illegitimate manner of opening doors to Gentiles. Stephen—whose death Paul seemingly approved—had, in Luke's telling (Acts 7), issued a strong indictment of the Jewish temple cult, ending with an accusation that the Jews who put Jesus to death did not keep the law. The representatives of Stephen's group, the so-called Hellenists, were then promptly expelled from Jerusalem (Acts 8:1, 4) and, according to Acts, set out for Antioch, where they preached to Gentiles (11:19–20). From Paul's later testimony it is evident that they succeeded in converting a number of Gentiles and that problems arose between Gentile and Jewish believers in Antioch over questions concerning the Jewish law and table fellowship (Acts 2:11–21). Perhaps the Christians of Damascus who instructed Paul after his conversion were related to this same group. The believers there, described as those belonging to the Way (Acts 9:1), were still members of

Saint Paul, a plaque from thirteenth-century France.   *(Courtesy of Bulloz Art Reference Bureau.)*

synagogues. But if such believers, who were open to fellowship with Gentiles on the latter's terms, were converting Gentiles without requiring them to become Jews, it was no wonder that they caused offense within the Jewish community. Paul's view of Jesus and his followers before his conversion remains largely hidden from us. In his letters Paul does not speak directly of the motivations that led him to persecute the church. We may only make inferences from his postconversion statements and from Acts.

The major watershed of Paul's life was, of course, this conversion, which changed him from persecutor of Jesus' followers to one of them. Although we must guard against viewing this event as a conversion from Judaism to Christianity, the controversy that marked Paul's career, and that followed him to the end of his days, centered precisely on the question of the relation and implications of Jesus and the claims made for him to traditional Jewish thought. Paul would later say that Christ was the end of the law (Rom. 10:4). What exactly he meant has been debated ever since, and is not entirely clear from his own writings. Nevertheless, it is beyond doubt that, at some point after his conversion, Paul began preaching a version of the gospel to Gentiles that did not require them to become Jewish. That is, his converts did not have to accept circumcision and the ritual provisions of the law. Thus Paul became the founder of predominantly Gentile churches. At the same time he desired to maintain communion with Jews, particularly Jewish Christians in the church. It was this loyalty to both commitments, to a Gentile mission and church and to historic Israel, that kept Paul at the center of controversy. We see that controversy reflected dimly in Acts, very much in the foreground of Galatians, 2 Corinthians, and Philippians, and rather more in the background of Romans and 1 Corinthians.

When we turn from the Gospels and Acts to Paul, we move to a different literary world, from narratives that deal with historical events to letters that were communications from Paul to churches he had founded or in which he had a strong interest. The analogy of modern letters is helpful as a beginning point in understanding Paul's, although there are differences of form and purpose. We should remember that Paul's letters are more than personal, occasional writings. They are means by which he intended to extend and exercise apostolic care and authority over the churches. Doubtless Paul expected each to be read before the entire church in solemn assembly (1 Thess. 5:27; cf. Col. 4:16).

The difference between Paul's letters and the Gospels are not, however, just literary. Although Paul speaks frequently of Jesus, Jesus Christ, or our Lord Jesus Christ, surprisingly he tells us little if anything about Jesus that we do not know from the Gospels. Indeed, there are only occasional allusions to sayings or incidents we know from the Gospels (e.g., 1 Cor. 7:10–11; 11:23–25; Gal. 4:4); if we were dependent on Paul for our knowledge of Jesus, it would be very slim indeed. This fact is all the more startling because Paul is our earliest witness to Jesus and the early Christian movement. His letters were written only a couple of decades after Jesus' death and a decade or two before the earliest Gospel, Mark. Doubtless Paul knew more about Jesus than he conveys in his letters, but how much more is a matter of uncertainty and debate. When he refers to his own missionary preaching, he underscores the centrality and importance of Jesus' death (1 Cor. 1:17–18; 2:1–2). Moreover, his account of the gospel tradition that he received, and passed on, reflects the centrality of Jesus' death and resurrection (1 Cor. 15:3–7). This focus mirrors Paul's theological interests as they are expressed in the Letter to the Romans (below, Chapter 9), where he expounds his views most fully. Paul there concentrates his attention on what God has done in Jesus, particularly by his death and resurrection.

Upon reflection, the disproportionate attention given Jesus' death in the Gospels, particularly in Mark and John, corresponds to Paul's emphasis. What is lacking in Paul, or at least in his letters, is equivalent attention to Jesus' life, teaching, and deeds. Remarkably, although Paul clearly knows of Jesus' teaching, he never mentions the miracles or mighty works of Jesus that loom so large in the Gospel narratives. In this respect Paul seems unique, but in all probability his intense concentration upon Jesus' death and resurrection as God's deed reflects the principal emphasis of the faith and preaching of many first-generation Christians. (This emphasis in turn accounts for the large role of the passion narratives in the Gospels.) In the narratives of the earliest missionary preaching in Acts, Peter and Paul are portrayed as concentrating mainly on Jesus' death and resurrection, although his mighty deeds, but not his teaching, are mentioned in passing (see Acts 2:22–36; but cf. 13:17–40, where Paul does *not* mention Jesus' deeds).

The Book of Acts gives us a clear picture of Paul and a blueprint—even an itinerary—of the course of his missionary career. It is possible to make an approximate correlation of the Acts account of Paul's career with the letters, to bring his life and work into relation with the main events of the epoch in which he lived, and thus to gain a general conception of Pauline chronology. On the basis of an ancient inscription found at Delphi in Greece, Gallio's proconsulship in Corinth can be dated about A.D. 51–52. According to the Acts report, while Paul was in Corinth for eighteen months on his second missionary journey (15:36–18:21) he was arrested and brought before this same Gallio (18:12 ff.). Thus we can arrive at an approximate date for Paul's first visit to Corinth, the surest fixed point of Pauline chronology. We may confidently place Paul's career in the middle third of the first century. Probably he was converted in the early thirties and died in the early sixties. Within this period there is less certainty about the exact dating of events. (For an approximate chronology of Paul and the Pauline letters, see the chart on p. xxviii.)[1]

More of the New Testament has been ascribed to Paul than to any other author. The Pauline authorship of Hebrews, which does not actually claim to be from Paul, is universally rejected among critical scholars, however, and that of the Pastorals (1 and 2 Timothy and Titus) generally so, with Colossians and 2 Thessalonians as well as Ephesians considered doubtful. Therefore, Luke would seem to have been the most prolific New Testament author. Yet slightly more than one-half of Luke's total work is about Jesus and therefore embodies much pre-Lukan tradition. Of the rest, more than one-half is about Paul. That so much later literature was ascribed to Paul and that his chief rival for literary productivity devoted a great part of his second work to a description of his career are accurate indications of the significance of the man. Paul was not only the most important missionary of the first Christian generation, he was also its most productive literary figure. Moreover, he was a notable organizer, man of affairs, and thinker. We would know a good deal about him if we had only the Book of Acts, in which he plays so large a role. Fortunately, we also have at least some of his letters, which reflect not only his activities and thought but also his own personality.

In this chapter, Paul's letters to churches he founded provide the basis for consideration of important aspects of his career, thought, and work. The Thessalonian let-

---

1. Something like the chronology reflected in our table has been widely accepted, but there is by no means universal agreement. Thorough treatments in English, which come to somewhat different conclusions, are Robert Jewett, *A Chronology of Paul's Life* (Philadelphia: Fortress, 1979), and Gerd Lüdemann, *Paul: Apostle to the Gentiles. Studies in Chronology*, trans. F. S. Jones (Philadelphia: Fortress, 1984).

ters reveal a Paul not yet at the center of controversy. Particularly 1 Thessalonians shows how Paul viewed the conversion of the Thessalonians and how he valued and nurtured their new life as a community of believers. Galatians reflects a Paul plunged into the heat of controversy and revealing his life and soul as testimony to the truth of the gospel as he understands it. Here we learn a great deal about Paul's personal history, self-understanding, and relation to the Jerusalem church. Also the clearest picture of the nature of the opposition Paul faced from the Jerusalem, or conservative, wing of the church emerges. There were many who assumed that believing in Jesus meant remaining, or becoming, Jewish, although Paul did not agree. The Corinthian letters do two extremely important things: 1 Corinthians provides insight into the range of problems and issues faced by the first Christians as they continued to live in a more or less inhospitable society; 2 Corinthians again reflects Paul's controversy with opponents and at the same time provides unparalleled insights into the self-consciousness of Paul as an apostle. Philippians is not a controversy letter. Paul is on good terms with the church at Philippi, as with that at Thessalonica, but—as chapter 3 makes clear—Paul's opponents still loom in the background, casting a pall over an otherwise friendly letter. Although it is difficult to arrange Paul's letters in chronological—and relative—order, the sequence of treatment here probably follows that in which they were written. Romans (Chapter 9) almost certainly followed all these letters except Philippians.

Thessalonians: Faith and the Future

Notes on the Thessalonian Letters

The Thessalonian letters are the earliest of Paul's letters and probably the earliest New Testament books. Thessalonica was an important and thriving seaport city and the capital of the Roman province of Macedonia; moreover, it was a business and trade center on the Egnatian Way that connected Rome with the East. Paul had founded a church there, as his letters make clear.

According to Acts(17:1), Paul and his companions arrived in Thessalonica after they had preached and been arrested in Philippi (16:12–40). Paul's preaching in the synagogue of Thessalonica is said to have been persuasive to some, but sharp opposition arose that resulted in his expulsion from the city, apparently after a period of less than a month (17:1–10, esp. vs. 2). Paul then set out for Athens in the province of Achaia to the south and, after a brief stay there (17:16–34), arrived in nearby Corinth (18:1), where he was joined by Silas (Silvanus) and Timothy (18:5). Some such travels are noted also in 1 Thessalonians (2:2; 3:1, 6), although the itineraries of Paul and his companions suggested there do not entirely agree with Acts. Nevertheless, we are probably reading about the same events in the two sources, and Acts helps fix the place of origin of the Thessalonian letters, namely at Corinth (18:5). In writing both letters Paul is joined by Silvanus and Timothy (1 Thess. 2:2; 2 Thess. 1:1), the companions named in Acts. Paul's stay in Corinth can be dated in A.D. 50 or 51, for it coincided with the proconsulship of Gallio (Acts 18:12).

The letters, especially 1 Thessalonians, suggest that Paul worked among his Thessalonian converts much longer than the few weeks mentioned in Acts (cf. 1 Thess. 1:5–6; 2:1–12). Otherwise, it is difficult to see how he came to know them so well. As in other cases where Paul and Acts stand in some tension, Paul's own account is to be preferred as the earlier and more direct testimony.

There are, however, reasons for doubting the authenticity of 2 Thessalonians. Its relationship to 1 Thessalonians is unclear and the apocalyptic mythology of 2:1–12 is unlike anything else we find in Paul. The emphasis upon the genuineness and authority of the letter (cf. 2:1; 3:14 f., 17) suggests that the author protests too much and thus arouses suspicion. Yet the supposition of pseudonymity (i.e., that another person wrote under Paul's name) does not immediately or completely clarify the situation and interpretation of the letter. It may be that 2 Thessalonians was written shortly after 1 Thessalonians and that it addressed the same situation and problems.

OUTLINE OF 1 THESSALONIANS

Salutation (1:1)
Personal and Related Matters (1:2–3:13)
    Thanksgiving (1:2–10)
    Paul's Missionary Work (2:1–16)
    Timothy's Mission (2:17–3:10)
    Prayer (3:11–13)
Exhortation and Encouragement (4:1–5:27)
    General Instructions (4:11–12)
    The Return of Jesus (4:13–5:11)
    Final Instructions and Prayers (5:12–27)
Concluding Benedictions (5:28)

THE RETURN OF JESUS (1 THESS. 4:13–5:11)

How is Paul's apocalyptic scenario relevant to the Thessalonians' situation?

As Paul's earliest letter, 1 Thessalonians offers valuable clues about the character of his missionary preaching and how conversion and belonging to the new community of Christians were understood. Paul speaks at the outset of how his converts turned from idols "to serve a living and true God" (1:9). This description obviously fits Gentile rather than Jewish converts. Despite the impression left by Acts, where Paul preaches in the synagogue in Thessalonica (Acts 17:1–3), we can only conclude that the Thessalonian church was made up mainly, if not exclusively, of Gentiles. Paul describes them as waiting for Jesus' return from heaven (1:10) and thus suggests concerns that are dealt with toward the end of the letter.

The Thessalonian Christians have become imitators of Paul, of his companions, and of the Lord, meaning Jesus (1:6), as well as of persecuted Christian churches of Judea (2:14). Thus there is solidarity among Christians, and this point is driven home by Paul's expressions of personal affection and concern for his converts (2:17–20). The Thessalonians themselves have proved their own affection and love (1:3; 4:9–12). The imitation of Paul (1:6) has as its end the perfecting and holiness of the Thessalonians—that is, their complete dedication to God. Paul reminds them that they learned from him and his companions how they ought to live and please God (4:1). The instructions he has given them are simple and unexceptional (4:2–8) and would likely have been approved by morally serious Gentiles as well as by Jews. There is no distinctly Christian ethic here.

In the midst of a lengthy exhortation, consisting of rather brief general admonitions and reminders only loosely tied together, we find a sustained discussion of the return of Jesus (4:13–5:11). The purpose of the discussion is similarly hortatory. That is, Paul intends to bolster and encourage the Thessalonians (5:11) by reminding them of a central aspect of his teaching, namely, hope.

There is not only discouragement but anxiety over Christians who have already died. Apparently in the earliest days of the new faith many thought that believers would not die until the Lord returned. As time passed, more and more Christians died, and their deaths could not be attributed to a fall from faith (cf. 1 Cor. 11:30). Paul reassures his readers that those members of the community who have died in faith are not lost (esp. 4:13–18). When the Lord (i.e., Jesus) returns, the "dead in Christ" (4:16) will rise and together with those who are left alive will ascend to meet the descending Lord in the air (4:17). Thus the dead in Christ, the believers who have died, suffer no disadvantage. With these words the readers may comfort one another (4:18).

If Paul is not quoting directly from Jesus himself (vs. 15: "by the word of the Lord"), he nevertheless intends to give the substance of what Jesus had said. The early Christians believed that Jesus had spoken of his return in glory and preserved sayings that expressed this intention (e.g., Mark 8:38; cf. Matt. 10:33; Luke 12:9). Moreover, collections of such sayings, attributed to Jesus, grew up among Christians (Mark 13 parr.). In these discourses Jesus described in detail his coming and the events leading up to it. Probably the brief word of the Lord to which Paul refers is an early form of this apocalyptic tradition, which, although it flowered quickly and luxuriantly, had roots in the authentic sayings of Jesus.[2] In 1 Corinthians 15:20–28 and 2 Thessalonians 2:1–11 we find other descriptions of the end time. Although neither of these is traced back to Jesus, in each case Paul seems to be drawing upon common Christian beliefs and perhaps traditions about the events leading up to the end.

The present passage is intended as a source of encouragement and hope for the Thessalonians. For unbelievers the day of the Lord may be wrath (1:10; 5:2 f.), but for those in Christ it is joy and vindication. In the second part of

---

2. On the eschatology of Jesus see pp. 224–233 above.

this rather long discussion of the coming of Jesus (5:1–11), Paul describes the way in which Jesus' imminent coming should affect not the dead but the Thessalonians who are alive. The day of the Lord will come suddenly, as a thief in the night (5:2; cf. Matt. 24:43; Luke 12:39; Rev. 3:3; 16:15; 2 Pet. 3:10), and its coming will clearly be a cause of dismay for those who have not believed or who are not prepared (5:2–4).[3] But the Thessalonians, like all those who believe in Christ, will understand that they already belong to that day.

Paul plays upon the technical, eschatological term *day of the Lord.* The day will not surprise the believers, for they are not in darkness as others are. Because they are children of the light, they are also children of the day (5:5); not children of daytime generally, however, but children of that particular day, the day of the Lord. Needless to say, the imagery of day and night is quite appropriate to Paul's hortatory purpose. Night is the time of sleep or drunkenness (5:6 ff.). Day is the time of wakefulness and sobriety. But Paul's exhortation turns upon the point that Christians already have the day of the Lord, at least in anticipation. That is, God has destined them for salvation, not for wrath (5:9). Therefore, their conduct should reflect who and what they are before God. "Belonging to the day" (5:8) is more than general metaphorical language. It has a specific reference in Paul's own thought: the day of the Lord's coming. This day is for his Christian readers an occasion for hope and therefore for encouragement. Such hope frees a person from despair, whether for himself or for his loved ones who have already died.

In 1 Thessalonians there is scarcely a suggestion of the distinctive theological themes and arguments found in Paul's later letters. There is as yet no hint of the great Pauline controversy over the role of the law; the Thessalonian community is predominantly Gentile.[4] Yet some typically Pauline emphases do appear. Faith, hope, and love are mentioned more than once, at the beginning as well as at the end (1:3; 5:8; cf. 1 Cor. 13:13), and Paul urges converts not to repay evil for evil (5:15; cf. Rom. 12:17), suggesting Jesus' own teaching (cf. Luke 6:27–36). Christianity seems to be essentially belief in the true God, the shunning of immorality and impurity, the solidarity of a love that forgoes the claims of self, and vibrant hope and the expectation of the imminent return of Jesus. Although in later letters joint authorship is scarcely more than a conventional form (cf. 1 Cor. 1:1), here Paul may actually speak in concert with his coworkers Silvanus and Timothy, as they remind the Thessalonian Christians of the essentials on which there is general agreement.

---

3. The Day of the Lord is, of course, the eschatological day or the day of judgment. The use of the term goes back to the preexilic prophets; see Amos 5:18–20.
4. Although the Book of Acts indicates that Paul made some converts in the synagogue (17:4), even Luke leaves the impression that most were not actually Jewish.

OUTLINE OF 2 THESSALONIANS

Salutation (1:1–2)
Thanksgiving (1:3–12)
Eschatological Teaching (2:1–17)
Instructions and Exhortations (3:1–16)
Conclusion (3:17–18)

ESCHATOLOGICAL TEACHING (2 THESS. 2:1–17)

How are the Thessalonians to act in the present?

Whereas in 1 Thessalonians Paul encourages the new believers to remain steadfast in their hope of Jesus' return (4:13–18) and to be alert for it (5:1–11), in 2 Thessalonians he faces a different problem. Now there are Christians who believe that the day of the Lord has already come (2 Thess. 2:2). Paul's earlier words of encouragement may have caused some members of the Thessalonian church to think that the end or goal had already been attained, and therefore that they might abandon all work and worldly responsibility (3:6–13). In any event, Paul must now dampen the enthusiasm that has apparently broken out in some quarters.

It is notable that Paul's earlier exhortations to alertness called not for idle waiting and watching but for responsible and upright living (1 Thess. 5:1–11). Had even these warnings been misconstrued so that expectations of the end have been further heightened? Whatever the answer, Paul now refutes the precipitous announcement of the advent of the day of the Lord by pointing out that the necessary conditions have not been fulfilled.

Paul's portrayal of the present situation and of the anticipated events of the future is painted in obviously apocalyptic language. That the figure or forces named (the rebellion, the man of lawlessness, the son of perdition, the one who restrains him) are not further identified in terms of historical persons or entities is typical of the apocalyptic style as we know it from such books as Daniel, Revelation, and the Qumran War Scroll. Paul is capable of thinking in similar fashion and terms. Apparently the one who is restraining the son of perdition or the lawless one is a person or force already present and at work as Paul writes. Perhaps he is making a veiled reference to the Roman Empire or to the emperor, or even to the preaching of the gospel; it is really impossible to know. What is certain is Paul's intention to check and refute apocalyptic enthusiasm and to encourage the Thessalonians to continue to live responsibly in the present.

Although in his other letters we find nothing comparable to the mysterious apocalyptic scenario that Paul suggests here, it is nevertheless quite clear that he expected a cataclysmic denouement of history (cf. 1 Thess. 4:13–18; 1 Cor. 15:20–28), perhaps within his own lifetime (but cf. Phil. 1:19–26). Because Paul's analysis of human experience and situations is often so acute, and closely paralleled in modern perceptions, we may be perplexed to find him thinking and speaking this apocalyptic language. Paul's thought, however, was deeply conditioned by scripture, ancient Jewish beliefs, and his vivid expectation of the return of Jesus; his world view was quite different from our own. That he did not refer to this sequence of apocalyptic events in 1 Thessalonians does not mean that he did not know it, or that he did not write 2 Thessalonians. There he was addressing a different problem; in 2 Thessalonians he speaks to a situation that may well have been created—quite without Paul's intention—by his own earlier words.

Galatians: Faith's Sufficiency

Notes on Galatians

The Galatian letter was written to combat the influence in the Galatian churches of so-called Judaizers—that is, believers who insisted that Christians be circumcised and keep the law. The exact location of these churches is in doubt. Either they were in the region of Pisidian Antioch, Lystra, and Derbe—which Paul evangelized on his first missionary journey, recounted in Acts 13–14—or they were located farther to the north in the ethnic region called Galatia, after its inhabitants (*Galatai*). The latter is probably the area referred to in Acts 16:6 and 18:23. In favor of the North Galatia theory is the fact that Paul calls his readers "Galatians," which he would be less likely to do if he were addressing the more heterogeneous population of the Roman province of Galatia.

The original Greek of Galatians 4:13 probably means "the first time" (NRSV, "first"), implying that Paul had made not one but two previous visits to Galatia. If the North Galatia theory is accepted and two previous visits to Galatia must be posited, then the letter cannot be earlier than the third missionary journey, for the two visits would be those noted in Acts 16:6 and 18:23. This would put the writing of the letter in the period of Paul's Ephesian ministry (Acts 19), as indicated on the chronological table, probably about A.D. 54. Moreover, such a setting is supported by the many affinities of Galatians with 1 and 2 Corinthians and Romans, which are more striking than any similarities to the early Thessalonian letters.

Galatians offers numerous points of contrast with the Thessalonian letters. Aside from the omission of the formal thanksgiving, the tenor of the letter is quite different, and the difference is immediately evident in the address. Paul no longer groups himself with other colleagues whom he names (as in 1 Thess. 1:1), but singles himself out as an apostle and indicates the divine origin of his apostolic calling, mentioning "all the brethren who are with me" as a kind of afterthought. After the salutation and benediction (vss. 3–5), occasioned by God's grace rather than by anything the Galatians may have done, Paul moves immediately to the business at hand without any customary thanksgiving for the Galatians, who in their behavior have given him no reason to offer thanks.

OUTLINE OF GALATIANS

Introduction or Salutation (1:1–5)
Paul's Defense (1:6–2:21)
    Paul's Charge against the Galatians (1:6–9)
    Autobiographical Section (1:10–2:10)
    Justification by Faith (2:11–21)
Law and Faith (3:1–4:31)
    Appeal to the Galatians (3:1–5)
    The History of Salvation (3:6–4:11)
    Personal Reminiscences and Appeal (4:12 20)
    The Allegory of the Two Women (4:21–31)
Freedom and Spirit (5:1–6:10)
    Freedom versus Circumcision (5:1–12)
    Living by the Spirit (5:13–6:10)
Conclusion (6:11–18)

APOSTLE BY GOD'S REVELATION (GAL. 1:6–2:10)

How does Paul's own story relate to his apostolic authority?

Paul's expression of astonishment at the speed of the Galatians' defection (vs. 6) is genuine and deep. They have deserted the one true gospel of Jesus Christ in favor of another, a pseudo-gospel, apparently proclaimed by intruders in the churches Paul had founded. That those who preached this other gospel boasted that their authority was above Paul's is suggested by what Paul writes: first, he underscores the source of his own authority (vs. 1); second, he dismisses the possibility that anyone could possess authority sufficient to contradict or pervert his version of the message (vss. 8–9). The one who called the Galatians in the grace of Christ (vs. 6) is, of course, God, but Paul may have also been alluding to the role he himself played in announcing the gospel in the first instance, particularly in view of the incursion of others who announced another gospel.

Paul's defense of his gospel as the one authentic gospel, authorized by God and agreed to by all the authorities of the church, takes the form of a narrative of his own career as an apostle (1:11–2:21). That narrative is in part a response to those who would accuse him, or who have accused him, to the Galatians of compromising the gospel in seeking human approval (1:10), presumably to make it more attractive and acceptable. Exactly how Paul is supposed to have done this is not said. Apparently those who preached another gospel attempted to discredit Paul by saying that he made confessing belief in Jesus easier and more palatable by not insisting on circumcision and the law. In 3:1–5:12 Paul argues against a version of the gospel in which both are necessary; he contends that such a gospel would be, in fact, no gospel at all. That is, it would reduce to insignificance what Jesus accomplished by dying upon the cross.

For the moment, however, Paul's principal concern is to establish his own authority as a preacher, and therefore the authority of the gospel he proclaims. He does this by narrating how he was called by God to be an apostle (one sent to preach the gospel) and by telling of his subsequent relations and negotiations with other, Jerusalem, apostles. The point he seeks to establish is that these negotiations in no way called into question or altered his gospel and his authority to preach it. In all essential respects the Jerusalem apostles—Peter, James the brother of Jesus, and John—approved what Paul preached as well as his authority to preach (2:6–9).

Paul's reaction to what he has learned about events in the Galatian churches seems defensive and angry. What was at stake was nothing less than Paul's life and work, which is intertwined with his faith and interpretation of the gospel. Certainly Paul's response is more than personal, but his person as well as his work was being challenged. Though Paul is on the defensive in 1:11–2:1, he is already moving to seize the initiative and to go on the attack. By chapter 3 he is fully on the offensive, attacking the rival gospel that has sought to displace his own.

Fundamental to Paul's defense is the account of his conversion or call (1:13–17). In the Book of Acts *conversion* seems an appropriate enough term, although it is a visionary and auditory event that surpasses ordinary religious experience (9:1–9; 22:4–16; 26:9–18). In 1 Corinthians Paul says that it is an appearance of the risen Lord (15:8; cf. 9:1). Here Paul emphasizes rather the purpose and call of God: that as apostle he might preach the gospel of Jesus Christ among the Gentiles. Thus Paul's conversion is his commissioning as apostle to the Gentiles. Paul makes clear that he needed no Jerusalem apostles nor anyone else to interpret the meaning of the experience (vss. 16–17). He consulted with no one, but, as he wants his readers to understand, he heard and obeyed God without the help of human mediation.

Paul's conversion, by whatever name it be called, doubtless played a fundamental role in his understanding of the gospel. He himself had been overtaken and overcome in a manner that contradicted his expectations and reversed the course of his life. God's action toward him was perceived by Paul as something prior to, and apart from, his own will. Probably Paul's experience became paradigmatic of the way he understood God's work in Christ. God worked upon him to effect a fundamental change in his perceptions and life, and Paul came to understand the gospel as God's prior action in Jesus Christ, to which a person must respond by faith or disobedience.

Although Paul strongly asserts his apostolic commission and independence of human authorization, he also believes that the gospel did not originate with him, but with God, and that it is not given to him alone, but to the church. Thus, although he insists upon his independence of those who were apostles before him (1:17), he is eager to show that these same apostles approved his preaching of the gospel (2:7–10). In fact, he candidly says that he put his gospel before them for their approval, as if everything depended upon that (2:2).

At first glance, Paul's assertion of his independence and his concern for apostolic approval may seem contradictory. Paul does not, however, want to say that his gospel is novel or unique, but to claim God's initiative in revealing it to him and commissioning him to preach it to the uncircumcised (2:7), that is, to Gentiles (cf. 1:16). For despite the claims for his own commission and authority, which he is not in the least embarrassed to make, Paul wishes to show that his gospel is the same gospel with which the church has been entrusted. The uniqueness of his commissioning lies in the fact that God has made him apostle to the Gentiles. Paul does not even put forward his central doctrine of justification by grace through faith as an original insight, but as an elementary aspect of the gospel itself, and one that anyone should have been able to make. Thus he can upbraid Peter for his dissimulation (2:11 ff.) rather than his ignorance.

Paul was a charismatic figure and an original thinker; yet he did not wish to set himself above, but only alongside, those who were apostles before him. Although not dependent on them, he actively sought their approval. For Paul was a churchman and was concerned for the unity of the church. He enthusiastically agreed to make a collection in his mission field for the poor in the Jerusalem church (2:10; cf. 1 Cor. 16:1–4; 2 Cor. 8, 9; Rom. 15:25–29). This act was more than charity. It was a visible and tangible expression of the oneness of the churches he had founded with the church at Jerusalem and, by implication, of the unity of the gospel.

FAITH (GAL. 2:11–21)

Why is circumcision such a crucial point of controversy?

That Paul had already been vigorously defending his own preaching and probably had to do so recurrently soon becomes apparent (2:11–21). Presumably the incident in Antioch had occurred some time before. There Cephas (i.e., Peter), Paul, Barnabas, and other Jewish Christians had been enjoying table fellowship among the Gentile Christians until some representatives from James appeared on the scene (2:11–13). They, and perhaps James also, represented the "circumcision faction," a powerful group of Jewish Christians, probably based in Jerusalem, who regarded circumcision as a necessity for Gentile Christians. Apparently for them, as for Paul, "circumcision" implied the obligation to keep the Jewish law and therefore entailed far more than the rite itself. They therefore refused table fellowship with nonobservant Gentile believers.

This same circumcision party had evidently made inroads into the Galatian church, occasioning Paul's letter. As one begins reading the letter it is not entirely obvious that this is what has happened, although Paul immediately denounces those who preach "another gospel" (1:6–9). The nature of that other gospel becomes clearer, however, in chapters 3–4. Paul asks the Galatians whether the new existence to which they were introduced by his missionary preaching was based on the works of the law or faith. Obviously, Paul is convinced it is based on the Spirit and faith, not the law (3:1–14). The law for Paul characterizes the older order that has passed away; it was always intermediate or provisional (3:15–29). In the beginning Abraham believed God—that is, Abraham had faith—and it was reckoned to him as righteousness (3:6, quoting Gen. 15:6). Faith defines the proper relation to God, whether in Abraham's time or Paul's. The Galatians are being urged by some to revert to a state from which they have been rescued by Christ (1:4). Apparently Paul equates a return to dependence on legal observance for salvation by the Galatians as a return to their pre-Christian enslavement to "elemental spirits of the world" (4:3, 9), presumably pagan religion or superstition. Such a reversion is the necessary consequence of acquiescing to the demand of the intruders that the Galatians submit to circumcision (5:2; 6:12). As Paul says (5:3), the whole legal system was bound up with this rite. It had become the fitting symbol of the problem of whether Christians must be held accountable for the Jewish law.

From a modern perspective, in which Christianity and Judaism are two different religions separated for over two thousand years, the position of the Judaizers seems to be an aberration. Why should they be conservative, or afraid of progress? Yet the question is misplaced or anachronistic. From their perspective Paul was the aberration. Jesus was accepted by all believers as the Messiah (or Christ) of Israel; why should this acceptance mean abandonment of the ancestral laws and customs? Obviously, Paul had theological reasons for believing that it should and he strongly argued his case in Galatians. Yet the Judaizers, or so-called circumcision party, had tradition on their side—or so they believed—and did not find Paul's arguments compelling.

The appearance of the circumcision party in Antioch (2:11) doubtless intimidated the Jewish Christians, including Peter and Barnabas, who had previously been exercising their freedom in Christ by disregarding Jewish restrictions against eating with Gentiles.[5] By eating with Gentiles the Jew inevitably exposed himself to the possibility of contamination by violating the Jewish laws concerning food and drink (cf. Lev. 11). Paul's reproach to Peter (2:14 ff.) has understandably been something of an embarrassment to later Christian interpreters. It surely shows Peter in a bad light vis-à-vis Paul, although admittedly we have only Paul's version of the story.

Paul's argument with Peter is based not so much on his own interpretation of the gospel as on what he plainly believes is the understanding of the gospel that Peter also accepts. The simple statement that Peter and the others "were not acting consistently with the truth of the gospel" (vs. 14) and the use of "we" (vss. 15–17) show that Paul was not trying to convince Peter of the truth of his own position, but recalling him to an agreement about the gospel that they had shared: the message of God's grace freely given. That this was more than merely intellectual assent is borne out by the fact (vs. 14) that Peter himself had been living like a Gentile. Whether Peter and company later began

---

5. On the historical background of this situation in the early church, see the excellent brief discussion of Hans Dieter Betz, *Galatians: A Commentary on Paul's Letter to the Churches in Galatia* (Philadelphia: Fortress, 1979), pp. 81–83.

trying to force Gentiles to live like Jews or only made this a prerequisite of continued table fellowship is uncertain. In any event the net result was apparently the same. Gentiles were forced to submit to Jewish regulations to participate in the life of the church on an equal footing. For Paul this development was unthinkable, despite the fact that he and Peter were by birth Jews (vs. 15), and not "Gentile sinners." It was unthinkable not because it was unnecessary or impolite but, rather, because Paul and Peter knew that a person is not justified (i.e., judged acceptable to God) on the basis of "works of the law" but by faith in Christ. At least Paul knew it, and he felt that Peter should.

From this point on it is clear that Paul does not entertain the possibility of two modes of salvation—one by the law, the other by faith in Christ (vss. 15–21). He is not just saying that one must choose one way or the other, although that is indeed necessary. In actuality there is only one way, because no one will be justified by works of the law. The important thing is that a new and viable access to God has been opened by his Son just when other avenues had shown themselves to be blind alleys. This conviction lies at the heart of Paul's gospel.

The objection that Christ was being made a servant of sin (vs. 17) had probably been raised by the circumcision party. It would have been directed against the doctrine of justification by faith and its corollaries of freedom from the law and uninhibited free association among Jewish and uncircumcised Gentile Christians. Paul categorically rejects the view that Christ is a servant of sin. Later, in the opening chapters of Romans, Paul will argue that all people, whether they claim to keep the law or not, are really sinners apart from the grace of God in Christ. Thus not surprisingly Paul concedes that people "have been found to be sinners" in seeking to be justified by Christ. Of course, it may by no means be inferred that those who seek to be justified by the law thereby escape the onus of sin. They simply do not understand their condition.

The real sin or transgression would be to go backward, to submit again to the law and to sin, after having escaped their grasp (vss. 18 f.). Paul has died to the law that he might live to God. Paul's dying to the law and his dying with Christ seem to be the same thing. He necessarily dies to the law that he may live to God and that Christ may live in him by faith (vs. 20). Paul ends this description of his encounter with Peter—somewhere along the way his focus seems to have shifted from the debate with Peter to the problem of the Galatian churches—with a succinct statement of his tight theological logic. Justification does not come through the law, or else Christ died to no purpose (2:21). If one insists on observance of the law as a prerequisite to salvation, one implies that faith in Christ is not enough and that the law supplies what is lacking. For Paul, who understands the gospel to be absolutely Christocentric, this suggestion is intolerable.

If for the moment we use the somewhat anachronistic term *Christianity*, which Paul never uses, we may say that for Paul Christianity is faith in Christ. On the other hand, faith in Christ makes possible the concept of Christianity as something new and distinct. For apart from the insistence that faith alone, not works of the law, justifies (i.e., makes one righteous before God), Christianity does not clearly distinguish itself from Judaism—as the Jewish Christians apparently did not. (Indeed, they did not intend to.) To believe that a particular person was the Messiah (Greek, *Christos*) was possible *within* Judaism. The Messiah, or Christ, would then be understood within the framework of Jewish messianism and eschatology. Paul's understanding of the essential meaning of the gospel of Jesus Christ, however, goes beyond this confession. For to say, as he does, that this faith alone is the crucial factor in the determination of a person's destiny breaks away from traditional messianic expectation and makes the Jewish legal requirements of no avail for salvation.

Christ has freed believers from sin, from "the elemental spirits of the world" (4:3), and from the law. All are a part of the older order. Thus Paul writes: "For freedom Christ has set us free; stand firm therefore, and do not submit again to a yoke of slavery" (5:1). As Paul lays out the practical implications of his theological position, he again addresses the specific and immediate problem in the church of Galatia. Should Christians accept circumcision? Paul reiterates in 5:2 the principle already enunciated in 2:21. Here circumcision stands in place of law, for to accept circumcision as the expression of membership in the Jewish community means to obligate oneself to the keeping of the whole law and to cut oneself off from the grace of Christ (vss. 3 f.). Yet circumcision is not in itself bad (vs. 6; cf. 6:11–16, esp. 15). Those who are already circumcised have nothing to fear (cf. 1 Cor. 7:18 f.). Rather, the desire to have circumcision or any mark of ethnic distinction or religious accomplishment after one has already been baptized into Christ (3:26 ff.) is blameworthy, for it is a movement away from grace to the law and away from the Spirit to the flesh (3:3; 5:4; 6:12). Paul regards such a retrogression as incredible and perverse. It is a negation of one's freedom in Christ.

Yet this freedom is not without responsibility. But the person of faith no longer experiences responsibility as a burden and no longer lives under the law to earn salvation. The believer is not a slave to the law or to anything else. At the same time the law continues to be the valid expression of the will of God (Gal. 5:14) and gives ethical content and direction for the new life in Christ under God. The freedom for which Christ sets humanity free is not anarchy or freedom to do as one pleases. Paul describes this freedom as faith working through love (5:6). He states the character and purpose of freedom most aptly and succinctly: "For you were called to freedom, brothers and sisters; only do not use your freedom as an opportunity for self-indulgence, but through love become slaves to one another" (5:13). So despite Paul's rejection of the law as the key to salvation, his strong sense of mutual human responsibility is grounded in the history of Israel, and specifically in Jewish scripture. In the Letter to the Romans, Paul will return to the question of the relationship of the gospel to Israel's history and scripture.

Corinthians: Love, Courage, and Authority

Notes on the Corinthian Letters

Quite in contrast to Galatians, in the case of the Corinthian letters we can be entirely confident of the destination and audience to which Paul writes. The description of Paul's founding of the Corinthian church in Acts 18 is sketchy, but there are several points of contact with 1 Corinthians. For example, Acts 18:8 named a Crispus who was ruler of the Corinthian synagogue and who was converted and baptized by Paul; the same Crispus is mentioned by Paul (1 Cor. 1:14) as one of only a few persons he baptized in Corinth. The Sosthenes who is spoken of in Acts 18:17 is perhaps the same person who appears with Paul in the salutation of the letter (1 Cor. 1:1). In Acts 19:21 the travel plans that Paul describes in 1 Corinthians 16:5–9 are suggested, as the latter passage clearly indicates (16:8) that Paul is in Ephesus (Acts 19) when he writes the letter.

The city of Corinth was the capital of the province of Achaia, and a major city of Greece. In this period Corinth was larger than Athens. The Greek city had been destroyed by the Romans in 146 B.C., and after a century it was rebuilt as a Roman colony. The population of the reconstituted city consisted of freedmen from Rome, as well as

Ruins of the ancient Temple of Apollo (sixth century B.C.) at Corinth, capital of the Roman province of Achaia.   *(Courtesy of Greek Press and Information Service.)*

Greeks, Orientals, and Jews—a cosmopolitan group. The religious life and traditions of Corinth were doubtless diverse. The city was new when Paul founded the church and later wrote his letters. There were no traditions or family connections going back for as much as a century.

Corinth was a center of trade, lying on the narrow isthmus between the Gulf of Corinth and the Saronic Gulf, across which flowed traffic between the Adriatic and Aegean seas. It was a manufacturing and banking town where social status was more likely based on economic or business achievement than on family history or connections. Perhaps too much can be made of the wide-open, immoral character of Corinth. "Not for every man is the voyage to Corinth," went the ancient proverb, presumably implying it was only for the experienced or jaded. Whether cultic prostitution was actually practiced in the temple of Aphrodite on the Acrocorinth overlooking the city is a matter of dispute. (The ancient geographer Strabo's statement to that effect would have applied to the Greek city, rather than to the Roman city of New Testament times.) Nevertheless, the problems and issues that Paul confronted in Corinth, as they are reflected in 1 Corinthians, bespeak its cosmopolitan character and tend to support the city's bawdy reputation. The ethos of the city was not Jewish, nor did it reflect the higher ideals of Greco-Roman culture.

Perhaps not surprisingly, we can deduce more about the character, as well as the problems, of the Corinthian church than about any other Pauline community. Not only do we know a great deal about the city of Corinth itself, but in 2 Corinthians the problems of the church get a thorough airing. Moreover, we can learn something from 1 Corinthians and related New Testament books about the people who made up the Corinthian church. In addition to those mentioned above, the Crispus mentioned in 1:14 was according to Acts (18:8) prominent in the Corinthian synagogue. Gaius, whom Paul also says he baptized, was evidently a householder of considerable means; the church could meet in his house (Rom. 16:23). Stephanus, whom Paul mentions by way of afterthought (1:16), was also a householder. Erastus (Rom. 16:23) was a city official in Corinth and therefore a prominent citizen. Paul describes the Corinthian Christians as lowly people according to worldly standards (1:26–31), and doubtless many were. On the other hand, some were obviously more well-to-do. When Paul calls the Corinthians rich (4:8), castigates them for going to court (6:1–8), and speaks of the houses they have to eat and drink in (11:22), he again reflects this fact. The church of Corinth was a mixed group, consisting of people from varied backgrounds, and its mixed character had something to do with the difficulties that arose within it.

The Corinthian letters were written from Ephesus in Asia (1 Cor. 16:8) and probably from Macedonia (2 Cor. 1:16; 2:13; 7:5; etc.) in the mid-fifties of the first century, during Paul's third missionary journey (see the time chart, p. xviii). 1 Corinthians was written before 2 Corinthians. This is clear not only from their order in the New Testament but also from their content. One finds in 2 Corinthians a much-deteriorated relationship between the Corinthian church and Paul, whose once-acknowledged status as apostle is now being challenged. In 1 Corinthians Paul was able to speak authoritatively; the church's acknowledgment of his apostolic authority was not yet the major question (although the problem does emerge in chapter 9). Moreover, 2 Corinthians assumes a second visit to Corinth (12:14; 13:1), which is not mentioned in 1 Corinthians. A date of 54 for the one and 55 for the other is likely.

1 Corinthians was at least the third letter in the correspondence between Paul and

Corinth. Paul had already written the Corinthians previously (cf. 5:9), and they him (7:1). Neither of these letters survive. Much of the latter part of 1 Corinthians (from 7:1 on) is devoted to answering questions raised by the Corinthians' letter. Chapters 1–4 deal with problems in the Corinthian church reported by Chloe's people (1:11). Chapters 5 and 6 are concerned with moral problems Paul has learned about from some undesignated source. It is sometimes suggested that 1 Corinthians is a composite of several letters,[6] but the original unity of the document is defended by most scholars. For further notes on the Corinthian correspondence, see pp. 323,327f.

> OUTLINE OF 1 CORINTHIANS
>
> Introduction: Salutation and Thanksgiving (1:1–9)
> Division in the Church (1:10–4:21)
> > *The Corinthian Situation (1:10–17)*
> > *Paul's Own Practice and Example (1:18–3:4)*
> > *Paul and Apollos as Servants (3:5–4:7)*
> > *Admonition to the Corinthians (4:8–21)*
> Immorality in the Church (5:1–6:20)
> > *Sexual Immorality (5:1–13)*
> > *Christians in Court against One Another (6:1–11)*
> > *Uses of the Body (6:12–20)*
> The Corinthians' Questions (7:1–15:58)
> > *Church Discipline (7:1–10:33, esp. 8:1–13)*
> > *Church Worship and Order (11:1–14:39)*
> > *The Resurrection (15:1–58)*
> Conclusion: The Collection and Other Church Business (16:1–24)

LOVE (1 COR. 8:1–13)

Why not eat meat offered to idols?

In Corinth Paul faced a situation quite different from that in Galatia. The Corinthian problem was not insistence upon the law but, if anything, just the opposite. Freedom had become license, at least in Paul's view.

1 Corinthians is valuable in understanding Paul, not only because it shows him approaching this major issue from the other side, but also because it reveals the many and varied questions to which he had to speak. The church in Corinth affords us, through Paul's letter, a priceless window into the situations the early church faced as the gospel confronted the mores and customs of a sophisticated ancient culture. 1 Corinthians thus shows how Paul's theological positions were hammered out in dialogue with a very real world. In several important respects 1 Corinthians will be for many readers the most interesting of Paul's letters.

---

6. For scholars espousing this position, see John Hurd, *The Origin of I Corinthians,* 2nd ed. (Macon, GA: Mercer University Press, 1983), p. 45.

In chapters 1–4 Paul is concerned with divisions or parties in the church. Behind this problem, however, lurks the question of the very character of Christian faith and life. Paul argues passionately that the Christian gospel is different from any worldly wisdom (chaps. 1, 2). At its heart is the word of the cross, the crucified Lord, folly to the Greeks and scandal to the Jews. This word shakes old confidences and offers new possibilities of life. Here and throughout this letter, however, there are indications that the Corinthians, or some people in the Corinthian church, take a different view of the matter. Some of them think that Christian faith centers in a privileged knowledge (Greek, *gnōsis*), beside which questions of ethics are of strictly secondary importance (cf. chap. 8). Therefore, various practical ethical problems have arisen that demand resolution, at least in Paul's view. A man is living with his father's wife, though presumably not his own mother (chap. 5); Christians are involved in lawsuits against one another (6:1–8); apparently some have not given up sexual intercourse with prostitutes (6:12–20). The existence of what Paul considers immorality in the church is understandable, if not excusable, because at least some of the Corinthian Christians had led immoral lives before their conversion (6:9–11). Their backgrounds would not predispose them to understand the Christian faith in ethical terms.

Over and above these morally dubious situations, of which Paul had evidently been informed by Chloe's people (cf. 1:11; 16:17), in a letter to Paul the Corinthians raised a number of knotty problems (cf. 7:1). The first concerns marriage and relations between men and women. In chapter 7 Paul offers his wisdom on the subject. From the Lord, Paul has the prohibition against divorce, which we find also in the Synoptic Gospels (7:10 f.; cf. Mark 10:2–9 parr.). Beyond that he is more or less on his own (1 Cor. 7:12), and he obviously exercises some freedom in interpreting Jesus' words (7:15 f.). Paul's advice in this chapter will not commend itself to modern men and women, inside the church or out. The contemporary minister or priest will scarcely counsel a couple contemplating engagement that, although total continence is preferable, it is better to marry than to be aflame with passion (7:9). Yet though Paul has a definite preference for the ascetic life (7:1, 6 f.), he grants the legitimacy of the married state and discourages celibacy within marriage (7:1–5) as well as undue suppression of strong sexual instincts (7:9). One very important factor in understanding Paul's attitude toward marriage is his anticipation of an imminent crisis culminating in the return of Jesus and the end of world history as we know it (7:29–31; cf. 16:22; 1 Thess. 4:13–18; Rom. 13:11 f.). In view of such times, marriage and the assumption of family responsibility were scarcely things to be sought. Paul does not, however, oppose marriage, even under these conditions. Yet it is probably true that Paul's own seemingly ascetic bent has contributed to the high premium placed upon celibacy in many quarters of historic Christianity.

The subsequent brief chapter (8) dealing with the question of what to do about meat offered to idols is even more useful than the interesting discussion of sex in revealing the fundamental character of Paul's problems at

Jesus and the disciples at the Last Supper by an unidentified Indian painter.
(Courtesy of Spartaco Appetiti.)

Corinth. On the face of it this question may seem an unlikely choice, inasmuch as the subject of sex is very much alive in Western culture, whereas the number of persons who either offer meat to idols or worry about the problem of whether to eat such meat is microscopic. (It may be an issue, however, for Christians in cultures where animal sacrifice is still practiced.) Yet a careful reading of chapter 8 reveals that far more is involved than the resolution of a practical problem faced by Christians in the ancient world. A fundamental theological and ethical question is raised. (See also Rom. 14:1–15:6.)

Christians living in a pagan world, among associates, relatives, and friends who were not Christian, were frequently placed in the position of having to eat, or refuse to eat, meat that had been offered to idols. Many poorer people could not as a rule afford meat, and could only eat it on public occasions. But even if Christians avoided such feasts in the temples of pagan gods, as Paul sternly admonishes them to do (1 Cor. 10:14–22), they could not entirely escape the problem. For in the ancient world, much of the meat sold in the markets had also been offered to idols, even if in a most perfunctory way. The slaughtering of animals was frequently accompanied by a quasi-religious rite or token sacrifice. Thus although Paul, in instructing the Corinthians, seems to assume that some meat had not been offered to idols, it is at the same time clear that Christians could scarcely have avoided the problem of whether to eat meat that had been so offered. It would sooner or later have been thrust upon them unless they withdrew from the world, an alternative that Paul does not recommend (1 Cor. 5:9 f.).

Paul concedes that the consecration of meat to idols has no theological significance, because the idols themselves are nothing (vs. 4). Thus, in principle, eating meat offered to gods that are nonentities should not affect one's relation to the true God (vs. 8). However, although Paul and some Corinthian Christians know this, others do not (vs. 7). Therefore, the knowledgeable believer should refuse to eat meat offered to idols out of respect for the weaker brother (cf. 8:11), who may follow him in eating the meat and think that it really has some special potency or sanctity because it has been offered to idols. Or the weaker brother may believe that he has incurred real guilt before God for eating the idol meat because he would not know that the idol has no real existence and that there is only one God, the Father, and one Lord Jesus Christ. Interestingly enough, Paul does not deny that other gods and lords exist (vs. 5), but only that they have any significance for the Christian.[7]

Although Paul has seemingly countenanced even eating meat in an idol's temple as a matter of indifference, except for the offense it might cause (8:10), when he returns to the subject (10:14–30) he issues a strict prohibition. Now participation in any cultic act at an idol's temple is prohibited on grounds of its conflicting with, and contradicting, the unity that believers have with Christ through participation at his table (10:16–22). Nevertheless, Paul continues to defend the believer's right to eat whatever meat is sold to him or set before him on other, noncultic, occasions (10:23–30), except that he must still have regard for the conscience of his sister or brother. Thus love takes precedence over knowledge.

Paul was aware of the potential danger of knowledge in a way that the Corinthians were not. He therefore makes it clear at the outset (8:1–3) that knowledge alone is a questionable gift. Some Corinthians were evidently so smitten with their newly found knowledge and consequent freedom that they identified knowledge and freedom as such with the essence of Christian existence. Paul found this intolerable.

At the beginning of this discussion Paul has put love and knowledge in proper perspective. Paul will go so far as to agree with the Corinthians that "all of us possess knowledge" (8:1). But he immediately issues a warning: knowledge, especially that knowledge that knows that it knows, and by implication takes pride in the fact, is a potential menace. The contrast between such knowledge and love is graphically put: "Knowledge puffs up, but love builds up." To be puffed up is obviously bad. (The same word meaning literally "to be puffed up" is translated as "arrogant" in 5:2 in the NRSV—an accurate translation that unfortunately loses the connection with chapter 8.) To be built up, on the other hand, implies inner and outer strengthening of the church and the individual (cf. 3:10–15). The priority of love over knowledge is driven home most memorably in 1 Corinthians 13, the famous chapter on love. At the beginning of this hymn in praise of love Paul accords it a place above prophecy, knowledge, and faith (13:2). Again in 13:8 and 9 he comes back to the theme of the superiority of love over knowledge. There

---

7. Paul would of course have denied that there were other gods and lords of equal power and authority with the one God and Father of Jesus Christ. That otherworldly and supernatural powers held sway over the heathen Paul need not deny. Indeed, he seems to assume their existence (cf. 15:24–27; Rom. 8:38 f.).

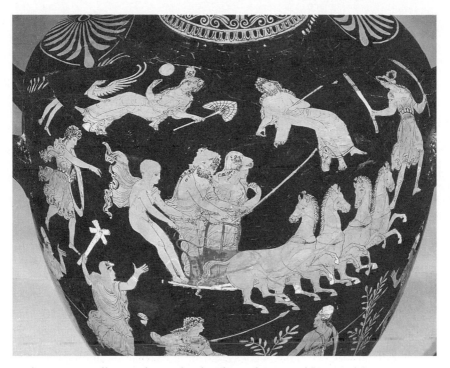

Hades carrying off Persephone, the daughter of Zeus and queen of the underworld. From a fourth-century B.C. Apulian vase.   *(Courtesy of Metropolitan Museum of Art. Gift of Miss Matilda W. Bruce, 1907.)*

is nothing wrong with knowledge per se, but in this world and this life it must give place to faith, hope, and love. Perfect knowledge will characterize the life to come, but in the present age the Christian must not make knowledge a primary concern (13:12 f.). The key to 1 Corinthians 8 is the supremacy of love over knowledge, not the impropriety of giving offense.

The character of the problems Paul faced in Corinth and his attitude toward them may be accurately assessed on the basis of this chapter. Thereafter, as before, Paul deals for the most part with specific issues. Chapter 9 is a defense of his apostleship and his conduct. In chapter 10 he returns, as we have seen, to the question of food offered to idols in the light of the danger of a return to idolatry. In chapter 11 there begins a discussion of matters pertaining to church life, which continues through chapter 14. Chapters 11 and 14 deal with worship and the Spirit; 12 is the well-known description of the church as the body of Christ; 13 is the chapter on love. A common thread can be seen, particularly in chapters 12 and 13, that runs back to chapter 8: the importance of love, respect, and unity within the Christian community. When Paul tells the Corinthians that they are members of Christ's body (12:27), the organic imagery expresses an ideal of human relationships in the church. The metaphor of the harmony of the body expresses the ideals of the attitude of respect and the relationship of love that should prevail among Christians. All are given equally necessary and important spiritual gifts. Thus quite naturally Paul continues by extolling love as the most important quality of the Christian community and the individuals that compose it (chap. 13). In speaking of love, Paul employs the Greek word *agapē,* which means a self-giving attitude or disposition, not physical passion, for which there is another Greek term (*erōs;* whence *erotic*).

Paul has already spoken of the Spirit to the Galatians (3:1–5) as if it were the vital reality that has profoundly changed their lives. Indeed, it was so perceived both by Paul and his converts. The Spirit was in effect the continuing presence of God among believers, a presence brought about by the crucified and risen Christ. Thus the very functions, capacities, and roles of the Corinthians could be described as gifts of the Spirit or spiritual gifts (chap. 12). They are not, or should not be, objects of either pride or scorn. As some Corinthian Christians have been puffed up (8:1) or arrogant (4:18), others have placed great emphasis on spiritual gifts or endowments, perhaps at the expense of fellow believers (chap. 12). In all probability some extolled speaking in tongues as the supreme, or essential, gift (13:1). Speaking in tongues was a kind of inspired but unintelligible utterance that many Christians took to be Spirit inspired, evidence of possession by the Spirit. The phenomenon has appeared often in Christian history and characterizes Christian charismatic movements in modern times. Paul's treatment of tongues in chapter 14 is carefully crafted so as to endorse the practice but at the same time to keep it under some control. Obviously, Paul does not approve unrestrained glossolalia in church services. If someone speaks in tongues, an interpretation (or translation) must be provided so that the people may understand and profit (14:5, 27). Otherwise, speaking in tongues becomes a demonstration of Spirit possession, but not an activity that builds up the church. In the context of the discussion of tongues, Paul admonishes women to keep silence in church (14:33–36). Since Paul elsewhere speaks of women praying and prophesying in church (11:5, 13), the admonition to silence may have been inserted by a later editor (cf. 1 Tim. 2:11–12, the work of a later Paulinist).

In chapter 15 Paul takes up the defense of the bodily resurrection of the dead, a doctrine that has at least been questioned, and perhaps denied, in Corinth. This view would accord with the attitude of the Corinthians, who fancied that they possessed superior knowledge. Against them Paul contends that to deny the bodily resurrection is to deny the resurrection of Jesus as well. Yet apparently in the face of incredulity about the concept of the resurrection as the resuscitation of so many corpses, Paul maintains a distinction between the present physical body and the future resurrection body, which is a spiritual body. Chapter 16, devoted to personal and business matters, includes Paul's plans for a collection for the Jerusalem church and his intention of visiting Corinth from Ephesus, where 1 Corinthians was doubtless written (vs. 8).

Notes on 2 Corinthians

Already in 1 Corinthians chapters 4 and 9 Paul has defended his legitimacy and pre-rogative as an apostle, as well as his conduct or lifestyle. His own submission to hard-ship and refusal to accept financial support betoken, in his view, the legitimacy of his apostleship. "Be imitators of me, as I am of Christ," says Paul (1 Cor. 11:1). We have the impression that Paul knows his apostleship and authority have been questioned in some quarters, but he seems to be confident that the Corinthians themselves will honor him (1 Cor. 9:2). On the other hand, 2 Corinthians mirrors a far more serious situation for Paul. His apostleship has been challenged, and the challenge has found a reception among at least some Corinthian Christians. Although in chapter 4 Paul's meditation on his apostleship is calm and not defensive, in chapters 10–13 his atti-tude is decidedly different. He refers explicitly to attacks upon him and sharply re-torts, pulling no punches in characterizing his opponents. That 2 Corinthians followed 1 Corinthians is clear from the general content. In addition, in 1 Corinthians Paul an-ticipates another visit (16:5); in 2 Corinthians he has apparently made that visit and anticipates a third (13:1).

OUTLINE OF 2 CORINTHIANS

Introduction: Salutation (1:1–2), Blessing (1:3–11), and Assurances of
     Concern (1:12–2:13)
Paul's Apostolic Service (2:14–5:21)
     Courage in Ministry (4:1–15)
Personal Appeals and Assurances (6:1–7:16)
Paul's Collection for the Jerusalem Church (8:1–9:15)
Paul under Attack (10:1–13:10)
Conclusion (13:11–14)

COURAGE IN MINISTRY (2 COR. 4:1–15)

How is Paul's ministry an imitation of Jesus?

Paul describes his apostolic ministry with moving eloquence (see 4:1–15). As a minister of Christ he is not relieved of the limitations and weaknesses of his human condition. Indeed, he is plunged farther into them. As he plainly reveals, his work is a trial as well as a joy. Yet he is not discouraged (vs. 1). His conduct is appropriate to his ministry (vs. 2). If in some cases his preach-ing of the gospel does not meet with approval and acceptance, the reasons lie outside his control (vss. 3 f.). Paul says the gospel is veiled (or concealed) to those who are perishing (picking up the imagery of chapter 3). The mean-ing of the veiling is then explained (vs. 4), but the explanation may raise more questions than it resolves.

   In speaking of the God of this world, Paul does not mean that there are two gods, the God of heaven revealed in Christ and another, equal God of this world. When he elsewhere speaks of many so-called gods in heaven and on earth (1 Cor. 8:4–6), and of the "elemental spirits of the world" (Gal. 4:3;

cf. Col. 2:8), he probably means supernatural beings, powers, or forces that influence human life. After all, for him Satan is a person, even as God is (2 Cor. 2:11). Paul is himself free from these powers because of Christ, whom he here calls the likeness or image (Greek, *eikōn*; cf. English icon) of God. Into the dark world controlled by the "god of this world," who is darkness, who blinds the eyes of those who do not believe so that they must live in darkness, the light of the gospel of the glory of Christ shines (vs. 4).

Not surprisingly, Paul emphasizes that he, as a minister, preaches Jesus Christ as Lord (vs. 5). This is the center and substance of the Christian message. But why does he say that he does not preach himself, stressing his servant role? Perhaps his rivals or opponents, who are apparently trying to seize the leadership of the church from him, extol themselves. This at least is Paul's opinion of them (see esp. chap. 11). In contrast to apostles or ministers who think they must impress the Corinthians by their letters of recommendations, mighty works, or spiritual virtuosity, Paul effaces himself to present Jesus Christ more adequately. In so doing Paul becomes, so to speak, transparent to the gospel he preaches (vs. 6).

Yet it is not only a matter of a successful missionary technique. Paul believes his conduct and attitude are both realistic and right. The fact that Paul is an apostle makes him no less subject to human limitations (vs. 7). Paul's own afflictions demonstrate this (vs. 8). But such afflictions (vss. 8 f.) do more than show that Paul is human; they recapitulate the death and resurrection of Jesus (vss. 10 f.). To suffer as Paul does is to carry in the body the death of Jesus, through which the life of Jesus becomes manifest (vs. 11). Paul means by the life of Jesus not just his earthly life, but the resurrection from the dead (cf. vs. 14). Because of Paul's dying—his giving up of himself for them—the Corinthians experience life, even as through Christ's death human beings gain life. His offering is therefore vicarious, on behalf of others.

Paul concludes this characterization of his ministry by referring to the scriptures (4:13), calling to mind his earlier discussion of Christ's crucial role in the proper interpretation of the Bible (3:16). Paul has the same spirit of faith as the psalmist who wrote, "I believed, and so I spoke" (Ps. 16:10). (Even though the coming of Christ marks the decisive turning point of history for Paul, the faith it calls forth is not different from the true faith of Israel.) Paul's faith, however, focuses primarily upon Jesus and here upon his hope in Jesus. Typically, Christian hope has found its basis and warrant in the resurrection of Jesus, and Paul is a pioneer in reflecting this fundamental pattern (vs. 14). The section is rounded off by the declaration "Yes, everything is for your sake" (vs. 15). Apparently, everything includes God's raising of Jesus, the gospel message, and Paul's affliction in his apostolic ministry. Its ultimate end is the glory of God himself, as God is extolled in thanksgiving by ever-increasing numbers of believers (vs. 15).

"The Apostle Paul" by Rembrandt (1606–1669).   *(Courtesy of National Gallery of Art, Washington, D.C. Widener Collection.)*

APOSTLESHIP UNDER ATTACK (2 COR. 10:1–13:10)

How does Paul's boasting of his weakness reflect his view of apostleship?

Paul's attitude as well as the subject matter change abruptly at the beginning of chapter 10. At first, Paul is restrained, although his anxiety and intense concern shine through the text. He earnestly entreats the Corinthians to attend to him, but assures them he does not intend to frighten them by his letters (10:9 f.). At just that point, however, Paul betrays his awareness of what his Christian opponents say about him, and cannot resist a derogatory characterization of them (10:12). But immediately he pulls back, both in tone and in his own estimate of his success (10:13–18).

Paul's feelings for the Corinthians and his unique relation to them become clear in chapter 11. He does not disavow his jealousy (11:2), which becomes almost painfully apparent (vss. 3 f.) as he compares himself with the "super-apostles" who have bewitched the Corinthians (vss. 5 f.). That the Corinthians have been exploited by those interlopers becomes evident, not only from Paul's explicit statements (vs. 20) but also from the contrast with Paul's own practice when in Corinth (vss. 7–11). The "super-apostles'" conduct and boasting lead Paul to speak unabashedly of the experiences that commend him, both as a Jew and as a servant of Christ (vss. 21–29). All the while Paul is aware of the dubious and self-contradictory nature of his own boasting. It contradicts his idea of Christian life according to the gospel, i.e., under the cross (vss. 21, 23); thus if he boasts Paul will boast of his weakness (vs. 30).

Yet before Paul boasts of his weakness he once again allows himself to speak of experiences that distinguish him from most of his colleagues and rivals (12:1–6). Presumably Paul here describes his own experience, although he speaks in the third person. He wishes to put distance between himself and the subject of his boasting (vs. 5), but quite clearly he believes he has ample reason to boast (vs. 6). His boasting is finally not limited by his own modesty. God has given him a reminder of his limitations—the "thorn in the flesh"—so that he may boast only in his weakness that the power of Christ may be manifest in him (vss. 7–10). This is a recurring theme of Paul's thought, especially in 2 Corinthians: "We have this treasure in clay jars (RSV: "earthen vessels") so that it may be made clear that this extraordinary power belongs to God and does not come from us" (4:7). In the midst of temptation to play his opponents' game, at which Paul is convinced he could excel, he restrains himself, or is restrained—by God or Christ himself, or by his understanding of the very nature of his message.

The gospel is God's power made manifest in human weakness, whether in the cross of Jesus or the life of the apostle. God makes himself known in this gospel, not in esoteric religious knowledge (1 Cor. 8) or spectacular demonstrations of Spirit possession (1 Cor. 14). Such revelation finds its natural counterpart in attitudes of humility and compassion among the faithful, for the cross of Christ is itself the ultimate expression of God's self-giving love (cf. Rom. 5:6–11). The pattern of the apostle's life expresses the nature of the gospel, as it reflects the cross of Christ, and affords a paradigm for every believer (1 Cor. 11:1).

Quite obviously, Paul's standards of what constitutes a true apostle of Jesus Christ are different from those of the "super-apostles." But at the same time Paul will not for one instant concede that he is inferior to them by any standard (vs. 11). His concern for the defense of his apostleship is, however, integrally related to his commitment to the Corinthian church (vs. 19). As in Galatians, so here: Paul's defense of the gospel, his insistence upon the validity of his apostleship, and his care for the welfare of his churches are of a piece. Thus at the conclusion of 2 Corinthians (12:14–13:14) we find Paul anticipating yet another visit to Corinth, a third, in which he hopes things will go well, although he is apparently wary, if not apprehensive (13:10). In Paul's view, the faithfulness of the Corinthians to the gospel is inseparable from their loyalty to him, not because of any proprietary rights but because he—in contrast to the "super-apostles" who have intruded or sent their agents into the church—represents in his conduct as well as in his preaching the one true gospel.

Note on the Literary Unity of 2 Corinthians

Because 2 Corinthians ends on a note of urgency, with Paul having dispatched Titus to Corinth (12:18) but remaining apprehensive about his approaching third visit, a comparison with the first half of the letter (chaps. 1–7) reveals a notable contrast. In the first part, Paul speaks of his past anxiety in anticipating another visit to Corinth, presumably his third (cf. 2:1). This attitude, which he now looks back on, corresponds with what he was presently experiencing as he wrote chapters 10–13. Paul's brief characterization of the letter he then wrote (2:3 f.) corresponds in part to the content of those final chapters. Moreover, Paul indicates that it was the return of Titus from Corinth that set his mind at ease and reassured him about the loyalty of the Corinthians (12:18; 7:5–16). There is, therefore, some reason to think that chapters 1–9 were written after chapters 10–13 and that the letter Paul describes in 2:3–4 is now found in those latter chapters. Yet the one matter that moved Paul to write the "tearful letter" (2:4), namely, the individual who has caused Paul or the community pain (2:5–8; 7:12), is not mentioned at all in 2 Corinthians 10–13. Because the evidence of Paul's correspondence is fragmentary, it may not be possible to reconstruct his itinerary and changing relationships with the church at Corinth.[8]

In addition to the tearful letter problem, there is the question of the character and origin of chapters 8 and 9. Both chapters apparently deal with the collection Paul was making for the Jerusalem church (cf. Gal. 2:10; Rom. 15:25–28). They do not, however, fit together very well. Paul introduces the subject in 9:1 as if he had not already been discussing it just previously; moreover, the content of chapter 9 seems somewhat repetitive. Further, the introduction of the subject (8:1) is abrupt, although not intolerable. Chapters 8 and 9 may be two separate letters that Paul sent to Corinth to pave the way for the consummation of the collection and its delivery to the saints (9:1) in Jerusalem. Alternatively, chapter 8 may have been a part of the letter comprising chapters 1–7 and chapter 9 a separate note. Although the unity of 2 Corinthians as a single letter is still defended, on close examination this unity tends to weaken, if not

---

8. V. P. Furnish, *II Corinthians* (Garden City, NY: Doubleday, 1984), pp. 35–41, 54–55, gives an excellent and judicious discussion of the literary problems.

dissolve. The most significant break is between chapters 9 and 10, at 10:1. Both tone and content shift abruptly and without explanation. It is difficult to believe that chapters 10–13 did not originally constitute some part of a different letter.

If 2 Corinthians is a composite document, i.e., made up of two or more earlier letters, this situation raises the question of the editing of the Pauline correspondence as in later years the letters were collected. The New Testament did not appear in anything like its present form until nearly 150 years after Paul wrote, and the history of the collection and circulation of the documents during that time is largely unknown. The simplest and most likely explanation of the editing of 2 Corinthians is that the process consisted of the joining together of two letters or parts of letters (chaps. 1–9 and 10–13) that had originally been written separately.

Philippians and Philemon: Personal Attitude and Relations

Notes on the Captivity Epistles

Ephesians, Philippians, and Colossians, as well as the brief personal letter to Philemon, are said to have been written by Paul from prison (Eph. 3:1; 4:1; Phil. 1:12–18; Col. 4:10; Philem. 1, 23). That this was actually the case with Philippians and Philemon is beyond reasonable doubt. Doubts about Colossians and Ephesians have to do with the question of whether they were written by Paul himself or by one or more of his disciples. In the latter case the prison setting may be a literary device.

We shall treat Colossians and Ephesians together (see pp. 371–383). Colossians may have been penned by Paul himself, or by a coworker in Paul's name. Ephesians is most likely the product of a later Paulinist. But even if Colossians was written by Paul, it is closely related to Ephesians in subject matter and style. In both there is a special emphasis upon the idea of the church as the body of Christ and upon Christians' being already raised with Christ, and in both are found the kinds of conventional ethical exhortations (Col. 3:18–4:1; Eph. 5:21–6:9) largely missing in Paul's uncontested letters, but characteristic of other early Christian writings (cf. 1 Pet. 2:18–3:7). Therefore, quite apart from questions of authorship, the letters are appropriately treated together. (Indeed, the author of Ephesians may have used Colossians as a principal source.)

Philemon and Colossians are closely related by many personal references (e.g., the slave Onesimus in Philem. 10 and Col. 4:9; Epaphras in Philem. 23 and Col. 1:7; 4:12) and by common destination (Colossae). If Colossians was written by Paul, they appear to have been dispatched at the same time, possibly by the same bearers (Col. 4:7–9). Philippians, on the other hand, stands somewhat apart.

Although the evidence is actually ambiguous, tradition has it that the so-called prison epistles were written from Rome during the two-year imprisonment of Paul recounted in Acts 28—that is, about A.D. 59–61. We know, however, that Paul was in prison at other times in other places (cf. 2 Cor. 11:23): in Caesarea (Acts 24–26), Philippi (Acts 16:19–40), and possibly Ephesus (1 Cor. 15:32; cf. Acts 19:28–41). It is, therefore, not impossible that one or more of the captivity epistles were written from prison elsewhere. Still, there is no compelling alternative to the long-standing view that the captivity letters were written in Rome toward the end of Paul's ministry. As a matter of fact, such general considerations as Paul's reminiscent frame of mind in Philippians suggest a late date and therefore point in the direction of a Roman origin. We shall proceed on the assumption that Philippians and Philemon are the last extant letters of Paul, probably written from Rome.

In Philippians Paul looks back over a long and arduous ministry with at least the intuition that it is now drawing to a close. Such resentment as he has toward his enemies and the enemies of the gospel is now overshadowed by his feelings of appreciation for the church that has supported him in bad times as well as in good. With the end perhaps in view (cf. Phil. 1:21 ff.), Paul never ceases to take seriously the task of caring for the churches that falls to him as an apostle of Christ, whether this task requires an expression of gratitude, a plea for personal reconciliation, or a sustained theological argument.

Perhaps the question of the place and date of origin of Philippians needs to be stated in the plural, because that loosely structured document (see outline) may be a composite of three Pauline letters or fragments. If so, the segments would be (1) 1:1–3:1; (2) 3:2–4:1; (3) 4:10–20, with the distribution of 4:2–9 and 21–23 uncertain.[9] Although this partitioning of Philippians is commended by breaks in the structure and flow of thought, it is not impossible that these irregularities stem from Paul himself and that the letter was an original unity. In any event, our text (1:12–26) was probably written from Rome during Paul's imprisonment there. There is no uncertainty about the Philippian destination of the letter (1:1; 4:15). According to the Acts account (16:11–40), with which Philippians 4:15 seems to agree, Philippi was Paul's first mission stop on his initial journey into Macedonia and Greece.

OUTLINE OF PHILIPPIANS

Introduction: Salutation and Thanksgiving (1:1–11)
Personal and Theological Communication (1:12–3:1)
    Personal Reminiscences and Reflection (1:12–26)
    Exhortation and Encouragement to the Philippians (1:27–2:18)
    Plans to Dispatch Emissaries (2:19–3:1)
A Warning (3:2–21)
    Paul's Own Life as an Example against the Evil Workers (3:2–17)
    Denunciation of the Evil Workers (3:18–21)
General Exhortation and Personal Matters (4:1–20)
Conclusion (4:21–23)

Joy in Hardship (Phil. 1:12–26)

How does Paul's attitude toward his own misfortune demonstrate his understanding of the gospel?

Paul is in prison (vss. 7, 13) on account of his preaching of the gospel (vs. 13; cf. Acts 21–28.) Despite his unfortunate circumstances, he is not de-

9. H. Köster, "The Purpose of the Polemic of a Pauline Fragment (Philippians iii)," *New Testament Studies,* 8 (1962), 317, especially n. 1 for the relevant literature.

spondent. Far from having impeded his work and the advance of the gospel, his opponents have done just the opposite (vs. 12), for by his very imprisonment Paul bears witness to Christ (vs. 13). In addition, and contrary to what might have been expected, Paul's coworkers have been emboldened rather than intimidated by the treatment accorded the apostle. Do these attitudes merely bespeak the foolhardiness, if not the foolishness, of these Christians?

The attitude that Paul expresses is at least no casual or passing foolishness, but a fundamental tenet of his faith. It is an aspect of the foolishness of God, which is the gospel of the crucified Messiah (1 Cor. 1:18–25). "My grace is sufficient for you," the Lord, the exalted Christ, had said to Paul, "for my power is made perfect in weakness" (2 Cor. 12:9; cf. 1 Cor. 1:27–29). His ultimate ground for this belief was the cross of Jesus, in which the humiliation of God's Son had become the demonstration not only of God's love but of his power. Likewise, for the apostle humiliation and even suffering might be expected to redound to God's glory in the spreading of the gospel; for through such unlikely means the church bore unmistakable and effective witness to the crucified Jesus. Paul not only could confess this as a matter of faith, he saw it actually coming about: through the suffering and hardship of the disciple, the cause of the gospel was being advanced.

Paul's realistic assessment of the motivations of his colleagues in preaching is striking (1:15–18). We know that Paul was not welcome everywhere, even among Christians in his own churches. Therefore it should not be surprising that his appearance among Roman Christians aroused not only love but also envy and rivalry. Paul was not modest about the importance of his own role in the apostolic preaching and suffered from no sense of personal inadequacy in comparison with his colleagues (cf. Rom. 15:17; 1 Cor. 15:10; 2 Cor. 11:5, 21 ff.). He was doubtless capable of arousing antagonisms. In all probability, therefore, he is here presenting a true picture.

Paul was able to rise above petty jealousies not because of superior personal or moral character, but on the basis of theological insight. The proclamation of the word of the gospel, not the personalities (cf. 1 Cor. 3) or even the motivations of the preachers, was for him primary. The gospel had a validity and an effect independent of the one who conveyed it. Thus, in spite of the intention of some rivals to harass him, presumably by making more converts than he could while he languished in jail, Paul was able to rejoice, for "whether out of false motives or true, Christ is proclaimed" (vss. 18 f.).

Paul had confidence in the Christian community and the Spirit. Therefore he had hope. The interdependence of one member of the community with another, so graphically portrayed in Paul's image of the body of Christ (1 Cor. 12; Rom. 12:3–8), finds practical expression in their prayers (vs. 19). The prayers of the church and the Spirit of Jesus work together for Paul's deliverance. Deliverance from what? It is by no means certain that Paul means just deliverance from the Roman executioner or from prison. The word *sōtēria*, translated "deliverance" in our English text, also means "salvation," and Paul's use of this and related terms usually has a future, eschatological reference. Paul can regard death as well as life as the fulfillment of his hope for deliverance (vs. 20). He does not, however, allow himself to yearn for death—a not uncommon attitude in the ancient world. He desires only to face either life or death with courage, so that Christ will be honored in his body (vs. 20). Here, moreover, is a good example of Paul's distinctive use of the Greek term *sōma,* "body." In this context it surely does not mean merely the physical shape and substance, but Paul's individual and personal presence in the world.

Paul next lays out the relative advantage of living or dying and indicates what he means by "dying is gain" (vss. 22–25). Life means labor (vs. 22), whereas death means being with Christ (vs. 23). Because of the continuing needs of the Philippians, Paul regards it as more urgent at the moment that he continue to live (vs. 24). This necessity is apparently the basis of his confidence that his life will now be spared so that he may visit the Philippians again (1:25 f.). Whether events proved him right in this expectation is debatable. If he was writing from Roman imprisonment, in all probability they did not. But the point is that Paul's eager expectation and hope of deliverance or salvation could by no means be disappointed, whatever the outcome of his situation, for he had hope because God had raised Jesus Christ from the dead. This Jesus, in his humiliation, death, and resurrection life, was for Paul the pattern of Christian existence and the ground of Christian hope. So at what was very likely the end of his ministry, with the possibility of his own death facing him, Paul had confidence and joy (1:4, 18, 19). This was not, however, the first time that Paul had faced death or mortal danger (cf. 1 Cor. 15:32; 2 Cor. 11:23 ff.).

In 1:27 ff. Paul makes an easy transition from encouragement to exhortation, and in 2:1–11 (esp. 5–11) he offers a Christological model for ethics. The pattern of humiliation, death, and exaltation found here is derived explicitly from Christ and is applied to the Christian. Paul may employ an earlier Christ-hymn in verses 6–11, though at least the ethical application is likely his own. This confession and its application are to be understood in conjunction with Romans 6. There Paul discusses baptism as the analogue of Christ's death and resurrection and interprets it in terms of its ethical implications. In both cases Paul assumes that there is, or must be, an integral relation between Christ and the Christian. The characteristic Pauline phrase *in Christ* also implies such a relationship, as do the concepts *body* and *body of Christ.*

The remainder, and thus the greater part, of the letter to the Philippians consists of words of encouragement, a warning against heretics (esp. in chap. 3), exhortation, personal reflections, and an expression of thanks. This last (4:14–20) may have provided the occasion for the entire letter. The tone of the letter, with the possible exception of chapter 3, is consonant with this expression of thanks. Indeed, Philippians shows an ease and familiarity not often found in Paul's letters. Even chapter 3 implies no division between Paul and the church, but warns against outsiders and intruders, who quite possibly had not yet appeared in Philippi. More is implied in 4:14 ff. than perfunctory thanks; there is a mutual sympathy and understanding between Paul and the first church he founded on the European continent.

Notes on Philemon

By far the briefest of Paul's letters, Philemon, unlike the other authentic letters, is a personal note addressed to an individual. Philemon was a member of the church at Colossae. Colossae is not mentioned in the letter, nor is Philemon mentioned in Colossians; but Archippus, who is mentioned in the greeting of Philemon, is named as a leader of the Colossian church (Col. 4:17). Much the same people send greetings in Colossians as in Philemon (Col. 4:10–17; Philem. 23–24) and, most importantly, Onesimus, concerning whom Paul writes to Philemon, is mentioned as having been sent to Colossae with Tychicus (Col. 4:7–8). The letters to the Colossians and to Philemon are thus closely related.

Whereas the authenticity of Colossians is debated (see pp. 328, 371 f.), no one doubts that Paul wrote Philemon. No canonical list of Paul's letters omits this letter, and it is difficult to conceive why some other person would have written such a brief personal note in Paul's name. If Colossians is deutero-Pauline (written by a disciple of Paul rather than Paul himself), the author either knew Paul's letter to Philemon or was otherwise familiar with the people mentioned in it.

Traditionally, Philemon has been assigned to the period of Paul's Roman imprisonment (ca. A.D. 60), even though the people named are mostly associated with Colossae and Asian Christianity. Moreover, Paul anticipates release from prison and the possibility of visiting Philemon in the immediate future (vs. 22). For him to have anticipated release and a trip to Colossae from Rome would not have been unthinkable, yet later local tradition attests to Paul's imprisonment in nearby Ephesus (cf. 1 Cor. 15:32; 2 Cor. 11:23), from which he could have more easily anticipated a visit to Colossae. In that case, Philemon would probably have been written in the early fifties.

SLAVERY AND FREEDOM (PHILEM. 4–20)

Did Paul insist on Onesimus' freedom?

Philemon does not tell a story, but implies a story, about Paul's relationship to Philemon and to Onesimus, Philemon's runaway slave. In the beginning Paul probably brought the good news of salvation to Philemon—that is, Paul converted him to the faith (vs. 16), whether at Colossae or elsewhere. (According to Colossians, at least, Paul had not yet visited Colossae.) Subsequently, Paul was arrested and imprisoned, whether at Rome or Ephesus. In the meantime, Onesimus, Philemon's slave, escaped or ran away (vs. 15, passim) and found his way to Paul in prison. (Again, nearby Ephesus would seem likely.) How he came upon Paul, or why he should have sought him out, we do not know. Conceivably, he was apprehended and put into prison with Paul, although if he was also a prisoner one wonders how Paul could have had the authority to send him back to Philemon (vs. 12). Perhaps Onesimus was not incarcerated. In any case, Paul apparently befriended Onesimus while in prison and brought him to faith in Jesus Christ (vs. 10). Rather than keep Onesimus as his own servant (vs. 13; Paul here avoids "slave" terminology), which he would have had some right to do, Paul elects to send him back to Philemon (vs. 12). With Onesimus Paul sends this letter (vss. 17–19a)—actually, a letter of recommendation for Onesimus—offering to compensate Philemon for any loss or damage (vss. 17–19a) and urging him to receive his slave back without penalty or recrimination (cf. vs. 16). We may imagine that Onesimus returned to Philemon and was received according to Paul's wish (vss. 8–10). Whether he was to be regarded as a slave or a freedman is not explicitly stated; this question has been the subject of much exegetical debate.

Paul obviously writes Philemon in order to persuade him to take Onesimus back as a brother (i.e., a fellow Christian), whatever his worldly status might be. Although careful to urge politely rather than command (vss. 8–10), Paul nevertheless reminds Philemon of the latter's debt to him (vs. 19b) and of his own (apostolic) authority. At the end he says that he is confident of Philemon's obedience (vs. 21) and instructs him to get the guest room ready for a visit (vs. 22)! There is little doubt that Paul knows what Philemon should do, and believes he has the authority to command it, because of both his apostolic status and their earlier relationship. Yet Paul recognizes that he cannot enforce his will and must draw on his powers of persuasion, using his own authority and Philemon's debt to him deftly and subtly, not rudely or blatantly.

Although Onesimus' status before God is that of a brother (fellow Christian), this does not necessarily mean Paul expected Philemon to manumit (free) him. Given Paul's understanding of the implications of baptism into Christ (cf. Gal. 3:27–28), one might think that he meant for Philemon to free Onesimus. The slavery question was, however, not as important for Paul, who expected the end of worldly conditions with the imminent return of Jesus, as it is for modern people, for whom the idea of slavery as an institution is abhorrent. Paul nowhere advocates the abolition of slavery, an enormously important institution in antiquity. Whether one is slave or free in this world is a matter of indifference (Gal. 3:28), for "the present form of this world is passing away" (1 Cor. 7:31). In 1 Corinthians Paul seems to recommend that Christians retain their present status (7:24), although he may quietly endorse a slave's making use of the opportunity to become free (7:21; but NSRV does not favor this translation). Paul was not a submissive, quiescent person (cf. 2 Cor. 11:23–29); nor can he be said to have actively supported slavery or the other oppressive social or political conditions of this world. Nevertheless, Paul does not say explicitly that he expects Philemon to grant Onesimus freedman's status. Conceivably his not commanding this action has something to do with the subtlety of Paul's rhetorical style, but it may have had more to do with his eschatology: God would soon end human slavery.

This brief letter reveals something about the constituency of Paul's churches, and presumably of others as well. Philemon was a householder (cf.

vs. 22) and a slave owner. The two usually went together in antiquity. The householder was not just a home owner; within his household were more than members of the nuclear family—there were also servants, slaves, more remote kin, and perhaps others. The householder was a person of acknowledged status and means. We know from Paul's letters that a fair number of householders had been converted to the new faith, for their houses served as gathering places for the Christian community. Thus Paul writes here, as he does often, of "the church in your house" (vs. 2). Not until much later did Christians have, or build, halls (i.e., "churches") in which to meet; they normally met in the homes of affluent members like Philemon (cf. Rom. 16:3–5, 23). As Paul's letter to Philemon clearly shows, slaves and poor people were gladly welcomed into the community of faith, and wealthier people were not excluded, but played an important role in the life of the emerging church.

Conclusion

We have now examined representative passages from letters written by Paul. As we saw, Paul had not been a disciple of Jesus during his life or at the very beginning of the new movement. If he had known Jesus, in all probability he would have opposed him, as did other Pharisees (cf. Phil. 3:5). Apparently there was no more vehement opponent of the first Christians than Paul (1 Cor. 15:9; Gal. 1:13). Nevertheless, after he became a follower rather than a persecutor of Jesus, Paul outdid all others in spreading the new faith. At least, so he believes (1 Cor. 15:10; cf. 2 Cor. 11:21–27), and the New Testament itself bears testimony to the validity of this claim.

Paul does not add much to our knowledge of Jesus, and does not appear interested in conveying the tradition about Jesus to the churches. Possibly Paul knew and conveyed more about Jesus than his writings indicate, although this is a subject of dispute that can scarcely be resolved on the basis of presently available evidence. All we can say with certainty is that Paul appeals frequently to the death and resurrection of Jesus, who is for him more the heavenly Lord than a historical figure. Paul often quotes the Bible (Old Testament) as authoritative, and he seldom refers to Jesus' teaching and never to Jesus' specific deeds. Paul, we must remember, did not know our Gospels, which were written some years after his letters.

In comparison with those who had been disciples of Jesus (cf. Acts 1:21–22) Paul was a latecomer, and in all probability he was suspect for that reason. Yet he was able to claim that he had seen the risen Jesus (1 Cor. 9:1; 15:8) and thus had legitimate status as an apostle, equal to those who had been apostles before him (Gal. 1:17). Even though Paul's claim was not taken at face value and the validity of his gospel was disputed, we are in a real sense beneficiaries of this fact. We have his letters, the source of our knowledge of him, mainly because he and his gospel message became a subject of contention in the early church.

Ironically, the one activity through which he is best known to us, letter writing, is not even mentioned in the extensive depiction of Paul in the Book of Acts. Either Luke did not know that Paul wrote letters, or conceivably he knew but did not consider it worth mentioning. Probably Luke had not read the letters themselves. Paul's justifiable reputation as a theologian, and in some sense the father of Christian theology, is based mainly on letters that occupied him for only a small fraction of his time and for which he was evidently not remembered in the immediately succeeding generation. This remarkable fact underscores the breadth and extent of Paul's work. He was a man for all seasons and tasks, a person of practical insight who possessed skills of leadership and organization. At the same time he was capable of theological reflection at a very sophisticated level.

As a rule, Paul's theological thinking arose out of practical situations. Perhaps his sharpest insights about faith come in response to a severe challenge. Those who have questioned Paul's own apostolic credentials claimed that male converts in the Galatian churches must undergo circumcision, the mark of membership in the Jewish community. In the Letter to the Galatians he rejects their claims, arguing that faith's acceptance of Jesus as God's grace is the heart and soul of the gospel. Faith is negated if one insists on circumcision, for circumcision implies acceptance of the law instead of grace as the way of salvation. Yet for Paul, the expression of faith in human relationships is love, not theological knowledge (1 Cor. 8:1–13). Love takes precedence over knowledge. Knowledge leads to the sort of confidence in one's own power that can defeat faith. Love honors the other person, whom God also loves, and is grounded upon faith. In one place Paul even gives love precedence over faith and hope (1 Cor. 13:13). By this statement he cannot mean that faith and hope are dispensable, but that they fail the test of genuineness apart from love.

Paul was a convert, a missionary preacher, an organizer of churches, an author and theologian, and, in a sense, a teacher and administrator for the churches he founded. His life was filled with hard work, travel, controversy, even physical punishment and imprisonment. Rarely, however, does any hint of what Paul endured, the fatigue he must have experienced, appear in his letters (but cf. 2 Cor. 11:23–29). Obviously, Paul's dedication was matched by a strong physical constitution. Not many people have the sheer energy to do what Paul did. When one considers that he did it in the face of hardship and opposition, his accomplishments become even more remarkable.

Suggestions for Further Reading

The Suggestions for Further Reading at the end of Chapter 9 include works on Paul's theology.

There are now two excellent brief treatments of the letters and work: C. J. Roetzel, *The Letters of Paul: Conversations in Context,* rev. ed. (Atlanta: John Knox, 1982), centers on the correspondence; while E. P. Sanders, *Paul* (Oxford: Oxford University Press, 1991), sets Paul's theology and ethics in the context of his mission. Recent works on Pauline chronology include R. Jewett, *A Chronology of Paul's Life* (Philadelphia: Fortress, 1979); and G. Lüdemann, *Paul, Apostle to the Gentiles: Studies in Chronology,* trans. F. S. Jones (Philadelphia: Fortress, 1984), which come to somewhat different conclusions on major issues. The conversion of Paul, as described by him and in the Book of Acts, is discussed by B. R. Gaventa, *From Darkness to Light: Aspects of Conversion in the New Testament* (Philadelphia: Fortress, 1986). Important moral issues with which Paul deals are taken up and analyzed by V. P. Furnish, *The Moral Teaching of Paul: Selected Issues,* rev. ed. (Nashville: Abingdon, 1985). For a somewhat different approach, see J. P. Sampley, *Walking between the Times: Paul's Moral Reasoning* (Minneapolis: Fortress, 1991). The sociohistorical context, constituency, and organization of Paul's churches are treated in the important and comprehensive study of W. A. Meeks, *The First Urban Christians: The Social World of the Apostle Paul* (New Haven: Yale University Press, 1983). Meeks has also collected a valuable anthology of essays, ancient and modern, on Paul: *The Writings of St. Paul* (New York: Norton, 1972). An informed treatment by a Jewish author, Alan F. Segal, *Paul the Convert: The Apostolate and Apostasy of Saul the Pharisee* (New Haven: Yale University Press, 1990), interprets Paul's career and thought in light of his conversion.

Paul's relation to Jesus and the Synoptic tradition has received thorough treatment in D. L. Dungan, *The Sayings of Jesus in the Churches of Paul: The Use of the Synoptic Tradition in the Regulation of Early Church Life* (Philadelphia: Fortress, 1971). Paul's apostleship is set in the context of modern sociological theory in J. H. Schütz, *Paul and the Anatomy of Apostolic Authority* (New York: Cambridge University Press, 1975). G. Lüdemann, *Opposition to Paul in Jewish Christianity,* trans. M. E. Boring (Minneapolis: Fortress, 1989), studies this important source of opposition to Paul and his mission.

1 AND 2 THESSALONIANS

Ernest Best, *A Commentary on the First and Second Epistles to the Thessalonians* (New York: Harper & Row, 1972), is a good and reliable guide. Best accepts 2 Thessalonians as Pauline. A. J. Malherbe, *Paul and the Thessalonians: The Philosophic Tradition of Pastoral Care* (Philadelphia: Fortress, 1987), sets 1 Thessalonians in its broader social and cultural context.

GALATIANS

H. D. Betz, *Galatians* (Philadelphia: Fortress, 1979), in the Hermeneia series, is now the standard commentary. Note also the commentaries of C. B. Cousar, *Galatians* (Atlanta: John Knox, 1982), and J. D. G. Dunn, *The Epistle to the Galatians* (Peabody, MA: Hendrickson, 1994). On theology and ethical issues in Galatians, see C. K. Barrett, *Freedom and Obligation: A Study of the Epistle to the Galatians* (London: SPCK, 1985), and J. M. G. Barclay, *Obeying the Truth: A Study of Paul's Ethics in Galatians* (Edinburgh: Clark, 1988).

THE CORINTHIAN LETTERS

The Harper commentaries of C. K. Barrett, *A Commentary on the First Epistle to the Corinthians* (New York: Harper & Row, 1968), and *A Commentary on the Second Epistle to the Corinthians* (1973), are still first-rate. H. Conzelmann, *I Corinthians,* trans. J. W. Leitch (Philadelphia: Fortress, 1975), is a standard work; but G. D. Fee, *The First Epistle to the Corinthians* (Grand Rapids, MI: Eerdmans, 1987), must now also be consulted. V. P. Furnish, *II Corinthians* (Garden City, NY: Doubleday, 1984), is an excellent commentary that, like Conzelmann and Fee, is a rich mine of information. J. C. Hurd, *The Origins of I Corinthians,* 2nd ed. (Macon, GA: Mercer University Press, 1983), argues that the Corinthian controversies were in large measure the result of Paul's own changing position. Sociological perspectives are invoked by G. Theissen, *The Social Setting of Pauline Christianity: Essays on Corinth,* trans. J. H. Schütz (Philadelphia: Fortress, 1982), while J. Murphy-O'Connor, *St. Paul's Corinth: Texts and Archaeology* (Wilmington, DE: Michael Glazier, 1983), is a valuable collection and interpretation of ancient evidence bearing upon the letters. Dieter Georgi, *The Opponents of Paul in Second Corinthians* (Philadelphia: Fortress, 1986), is a translation and revision, with a new epilogue of over one hundred pages, of the author's important monograph of 1964, in which he attempts to deduce the nature of the opponents from Paul's statements.

PHILIPPIANS

The work of F. W. Beare, *A Commentary on the Epistle to the Philippians* (New York: Harper & Row, 1959), is still worthwhile. The Christ-hymn in Philippians is treated by R. P. Martin, *Carmen Christi: Philippians 2:5–11 in Recent Interpretation and in the Setting of Early Christian Worship,* rev. ed. (Grand Rapids, MI: Eerdmans, 1983). Note also Martin's commentary, *Philippians,* rev. ed. (Grand Rapids, MI: Eerdmans, 1983).

PHILEMON

For commentaries on Philemon, see under Colossians (Chapter 10). The most recent thorough study of this briefest of Paul's letters is N. R. Petersen, *Rediscovering Paul: Philemon and the Sociology of Paul's Narrative World* (Philadelphia: Fortress, 1985), in which the author finds Paul's narrative world to have been integrally related to the actual circumstances of his historical relationships.

Chapter 9

Romans: The Righteousness of God

Notes on Romans

*P*aul's Letter to the Romans was probably written during, or shortly after, his last visit to Corinth, following the resolution of the problems of the Galatian and Corinthian churches and the completion of the collection for Jerusalem (cf. Rom. 15:17–29; 2 Cor. 1:16; 8; 9; Acts 20:2 f.). Paul was clearly heading for Jerusalem when he wrote this letter (Rom. 15:25, 28, 30 f.). Romans was thus written in the mid- to late fifties of the first century, probably in A.D. 56. Paul regarded his work in the eastern part of the Mediterranean world as complete and was looking forward to a subsequent journey to Spain, but his plans were to be foreclosed by his arrest and imprisonment (cf. Rom. 15:23–29 and Acts 20:25, 38). Romans is not addressed to a church lying within what had heretofore been Paul's missionary orbit, but rather to an already established church that Paul expected to visit. Paul wished to present himself and his gospel to the church or Christians at Rome. He also hoped to use Rome as a center for his future missionary endeavors in Spain and thus sought the approval of the Roman church (15:24). Romans is the fullest presentation of Paul's theological views that we possess.

Galatians, especially the account of Paul's earlier conversation with Peter (Gal. 2:11–21), indicates that the seeds of Romans had already been planted in Paul's thought long before. Yet Paul was likely driven by experiences with his churches in Galatia and Corinth to formulate more carefully his understanding of the gospel. The basic theological themes set forth in Galatians receive more extensive and considered treatment in Romans, whereas some of the themes as well as the practical counsel of the Corinthian correspondence also appear here (e.g., the body of Christ in Rom. 12:3–8; love in 12:9 ff., 13:8 ff., and elsewhere; conscience and the weaker brother in chap. 14). One has the distinct impression that Romans embodies Paul's relatively later and more considered reflection, a judgment borne out by other evidence for dating the letters.

OUTLINE OF ROMANS

Introduction: Righteousness by Faith (1:1–17)
God's Wrath: The Problem of Sin (1:18–3:20)
God's Righteousness and the Response of Faith (3:21–4:25)

Introduction: Righteousness by Faith (1:1–17)

How does Paul use the introduction of Romans to introduce his message?

Romans opens with a long, formal salutation (1:1–7), containing a confessional statement (vss. 2–4) as well as Paul's description of his apostolic office. Non-Pauline elements such as the reference to the Davidic sonship of Jesus and the term "Spirit of holiness" suggest that the confessional statement may represent an earlier tradition. On the other hand, the equally rare phrase "obedience of faith" (vs. 5) sets out an important emphasis of Romans. By it Paul means the obedience to, or acknowledgment of, God accomplished through faith.

The customary thanksgiving (vss. 8–15) builds toward the statement of the theme of the letter (vss. 16–17). In it Paul praises the Romans' faith and gives elaborate assurances about his own prayers for them. Although such expressions were conventional in Hellenistic correspondence of the time,[1] Paul is not merely engaging in conventionalities, as is shown by the specific content of his prayers (vs. 10) and by the appropriateness of his praise for the Roman Christians.

The full meaning and import of the thematic statement (vss. 16 f.) can only be seen in the light of the entire letter. Yet several points stand out. Paul's interpretation of the Christian gospel is here summed up in a kind of theological shorthand: "the power of God for salvation" (vs. 16). The gospel is God's grace, something freely given rather than earned. The pairing of Jew and Greek is a further extension of the same line of thought. God grants salvation without regard for merit or national origin, without regard even for special religious distinction. It is bestowed universally. Although *Jew* means for Paul "an Israelite according to the flesh," *Greek* is virtually a synonym for

---

1. Cf. A. S. Hunt and C. C. Edgar, eds. and trans., *Select Papyri,* I (London: Heinemann, 1932–1934), pp. 339, 369, for examples of conventional thanksgivings.

Gentile. The substance of Paul's gospel is then spelled out more fully (vs. 17). It is the revelation of the righteousness (Greek: *dikaiosynē*) of God. By this Paul might mean a doctrine or fact about God, that he is righteous rather than unrighteous, which Paul would have by no means denied. But for Paul the term *righteousness of God* has a specific dynamic meaning (cf. Rom. 3:26). It refers primarily to how God acts and relates to human history.

The gospel displays and interprets God's righteousness, and it is this theme that Paul develops in Romans. His righteousness is made known to, and appropriated by, faith; faith has now become a universal possibility. As we have already noticed in Galatians, emphasis on the importance and indispensability of faith is characteristic of Paul. The theme of the righteousness of faith will be developed and refined in Romans.

God's Wrath: The Problem of Sin (1:18–3:20)

How does homosexuality, in Paul's view, typify the sinful human condition?

Paul speaks of the revelation of God's righteousness in 1:17; in 1:18 he turns to the revelation of God's wrath. Both terms, *righteousness* and *wrath,* are eschatological. That is, they refer to revelations expected in the last days of this world as signs that God is bringing human history to a climactic and perhaps catastrophic conclusion. Paul places God's righteousness and his wrath over against one another as if he believed that their presence already marked the final turning point of world history. Indeed, Paul can refer to Christians as those upon whom the end of the ages has come (1 Cor. 10:11) and can advise against marriage or any other too close attachment to this world on the grounds that it is passing away (1 Cor. 7:31).

Although the primary tension in 1:17 f. is between God's righteousness and his wrath, Paul introduces a secondary tension between the righteousness of God and the wickedness of humanity. Paul plays upon the *dikaiosynē* ("righteousness") of God and the *adikia* ("wickedness") of humanity. With the setting up of these tensions or polarities, the problem of Romans is posed, and the fundamental theological questions are raised. What is the relation between God's wrath and his righteousness? Moreover, how is it possible for humanity, characterized by *adikia,* lack of righteousness, to stand before a holy God, whose very essence is righteousness?

Paul does not yet deal fully with these questions. He will first characterize humankind as the object and occasion of God's wrath (Rom. 1:18–3:20). At the outset (vs. 18) he makes clear that the characterization will not be favorable, even though he does not yet indicate the extent of wickedness. Paul speaks of a present outpouring of God's wrath, parallel with the revelation of his righteousness just mentioned. Actually he describes the condition of

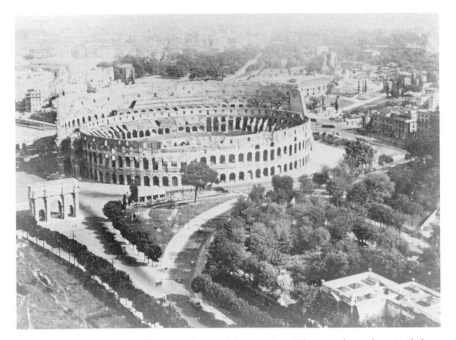

The Colosseum at Rome, frequently used for gladiatorial, mortal combat. Built by Vespasian and Titus about A.D. 80 as an outdoor theater, before the time of the emperor Constantine it was the scene of the persecution of Christians.   *(Courtesy of Lufthansa German Airlines.)*

humankind from the standpoint of the revelation of God's righteousness and wrath in and through the gospel. He does not present the human condition from the perspective of the neutral and strictly objective onlooker. Thus Paul could scarcely have expected everyone to subscribe to his description. The wrath of God against human wickedness accompanies the revelation of his righteousness, and only against the background of this norm—the righteousness of God as revealed in Jesus Christ—does human wickedness stand out in bold relief.

This wickedness is first said to be suppression of the truth (vs. 18), that is, failure to recognize the truth about the Creator implicit in the creation (vss. 19–20). It is not as if the world had no access to knowledge of God. In fact, precisely the opposite is true. Therefore Paul can say, "They are without excuse" (vs. 20). Not only do people generally have the possibility of knowing God and fail to exercise it, Paul goes so far as to attribute to them an actual knowledge of God (vs. 21). They lack, however, a proper *acknowledgment:* "They did not honor him as God or give thanks to him." Instead they became senseless and practiced disobedience—namely, idolatry (vss. 22 f.)—with the resulting defilement or dishonoring of their bodies (vs. 24). The grounds for the existing state of affairs lie in the fact that the values and loyalties of people have become perverted, even inverted, since they "exchanged the truth about God for a lie and worshiped and served the creature rather than the Creator" (vs. 25). This inversion of the "natural order" (worship of the Creator) concludes the first stage in the development of Paul's description of the human situation.

Three important points are now emerging. First, Paul speaks of wickedness, or unrighteousness, without yet saying that it is universal. Paul leaves open the option of extending the condemnation of human wickedness to include all people but does not yet explicitly do so. Second, although Paul speaks initially of the present revelation of the wrath of God (vs. 18), he changes over to the past tense in describing the course of sin in the human race. Thus he indicates that the present situation, against which God's wrath is directed, did not come about in a day, but has a long and significant past. Third, Paul asserts that God gives people up to their lusts, an idea that occurs first in verse 24 and recurs in verses 26 and 28. He does not mean that God is the cause of sin but, rather, that God allows people to fall prey to the overt sinning that is already implicit in their misdirected loyalty and worship.

Paul's singling out of homosexuality as typical of the inversion of the natural order is not accidental. The Bible condemns homosexuality in the strictest terms (cf. Lev. 18:22; 20:13), which in itself indicates it was not unheard of in Old Testament times (Gen. 19:4–8; Judg. 19:22–26). Apparently, this practice was fairly prevalent in the Greco-Roman world, as, for example, Plato's *Symposium* implies. Paul, however, does not speak simply as a pious Jew enraged at what he regards as a most heinous violation of law and nature. Paul has already argued that people's lack of righteousness results from their lack of a proper knowledge of God—a failing that bears its expected fruit in idolatry. For him idolatry, as a worshiping and serving of the creature rather than the Creator (vs. 25), is literally a perversion or, as we have already suggested, a glaring manifestation of the inversion of the order of things that God created. The result of this reversal of the created order is the disordering and confusion of human life in general. Homosexual practices also appear to reverse the order in which sexual relations were intended. Thus in antiquity, as today, "unnaturalness" is the basis for the condemnation of homosexuality. Therefore not a puritanical disposition but Paul's understanding of wickedness and idolatry as inversion or perversion of a God-given order suggests homosexuality as the best outward example of human sinfulness. Sin is not merely the breaking of commandments or laws, although it certainly involves that; rather, sin is a complete disorientation of life such that human existence and behavior become completely divorced and estranged from the ground of their being, the God who creates and orders all things. Yet it cannot be emphasized too strongly that Paul does not cite homosexuality specifically because it is the worst of sins, but because in his view it best exemplifies the nature of sin.

Such disorientation does not stop with sexual aberrations, but extends to all life. "Things that should not be done" (vs. 28) translates a Stoic expression (*ta mē kathēkonta*) meaning things out of accord with the proper nature of humanity. Human perversity in refusing to acknowledge God is thus manifest in homosexuality and no less strikingly in the general disordering of life, most especially of human relationships, the subject of the catalog of vices (vss. 29–31). Paul describes people turned toward one another in animosity and suspicion rather than love. This unnatural way of relating to others is a violation of the intended order of creation.

Paul has not yet explicitly extended his condemnations to include all of humanity. From the prominence given to homosexuality and the subsequent catalog of vices, the Jewish reader would be justified in suspecting that Paul has in mind the Gentile and is making an exception of the Jew. After all, Paul was not above referring disparagingly to "Gentile sinners" (Gal. 2:15), as if the terms were practically synonymous. Probably Paul does have in mind here the sinful conduct of the Gentile. For the Jewish or Jewish–Christian reader, what he has to say might seem quite convincing. In fact, in the apocryphal book of the Wisdom of Solomon one can find ideas akin to those that Paul sets forth here. For example, the author, in agreement with Paul, seems to assume that knowledge of God should be attainable from creation, although people by and large do not attain it (Wisdom 13:6–9). He gives a similar assessment of the relation between idolatry and immorality (Wisdom 14:12) and presents a catalog of specific sins (Wisdom 14:22 ff.) not unlike that of Romans 1:29 ff.[2] So far in Romans there is little to make the Jewish reader uneasy, for Paul has written an eloquent condemnation of Gentile sin.

That Paul intends something more, however, is already clear from the first few verses of chapter 2 (vss. 1–4). As Paul has the Gentile in the back of his mind in 1:18–32, so he seems here to be thinking of the Jew. That Paul would apply his hard words to any presumptuous and self-righteous human being need scarcely be said, but that he specifically intends them for the Jew as well as the Greek soon becomes apparent (2:6 ff.). The idea that God shows no partiality (2:11) means that the Jew is brought to judgment on the same basis as the Gentile, as Paul in fact makes quite explicit (vss. 9–10). This naming of the Jew alongside the Gentile probably indicates that the Jew has been in mind from the beginning of chapter 2.

What Paul has already stated (vss. 9–11) he now develops by setting forth the basis for God's impartial judgment of Jew and Gentile (vss. 12–16). Interestingly, the law—and Paul means here scriptural, Jewish law—is accepted as the definitive expression of the will of God, according to which he will judge all people on the last day (but cf. vs. 16). Mere possession of the law has, however, no particular value. Therefore, if any Gentile fulfills the requirements of the law, even without knowing its concrete form (vss. 14–15), that obedience is perfectly acceptable. The idea that God's election of Israel constitutes a special privilege and advantage even if Jews do not respond ap-

---

2. The New Testament, and especially Paul's epistles, are full of these catalogs of vices (e.g., Rom. 13:13; 1 Cor. 5:10 f.; 6:9 f.; 2 Cor. 12:20 f.; Gal. 5:19 ff.; Eph. 4:31; 5:3 ff.; Col. 3:5, 8; 1 Tim. 1:9 f.; 2 Tim. 3:2–5).

propriately is already rejected (vss. 12 f.). In the two closing paragraphs (vss. 17–24 and 25–29) this point is driven home with the clear implication (esp. in vss. 17–24) that the Jews by and large stand condemned. Despite their advantage as the recipients and bearers of God's law, they do not in fact do what the law commands. Thus their desire to instruct or reprove others is sheer presumption. Really to be a Jew is to obey God. Such obedience is not a matter of outward show, but "a matter of the heart . . . spiritual and not literal" (vs. 29). This statement, of course, does not mean that obedience has no visible form or tangible expression. The true Judaism of which Paul speaks can be nothing less than obedience to God in the real world, not a specious and amorphous spirituality without concrete manifestations. Yet quite clearly being a real Jew cannot be identified with belonging to an institution or nation, or with fleshly marks of the same, such as circumcision. Significantly, "Jew" is still a positive term in Paul's vocabulary.

Paul's questions (3:1) are now well motivated, and from what has so far been said, we might expect negative replies: the Jew has no advantage. In a sense such an assertion would be fitting, because the Jew has no advantage just because he is a Jew, and circumcision, the distinguishing mark of every Jewish male, has no merit in and of itself. Yet the Jewish possession of the scriptures (the "oracles of God," vs. 2) is in and of itself a great advantage. Paul mentions this benefit as the first of what was apparently intended to be a series of items. But he immediately becomes sidetracked and does not mention the remaining advantages in this context (graphic proof of the more or less occasional character of even Romans). For the moment (vss. 3–8), Paul is obviously concerned with matters about which he has probably been challenged or attacked. We thus encounter a series of embarrassing questions (vss. 3, 5, 7) that Paul was probably not the first, or the last, to ponder. The unfaithfulness of the Jews constitutes a problem, because they do not now receive the promises vouchsafed to them (vs. 3): "Will their faithlessness nullify the faithfulness of God?" To resolve this problem by blaming Israel rather than God so that God's righteousness is not impugned but rather established (vs. 4) raises the further problem of how God can justly condemn the transgressor when the wickedness really serves to vindicate God's righteousness (vs. 5). In other words, "if through my falsehood God's truthfulness abounds to his glory, why am I still being condemned as a sinner?" (vs. 7). Paul hardly answers these questions at this point. Indeed, he dismisses the questioner rather rudely (vs. 8). Yet, as we shall see, these questions are pivotal points in Paul's argument in Romans, and at length he returns to them in chapters 9–11.

The argument concerning the universality of sin that Paul has been developing since the introductory part of the letter (3:9–20) is now concluded. Uncertainty about the meaning of the particular form of a Greek verb makes it unclear whether in verse 9 Paul is asking whether the Jews are better or worse off than others. Whatever the question, however, Paul's basic contention is unaltered, as his positive statement shows (vs. 9). The Jews are actually no better off. To clinch his demonstration Paul characteristically calls upon the scriptures (vss. 10–18). If there has been any doubt about what Paul is trying to prove, these verses dispel it. Scriptural quotations from many different sources have been skillfully woven together to describe the general state of humanity (vss. 10–12) and to specify the details of that condition (vss. 13–18). Next comes an interpretative clarification (vs. 19) to remove any uncertainty as to their applicability, for they apply not only to Gentiles but particularly to those under the law, that is, to Jews. Finally, Paul makes his own theological statement about what the law can and cannot do (vs. 20; see also 4:15; 5:20; 7:8, 10 f.). Clearly this long section, extending from 1:18 to 3:20, is intended to show the universal sinfulness of humanity as the backdrop for the proclamation of the gospel (cf. 3:23), which reveals God's righteousness and also his wrath (1:17–18).

At first glance it may appear that this lengthy prolegomenon is only a frightening diagnosis intended to induce the patient to accept the radical new cure. Yet Paul has already referred to the present, rather than the past, revelation of the wrath of God (1:18) precisely as proof that the revelation of God's righteousness is also taking place. For Paul human sinfulness becomes fully apparent only now with the revelation of the righteousness of God in Christ (see 3:26). Paul did not understand his own pre-Christian life as a period of disappointment over sinful humanity and disillusionment with his own sin (cf. Gal. 1:14 and Phil. 3:4–6). His darker view of the predicament of humanity and his own past situation apparently arose only after his conversion. Thus Paul does not think the hearer of the Christian preaching could be convinced of the seriousness of his plight apart from the message that the crucified one was the Christ. Because the world did not recognize in Jesus the Messiah, God's Son, but crucified him, the depth of its wickedness is revealed.

On the other hand, we cannot maintain that nothing in this section (Rom. 1:18–3:20) could have been said by Paul except in the light of the Christian revelation and on the basis of Christian faith. His condemnation of Gentile sinfulness and his admission of the theoretical possibility of Gentile righteousness apart from the law are not unique to Paul the Christian. Probably he could have said as much before his conversion. Jewish condemnation of Gentile sin was not uncommon in New Testament times and in the New Testament itself (cf. Matt. 5:47; 6:7; Gal. 2:15). More unusual are Paul's inclusion of the Jew and Gentile under the same standard of judgment and his view that, when the Jew and Gentile are judged on the same basis before God, the Jew will have no particular advantage. And even this assertion might not have seemed so offensive to his fellow Jew had Paul not gone on to say that the Jew actually falls short of fulfillment of the will of God and consequently stands condemned with the Gentile. In the light of the revelation of God's righteousness in the gospel of his Son, all are sinners. Paul's affirmative answer to the question about the advantage of the Jew (3:1) scarcely seems convincing in the light of his wholesale condemnation of Jew and Gentile.

Even if we grant that Paul's condemnation (or, as he understands it, God's condemnation) of human sinfulness is just (given his unique perspective), the origin of sin remains a mystery. Paul could have maintained that human nature in and of itself is evil. If so, what Paul calls wickedness, unrighteousness, or sin would be not a human possibility but a necessity. There would then be no such thing as meaningful human responsibility. Such a position with respect to a part of humanity may have been possible for some of Paul's contemporaries, but this sort of determinism does not explain Paul's thought. On the one hand, the corruption of which he speaks extends to all humanity, not just a portion. On the other, Paul goes to great pains to maintain that the plight of humanity is the result not of a corrupt nature but of concrete sinning. Thus the point of verse 1:19 is, as we have seen, the establishment of humankind's responsibility for the human condition. God's giving people over to certain forms of wickedness (1:24, 26, 28) does not mean that God causes them to be evil, but that he allows them to be. Therefore Paul proclaims that humanity stands in a state of universal sinfulness because of actual sinning. That specific acts of sinning carried with them ominous consequences for the future and future generations is implied by verses 1:24, 26, 28, where Paul doubtless has more than one generation in view. Is sin then some disease that has infected the human race at the outset and been passed on from one generation to the next? If so, then every person would be born with an inclination toward sin. Perhaps Paul would have agreed that this is the case. But he does not set out that venerable conception of original sin, according to which a sinful nature is inherited by each generation from its predecessor. That is a later development in the history of Christian doctrine.

Still Paul obviously does not regard sin simply as personal wickedness or transgression resulting from the ill will of individuals. Although he indicates that individuals are responsible for their sin and do not sin inevitably or by

"The Fall of Man" by Albrecht Altdorfer (1480–1538).   *(Courtesy of National Gallery of Art, Washington, D.C. Samuel H. Kress Collection.)*

nature, he is quite aware of the suprapersonal character of evil among the human race. Specifically, he traces the origin of this evil or sin to Adam (Rom. 5:12–21; cf. 1 Cor. 15:45 ff.). Elsewhere he can refer to the bondage of the creation to decay (8:21) or to the present evil age (Gal. 1:4) without ever mentioning Adam. Also without mentioning him, Paul speaks of sin as an external power that can enslave humanity (chap. 6) and describes how it insidiously attacks through the law (chap. 7). Yet in view of his specific references to Adam it is probable that Paul's understanding of the corporate character of sin owes much to the strand of Jewish thought that laid responsibility for the corrupt state of humanity at Adam's doorstep (esp. 4 Ezra 3:20-21; 7:116–126; cf. Baruch 54:15–19).

Paul's conception of sin has then two foci, which remain in paradoxical and unresolved tension with one another: people sin willingly, but inevitably. Paul can never speak of sin in such a way as to relieve all of humanity, and indeed the individual, of responsibility for it. Yet he would by no means subscribe to a purely personal or individualist concept of sin. Like his predecessors among the ancient prophets of Israel, Paul was fully aware of both its individual and corporate dimensions.

Paul's conceptual categories may seem foreign to us. We like to "explain" human evil in terms of historical cause and effect and environmental influence. Generally, we do not describe our own situation, no matter how evil or dangerous, in terms of oppression by mythological demonic powers (Rom. 8:38). Yet awareness of the awful depth and mystery of human evil, illumined but by no means exhausted by historical and sociological explanation, comes to expression in works of art, literature, and the theater. Rational efforts, significant as they may be, do not suffice to exorcise or even comprehend the demonic dimensions of our society and our world. Paul's awareness of being beset by mysterious forces outside human control, far from being utterly strange, corresponds to the experience of our contemporary existence. Moreover, his refusal to release humanity from responsibility for sin, paradoxical as it may appear, also characterizes our apprehension of life. We know that injustice, violence, racism, and sexism are our heritage, but are also our responsibility.

God's Righteousness and the Response of Faith (3:21–4:25)

According to Paul, God's wrath is not his last word. Although God has every reason to display righteous wrath against human rebelliousness and perversity, he does not leave the human race to its deserved condemnation. Instead, he turns in mercy and compassion, and, according to Paul, the evidence of this grace is Jesus Christ. The historic and public crucifixion of the expected Jewish Messiah reveals God's righteousness and his power for salvation (1:16). At a pivotal point of Romans, Paul announces this manifestation of God's righteousness in terms drawn largely from the Jewish sacrificial system (3:21–31). In a world gone wrong, God sets things right.

JUSTIFICATION BY FAITH (3:21–31)

Why is Jesus Christ offered as a sacrifice to God for human sin?

Paul now spells out his concept of God's righteousness and how it is effected through Jesus Christ. In this discussion the bleak picture of humankind held captive under the power of sin set forth in the preceding chapters is presupposed. Although knowledge of God is given to everyone in creation (1:19 ff.), and despite the fact that knowledge of God's will is accessible to Jew and Gentile (2:12 ff., 17 ff.), the plight of both is a dire one (3:19 f.). Paul challenges fundamentally those who consider themselves righteous by virtue of their own accomplishments. That righteousness is shown to be unrighteousness. For "now apart from the law the righteousness of God has been disclosed, and is attested by the law and the prophets" (Rom. 3:21).

Paul is intrigued by paradox. The revelation of God's righteousness is attested in advance by the law and the prophets (the Old Testament), although the revelation does not come through the law. Neither is this righteousness gained through works of the law. Rather, it is accessible through faith in Christ (vs. 22). Human wisdom, power, and righteousness all stand in opposition to the cross of Christ, because they represent the attempt to establish life as secure apart from God (cf. 1:25). Faith is the means by which one may receive God's righteousness. That this is the only possibility of righteousness and life is clearly spelled out by Paul (3:22b–23) in a summation of Paul's argument of the preceding section (1:18–3:20). In verse 24, Paul then specifies how God makes his righteousness accessible as a gift, that is, "by his grace." Only now does Paul refer to the historic event of the cross of Christ, in which, according to his gospel, this grace is bestowed.

This brief series of assertions (vss. 24–26) is as difficult as it is important, for here (and especially in verse 25) Paul introduces unfamiliar terminology taken largely from Jewish sacrificial practice. The word *redemption* (vs. 24), however, means literally a buying back from slavery, although the specific meaning in this context is not certain. Redemption may simply have the general meaning of deliverance, for in the next verse Paul quickly drops this legal term and changes back to a sacrificial vocabulary. Thus (vs. 25) he says that God put Christ forth as a sacrifice of atonement by his blood (vs. 25). The conviction that sin must be dealt with concretely is deeply embedded in biblical religion and doubtless in the consciousness of Paul and the earliest Christian community. Paul's reference to blood makes clear that the sacrifice of the altar is in view. The model for conceiving the significance of Christ's death is the sacrifice of the animal on the altar and the sprinkling of his blood. Paul, however, qualifies this idea of ritual sacrifice with the phrase "effective through faith," showing that for him the effect of the sacrifice is dependent upon the manner of its reception. Christ is an expiation—but for faith alone.

Yet the power of the sacrifice itself is not thereby dissipated. The event of Christ's death, understood as a sacrifice, shows God's righteousness (vs. 25). This righteousness needed to be demonstrated or vindicated, because God had not dealt with sin in the past (vs. 25b). This is apparently what was meant by his divine forbearance in passing over former sins. God exercises patience with sin, but not tolerance. In the face of human sin and evil, which has been allowed to go unchecked and unpunished, God must act to demonstrate his righteousness (vs. 26). This could only have been done by an event within human history. It is done in the cross of Christ, which God set forth as an expiation—literally, a means of dealing with sin.

Not only the word translated "sacrifice of atonement" (Greek: *hilastērion*) but a number of other words and expressions found in verse 24 are rare in Paul. For example, even the term *redemption* is not common in his letters. Moreover, Paul does not often speak of the blood of Christ, but of the cross, death, or body of Christ. Paul has probably drawn upon traditional terms and concepts in this definitive statement of the nature and effect of the work of Christ. The source of his language may be the words of institution of the Lord's Supper (1 Cor. 11:23–26; Matt. 26:26–28; Mark 14:22–24; Luke 22:17–19), where Jesus interpreted his own coming death as a sacrifice. Jewish sacrificial, cultic language was used early on to explain Christ's death. Indeed, the belief that Christ's death was a sacrifice for sin is quite common in the New Testament (cf. 1 Cor. 15:3; John 1:29; 1 Pet. 2:24; 1 John 2:2; and the theme of the entire Epistle to the Hebrews). Paul here identifies his own view of the work of Christ with commonly accepted ideas (cf. also 2 Cor. 5:21; Gal. 3:13), if he is not drawing directly upon earlier creedal or liturgical formulations. Elsewhere he was able to develop other interpretations of the significance of Christ's death independent of the sacrificial imagery (cf. 1 Cor. 1:18–25; 2 Cor. 5:16 ff.). Already in this passage he places emphasis on faith (vs. 25). Although the first clause of verse 26 only reiterates what has been said in the previous verse, the second and concluding clause takes the thought further and in a decidedly Pauline direction. God shows himself to be righteous in justifying the person of faith.

The Greek verb translated "justify" (*dikaioun*) has exactly the same stem as the Greek noun translated "righteousness" (*dikaiosynē*). Therefore, according to the literal sense of the Greek word, to justify means "to make righteous." In Paul's thought, however, this process is not simply an infusing or a miraculous re-creation or transformation, but is in the first instance a reckoning. As one can see (chap. 4), God reckons faith as righteousness and thus puts the believer in the right before him.

The model that Paul has in mind is the law court, with God the righteous judge. Thus it is a *forensic* righteousness, the verdict of righteousness pronounced over a person on trial. Quite clearly, then, this righteousness is less an ethical quality than a relationship. A person who is righteous in this sense

Sacrifice of a bull. To the left is Nike and in the center stands a beardless figure, probably Heracles. Pre-350 B.C.   *(Courtesy of the British Museum.)*

is one who is vindicated in the court of law, or acquitted. That person is declared righteous. He is put in the right before God.

That *righteousness* has this forensic meaning in Paul is plain in such passages as Romans 3:4, where Paul quotes Psalm 51:4 (here we find the verbal form translated "justified"), and 8:34, where the act of justifying is set over against that of condemning in the context of a court scene when the

judge pronounces a verdict. (Cf. Gal. 3:11 and Rom. 3:20, where the forensic meaning is also clear, and 1 Cor. 4:4, where the verb *dikaioun* is best
translated "acquitted," as in NRSV.) The scriptural precedent for this understanding of righteousness in the sense of "to pronounce righteous" can
be seen in Isaiah 43:9:

> Let all the nations gather together, and let the peoples assemble . . .
> Let them bring their witnesses to *justify them* [that is, pronounce them
> righteous],
> and let them hear and say, "It is true."[3]

Although this quotation shows a certain agreement between the Pauline
and older biblical understanding of righteousness, there is also an important
difference with respect to the righteousness of God. For the Old Testament
and Judaism generally it is self-evident that the *sinner* is not to be acquitted
("justified"), but the *righteous person* (Exod. 23:7; Prov. 10:27 ff.; Ps. 1). Paul,
on the other hand, maintains that God pronounces precisely the ungodly as
righteous (Rom. 4:5; 5:7 f.) and this is the marvel of the gospel.

Paul does not, however, envision God merely as a judge who sits somewhere in heaven, aloof from human affairs, holding court and pronouncing
verdicts. The righteous God is a saving God, and his righteousness and salvation are closely related. The scriptural background of this relationship can
be seen in the Hebrew literary construction known as synonymous paral-
lelism, in which the second line of a couplet is synonymous with the first:

> The Lord has made known his victory, he has revealed his vindication
> [Septuagint *dikaiosynē* = righteousness] in the sight of the nations. (Ps. 98:2)
> I bring near my deliverance [righteousness], it is not far off, and my salvation
> will not tarry. (Isa. 46:13)
> I will bring near my deliverance [righteousness] swiftly, my salvation has gone
> out. . . . (Isa. 51:5)

In such passages God's righteousness is understood as a saving act or
event. Similarly, God *reveals* his righteousness in the gospel (Rom. 1:17)
while at the same time manifesting his wrath against sin (1:18). Thus, for Paul
God's righteousness is not primarily an abstract quality. Although a judgment, it is not a disinterested judicial pronouncement. It is an event in which
God goes forth to judge and save—indeed, the climactic deed of salvation in
the history of God's dealing with humanity.

That verdict of righteousness that was expected or hoped for in the final
judgment (cf. Rom. 2:12) has already been spoken in favor of humankind
through Jesus Christ. Although Paul believes that salvation is only consummated at the day on which the Lord returns in judgment (Rom. 13:11; cf. 2
Cor. 5:10), he nevertheless maintains that those who trust in what God has

---

3. Cf. Isaiah 50:8 f.; 58:2. The terms used in the Septuagint are exactly those which Paul
   employs. This is particularly significant in view of the fact that when Paul quotes scripture
   (Old Testament) he usually uses the Septuagint.

done already find themselves in a decisively new situation. Thus they live in a creative tension characterized by past assurances and hope for the future.

Since Paul is here dealing with such central biblical motifs as God's righteousness and human sin, it may seem surprising that he has so little to say about repentance and even forgiveness. The absence of these themes is not coincidental. They are important not only in the Bible, the Old Testament, and Judaism, but for much of early Christianity. (In Luke 24;47, for example, the Christian message is understood to be the proclamation of repentance and forgiveness in Jesus' name.) For Paul, however, human sin requires a more radical change than repentance can bring about. Indeed, the human situation is so dire that a true repentance is virtually impossible. Therefore, God's forgiveness comes not in response to such repentance but only as a sheer act of grace. Only God can rectify the fallen state of the human race. Thus God takes the initiative where human initiative is no longer possible and creates a new situation and relationship.

ABRAHAM AND THE PROMISE TO FAITH (4:1–25)

Why does Paul use Abraham rather than Jesus as the example of faith?

God's saving act in Jesus Christ is appropriated by faith rather than by works of the law (3:27 ff. and chap. 4). That this is no novel idea is shown by the example of Abraham, the father of Israel (chap. 4; cf. Gal. 3). Long before the law was given or even the requirement of circumcision established, "Abraham believed God and it was reckoned to him as righteousness" (4:3; cf. Gen. 15:6). As Paul has already argued in the letter to the Galatians (see pp. 311–314), a person is accounted righteous before God by faith, not works. One is pronounced righteous before God not on the basis of the character or quantity of his deeds—much less the accident of birth—but on the basis of that fundamental conviction or allegiance that determines life.

Now in view of Christ's crucifixion and resurrection this allegiance must focus upon a specific historical person and event. Paul sees Abraham's faith as a general prototype of specifically Christian faith and the righteousness reckoned to him as the model of what the Christian receives by faith—that is, apart from works. Abraham, the father of Israel, shows that faith in God's promise has from the beginning of the story of salvation been the proper attitude before God.

God's Grace and Human Freedom (5:1–8:39)

Faith for Paul is not just believing a set of facts, much less adhering to a theory. Faith is trust in God's faithfulness, living in the new situation that God has created. After having shown the appropriateness and indispensability of faith by his argument based upon Abraham (chap. 4), Paul underscores the reality of this new situation (chap. 5). In fact, chapters 5–8 can profitably be viewed as Paul's effort to show that such a new situation actually exists, despite indications to the contrary.

THE NEW SITUATION (5:1–21)

How has life been changed by the coming of Christ?

As he speaks of this new reality (5:1–5), Paul's writing style changes. To this point he has set forth the revelation of God's wrath and righteousness and argued that the latter can be apprehended only in faith. Now he speaks from the standpoint of the community of faith and in the first person plural. What he has previously sought to establish now becomes his working assumption: "Therefore, since we are justified by faith. . . ." On the basis of the new reality Paul can now speak of "this grace in which we stand." Having been put in the right through God's act in Christ, the person of faith has peace with God and enjoys his grace. For Paul "grace" encompasses the entire Christ event and its effects. Grace is the mode of God's working and the resulting state in which believing humanity is placed. Grace is God's benevolent disposition and action on humanity's behalf, prior to and apart from any human effort and accomplishment—the framework, so to speak, for the response of faith.

The nature of grace is then spelled out (vss. 6–11). Not merely an abstraction, grace has to do with a real and specific event in human history, and recent history at that. Moreover, this event, the death of Christ, took place for the sake of sinful people (vss. 6–8). The pathos of this death is deeply felt by Paul himself (vs. 7). Significantly, Paul does not reckon Christ's death as showing his own love for us, but God's (vs. 8). Paul thus emphasizes not the personal motivation of the man Jesus as he went to the cross but the underlying purpose and disposition of God. For God, even the cross is not wanton and meaningless violence; it is rather the means by which judgment and salvation are made known to and for sinners.

The distinction between salvation as future fulfillment and justification as the present assurance of this future reality now comes to light (vs. 9). "Blood" refers to the death of Christ, again alluding to the sacrificial system. Between verses 9 and 10, however, a subtle shift of terminology occurs. Paul first speaks of being justified (vs. 9), the term used in the key statement of 3:21–23 and in the discussion of Abraham in chapter 4. Now, however, the key words for the same state of affairs become "reconciled" and "reconciliation" (vss. 10 f.). The work of Christ is no longer described in terms of the sacrificial cultus, but of the reorientation of the person. The one who was at odds with God is put in the right ("justified"), thereby at peace with God (5:1) and no longer under the dire threat of his wrath (1:18; 5:9). Paul thus maintains that the death of Christ directly affects the individual, who is transformed from a state of hostility to one of reconciliation and peace. Because the future is no longer in jeopardy, but secure by virtue of the accomplished work of Christ, the believer already has grounds for rejoicing in God through the Lord Jesus Christ (vs. 11). Yet Paul carefully avoids saying that salvation is already present (cf. Rom. 13:11).

In Romans 5:12–21 Paul completes the transition from the discussion of the righteousness of faith (3:21–4:25) to the exposition of the new life that results from God's power and grace. The sentence structure and train of thought break off abruptly at the end of verse 12, but the basic idea is picked up again in verses 15–18. The digression of verses 13 f. is puzzling, because Paul's relatively simple earlier statements about Christ and Adam (1 Cor. 15:21 f. and 45 ff.) seem needlessly complicated by the introduction of the ideas of sin and the law. Paul, however, introduces the complication because he does not see the human problem as one of mortality and its solution as resurrection or the assurance of eternal life. The intrusion of sin and the law, which are integrally related to death (cf. 1 Cor. 15:56), render the human problem more complex, and more deadly.

Death is not simply the termination of vital bodily functions. Instead death follows from sinfulness and ultimately negates and condemns human life. In turn, sin is accentuated rather than removed by the law (vs. 13; cf. Rom. 3:20). Over against this hopeless oppression and bondage Paul places the assurance of God's all-sufficient grace in Jesus Christ. This power (cf. 1:16), effective for humanity in the righteous obedience of Jesus, frees people from the oppressive and enslaving bondage of sin, death, and law. Against this triumvirate are arrayed righteousness, life, and grace. As through one man, Adam, humanity was bound, so in one man, Jesus, humanity is set free. If condemnation and death could follow from one man's disobedience, then freedom and life can follow from one man's obedience.

Paul sees death as the ultimate threat to human life, and sin as the ultimate problem, and knows that the two are interrelated. The human predicament is not just death, for death occurs in a state of rebellion against the Creator and in alienation from one's fellow human beings. This plight is not helped, but worsened, by the law, which says what to do but cannot give the power to do it. Thus not only death but sin and dying in sin become the human fate, without God's ceasing to hold people responsible for their waywardness. One is at the same time responsible for sin and fated to die in it.

Paul has first testified that those who are accounted righteous by faith can live in grace with confidence about their ultimate destiny (5:1–11). Now he has declared that those powers that oppressed humanity are overcome (5:12–21). Thus the rejoicing and reigning of the justified (see 5:2, 3, 11, 17) are not a fancy but a genuine, palpable reality. Whether this assertion can be maintained in the face of life's hard facts and whether conditions have actually changed so that the power of sin, law, and death are overcome are the fundamental questions to which Paul next addresses himself (chaps. 6, 7, and 8).

This entire section (chaps. 5–8) is the center and the heart of Romans, for here Paul sets forth and describes "this grace in which we stand" (5:2). Chapter 5 dealt with this new state in a more or less general way. Now chapters 6–8 take up specific problems and objections, phrased by Paul in the form of a battery of questions that punctuate these chapters: "Should we continue in sin in order that grace may abound?" (6:1); "Should we sin because we are not under the law but under grace?" (6:15); "Do you not know . . . that the law is binding on a person only during that person's lifetime?" (7:1); "What then shall we say? That the law is sin?" (7:7); "Did what is good, then, bring death to me?" (7:13); "Wretched man that I am, who will rescue me from this body of death?" (7:24); "What then are we to say about these things? If God is for us, who is against us?" (8:31); "Who will separate us from the love of Christ?" (8:35). From these questions the reader may correctly infer that chapter 6 deals with the new life under grace and the problem of sin, chapter 7 with the newly found freedom from the oppression of the law, and chapter 8 with the role of the Spirit and the ground of the believer's hope.

Freedom from Sin (6:1–23)

Why not sin to increase God's outpouring of grace?

Paul now poses a problem that probably had already been raised by others. If the believer receives grace in proportion to the sin that must be overcome (5:20 f.), why should one not go on sinning to increase the supply of grace (6:1)? Paul understands the question, but not the motivation of the questioner (6:2 f.). The grace of God in Jesus Christ is indeed freedom (6:15 ff.; cf Gal. 4–5), but freedom *from* sin, not freedom *for* sin. Paul understands sin as an oppressive and finally fatal enemy of humankind, a bondage and a burden. Therefore, he declares that baptism, understood as dying and rising with Christ, is a dying to sin and a rising to "newness of life." Paul assumes that all believers have been baptized and that baptism is the event through which the new believer is united with Christ, particularly with his death and resurrection. Evidently he can presuppose this understanding of baptism among his readers (vss. 3, 6). Taking this concept of baptism as dying and rising with Christ, he gives it his own, ethical, interpretation. For Paul it is most important that baptism not be an end, but a beginning. Anyone who has in baptism died to sin is henceforth freed from it. Life is no longer under sin's dominion. Of course, sin continues to exist as a power and a reality. But to return to sin after having been freed from it in Christian baptism would be a contradiction of the new basis of one's existence. Such a reversal is for Paul unthinkable (vs. 2).

Even though newness of life is already a reality, it calls forth a personal human response. Paul does not believe that this response is automatic; an automatic response would nullify human freedom and genuine responsibility. He therefore exhorts his readers not to let sin reign over them (vs. 12), not to yield themselves to sin (vs. 13); instead they should yield themselves to God as instruments of righteousness and not allow sin to have dominion over them (vs. 14). For Paul there is no question of obtaining newness of life through right behavior, as a reward. What God gives in Christ he gives freely. Further, the acceptance of that free gift takes the form of yielding one's own life to the power and reality to which one has been joined in baptism—that is, to God's redemptive act in Jesus Christ.

Significantly, although Paul speaks of believers' having died with Christ and having risen to "newness of life," he does not say that they have already risen with Christ, that is, experienced his resurrection (cf. also Phil. 3:10–11). In Colossians (2:12) and Ephesians (2:4–6), however, believers are said to have already risen with Christ. Admittedly, the difference is not absolute, for in Colossians and Ephesians ethical implications are drawn from Christians' new, risen status, while clearly in Romans Paul believes that believers are now empowered in ways they had not been previously.

FREEDOM FROM THE LAW (7:1–25)

Why, if the law is from God, does it not save?

A question repeatedly implied, if not explicitly stated (cf. 3:31), in Paul's discussion so far concerns the place of the law. Paul's statements about the law seem to contradict one another. On the one hand, he obviously takes the law (i.e., the law as contained in the Hebrew scriptures) to be the definitive expression of God's will for the ordering of human life (Rom. 2; 3:31). On the other, he maintains that the law does not enable one to escape the sinful and death-oriented existence that is now the human lot (cf. 3:20; 4:15; 5:13, 20). Moreover, as we shall see, the law itself becomes an oppressive factor in humankind's plight.

Paul begins his extended discussion of the law by describing how death sets aside a former legal obligation (7:1–6). The marriage analogy that Paul introduces in verses 1–3 is not completely appropriate for the point he wants to make and, therefore, must not be pressed. What Paul says here makes sense when we see that his argument is simply that a legal obligation is set aside by means of a death. Therefore, as the law binding a woman to a man is set aside by his death, so the law to which allegiance was once owed is set aside through dying with Christ (7:4).

The subsequent discussion of the law (vss. 7–25) ought to be understood in the light of the basic contention that death sets aside the law. Why should this fact be so important to Paul? This long excursus answering the question of whether the law is sin implies the prior question of why one must die to the law, or, conversely, why one may not be saved by it. Why does not life, in the fullest sense of the word, result from keeping the law? The Jew believed that it did, and Paul, as a Jew, had once believed this too. Because his own view of the law's effect had been reversed so radically, however, he has a great deal at stake in showing that death cancels law. After having shown this annulment (vss. 1–6), he proceeds to explain why the law cannot bring about the life it intends (7–25). Paul's question (7:7) introduces this explanation. Is the law sin? To maintain his position and avoid the charge of an-tinomianism, he must answer in such a way as to maintain the integrity of the law (3:31), but at the same time he must refuse to concede that the law in the present situation can rescue humankind from its predicament.

Paul's position is that the law is good, but sin subverts it. This subversion of the law takes place because people are under the power of sin that works in their flesh (7:14). Yet this flesh is not simply to be equated with the phys-ical side of being human any more than is the body of death from which one yearns to be free (7:24). Sin has laid claim upon the intangible as well as the tangible aspects of life. When Paul says that "nothing good dwells within me, that is, in my flesh" (vs. 18), the "me" he speaks of is the fleshly person in Adam, as contrasted to the person in Christ. This individual knows that the law is good, but cannot keep it. Life is a conflict between what is intended and what is actually accomplished (7:13 ff., 21 ff.). Entrapped under sin and flesh, the law only adds to the predicament, because in the very hearing of the law one disobeys and is led further into sin. So, although the law con-tinues to be holy and just and good (7:12), for the person "under the law" in the specifically Pauline sense it is nevertheless fatal (vss. 11, 13).

Significantly, Paul can also relegate religious acts and attitudes to the realm of the flesh, as in Philippians 3:4–6, where he refers to his own Jewish back-ground as "reason for confidence in the flesh" (vs. 4). Moreover, the Judaiz-ers' demand that the Galatian Christians accept circumcision is due to their desire to make a show in the flesh (6:12 f.). Here the twofold connotation of *flesh* is apparent: on the one hand, the physical substance of the body (2 Cor. 12:7), on the other, a way of life (Gal. 3:3). "Flesh" can also be a way of re-ferring to humanity, in the style of the Hebrew scriptures (cf. Rom. 3;20, where NRSV's "no human being" aptly translates what is literally "no flesh").

A central problem of 7:7–25 is that Paul everywhere speaks in the first per-son singular and even in the present tense. Is he, as at first we might think, recounting his own present experience, or does 7:9 indicate that he is speak-ing of his earlier life as a Jew under the law? Or is it possible that by "I" Paul does not really refer to himself at all? In Paul's speech "I" may not mean the speaker or writer personally, but could mean people generally ("one," the German *man*; or the French *on*). Paul uses the first-person pronoun in some such sense in 1 Corinthians 13, where the "I" includes himself but is not lim-ited to him personally. In spite of a long history of interpretation that sees Paul grappling with his own inadequacy and sin in 7:7–25, nothing else in the context or in Paul's letters generally indicates that he had such a pessimistic view of his own possibilities *in Christ.* Quite the contrary; moreover, it is un-likely that this description is a passing moment or phase of his conscious-ness. Further, the passage hardly refers to his previous experience as a Jew, for in Philippians 3:4 ff. and Galatians 1:14 Paul talks about his earlier life and does not indicate that he was anxious or depressed.

Probably the correct explanation of this difficult passage is that Paul writes of his own, or any person's, experience under the law, but that he now sees it from a new, Christian perspective. Thus, Paul speaks of this experience as he could not have before his conversion. Paul the believer writes about his earlier, preconversion experience as he now sees it, not as he understood it at the time. Although the passage cannot apply to Paul's Christian awareness, many Christians have since found their own experience echoed in it. This viewpoint is not surprising, for to retreat into a life under law, rather than under grace, remains a possibility for the believer.

LIFE IN THE SPIRIT (8:1–39)

How does the Spirit affect the believer?

If we understand Romans 7:7–25 as a description of the way in which sin works through the law, rather than as an autobiographical confession or reminiscence, the problem of how to fit it (esp. 7:14) into Paul's personal experience disappears. This reflection is not about something he has felt; Paul is analyzing law, sin, and existence under their dominion rather than portraying his own state of mind. The opening of chapter 8 bears out this interpretation, for here the reverse of the situation described in chapter 7 is presented as typical of Paul and others in Christ. For them a great revolution has occurred (vss. 1–4). Life is no longer dominated and defined by flesh, sin, law, and death—that is, by the old Adam—but by Spirit, righteousness, grace, and life—that is, by the new Christ. God himself has brought about this revolution in the human estate, for the Spirit is God's Spirit. (Paul also speaks of the Spirit of Christ and he does not distinguish between them; see vs. 9.)

The conviction that God has acted decisively on humankind's behalf in the historical appearance of Jesus as the Christ leads Paul to encourage his fellow Christians. He speaks of the Spirit and its assuring role (vss. 16, 23, 26 f.), of the hope that lies ahead (vss. 18–25), and of the invincible plan and purpose of God (vss. 28–30), grounded in God's love (vss. 28, 35, 37, 39). With the magnificent peroration of verses 35–39, Paul ends this central section of his letter, having maintained that the revelation of God's grace as righteousness in Christ has brought about a truly new situation in which the bondage of the old age has been broken and the promise of a new age is finding fulfillment. For Paul the knowledge of this new reality is given in and by the Spirit. The term *spirit* translates the Greek *pneuma,* which, like the Hebrew *ruach,* can also mean "wind" or "breath." Accordingly, in the Old Testament and earliest Christianity the appearance of the Spirit implied the advent of extraordinary divine power (cf. Acts 2 and the discussion in chap. 6; also 1 Cor. 14). Usually Paul means by *spirit* the Spirit of God or Christ, although he also uses the word in a somewhat more general sense of the human faculty (body, soul, and spirit), so it is sometimes difficult to know whether one should speak of spirit with a small or capital letter. For Paul the Lord is the Spirit (2 Cor. 3:17); that is, he does not differentiate precisely between the risen Lord Jesus Christ and his Spirit. The Spirit is Christ's and

"The Sacrament of the Last Supper" by Salvador Dali (1955).   *(Courtesy of National Gallery of Art, Washington, D.C. Chester Dale Collection.)*

God's active and supporting presence in the individual believer and the whole community. As such, the Spirit is also the first fruits (Rom. 8:23) and guarantee (2 Cor. 1:22; 5:5) of the salvation that lies just ahead. In the interim between the earthly appearance of Jesus the Messiah and his coming in glory, the Spirit is given.

In Paul's view the Spirit is both the life-giving power and the ethical guide for the believer's life (Gal. 5:25). Elsewhere Paul contrasts Spirit and letter as if the Spirit had taken over the role of the law (2 Cor. 3:7 f.). Those who live in or by the Spirit live out of God's resources rather than their own and are able to break free from the power of the flesh, that is, the fate of human existence estranged from God ("the law of sin and death" of Rom. 8:2), and to attain life (Rom. 8:9–11). Paul's comprehensive view of the functioning of the Spirit allows him to understand the believer's whole life in terms of the Spirit (Rom. 8:3–8) and its gifts (1 Cor. 12–14, esp. 12:4–11; cf. Gal. 5:22 f.). Thus, he can also think of human spirits as attuned to God's Spirit (Rom. 8:16) and of Christians as "spiritual" in this sense (Gal. 6:1). Nevertheless, Paul does not portray life in the Spirit as invulnerable to sin. One's willing and doing must be in accord with the Spirit in its particular character as the Spirit of God and Christ. Spirit is not merely God's power in the eschatological age. The presence of the Spirit is marked by such qualities as love, joy, peace, and patience (Gal. 5:22) in human relationships. Whatever may be said or claimed, the opposite qualities in human relationships are a sign of the dominance of the flesh (Gal. 5:19 ff.). Paul exhorts his readers not to live according to the flesh (Rom. 8:12 f.), but with the Spirit which is given in the new age for a new obedience (see 12:1 ff.).

God's Faithfulness (9:1–11:36)

Why does Paul not concede that God has abandoned the Jewish people?

With the coming of the new age in Christ and the consequent fulfillment of God's promises in the new Christian community, a serious question is raised about the promises of God to the old community, Israel (see 3:1 ff.). Paul sees the event of Christ's coming within the framework of a larger history of interaction between God and humanity that centers in Israel and is recorded in the Hebrew scriptures. For him the question now revolves about that history and those promises. Were they meaningless and are they now null and void?

Before Paul seriously tackles this question he makes clear by way of introduction (9:1–5) his abiding kinship with Israel, the Jewish people. He as-

This wall is part of the original wall of Herod that enclosed the temple area. Known as the "Wailing Wall," it has become sacred to adherents of Judaism. *(Courtesy of Israel Information Services.)*

sumes, however, that the Jews have not, for the most part, accepted Jesus as the Messiah; thus they remain outside the circle of the new community (vss. 1–3). This situation is the crux of the problem with which Paul wrestles in Romans 9–11. Paul will not write off his kinsfolk, nor will he concede that God has written them off. Although because of Christ Paul discounts his own Jewish religious pedigree and accomplishments (Phil. 3:7), he is unwilling to discount the distinctive position of Israel as a people before God (9:4 f.; cf. 3:1 ff.).

Yet Paul's fundamental reason for regarding the given situation as a problem has to do with God, not Israel. For if the word of God has in fact failed, if God has simply canceled his promises, then everything that has been said by Paul up to this point is called into question, for God's righteousness is then jeopardized by his unfaithfulness (9:6). Paul will not countenance such blasphemy (cf. 3:3 ff.). If God were unjust (9:14), the note of supreme confidence struck in chapter 8 would be undermined. To put it bluntly, if God had reneged on his promises to Israel, how could the Christian be certain that God would not change his mind again? At stake is nothing less than the validity of the promises of God and by implication the character of God as righteous deliverer. For if the promises of God are revocable, then how can one have faith in his righteous judgment on humanity's behalf in Jesus Christ? Paul now turns to the questions of the faithfulness and righteousness of God in history (cf. Rom. 3:1–8). Thus Romans 9–11 is not an appendix dealing with a question that has become peripheral. Rather, for the gospel to make sense, Paul must show that God's faithfulness vindicates itself in history.

In four different ways Paul meets the implied charge that the word of God has failed. In the first place, he argues that God's promise was always based on the principle of election or choice (9:5–26). Moreover, this promise is not automatically passed down from one generation to the next, but is a dynamic process in history by which God continues to call and to choose (9:6b–13). It might appear that Paul thought God somewhat capricious in this respect (vs. 5:18). Indeed, he seems to defend that capriciousness (vss. 19 ff.). Yet here Paul grounds election in a prior faith in God as Creator and Lord of creation (vss. 20 ff.), for what Paul ultimately has in view is not God's arbitrary rigor but his mercy (vss. 22 ff.). Moreover, the rejection of large numbers of the children of Israel is predicted by the prophets Hosea and Isaiah (vss. 25–29). Thus God himself has declared that it must occur.

In the second place, sufficient grounds for the rejection of Israel can be found in her own misguided effort to please God. In 9:30–10:4 Paul clarifies the concept of the righteousness of God. Because Israel has not understood that God's righteousness is to be received by faith (9:30 ff.), she has sought to establish her own by works (10:3). But Paul insists that God's righteousness cannot be earned. God pronounces people righteous and thus brings them into the right before himself through the cross of Jesus. Christ becomes "for us . . . righteousness" (1 Cor. 1:30), and in the apostles' preaching the cross of Jesus is said to be the revelation of God's righteousness (1:16 f.; cf.

1 Cor. 1:18 ff.). If there is any effort to establish one's own righteousness, then the gift of God is refused.

Israel thus brings reprobation upon herself (9:30–10:4; cf. 3:3 f.). To make clear that the responsibility rests fully upon Israel, not God, Paul contends that Israel has in fact heard the preaching of the gospel and rejected it (10:5–21, esp. 14–21). He drives home this point not by making specific references to the preaching of good news to the Jews, as he certainly could have, but by once again referring to scripture (10:18–20).

So far Paul has assumed the unbelief of Israel as a condition calling for explanation. Beginning with chapter 11, however, Paul's argument takes a new tack as he makes his third point. To the question of whether God has rejected his people, Paul now says no. He himself is an Israelite (11:1). The example of Elijah (vss. 2–4) serves to show that Paul is not alone: "So too at the present time there is a remnant, chosen by grace" (vs. 5). Paul combines Isaiah's concept of the remnant with the idea of election already set forth in chapter 9 and his own understanding of the gospel as God's grace. Actually what Paul says here fits well with the election doctrine of chapter 9. God's grace in Jesus Christ becomes the point at which the process of election in history takes another step forward, while the remnant from Israel provides continuity with the Old Testament people of God. So far, Paul's exposition of the way in which God works in history does not differ in principle from the Hebrew scriptures' understanding, or at least his interpretation of them. God elects according to his own free choice rather than according to national, ethnic, or familial principles. The only unhappy aspect of this doctrine is that God's election seems to work through a process of elimination, whereby the number of the elect becomes progressively fewer—not exactly a happy outcome except that presumably God could have elected to save no one at all.

The discussion then takes another decisive and surprising turn as Paul makes his fourth point (11:11). The prospect is not pessimistic, as we might have been led to expect. Paul now expounds his expectation of God's continuing work in history for the salvation of Jew as well as Greek (vss. 11–32). The salvation of the Gentiles is to make the Jews jealous and thus to bring them back into the fold.

How seriously one can take this view of history is at least a legitimate question. For one thing, Paul did not anticipate an indefinite continuation of world history (see Rom. 13:11 f.). He thought history was coming rapidly to a close, and that Christ would soon return. Of course, the sequence of eschatological events that Paul anticipated has not occurred. The conversion of the Gentiles does not seem to be complete, although "the full number of the Gentiles" (vs. 25) may not mean every Gentile. Moreover, there is not yet any indication of the conversion of Israel. Paul's image of the olive tree (vss. 17–24; cf. Jer. 11:16) nevertheless provides a graphic picture of his understanding of Gentile Christianity's relationship to contemporary Judaism and to the true Israel of God represented by the root of the tree. Gentile Christians are branches grafted in only because some original branches were broken off. The olive tree itself is the new universal people of God intended to comprise both Jew and Greek. The imagery ought not to be interpreted as Paul's attempt to predict the future; instead we have here an affirmation of faith in the ultimate fulfillment of God's purposes.

In concluding his argument, Paul here neatly summarizes an important paradox of Christian faith: "For God has imprisoned all in disobedience, so that he may be merciful to all" (11:32). This astounding statement is neither a passing thought nor a means of easing a difficult predicament into which Paul's argument has led him (cf. the occurrence of the same basic idea elsewhere, notably in 5:18–20 and Gal. 3:22). Even in the extremity of his severity, God's purpose, the end and goal of his activity, is mercy. In the history of peoples, as of individuals, God's saving activity is grace, surpassing and contradicting human expectation and hopes, appearing where least expected and on behalf of the ungodly (4:5). For Paul, the ungodly are in the end all people; ". . . so that he may be merciful to all" (vs. 32).

The final paragraph of this chapter and of this section of Romans is a confession in almost hymnic form (vss. 33–36). Paul wishes to emphasize the continuing mystery, which his elaboration has only partly exhausted. The seeming triumph of iniquity in the human race is deceptive. The complete revelation, which is God's to give, is not yet fully disclosed. God continues to work in history to the end that he may have mercy upon all. Yet Paul's faith is not in his own theology of history, but in the God who makes his mercy known in Christ: "For from him and through him and to him are all things. To him be the glory forever. Amen" (11:36).

The Obedience of Faith (12:1–15:13)

Why not just accept God's grace and be done with moral striving?

A major division in the structure of Romans occurs after the hymn of praise that concludes Paul's discussion of the destiny of Israel (11:33–36). With a general exhortation (12:1–2) Paul introduces a series of ethical instructions that concludes at 15:13. The character of this long section and its relation to what precedes can best be grasped by looking closely at the introductory exhortation.

Paul bases his appeal (vs. 1) on the "mercies of God." The most likely clue to the meaning of this term is to be found in the word "therefore," which suggests that Paul grounds what he now proposes to say in what has gone before. Chapters 1–11 might then be understood as an exposition of the mercies of God, in the sense of the merciful activity of God on behalf of sinful and wayward humanity. Paul is basing his ethical exhortations on the prior claim that God has on believers by virtue of the grace shown them in Jesus Christ. The indicative ("what God has done for you") becomes the ground for the imperative ("what you must do for your fellow human being"); moreover, this is altogether characteristic of Paul's thought. This interpretation of the mercies of God also suggests that Paul is picking up in 12:1 the theme of mercy from 11:32: "For God has imprisoned all in disobedience so that he may be merciful to all."

"To present your bodies as a living sacrifice" and "spiritual worship" (vs. 1) are perplexing phrases. Here, as previously (cf. 3:21 ff.), Paul appropriates the language of the sacrificial cult at a crucial point of his exposition. Obviously, such language cannot be taken literally, for it is quite clear that Paul is not talking about a material sacrifice when he speaks of "spiritual worship." Paul means a personal commitment or offering to God in response to his mercy in Jesus Christ. By the sacrifice of the body Paul means the surrender of the self, which has heretofore been subjected to sin, flesh, and death (cf. 8:9–11; 7:21–25). Thus the sacrificial language is quite appropriate when understood in terms of "spiritual worship."

Paul next introduces the tension between present and future that is characteristic of early Christian eschatology (vs. 2). The NRSV's alternative translation, "Do not be conformed to this *age*," is almost surely more accurate than "this *world*." As we have already seen, the coming of Christ has inaugurated a new age, even though the old age continues. Believers must no longer conform to the old age as the regulative principle of life, but to the new, which they have entered. They should be transformed by the *renewal* of the mind.

The mind here evidently means both the knowing and willing faculties, but the importance of the mind as the seat of intelligence and common sense should not be understated. Paul does not believe that anyone can come to God through rational means alone. Nevertheless, he deems it possible and necessary for the one who has come to God in faith to exercise his mind in God's service to discern God's will. "What is the will of God . . . good and acceptable and perfect" is to be discerned and then proved (cf. RSV) in the doing of the deed as well as in contemplating it.

This appeal (12:1–2) forms the connecting link between Paul's long theological discourse in chapters 1–11 and the ethical exhortations of chapters 12–15. These exhortations are of a general and more or less stereotyped nature, but whether they reflect Paul's own firsthand knowledge of the situation among the Christians in Rome is a good question. Doubtless they indicate the state of Paul's own thinking and perhaps to a considerable degree the problems that he encountered in other churches. Probably they also contain certain pre-Pauline traditional materials.

The use of the image of the body to illumine the relation of Christians to one another and to Christ (12:3–8) recalls its earlier and more extensive elaboration in 1 Corinthians 12 and forms the basis for further exhortations (vss. 9–13). The general ethical injunctions of 12:14–21 recall the Old Testament and (vs. 20) the words of Jesus (Matt. 5:44 and Luke 6:27). Yet Paul may actually be quoting directly from Proverbs 25:21 f. rather than giving Jesus' own words. This would account for the inclusion of the "burning coals" clause, which is not found in Jesus' sayings.

The discussion of the governing authorities (13:1–7) is strikingly similar to 1 Peter (2:13–17) and, if 1 Peter is not dependent upon Romans, probably indicates the existence of a common viewpoint and tradition regarding the relation of the church to worldly authority (cf. 1 Tim. 2:1–2; Tit. 3:1). In 13:7 we may see a dim reflection of the teaching of Jesus of Mark 12:13–17. Similarly, 13:8–10 evokes Mark 10:19, especially 12:31, but without conforming closely enough to suggest any direct dependence. The eschatology of 13:11 ff. is quite Pauline (cf. 1 Cor. 7:31; 1 Thess. 4:13–18), as is the manner in which eschatology and ethics are combined (cf. 12:2).

Chapter 14 continues the ethical reflections about the Christian's responsibility to his brother or sister that we have already studied in 1 Corinthians 8 and 10. Paul takes the theological position of the strong (15:1) to be correct, as he does in 1 Corinthians, but admonishes others who consider themselves strong on their responsibilities to the weak, who have dietary or similar scruples. In 15:1–3, as he is bringing his exhortations to a close, Paul introduces the example of Christ himself (Phil. 2:5–11; cf. 1 Pet. 2:21; Mark 8:34, 10:38 ff.). The principle of scriptural interpretation enunciated here (vs. 4) is stated more extensively in 1 Corinthians 9:8–10; 10:6, 11; and 2 Corinthians 3. Paul then introduces the subject of the Gentile mission by means of further scriptural quotations (15:7–13) and thus prepares the way for his reflections upon his own missionary accomplishments and plan (15:14–33).

These hortatory chapters of Romans are not merely perfunctory admonitions. Faith for Paul is not abandonment of moral responsibility, but the way to come to obedience to God (Rom. 1:5; 15:18). As he stresses repeatedly, faith in Christ does not overthrow the law but upholds it. Paul has absolutely no tolerance for a Christianity that is morally lax or indifferent. That would be as much "another gospel" or "no gospel" as the legalism of the Judaizers in Galatia. Thus the concrete ethical exhortations and advice in Romans 12:1–15:13 are entirely in accord with—in fact, the outgrowth of—Paul's fundamental theological stance. The gospel must elicit a faithful response that is obedience to God, and this obedience of faith must have specific relevance for the actual situations of life.

Closing (15:14–16:27)

How does the closing relate to the rest of Romans?

Paul's discussion of his accomplishments and plans for the immediate future is important for setting Romans in its *historical context* (see "Notes on Romans"). Paul obviously regards his work as entering a new phase, to be marked by a visit to Jerusalem (vs. 25), his long-awaited journey to Rome (vss. 28–29), and ultimately further missionary endeavors in Spain (vs. 28). The concluding chapter of Romans (16) is a series of personal greetings and commendations to and from Christians either in Rome or with Paul.[4] In this letter Paul gives the Romans an introduction to his theology, his understanding of the gospel, while at the same time correcting misinterpretations by his opponents within the church. He clearly intends to gain their approval and moral support—perhaps also their financial or logistical support—for his mission to Spain. Thus Romans apparently was written after the Corinthian crisis was resolved, probably while Paul was on the road between Corinth and Jerusalem, in the act of bringing the collection to the poor among the saints in Jerusalem (Rom. 15:25–26; cf. Acts 20:2–6; 21:4, 11–19; 24:17). Indeed, as we have noted, there are in Romans traces of the Corinthian, as well as the Galatian, conflicts and correspondence.

Conclusion

We have just considered the *historical context* of Romans, which is closely related to its character and purpose. In Romans more than in any other letter, Paul is in conversation and debate with his Jewish heritage and theological background. Not surprisingly, then, Paul makes a concerted effort to do justice to his traditional roots, both Jewish and Jewish Christian. Thus Romans contains a considerable amount of traditional material of which 1:2–4 and 3:24–26, as well as much of the hortatory material of chapters 13–15, afford good examples. Yet one cannot make much headway in distinguishing *tradition* from *redaction* in Romans, for Paul is more likely to pick up traditional language and concepts than to use extended sources. Moreover, such traditional materials or concepts as he adopts have been well assimilated to his thought. It is more profitable simply to ask what Paul has stated and what he intended. Although there are real difficulties of interpretation, the broad outline of his thought are clearly discernible from the structure and emphases of Romans.

The *structure* of Romans is actually a kind of theological argument, and in that respect unlike any other book in the New Testament. It has to be studied in its entirety to be understood, and such a study has been outlined in this chapter. After a long introduction, in which the themes of the letter, especially the righteousness of God, are set forth, Paul gives an extensive account of the human condition, in which he concludes that sin has pervaded

---

4. Because of certain manuscript evidence and the known relation of a number of the persons named in this chapter to the Ephesian or Asian churches, some scholars have proposed that Romans 16 was originally a separate note to Ephesus, or that it was attached to a version of Romans sent to that destination. As intriguing as this thesis is, it is no longer regarded as likely. A Roman destination makes good sense of the letter as a whole, and the textual evidence against it is slim and can better be explained in other ways. That chapter 16 (but not the doxology of 16:25–27) was an authentic part of the original letter to Rome has been convincingly argued by Harry Gamble, Jr., *The Textual History of the Letter to the Romans: A Study in Textual and Literary Criticism* (Grand Rapids, MI: Eerdmans, 1977).

the entire human race and has left all Jews as well as Gentiles in need of redemption (1:18–3:20). Paul then turns to the sacrificial and saving death of
Jesus (3:21–26) and to the necessity of faith as the only way the benefits of
that death can be appropriated. Abraham is brought forth as the prime example and the confirmation of the saving efficacy of faith: "Abraham believed
God, and it was reckoned to him as righteousness" (Rom. 4:3; cf. Gen. 15:6).

The beginning of chapter 5 marks a turning point in the letter. Paul shifts
from an argumentative to a confessional style and from the second and third
persons to the first. Chapters 5 through 8 are concerned with the question
of whether and how the conditions of human existence have been changed
by Christ's coming. According to Paul, because of God's love and deed in
Christ (chap. 5), believers live a new life in this world even before salvation
has fully arrived and while the world continues to decay. They are able to
overcome sin (chap. 6); they are no longer under a law they cannot fulfill
(chap. 7); and they are full of the Spirit of life and free from death (chap. 8).
Thus in chapters 5 through 8 Paul spells out the nature and effects of "this
grace in which we stand" (5:2).

Chapters 9 through 11 are concerned with the question of God's faithfulness to his promises to Israel, a question lurking in the background since
3:3 f. This is an urgent matter, because on Paul's own terms Israel does not
seem to be inheriting the promise. If God has been faithless with Israel, can
he be counted on to be faithful to the Christian church? Yet it is not God but
Israel who has defected on the terms of the promise. Moreover, Paul maintains that at length even a wayward Israel, whose seeming apostasy will lead
to the salvation of the Gentiles, will return to God's favor and be saved.

The final major section of the letter spells out the meaning of Christian
faith for life's various circumstances (12:1–15:13). Paul scarcely strives for
comprehensiveness; rather, he lays down guidelines and directions, often relying on earlier and traditional formulations to specify what the obedience
of faith (1:5) demands in concrete situations. Here as elsewhere the imperative, what the person in Christ is to do, flows from the indicative, what God
in Christ has done. Thereafter, Paul gives an insight into his view of his own
groundbreaking apostolic work, sketches out his plans to visit Rome and
eventually to go to Spain (15:14–33), and ends with sundry words of personal
greeting and a final general exhortation (chap. 16).

The principal *emphases* of Romans should already be apparent from our
study of the text and its structure, but they can now be stated more succinctly.
Romans concerns the meaning of the event of the Messiah's coming, particularly the fact of his death and the faith that he is risen. This event sheds light
backward, so to speak, to show the enormity of human sin, and forward to
show the richness of human freedom and life under grace. Paul carries on his
discussion against the background of problems and assumptions arising out
of his Jewish heritage. Thus the meaning of Jesus' coming as the Christ is not
discussed in abstraction, nor simply over against the problems of human existence in general, but primarily with the history of Israel and her under-

standing of God and humanity in view. The principal question arising out of that heritage in the light of the revelation of God's righteousness and wrath in Christ is how sinners can be accounted righteous before God. For Paul, the righteousness of God is revealed in Jesus Christ; it is an action and pronouncement of God. God bestows his righteousness freely. Thus he shows himself to be a righteous and gracious God. Faith is the proper response to God's graciousness. This means, first of all, that one must trust in what God has done in Jesus Christ. But this trust is not intellectual assent in the abstract. It finds expression in a new life. The possibility and power of the new life are already given. Still, life must actually be lived out in the community of faith and love. Thus Paul not only speaks to his hearers in the indicative mood to tell them what God has done, he also appeals to them in the imperative mood to make their lives conform with this new reality. Meanwhile God continues to work, sometimes in mysterious ways, for the salvation of Jew and Greek.

Suggestions for Further Reading

ROMANS

C. K. Barrett, *A Commentary on the Epistle to the Romans* (New York: Harper & Row, 1957), is still useful. E. Käsemann, *Commentary on Romans,* trans. G. W. Bromiley (Grand Rapids, MI: Eerdmans, 1980), is a major exegetical–theological work, but will be of limited use to the student who does not know Greek. The same is true of C. E. B. Cranfield's two-volume commentary on Romans in the International Critical Commentary's new series (Edinburgh: T. & T. Clark, 1975, 1979), as well as J. D. G. Dunn's two-volume commentary in the Word Biblical Commentary series (Dallas: Word Books, 1988). There is, however, a more popular commentary by Cranfield, *Romans: A Shorter Commentary* (Grand Rapids: Eerdmans, 1985). Also accessible to the general reader is the reliable commentary of P. J. Achtemeier, *Romans* (Atlanta: John Knox, 1985). More technical, but not presuming Greek, is J. A. Fitzmyer, *Romans: A New Translation with Introduction and Commentary* (New York: Doubleday, 1993).

For a collection of significant essays, see K. P. Donfried (ed.), *The Romans Debate,* rev. ed. (Peabody, MA: Hendrikson, 1991). On Paul's purposes in writing to Rome, see A. J. M. Wedderburn, *The Reasons for Romans* (Edinburgh: Clark, 1988), On the Roman church to which Paul wrote, see R. E. Brown and J. P. Meier, *Antioch and Rome: New Testament Cradles of Catholic Christianity* (New York: Paulist, 1983).

PAULINE THEOLOGY

Romans sets in clear focus issues of Paul's theology, and indeed is climactic and central in the development of Paul's thought. Still an important treatment of that theology is R. Bultmann, *Theology of the New Testament,* vol. 1, trans. K. Grobel (New York: Scribner's, 1951–55), pp. 185–352. V. P. Furnish, *Theology and Ethics in Paul* (Nashville: Abingdon, 1968), makes a useful contribution, including a survey of modern interpretations of Paul's ethic. J. C. Beker, *Paul the Apostle: The Triumph of God in Life and Thought* (Philadelphia: Fortress, 1980), deals with Paul's theology in its Jewish apocalyptic framework and addresses the problem of drawing out the coherence of thought from letters that are addressed to specific occasions and problems. The central motif of Pauline theology is illumined by C. B. Cousar, *A Theology of the Cross: The Death of Jesus in the Pauline Letters* (Minneapolis: Fortress, 1990). Important scholarly works that view Paul against a contemporary Jewish background include A. Schweitzer, *The Mysticism of Paul the Apostle,* trans. W. Montgomery (New York: Holt, 1931); W. D. Davies, *Paul and Rabbinic Judaism,* 4th rev. ed. (Philadelphia: Fortress, 1980); K. Stendahl, *Paul Among Jews and Gentiles and Other Essays* (Philadelphia: Fortress, 1976); and E. P. Sanders, *Paul and Palestinian Judaism* (Philadelphia: Fortress, 1977), who enters into dialogue with Schweitzer, Bultmann, and Davies. The Pauline Theology Group of the Society of Biblical Literature is producing a series of volumes treating aspects of Pauline theology and its formulation. J. M. Bassler (ed.), *Pauline Theology, Volume 1: Thessalonians, Philippians, Galatians, Philemon* (Minneapolis: Fortress, 1991), and D. M. Hay (ed.), *Pauline Theology, Volume 2: 1 and 2 Corinthians* (Minneapolis: Fortress, 1993), have already appeared.

For Paul's use of scripture (i.e., the Christian Old Testament) there is a clearly written introduction, J. W. Aageson, *Written Also for Our Sake: Paul and the Art of Biblical Interpretation* (Louisville, KY: Westminster/John Knox, 1993). Important also for its contemporary literary–critical, as well as theological, insights is R. B. Hays, *Echoes of Scripture in the Letters of Paul* (New Haven: Yale University Press, 1989).

Chapter 10

Pauline Letters:
The Emerging Church

Colossians: Steadfastness against Heresy
        Warning against Erroneous Teaching (Col. 2:8–15)
Ephesians: Looking to the Foundation
        The Unity of the Church (Eph. 2:11–22)
The Pastorals: The Community as Institution
        Care of the Church (1 Tim. 4:1–16)
Hebrews: The True High Priesthood
        Jesus' Qualifications as High Priest (Heb. 4:14–5:10)

*E*ven the most casual reader must be impressed with how much of the New Testament is in one way or another related to the apostle Paul. Thirteen letters are ascribed to him. Another letter or treatise, Hebrews, came into the New Testament under his banner, and more than half the Book of Acts is devoted to his missionary work. Paul is the apostle to the Gentiles, not only according to his own claim but also by virtue of the place he holds in the New Testament. The reader who goes straight through the New Testament first encounters Paul in Acts, then after Romans reads the numerous letters addressed to special situations and crises of Paul's churches, and finally in the Pastorals meets the ministerial Paul, concerned with church office and administration. Hebrews, which deals so extensively with the sacrificial work of Jesus—also a theme of Paul's theology—and exhorts believers to continued faithfulness, stands at the boundary of the Pauline corpus.

We have already considered the letters that Paul himself wrote. (Of these, only 2 Thessalonians is at all questionable.) In this chapter, we treat the Pauline letters that are more doubtful (Colossians and Ephesians) and those that he almost certainly did not pen (the three Pastoral letters as well as Hebrews). For several reasons, however, these letters can be considered Pauline. They have obviously been ascribed to him by tradition. (This is true even of Hebrews, which nowhere claims Pauline authority.) Moreover, important themes of Pauline theology are developed, or altered, in them, and matters that might have concerned Paul had he lived into the subsequent generation or generations are addressed. These later Pauline letters, as well as the Book of Acts, attest the existence of a Pauline tradition or school that flourished long after Paul had passed from the scene.

Because Paul had Christian opponents during his lifetime, his legacy was not at first universally accepted. In the Epistle of James (2:8–26), perhaps even in parts of the Sermon on the Mount (Matt. 5:18–19; 7:13–23), we may well find polemic against a Pauline point of view. Ebionite (derived from the Hebrew word for "poor"; cf. Gal. 2:10) Christians, who survived into the second century and later, apparently represented a Jewish version of Christianity that was unfriendly to Paul. Clearly anti-Pauline sentiments and statements are also found in the so-called Clementine Christian literature of the second and third centuries. Against such a background, consisting of pro-Pauline and anti-Pauline forces, we should read these later letters ascribed to him.

These letters are treated in roughly their chronological sequence, which is also the descending order of proximity to Paul. That is, the order runs from Colossians, which is closest chronologically and substantially (and is still widely regarded as authentic), to Hebrews, which no one any longer takes to be Pauline, although it may have actually been composed earlier than the Pastorals.

Colossians: Steadfastness against Heresy

Notes on Colossians

There are several kinds of arguments against the authenticity of Colossians: (1) differences in style from the undoubtedly Pauline letters, (2) differences in development of theological thought, (3) the complex character of the erroneous teaching that Paul combats (could it have developed in Paul's lifetime?), and (4) the close relation both in style and thought to Ephesians, which is probably the work of a later Paulinist rather than of Paul himself.

Although none of these arguments taken singly is decisive, taken together they constitute strong grounds for doubting that Paul himself wrote Colossians. That Paul had never visited Colossae (5:4) does not speak decisively on either side, for neither had he visited Rome. In recent scholarship, however, Pauline authorship has been increasingly rejected, without Colossians' necessarily being dated much later than Paul. One of the problems in denying Pauline authorship is to find an alternative setting a generation or so later. The question naturally arises whether Colossians was actually composed by one of Paul's fellow workers in his name. (Timothy joins him in the salutation, but that is commonplace; cf. Phil. 1:1). We shall continue to refer to the author as Paul, despite the valid reasons for doubting the traditional claim.

Stylistic considerations raise doubts about Pauline authorship that even a reading of the English text will sustain. Colossians contains a number of long and well-rounded Greek periods, or sentences, unlike the rough-hewn eloquence of the unquestioned letters. Such differences, which could scarcely be the result of a difference in secretarial styles, are impressive, especially because they seem to be shared by Ephesians. There is another simple but telling bit of evidence. In neither Colossians nor Ephesians does the author address his readers as *brethren* (NRSV: "brothers and sisters"; Greek: vocative plural, *adelphoi*), a form of address found in all the genuine letters.

If Colossians was written by Paul himself, or by one of his associates in his name, it was apparently occasioned by the return of Epaphras from Colossae to Paul in prison, bearing news of the situation of that church (1:7; 4:10, 12 f.). That Archippus is mentioned (4:17) suggests a relationship to the letter of Philemon, where a person of the same name is addressed in the salutation (vs. 2). In fact, a number of the same persons are mentioned in Philemon (vss. 23–24) and Colossians (4:10–17). If Colossians is a later pseudonymous letter, it is difficult to conceive of its setting except in very general terms.

OUTLINE OF COLOSSIANS

Introduction: Salutation and Extended Thanksgiving (1:1–14)
Doctrine of Christ (1:15–2:7)
    Christ's Status (1:15–20)
    Christ's Saving Work (1:21–23)
    Christ's Ministry—Paul's Service (1:24–2:7)
Warning against Erroneous Teaching (2:8–23; esp. 2:8–15)
Exhortation to Good Conduct (3:1–4:6)
    Death and Resurrection the Basis for Christian Conduct (3:1–11)
    General Advice (3:12-17)
    Advice to Families (3:18–4:1)
    Further General Admonitions (4:2–6)
Conclusion: Instructions and Personal Matters (4:7–18)

WARNING AGAINST ERRONEOUS TEACHING (COL. 2:8–15)

Why is the heresy that Paul attacks harmful?

Colossians appears to have been written in part to warn the church of Colossae against the dangers inherent in a certain aberrant form of Christianity, which, for want of a better term, we shall call the Colossian heresy. (*Heresy* and *heretic* are somewhat anachronistic terms, as they presuppose a creedal orthodoxy that did not exist at the beginning of the development of Christian thought, but they are nevertheless useful in describing Paul's Colossian opponents, who seek to put obstacles in the way of true faith.) Our knowledge of this heresy has to be gleaned from the letter's own statements. So the task of understanding it, and of fully understanding Colossians, is a difficult one. But in 2:8–15 Paul gives some hints about its nature. (Although verses 16–23 enlarge upon the description of the Colossian heresy, for the sake of brevity we concentrate here upon 2:8–15.) He characterizes it as "philosophy and empty deceit" having to do with "human tradition" and the "elemental spirits of the universe" and not with Christ (vs. 8.). There is a fundamental opposition between this teaching and the Christian gospel as Paul understands it.

The key phrase (vss. 8, 20) seems to be "elemental spirits of the universe" (Greek, *kosmos*). Paul uses the term elsewhere only in Galatians 4:3, 8 ff., where he apparently regards the observance of Jewish ceremonial law as submission to such spirits. This may also be the case in Colossians (2:20 ff.).

But in Colossians such observance is also an expression of a philosophy or world view in which Christ has a subordinate place. In it the elemental spirits of the universe may have been natural phenomena that were thought to sustain or determine life and therefore were endowed with a semireligious aura—for example, the heavenly bodies, which, like the sun, sustain life, or, like the stars, determine it. Within these natural phenomena the divine influences that work upon humanity were deemed to be active and accessible. Ritual demands and taboos and calendar observances accompanied this "philosophy" (2:16 ff., 20 ff.). For as the universe was filled with such numinous powers, it behooved people to propitiate them through the appropriate ritual. Paul seems to be dealing with what we understand as astrology.

Most disturbing was not ritual observance per se, although Paul would have rejected any insistence upon that, but the heretics' apparent willingness to subsume Christ under the system of elemental spirits. Ancient religious syncretism was in the habit of absorbing strange deities, and Christ presented no special problem. Paul seems to counter the Colossian heretics' claim that the deity dwelt or subsisted in the elemental spirits of the universe when he asserts that the whole fullness of deity dwells in Jesus Christ (vs. 9). The term *bodily* in this connection probably does not refer to the earthly body of Jesus Christ but to the dwelling of the deity in Christ, understood as the body of the church or universe. For in Colossians both church (1:18) and the universe (1:15–17; 2:10) are described as the body of Christ, or the body of which Christ is the head.

"Fullness" (vs. 10) may have been offered by the heretics through subservience to the elemental spirits of the universe. Against this contention it is argued that such "fullness" comes only from Jesus Christ. Far from being subordinate to these elemental spirits, he is the head of every ruler and authority. Paul does not directly deny the existence of such beings, but only insists that they have been subordinated to Christ. Therefore there is no reason for the Christian to have any regard for them. In a different context Paul has already stated the same basic idea (see 1 Cor. 8:5 f.).

Colossians reminds the readers, who may be about to succumb to this misleading teaching, of the real ground of their hope and confidence (vss. 11 ff.). The reference to "circumcision made without hands" (vs. 11; NRSV: "spiritual circumcision") may imply that the Colossian heretics, like the so-called Judaizers of Galatia, demanded that Christians submit to circumcision in the flesh. Christian circumcision, replies Paul, is not "in the flesh" but has the effect of "putting off the body of flesh" (vs. 11). This does not mean leaving this mortal life, of course, but putting off the life that is determined by the flesh. (See the discussion of flesh and spirit, pp. 357 ff. and the reference to "a human way of thinking," literally "mind of the flesh," in 2:18.) The death of the body (and mind) of the flesh occurs in baptism, where the new believer is buried and rises with Christ in a recapitulation of Christ's death and resurrection (vs. 12; cf. Rom. 6). Typically, Paul does not claim that this dying and rising is an automatic or magical occurrence; rather, it takes place through faith. Notice the close relation between sin and death, forgiveness and life (vs. 13), a pattern typical of Paul, who nevertheless usually speaks of righteousness or justification rather than forgiveness.

Although Paul suggests his familiar interpretation of Christ as God's saving act, in verse 15 he introduces another interpretation of Christ's work, one better adapted to the situation in Colossae. Christ, he says, has decisively triumphed over the "rulers and authorities." These are doubtless included among the elemental spirits of the universe, if not identical with them. His redemptive work means not only freedom from flesh, sin, death (vs. 13), and the law (vs. 14) but freedom from the oppressive powers of the universe that have held humanity under their dominion (cf. also Gal. 4:1 ff.). For the baptized believer subjection to such worldly spirits, powers, or authorities was a thing of the past; they had been conquered and rendered harmless or "disarmed." Christ is the universal or *cosmic* redeemer.

Paul now draws the ethical implications of his theological argument, and most of the remainder of the epistle (2:16–4:6) is concerned with them. In 2:16–23 he rejects the spurious asceticism of the Colossian heretics, which does not take account of Christ's lordship over the world but is simply subservience to the things that Christ has already overcome (2:20). Such religiosity, ascetic though it may be, does not finally escape the lordship of the flesh (2:23; note esp. the NRSV's alternative reading). The believer is not, however, subject to the elemental spirits of the universe. He is instead in the realm of the resurrected Christ (3:1 ff.). With Christ and the believer now portrayed as sitting at the right hand of God, Paul seems on the verge of speculative fancy. But such resurrection life is interpreted as this-worldly existence free from the power of sin, death, and "things that are on earth" (vs. 2; Paul probably has in mind those elemental world spirits of which he has already spoken). To all these the believer has died. Life is now secure with God (vs. 3), and the believer hopes to share in the eschatological glory of Christ (vs. 4).

Emphasis on the present reality of resurrection life is nevertheless somewhat strange in Paul, who elsewhere hesitates to speak of believers as if they had already attained resurrection glory (cf. Rom. 6:5 and the future tense as applied to resurrection; also 1 Cor. 4:8). On the other hand, this idea is common in Ephesians (2:4–9), where believers are also said to *have been* saved (2:8). In the uncontested letters of Paul, salvation is reserved for the eschatological future (Rom. 13:11). Believers are in this age justified and reconciled to God so that their future salvation is assured.

Like Ephesians, Colossians makes much of the church as the body of Christ (Col. 1:18, 24; 3:15), an idea that is surely rooted in Pauline thought (1 Cor. 12; Rom. 12:4–8). Yet it is an interesting and perhaps significant fact that the earlier Paul says, "You are the body of Christ" (1 Cor. 12:27) or, "We are one body in Christ" (Rom. 12:5), but never makes the more abstract statement that the church is the body of Christ, although the latter is at least the apparent meaning of his conception. It is as if Colossians and Ephesians are developing a doctrine of the church as the body of Christ from a Pauline metaphor. In Colossians (3:18) and Ephesians (5:23) the metaphor is extended as Christ becomes the head of the church, which is his body.

Ephesians: Looking to the Foundation

Notes on Ephesians

Although Colossians does not clearly imply a time and church situation subsequent to Paul's ministry (unless the erroneous teaching is regarded as post-Pauline Gnosticism), Ephesians does seem to presuppose a different and later setting and manifests other points of divergence from Paul. The indications of this changed situation are subtle, but nonetheless real.

The style of the author's Greek, which is clearly reflected in a good English translation (especially the RSV), is elaborate to the point of ostentation (cf. especially 1:5–23, which the RSV preserves in one sentence, as it is in Greek, while the NRSV breaks the passage down into several English sentences). The sentences also lack the pungency, abruptness, and punch of Paul's rough, but eloquent, style. In this respect Ephesians is farther removed from Paul than Colossians, while at the same time bearing such a close resemblance to it at a number of points that the possibility of literary dependence on Colossians cannot be dismissed (Col. 1:21–22 and Eph. 2:11; Col. 1:25–27 and Eph. 3:4–7; Col. 2:19 and Eph. 4:15–16). Paul sometimes has difficulty ending a sentence (cf. Gal. 2:6–10) because so many thoughts and considerations pile into his mind; in Ephesians, however, the long sentence seems to be a deliberate and eloquent development based on the study of Paul.

There are other differences, which betray a somewhat different theological perspective. For example, the "mystery" spoken of in Ephesians (3:3) is the incorporation of Gentiles, along with Jews, into the body of Christ (3:6), whereas the "mystery" of which Paul speaks in 1 Corinthians (15:51) is apocalyptic; it concerns the transformation of the resurrection. When Paul uses the term in 1 Corinthians 4:1, its meaning is scarcely the same as in Ephesians. This apparent shift in terminology typifies the ecclesial focus of Ephesians; that is, emphasis shifts toward the church as the center of theological interest. This shift is clearly evident in the text that we treat below (2:11–22). There the church is said to be founded upon the apostles and prophets, as if these were ancient worthies rather than contemporaries.

A final characteristic of Ephesians sets it apart from the other Pauline letters: it is a general epistle, not a letter written to a specific church. The oldest manuscripts did not contain "Ephesus" in the salutation, and this omission corresponds with the lack of specific reference to persons and places at the end of the letter. (The RSV's omission of "in Ephesus" better represents the textual tradition than the NRSV's inclusion of it.) Aside from Tychicus (6:21) the conclusion contains no references to persons or

The Marble Street of Ephesus, where modern excavations are uncovering the grandeur of that ancient city. Paul and other Christian leaders founded an important church here.   *(Courtesy of D. Moody Smith.)*

events (cf. Col. 4:7–8). When "Ephesus" falls out of the salutation, Ephesians becomes a letter addressed by Paul to all Christians. Its general, even universal, salutation then corresponds to its content. It is a compendium of Pauline ideas and theology, having close parallels not only with Colossians but also with the other, genuine Pauline letters (cf. Eph. 1:3 and 2 Cor. 1:3; Eph. 4:4, 11 and 1 Cor. 12 or Rom. 12:5; Eph. 6:13–17 and 1 Thess. 5:8).

We can no longer say for what specific purpose Ephesians was written. The suggestion that it was written as a covering letter for the first, or an early, collection of Paul's letters is plausible, but cannot be proven.[1] The earliest-known collection of Paul's letters, that of Marcion (ca. 140), whose views came to be regarded as heretical, contained Ephesians (although not Hebrews or the Pastorals). Thus we can be certain that its reputation and authority had been established less than a century after its composition.

OUTLINE OF EPHESIANS

Address (1:1–2)
Thanksgiving and Praise of God and Christ (1:3–23)
Christ's Work and Its Results (2:1–3:21)

1. Goodspeed sets forth this proposal in *The Meaning of Ephesians* (Chicago: University of Chicago Press, 1933). For a criticism of Goodspeed's position see C. F. D. Moule, *The Epistles of Paul the Apostle to the Colossians and to Philemon* (New York: Cambridge University Press, 1957), pp. 14–18.

THE UNITY OF THE CHURCH (EPH. 2:11–22)

How are the themes of Jew, Gentile, and church related?

The hymn of praise (1:3–23) takes up and elaborates the characteristic Pauline thanksgiving. Whereas the typical thanksgiving makes contact with the concrete situation of the church Paul is addressing, the Ephesian thanksgiving does not. It is long, solemn, and liturgical. The thanksgiving ends with chapter 1, and the second major phase of the letter begins. It is a kind of declaration or address to the readers. The author starts in the second person, "you," but more than once slips over into the confessional first person plural, "we" or "us" (cf. 2:3–7, 10).

The next section (2:1–10) relates God's saving act in Jesus Christ, already set forth in Old Testament imagery (1:15–23; cf. Ps. 110), to believers. The Pauline language and conceptuality are clearly visible. No single passage from Paul's epistles is the source or model of this passage, but many familiar Pauline themes appear. For obvious reasons, 2:8 f. is often quoted as a succinct statement of Pauline theology, and it is, even though it was probably not written by Paul. This whole section is to be placed alongside others in the genuine letters (Rom. 3:21–31; 5:1–11; 1 Cor. 1:18–25; 2 Cor. 5:16–21; and Gal. 2:14–21) as a classical summation of Pauline theology.

The same solemn tone that has so far dominated the letter continues, but in 2:11–22 a subtle shift of emphasis occurs. Whereas 2:1–10 deals with the work of Christ on behalf of individuals, in 2:11–22 attention shifts to the church. Of course, the church was already in view (cf. 1:22 f.), and the individual is not now lost from sight. Nevertheless, in a special sense the passage in question (2:11–22) focuses upon the church. Even though the word *church* does not appear, emphasis falls upon the idea of community and the creation of this community through the death of Jesus.

The author envisions the church as composed primarily of Gentiles rather than Jews (2:11, see also 3:1; cf. 4:17). Inasmuch as he speaks for Paul, he naturally takes the position of the Jew. Already in this verse we read of the existence of two groups, distinguished by their circumcision or lack of circumcision in the flesh. They are both communities in and of the flesh, that is, ethnic communities. As far as the author is concerned, the circumcision made in the flesh by hands does not give the circumcised any particular advantage. Yet this does not mean that Israel as God's people has no theological significance. Here the author remains quite close to Paul's own thought. Israel as an ethnic group, as the circumcision, has no particular advantage, but the same may not be said of Israel as the inheritor of God's promises. The advantage of the Jew or of Israel in the latter sense (cf. Rom. 3:1, 9, and 9:1 ff.) is apparent in the statement that follows immediately (vs. 12). Even the phrase "without Christ" implies the advantage of the Jew over the Gentile, because the Messiah is promised to Israel. To be "aliens from the commonwealth of Israel" is also to be separated from the messianic hope, as is indicated by the phrase "strangers to the covenants of promise." Obviously what is meant are the covenant promises to Israel. Significantly, Gentiles are characterized as "aliens" and "strangers." Their situation is one of being alone, cut off, lost in the most profound and far-reaching sense of the word. Moreover, they are hopeless and godless. Although the author does not grant any particular advantage or significance to fleshly circumcision per se, he ascribes the greatest significance to Israel as the object of God's redemption and the community of God's people. To be alienated from Israel is to be without hope and without God in the world.

The work of Christ is interpreted as the recovery of the estranged (vs. 13). "By the blood of Christ" refers to Christ's death understood as a sacrifice on behalf of humanity. The concept of being "far off" can be understood in the light of what immediately precedes (vss. 11–12). But what is meant by "have been brought near"? Naturally, one would suspect that, since the estrangement was defined in terms of separation from Israel, reconciliation and salvation would be described as union or reunion with Israel. Thus "being brought near" would mean the Gentiles' association, or incorporation, with the covenant people. This is partly what is meant; however, Christ is peace for both Jew and Gentile (vs. 14). He effects reconciliation (vs. 16) between them, making them one (vs. 14) by breaking down the "dividing wall, that is, the hostility between us."[2] Moreover, he sets aside the Jewish law, the commandments and ordinances (2:15). Jesus' abolishing them in his flesh doubtless refers to his death. The author has in mind other similar Pauline statements (cf. Gal. 3:13; Rom. 7:4 and 8:3).

Jesus' death marks the end of the period in which the law holds sway. Thus Christ is the end of the law (Rom. 10:4). By bringing the law to naught Christ does away with the hostility that separates Jew from Gentile, and thus becomes

---

2. The breaking down of the dividing wall of hostility (2:14) is often taken to be an allusion to the destruction of the wall of the Jerusalem temple that separated the court of the Gentiles from the inner court open only to Jews. This would allow those who were far off (the Gentiles) to be brought near (2:13). The destruction of Jerusalem in A.D. 70 and the consequent demolition of the temple walls may have suggested this way of describing the work of Christ. That this allusion to the temple is intended is suggested by the extensive use of temple imagery in verses 20–22.

their peace. It is not simply a matter of Gentiles becoming Jews, for the fundamental status of the believing Jew is also changed. The author's careful qualification of the law as the "law with its commandments and ordinances" implies that Christ sets aside the particular, Jewish formulation of the law of God, but not that he introduces an era of lawlessness. The result of the abolition of the distinction between Jew and Gentile is the creation of "one new humanity" in Christ (vs. 15). The creation of the "new humanity" is the prerequisite for peace among all peoples (vs. 15), as well as with God (vs. 16). This new human being (4:24; NRSV: "the new self") can obey God. (The same Greek word, *anthrōpos,* whence the English *anthropology,* is used in 2:15 and 4:24.) The idea of the *creation* (vs. 15) of the "new" man in place of the "old" man probably intentionally recalls 2 Corinthians 5:17: "So if anyone is in Christ, there is a new creation; everything old has passed away; see, everything has become new!"

The idea that reconciliation comes through the cross of Christ is what we might have expected from a Paulinist (vs. 16), and the term *body* (Greek, *sōma*) is thoroughly Pauline. In fact, Ephesians here combines different Pauline uses. Obviously the primary reference is to the crucified body of Jesus, who becomes a curse for us (Gal. 3:13), who becomes sin, or a sin offering, for our sake (2 Cor. 5:21), who died for our sins (1 Cor. 15:3), whose death is our reconciliation: "while we were enemies, we were reconciled to God through the death of his Son" (Rom. 5:10). In addition, the peculiar wording of Ephesians 2:16, "in one body," implies an identification of those being reconciled with the reconciler. Again the union of the believer with the crucified is a typical Pauline motif: "I have been crucified with Christ" (Gal. 2:19); "you have died to the law through the body of Christ" (Rom. 7:4). Moreover, the body is an important Pauline image signifying the unity of Christians in Christ—that is, the church (Eph. 1:22; 1 Cor. 12; Rom. 12:3–8; see pp. 321–323 above). The initial theme of this passage was community, and the recitation of Christ's work has focused upon its effect in reconstituting unity or community between God and humanity and, especially, among different peoples.

This emphasis on restored community is reiterated (vss. 17 f.). Those who are far off are doubtless Gentiles, and those who are near, Jews (vs. 17). The present unified status before God of both Jew and Gentile is described as "access in one spirit" (vs. 18). Once again, the thought is a legitimate echo of Pauline theology. The idea of a new access to God through Jesus has appeared already (Rom. 5:2). That the mode of this access to God is the Spirit is a thought that pervades Paul's writings (cf., for example, 1 Cor. 12; Rom. 8). The Spirit assures the reality of the new condition enjoyed by the believer. The Spirit and Christ are not to be identified, but the Spirit is the means or mode of Christ's presence, and therefore of access to God.

Mention of the one Spirit leads to the theme of the unity of the new community (vss. 20–22) constituted by the new humanity. Again we have a Pauline web of ideas. For the new community is characterized by the possession of the Spirit, and the Spirit-possessed community is the body of Christ (cf. vs. 16

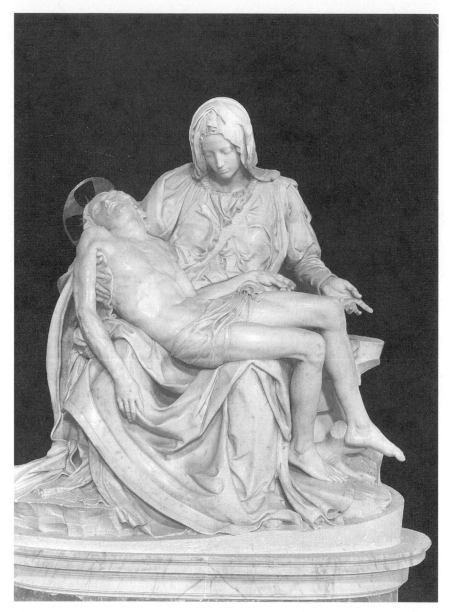

The "Pieta" by the Italian sculptor Michelangelo (1475–1564).   *(Courtesy of Alinari Art Reference Bureau.)*

and 1 Cor. 12:12 f.). The idea of Spirit and body is not developed immediately, however. Instead, another typical Pauline image, that of the house or temple, is invoked, but with some uncharacteristic variations, as we shall soon see.

The author solemnly declares (vs. 19) that the situation of separation (vss. 11 f.) is no more. The Gentiles have been incorporated into the reconstituted humanity that is the church. They are now "citizens with the saints"—that is, Israel. Yet as we have seen, "Israel" herself has been thoroughly redefined through Christ, who puts an end to the law and by implication to the "circumcision made in the flesh by human hands" (2:11). "Saints" (vs. 19) now simply means "those consecrated to God," a biblical idea and a common Pauline designation of Christians (1 Cor. 1:2).

"Household of God" (vs. 19; literally "householders of God") evokes the temple imagery, which is developed in verses 20–22. The foundation of the building that is to be the temple is first described (vs. 20). The description given here may be contrasted to 1 Corinthians 3:11, where Paul emphatically maintains that Jesus Christ alone is the foundation of the building that is the church. Although the sharpness of the disagreement is softened by the designation of Christ as the chief cornerstone (probably the keystone that holds the entire structure together, as in an arch; cf. vs. 21), there is still a considerable and important difference. This difference is heightened when the prophets and apostles are called "holy" (3:5). In contrast to Paul, for whom every true member of the church is holy or a saint (the two words are the same in Greek), the word is here used to set apart the apostles and prophets as a special and superior group within the church—much in the manner in which the words are used in medieval and modern ecclesiastical parlance. The prophets and apostles appear to be elevated as a special group (vs. 20). Even though in Paul's own thought the apostle plays a key role and the prophet is second only to him (1 Cor. 12:28), Paul goes out of his way to maintain that there are no fundamental distinctions among the members of Christ's body (1 Cor. 12, esp. 12:13). Probably the author of Ephesians would not have denied this. Yet the idea of a special status of the apostolate slips into his understanding of the structure of the church.

Ephesians does not, however, consciously downgrade the role of Jesus Christ in favor of the apostles (cf. vs. 21). The church holds together in Christ and grows in him. Although being in Christ is a Pauline concept, there is a new twist here in that the church grows in Christ (vs. 21; cf. 4:13, 15). Again, the Pauline imagery is developed further in Ephesians, and in this passage, by a process of combining motifs. For actually the temple, not the body, is the explicit subject. Yet obviously the concept of growth relates to the body, as is made plain at other points in this letter (cf. esp. 4:12, 16, where the building imagery also appears). Apparently the image of the body is in the background (cf. 1:22 f.; 2:16) and enriches the temple image.

The Gentiles, who at one time were aliens and were brought near and made fellow citizens, are now actually built into a new building or structure, which is to be a dwelling place for God (vs. 22). That God or his glory dwells in his temple is an Old Testament and Jewish idea that was applied to the Jerusalem temple until its destruction. Although that temple had probably been destroyed by the time Ephesians was written,[3] making way for the designation of the church of Christ as the new temple, Paul had already anticipated this event by his use of the temple imagery in relation to the new community and its members (1 Cor. 3:16 f.; 6:19 ff.; 2 Cor. 6:16). Whereas the older view of God's dwelling in his temple envisioned his abiding in a building, in the new conception the "building" is the community of persons, the church. In 1 Peter 2:4 ff., the figure of the building or temple is taken yet a step farther, and the individual Christians, like Christ, are described as "living stones."

The passage we have considered (2:11–22) marks the culmination of the theological themes that the author has been developing. Formally, the theological section of the epistle continues to the benediction at the end of chapter 3. But that chapter is basically a recapitulation of what has gone before, with special reference to the ministry of Paul.

Significantly, the drama of salvation just narrated is now described as Paul's insight into the mystery of Christ (vs. 6): "that is, the Gentiles have become fellow heirs, members of the same body, and sharers in the promise in Christ Jesus through the gospel." Clearly the author regards this as the peculiarly Pauline understanding of the gospel. It is true that for Paul the gospel implies the church, and the church abolishes the distinctions of an age that is already passing away. Moreover, the scriptural prophecies are directed to persons of faith, not to Israel according to the flesh. But Paul does not regard the incorporation of the Gentiles into the body of Christ as his *central* insight into the mystery of the gospel. The elements of the thought are Pauline, but somehow the focus has shifted. There has been a subtle change in the center of interest and emphasis in Ephesians from Christ to the church. This does not mean that the importance of Christ is lessened, or that the church was unimportant to Paul, but that the church as the result of Christ's work and the historical embodiment of Christ increasingly becomes the main subject of the author's theological concern. Hence he takes Paul's central insight to be an ecclesiological one. He returns to the theme of the church again and again (1:22 f.; 2:11–22; 3:6, 10; 4:1–16; 5:21–33; 6:10–20). After chapter 2 what is not explicit discussion of the church is exhortation to the church. This exhortation seems not to be directed to specific, individual problems and situations but to the church in general. Even the practical instructions regarding the relationship of husband and wife are to be seen as expressing the exemplary relation of Christ and the church—"the two shall become one" (5:31 f.).

Ephesians is an exposition of Paul's thought in the light of a new situation. Its concentration of interest upon the church is not un-Pauline so much as it is a development on the basis of Paul. It is, moreover, a development in the light of a peculiar state of affairs that Paul did not anticipate and that, in

3. See note 2, p. 378. If, as we suggest, Ephesians is pseudonymous and not the work of Paul, a date before the destruction of the temple becomes highly unlikely.

a certain sense, makes us and the author of Ephesians closer to each other than to Paul. Paul anticipated the imminent return of Christ and the end of the age. No such urgent anticipation is reflected in Ephesians. The church will have to exist as an institution in this world for quite a while. The solemn injunction to put on the whole armor of God indicates that the author expects a long fight. (Similar imagery appears in 1 Thess. 5:8, but in an eschatological context missing in Ephesians.) Yet Ephesians manifests no weakening of conviction or attenuation of the faith.

The Pastorals: The Community as Institution

Notes on the Pastorals

Whereas Ephesians was originally addressed to Christians generally, the Pastorals are cast in the form of letters to Timothy and Titus, Paul's fellow workers, who are mentioned frequently in the other Pauline letters. According to Acts, Paul found Timothy in Lystra in Asia Minor (16:1; cf. 2 Tim. 3:11). Because his mother was a Jewish believer, and thus Timothy was considered Jewish, Paul circumcised him (16:3). Titus was a Gentile, according to Paul, and was not required to be circumcised (Gal. 2:3). He is not mentioned in Acts.

Unlike the letters previously considered, the Pastorals do not quite fit any situation described in the Book of Acts. According to 1 Timothy, Timothy is in Ephesus, where he has been urged to remain (1:3). Paul himself seems to write from Macedonia (1:3). Possibly the situation envisioned corresponds to 1 Corinthians 16, where Paul plans to travel to Macedonia (vs. 5) and anticipates Timothy's return to Ephesus (vs. 11), although this is entirely hypothetical.

In 2 Timothy Paul is in prison in Rome (1:17), where he has survived one trial (4:16–18), but apparently awaits further proceedings and his own death (4:6–8). Various coworkers of Paul are located, but we are not told Timothy's whereabouts. Quite possibly he is still in Ephesus (1:15, 18). In any event, Paul urges him to join him (4:9).

Titus is in Crete when Paul writes him (1:5), and Paul in Nicopolis (3:12) on the Adriatic shore of Greece, a city mentioned in neither Acts nor the other Pauline letters. According to Acts, Paul did not visit Crete until the final journey to Rome (27:7), and there is no mention of Titus' accompanying him on that journey. Titus might have been composed during a period of Paul's ministry not recorded in Acts, perhaps after his "first defense" (2 Tim. 4:16), assuming he then gained his freedom temporarily. Such reconstructions are highly speculative, however, and are probably unnecessary, for there are significant grounds for doubting that the Pastorals were composed during Paul's lifetime.

The Pastorals were not included by Marcion in the first-known collection of Paul's letters (ca. 140), and one of the earliest papyrus manuscripts of the Greek New Testament (P[46], dating from the end of the second century) does not have, and perhaps never contained, them. Of course, Marcion was condemned as a heretic because he believed that the God of the Old Testament was not the Father of Jesus Christ, and he denied the goodness of creation. He might have rejected the Pastorals as inauthentic for theological reasons, had he known them. We cannot be certain he knew them, but even if he was acquainted with them, he felt that he could reject them without sacrificing his own credibility.

The Greek style and especially the language of the Pastorals are markedly different from the other Pauline letters, including Colossians and Ephesians. The Pastorals have a vocabulary of just over 900 words, 848 exclusive of proper names. Of these, 306 are not found elsewhere in the Pauline letters (as compared with 177 in the genuine 2 Corinthians, which is a bit longer). About 175 words are not found elsewhere in the New Testament; 211 are common to second-century Christianity; only about 50 are distinctly Pauline.[4] There are no dialogues with an imaginary opponent. The syntax does not reflect Paul's emotional involvement. Occasionally there is an obviously poor imitation of Paul (1 Tim. 2:7, where Paul's claim that he is not lying seems pointless; cf. Gal. 1:20). Style, as well as language, are somewhat different from the other Pauline letters.

Moreover, the theology of the Pastorals differs from that of the other letters even, and perhaps especially, where the same words are used. For example, *faith* (Gr. *pistis*) in Paul means the acceptance of God's grace, trusting what God has done in Jesus (see also pp. 311–314). It refers primarily to a believing, faithful relationship. In the Pastorals, however, *faith* means primarily the content or object of belief. Thus the author can speak of "the faith" (1 Tim. 3:9; 4:1; 2 Tim. 4:7), meaning a body of doctrine. This change signals a significant theological difference and suggests a later time, in which the defense of correct belief had become a primary concern; indeed, the danger of heresy has become acute (1 Tim. 6:20–21). Also, righteousness has become a virtue (1 Tim. 6:11), along with godliness, faith, love, steadfastness, and gentleness (cf. 2 Tim. 3:16: "training in righteousness"). It is no longer tied to an action or revelation of God. The statement about the law in 1 Timothy 1:7–11 may sound Pauline but on closer examination is unlike what Paul elsewhere says. The Spirit is spoken of rarely (cf. 2 Tim. 1:14) and the body (or body of Christ) not at all. Religion or godliness (*eusebeia*) plays an important role; by contrast the term does not figure in Paul's other letters.

OUTLINE OF 1 TIMOTHY

Address (1:1–2)
Warning against Heresy and Heretics (1:3–20)
Manual of Church Order (2:1–4:5)
  Worship (2:1–15)
  Qualifications and Duties of the Clergy (3:1–16)
  Appearance of Heresy (4:1–5)
Manual for Ministers (4:6–6:19)
  Teaching in the Church (4:6–16)
  Dealing with Elders and Widows (5:1–22)
  Personal Advice (5:23–24)
  Advice to Slaves (6:1–2)
  Dangers of False Teachers and Teachings (6:3–10)
  Exhortation to Ministers (6:11–19)
Conclusion (6:20–21)

---

4. See P. N. Harrison, *The Problem of the Pastoral Epistles* (Oxford: Humphrey Milford, 1921), pp. 18–86.

CARE OF THE CHURCH (1 TIM. 4:1–16)

Why was an ordained ministry necessary and important?

In the Pastorals the development of church organization or order runs parallel to the development of doctrine. In the other Pauline letters there are various functions and offices in the church, all of which are equally gifts of the Spirit (1 Cor. 12). Although Paul singles out apostles, along with prophets and teachers, as having priority (12:28), he does not distinguish clergy from laity. Apparently, he does not know an ordained clergy, and even where he mentions deacons and bishops (Phil. 1:1) it is not clear he regards them as such a distinct group. In the Pastorals, on the other hand, specific qualifications for bishops and deacons are set forth (1 Tim. 3:1–13). Timothy himself is called a servant of Jesus Christ (1 Tim. 4:6; *diakonos* or deacon) and his ordination by elders is mentioned (1 Tim. 4:14). Yet directions concerning "elders who rule" are given to him, and he is in charge of their ordination (5:17–22). Timothy is obviously a church officer of the highest rank who presides over bishops and elders (cf. Titus 1:5). As such he is the guardian of the faith and doctrine of the church (1 Tim. 6:20–21; 2 Tim. 1:13–14).

That the faith has attained credal formulation is evident from several statements in the Pastorals (e.g., 1 Tim. 2:4–6; 2 Tim. 2:11–13). Possibly distinctively Christian writings are used and extolled in the churches of the Pastorals (2 Tim. 3:15), and all scripture, including the Old Testament, is commended (2 Tim. 3:16). Timothy's faith began with his grandmother Lois, and apparently came down to him through her and his mother Eunice (2 Tim. 1:5). This does not necessarily mean that Timothy was a third-generation Christian, but when we first meet him in Acts (16:1–3) he is already a believer, as was his mother. There is in Acts no mention of his grandmother, but the picture of Timothy as the descendant of a Christian family of long standing fits what the Pastorals otherwise convey: the church is well established, and has been for some time. It is girding itself to live in the world for a period of indefinite duration. This attitude contrasts sharply with that of Paul himself, who thought the day was at hand (Rom. 13:12) and prayed for Jesus' return (1 Cor. 16:22).

The concern to establish church order and church office and to ensure the continuity and stability of church doctrine against heresy or aberration reflects the recognition of the changed conditions under which the church was living. 1 Timothy 4 is a good cross section of the letter, as it reveals most of the distinguishing features of the Pastorals. The first five verses deal with heresy, false teaching, that has arisen within the Christian community. The remainder of the chapter is the opening of the section designated in the outline as a manual for ministers.

When the author says of the heretics against whom he struggles that they were to be anticipated (4:1), the edge is taken off the hard and discouraging fact that even within the community of faith error persists. This unhappy circumstance occurs with the foreknowledge of God; the Spirit predicts it. The same motif appears elsewhere in the New Testament (Acts 20:28–30; Mark 13:5 f.; Jude 18; 2 Pet. 3:3; and 1 John 2:18). The common element in these texts is the fact that the church has been duly warned of the appearance of evil persons within her midst. At an earlier period Paul recognized the existence and danger of such persons (Phil. 3:1 ff.) but said nothing about their having been predicted.

The attitude of our author is intolerant because the heretics have "renounced the faith" by attending to "deceitful spirits" and "teachings of demons" (cf. vss. 1–2). The luxury of allowing each his or her own view in religious matters is impossible for the author. The writer is a churchman concerned about the truth of the Christian message, the church's proper preservation of it, and the obedient ordering of church life in the light of the gospel. The false doctrine that he denounces and deplores has immediate practical ramifications, for the beliefs of the heretics lead inevitably to the wrong ordering of life (vss. 3–5).

The ascetic, world-denying character of their heresy is apparent (vs. 3). Their asceticism—avoidance of sex and certain food—suggests that the opponents are closely related to, if not identical with, the Gnostics denounced by the Christian Fathers in the second century. The earlier description of the false teachers (1:3–7) corresponds rather well with this aberrant form of Christianity. Confirmation is also found at the end, where Timothy is advised to "avoid the profane chatter and contradictions of what is falsely called knowledge" (6:20). The Greek word translated *knowledge* is *gnōsis,* whence the name of this heresy, Gnosticism. The widespread appearance of this heretical version of the Christian gospel, which defined the Christian message as a program of escape from this evil world to a good one above, was one of the most important developments in the history of second-century Christianity. 1 Timothy probably represents an early stage in the emergence, identification, and rejection of the Gnostic viewpoint. Perhaps an even earlier stage of the heresy is resisted in Paul's own writings, possibly in the Corinthian correspondence (and very likely in Colossians). We cannot assume, however, that Gnosticism is the only heresy attacked in the Pastoral letters.

In opposition to this specious and harmful asceticism, the author lays out his own position (vss. 4 f.). His view had already been adumbrated in verse 3 ("received with thanksgiving"; cf. the same phrase in vs. 4), where the phrase "by those who believe and *know the truth*" may be consciously formulated in opposition to the claims of the Gnostics. 1 Timothy (4:4 f.) vigorously reasserts the claim of the Hebrew Bible (Genesis 1:29), Judaism, and Jesus himself that God's creation is fundamentally good. This belief, though not denied by the earliest generation of Christians, was relegated to the periphery because of eager expectation of further revelations from the Lord and a correspondingly low estimate of this world.[5] What has become the classi-

---

5. The apocryphal Acts of Paul presents a contrary view of the apostle, for "in practically every episode the motif of sexual continence plays a dominant role. . . . The basis of this attitude

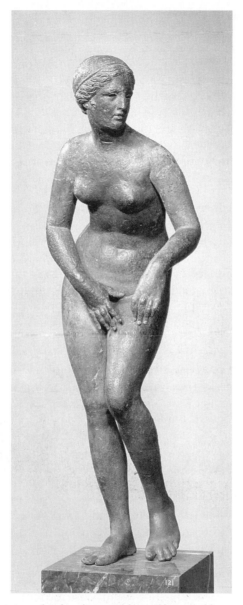

A classical Greek statue of Aphrodite, goddess of love and beauty (*ca.* fourth century B.C.).   *(Courtesy of Metropolitan Museum of Art. Rogers Fund, 1912.)*

is the conviction that the goods of this world are worthless and unprofitable, that salvation lies in the world to come, and that all depends on the securing of this other-worldly salvation. . . ." See E. Hennecke, *New Testament Apocrypha,* II, ed. W. Schneemelcher and trans. R. McL. Wilson (Philadelphia: Westminster/John Knox, 1992), p. 234.

cal Christian position is clearly formulated in 1 Timothy: "Everything created by God is good, and nothing is to be rejected, provided it is received with thanksgiving." "Thanksgiving" involves consecration by God's word and by prayer (vss. 4 f.). What "God's word" means in this context is not obvious; possibly it signifies scripture. Although the New Testament per se had not yet been formed, the Old was the Bible of the Christian community.

The next two paragraphs (vss. 6–10 and 11–16) instruct Timothy, and therefore the clergy, about the ministry and administration of the church. The following section (5:1–6:2) contains specific guidance for dealing with various groups in the church, especially widows, who were considered the responsibility of the community. We have then a kind of manual for the minister.

"These instructions" (4:6) may refer to all that has preceded in the letter or to what follows. Either makes good sense. The term *servant* or *minister* apparently designates an office or class of offices in the church. In chapter 3 the qualifications for the ministry, the offices of bishop and deacon, have been outlined. "Timothy" is himself such a "minister" in the official clerical sense. He has been ordained to this ministry through the laying on of hands (vs. 14). The investment of the historical Timothy by a board of elders seems unlikely and does not agree with the account of Paul's enlistment of Timothy in Acts 16:1–3. This section of the letter is more intelligible on the assumption that it was written for the benefit of the nascent official ministry of the church a generation or two after Paul.

The emphasis on right doctrine (vs. 6b) supports this view. "The words of the faith," an un-Pauline expression, refers to the right formulation of the confession of faith, as the immediately succeeding mention of sound teaching (or doctrine) shows. For Paul, faith is belief, trust, obedience, an orientation of life, a relationship. Of course, faith for Paul has an object toward which it is directed and about which intelligible things can be said. Yet Paul does not emphasize the correct doctrinal formulation in the way in which the Pastorals do. Much less does he understand faith in the sense of "the faith"—the correct doctrinal formula.

A major reason for this difference between Paul and the Pastorals appears in the reference to profane myths and old wives' tales (vs. 7). Doubtless the rise of strange teachings leads to the emphasis upon right doctrine that we find in the Pastorals. The appearance of contradictory beliefs necessitates the definition of the true teaching. Now we may use the term *heresy* in its proper sense, as a contradiction of, or departure from, established doctrine (cf. pp. 452 ff.). The false teachers are considered beyond the pale (cf. 4:1–5; 6:3 ff.); indeed, there is no question of discussion with them, much less of winning them back. They must be prevented from contaminating the church and pulling others down with them. It is a good question whether the difference between the Pastorals and their opponents and Paul and his foes is more than one of degree. In any event the gulf that separates them is deeper and the lines of separation are more sharply drawn.

Attention next focuses upon the relative merits of physical training and training in godliness (vss. 7b–10). The Pastorals regularly underscore an important saying with some such assertion as "the saying is sure" (vs. 9; cf. 1:15; 3:1; 2 Tim. 2:11; Titus 3:8). Probably this formula indicates a traditional saying. The KJV's "bodily exercise profiteth little" is closer to the Greek original than is the NRSV (vs. 8); 1 Timothy wishes to contrast the little profit of bodily training with the great values of training in godliness. "Godliness" (*eusebeia*) is a word found not at all in Paul, and quite rarely in the New Testament outside the Pastorals and 2 Peter. It is, in fact, a term at home in ancient Hellenistic piety rather than in specifically biblical or Christian faith. "Piety" might be an equally good translation of the Greek word in question. The high value that the Pastorals plainly ascribe to this quality is significant, underscoring how the thought of the Pastorals differs from the outlook of Paul. For Paul the mode of Christian existence is faith, life in Christ or in the Spirit, and the term for godliness or piety does not occur. In the Pastorals the mode of Christian existence is godliness and piety, and faith is the body of right doctrine. The concepts of "in Christ" and "in Spirit" play little or no role in the Pastorals. It is typical of the Pastorals that the promise for the present life and the life to come is not related directly to Christ and the Spirit but instead to godliness (vs. 8b).

The toiling and striving of those whose exercise is godliness have as their end and goal the believers' hope in the living God and Savior (vs. 10). The anti-Gnostic character of the Pastorals' polemic may appear again in this affirmation of God as the Savior of all. Commonly in Gnosticism only an elect group with a disposition for and capability of possessing knowledge could attain salvation. Here God in intention is the Savior of all, not a special class. That God actually saves only those who believe is the probable meaning of the last clause (cf. 2:1–6). But 1 Timothy declares quite clearly that no one stands *a priori* outside the potential realm of God's redemption.

The specific referent of "these things" in the following exhortation is unclear (vs. 11; cf. vs. 6). Does it refer to what precedes or what follows, or is it a general exhortation without any specific point of reference? The latter is more likely. At any rate, what immediately follows (vss. 12–16) is not material that Timothy would command and teach, but advice to him personally. The injunction to Timothy to let no one despise his youth (vs. 12) and the indication that Paul plans a visit (vs. 13) lend a note of genuineness to the correspondence, but they are probably a part of the cloak of pseudonymity in which the letter is clad. The rest is general instruction to the pastor, like much of the Pastorals. We have already noted that verse 14 presupposes the existence of an ordained ministry.

The word here translated *gift* is the Greek *charisma*, which implies a special spiritual endowment. Paul held that the *charismata*, "spiritual gifts," were distributed among all the members of the community, so that, although there are varieties of gifts and services, all Christians are, so to speak, gifted (1 Cor. 12). Here, however, the charismatic gift is limited, whether consciously or not, to the particular power and authority of an all-male ministerial office.[6] It is granted by the laying on of hands as well as by prophecy. "Prophecy" is probably an allusion to the Spirit-inspired designation of people for certain tasks, which was characteristic of earliest Christianity (Acts 13:12; cf. 1 Cor. 12:28; 14:1). But in spite of the continuation of prophetic utterance, the dispensation of the Spirit is apparently being tied to institutional office and ordination. What then of the free movement and authority of the Spirit in the community? Is spontaneity being sacrificed to the need for unity and order in the community? If so, is this necessary, or is the price too great to pay? The Pastorals do not represent the only period in the history of the church that has entertained such questions as these.

The other injunctions (vss. 12 f. and 15 f.) mirror the continuing life of the community, now a religious institution. The official leaders are to set the example in faith, conduct, and related matters (vs. 12), seeing after their duties of conducting public worship (vs. 13) and supervising the education of the people in sound doctrine (vss. 13–16), to the end that both minister and people will be saved (vs. 16). The model of the church as a continuing community composed of leaders and followers, clergy and laity, making its way through the world toward greater things that God has in store, is the legitimate legacy of the Pastoral epistles.

The reader is left finally with the impression of Paul as pastor. This Paul cares for and provides for the indefinite continuation and survival of the church. He instructs Timothy, his coworker, to establish the clergy, to guard the true doctrine, to resist error, and to preserve discipline and order among the faithful. This Paul is not without strong positive ties to the historical Paul of the genuine letters. The Paul of the Pastorals extends his authority and ministry to the continuing church.

Expectations had changed as conditions had changed, and it was tacitly acknowledged that although Jesus would return (1 Tim. 6:14; 2 Tim. 4:1), in the meantime generations might come and go, as perhaps they already had (2 Tim. 1:5). In 1 Timothy, chapter 4, we find an excellent sample of the concern for the continuing life and teaching of the church that characterizes these letters.

---

6. In some contrast to 1 Timothy 2:11–15, where the exercise of authority or any teaching role is denied women, Paul himself refers to a Phoebe as a deacon of the church at Cenchreae (Rom. 16:1; cf. 1 Cor. 11:5).

Hebrews: The True High Priesthood

Notes on the Letter to the Hebrews

Traditionally Hebrews has been ascribed to the apostle Paul, but Origen, the great theologian and scholar of the third-century church, knew that it was not his work. Indeed, Origen stated that only God knew the identity of the author of Hebrews. The letter itself does not claim Pauline authorship. Even less than the Pastorals, and far less than Ephesians, does it express typically Pauline ideas and interests. For example, in the Pastorals faith has become belief in doctrine about Jesus instead of a relationship to Christ; in Hebrews faith is simply steadfastness. Neither expresses Paul's view of faith as the acceptance of God's grace in Christ. The personal allusions and the mention of Timothy (13:23) have perhaps suggested that the letter is Paul's. The identity of the author remains unknown. Apollos, coworker with Paul (Acts 18:24; 1 Cor 1:12; 3:4 ff.), has been suggested by some, including Martin Luther in the sixteenth century. The suggestion is reasonable but can scarcely be either proven or disproven.

The readers suggested by the title would be Jewish Christians, not Jews. The title is a later addition, however, and the author's argument does not necessarily demand a Jewish background for his readers, only a Christian one. The reference to those from Italy sending greetings (13:24) suggests that Rome may have been the destination of Hebrews, as does its use in the late first-century letter of Clement of Rome. Because of the similarities in biblical exegesis and thought patterns between Hebrews and Philo of Alexandria, it is often conjectured that the document was composed in or near Alexandria in Egypt. References to persecution (10:32–34; 12:4) do not help very much in placing or dating the letter.

The situation and mood of the intended readers and the kind of ethical exhortations suggest second-generation Christianity, perhaps about A.D. 80–90. Yet Hebrews does not mention the destruction of the Jerusalem temple (A.D. 70) in the course of the argument concerning the new priesthood in Jesus Christ, and an earlier date is therefore sometimes proposed. Its concern with the Old Testament tabernacle, and not with the contemporary temple, may explain this silence.

Despite the lack of an epistolary salutation, Hebrews concludes as if it were a letter (cf. 13:22–25). Yet without chapter 13 Hebrews would probably be taken for a tract or perhaps a sermon. Extensive hortatory passages or exhortations are scattered throughout the book. Hebrews differs from many other New Testament books, however, in that such passages are integrally related to the author's theological thought. They do not appear to be merely traditional or conventional bits of ethical wisdom and admonition.

The thought of Hebrews is complex, subtle, and sophisticated. The author was skilled in the use of the Greek language and the then-current methods of biblical interpretation. We should not expect to grasp the full range and complexity of Hebrews on first reading. Despite its obvious qualities, Hebrews was not everywhere accepted as Pauline or authoritative in the early church. Particularly in Western Christendom, it was slow gaining recognition as canonical.

OUTLINE OF HEBREWS

Prologue: God's Final Word (1:1–2)

Argument: Jesus as Son and High Priest (1:3–10:18)
    The Person of the Son (1:3–4:13)
        His Superiority to Angels (1:3–2:18)
        His Superiority to Moses (3:1–6)
        Warning and Admonition (3:7–4:13)
    The Son as High Priest (4:14–10:18)
        Jesus' Qualifications as High Priest (4:14–5:10)
        Exhortation to Maturity (5:11–6:20)
        The Superiority of Christ's Priesthood (7:1–28)
        The High Priestly Work of Jesus (8:1–10:18)
Application: The Necessity of Faithfulness (10:19–12:29)
    The Response of Faith (10:19–39)
    Forerunners in Faithfulness (11:1–12:11)
        Examples from Israel (11:1–40)
        The Example of Jesus (12:1–11)
    Exhortation and Warning (12:12–29)
Conclusion: Final Exhortation, Personal Matters, and Benediction
(13:1–25)

JESUS' QUALIFICATIONS AS HIGH PRIEST (HEB. 4:14–5:10)

Why is the humanity of Jesus indispensable to his high-priestly work?

Because Hebrews deals extensively and repeatedly with Jesus' sacrifice, his crucifixion, it has some common ground with Paul, for whom Christ's death on the cross is of central importance. Yet Paul does not present Christ as high priest; that theme belongs only to Hebrews, where Christ is both priest and sacrifice. There is, nevertheless, a certain kinship that makes the notion that Paul wrote Hebrews at least intelligible. Both Paul and Hebrews place Jesus' death as a redemptive sacrifice at the center of their respective theologies. At least two aspects of the thought of Hebrews differentiate it, however, from Paul: the presentation of the relation of Jesus to the old covenant and the apparent belief that if believers sin, they cannot again obtain forgiveness.

For Paul the advent and death of Christ are foretold in the prophetic scriptures. These events appear as the fulfillment of prophecy. There is a subtle but significant difference in Hebrews, where the old era and its scriptures are only a foreshadowing of the new. Hebrews goes to great lengths to show that the old priesthood and all that went with it have been displaced by Christ the true high priest. Without disparaging Abraham, Moses, or other worthies who became examples of faith (chap. 11), Hebrews insists that the old covenant with its system of sacrifices has not only been superseded but was never effective in the first place. Psalm 95:7–11 is applied to the wilderness generation of the exodus from Egypt (3:7–11) with the conclusion that they may not enter the promised rest because of their unbelief (3:18–19; cf. 4:8). The present generation of Jesus' followers has come into the promised salvation because of the defection of the older one. Because the wilderness generation missed its chance, the readers are warned lest a similar fate overtake them (3:12; 4:11).

The disobedience and failure of the wilderness people prepare the reader for what is said about the old covenant and priesthood. Hebrews never tires of asserting that the tabernacle priesthood established under the old covenant, of which the temple priests were the successors, was unable to deal adequately with sin (9:6–10, 23–28). The covenant under which it was established has, in fact, now been superseded. Drawing upon Jeremiah 31:31–54, the author declares the establishment of a new covenant, better than the first (8:8–12). Of this covenant Christ has been appointed high priest. The major theological theme of Hebrews is the explanation and justification of the superiority of Christ's high priestly work.

The Christological statement of the first two chapters deals with the exaltation of Jesus to heaven (cf. 1:3 f.). There as the Son of God he reigns above all the angels (1:4 ff.), that is, above all heavenly and earthly powers. The exaltation of Christ is grounded in his preexistence and role in creation (1:2; cf. 1 Cor. 8:6; John 1:1 ff.). Already the Christological confession contains a word of warning and admonition to the reader (2:1–4). Moreover, not just the heavenly exaltation of the Son but also his earthly ministry comes into view (2:5–9), and the essential aspects of that ministry are emphasized. The example of Christ's faithfulness (3:6) leads to an extended exhortation to the readers about their own faithfulness (3:6–4:13). But this section is not just a series of exhortations; Hebrews unfolds a careful and elaborate argument in which the church's situation is compared with that of Israel in its forty years of wandering in the wilderness. Although this conception is based on an interpretation of the Old Testament, it is also related to the actual situation of the church to which the author wrote. That church is in need of challenge and in danger of losing faith and never reaching the promised rest (2:3 and 4:1–11; cf. 5:11–6:12; 10:19–12:29). It faced the danger of weariness after the enthusiasm and hope of the earliest days had faded—perhaps when the first apostles had died. The road ahead was long, and many were tempted to abandon the journey. There was a danger that they would retreat into Judaism or perhaps merely into conventional, lifeless piety.

The author's method of paralleling the Christian church with the Old Testament is typological; that is, an Old Testament figure or institution is understood as the type or prototype of some aspect of Christian revelation. Still, the moving force of his appeal is not the Old Testament, but Jesus. Yet faith is mentioned quite apart from Jesus (cf. chap. 11) and faith is not related to Jesus in the way we would expect in the light of Acts, Paul, the Gospels, and even James. For Hebrews faith is steadfastness or persistence in hope; this is clear here as well as in chapter 11, where faith is not specifically faith in Jesus Christ. Indeed, Jesus is himself the prime example of faith.

Ultimately the ground of faith is Jesus Christ, however, for the "holding fast" of faith (4:14 ff.) would be pointless apart from him. Central to the author's presentation of Jesus is the concept of the "great high priest who has passed through the heavens." He is the guarantor of the salvation that is promised. The description of the heavenly enthronement of Jesus as the Son (chaps. 1 and 2) precedes an extended discussion of the high-priestly activity of the heavenly Christ. The explanation and exposition of his high-priestly ministry is the subject of much of the remainder of the letter, especially chapters 7–10. Hebrews thus seeks to show in detail how Jesus' heavenly high priesthood directly affects the church and the Christian. It is the surety supporting the Christians' life in the world and sustaining their hope. With such encouragement they can hold fast the confession (4:14), which is the church's expression of faith and hope in God through Jesus Christ.

The high-priestly ministry of Jesus is the basis for renewal of confidence and hope (succinctly stated in vss. 4:15 f.). The Christology of Hebrews is well summarized in 4:14–16, especially in the two very different assertions about Jesus in verses 14 and 15—namely, that he is the great heavenly high priest (vs. 14) and at the same time the "one who in every respect has been tested as we are, yet without sin" (vs. 15). It is not sufficient to ground the church's confidence in the heavenly ministry of Jesus. This alone could have no effect, no relevance for people on earth. Already the author's logic impresses itself upon the reader: Christ could not act for others unless he sympathized with them and he could not sympathize unless he had really shared human nature and experience (cf. 2:14). The heavenly high priesthood of Jesus is relevant to humankind because it is the high priesthood of a real human being. Hebrews contains perhaps the earliest clear, straightforward New Testament statement of what later came to be called the Incarnation—God's human presence in Jesus of Nazareth. God is present in Jesus, in his earthly and in his heavenly ministry, but not in such a way that Jesus ceases to be a man and becomes by this fact a heavenly supernatural being, unbelievable or irrelevant to ordinary mortals. Yet in spite of Jesus' full participation in human life, he is not overcome by its temptation; he does not sin. "Without sin" means that Jesus did not succumb to the fundamental temptation to abandon God in faithlessness. Rather, he becomes the model of faith (12:2).

The twofold assertion that Christ has passed through the heavens and yet is like other human beings (4:14–15) lays the basis for the following exhortation and invitation (vs. 16). The term *throne of grace* implies the presence of Christ the high priest at the right hand of God (1:3). The understanding of the gospel as God's grace is, of course, thoroughly and typically Pauline. The fact that the concept of grace was from the first recognized as Pauline is shown by its presence not only in the genuine Pauline letters but also in the Pastorals, Ephesians, and Acts, especially the chapters dealing with Paul. The use of *grace* in 1 Peter and Hebrews may indicate that these documents also belong within the Pauline sphere of influence, for elsewhere in the New Testament the term is surprisingly infrequent.[7] Although in Hebrews *grace* is

7. The Greek *charis*, grace, occurs not at all in Matthew and Mark, a few times in Luke (but more often than not without theological meaning), only in the prologue of John, twice in

not the object of theological discussion, it seems to have Pauline roots. It is God's graciousness, his love freely given. As in the case of faith, however, in Hebrews grace does not appear to be tied explicitly to the event of Christ's coming. Instead, it signifies the continuing availability of God's strength, making faith, understood as faithfulness, possible.

The people of God must not lose their will or way; therefore, they must be reminded of the sure hope of reaching the goal. Although the general theme of the wandering people of God gives continuity to the entire book, the climactic theological moments have to do with Christ himself, the heavenly high priest. An extensive statement of Jesus' qualifications for the high priesthood now appears (5:1–10). It falls into two distinct parts: first, a general statement of the qualifications for the high priesthood (5:1–4); second, a declaration of the way in which Jesus corresponds to these qualifications (5:5–10).

The model of the high-priestly ministry (5:1–4) is the biblical priesthood. Jewish priests in this tradition administered the temple cult in Jerusalem according to the mandates of the Old Testament until the siege and ultimate destruction of the city and the temple in the Roman war. The author could assume his readers' familiarity with the concept of a priest as a mediator between God and humanity, especially in matters of sin and purification, if only from the Old Testament. Moreover, the concept and office of priest as one who performs ritual sacrifice for the community are widespread in the history of religions. The function of the priest was to maintain an open channel of communication with the divine and, by offering sacrifice for sin and abolishing impurity, to ensure the divine favor.

The succinct, clear definition of the high priest's office and function (vs. 1) could equally apply to the entire Levitical priesthood. Although the high priest had a special office, he could effectively exercise this office only because of his common lot with the people (vs. 2). This is, in effect, the first qualification of the high priest. But because what he shared with the people led him to sin, he had to offer sacrifice on his own behalf (vs. 3). Christ, on the other hand, although subject to human temptation, was without sin (4:15). The second qualification of the high priest (vs. 4) was the divine calling.

In showing that Christ fulfills both qualifications for the high priesthood (vss. 5–10), the author begins with the second. He affirms with the New Testament generally that the significance, honor, and glory of Christ are not things he claims for himself. Quite the contrary, Jesus' own life is one of self-giving service, not arrogance. His peculiar dignity has no human basis, but stems from the call and appointment of God. As proof the author turns once again to the Old Testament, which he regards as the definitive expression of the will and purpose of God, when rightly understood and interpreted. Psalm

---

one verse and nowhere else in James, twice each in 2 and 3 John and Jude, but not at all in 1 John. By contrast *charis* occurs in every Pauline and deutero-Pauline letter, including the brief note to Philemon, and is quite frequent—for example, twenty-two occurrences in Romans and eighteen in 2 Corinthians.

2:7, quoted in 5:5, appears also in 1:5 and in Acts 13:33 and seems to have been an important Christian proof-text. However, the quotation from Psalm 110:4 (Heb. 5:6) is even more important for the author's argument. For the theological exposition from this point through chapter 10 (as distinguished from the exhortation) is devoted to the theme of Jesus as high priest after the order of Melchizedek.

In describing Jesus' human nature (vss. 7–9), the author takes up and develops ideas already set forth (2:9, 11, 14, 17 f.). Undoubtedly there is here an intentional reference to the agony of Jesus in the Garden of Gethsemane (Mark 14:32–42 parr.), although the details may not correspond exactly to the Synoptics (cf. John 12:27).

The allusion to the Gethsemane story is indicative of another characteristic of Hebrews. The author seems to know historical tradition about Jesus without, in all probability, knowing the canonical Gospels. In speaking of Jesus' death, Hebrews states that he "suffered outside the city gate" (13:12), apparently a reference to the place of crucifixion. This detail agrees with John 19:20 (cf. 19:17), where Jesus is said to have been crucified "near the city." Probably executions were not ordinarily carried out within the city walls (cf. Acts 7:58); quite likely, then, Hebrews gives accurate information. As our reading of the text shows, the author has a distinctive grasp of the character of Jesus' earthly ministry. It is quite probable that he also had access to genuine historical traditions and data. Although Hebrews' presentation of Jesus was informed by the author's theology, it was apparently not simply created by and for it. Hebrews' portrayal stresses what Jesus holds in common with humanity, not what distinguishes him from others. Thus Jesus, the pioneer of salvation, was made perfect through suffering (2:10). The term *pioneer* in 2:10 is well chosen, for the author looks upon Jesus not only as the heavenly high priest above and beyond the people but as the one who leads them to salvation, undergoing the same experience as they (cf. again 2:10; also 2:14 ff.).

Jesus now lives and works at God's right hand as the superior high priest according to the order of Melchizedek (5:10; cf. 6:19–20). Yet why should the author attempt to explain the relatively better-known Jesus by means of the lesser-known Melchizedek (cf. Gen. 14:17–20; Ps. 110:4)? The key is concealed in the quotation from Psalm 110:4 in Hebrews 5:6. When this Psalm is read in its entirety, the reason for the author's preoccupation with Melchizedek comes to light.[8] The Psalm is addressed to David, the king, the Lord's anointed (the Messiah), and he is called a priest forever according to the order of Melchizedek (vs. 4). Since Jesus was believed to be the Davidic Messiah, the Christ, what is said of the Messiah in Psalm 110 is said of him. Thus the Melchizedek title is taken to be a messianic designation applying to Jesus. Genesis 14:17–20, the brief Old Testament story of Melchizedek,

---

8. Traditions about Melchizedek were current in his day. See F. L. Horton, *The Melchizedek Tradition: A Critical Examination of the Sources to the Fifth Century* A.D. *and in the Epistle to the Hebrews* (New York: Cambridge University Press, 1976).

Seven-branched Menorah found on the northern entryway to synagogue at Khirbet Shema, Galilee—one of the largest candelabra ever recovered from an ancient Jewish site.   *(Courtesy of Eric M. Meyers.)*

then serves to demonstrate that the Melchizedekian (i.e., messianic) high priesthood is superior to the Levitical (cf. Heb. 7:1–10). It is the true, real, and effective priesthood. This point is elaborated and supported by additional Old Testament evidence and other arguments, which comprise the greater part of chapters 7–10. The author does not wish to say anything about Melchizedek per se, but the concept of his priesthood provides a means of showing from scripture that the Levitical priesthood and sanctuary are only a shadow and prototype of the one great High Priest in his heavenly sanctuary (9:24).

The central fact is the eternal validity and effectiveness of the ministry of Jesus, the exalted Lord, as heavenly High Priest (8:1 ff.) The discussion of the nature of the Old Testament Levitical high priesthood serves indirectly to illumine it. That high priesthood, although not fraudulent or unnecessary, was finally ineffectual. In retrospect, it was only a shadow and a copy (8:5) of Jesus' heavenly high priesthood, and it had to be replaced by him. The author seeks to make the death and heavenly ministry of Christ intelligible through the biblical descriptions of the purpose and practice of the Levitical high priesthood. The sacrificial system then becomes a means of understanding and interpreting what Christ accomplished and accomplishes. What other priests did over and over again in a vain attempt to deal with sin, Christ has done once and for all (9:25–10:10).

The assertion of the sufficiency of Christ's work, in contrast to the work of other priests, leads to an exhortation to those who have benefited from his priestly offering (10:19 ff.). Here again there is the alternation between Christology and exhortation typical of Hebrews. In this case the exhortation includes a threat of judgment (vss. 26–31), followed by a recollection of the readers' earlier courage and confidence (vss. 32–39). The latter passage amounts to an encouragement to keep the faith, and leads into a kind of historical summation (Heb. 11), in which numerous examples of faith are brought forward from the Old Testament. The example of the faithful worthies of biblical history, culminating in Jesus the pioneer and perfecter of faith (12:2 f.), leads to yet a further exhortation to the readers (chap. 12).

The final section of Hebrews (chap. 13) evokes an epistolary style reminiscent of Paul. In it there is a rather long hortatory section (vss. 1–18), which differs from the exhortations found earlier in the epistle in that instructions are diverse and disconnected and are not directly related to Hebrews' theological themes. After a benediction (vss. 20 f.) comes an epistolary closing (vss. 22–25). This final chapter thus sounds more like Paul than the rest of Hebrews and doubtless led to the traditional view that the letter was Paul's own work.

Despite the fact that most of the letters treated in this chapter—probably all of them—were not written by Paul himself, they bear unmistakable marks of Pauline influence. We legitimately count them a part of the Pauline heritage. They complete the New Testament depiction of Paul that begins in the Book of Acts. There the reader finds a Paul concerned with missionary preaching and the establishment of churches. In the genuine letters Paul's pastoral, apostolic care for these churches was manifest. At the same time the basic lineaments of his theological thought emerged into the foreground. In the last letters, those in the Pauline tradition, the missionary and apostle has become the pastor, more and more concerned with the structuring of the church and with making provision for its life as an institution of salvation in the world. This is even true of Hebrews, which is nevertheless filled with its own profound theological reflection.

Conclusion: Note on Pseudonymous Writings

A pseudonymous writing is one written under the name of someone other than the actual author. All the Pauline letters treated in this chapter are probably pseudonymous, with the exception of Hebrews, which makes no explicit claim of authorship by Paul or anyone else.

So far, only in this chapter have we encountered pseudonymous writings, for the Gospels and Acts are instead anonymous. That is, within the documents themselves no one is actually named as author. This is true even of the Gospel of John, where the anonymous Beloved Disciple is never identified with John, and of Luke–Acts, where the author's identity is never revealed, although he refers to his own literary work in the prologues of those books. The traditional titles of the Gospels were apparently added only as the books were incorporated into the New Testament. The title of the Acts of the Apostles does not, of course, reveal the name of the author.

In Chapter 11 a number of other writings whose authorship is uncertain are treated, but only a couple may be clearly pseudonymous, namely 1 and 2 Peter, both of which contain explicit references or allusions to the apostle Peter as their author (e.g., 1 Pet. 1:1; 5:1; 2 Pet. 1:1; 1:17 f.). The letters of James and Jude seem to be represented as the work of brothers of Jesus, but this is only probable, not certain, since the names are common and no fraternal connection with Jesus is claimed (although Jude identifies himself as a servant of Jesus Christ and brother of James in Jude 1). Similarly, the

Revelation to John explicitly names a John as author (1:1), but does not identify him as the disciple of Jesus or as an apostle. The Johannine letters, unlike the Pauline, do not name an author, although in 2 and 3 John the author is identified simply as "the elder," as if he were well known to his readers.

The most acute problems are found in the Pauline and Petrine letters. Of these as many as eight may be pseudonymous (2 Thessalonians, Colossians, Ephesians, and the three Pastorals, as well as both 1 and 2 Peter). According to the current consensus of biblical scholarship, at least five are pseudonymous (Ephesians, the Pastorals, 2 Peter). These not only name Paul or Peter as author but contain a number of self-references or allusions apparently intended to underscore their authorship. Not surprisingly, it has been maintained that if they are pseudepigrapha (written under an assumed name), they are forgeries, with all that implies.[9] Most critical scholars have, however, been reluctant to go so far, although it is the case that literate people in antiquity were aware of forgeries. In fact, some later Christian books written under the names of apostles, but known to have been written by others, were eventually rejected by the church as apocryphal.

New Testament pseudepigrapha should be viewed in light of Old Testament and ancient Jewish practice and tradition.[10] All law was ascribed to Moses, although he did not write the Pentateuch in its present form. Similarly, wisdom books were ascribed to Solomon and Psalms to David. Also, prophetic books such as Isaiah contain material originating with the eighth-century prophet, but literary layers from later centuries as well. Jewish apocalyptic books were characteristically written under the names of ancient worthies rather than their actual authors (e.g., Daniel, Enoch).

Obviously, these Hebrew and Jewish scriptures establish a precedent, not of forgery, but for the ascription of sacred writings to an ancient figure whom tradition holds to be their source. For example, that Paul is the source of Ephesians there can be no doubt, for apart from Paul Ephesians would be inconceivable. The same may be said of the Pastorals, although their differences from the writings of the apostle himself are more pronounced. Yet the Pastorals clearly intend to apply the Pauline message and tradition to a later generation, when matters of church organization and ministerial office have become increasingly crucial. The many personal details of the Pastorals establish them as Pauline; this is particularly true of the relationship of Paul to his subordinates Timothy and Titus. Paul is not only a source of tradition but in the Pastorals becomes a part of the tradition itself, which is literally unthinkable apart from him. For the early Christians, like their Jewish forebears, literary origin was less important than continuity of tradition. In other words, Paul and Peter continue to speak to new situations in the life of the church through letters ascribed to them, as Moses or Isaiah continued to speak to Israel.

Although questions of literary authorship and ownership were, so to speak, put in second place, they did not disappear from Christian consciousness. Thus in the

9. See E. Earle Ellis, "Pseudonymity and Canonicity of New Testament Documents," in *Worship, Theology and Ministry in the Early Church: Essays in Honor of Ralph P. Martin*, ed. Michael J. Wilkins and Terence Page (Sheffield, England: JSOT Press, 1992), pp. 212–224.

10. See David G. Meade, *Pseudonymity and Canon: An Investigation into the Relationship of Authorship and Authority in Jewish and Earliest Christian Tradition* (Tübingen: Mohr, 1986). Our discussion is much indebted to his proposals. His monograph also contains an excellent bibliography.

second and third centuries false claims of apostolic authorship were recognized, and writings such as the Gospel of Peter and 3 Corinthians were discredited on such grounds.

Suggestions for Further Reading

M. Y. MacDonald, *The Pauline Churches: A Socio-historical Study of Institutionalization in the Pauline and Deutero-Pauline Writings* (Cambridge: Cambridge University Press, 1988), uses the insights of Peter Berger and Thomas Luckmann (*The Social Construction of Reality,* 1966) to provide a basis to account for the similarities as well as the differences of the Pauline and deutero-Pauline letters. Her book is a valuable introduction to this approach as well as to the letters and communities in the Pauline tradition.

COLOSSIANS

Edward Lohse, *Colossians and Philemon* (Philadelphia: Fortress, 1971), in the Hermeneia series, is the standard commentary. Lohse concludes (p. 18) that Paul is not the author of Colossians. (The Pauline authorship of Philemon is not contested.) For a judicious espousal of Pauline authorship, see the commentary of J. L. Houlden, *Paul's Letters from Prison: Philippians, Colossians, Philemon, and Ephesians* (Philadelphia: Westminster, 1970), pp. 134–139. While accepting the authenticity of Colossians, Houlden regards Ephesians as non-Pauline. E. Schweizer, *The Letter to the Colossians: A Commentary,* trans. A. Chester (Minneapolis: Augsburg, 1982), raises the possibility that Timothy, named as coauthor, actually wrote the letter while Paul was in prison. Thus a post-Pauline setting does not have to be sought. P. Pokorny, *Colossians: A Commentary,* trans. S. S. Schatzmann (Peabody, MA: Hendrickson, 1991), p. 4, quoting Käsemann to the effect that if Colossians is by Paul it must be as late as possible in Paul's career, but if not it must have been written as early as possible afterwards, nevertheless decides in favor of a deutero-Pauline author. A more conservative viewpoint on authorship is represented by F. F. Bruce, *The Epistles to the Colossians, to Philemon, and to the Ephesians* (Grand Rapids, MI: Eerdmans, 1984).

EPHESIANS

Representative commentaries are C. L. Mitton, *Ephesians* (Grand Rapids, MI: Eerdmans, 1973), and M. Barth, *Ephesians,* 2 vols. (Garden City, NY: Doubleday, 1974). Mitton belongs to the critical majority who reject authorship by Paul himself. Barth, while acknowledging problems with that ancient tradition, believes that the case for pseudonymity has not been convincingly made. The case against Pauline authorship has been set out by Mitton in an earlier monograph, *The Epistle to the Ephesians: Its Authorship, Origin, and Purpose* (Oxford: Clarendon, 1951). See also works cited under Colossians.

PASTORALS

A thorough commentary is M. Dibelius, *The Pastoral Epistles,* rev. by H. Conzelmann and trans. P. Buttolph and A. Yarbro (Philadelphia: Fortress, 1972). The analysis is technical, but as in all Hermeneia commentaries the Greek is translated. Shorter and less technical are C. K. Barrett, *The Pastoral Epistles* (Oxford: Clarendon, 1963), and

J. L. Houlden, *The Pastoral Epistles: I and II Timothy, Titus* (Philadelphia: Trinity Press International, 1989). P. N. Harrison, *The Problem of the Pastoral Epistles* (Oxford: Humphrey Milford, 1921), has demonstrated why on linguistic grounds the Pastorals in their present form can scarcely be considered the writings of Paul. L. R. Donelson, *Pseudepigraphy and Ethical Argument in the Pastoral Epistles* (Tübingen: Mohr, 1986), sets the Pastorals in the broader context of pseudepigraphal letters of antiquity and seeks to reconstruct their theological and ethical point of view.

HEBREWS

H. W. Attridge, *The Epistle to the Hebrews: A Commentary on the Epistle to the Hebrews* (Philadelphia: Fortress, 1989), is now the standard commentary. Other worthwhile commentaries include F. F. Bruce, *The Epistle to the Hebrews* (Grand Rapids, MI: Eerdmans, 1964); H. Montefiore, *A Commentary on the Epistle to the Hebrews* (New York: Harper & Row, 1964); and D. A. Hagner, *Hebrews* (San Francisco: Harper & Row, 1983). G. Hughes, *Hebrews and Hermeneutics* (New York: Cambridge University Press, 1979), sets Hebrews in the context of a discussion of significant theological issues. The older, but still noteworthy, monograph of E. Käsemann, *The Wandering People of God: An Interpretation of the Letter to the Hebrews,* trans. R. A. Harrisville and I. L. Sandberg (Minneapolis: Augsburg, 1984), is available in English translation. B. Lindars, *The Theology of the Letter to the Hebrews* (Cambridge: Cambridge University Press, 1991), offers a valuable, succinct treatment of the subject in its literary and historical contexts.

Chapter 11

Apostolic Writings: Faith, Order, and Vision

*J*ames, 1 and 2 Peter, Jude, and the Epistles of John are all in different ways concerned with the life, doctrine and discipline of the early Christian communities. Because they are not addressed to individual Christian churches, they are traditionally called the Catholic (general) Epistles. James insists that faith should be accompanied by good works, and lays heavy emphasis on the ethical demands under which Christians should live. Like the writer of the Pastoral letters, the author tends to construe faith as believing in certain doctrines.

1 Peter addresses itself to similar moral concerns, but is much more directly Christological—that is, a doctrine of Christ is fundamental. At the same time the author shows a distinct consciousness of the unfriendly environment in which believers must live. Christians are to give no cause for offense, and at the same time they are to live courageously in the face of external hostility. A similar attitude was found in Hebrews.

In different ways both 1 Peter and James, as well as 2 Peter and Jude, deal with the threat posed by false doctrine and false teachers within the church. Such interests have already been encountered in the Pastorals and Colossians, and recur also in the Johannine letters. Possibly forms of the ancient Gnostic heresy constitute the opposition against which most of these letters warn. The Johannine letters are, however, principally concerned with the quality of the community's inner life—whether it is characterized by love. In this respect as in others they stand very close to the Gospel of John, where there is also a striking emphasis on the unity of the community that finds expression in mutual love among the members.

All the writers of the New Testament share a lively hope for the future, in which God will visit and redeem the faithful. This hope is, however, most vividly depicted in the Book of Revelation, or the Revelation to John. The apocalyptic perspective, characteristic also of parts of the Synoptic Gospels and Paul, comes to most graphic expression here. At the same time, the author obviously shares a broad range of theological beliefs and concerns with other early Christian authors.

James: Inner Discipline

Notes on the Letter of James

The very first verse of the letter of James presents problems. Who is James? There are several possibilities: the brother of Jesus himself, one of the two disciples of Jesus bearing that name, or someone else. Who or what are the twelve tribes in the Dispersion (1:1)? The reference is obviously to the twelve tribes of Israel dispersed around the Greco-Roman world, but James is not a letter to Jews (cf. 1:1; 2:1; 2:14–26). Apparently Christians could also be referred to as the "Dispersion" (1 Pet. 1:1). The letter is addressed to Christians but to no single Christian congregation. The conditions existing in a single congregation or in specific congregations are no more reflected in the letter as a whole than in the salutation. The conclusion tells us nothing; the "letter" stops quite abruptly.

Although tradition has ascribed the book to James, the brother of the Lord, it does not seem to have been known and quoted by other Christian writers until the early third century. The fourth-century church historian Eusebius of Caesarea indicates that some Christians of his day doubted that it belonged in the New Testament at all. The Protestant reformer Martin Luther criticized the letter because of its emphasis on good works at the expense of faith, and apparently did not regard it as the work of Jesus' brother. In fact, the letter itself nowhere explicitly claims to be the work of this particular James. Nor is the ascription to Jesus' brother supported by considerations of language and style. The style and quality of the Greek are reasonably good, probably better than what an Aramaic-speaking Galilean would produce. The content is nevertheless Jewish. The law and moral rectitude are extolled. Furthermore, the address to "the twelve tribes in the Dispersion" implies a Hellenistic Jewish readership. The ascription of the letter to James is intelligible, even if it should turn out to be incorrect.

Plainly, little is known about the origin of the letter of James. Probably James represents a form of Jewish Christianity at the end of the first century or the beginning of the second. Its ethical exhortations reflect a knowledge and use of what had by then become an extensive ethical tradition. The best-known section (2:14–26) betrays a knowledge of Pauline theology, perhaps of Galatians and Romans. If so, then the author very likely knew the collected Pauline corpus, which would date his writing toward the end of the first century at the earliest. On the other hand, Paul or the views of Paulinists are not above criticism (contrast 2 Pet. 3:15–17), making a much later date seem unlikely. Because the kind of Judaism that formed the background of James existed in many parts of the Hellenistic world, it is futile to try to locate the book's place of origin.

Despite the Jewish cast of James, references and quotations from the Old Testament are not frequent. There are, however, a number of possible references or allusions to Jesus' sayings and teachings, particularly the Matthean version (e.g., 5:12; cf. Matt. 5:34-37). Whether these indicate a knowledge of any of our Gospels, or only of an independent tradition, is uncertain.

OUTLINE OF JAMES

Address (1:1)
Exhortation to Christian Practice (1:2–27)
Faith and Ethics (2:1–26)
    Faith and the Poor (2:1–7)
    The Importance of the Law (2:8–13)
    Faith and Action (2:14–26)
Teaching and Wisdom (3:1–18)
Condemnation of Pride and Passion (4:1–12)
Concluding Exhortation (4:13–5:20)
    Warning against Boasting and Riches (4:13–5:6)
    Exhortation to Practice, Prayer, and the Restoration of the Sinner
    (5:7–20)

FAITH AND ACTION (JAMES 2:14–26)

In what sense does James oppose Paul in emphasizing works?

The letter of James seems to have been written to meet the actual needs of the expanding and consolidating Christian church, even though it is addressed to no specific congregation. Members of the newly formed churches needed concrete guidance about what to do in actual life situations in which ethical decisions were required. For the Christian converted from Judaism, the problem was less acute, because such a person possessed the powerful and comprehensive tradition of the biblical and Jewish law. In addition, in wide circles of the early Christian church, the teachings of Jesus were circulated and used for moral and spiritual guidance.[1] The existence of a substantial tradition of Jesus' teaching in the Gospels, especially Matthew and Luke, is ample testimony to this fact. The appropriation of the Jesus tradition in the Gospels and the incorporation of all four Gospels into the canon of the church naturally resulted in the increasing availability and use of the tradition of Jesus' ethical teaching as a norm and guide for Christian life. Already in James we may see this development in those passages that are similar to sayings of Jesus known from the Synoptic Gospels, although James seems to have known the earlier tradition rather than the Gospels.

From Paul's letters we can already see that there were various ideas about what it meant to be Christian. The character of Christian life had to be defined, and for the individual this definition by and large took place after, not

1. The literature on this subject is immense. Still illuminating is M. Dibelius, *From Tradition to Gospel,* trans B. L. Woolf (New York: Scribner, 1934), esp. pp. 9–132.

St. James on a plaque of a French altar frontal—second half of thirteenth century.
(Courtesy of Metropolitan Museum of Art. Gift of J. Pierpont Morgan, 1917.)

before, the experience of conversion. James helps to define Christian life by concrete advice and admonition. The ethical exhortations of James have much in common with those of other Christian documents, such as the Pauline epistles (cf. 1 Thess. 4:1–12), Ephesians (4:25–6:20), 1 John (3:11–18), and Hebrews (13:1–8), as well as the Letter of Barnabas and the Didache of the so-called Apostolic Fathers.

Perhaps the ethical interest and character of James are portrayed most graphically at the point at which the author evidently combats what he considers to be a dangerous form of Christianity, which holds that a person is justified before God by faith alone rather than by conduct as well (2:14–26). The initial hypothetical situation (described in vss. 14–17) and the moral lesson drawn from it have a timeless appeal to pious, practical Christian people. On the other hand, a quite narrow understanding of faith is presupposed; for James, faith equals belief (vs. 19). This view of faith, similar to that of the Pastorals, takes faith to be primarily assent to certain propositions. This understanding is different from that of Paul, for whom faith is the *act of believing* and the *relationship* between the believer and the one believed.

The contrast between faith and works reminds the reader of Paul's intense theological discussion of this subject. Possibly James's arguments are directed against the position of Paul. Paul would have surely agreed with the intention of James (cf. vss. 18 and 20). Yet the use of the example of Abraham (vss. 21 ff.), as well as the citation of the same Old Testament passage (Gen. 15:6) that Paul used to prove a quite different point (Rom. 4 and Gal. 3), suggests some sort of contact and disagreement with Paul or an interpretation of him. The disagreement, of course, concerns the relationship of faith and works and the place of works in the economy of salvation (vss. 21–24).

We have already noted the discrepancy between James's and Paul's views of faith. We must now ask how James understands works and in what sense they are necessary for salvation. Paul, of course, espouses justification by faith alone and excludes "works of the law" as a means of justification before God (Gal. 2:15–16). James, on the other hand, does not oppose justification by works to justification by faith. He does not accept Paul's posing of the alternatives. Rather, he regards the performance of works of the law, along with faith, as indispensable for justification (2:24; cf. 2:10). Interestingly, James (2:8) brings forth the same scripture passage (Lev. 19:18) with which both Jesus (Matt. 22:34–40; Mark 12:28–31; Luke 10:25–28) and Paul (Rom. 13:8–10; Gal. 5:14) sum up the law and, like Paul, he does not attribute it to Jesus.

Paul's actual controversies over "works of the law" had to do with the specifics of food laws and circumcision, which apparently no longer concern James, who is interested in the necessity of good conduct as well as belief. Still, Paul and James really differ on the question of justification. Whether James would have expressed himself in this fashion had he understood Paul's view of faith or faced Paul's situation in the controversy with Jewish Christians is a moot question. There is, however, a kind of practical agreement between them. James says (vs. 24) that belief alone is not enough, that pure religion, as he styles it (1:27), involves faith and ethics. Paul would have quite agreed: "For in Christ Jesus neither circumcision nor uncircumcision counts for anything; the only thing that counts is faith working through love" (Gal. 5:6). James insists on works as the proof of faith (vs. 18): faith without works is dead. Paul would prefer to say that faith without obedience is not genuine faith.

It is not clear that James intends to oppose Paul directly. He seems to be fighting a misunderstood Paulinism—whether his own or someone else's— that separates faith from life. Such a misunderstanding of Paul's thought may have been prevalent in the church of his day (cf. 2 Pet. 3:15–17). Paul encountered in Corinth among his own converts those who thought that their knowledge or possession of the Spirit put them beyond any paltry considerations of right and wrong, sin and righteousness. They separated faith or piety from this-worldly ethical questions. Thus Paul had to exhort the Corinthian Christians to abstain from, or give up, immoral practices. It would therefore not be surprising if the subtleties of Paul's theological and ethical reflection were lost on a later generation of Christians.

Whether the simple paralleling of faith and works in James is satisfying depends on how one understands the human situation and what one takes to be the essential problem in human life. If one is free to do and to believe according to one's own choice and without any predisposition to good or evil, then James certainly does make more sense than Paul. On the other hand, if present existence in the world is to be understood in terms of oppressive bondage to sin, as alienation and rebellion, then the simple view of James does not suffice, at least not as a theological analysis of the state of humanity in the world and the manner of redemption. In the final analysis, however, James is a manual for Christian behavior, not a fundamental theological treatise.

The Letters of Peter and Jude: Continuing Struggle for the Faith

Notes on 1 Peter

1 Peter presents itself as the work of the great disciple and apostle, and no grounds for doubting this claim were advanced until modern times. Yet there are at least three reasons for questioning this tradition:

1. The Greek of 1 Peter is very good. Could a Galilean fisherman have written it? Aramaic, Peter's native tongue, differs at least as much from Greek as Greek differs from English.

2. 1 Peter contains many Pauline motifs and ideas, especially the concept of Jesus' death atoning for sin and effecting righteousness (1:18 f.; 2:24). The Pauline expression "in Christ" also occurs in 1 Peter (3:16; 5:10, 14), and there is a striking similarity between the view expressed in 2:14 ff. and the attitude toward

the state commended by Paul in Romans 13:1–7. If the author knew the collected Pauline letters, such knowledge would imply that 1 Peter was written perhaps a generation later and could not be the work of Peter, who is reported to have died in the sixties in Rome. Still the possibility that Peter, in Rome (5:13), might have known only the letter to the Romans cannot be excluded.

3. 1 Peter contains no indication of acquaintanceship with the historical Jesus of the sort we would expect from the man who in many ways was closest to him. The claim to be a witness of the suffering Christ (5:1) does not necessarily mean an eyewitness. According to the Gospels, Peter fled Jesus on the night he was betrayed and presumably did not see the crucifixion. Moreover, the passage that deals with Christ's suffering and death (2:22 ff.) is apparently based on the suffering-servant passages of Isaiah rather than on historical observation. Although this observation does not disprove Peter's authorship, for he was not present at the crucifixion, the text can scarcely be taken as evidence for it.

Modern defenders of Petrine authorship acknowledge the weight of at least the first and second arguments and offer the explanation that these factors are due to the role played by Silvanus (5:12), a coworker of Paul (1 and 2 Thess. 1:1), who as secretary actually composed the letter in its present form. But if Silvanus is the same as the Silas of Acts, as is usually supposed, he too was originally an Aramaic-speaking Palestinian (Acts 15:22, 27, 40); therefore, the first difficulty would not be entirely removed.

If the letter is by Peter, it must date from about A.D. 60, or a few years later. The suffering of Christians to which the letter refers would be the persecution of the Emperor Nero. In that case the warnings and admonitions would seem misdirected, for Nero's persecution took place in Rome (the probable place of origin; "Babylon," 5:13; cf. Rev. 18), not in Asia Minor, to which the letter is addressed. If the letter is not Petrine, the period of the Emperor Domitian's persecution would be the probable time of composition. This situation would date 1 Peter in the last decade of the first century and also make knowledge of the Pauline letters a possibility. Whatever the conclusion concerning the origin of 1 Peter, the purpose of the author was to encourage early Christians in their faith.

Structurally, 1 Peter presents some peculiarities. The salutation (1:1–2) and epistolary conclusion (5:12–14) easily fall away. At 4:11 there is a conclusion of sorts and 4:12 makes a new beginning. The fact that in 4:12 ff. persecution seems an imminent possibility, whereas in the preceding part of the letter it is more remote, has led to the suggestion that the different parts were written at different times. The hortatory and even homiletical character of much of the letter suggests that its basis may be a baptismal sermon, with the epistolary form a later editorial addition. The explicit reference to the hearers' or readers' baptism (3:21) is accompanied by several other baptismal allusions (1:3, 8–9, 22–23), and the entire piece makes sense as an address to newly baptized converts. Although plausible, the hypothesis falls short of proof, however, and the book is known only in epistolary form.

OUTLINE OF 1 PETER

Address (1:1–2)
The Hope of Salvation (1:3–12)
The Holiness of Christians (1:13–2:10)
Instructions and Appeal for Good Conduct (2:11–4:11)

THE SUFFERING SERVANT (1 PET. 2:11–25)

Why should Christians accept persecution?

Whether or not one reckons it to be the work of the apostle Peter, 1 Peter is one of the choice writings of the early Christian period and of the New Testament. 1 Peter is written with good taste and restraint, and bespeaks a realistic, if critical, understanding of the world. The author calls Christians to obedient work and witness in the world without surrendering to its standards and demands.

The main body of the document falls into four sections, the last three having to do with conduct. Of these the first (1:13–2:10) is more explicitly theological, dealing with the basis of the ethical demand of the gospel, and culminating in the hortatory use of the image of building or temple (2:4–10), an image already noted in Ephesians and 1 Corinthians. The second (2:11–4:11) is specific and practical, without losing contact with its theological roots or becoming banal or trivial. Throughout this section the theme of submissiveness recurs (2:13, 18; 3:1). This submission is no cowardly groveling before worldly power, but an acceptance of the divinely ordained structures of order and authority in the world. Christians submit without capitulating and without surrendering their conscience. That they may have to suffer is a real possibility reflected throughout the letter. The final section (4:12–5:11) deals specifically with conduct in the face of persecution. The central point is that Christians should be obedient to God, conducting themselves in a manner beyond reproach and enduring with patience and courage the evil that unrighteous people may inflict.

In our passage (2:11–25), the author writes clearly and impressively. There is first a general introductory exhortation (vss. 11–12). "Aliens and exiles" possibly alludes to Genesis 23:4 (LXX), where Abraham calls himself an alien and exile (cf. also Heb. 11:13 and Ps. 39:12). The Christian church is a pilgrim people, as was the people of Israel. The language and conceptuality applied to Israel in scripture are adopted for the Christian community, which regards itself as heir to those ancient promises of God. The author's main interest (cf. vs. 12), however, is that Christians' behavior before the world should be above

"Repentant Peter" by Francisco de Goya (1746–1828).   *(Courtesy of the Phillips Collection, Washington, D.C.)*

reproach. It is anticipated that Christians will be denounced by the Gentiles. "Gentiles" here seems to mean non-Christian rather than non-Jew, an indication that the church regards itself either as a "third race" distinguishable from both Jew and Gentile or as the true Israel. In any case, the church sees itself against the background of a largely Gentile culture, and the problem of Jew and Gentile within the church seems to have been left behind. This viewpoint bespeaks a second- rather than first-generation origin for 1 Peter. "When he comes to judge" refers to the last judgment, an event still anticipated in the near future (4:7). It is implied that there may be some hope for those Gentiles who have previously maligned Christians if in the end they are led by their good works to an acknowledgment of God (which seems to be the meaning of "glorify"). Such a humane and hopeful view would accord with 1 Peter's doctrine of Christ's preaching to the dead (i.e., "the spirits in prison"; cf. 3:19; 4:6).

In line with the kind of conduct expected of Christians in this world, the author urges subjection to and support of civil authority (2:13–17). This passage finds a close parallel in Romans (13:1–7). If the author of 1 Peter did not know Romans, the similarity may rest on a common tradition concerning church and state reflected also in 1 Timothy (2:1 f.) and perhaps going back to Jesus himself (Mark 12:17). In any event, 1 Peter makes clear that Christianity is not a politically revolutionary movement. The government is ordained by God for the enforcement of order and justice (2:14; cf. Rom. 13:1–5). Whereas Paul assumed that the civil authority would carry out this function, such an assumption is not quite so clear in 1 Peter. Nevertheless, fundamental confidence in the emperor is affirmed (vss. 13, 17).

Obedience is not urged for the sake of sheer conformity, however, and is therefore not fundamentally self-serving. It is intended to silence the calumnies against the church and to contribute to its inner stability and unity. Moreover, its ultimate end is not that Christians should be docile and enslaved to whatever worldly order exists at any given time or place. The twofold injunction, "As servants of God, live as free people, yet do not use your freedom as a pretext for evil" (vs. 16), exhorts Christians to blameless behavior

Mocking and flagellation of Christ from French painted enamels by Pierre Reymond (sixteenth century). *(Courtesy of Metropolitan Museum of Art. Fletcher Fund, 1945.)*

in the world so that charges brought against them from any quarter may be shown to be palpably false. The author does not blandly assume that all will be well in this world for Christians whose conduct is unexceptionable. The prospect of unmerited punishment and suffering is already a real one (1:6; 4:12 ff.; 5:9 f.). The Christian is to *respect* the secular ruler, along with all people, and to *fear* only God and to *love* fellow Christians in the church (2:17).

The following paragraph (vss. 18–25) is directed specifically to slaves, but has implications for other Christians that extend beyond the institution of slavery. Within the established order, Christians conform to the legitimate demands that are placed upon them. Yet even in the face of illegitimate demands and punishment they accept their lot without rebelling. The person who has done wrong and suffers has nothing of which to boast. Rather, the righteous one who suffers unjustly has God's special approval (vss. 19, 20). The warrant for such an assertion is the example of Jesus Christ. Because Christ has suffered for them, believers follow in his steps (vs. 21) by suffering willingly also.

The mention of Christ's suffering leads into a series of descriptive and theological statements about the suffering of Jesus (vss. 21–24). These are largely constructed out of the Septuagint version of the servant songs of Isaiah. If they seem appropriate when applied to the suffering and death of Jesus, it is partly because from 1 Peter on—and perhaps earlier—these Isaiah passages have been used in describing and interpreting Jesus' death. We have in 1 Peter the *locus classicus* for the interpretation of the death of Jesus in terms of suffering, and with reference to Isaiah's suffering servant. Indeed, in relating Christ and Christians this passage marks an important point in the development of Christological thought and its ethical implications—the recognition that Jesus' death is the norm and model for Christian conduct.

The author's immediate purpose, to speak a redeeming and comforting word, a word of encouragement, is accomplished by pointing to the real and meaningful relation between the slave who is unjustly beaten and Christ, who was also unjustly punished, but by whose wounds the same slaves are healed. As they are united with him in suffering, so they will be united in his glory (1:3–9; 5:10). The relevance of the suffering of Christ is not, however, limited to slaves who are being unjustly punished. Any person of faith who suffers evil unjustly for righteousness' sake will be blessed (3:14), for it is better to suffer for doing good than for doing evil (3:17). Such a one, who suffers according to God's will, is comparable to Christ himself (3:18). Indeed, that person may be said to share in the sufferings of Christ (4:13).

The question of what historical circumstance evoked this emphasis on suffering (cf. also 1:6) has already been suggested (see Notes). The harassment of the readers *as Christians* is anticipated in 1 Peter, although it is uncertain whether the author expects a general state-sponsored persecution of Christians. The references to suffering as a Christian (4:14, 16) and the coming "fiery ordeal" (4:12) suggest as much. Yet the positive attitude to Roman authority expressed in 2:13–17 implies that the authority of the state is not behind the persecution of Christians, or at least the state is not recognized as hostile.[2] Clearly 1 Peter intends to encourage Christians and to promote their sense of inner strength and cohesiveness in the midst of an unfriendly environment.

To this end, much of the letter concerns the normal day-to-day business and behavior of individuals and church congregations. Thus we find in 1 Peter something already seen in Colossians, Ephesians, and James: the more or less stereotyped and probably traditional ethical exhortation directed to various persons or groups. In fact, despite its originality in appealing to the suffering of Christ, this passage (2:18–25) is just such an exhortation addressed specifically to slaves. Similar exhortations to wives (3:1–6), husbands (3:7), and the whole congregation (3:8–12) follow. Possibly also the exhortations to patience, courage, and steadfastness in the face of suffering are of a traditional nature.

Notes on 2 Peter and Jude

The second letter attributed to Peter, which follows 1 Peter in the New Testament, is now almost universally regarded as pseudonymous. 2 Peter contains material remarkably similar to the Epistle of Jude and is probably an elaboration of the content of that brief letter. Moreover, the author struggles against skepticism about the return of Jesus in light of its delay (3:3–10). He also knows a collection of the apostle Paul's letters, which he apparently regards as scripture (3:15–16), and may know one or more of the Synoptic Gospels (cf. 1:17–18), as well as John (1:14; cf. John 21:18). All these facts point in the direction of composition in the first half of the second century rather than during the apostle Peter's lifetime.

The Epistle of Jude, probably earlier than 2 Peter, is a writing of the late first century at the earliest. The "false teachers" (2 Pet. 2:1) who bring in heresies are likely the same as Jude's ungodly people "who pervert the grace of our God into licentiousness and deny our only Master and Lord, Jesus Christ" (Jude 4). Jude's denunciation accurately, if generally, describes what certain early Gnostic groups would have been perceived as doing and probably attests to their existence (cf. 1 Tim. 6:20–21), although the term is not used. The invective of 2 Peter is directed at similar opponents. Such Gnosticism became an important force in the second century, although it had roots in the first. By the explicit linkage with James (Jude 1), Jude is tied to the Letter of James as well. Prob-

---

2. It is sometimes suggested that 1 Peter reflects a situation similar to that described in the correspondence between the Roman governor Pliny and the Roman emperor Trajan (*ca.* A.D. 112). Pliny writes Trajan asking for instructions on handling the problem presented by Christians, and although both display an admirable desire to act fairly, it must also be noted that Romans preside over the execution of Christians who refuse to recant. But does such a policy and procedure admit of the kind of approbation found in 1 Peter 2:13–17? (The correspondence between Pliny and Trajan is available in English translation in H. Bettenson, ed., *Documents of the Christian Church,* 2nd ed. [New York: Oxford University Press, 1963], pp. 3 f.)

ably the reader is to understand it as emanating from the brother of James of Jerusalem, and therefore also from a brother of Jesus. This implied identification is difficult, however, given the character of the letter, especially its opposition to Gnosticism. There is no way of knowing where Jude and 2 Peter were written. Although the two letters are related, they are separated in the New Testament by the Johannine epistles.

Historically, neither Jude nor 2 Peter has played an important role in later interpretation of the New Testament. Indeed, there were doubts about the authenticity and authority of both in antiquity—of 2 Peter even more than of Jude. Possibly their eventual acceptance as authoritative and canonical had something to do with their vigorous, and useful, denunciation of the Gnostic or other aberrations from the faith. Such denunciation, which shades into a vilification of opponents unexampled elsewhere in the New Testament, could easily be applied by later interpreters to other opponents. In the history of polemics, therefore, 2 Peter and Jude have, unfortunately, provided controversialists with a rich source of fierce invective.

OUTLINE OF 2 PETER

Address (1:1–2)
Exhortation and Reminder (1:3–21)
Warning and Condemnation of False Teachers (2:1–22)
The Coming of the Day of the Lord (3:1–13)
Concluding Exhortation (3:14–18)

THE SECOND COMING AND THE TRUE FAITH (2 PET. 3:3–10; JUDE 3)

What is the relation between the delay of Jesus' return and the importance of true doctrine?

The third chapter of 2 Peter reveals a great deal about the situation and purpose of the letter. At the outset the author speaks of a previous letter, presumably 1 Peter, which he may have known as an authoritative book. Toward the end his reference to Paul clearly indicates that he knows a collection of the apostle's letters that have the status of holy scripture (3:16).

We have already noticed some indications that 2 Peter presupposes knowledge of the Synoptic Gospels, and even the Gospel of John. The reference to Jesus' having spoken of Peter's death (1:14) seems to reflect knowledge of John 21:18 or of a related tradition in which Jesus gives Peter to understand that he will die a martyr's death. Immediately thereafter the Johannine narrative deals with the question of the Beloved Disciple's fate (21:20–23). The reader discovers that some Christians believed that he would not die, but would live to see Jesus' return in glory (vs. 23). John, however, goes out of his way to make clear that Jesus did not actually say that. Apparently, the Gospel writer here deals with a real or potential disappointment at the failure of Jesus to appear (see Glossary: *Parousia*).

A similar concern is met in 2 Peter 3:3–10, where the "scoffers" who raise questions about the return of Jesus are probably Christians who have become disillusioned (vss. 3–4). Perhaps some were beginning to think that the

promise of Jesus' return had somehow already been fulfilled. In this connection, 2 Thessalonians 2:1–2 and 2 Timothy 2:17–18 give evidence of such
belief, as do some of the words of Jesus in the farewell discourses of the
Gospel of John (chaps. 14–17). In any event, we are confronting an understandable problem among Christians living a generation or more after Jesus'
death. Clearly, many of the first Christians believed that Jesus would return
before they, or at least their generation, had died out (cf. Mark 9:1; 1 Cor.
11:30; 1 Thess. 4:15). When he did not, troubling doubts arose.

The author of 2 Peter answers the questions raised by the so-called scoffers
on the basis of scripture or scriptural exegesis. First, he maintains that all
things have not continued "as they were from the beginning of creation" (3:4)
and points to the destruction of the world by flood (in the time of Noah; Gen.
7:11–21). Then he reiterates that a fiery judgment is still to come (vs. 7). Its
seeming delay has resulted from a failure to reckon according to God's time
(vs. 8). The basis for this reckoning is Psalm 90:4, although it is not explicitly
cited, where one day is equated with a thousand years. The author thus
shows that the scoffers do not know or understand scripture. Moreover, if
the Lord seems slow—actually he is not—it is just another manifestation of
his patience (vs. 9). In the meantime, let the scoffers and all others take warning! The comparison of the coming of the Lord to a thief (vs. 10) presupposes the motif of "a thief in the night" found in earlier New Testament
traditions (Matt. 24:43–44; 1 Thess. 5:2, 4; Rev. 3:3; 16:15).

In 2 Peter the typical concern of early Christians for pure doctrine, which
we have already observed in the Pastorals, comes to expression quite openly.
This letter reflects a situation in which the church had begun to think in terms
of a very long, indeterminate future. For such a future the church needed to
ready itself by emphasizing inner discipline, correct doctrine, and the rejection of heresy.

Both 2 Peter and Jude share these emphases, with the latter two becoming particularly clear in Jude, where the author appeals to his readers or hearers to defend "the faith that was once for all entrusted to the saints" (Jude
3). Such defense is necessary in the face of what both authors would consider the rankest heresy.

Jude, like 2 Peter, is convinced that the church, or Christians, must dig in
for a long siege. The concept of faith as "the faith" (i.e., doctrine), already
found in the Pauline Pastorals, here comes to completion: "faith" is understood as a deposit of doctrine given to the church ("the saints") at the beginning of the Christian era. The word *orthodoxy* is not used, but the author
is plainly thinking in terms of the opposition of orthodoxy and heresy that
has characterized the development of Christian doctrine during much of its
history. Interestingly, whereas the concept of faith foreshadows later developments, the designation of the church as "the saints" reflects a very primitive manner of thinking and speaking (cf. Rom. 1:7). Saints are not yet a

special or elite group within the church. All true believers are saints; that is, they are holy and dedicated to the Lord.

The Letters of John: Love, Doctrine, and Church Politics

Notes on the Johannine Letters

Although 2 and 3 John seem to be genuine letters, it is not clear that 1 John was conceived originally as a letter. It lacks the customary epistolary introduction as well as a conclusion. In fact, 1 John seems to end in midair with no conclusion at all. Nevertheless, the text more than once indicates that the author is writing to someone (2:12 ff., 26; 5:13); thus at least in this respect the document has the appearance of a letter.

Significant similarities of 1 John to the Gospel of John are pointed out in the discussion of the text. They are both formal and substantial, stylistic and theological. Although there are also some differences, the close relation of the Gospel and letters cannot be denied. In all probability the letters were written after the Gospel; 1 John in particular seems to presuppose the teaching of the Gospel. Its prologue is immediately intelligible in light of John 1:1–18, especially verse 14. The play on old and new commandments (2:7–8) seems to presuppose John 13:34. The problem posed by heterodox teachers or prophets claiming to speak through the Spirit may result from the promise of the Spirit (or Paraclete) as given by Jesus in the Fourth Gospel (cf. 14:15–17, 26; 16:12–15). The writer of 1 John has learned that the claim to be spiritually inspired does not guarantee orthodox teaching. In all probability 1 John was written to clarify the message of the Gospel of John and to make sure that it was not misinterpreted by those whom the writer considered false prophets.[3]

The place and date of origin of the Johannine letters are uncertain. According to ancient church tradition, both the Gospel and the letters were written in Ephesus by the apostle John. But most of the same reservations cited in connection with the tradition of the Gospel's origin and authorship apply also to the letters. There was a noted Asian churchman called the Elder John who flourished at the end of the first century or the beginning of the second and may have been confused with the apostle John in ancient times (Eusebius, *EH,* III, 39). It is tempting to suggest that he is the "John" who wrote the Gospel and letters, as the author of the brief second and third letters identifies himself as "the Elder." At best the evidence for identifying the author of 2 and 3 John with this ancient and largely unknown man is inconclusive. *Elder* was a common ecclesiastical title and *John* a common name. (The Greek noun *presbyteros,* elder, yields the term *presbyterian* to designate churches governed by elders.)

---

3. See Raymond E. Brown, *The Community of the Beloved Disciple* (New York: Paulist, 1979), pp. 93–144, as well as his *The Epistles of John,* The Anchor Bible, 30 (Garden City, NY: Doubleday, 1982), *passim.*

2 and 3 John, however, are so brief as to yield little data about their origin. Their obvious theological and stylistic similarities to 1 John strongly suggest that they were written by the same author. Although 2 John seems to presuppose and resist the same heretical views opposed by 1 John, this problem is not discussed in 3 John. Rather, some question of ecclesiastical politics seems to be the center of attention. Obviously, Diotrephes (vs. 9) is resisting the spiritual authority of the Elder. Unlike the Gospel and Revelation, 1 John has little distinct structure or pattern. Nevertheless, the identification of the following major thematic units may assist the reader in understanding the book.

OUTLINE OF 1 JOHN

Prologue: Christian Fellowship (1:1–4)
The Nature and Essence of Christianity (1:5–2:29)
The Marks of True Life in the Community (3:1–24)
Criteria for Certainty and Assurance Among the Faithful (4:1–5:12)
> *The Spirit of Jesus as Love (4:1–21)*
> *Obeying the Commandments (5:1–5)*
> *The Three Witnesses (5:6–12)*
Postscript: Sin and Forgiveness (5:13–21)

THE SPIRIT OF JESUS AS LOVE (1 JOHN 4:1–21)

How does one distinguish the bad spirit from the good?

After the introductory prologue, which is strikingly reminiscent of that of the Fourth Gospel, the author treats two basic themes, Christian life and Christian faith. He defines Christian faith so as to exclude certain erroneous views, including the notion that it is possible to have faith without its taking concrete form in a distinct manner of life.

Chapter 4 is typical in that it treats the major themes. First, there is a warning to test the spirits (vss. 1–6). The spirits are ultimately only two, the spirit of truth and the spirit of error (vs. 6). The spirit of error manifests itself in false prophets (vs. 1). This is the spirit of the antichrist, whose coming was predicted (vs. 3; cf. 1 Tim. 4:1; also pp. 385 f.). It is now in the world, and those who obey it are of the world (vss. 4 f.), whereas the intended readers are of God (vs. 6). The opposition of world and God in 1 John is irreconcilable (cf. 2:15–17).

A fuller understanding of this passage necessitates some acquaintance with the phenomenon of prophecy in the early church. The role of the Christian prophet has probably been underestimated, because none of the New Testament books except Revelation seems to have been written by a person who was primarily a prophet. Yet Paul ranks prophets immediately after apostles in importance (1 Cor. 12:28). When the author of Ephesians speaks of the church's being built upon the foundation of the prophets and the apostles (2:20), he may mean not Old Testament but Christian prophets. Although prophets were doubtless important figures (cf. also Acts 11:27 ff.; 21:10 ff.), they constituted a potential problem. Their claim to speak inspired words of Christ or the Spirit (cf. Rev. 1:1–3; 22:18 f.) might result in confusion, especially if divinely inspired prophets disagreed. Thus, the early Christians saw the necessity of distinguishing among them— "test the spirits" (4:1). The idea of discerning among the spirits, or among the prophets claiming to speak in the Spirit, is already present in Paul (1 Thess. 5:19–22), who laid down some fundamental rules for distinguishing the inspiration of the Holy Spirit in 1 Corinthians 12:3 and went on to outline procedures for regulating Spirit-inspired prophecy (1 Cor. 14). A half-century or so later the author of the Didache was to suggest that prophets who stayed in one place for longer than a brief period, sponging off the community, were very likely false prophets— not to mention those who, while purporting to speak in prophetic ecstasy, ordered a meal or demanded money (cf. *Didache* xi, 7–12; xii–xiii).

John's criterion for distinguishing the Spirit of God from that of the antichrist (4:2 f.) reveals a great deal about the understanding of Christianity that he opposed. His own positive affirmation or confession is apparent (vs. 2): the person inspired by the Spirit of God confesses that Jesus Christ has come in the flesh. The contrary confession would then deny that Jesus had come in the flesh, presumably in favor of the view that he was actually a spirit or matterless manifestation that had only appeared to take on an actual human body. In the apocryphal New Testament literature of the second century one may clearly see the burgeoning of this docetic view (*docetic* from the Greek verb *dokein,* meaning "to seem or appear"; that is, Christ only seems to be human). It was characteristic of Gnostic Christianity and went hand in hand with an abhorrence of this world and all things material (cf. 1 Tim. 4:3–5; pp. 386 ff.). John rejects such Christology as the work of the antichrist. Not confessing Jesus means to deny the genuinely human dimension of the Christ event. An important textual variant (vs. 3) reads "dissolves Jesus" instead of "does not confess Jesus." It was understood by the interpreters of the ancient church to refer to the gnosticizing division between Jesus and the Christ. Although this reading is probably not original, it would be an accurate commentary on our text, if the heretics denied that God had really revealed himself in Jesus—that the Word had become flesh (John 1:14).

The antichrist (vs. 3), whose spirit speaks through the false prophets, is the antithesis of God's revelation in Jesus. Therefore the typically Johannine dualism or polarity of God and world can be used in describing him and his adherents (vss. 4 ff.). The world in this sense is not the good creation of God but the bad creation of human beings. The world represents human society organized and operating without reference to, or concern for, the existence and will of God. World and Christ, world and church, are placed sharply over against one another. We have observed that in the Fourth Gospel this world is nevertheless described as the object of God's love (3:16 ff.); 1 John is not so explicit, yet even here Jesus is called "the Savior of the world" (4:14).

The antichrist is an apocalyptic figure, whose traces appear elsewhere in the New Testament. Although the actual term *antichrist* is found only in the Johannine letters, the idea of an individual or collective opponent of God's purposes, especially of his Messiah, appearing as a prelude to the winding up of world history, is not uncommon in Jewish and early Christian apocalyptic literature (cf. Mark 13:5 f.; 2 Thess. 2:1-12; and Rev. 20:7-10). Both 1 and 2 John (cf. 1 John 2:18–25; 2 John 7) apparently presuppose a tradition concerning the appearance of the antichrist at the last hour. But rather than seeing the antichrist as a purely supernatural, apocalyptic being, the author now equates this figure with the emergence of false teachers (2:18) or false teaching—that is, with historical events or personages. The teaching that denies the humanity of the Son of God, and in effect denies Jesus, is the spirit of the antichrist.

In the face of this powerful movement, represented by the antichrist, which is "of the world" (vs. 5),[4] the believer can be of good courage. The true believer has overcome the spirits (vs. 4), for as the author elsewhere says, "the darkness is passing away, and the true light is already shining" (2:8). The effective power of the new life that God gives through Christ is already present and available. With Christ, the believer has already overcome the power of the world (cf. John 16:33). The concept of the world develops (vss. 3ff.) from the simple statement that the antichrist is in the world, and a neutral concept of world, to an idea of the indwelling of the antichrist (or perhaps of Satan) in the world analogous to God's dwelling in the believer (vs. 4). Now the world becomes a hostile power. Thus it can be said that those heretics who have the spirit of the antichrist are "of the world" in the negative sense so characteristic of John's understanding of the term. As they are of the world, so the Christian is of God (vs. 6). Those who do not "listen to us," but instead presumably listen to the heretics (that is, those who do not accept the orthodox teaching about Christ), thereby show themselves to be not of God, but of the world.

A second major motif is now introduced (4:7–12). Being born of God is joined to the exhortation to love. The act of love determines one's relationship to God. Who is born of God and knows God? The person who loves. The possibility of knowing God in lovelessness is absolutely excluded (vs. 8): "God is love." The very character of love is to be understood with reference to the way in which God has shown love by sending his Son as the expiation for sin (vs. 9; cf. John 3:16 ff. and Rom. 3:25). Love is not a quality by which God is to be defined. Rather, God, in the sending of the Son, is the active subject by whom love is to be defined. Therefore, the question of human love toward God is secondary (vs. 10). Yet human love is certainly not a matter of indifference. Because God loves, Christians ought to love one another (vs. 11). The primary responses to God's love are faith in Jesus, as God's revelation in the flesh, and love for the other person. The real Christian, as distinguished from the pretender, is the one

4. NRSV translates "from the world" and "from God," but RSV's "of the world" and "of God" seem preferable.

who believes in Jesus and practices love. Through such human love God and his love become real and accessible, despite the fact that no one sees God (vs. 12; cf. John 1:18). The characteristically Christian belief that human love is grounded in the love of God finds no clearer expression than in 1 John.

The assurance that God abides in the believer and the believer in God is the possession of the Spirit (vs. 13). Obviously, one cannot possess the Spirit without love. What is more, neither love nor Spirit are abstract qualities or concepts. They are based upon a particular confession of Jesus. The confession of Jesus, or of God's action toward the world in Jesus (vss. 15 and 14, respectively), is the basis for the true understanding of both love and the Spirit. Of course, no one can truly claim the Spirit who does not believe in Jesus and live in love. The Spirit gives the believer assurance (vs. 13), but not in abstraction from faith and love (vs. 16). Those who lack faith and love can only be possessed of the spirit of the antichrist (4:1, 3; cf. 2:18–19).

John refers again (vs. 17) to the ground of the Christian's confidence, which is ultimately confidence before God in the day of judgment. Presumably, the perfecting of love of which he speaks is based upon a relation to Jesus: as Jesus is in this world, so is the Christian. One's pattern of life is modeled after Christ's (cf. John 13:12–17). The thought of confidence is carried a step forward by the introduction of a new idea, the incompatibility of love and fear (vs. 18). The perfecting of love means confidence in the day of judgment, because love excludes fear. One could, of course, think that perfect love casts out fear because it does away with the danger of judgment. Yet the author's initial statement, "There is no fear in love," indicates an intrinsic incompatibility between fear and love. "Perfect love casts out fear," because the one who loves is born of God and knows God (vs. 7), and because love eliminates the concern for self that breeds anxiety. Therefore, the presence of fear means that one is not perfected in love. Here the terms "perfected" (vs. 17) and "reached perfection" (vs. 18) are based on a Greek stem meaning "complete" in the sense of finished. In the person who is perfected, love has reached its desired fulfillment: it determines life.

John returns to the theme of God's prior love and the way in which it motivates people to love (vs. 19). The chapter ends with a simple but pointed statement on the relationship of love of God and love of other people (vss. 20 f.); the author puts matters succinctly and pungently. The commandment (vs. 21) is presumably Jesus' "new commandment" of John 13:34, which the author sometimes calls the old commandment (e.g., 2:7). The commandment is old from the author's perspective because it goes back to the beginning, i.e., to Jesus. In either case the commandment concisely conveys the burden of Jesus' teaching. At the same time it effectively reiterates a central conviction of our author, that faith and obedience, religion and ethics, must not be separated from one another, but always belong together.

The similarities of 1 John 4 to the Gospel of John are numerous. Some have already been noted; in conclusion, however, it will be helpful to call attention to the most prominent. The concept of the Spirit (1 John 4:1 ff.) plays a prominent role in the Gospel. "Spirit of truth" (1 John 4:6) occurs several times in the farewell discourses (John 14–16), although it is not set over against the spirit of error or the antichrist as in 1 John. The idea of Jesus' coming in the flesh (1 John 4:2) is reminiscent of John 1:14. The negative valuation of the world (1 John 4:5) is typical of the Fourth Gospel (John 4:6; cf. esp. John 17). The idea of birth (1 John 4:7) as spiritual regeneration also appears in John (esp. chap. 3). We have already noted the importance of the theme of love (1 John 4:7 ff.) in the Fourth Gospel. Most remarkably, 1 John 4:9 reflects the basic motifs and even the language of John 3:16. That no one has ever seen God (1 John 4:12) is also an affirmation of the prologue of the Gospel (1:18). The concept of abiding in Christ (1 John 4:13, 15 f.) and the themes of seeing and testifying or witnessing (4:14) are commonplace in John, and the connection of "this commandment" (1 John 4:21) and the "new commandment" of the Fourth Gospel has already been noted. Furthermore, the Greek text reveals many common stylistic traits that cannot be reproduced easily in English.[5]

CHURCH DOCTRINE AND POLITICS (2 AND 3 JOHN)

Why is hospitality to be tied to right doctrine?

These briefest letters of the New Testament deal with different problems. One (2 John) is theological and ethical; the other (3 John) more practical or political. Although they are similar in style and vocabulary to 1 John, because of their brevity one cannot be absolutely certain that they were written by the same author. In both letters, the author identifies himself as the Elder, although in 1 John there is no salutation and therefore no title.

The "elect lady and her children" addressed in the salutation of 2 John are often taken to be a church. (The Greek word *kyria* is the feminine form of *kyrios,* the title applied to Jesus and usually translated "Lord.") This seems to be confirmed by the reference to "the children of your elect sister" in the conclusion (vs. 13)—that is, the church from which the Elder writes.

The very brief 2 John takes up the two principal concerns of 1 John: love within the community (vss. 5–6) and the threat of false teaching (vss. 7–11). Once again the readers are reminded of the commandment they have had

---

5. Nevertheless, 1 John, and the Johannine letters generally, seem to embody a perspective and interests different from the Gospel. H. Conzelmann has pointed to the interest in guarding the tradition that pervades 1 John and distinguishes it from the Gospel; see "'Was von Anfang war,'" in *Neutestamentliche Studien für Rudolf Bultmann* (Berlin: Töpelmann, 1957), pp. 194–201. Reasons for this have been deduced and elaborated by Raymond E. Brown (above, p. 416, n. 3).

"from the beginning" to love another (cf. 1 John 2:7–11; 3:11). Clearly this is understood as the fundamental teaching of Jesus himself (vs. 6; cf. John 13:34), the commandment that defines the community in its conduct over against the world. The true community is, however, also defined by its correct doctrine, which begins with the affirmation of "the flesh," the real humanity of Jesus (vs. 7; cf. 1 John 1:1–3; 4:2–3; John 1:14). From this doctrine "the deceivers" have departed (cf. 1 John 4:1, 3), and such persons are to be shunned personally as well as theologically. They are not to be received or given hospitality (vs. 10). Whether or not 2 John was actually written by the author of the First Epistle, it seems to have been written subsequently to reinforce its teaching. Even as 1 John seems to presuppose, or to be based upon, the Fourth Gospel, so 2 John seems to presuppose 1 John.

The equally brief note known to us as 3 John is somewhat different, in that it does not address theological or ethical matters. It begins with a relatively lengthy, and genuinely personal, salutation addressed to a Gaius, who is a church leader loyal to and dependent upon (vs. 4) the Elder. Obviously, the Elder has just received a reassuring report about Gaius from traveling Christians (vs. 3).

Indeed, the burden of the letter has to do with such travelers and the obligation of offering hospitality to them (vss. 5–8). After reading Acts and Paul's letters, it comes as no surprise to learn that Christians, particularly some church leaders, frequently traveled from church to church or from city to city exercising apostolic or pastoral oversight and preaching the gospel. Hospitality to such travelers ("strangers," vs. 5) was therefore more than a matter of courtesy, although it was that as well.

The background of 3 John seems to have involved the refusal of one local church leader, Diotrephes, to receive the emissaries of the Elder (vss. 9–11). Quite plainly, no love is lost between the Elder and Diotrephes. Whether their conflict was based on theological or ethical matters, on questions of church polity or leadership, or merely on personal distaste, we are not told. Presumably the dispute did not have to do with the substance of the gospel; otherwise Diotrephes would have been denounced on these grounds. Nor does the Elder defend himself against charges made by Diotrephes. Probably this letter attests a struggle over jurisdiction and authority between church leaders. Interpreters have devoted a great deal of energy and imagination to the reconstruction of the circumstances or causes of this dispute, but the reasons are, unfortunately, hidden.

One specific purpose of 3 John is to commend Demetrius (vs. 12), who seems to be the bearer of the letter. The Elder apparently anticipated that while his emissary would not find the welcome mat out at Diotrephes' doorstep, Gaius would take him in. Clearly, 3 John again shows the importance of the house church and householder, which we have already encountered in Paul's letters. The relatively well-off Christian who possessed a house was an important figure who could not only host a church meeting but who could also provide hospitality for traveling missionaries and others. The letter also raises the question of itinerant versus local leaders in the early church. Obviously, Paul as an apostle was an itinerant leader, traveling from city to city and church to church, but he and the churches he founded had to rely on local, indigenous leadership as well (cf. Phil. 1:1). In 3 John we may well see evidence of conflict between a traveling leader, the Elder (and his emissaries), and a local church authority, Diotrephes. Such tensions would have developed as the church organized itself to live and work in the world.

The Revelation to John: Faith's Vision of a New Order

Notes on Revelation

The last book of the Bible, the Revelation to John, belongs to the genre and thought-world of apocalypticism, to which it has given its name. The term *apocalypticism* comes from the Greek word *apokalypsis,* which is the Greek title of the book and means "revelation." Thus Revelation is rightly said to be an apocalypse, and its thought is apocalyptic.

The literary genre of apocalypse is marked by four features: (1) the revelation itself, which is given by God; (2) a mediator between God and the world (in Revelation either Jesus Christ or an angel); (3) a prophet or seer who receives the revelation (in Revelation, John of Patmos); (4) disclosure of future events. This definition is actually based on Revelation, but it fits a number of documents, Jewish and Christian, written before and since. In the Hebrew Bible one thinks particularly of Daniel 7–12 and of Isaiah 24–27; in the Pseudepigrapha, parts of 1 Enoch (chaps. 14–15), 4 Ezra, and 2 Baruch. In early second-century Christianity, the Shepherd of Hermas followed Revelation, as did the Apocalypse of Peter.

Although in popular, as well as most scholarly, understanding, eschatology and therefore disclosure of the future belongs to the essence of apocalyptic thought, it can be argued that the revelation of heavenly, divine secrets rather than future expectation lies at its heart. Certainly in the New Testament, however, both the role of unfolding history and the revelation of knowledge about it are quite central and important. This is also the case in Daniel, the most prominent Old Testament apocalypse.

Apocalyptic eschatology was much more widespread in antiquity than the apocalypse as a literary genre. The entire New Testament, or most of it, is either written from the standpoint of apocalyptic eschatology or takes a position with respect to it. That is, it relates the dawning of a new age, commencing with Jesus (or John the Baptist) and inaugurated by God, who will bring it to completion in order to save the elect, or those who believe and obey. The New Testament can thus be said to be based on an apocalyptic eschatological outlook. But within the New Testament only Revelation is

The Emperor Domitian (A.D. 81–96), on a Roman coin.   *(Courtesy of American Numismatic Society.)*

an apocalypse, belonging to that literary genre. Because biblical apocalyptic presupposes the Old Testament, especially the prophets, it is fitting that Revelation is shot through with Old Testament language, though without explicit quotations.

The origins of the apocalyptic view of the world and history have been much debated, with several possibilities proposed. Persian dualistic influence on late biblical thought; the disappointment of this-worldly hopes for a free Jewish state; the impetus of ancient Hebrew prophecy. Without doubt apocalyptic ideas appear in Judaism as a consequence of the Exile, and under foreign influence and the pressure of the disappointment of worldly, historical hopes. Daniel, for example—at least the Daniel apocalypse—was written under the influence of the Seleucid repression of Jewish religion in the early second century B.C. The Qumran community felt oppressed by the Hasmonean dynasty, which it considered illegitimate, and produced its own, sharply dualistic, apocalyptic writings, perhaps under Persian (Iranian), Zoroastrian influence.

To what extent the entire Christian movement is a response to a sense of oppression and alienation—first, as experienced by (and within) Judaism; second, as experienced in the wider Roman world—is an important historical and theological question. The Gospel of John, which reflects a profound alienation of Jesus' followers from Judaism, does not promote an apocalyptic eschatological point of view. Instead, John reinterprets apocalyptic eschatology. Jesus' own proclamation of the coming of God's kingdom, as it is presented in the Gospels, can be understood as an expression of apocalyptic thought. Yet Jesus' kingdom proclamation does not share the dismal alienation from this world fostered by apocalyptic assumptions. Nor does the Jesus of the New Testament create the detailed symbolism of apocalyptic imagery. Still, Jesus' own kinship to the apocalyptic perspective is apparent, as can be seen from his words about the kingdom and judgment (see pp. 224–233). Paul also expects God to intervene decisively within history in a very short space of time (1 Thess. 4:13 ff.; 1 Cor. 15). Yet Paul, like Jesus, for the most part avoids detailed apocalyptic symbolism.

To understand and appreciate Revelation, we need to read it within the context of biblical and early Christian thought. Revelation echoes the language of scripture, especially the prophetic books of the Old Testament. Although its world may seem strange, it was not foreign to early Christian readers. It stands much closer to the world and thought of first-century Christians, and to Jesus, Paul, and even John, than modern Christians are likely to suppose.

The Book of Revelation itself was undoubtedly written during a period of crisis in the church, brought about by the active opposition of the Roman government. Tradition ascribes its message of resistance and hope in times of hardship and persecution to the reign of the Emperor Domitian, near the close of the first century (Eusebius, *EH*, III, 18, 3, citing Ignatius). As to the place and conditions of writing and the identification of those addressed, there is no reason to doubt its own statements (1:9). Nor is there any reason to doubt what the author says about himself in the same chapter. He is clearly an important church figure of Asia, a prophet, whose name is John. The traditional identification with John the son of Zebedee is not impossible, but nothing in the book itself either demands or indicates this. This John does not call himself an apostle; rather, he seems to refer to the apostles as revered figures of the past (18:20; 21:14). Moreover, he gives no indication of having accompanied Jesus or having known those who did. Nevertheless, the later identification of this John with the apostle and author of the Gospel paved the way for Revelation's acceptance into the canon of the New Testament.

The structure of Revelation is complex, and there is some reason to suspect that the original order has at points been disrupted or augmented. The following outline is developed in terms of a simple time scheme.

OUTLINE OF REVELATION

Introduction: The Vision of the Prophet on Patmos (1:1–20)
The Present Time of the Church Struggle: The Letters to the Seven
      Churches (2:1–3:22)
The Time between the Present and the End (4:1–18:24)
    The Vision of Heaven (4:1–5:14)
    The Opening of the Seven Seals (6:1–8:1)
    The Blowing of the Seven Trumpets (8:2–11:19)
    Apocalyptic Vision of Happenings on Earth (12:1–13:18)
    Preparatory Vision of the End (14:1–20)
    The Pouring Out of the Seven Bowls of Wrath (15:1–18:24)
The End: Future Victory (19:1–22:5)
    The Judgment and Christ's Return (19:1–20:15)
    The New World (21:1–22:5)
Conclusion: Present Time and the Prophet on Patmos (22:6–21)

THE VISION OF THE PROPHET ON PATMOS (REV. 1:1–20)

What is the relationship of the present to the future?

Although chapter 1 is not altogether typical of Revelation, because it contains hints and indications of what is to come it affords a springboard for understanding the entire book.

From beginning to end this is an apocalyptic work, a revelation. Thus John declares that his book will show the servants of God what must soon take place (vs. 1). The author of the revelation is God, who apparently gives it to

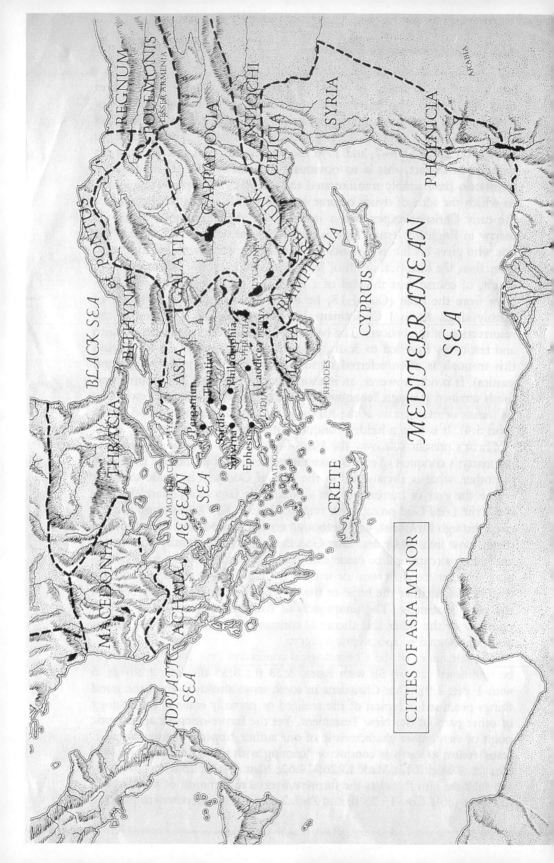

CITIES OF ASIA MINOR

Jesus Christ, who gives it to his angel, who in turn delivers it to John (cf. 22:6, 8, 16). John has borne witness or testified (1:2), a reference to the writing of this book; the object of this witness is the word of God and the testimony of Jesus Christ—that is, the revelation (cf. vs. 1), as is clear from the explanatory phrase "even to all that he saw." The same Greek word, or stem (*martyr-*), may be translated by the English words "witness" or "testimony." A blessing is pronounced on anyone who reads aloud, hears, and keeps (obeys) this prophecy about the future (vs. 3), and the imminence of what is to be narrated is again emphasized.

Several important characteristics of Revelation may be observed in this brief paragraph. The author's own title, "the revelation of Jesus Christ," reveals the apocalyptic character of the book. This emphasis is indicated also in several other ways: the content is to be revealed only to the faithful ("his servants"); it has to do with things that are soon to take place; the mediator between the divine realm (represented by God and Christ) and the human (represented by John and the other servants of God) is an angel; what the angel communicates, John somehow sees, presumably as a vision. All these traits are typical of the Jewish–Christian apocalyptic tradition. Furthermore, in the apocalyptic understanding of history, events unfold according to the plan and purpose of God ("what *must* soon take place"). John sees a preenactment of the unfolding culmination of world history. In keeping with the apocalyptic character of the book, Jesus Christ (vs. 1) is primarily the heavenly Christ, who later appears in great splendor (1:12 ff.) and is to return from heaven at the end of the age (22:20).

John next addresses himself to the seven churches of Asia (vss. 4 ff.; cf. 1:11 and see map, p. 426) with an epistolary salutation. This mixing of apocalyptic and epistolary form is not unprecedented. (The pseudepigraphical 2 Baruch chapters 76–87, although apocalyptic, are also in the form of a letter.) It is unusual, however, that John writes in his own name, in sharp contrast to most authors of apocalypses, who adopted names of famous persons out of the past (e.g., Ezra, Baruch, or Peter). By assuming the stance of an earlier figure, the writer could "predict" the intervening events, which had actually already occurred, thus lending credence to his predictions of the actual future. John, however, writes confidently under his own name and from the standpoint of his own time to the churches of Asia. Although he is an authoritative figure, his confidence lies not in himself but, rather, in his conviction that prophetic inspiration has been reborn in the church. He seems to have been a Christian prophet in the tradition of those mentioned in the letters of Paul, Ephesians, 1 John, and the Didache. As the Lord of Israel spoke through prophets in ancient times, so the Lord Jesus Christ speaks through prophets to the church and to the world. Although the prophet is addressed through angels, this mediation does not dilute his own experience and awareness of the powerful presence of the Lord.

The greeting "Grace to you and peace" (vs. 4) is typical of the New Testament, especially of Paul. "Who is and who was and who is to come" is God.

Judaism and the pagan world, as well as Christianity, afford examples of such speaking of God in the past, present, and future tenses. As for the seven spirits, they are probably the author's unique way of referring to the Holy Spirit. The number seven may be suggested by the seven churches to which John addresses the letters (chapters 2–3), but elsewhere (4:5; 5:6) he can speak of seven spirits, where the context excludes any reference or even allusion to the churches. Perhaps the seven spirits can be explained on the basis of John's fondness for the number seven, a symbol of completeness in antiquity. In later chapters Revelation speaks of the seven seals, trumpets, and bowls (see outline, p. 425.).

The description of Jesus as a faithful witness (vs. 5) recalls the "testimony" or "witness" of Jesus (1:2; Greek, *martyria*). Witness is the term used of a person who bears witness or testimony in the sense either of witnessing an event or witnessing on behalf of someone. In early Christian usage, however, it soon took on a specific connotation. For example, in Revelation (see 2:13, 11:3–7, and 17:6), the witness has often died as a result of witnessing. The extent to which the idea of dying became integral to the term itself because of the early Christian experience is indicated by the meaning of the word *martyr* in English. Jesus Christ is the archetypal witness and martyr, the one who gives his life as his testimony, and others follow in his footsteps. Thus the historical death of Jesus is crucial for John.

His martyrdom is not, of course, just the end of a great and good person. As the first-born from the dead (cf. Col. 1:18) he is the exalted Messiah, the ruler of earthly kings. Moreover, his resurrection is related to the resurrection of the believer (cf. 2 Cor. 15). The believer, especially the person whose faith and testimony have led to death, is to share Christ's glory. In Revelation this triumph is often referred to simply as conquering (cf. 2:26 and *passim*). It is not, however, an immortality easily gained. The resurrection life is attained through conquest of the power of this world, especially by means of martyrdom at the hands of the world (cf. John 16:33 and 1 John 5:4). It is then a hidden conquest, at least to the eyes of the world.

Christ's present rule over the kings on earth (vs. 5) is as hidden as is the martyr's conquest. Yet it is nonetheless real. And in the one case as in the other, what is already real in the eyes of God will be made manifest before the eyes of humankind. In words made famous by Handel's *Messiah*, "the Lord God omnipotent reigneth" (19:6 KJV). God's reign is exercised through Christ, who, although crucified, dead, and buried, nevertheless now lives and rules. That God through Christ actually does reign, and that this reign will be made manifest to bring all peoples into subjection, whether for their weal or woe, is the basic theme of Revelation. Of course, this message is either the hope or the assumption of almost every book in the New Testament. The uniqueness of Revelation, however, is that in one way or another this theme is constantly in the foreground and is always presented in apocalyptic imagery.

The remainder of the Christological confession (vss. 5b–7) appears to be traditional (cf. vs. 5b with Rom. 3:23 ff.; 8:35 ff.; Gal. 2:20; vs. 6 with 1 Pet. 2:9). That Christians in some sense already possess the good things promised is typical of the realized or partially realized eschatology of other parts of the New Testament. Yet the future-oriented apocalyptic point of view, more characteristic of this author, appears again in verse 7. Jesus' return to earth as conqueror "coming with the clouds" is not a new idea (cf. Daniel 7:13; Mark 13:26; 14:62; Matt. 24:30; 25:31). That every eye shall see him forecasts the future universal recognition of the lordship of Christ (cf. 1 Cor. 15:25 ff. and Phil. 2:10 f.). The references to piercing and wailing allude to the crucifixion (cf. Zech. 12:10 and John 19:37) and the implied future judgment of the nations.

The end of the epistolary salutation is indicated by the "So it is to be. Amen," a liturgical formula. The prophetic word (vs. 8) has no obvious connection with what precedes or follows. In a sense the verse is related to the prediction of the coming of Jesus (vs. 7), because it affirms that God is the sure ground of this hope. The first and last parts of the statement, the word of the Lord God ("I am the Alpha and the Omega") and the description of him in terms of past, present, and future, are more closely related than may initially appear. Alpha and omega are the first and last letters of the Greek alphabet, the equivalent of the English expression "from A to Z." God is the first and last (cf. 22:13, where this explanation is given), the one who was and is and is to come. Thus he is the Lord of history at the beginning, at its end, and in the interim.

The apocalyptic character of the book and its abuse by ancients and moderns obsessed with predicting the future have obscured the indispensable link with the past and the significance of the present as real and important aspects of the author's thought. We have already observed the importance of the past (vss. 4–7): church tradition, the historical Jesus, and the Old Testament. As for the present, the author's message for the contemporary churches of Asia unfolds in the next chapters (2–3). Although chapters 19–22 plainly have to do with the future return of Christ and the end of the world history, the long central section (chaps. 4–18) does not deal solely with the end time. Although the end is constantly in view, the author is also concerned with his own period. For example, John's apocalyptic interpretation of past and present historical events can be seen in the portrayal of the destruction of Jerusalem (chap. 11), the destiny of the Messiah and the church in the world (chap. 12), and the depredations of the Roman Empire (chaps. 13, 17, and 18). All history—past, present, and future—is under the sign of the Alpha and the Omega, the lordship of the God who was and is and is to come; nothing falls outside the scope of his revelation.

John's own involvement in that history becomes clearer in the following paragraph (1:9–11), where the reader learns that it includes participation in the events of the world as well as in the life of the church. This section marks the beginning of the revelatory book proper, for it serves to introduce the visions, which comprise chapters 2 and 3 as well as the rest of his work. The

"Saint John the Evangelist on Patmos" by Titian (1490–1576).   *(Courtesy of National Gallery of Art, Washington, D.C. Samuel H. Kress Collection.)*

so-called letters to the seven churches are no less visions (1:11–20) than the sighting of New Jerusalem (chap. 21). Yet the naming of the locations of the churches (vs. 11) makes graphic and concrete the this-worldly dimension of Revelation.

Crucial for grasping John's situation as he writes, and therefore for understanding this book, is the statement that he was on Patmos "because of the word of God and the testimony of Jesus" (vs. 9). Probably he means that he was on Patmos as punishment for preaching the word of God and testifying to Jesus; this is especially likely in view of the fact that such preaching and testifying had led to martyrdom (cf. 6:9 and 20:4). John speaks of sharing not only the kingdom but the persecution and the patient endurance.

The persecutions perpetrated against God's people call for steadfast endurance. Hebrews also mentioned the need for endurance with the possibility of persecution already in view (10:34 f.; 12:4). In Revelation persecution seems to have become the predominant reality. Moreover, we know that Patmos was used as a penal colony, a place of banishment, by the Romans. Ancient church tradition also understood John to have been in prison because of his Christian preaching.[6] We are justified in accepting this tradition as an accurate interpretation of Revelation 1:9.

John receives his revelation "in the Spirit" (vs. 10); the association of the Spirit with visions and ecstatic utterances is common to primitive Christianity. The speaking in tongues that Paul discusses in 1 Corinthians (chap. 14) is called the utterance of mysteries in the Spirit (cf. Acts 2:1 ff.). By "the Lord's day" John evidently means Sunday. If so, this is one of the earliest references to Sunday as the distinctly Christian holy day. "The sabbath" in the New Testament as in the Old always means the Jewish Sabbath, Saturday. Sunday has appropriately replaced Saturday as the Christian Sabbath, for according to tradition it was on Sunday (the third day after, and including, Friday) that Jesus rose from the dead. The voice like a trumpet that John hears is that of the Son of Man (vs. 13), the heavenly Christ.

John writes by divine command (vs. 11) and by command sends what he writes to the seven churches of Asia. The command is to "write in a book what you see" rather than what you hear. The mode of the communication of revelation is not verbal, as is usual in the earlier Old Testament prophets, but visual, as in the tradition of Ezekiel, the later, postexilic prophets, and, above all, the Jewish apocalyptic writers.

The visionary scenes now begin (vs. 12) and we encounter for the first time the problem of how to understand them. On the one hand, the narrations of the visions seem to be carefully constructed literary works, replete with scriptural allusions and language. (It is all the more remarkable that John does not cite scripture explicitly, as other major New Testament writers do.) On the other hand, the possibility that ecstatic or visionary experiences were the basis for what the author has written cannot be excluded. Evidence of the genuineness of the experiences is the absence of certain conventionalities of literary form that appear in most late Jewish apocalyptic. As we have observed, John is not pseudonymous and does not utilize the fiction of prophecy written in an earlier era. In other words, he does not find it necessary to accredit his message by concealing himself; nor does he attempt to gain credence for his prophecy of things to come by dressing out as predictions the recitation of generally known historical facts.

The seven golden lampstands (vs. 12) recall the seven-branched lampstand (Hebrew, *menorah*) that was said to stand outside the second veil of the Israelite tabernacle (Exod. 25:31–40; cf. Zech. 4; a passage dealing with

---

6. R. H. Charles, *A Critical and Exegetical Commentary on the Revelation of St. John* (Edinburgh: T. & T. Clark, 1920), I, 23, cites the relevant passages from Pliny, Tertullian, Clement of Alexandria, and Origen.

the messianic hope). In all probability the allusion is intentional despite the fact that we here seem to be dealing with seven separate stands, not one. The presence of the lampstands indicates an approach to the holy place. But John's explicit interpretation is that the seven lampstands represent the seven churches soon to be addressed (chaps. 2 and 3).

The appearance of the Christ (vs. 13) evokes Daniel 7:13, "one like the son of man." We are not told that this figure is the Christ, and John does not favor Son of Man as a messianic title (but cf. 14:14); yet 1:17 ff. makes this identification with Christ certain. The clothing of this still-mysterious figure (vs. 13) may have been suggested by Ezekiel 9:2 and 11 and Daniel 10:5. The remainder of the description (vss. 14–15) is for the most part derived from the appearance of the one who was the Ancient of Days or an Ancient One (Dan. 7:9, NSRV), although the comparison of his voice to the sound of many waters probably comes from Ezekiel 1:24 and 43:2. Obviously John's mind was steeped in the language and imagery of the Old Testament.

The seven stars (vs. 16) are interpreted in verse 20. The sharp two-edged sword recalls Genesis 3:24 (cf. Ezek. 21:9–10) and especially Hebrews 4:12. In the latter passage, as apparently here, the sword symbolizes the word of God. Christ's shining face indicates nearness to, if not possession of, the glory of God himself (cf. 2 Cor. 3:7–18; 4:6). With this verse the description of the vision of the Son of Man is complete. John's reaction and Christ's response in identifying himself and explaining the vision to John follow (vss. 17–20).

John's prostration at his vision of the heavenly Christ (vs. 17) is not only understandable but also liturgically appropriate. Daniel 10:7–10 is evidently the immediate background if not the direct inspiration of this verse. Christ reaches out, restores John (vs. 17), and identifies himself to him (vss. 17b–18). That Christ is the first and the last implies that like God, and with him, he exercises lordship over history from beginning to end. "Living one" and "alive forever and ever" in conjunction with the statement "I was dead" refer unmistakably to the crucifixion and resurrection. The power of the keys (in Matt. 16:19 given to Peter) is here reserved for Christ. As a result of his own death and resurrection Christ assumes power over death and Hades (cf. Rom. 6:9 f.), for his resurrection is no mere resuscitation, but an exaltation to supreme power and authority. The divine ascriptions and prerogatives applied to Christ imply that humanity's ultimate destiny depends upon and is assured by him. The claim to possess the keys of death and Hades (vs. 18) may also be related to the primitive Christian concept of Christ's descent into hell and his freeing of the captives there (1 Pet. 3:18–22; 4:6; cf. Eph. 4:8–10).

Attention turns once again to the prophet's task as Christ commands him to write (vs. 19). The Book of Revelation concerns not only the unfolding of the future but also the interpretation of present events: "what is" as well as "what is to take place after this." Christ interprets the seven stars and seven lampstands to him (vs. 20). The notion that nations, communities, or even individuals had guardian angels was not uncommon in the ancient world (cf.

Ancient tomb at Beth She'arim with the seven-branched menorah.   *(Courtesy of Israel Government Tourist Office.)*

Tob. 5:21); so each church has its angel, who serves it as a medium of revelation or communication with God. The letters to the seven churches (chaps. 2 and 3) are then directed to them through these guardian angels.

The seven letters are no ordinary letters at all, but are as much supernatural in their source and delivery as the rest of the book. Nevertheless, they again show the author's concern, not only with heavenly things and things to come, but with the this-worldly life and problems of the churches. This concern is directed both toward the inner life of the church and toward its witness to a hostile world. Naturally, the two are related, for no church with chinks in its moral armor would be strong enough to stand before such a world and resist the demand to worship its gods.

The remainder of Revelation presents a jarring juxtaposition of the heavenly and the earthly, the historical or worldly and the eschatological. Chapters 4 and 5 picture the heavenly court. The seer describes the throne of God himself and the momentous events taking place there, particularly the designation of the Lamb who had been slain as worthy to open the scroll. The Lamb is, of course, Christ. The opening of six of these seals is described in chapter 6. Heavenly events and realities have their earthly counterparts and consequences. With the opening of the seals catastrophes break out across the earth. Then there follows an interlude (chap. 7). The first part (7:1–8) shows the gathering of the elect from the four corners of the earth and the latter (vss. 9–17) their appearance in heaven. At the beginning of chapter 8 we have the opening of the seventh seal—and silence. After about half an hour of silence, the sounding of the seven trumpets begins (chaps. 8 and 9; 11:15–19) with disasters erupting upon the earth.

Chapters 10–13 deal with contemporary events or those of the recent past. The prophet's own experience (chap. 10) is like that of the prophet Ezekiel (Ezek. 2:8–3:3). Since Ezekiel's word of the Lord had to do with lamentations and woes, especially against Jerusalem (cf., e.g., Ezek. 4:1 ff.), not surprisingly Revelation 11 reflects the devastation of that same city. The birth and persecution of the Messiah and of his church are envisioned in chapters 12 and 13. In chapter 12 the heavenly dimension of the conflict is paramount, whereas in 13 attention focuses on Rome, described under the apocalyptic symbol of the beast. The sounding of the seventh trumpet is delayed by intervening scenes, just as the opening of the seventh seal was delayed. The seventh and final stage of each sequence has a peculiar significance, for apparently it stands symbolically at the borderline between the apocalyptic and catastrophic dissolution of this world and the coming of God's kingdom. The events following upon the sounding of the trumpets recapitulate those following the opening of the seven seals. Yet there may also be a progression. After the seventh seal there is only silence, but after the seventh trumpet we get a preview of the glory that is to come (11:15–19).

From chapter 14 onward there are no longer apocalyptic interpretations of the immediate past or present, but of the future. Again the seer has a vision of heaven (14:1–5), this time followed by a series of warnings from angels flying in heaven and the command that the heavenly Christ reap the harvest of the earth (14:14–20). Chapters 15 through 18 describe in appropriately symbolic terms the final upheavals to be wrought on earth by the outpouring of the bowls of divine wrath.

The seer's prophecy about the remainder of world history is completed with the outpouring of the seventh bowl of wrath and the destruction of Babylon, which is persumably Rome (chaps. 17 and 18). Yet we can actually discern no clear distinction between world history as we understand it and the last days. John understands his own time to be the last days. He does not conceive the present as a period of secular history where everything is governed by natural, social, or psychological laws of cause and effect. There is for him no secular history, for all time is ultimately under the lordship of God. Nevertheless, the immense powers of evil, with otherworldly origins and dimensions (e.g., the beast, the dragon or serpent, who is called the Devil and Satan, 12:9), presently hold sway in the world. Their lordship is, however, ephemeral. God's wrath is directed against them and they are overthrown.

Yet victory does not occur easily or without vast repercussions. Chaos and disaster break out upon the earth as the power of God overwhelms the forces of evil. Even the advent of Christ, traditionally called the second coming, does not put an end to the struggle once and for all (chap. 19). After the thousand-year reign of Christ, the millennium (after the Latin word for thousand), there is still another outbreak of evil, led by Satan himself (chap. 20), before God finally brings everything into subjection (21:1–22:5). Nevertheless, the substance of the seer's message is not that the end is a long way off, but that the night is already far spent, the day is at hand (cf. Rom. 13:12). The apocalyptic drama is underway and moves inexorably toward its conclusion. "Surely I am coming soon. Amen. Come, Lord Jesus!" (22:20).

Christians of John's day were willing at the risk of their lives to resist the demand that they worship the Roman emperor (13:1–15; cf. 18:24), the incarnation of worldly order and power, the epitome of a man's deification of himself. Why did they dare to do so? Such worship seems little more than a perfunctory gesture, although it was a significant token of subjection to the power and authority of this world. These Christians resisted because they believed in an authority that transcends this world, an authority revealed in the death of Jesus upon the cross and in his exaltation from the dead to God's own right hand. The Book of Revelation shows that for many, if not most, of them this conviction and the refusal to fall down and worship the beast were set in the context of a lively future hope, not primarily for their own personal survival of physical death, but for the manifestation of God's authority and rule before all humanity. God's Christ and his saints were to be vindicated before the eyes of a skeptical and evil world.

Thus Revelation gives testimony to faith in the lordship of God over history. The author is convinced that the apparent confusion of events does in fact lead somewhere; it is not meaningless. Yet such meaning is not apparent in individual events, for it can only be grasped when history is viewed in its entirety—that is, from the standpoint of its expected end. Christ is the light by which all history is illuminated for John. The Old Testament provides the imagery by means of which he portrays the end. Of course, Revelation's interest in the final days is not unprecedented in the New Testament. Already Paul's correspondence testifies to his conviction that the projected end provides the key to understanding the present. The various apocalyptic discourses of the Gospels (Mark 13 parr.) disclose the existence of widespread early Christian concern about the end time, its signs and warnings. For the early church and the writers of the New Testament, faith meant not only looking upward to God and Christ, and backward to the manifestations of God's reality in the past, but forward in expectation to his further and final revelations in the future.

Revelation's concentration upon the eschatological future and its use of vivid apocalyptic language seems to stand in sharp contrast to the Gospel of John, in which eschatological fulfillment is emphasized and apocalyptic imagery is avoided. We have seen that the language and theology of the letters of John are closely related to the Gospel. Although the Revelation to John, traditionally ascribed to the same author, seems remote from the other Johannine writings, some important points of similarity or lines of connection exist. There is in 1 John still an expectation of Jesus' return (2:8, 18, 28), and the circle of disciples that preserved and published the Gospel of John evidently had at one time cherished the hope that he would return before the death of the Beloved Disciple (21:23). Moreover, in Revelation, as in the Gospel and 1 John, Jesus is called the word, *logos* (Rev. 19:13). *Witness* (or testimony) and *witnessing* are also important concepts in all these writings. In the Gospel, Jesus promises the Spirit to his disciples (e.g., in 14:15–17), but in 1 John the claim of spiritual inspiration by those who espouse erroneous doctrine is challenged (4:1–3), whereas the Revelation to John claims to be a Spirit-inspired book in its entirety (1:10). Only in the Gospel of John (19:37) and Revelation (1:7) is Zechariah's prophecy (12:10) applied to the crucifixion of Jesus. One could go on, but these instances are enough to indicate that the Johannine writings—Gospel, letters, and apocalypse—are related by content and perspective as well as by tradition.

Suggestions for Further Reading

JAMES

Martin Dibelius, rev. by H. Greeven, *James,* trans. M. A. Williams (Philadelphia: Fortress, 1976), is a classic commentary dating from 1920 but revised as recently as 1964 before being translated for the Hermeneia series. A good shorter, less technical, commentary is S. Laws, *The Epistle of James* (San Francisco: Harper & Row, 1980).

1 PETER, 2 PETER, JUDE

E. Best, *1 Peter* (Grand Rapids, MI: Eerdmans, 1971), is a helpful and reliable commentary. L. Goppelt, *A Commentary on 1 Peter,* trans. J. E. Alsup (Grand Rapids, MI: Eerdmans, 1993), although originally completed two decades ago, remains an important work. Because of their close literary relationship, 2 Peter and Jude are usually treated together, as in J. H. Neyrey, *2 Peter, Jude: A New Translation with Introduction and Commentary* (New York: Doubleday, 1993). R. J. Bauckham, *Jude, 2 Peter* (Waco, TX: Word Books, 1983), is conservative (the authenticity of Jude but not 2 Peter is accepted) but also a serious commentary on those two letters. Although based on the Greek text, the introductions are accessible to the English reader. On 1 Peter see also J. H. Elliott, *A Home for the Homeless: A Sociological Exegesis of 1 Peter, Its Situation and Strategy* (Philadelphia: Fortress, 1981).

THE JOHANNINE LETTERS

The standard commentary is still R. E. Brown, *The Epistles of John* (Garden City, NY: Doubleday, 1982), although the commentary of Rudolf Schnackenburg, *The Johannine Epistles: Introduction and Commentary,* trans. R. and I. Fuller (New York: Crossroad, 1992), has at length been made available to the English reader. K. Grayston, *The Johannine Epistles* (Grand Rapids, MI: Eerdmans, 1984), is briefer in scope and differs from most other commentaries in dating the letters earlier than the Fourth Gospel. On the theology of the letters, see J. M. Lieu, *The Theology of the Johannine Epistles* (Cambridge: Cambridge University Press, 1991). For further suggestions see the bibliography at the end of Chapter 5.

THE REVELATION TO JOHN

Commentaries include G. R. Beasley-Murray, *The Book of Revelation* (Grand Rapids, MI: Eerdmans, 1974); M. E. Boring, *Revelation* (Louisville, KY: Westminster/John Knox, 1989); and J. Roloff, *The Revelation of John: A Continental Commentary,* trans. J. E. Alsup (Minneapolis: Forress, 1993). There are also the recent studies of A. Y. Collins, *Crisis and Catharsis: The Power of the Apocalypse* (Philadelphia: Westminster, 1984), and E. S. Fiorenza, *The Book of Revelation: Justice and Judgment* (Philadelphia: Fortress, 1985), the latter a collection of essays. C. J. Hemer, *The Letters to the Seven Churches of Asia in their Local Setting* (Sheffield, England: JSOT Press, 1986), deals with historical connections and archaeological evidence, and R. J. Bauckham, *The Theology of the Book of Revelation* (Cambridge: Cambridge University Press, 1993), with theology. A. W. Wainwright traces the history of interpretation in *Mysterious Apocalypse: Interpreting the Book of Revelation* (Nashville: Abingden, 1993).

The Book of Revelation represents the literary genre and mode of language and thought that is called apocalyptic, after the Greek title of the book (*apokalypsis,* which means "revelation"). There are several extensive studies of apocalyptic. Among the more recent and important: P. D. Hanson, *The Dawn of Apocalyptic: The Historical and Sociological Roots of Jewish Apocalyptic Eschatology,* rev. ed. (Philadelphia: Fortress, 1979); C. Rowland, *The Open Heaven: A Study of Apocalyptic in Judaism and Early Christianity* (New York: Crossroad, 1982); J. J. Collins, *The Apocalyptic Imagination: An Introduction to the Jewish Matrix of Christianity* (New York: Crossroad, 1984). Rowland is distinctive in questioning the longstanding assumption that imminent futurist eschatology defines the essence of apocalyptic thought.

Chapter *12*

The Community of the New Testament

*T*he New Testament is a book, or a collection of books. To study the New Testament is, as we have seen, to endeavor to understand these books individually and as a whole. New Testament study is then the study of literature, a body of ancient religious literature. The study of any literature is impoverished if history is ignored. One may watch or study Shakespeare without knowledge of Elizabethan England and be fascinated, amused, and moved. Yet one's understanding and appreciation will be greatly enhanced by knowledge of the period from which the plays stem. The same is true for the Bible in general and the New Testament in particular.

The desire to know about Jesus, the earliest Christians, and their writings is, however, usually motivated by something other than sheer antiquarian interest. Although historical knowledge may illumine Shakespeare's plays, it makes little difference for the appreciation of Shakespeare whether or not his characters ever actually existed, though many of them did. For vitally interested readers of the New Testament, however, that sort of historical question is more than a matter of academic interest. The New Testament writers believe and claim that in Jesus, and among the events and disciples clustered about him, God was active and making himself known. Moreover, they invite the reader to decide about their claim, which extends to the history following the active ministry of Jesus as well as to that ministry itself. If we had reason to ask what really happened with Jesus, we have equal reason to ask about what happened with the early church. It belongs to the nature of the New Testament, as well as to the character of Christian faith, that readers should be concerned with its history.

The Emergence of Early Christianity

Basically, the order of the New Testament books does not mislead us about early Christian history, which was, however, more complex than at first appears. The earliest Christians had little interest in recording history, in part because of their expectation of its imminent end. The Book of Acts, for example, was in all probability written a half-century or more after the crucifixion of Jesus and a quarter of a century after the death of Paul. Likewise, the canonical Gospels were not written down until the original eyewitnesses and apostles had virtually died out. This is certainly true of Luke (1:1–3), and in all probability also of Matthew. John is explicitly traced to one of the last surviving disciples of Jesus (21:23–24), but whether he wrote the Gospel in its present form remains questionable. Mark, the earliest Gospel, was not written by one of the Twelve, although ancient church tradition links the evangelist with Peter and implies that it was written either toward the end of his career or soon after his death.

The earliest Christian writings of which we have any knowledge were Paul's letters, written out of the pressing demands of the moment. Indeed, when the Gospels appeared, they were written primarily for religious, theological, inspirational, and instructional purposes. That they were about a real person was certainly important, and they are valuable as historical sources. Nevertheless, they were not written to record history for the sake of history. Perhaps Luke comes closest to matching the purpose or intention of an ancient, if not a modern, biographer or historian. Significantly, it was Luke who in Acts first wrote about the life of the early church. It is quite clear, as we have seen, that Luke intended to describe a historical movement, namely, the progress of the gospel across the known world, from Jerusalem to Rome. But his purpose, though historical, was charged with theological motivation.

Having read Acts, we know Luke's version of the history of the early church. As we have already noticed, however, some things were occurring that Luke does not describe or even mention, and some things that he does mention create as many problems for the historian as they solve. Luke's portrayal of the gospel's progress fixes primarily upon the missionary work of Paul.

Where Paul goes, the gospel goes. We do not learn, however, how Christianity reached Rome or Egypt, although it got there prior to and apart from Paul's efforts. We do not learn from Acts about the transmission and preservation of tradition about Jesus, although Luke's Gospel attests to its existence. (Luke does, however, portray the apostles as referring to Jesus' ministry in their missionary preaching.) We gain from Acts little sense of the lively expectation of Jesus' return and the coming of God's kingdom that we find in the Gospels and Paul's letters.

Luke gives in Acts a great deal of data about Paul's missionary work that makes contact with what we can glean from Paul's letters. Obviously, the information found in Acts is not fabricated. Positive correlations can often be made between the Acts narrative and Paul's letters (see pp. 267–268). On the other hand, there are also difficulties. Although much of what Paul says in Galatians (chaps. 1 and 2) about his second visit to Jerusalem corresponds to the narrative of the Jerusalem Council (Acts 15), there are also differences. For example, the Jeruslem Council is Paul's *third* visit to Jerusalem according to Acts, not his second (Gal. 1:20). That complete tranquillity on the issue of Gentile Christians did not, as Acts implies, result from the council is already clear in Galatians (2:11–21). Despite these problems, in Acts as well as the Pauline letters we have important sources for understanding earliest Christianity, even though they must be used with critical care.

For the latter part of the first century, valuable information can be gleaned from Ephesians, the Pastoral and Catholic Epistles, and Revelation, as well as from 1 Clement of the so-called Apostolic Fathers (see the Glossary). Of course, it is still arguable that certain of these letters, namely, Ephesians, James, and 1 Peter are the work of the apostolic authors to whom they are ascribed. Hebrews is sometimes taken to be earlier than the Roman war (A.D. 66–70), although this writing cannot any longer be ascribed to Paul. But at the least the Pastorals, the Johannine Epistles, 2 Peter, Jude, and Revelation, along with 1 Clement, inform us about conditions in the churches toward the end of the first century or even later. They are second- or third-generation documents, concerned with church order, organization, discipline, and leadership, and also with the appearance of what seems to them to be obviously erroneous and dangerous teaching—often accompanied by moral degradation. Strong church leadership and strict adherence to firm doctrinal and moral standards are enjoined in the face of such aberrations.

The question of whether Christians must observe the Jewish ceremonial law and males must be circumcised is apparently settled: they need not. Yet the Old Testament and its Decalogue continue to carry authority. The relationship of Christianity to Judaism is still an issue, but the separation of church and synagogue (cf. John 9:22; 12:42) seems to have taken place. The danger of persecution by the Roman state is by now increasing. The books of 1 Peter, Hebrews, and Revelation, especially, are concerned with this problem and what the Christians' attitude toward it should be. Both persecution and the problem of heresy continued to occupy the church far beyond the

New Testament period, as did the question of the relationship of Christianity and Judaism.

Just such problems or situations as these are not foreign to the Gospels, most of which were probably written nearer the end than the middle of the first century. That the Gospels are primarily sources for the history of the church of their times and only secondarily sources for Jesus' own ministry may be an overstatement. Yet the very existence of the Gospels is unthinkable apart from the interests of the churches that produced them. Their interests were not completely different from those of Jesus and the earliest apostles, but neither were they identical. The impact of Jesus upon subsequent generations has been filtered mainly through the New Testament, especially the Gospels. It was transmitted initially through those followers who recalled his words and ministry and spoke of them to others. In doing so they exercised a significant and selective role in shaping the tradition and, ultimately, the Gospels. Of course, in selecting, editing, and arranging such tradition the evangelists further influenced, directed, and in a sense enhanced the historic impact of Jesus.

Having studied the Gospels and other documents of the developing Christian movement, we now consider briefly how in the life of the church the influence of Jesus himself maintained itself and grew, even before the Gospels were written. We then examine the reasons for the missionary thrust and success of early Christianity and the ways in which it established its own identity in the New Testament period and thereafter. The continuing need for self-definition was an important factor in the development of the New Testament.

THE PRIMITIVE CHURCH AND JESUS

The execution of Jesus was the pivotal point in the transition from the movement he led among Palestinian Jews to the community we know as the Christian church. Whether or in what sense Jesus founded the church is a difficult and debated question. We do know that the church, properly speaking, only came into being in the aftermath of his ministry and death. Closely related to his death was the conviction that he had risen from the dead and would soon return to reign in power. Belief in Jesus' resurrection and his glorious return and rule were at first closely related, although they soon became separate articles of belief, as they are in the historic Apostles' Creed. Such a relationship is assumed in the question of the disciples to the risen Jesus: "Will you at this time restore the kingdom to Israel?" (Acts 1:6). The Risen Jesus, as Messiah, is expected immediately to establish his rule over Israel. The New Testament's emphasis on Jesus' death, and the consequent belief in his resurrection, exaltation, and return, is, however, unmistakable. Although Jesus himself was a memorable and impressive person, and he obviously said and did things that elicited both a following and an opposition, it is clear from the Gospel accounts that Christianity as a religion, as a gospel (i.e., a message of good news), began with the death and resurrection of Jesus rather than with his historic life. Still, his life was not irrelevant to the beginnings of the new religion.

Undoubtedly, one of the major problems in understanding Jesus and the origins of Christianity lies in their relationship to Judaism. There is a central and important sense in which the mission and message of Jesus himself lies at the very heart of this problem. It is sometimes said that Jesus was a Jew, not a Christian. That is certainly true, but it is also true of Paul, Peter, John, Jesus' brother James, and all the original disciples. We have seen that the self-awareness of Christianity as a religion separate from Judaism emerged only over a period of years, indeed, decades. Paul and the author of the Gospel of John were major figures in this separation, Paul in the fifties and John as late as the nineties of the first century. Jesus' brother James lived in Jerusalem until his death in the early sixties, shortly before the Roman war, and was not only recognized as the head of the Jerusalem church (cf. Acts 15) but was revered among his fellow Jews (cf. Acts 21:20–21). (On the esteem in which James was held, and his martyrdom, see Eusebius, *EH,* II, 23.) The pictures of James in early Christian sources make him out to be a more conservative Jew than Jesus. Of course, the portrayals of Jesus in the New Testament Gospels are all done from a Christian point of view. Yet even there Jesus' basic Jewishness is quite evident. The Gospel of John comes closest to presenting a Christian Jesus, in that Jesus debates Christological issues that had already begun to separate Christians from Jews. Even in John, however, Jesus is not dissociated from Judaism. He is the Messiah, the one prophesied in scripture (John 1:41, 45), and the Samaritan woman immediately recognizes him as a Jew (4:9).

Our portrayal of Jesus (Chapter 6, above) has tended to highlight his distinctive characteristics without claiming for him uniqueness, except in the way that various aspects of his career come together. We have portrayed this uniqueness within the context of Judaism, without claiming for Jesus an absolute, or Christian, uniqueness. Earliest Christianity itself, like Jesus, was grounded in Judaism, and, where it differed, differed on questions of Jewish theology: e.g., the place of Jewish law and Jesus' rule as Messiah of Israel. Admittedly these questions were fundamental, but such issues are literally unthinkable apart from Judaism. The emergence of the Christian church on the basis of the miracles, teaching, death, and resurrection of Jesus is, generally speaking, a plausible outcome in a Jewish context.

The miracles of Jesus doubtless contributed to the Christian belief that he was God's emissary, the Messiah and Son of God. Yet for Paul, the earliest preacher and apostle of the New Testament, the miracles of Jesus seem to play no role, although Paul knows of similar deeds, including his own, within the Christian church (1 Cor. 10:9–10, 28; 2 Cor. 12:12). Miracles and healings were apparently a fact of early Christian life, as of Jesus' ministry, before they entered the Gospel tradition. When they were incorporated into the Gospels, there was still some residual reservation about them, manifest in the questions of Jesus' opponents (Mark 3:22; John 9:16). The fact of Jesus' miracle activity could be seen as an oddity, if not an embarrassment. Such activity

A Byzantine medallion with Christ enameled on gold (eleventh century).
(Courtesy of Metropolitan Museum of Art. Gift of J. Pierpont Morgan, 1917.)

was not unknown in Judaism or the Gentile world (see above, p. 215), but it
was not a part of the practice of most rabbis of Jesus' day—and presumably
also not of Paul until after his conversion. In all likelihood the miraculous
charismatic dimension of Jesus' ministry caused him to stand out within Judaism and carried over into the early church.

Jesus' teaching was thoroughly rooted in Jewish scripture and tradition,
as the Gospels show, but aroused opposition among his fellow Jews in his
own day. In the Gospel of John that opposition becomes acute and centers
on the question of Jesus' own claims, or the claims made for him. Yet the fact
that the same Pharisees who question Jesus on issues of the law in the Synoptics are his principal opponents in John is scarcely coincidental. Modern
interpreters still debate Jesus' own view of the law; he seems to have taken
it seriously but unconventionally. That is, Jesus' concern for obedience, and
his understanding of obedience, differed from that of many of his contemporaries. Doubtless Jesus' own attitude toward the law is somehow related
to Paul's view that Christ was the end of the law (Rom. 10:4). Even Paul, however, was unwilling simply to dismiss the law, but insisted that it was God-
given (Rom. 7:12), although its status and meaning had to be revised in view
of the coming of the Messiah and his death and resurrection.

Jesus' proclamation and promise of the coming kingdom of God (Mark
1:14–15) seems not to have been fulfilled in the way many early Christians
anticipated. Nevertheless, its very nonfulfillment marks it as historically authentic. Yet for Jesus' followers there was an important fulfillment in the appearances of the risen Jesus, the dramatic onset of the Spirit, and the
gathering of the disciples as a new, eschatological people of God, still look-

The south wall of the Jerusalem Temple. Excavations have exposed the enormous stones of the Herodian reconstruction at the base (cf. Mark 13:1–2).   *(Courtesy of D. Moody Smith.)*

ing toward the future for God's redemption. The atmosphere of anticipation and hope that characterized primitive Christianity would be hard to understand apart from Jesus' proclamation of the coming kingdom of God.

Finally, in ways that are obvious in the New Testament, Jesus' own death was fundamental to early Christian views of him. Understandably, the Gospels unanimously ascribe to Jesus advance knowledge of his death and its redemptive purpose (Mark 8:31; 14:22–25; cf. John 10:18). This death and the subsequent resurrection appearances and resurrection faith were the cornerstone of early Christian belief. To what extent, if at all, Jesus anticipated his death can probably never be determined. At the same time, it is as hazardous to assume that Jesus took no thought of his own death and its consequences as to make the opposite assumption. Martyrdom was not an uncommon fate of prophets or messianic claimants. Moreover, his earliest followers had no problem in interpreting Jesus' ministry and teaching in light of his death, just as they seemed to find in his resurrection appearances a fulfillment of his kingdom proclamation.

Christianity as a message of good news (i.e., "gospel") about what God had done and was doing gave birth to a new pattern of religion, separate and distinct from Judaism.[1] Yet the roots of that religion, and even the gospel, lay

1. See E. P. Sanders, *Paul and Palestinian Judaism: A Comparison of Patterns of Religion* (Philadelphia: Fortress, 1977).

in contemporary Judaism, particularly as Judaism was filtered through the ministry and teaching of Jesus himself. As important as Jesus' death and resurrection were, for historical as well as theological reasons, they should not be separated from his earthly career, which in ways we cannot fully know influenced the shape of early Christianity.

THE MISSION AND SUCCESS OF CHRISTIANITY

The parent religion of Christianity was, then, Judaism. Although Judaism made converts in antiquity, as it does still, it was not principally a missionary religion. On the other hand, Christianity was distinguished by its emphasis upon conversion.[2] It is not coincidental that the English word *evangelism* is derived from the Greek word for gospel. As far as we know, an important aspect and activity of early Christianity was its preaching of the gospel in the hope and expectation that people would hear, repent, and believe (see Rom. 10:11–21; Acts 2:14–41).

The fact that Christianity was from the beginning such an outward-oriented or missionary movement merits critical reflection. Any understanding of it as an ethical system or way of life based on the teaching of Jesus misses the point, as important as Jesus and his teaching may have been. It was a gospel (good news), with many of the connotations that the word still evokes. If it had not been, many of our New Testament books would have been vastly different, or would not have existed at all.

What, then, was the gospel? The study of the New Testament implies that for different people it meant somewhat different things. For all, however, its center was Jesus, whether he was viewed as the Son of Man, the Messiah who would soon return to judge the world, punish the enemies of God, and save the elect, or the exalted Lord whose rule would soon be extended from the church throughout all creation. Thus it was appropriate that books describing the ministry of Jesus should have been called Gospels. (In the New Testament, however, the term is used of the document itself only in Mark 1:1—"good news" in NRSV—and even there its application to the book is uncertain.) With the exception of Mark (but see 13:10), the conclusion of each of the Gospels contains a distinct missionary thrust. Matthew ends with the so-called Great Commission (28:16–20). Similarly, Luke has Jesus tell his disciples they are to bear witness to him (Luke 24:45–49; Acts 1:8); in fact, the entire book of Acts is a description of this missionary appeal. John's Gospel

---

2. For a discussion of the phenomenon of conversion in late antiquity and its bearing upon early Christianity, see A. D. Nock, *Conversion: The Old and the New in Religion from Alexander the Great to Augustine of Hippo* (Oxford: Clarendon, 1933). For the New Testament, especially Paul and Acts, there is now the helpful study of B. R. Gaventa, *From Darkness to Light: Aspects of Conversion in the New Testament* (Philadelphia: Fortress, 1986).

is said to have been written to elicit faith in Jesus (20:30 f.) and Jesus tells his disciples that he sends them out just as the Father has sent him (20:21).

Since the earliest Christian missionary preachers expected the return of Jesus soon, they felt under some constraint to gather the believers from among Jews and also, and especially, Gentiles before the end should come (cf. Mark 13:10 and Rom. 11:25–32; 15:17–19). Those who opposed the Gentile mission likely thought that the Gentiles would be brought in only after or with Christ's return (cf. Matt. 10:5 f., 23; 25:31 f., 46). The missionary preachers, therefore, had a strong sense of urgency about their work. Such urgency is mirrored in Paul's letters, and especially in the way he hurried about the eastern half of the Mediterranean world.

As we have seen, the New Testament contains the documents of a movement that is obviously succeeding. Of the religions of that period and place, only Judaism and Christianity survive. In view of the Roman persecution that the church faced until the fourth century, and that Judaism has endured both before and since, it is remarkable that either has survived from antiquity. Even before Christianity became the official and dominant religion of the Roman Empire under the emperor Constantine, it flourished and grew rapidly. Can the reasons for this advance be understood and described? Most Christians have believed that the real reason was the providence or purpose of God, the work of the Holy Spirit, a factor that lies beyond the purview and grasp of a study such as this. But there are other causes that involve the quality of community and the sense of personal worth and destiny that the new faith imparted.

EXCLUSIVENESS

Quite possibly the exclusiveness and seeming intolerance with which Christianity (and Judaism) insisted upon total and individual allegiance was a factor that abetted survival and success. To many people, modern and ancient, this attitude seems unnecessarily harsh. It is entirely clear from later as well as New Testament sources, however, that Christians were anything but tolerant of pagan religion, which they regarded as pernicious, standing in the way of the truth, and immoral.

In an age when people tended to divide or combine religious allegiance and when religions themselves were syncretistic (i.e., tending to borrow from one another), Christianity and Judaism testified to their seriousness and self-confidence by expecting the complete and undivided devotion of their followers. To be sure, there were defections from both, and strong influences from surrounding culture and religions affected each faith, but neither religion had any doubts about its identity and distinctiveness *vis-à-vis* a pagan world.[3] The only point at which this sense of identity became blurred was in

---

3. The word *pagan* is not used in any pejorative sense, but with its proper meaning as a designation of religious phenomena lying outside the Jewish, Christian, or Islamic religious traditions.

their interrelation. As we have seen, the question of whether Christianity and Judaism were mutually incompatible was debated during the first Christian century and for some time thereafter.

HOPE

Along with its sense of exclusiveness early Christianity embodied and offered to people a profound and pervasive hope. Together with the community's hope for Jesus' return and the establishment of God's kingdom, there was a trust and confidence in the individual's destiny with which each Christian seems to have been imbued. The prospect of death is depressing, particularly when death implies isolation, meaninglessness, nothingness, or futility. Such anxiety was at least as real in antiquity as it is in the modern world, where the prospect of death is often disguised or ignored because it can be postponed. For the early Christians the consciousness of having overcome the prospect and present oppressive power of death was strong; this confidence is reflected particularly in Paul's letters and the Gospel of John. The idea that a person survives death in some manner was widely held by pagans as well as Jews. But Christians were distinguished by their belief that Jesus had already conquered death, as living witnesses to his resurrection could testify, and that by faith in him or through unity with him they too could overcome its power. Although the resurrection of Jesus in the New Testament meant more than that the believer would also conquer death, it meant at least that to Christians.

COMMUNITY LIFE

The early Christian hope was not simply a hope for individual survival after death, but was tied to the hope for the kingdom of God, a corporate or collective concept. Moreover, it was a hope held in the context of a community of hope. Paul uses the image of the body, an organic unity, to describe the Christian community (1 Cor. 12 and Rom. 12). All the members are interrelated. This interrelationship or community was an extremely important aspect of the strength of primitive Christianity.

Not coincidentally it found adherents among urban people, who gained from their faith and participation in the church a sense of identity and belonging (cf. 1 Pet. 2:9 f.). Primitive Christianity, particularly in the Gentile world, was an urban religion. Country folk were not excluded, but the missionary preaching seems to have had its most notable success in cities. Doubtless it spoke to the issues or problems of people living in proximity to one another, many of whom experienced a sense of dislocation or meaninglessness in the face of the pressures of urban life. Strikingly, Paul describes the Corinthians as marginal people in society (1 Cor. 1:25–31). Further, Christians gained a sense of belonging from their faith in Christ and participation in the new community (cf. 1 Pet. 2:9 f.). The Christian gospel and community met a fundamental and, in a sense, this-worldly need of people who felt alone and rejected among masses of their fellow human beings. The early Christian movement has sometimes been described as lower class, in the sense of proletarian. Although the poor, as well as slaves, were welcomed, some of the earliest Christians were obviously people of means. In Romans 16:23 Paul mentions a Gaius who owned a house big enough for the whole church to meet in and an Erastus who was an important city official.

The existence of the church, of concrete communities, meant that some organization and regulation of life was necessary. Except for the early Jerusalem church, described in the first chapters of the Book of Acts, we do not hear of Christians' living together in communes, although perhaps they sometimes did. Christians gathered at least weekly for worship, usually on Sunday (1 Cor. 16:2; Col. 3:16) as is still the custom, although Jewish Christians probably continued to observe the Sabbath. Doubtless they also had considerable contact with one another and showed concern for each other during the week.

MORAL CONDUCT

Although rules for communal living were usually not necessary, the church had to be organized for worship, instruction, and the care of its ill or impoverished members (cf. James 5:13–18; 1 Tim. 5:3–5). Moreover, matters of conduct could not be left to chance or private taste. Jesus was a Jew, recognizing the full authority of the law of God, as radically as he may have interpreted it. So were the first apostles, and so was Paul. From the beginning the people associated with Jesus had been attracted to and directed by the moral attitude and demand that suffused his teaching and conduct. Whatever may be said of the relation of Jesus and the church, this attitude clearly carried over into the community that stemmed from him.

This emphasis on morality is nowhere clearer than in Paul, the apostle of Christian freedom. Although Paul stoutly maintained that the Jewish law by itself could not save a person from sin and death, he also insisted that freedom is not license (Gal. 5:13). Freedom cannot contradict the nature of the gospel itself, for the gospel is not the negation of God's law but its fulfillment. Doubtless Paul goes out of his way to portray the sad state of morality in his own day (Rom. 1–3). Although we may doubt that he gives an entirely fair picture, in all probability a part of Christianity's attractiveness lay in the fact that, like Hellenic Judaism, it offered a refreshing moral alternative in a world where sordidness and degradation had grown tiresome to many people.

The intrinsically moral character of primitive Christianity manifests itself in a variety of ways in the New Testament. Unlike Paul's letters, the Gospels spell out the new life in Christ primarily by remembering and repeating the teaching of Jesus, which becomes a source book of Christian ethics, if not a new law. Paul and particularly his later disciples sometimes resort to stereotyped or set forms of moral exhortation, principally the expression of commonsense wisdom. The Pastoral Epistles (1 and 2 Tim. and Titus) are full of this sort of ethical exhortation, which the author is intent on applying to the establishment of suitable standards for the Christian ministry.

WORSHIP

That the early Christian churches worshiped as congregations is evident from the New Testament.[4] Paul discusses the conduct of the Lord's Supper (1 Cor. 11:17 ff.) and other aspects of worship (1 Cor. 14) with his fellow Christians. The prominence of the Lord's Supper in Paul, as well as in the Synoptic Gospels, indicates that it was an important part of worship. Baptism was also practiced by the early Christians (Gal. 3:27; Rom. 6:1 ff.). In the view of these Christians its practice was rooted in Jesus' own example and command, as was the Lord's Supper. It appears that these were the two most widespread and significant cultic acts performed among Christians. (Perhaps significantly, they are not called sacraments in the New Testament, nor are they grouped together as though they belonged in the same category.) From 1 Corinthians 14 and other New Testament passages it appears that worship also included prayer, prophecy or a sermon, speaking in tongues, the reading of scripture, and the singing of hymns. If Christian worship to some extent paralleled synagogue worship, this should not be surprising. In many instances Christian groups developed in or from a synagogue (cf. James 2:1, literally "your synagogue," although NRSV translates "your assembly").

In Christian worship, the principal liturgical acts, the Lord's Supper and baptism, although rooted in Judaism, had obvious appeal to Gentiles, many of whom were familiar with similar initiation rites and sacred meals, perhaps from the mystery religions (see pp. 44–47). Such ritual acts also promised individual immortality by participation in the cult.

ECONOMIC STATUS

There were no church buildings in the first century, and church building on a large scale did not take place until Christianity became an official religion in the fourth century. As we have observed, Christians characteristically met in the homes of more affluent members. The presence of such persons says something about the scope of the church's appeal. The social world of antiquity was in some ways reflected, in other ways contradicted, in the life and ethos of the early Christian communities. Although it was once widely believed that the first Christians were mainly the poor, the outcasts of society (cf. 1 Cor. 1:26–31), recent studies focusing upon the persons identified in Paul's letters have shown that this was not the case. The constituency of early Christianity was from the beginning something of a cross section of ancient society. There were among the Christians in Paul's churches people of means and status, as well as the poor and slaves. Indeed, there were slaveholders as well as slaves,

---

4. The importance of worship for the development of the New Testament writings is underlined by C. F. D. Moule, *The Birth of the New Testament,* 3rd rev. ed. (London: Black, 1981), esp. pp. 19–43.

as the letter to Philemon most clearly attests (cf. Eph. 6:5–9). Churches met in houses owned by members, and Christians of means went to law courts, bringing suit against each other (1 Cor. 6:1–8), apparently confident of their ability to prevail. Some could attend public feasts (1 Cor. 8) and were invited to dinner by well-to-do people who could afford to serve meat (1 Cor. 10:27), not the fare of the poor. The Christian message had a broad appeal.

The injunctions of later New Testament writings reveal the presence of people explicitly called "rich" in the Christian community (1 Tim. 6:17–19; James 1:10; 2:1–7). Obviously, they are to be warned about the dangers of riches, but they have been accepted into the community and are not to be excluded because of their wealth. At the same time, membership in the church was viewed as a gift from God and not something that could be purchased. The basis of the common life was given in what God had already done. People were called upon to respond appropriately, in faith, generosity, and concern for their fellows.

The organization of churches developed necessarily as a way to order and preserve the Christian community over the years within the wider world. Not surprisingly, a regular leadership, or clergy, was established, although the full development of an ordained priesthood or ministry did not occur until after the New Testament books were written. One sees provision for leadership being made in such documents as the Pauline Pastorals (see pp. 388–390). Probably such church leaders were not infrequently of higher social or economic status (1 Tim. 3:1–7; cf. Rom. 16:3–5; 16:23).

THE ROLE OF WOMEN

When the genuine Pauline letters and the Gospels, particularly Mark and John, are considered, the reader is struck with the role played by women among the disciples of Jesus and in the first churches. Paul speaks of a Phoebe, a deacon (or minister) of the church of Cenchreae, near Corinth (Rom. 16:1), who has been of great assistance to himself and others. Prisca, or Priscilla, with her husband Aquila, is mentioned a number of times in Paul's letters and Acts, where she is associated with Paul in his missionary work. According to Romans 16:3–5, a church meets in the couple's house. The fact that Prisca is usually mentioned before Aquila may mean she was a more important figure in the church than he. Paul's strictures against women speaking in church (1 Cor. 14:34–36) seem to stand in contradiction to his assumption that they will pray and prophesy publicly (1 Cor. 11:5, 13). In fact, 14:33b–36 breaks the chain of Paul's thought and the NRSV puts it in parentheses. Although the passage is found in all manuscripts, it may be a later interpolation.

The role of women in the early church doubtless followed from their prominence among Jesus' followers. With the exception of the Beloved Disciple of John's Gospel, only women, particularly Mary Magdalene, witnessed his death, and they are described in Mark (15:41) as those who followed him in Galilee (cf. Luke 8:13). These faithful women became the first witnesses to the resurrection when they discovered Jesus' tomb standing empty. John (20:14–18) describes a poignant scene near the tomb when Mary Magdalene first encounters, and ultimately recognizes, the risen Jesus. Even though the twelve disciples were men, the Gospels make clear that Jesus had other followers, prominent among whom were the women who figure so largely in the passion and resurrection narratives.

The later New Testament writings reflect what has been called the increasingly patriarchal nature of early church organization and ministry. Apparently the author of the Pastorals assumes that the general leadership of the church will be male (1 Tim. 2:11–15), although he envisions a situation in which older women teach younger ones (Titus 2:4–5). The recollection of an earlier day, in which women played a much broader role, lives on; in the Pauline-sounding conclusion of 2 Timothy, the author sends greetings to Prisca as well as Aquila and conveys the greetings of a Claudia, among others (4:19–21). Moreover, Timothy's faith is traced back two generations to his grandmother Lois and his mother Eunice (2 Tim. 1:5). It is significant that women are named as the hearers and conveyors of the faith, for it doubtless reflects their prominence in the early church. (In Acts 16:1 Timothy's mother, not his father, is described as a believer.) In 1 Timothy and Titus, however, only male disciples are mentioned. When one compares the Pastorals with the earlier, authentic Pauline letters, it is clear that the process by which church leadership became increasingly male and male-oriented is well underway. Although the leadership of the church was never predominantly female, women had played a much larger role among Jesus' followers and in the Gentile Christian churches than they were to play in subsequent generations.

What happened to the role of women is perhaps typical of the direction of developments in the early church. The first Christian communities obviously lived within, but in some ways—as is seen in the prominence of women—stood out from, the larger societies of which they were a part. As their numbers grew and decades passed, it became increasingly evident that Jesus would not soon return to inaugurate his kingdom in any tangible or visible way. The church, whether consciously or not, prepared to live as a community or religious institution within a larger society that it eventually came to dominate. Ironically, as the church conquered the Mediterranean world in the second, third, and fourth centuries, it gradually, perhaps necessarily, became more closely conformed to that world (contrast Rom. 12:2) in which male domination was the rule. The fact that its leadership became increasingly male should be seen against that background; it is an example of how living in the world, and especially enjoying success, presents the church with the danger of succumbing to the world's values.

Christianity's Identity

The rapid spread of Christianity across the Roman Empire would hardly have been possible without the synagogue (cf. pp. 50–52). The earliest Christians were Jews who claimed that Jesus was the Messiah; thus the synagogue would have been the obvious place for them to expound their views. By the same token, Christianity's greatest difficulty in securing an identity lay in its relation with Judaism. In some ways this relation has yet to reach a mutually satisfactory solution. As we have seen, the study of the New Testament leads to this problem time and again. Before the end of the New Testament period, however, the problem of Christian identity arose in other ways and in other connections.

THE DISTINCTION OF ORTHODOXY AND HERESY

In the second century the relationship of Christianity to forms of pagan piety, and also particularly to Gnosticism, became an important issue. Undoubtedly the roots of this problem lay in the first century, although the connections are hard to trace with certainty. Already Paul faced a kind of religious enthusiasm among the Corinthians that he regarded as foreign and harmful to Christian faith and community. Other, perhaps related, phenomena appear in Colossians, the Pastorals, and the Johannine Epistles; also in the letters to the seven churches (Rev. 1:1–3:21) specious forms of Christianity are vehemently denounced.

The New Testament contains evidence of the importance of the recurring and ever-pressing task of attempting to say what Christianity is and what it is not. In the controversies of the Galatian and Corinthian letters Paul addressed this problem when he asserted the authority of his gospel, backed by his own status as an apostle. In his own way the author of the Epistle of James addresses the question of Christianity's identity when he argues against an important Pauline saying and insists that both faith and works—not faith alone—are necessary for salvation. Mark may well have been moved to write his Gospel because of what he regarded as inadequate ways of understanding Christianity in the church or churches that he knew. Matthew and Luke apparently felt the need of improving upon Mark, or at least of speaking to different situations. Matthew is less explicit on this point than Luke (1:1–4), but his intention to embody the proper understanding of Christianity within the framework of a Gospel is clear enough. In fact, in Matthew's Gospel Jesus goes out of his way to reiterate that his real disciples are not those who just call upon his name and hear his words, but those who keep them and do them (7:21–27; cf. 25:31–46; 28:16–20). Clearly he has in view those who say "Lord, Lord" but do not obey Jesus. Whereas for Paul the word of the apostle himself seems to have had a special authority, for Matthew the word of Jesus—hearing and doing it—is all important. Something essential is thereby said about what is Christianity and what is not. By the same token, the hall-mark of Christian community is established. The church of Jesus' true disciples is the community in which his words are heard and obeyed.

The author of the Pastoral Epistles, someone endeavoring to follow in Paul's footsteps, appears certain enough of his own orthodoxy that he can denounce those whom he regards as corrupters of the faith and place a ban of excommunication upon them (see Titus 3). Similarly, the Johannine Epistles face a crisis in which wrong doctrine is being taught in the name of Christ by some, and the author, like the author of the Pastorals, wants to put those who persist in their error beyond the pale (cf. 1 John 2:18–19). If those whom Matthew deprecates for saying "Lord, Lord," but not doing God's will as Jesus taught it, can be called heretics only by stretching the usual meaning of the term, it is clear enough that in the Pastorals and the Johannine Epistles the distinction between orthodoxy and heresy is already being formulated.

ORGANS OF AUTHORITY

In the face of widely differing understandings of the nature of Christianity, the pressure to define the new religion and its beliefs grew. The situation was perhaps analogous to contemporary North America, where groups of widely divergent, and even opposing, views style themselves Christian, and there is no overall authority to adjudicate differences. To deal with this problem three organs of authority emerged: clergy, creeds, and scripture.

CLERGY

During the course of the second century and thereafter, standards of orthodoxy in faith developed as the various churches, which had from the beginning a sense of their unity of origin and purpose, began to express that sense through organizational structures with clearly designated leaders who held positions of authority. The resulting distinction between church leaders, ordained and set aside for their tasks, and the rest of the congregations proved to be a momentous one. Already the Pastoral letters show an explicit awareness of this distinction between ordained clergy and laity; moreover, they imply that the authority of the apostle Paul is exercised through Timothy and Titus, who in turn delegate it to ordained bishops and elders. Even today the language of the Pastorals appears in the liturgies and certificates of ordination of some denominations.

Already in the Pastorals the bishop seems to be the highest church official, after the apostles and their personal emissaries. As it developed, the bishop, who was the leader of the church in a given city or locality, quickly gained recognition as the guardian of tradition and the custodian of the true faith. The letters of Ignatius of Antioch, a bishop of the early second century, and Clement of Rome, a bishop in the last decade of the first century, reveal the growing importance of the office. In Ignatius' letters the essence of the church resides, so to speak, in the person of the bishop. In 1 Clement the concept of apostolic succession begins to attain clarity. The bishops are appointed by the apostles to succeed them and, in effect, to continue and extend their authority in the church through time and space.

CREEDS

Christian authors of the second century, such as Justin Martyr and Irenaeus, give indication of the development of creeds as the church sought to unify itself around certain basic beliefs. The well-known Apostles' Creed has its roots in this period, although it was not composed by the apostles of the first generation and is not found in its present form until many centuries later. We know of no creed plainly identified as such from the New Testament period, but the seeds of creeds and creedal formulation are already found there. In 1 Corinthians 15:3–5 Paul repeats the main points of his initial proclamation of the gospel by way of underlining the essential points of Christian belief. Similar summaries of early Christian preaching appear in the Book of Acts (see 2:22–36). The liturgy of the institution of the Lord's Supper, found in Paul (1 Cor. 11:23–26) as well as the Synoptics (Mark 14:22–24), embodies certain basic elements of Christian belief pertaining to Jesus' death. We may have in Matthew 28:19 (". . . baptizing them in the name of the Father and of the Son and of the Holy Spirit") an early baptismal formulation or creed. Another early creedal (or hymnic) formulation may be found in 1 Timothy 3:16, introduced by the rubric, "Great indeed, we confess, is the mystery of our religion."

In 1 John heavy emphasis falls upon the right and true confession (2:21–23; 4:1–3, 15). The author of the brief Letter of Jude writes of "the faith which was once for all delivered to the saints" (vs. 3) as if it were a creed or a body of doctrine. Indeed, the understanding of faith as doctrine is found already in the Pastorals (1 Tim. 3:9; 4:6), clear evidence that true Christianity is to be equated with something like creedal orthodoxy, true confession. Creed-making was related to preaching, baptism, and the Lord's Supper (i.e., liturgy), as well as controversy over the nature of Christian belief. Early Christians did not all say and believe the same things. As it became increasingly apparent that they did not, adequate statements of common belief were hammered out. The original purpose or function of creeds was as much to exclude the erroneous as to state the true faith. Just for this reason they were valuable weapons in the struggle to define orthodoxy and rule out heresy.

SCRIPTURE

Alongside creeds stood scripture, and the creeds were early understood as statements of scriptural teaching. The collection of a canon (Greek, *kanōn*, meaning rule) of books that could be regarded as holy scripture was itself a process that spanned the second and third centuries. But as we have already suggested, its roots lay farther back.

We have seen that the need for a norm or rule of faith and life was already at work in the writing of many of the New Testament books. During the period of the formation of the New Testament, as various books were sifted and collected, this need only became more explicit. Some early writings were eliminated because they were deemed not the work of apostles or authors with apostolic connections; others fell into disuse or were considered less profitable, unsound, or even dangerous. Gradually a consensus developed on the need for a canon and on the books to be included in it.

Two approximate dates, the end of the first century and the end of the second or the beginning of the third, are most important for the development of the New Testament. By the end of the first century, or soon thereafter, most of the books now in the New Testament had been written. A century later the principal books of the New Testament were already widely recognized as authoritative, although others were also used. For example, the Epistle of Barnabas and the Shepherd of Hermas appear in the great fourth-century Bible Codex Sinaiticus.

We learn from a number of different sources dating from about the end of the second century or the early third that many Christians throughout the world were using the same authoritative books. These writings, which now comprise the major portion of the New Testament, are the four Gospels, the Acts of the Apostles, the thirteen Pauline letters, and at least two of the Catholic or general letters, 1 Peter and 1 John. Consensus was lacking on the Letter to the Hebrews and the Revelation to John. The apostolic origin of Hebrews was doubted in Western Christendom for a long time but it was eventually accepted as the work of Paul. The Revelation to John was suspect in the East but was eventually accepted as the work of the apostle. Although such omissions are significant, it is perhaps more important that about twenty of the twenty-seven books that were eventually to compose the New Testament were widely accepted as authoritative by about the end of the second century. The Muratorian Canon, which lists the books accepted by the Roman church; Irenaeus, representing Gaul and the West; Tertullian, the fiery North African; and Clement, the learned bishop of Alexandria, all testify that by and large the same books were in use. A scant half-century earlier Justin Martyr, living in Rome, does not attest a well-defined New Testament canon, although he apparently knew all four Gospels. A list of canonical books identical with the twenty-seven accepted by almost all churches does not appear until the latter half of the fourth century, but after A.D. 200 the differences were smaller than was the amount of basic agreement among most Christians.

The history of the New Testament canon from the end of the first century to the end of the second, or from the writing of the individual books until the first sign of the emergence of an accepted collection at about the end of the second century, is quite obscure. During this time the history of the canon is mainly the history of its two primary parts, the Gospels and the letters of Paul. Concerning the collection of these two sets of documents, however, we actually know little.

Some of the letters of Paul seem to have circulated during his own lifetime and at his direction (see Col. 4:16). How soon after his death an effort was made to collect his letters is uncertain. If, as has been proposed, Ephesians was written as an introduction to a collection of ten of Paul's letters, the collection itself would have to be dated within the first century. This plausible hypothesis cannot be proved, however, for clear evidence is too slim. It is true that about the middle of the second century Marcion, who espoused doctrines later condemned as heretical, put forward a canon consisting of the Gospel of Luke and ten of Paul's letters. Yet this bit of information is not conclusive, for it is uncertain whether Marcion's canon was the first ever to have been proposed or merely an adaptation of an already existing collection—probably the latter. Clearly between the end of the first century and the middle of the second Paul's letters began to circulate and were regarded as fruitful for reading if not as holy scripture. Ignatius, the bishop of Antioch (*ca.* 115), mentions "all the letters of Paul" in his own letter to the Ephesian church (12:2), and all Paul's letters are also spoken of in 2 Peter 3:16 (written *ca.* 125). Moreover, the collection of Ignatius' letters soon after they were written may well have been inspired by the existence of a Pauline collection.[5]

As for the Gospels, we again know little about the circumstances of their collection. Ignatius seems to have known Matthew and perhaps John. Marcion at mid-second century knew at least Luke. At the same time Justin Martyr knew the Synoptic Gospels, and probably the Gospel of John also, but he betrays a curious reticence in referring to the latter. His disciple Tatian somewhat later in the second century combined the four canonical Gospels into one unified account of Jesus' ministry called the *Diatessaron* (the Greek name indicates that it has been composed out of four other documents). In the last quarter of the second century, Irenaeus wrote at some length about the four Gospels and made a point of stressing the appropriateness and the necessity of four, as if he were addressing himself to people who did not think that four were needed. And, in fact, there were those in the early church who questioned the right of the Fourth Gospel to be regarded as apostolic and authoritative. In all probability, Marcion, whose canon contained only one Gospel, reflects the earlier practice. For in the beginning an individual church, or even a geographical area, would have used only one Gospel. A multigospel canon would have come into use only as the Gospels of various churches were combined. In the process of combination some Gospels doubtless fell by the wayside. In the early Christian writers we catch glimpses of some of these other Gospels, which for one reason or another were rejected in the process of sifting and choosing that led to the formation of what we know as the New Testament.[6]

5. That Ignatius' letters already existed as a collection in the early second century is indicated by Polycarp (died *ca.* 155), Epistle to the Philippians 13:2.
6. Portions of these Gospels that survive have been conveniently collected and analyzed in E. Hennecke, *New Testament Apocrypha,* vol. 1.

Suggestions for Further Reading

Important older treatments of the history of early Christianity are H. Lietzmann, *The Beginnings of the Christian Church,* trans. B. L. Woolf, 3rd ed. (London: Lutterworth, 1953; paperback, Meridian), and J. Weiss, *Earliest Christianity,* 2 vols., trans. F. C. Grant et al. (New York: Harper Torchbook, 1959), both of which were written in German in the earlier part of this century. Two more recent such histories are typical in that they represent opposite poles: F. F. Bruce, *New Testament History* (Garden City, NY: Doubleday, 1972); H. Conzelmann, *History of Primitive Christianity* (Nashville: Abingdon, 1973). Bruce may be described as conservative in his positive use of New Testament data in historical reconstructions, while Conzelmann is much more guarded and skeptical. J. Becker (ed.), *Christian Beginnings: Word and Community from Jesus to Post-Apostolic Times,* trans. A. S. Kidder and R. Krauss (Louisville, KY: Westminster/John Knox, 1993), contains more recent essays by several scholars covering the various periods and aspects of New Testament Christianity.

Most recent work is, however, found mainly in monographs. The series edited by W. A. Meeks, Library of Early Christianity (Philadelphia: Westminster, 1986–) covers a variety of important topics. Volumes published (dates in parentheses) in the series include: *Gods and the One God* by Robert M. Grant (1986); *The New Testament in Its Social Environment* by J. E. Stambaugh and D. L. Balch (1986); *Early Biblical Interpretation* by J. L. Kugel and R. A. Greer (1986); *Moral Exhortation, A Greco-Roman Sourcebook* by A. J. Malherbe (1986); *Letter Writing in Greco-Roman Antiquity* by S. K. Stowers (1986); *The Moral World of the First Christians* by Meeks (1986); *From the Maccabees to the Mishnah* by S. J. D. Cohen (1987); and *The New Testament in Its Literary Environment* by D. E. Aune (1987). E. S. Fiorenza, *In Memory of Her: A Feminist Theological Reconstruction of Christian Origins* (New York: Crossroad, 1983), attempts to discern in the already fragmentary and muted records of the New Testament a primeval period in which the participation of women in the leadership of the church was much larger and more significant than it became in immediately succeeding generations. R. E. Brown and J. P. Meier have analyzed and reconstructed the earliest period of two most important churches in *Antioch and Rome: New Testament Cradles of Catholic Christianity* (New York: Paulist, 1983), and Brown has published studies of postapostolic New Testament Christianity in *The Churches the Apostles Left Behind* (New York: Paulist, 1984). A. J. Malherbe, *Social Aspects of Early Christianity,* rev. ed. (Philadelphia: Fortress, 1983), is a good, brief statement of advances in our knowledge about the social world and setting of the New Testament.

On the diversity of early Christianity as it developed in various places, one should consult W. Bauer, *Orthodoxy and Heresy in Earliest Christianity,* trans. and ed. R. A. Kraft and G. Krodel et al., 2nd ed. (Philadelphia: Fortress, 1971). A more conservative approach to the origin and history of Christian doctrine is represented by H. E. W. Turner, *The Pattern of Christian Truth: A Study in Relations between Orthodoxy and Heresy in the Early Church* (London: Mowbray, 1954; reprinted, New York: AMS, 1978), esp. pp. 39–80, where Turner debates with Bauer.

On questions of church–state relations, persecution, and martyrdom, note O. Cullmann, *The State in the New Testament* (London: SCM, 1963); R. M. Grant, *The Sword and the Cross* (New York: Macmillan, 1955); and W. H. C. Frend, *Martyrdom and Persecution in the Early Church* (Oxford: Blackwell, 1965; paperback, Anchor).

K. Wengst, in his fascinating essay *Pax Romana and the Peace of Jesus Christ,* trans. J. Bowden (Philadelphia: Fortress, 1987), portrays the two as finally antithetical.

The development of the Christian canon of scripture is comprehensively treated by H. von Campenhausen, *The Formation of the Christian Bible,* trans. J. A. Baker (London: Black, 1972), as well as by B. M. Metzger, *The Canon of the New Testament: Its Origin, Development, and Significance* (New York: Oxford University Press, 1987), both of which are standard works.

There is also an excellent short study: H. Y. Gamble, *The New Testament Canon: Its Making and Meaning* (Philadelphia: Fortress, 1985). In *Books and Readers in the Early Church: A History of Early Christian Texts* (New Haven: Yale University Press, 1994), Gamble turns his attention to questions of the actual production, circulation, and reading of texts in early Christianity. D. G. Meade, *Pseudonymity and Canon: An Investigation into the Relationship of Authorship and Authority in Jewish and Earliest Christian Tradition* (Tübingen: Mohr, 1986), confronts an issue that has troubled many Christians since the rise of historical criticism.

Primary sources pertinent to the New Testament period are mentioned at the end of Chapter 1, pp. 56–57. Early Christian writings not found in the New Testament or Apostolic Fathers, but in many cases ascribed to apostolic figures, have been collected and discussed in W. Schneemelcher (ed.), *New Testament Apocrypha,* trans. R. McL. Wilson, 2 vols., rev. ed. (Philadelphia: Westminster, 1991–92). See also J. Stevenson (ed.), *A New Eusebius: Documents Illustrative of the History of the Church to* A.D. *337,* rev. by W. H. C. Frend (London: SPCK, 1987).

Non-Christian evidence concerning the relationship of nascent Christianity to the surrounding culture begins to surface in the second century. R. MacMullen, *Christianizing the Roman Empire (A.D. 100–400)* (New Haven: Yale University Press, 1984), and R. L. Wilken, *The Christians as the Romans Saw Them* (New Haven: Yale University Press, 1984), deal with the centuries immediately following the writing of the New Testament books, but are nevertheless valuable for the light they shed on the first century of Christianity.

Epilogue: The Anatomy of the New Testament— Meaning and Structure

The *meaning* of the New Testament as a whole is more than that of each of its parts, but different levels of meaning within the New Testament are not unrelated. The New Testament as a collection of authoritative books, a canon of holy scripture, was born out of theological interests and practical needs of the second and third centuries. But these interests and needs were not simply imposed from without upon the New Testament books. Doubtless the apostle Paul, for example, did not think that he was writing holy scripture when he wrote to the Corinthians or even to the Romans. Yet he was quite consciously asserting his apostolic authority to say what distinctively Christian faith was and what it implied for the life of believers under certain specific circumstances. Similarly, those who preserved the sayings of Jesus may not have thought of themselves as setting up a rival to Moses. Nevertheless, they believed in the sayings of Jesus as faithful guides to the will of God and applied them like holy scripture to the situations that arose in the life of the church. The impulses to establish a canon and thus to provide resources for the guidance and enrichment of the church did not begin long after the writing of the last New Testament book, but in some form actually preceded and motivated the writing of many of those books. In the long run the purposes of a Matthew or a Paul found fulfillment when their books were incorporated into a larger whole.

Of course, the various New Testament books do not all say the same thing. In fact, there are real differences and even disagreements among them. For the most part, however, the New Testament books show an interest in what is apostolic, authoritative, and original. They attach importance to the earthly life and ministry of Jesus, even if, as in the case of Paul, that interest concentrates mainly upon his death. They regard the death and resurrection of Jesus as the central saving event. They look upon Christ and the church as the fulfillment of Old Testament prophecy, and they look forward to the final revelation of God's power and glory. Moreover, they agree in attaching fundamental importance to the moral life. It is by no means a safe assumption, however, that all early Christians or their literature agreed on these points. Increasing evidence that they did not continually comes to the fore. We have discovered that Paul encountered Christians who thought the gospel presumed acceptance of the traditions and scriptures of Israel as binding law, and others who found in it a license to do as they pleased. The Pastoral Epistles, 2 Peter, and Revelation all lash out at wrongheaded and dangerous ideas held by Christians. The Christian Gnostic texts recently discovered in Egypt reveal a divergent form of Christianity with ancient roots. Significantly, some words of Jesus in the Synoptic Gospels, especially Matthew, are applied against misguided Christians.

The New Testament itself is a result of the effort of the early Christian church to define the faith and indicate its consequences for life. Intended to lay down certain directions and set boundaries, it is not simply a random or even a representative specimen of opinion. In going beyond the purposes of the individual books or writings, it embodies and affirms them. When we think of the meaning of the New Testament, therefore, we concern ourselves not only with what the authors intended but with the canon as a whole.

The *structure* of the New Testament is simple. The twenty-seven books are divided into four Gospels, the Book of Acts, twenty-one Epistles, and the Revelation to John. Ancient canonical lists give different orders within the Gospels and Epistles, but the integrity of the groupings is always observed. As we have noticed already, the canonical order makes a certain sense and is therefore helpful to the reader. Although the genuine Pauline letters were written first, the Gospels stand at the head of the canon. From a historical perspective on the beginnings of Christianity this may be misleading, but for the Christian churches that over a period of many years brought the New Testament to its present shape this order makes sense. Jesus is primary, theologically as well as chronologically, for Christian faith.

Within the fourfold Gospel canon, Matthew stands first. Despite tradition and occasional scholarly theories supporting the priority of Matthew, Mark was likely the first Gospel written. Yet Matthew's primacy in the Gospel canon and in the New Testament is understandable, and, from the standpoint of the church that formulated the New Testament, quite proper. Matthew presents Jesus as the fulfillment of the Hebrew scriptures and the founder and teacher of the church. The final Gospel, John, may well have been the last of the four to have been written; its character as a theological reflection in narrative form suits it admirably for the final position in the Gospel canon. For most of the church's history John has provided the theological and Christological perspective for understanding Jesus, the key to the other Gospels, as the Protestant reformer John Calvin put it.

Although Acts was written after at least two of the Gospels, and at least a generation after the genuine Pauline letters, it appropriately bridges the gap between Gospels and Epistles. Although the Pauline letters are to be preferred to Acts as historical sources, those letters provide only bits and fragments of each church's history. The Book of Acts is the first attempt to write a continuous account of the earliest church. As such it provides a rudimentary framework and background for reading and understanding the Epistles. Its emphasis upon the missionary work of Paul, to whom fourteen of the New Testament Epistles have traditionally been ascribed, is quite appropriate.

Among the Epistles Romans stands first in the order that has become standard among Christian churches. Again, it was not written first, but it has valid claim to that position as the most thorough exposition of Paul's theology. After Romans the Pauline letters tend to group themselves in descending order of length or importance. Not coincidentally the Pastorals, written a generation or so after Paul, come near the end, and Hebrews, whose ascription to Paul was seriously doubted in antiquity, is last of all. The Pauline corpus is then followed by the Catholic Epistles, all of which are in fact later than Paul and represent the interests of emerging, institutional Christianity.

As though the claims and interests of the institution should not have the last word, the New Testament concludes with Revelation. In all probability its position in the canon is related to the fact that in antiquity serious doubts were raised about its apostolicity and therefore its right to be included. Apart from such considerations, however, its position at the end is quite appropriate. Revelation points toward the future, toward the end or goal of history, and expresses in terms of apocalyptic imagery the fundamental early Christian conviction that God rules, appearances to the contrary notwithstanding.

That the New Testament as a whole embodies certain *emphases* that to a considerable extent determine its meaning is quite apparent. Some things were underscored, whereas others were omitted. That we have in the New Testament no letters from Paul's converts in Corinth (1 Cor. 7:1), much less his opponents, is not coincidental. Certain viewpoints were ruled out in the course of the doctrinal development that produced our New Testament canon, the ancient creeds of the church, and the carefully articulated sacramental and clerical organization. Nevertheless, theological viewpoints that at one time seemed at odds with one another gained representation within the canon. Thus the Epistle of James, which in fact and perhaps intentionally differs from Paul, stands in the same New Testament with Romans and Galatians. If the opponents of Paul in 2 Corinthians were miracle-working charismatics, their opposition to him did not prevent a similar point of view from finding expression in the miracle traditions of Mark and John, though even there the tradition is modified and redirected. The New Testament rep-

resents no strict doctrinal unity. Be that as it may, there is nevertheless a remarkable continuity of perspective and emphasis in most of the canonical
writings.

Not only was Jesus a Jew, but Christianity began as a Jewish sect. From this
origin it rather quickly branched off into a separate religious group. Yet basic Jewish assumptions, drawn from the Old Testament, continued to inform
the new religion and were in fact fundamental to its development and shape.
For one thing, the Old Testament itself was retained in the Christian canon,
despite the efforts of some early Christians to set it aside or overthrow it. Re-
tention of the Old Testament signified Christianity's continuing commitment
to what it represents and embodies: law, as well as prophecy; history, especially eschatology; and community, the church as the people of Israel.

Although Paul's controversy with Jewish Christians over the observance of
the law resulted in his vindication, early Christianity did not lose touch with
the fundamental moral emphasis of the law. Ritual law was quickly allegorized, forgotten, or replaced by the new liturgical life of the church, but the
basic moral commandments of the Hebrew Bible, epitomized in the Ten
Commandments, continued to be honored. In this respect the emerging orthodoxy was perhaps a bit more conservative than either Jesus or Paul, although neither of them had denied the validity of the law as an expression
of God's will, much less the general thrust or intention of the law.

Even though the character of the scriptures as law was not denied by Christians, they read them also as prophecy of Christ. Thus from the beginning
the revelation in Christ was seen and interpreted as the fulfillment of scripture (1 Cor. 15:3 ff.). The scriptures provided the conceptual categories for
the gospel. This is nowhere clearer than in the title Christ itself, which is simply the Greek translation of Messiah, the Hebrew word meaning "[the Lord's]
anointed." Thus the New Testament was meant to be the affirmation and fulfillment of the Old.

Precisely the Jewish heritage and scriptural foundation of earliest Christianity explain the tenacity with which it clung to and emphasized the importance of history, especially eschatology. This was by no means a
happenstance. As the new faith broke with Judaism and spread across the
Hellenistic world, becoming mostly Gentile in constituency, many saw no
real point in such insistence upon God's revelation in a historically real past
and future. In some areas many, if not most, Christians were Gnostic. The
Gnostic Christians characteristically rejected the Old Testament (except insofar as they might interpret it in an idiosyncratic or esoteric way), had little
interest in Jesus as a historical and human figure, and looked above for individual salvation rather than to any meaningful future. In response to and
rejection of such a theological stance, other early Christians harked back to
writings and traditions that emphasized fulfillment of (Old Testament) scripture in Jesus, his historical and human reality, and his return and the coming of God's kingdom. The Gnostic idea that this world was not the creation
of the true God and Father of Jesus Christ was also rejected, despite the trou-

bles and adversity that Christians encountered in this world. Thus the most Gnostic sounding of the major New Testament books, the Gospel of John, insists that the God of Jesus Christ is the Creator (1:3), and that Jesus himself was truly human, "flesh" (1:14; cf. 1 John 1:1–3). Even the miracles of the Gospels indicate the seriousness with which Jesus and his followers in the first and second centuries took this world and its conditions.

Christianity was never at any point sealed off from the secular and religious world of its time. Its language, cultic practices, and ethics were inevitably influenced by the surrounding culture. Because from earliest times this cultural environment was increasingly Hellenistic and Gentile, it is not surprising that early Christianity began to absorb its coloration. This fact is clearly discernible in the Christian creedal statements of the fourth and fifth centuries, which presuppose and are set forth in terms drawn from Greek philosophy rather than the Hebrew scriptures. In the New Testament period the transition from Jewish to Gentile environment was greatly facilitated by Judaism's own accommodation to the surrounding world. Most Jews no longer lived in Palestine or spoke Hebrew as the language of ordinary intercourse. In making the transition the gospel did not always break new ground, but often followed well-established paths.

Although the Jewish basis was not forgotten, other factors came to play a large role. In all probability the intense concentration upon the person of Jesus Christ in Christianity is related to the role he played in worship. For Paul, his churches, and even his Christian opponents (cf. 2 Cor. 13:3a), Jesus Christ is a living reality, not just a figure of the past. Christians call upon his name (1 Cor. 1:2). In effect, they worship him, not to the exclusion of the God of Israel, but alongside him as God incarnate. In this way the Christian faith appeared to be similar to Greek religions in which gods manifested themselves in human form. The seeds of an irrevocable split with the parent religion were thus planted, as in a Gentile environment Christianity became liturgically, as well as theologically, increasingly Christ-centered.

Thus before the end of the first century Christianity was a distinct and different religion, taking varied forms as it spread across the Mediterranean world, appealing to large numbers of people in different walks of life. Of course, the New Testament did not produce Christianity; rather Christianity produced the New Testament. Yet the anatomy of the New Testament reflects the origin and growth of Christianity: first the Gospels, the church's testimony to its founder, Jesus; then the Book of Acts, a story of the church's beginnings and universal mission; next, letters that testify to the vitality, as well as the problems, of the Christian community; finally, the Book of Revelation, which looks to heaven and to the future to reveal the coming of a new community, the city of God.

The *meaning* of the New Testament is more than its *structure*, but its meaning cannot be separated from the structure, which expresses the shape of Christian revelation and belief. Christianity began with Jesus' ministry to Israel, but with his death and the reports of resurrection appearances, faith quickly spread beyond the ethnic, geographic, and religious bounds of Judaism. Thus the new religion eventually established itself as a distinct confession and people with ancient, traditional roots and hopes represented by its holy scripture, Old Testament and New. Yet the new faith looked finally not to the past for its vindication but to the future advent of God's salvation. Thus the New Testament ends fittingly with an apocalypse, the Revelation to John. The fulfillment of hope that Revelation portrays in such graphic imagery does not, of course, misrepresent the Gospels and Epistles, for an evangelist (Mark 13 parr.) or an apostle (1 Cor. 15) could speak with equal assurance of the coming of God's deliverance.

Glossary

Abba: the intimate, familiar Aramaic word for father. In the normal piety of first-century Judaism this form of address was too intimate to be used of God. But Jesus (Mark 14:36) and the early Christians (Rom. 8:15; Gal. 4:6) used it in this way.

A.D.: abbreviation of the Latin *Anno Domini*, which means "in the year of our Lord." In the Western world the birth of Christ is the point of reference for dating events. Events occurring before the birth of Jesus are indicated by the abbreviation B.C., "before Christ." Alternatively, one may speak of C.E. (Common Era) or B.C.E. (Before the Common Era).

Agrapha: literally, unwritten words or sayings. The term refers to words and sayings of Jesus not contained in the canonical Gospels.

Allegory: a story whose details or actions illustrate or tell about something quite different. Each element of an allegory possesses its own distinct meaning, which is determined by something outside the story, for example, the Christian faith in the case of Bunyan's *Pilgrim's Progress.*

Amen: the transliteration of a Greek word that in turn transliterates a Hebrew word. In common usage *amen* is either a solemn confirmation of what has been said or a response of assent to words of another.

Antichrist: an apocalyptic figure, the archenemy of Christ, who will appear shortly before the parousia to wage war against the friends of Christ. (*See* Parousia.)

Antinomianism: the belief that the Christian who has been freed by Christ has no ethical or moral obligations at all.

Antitheses: the six contrasts with ancient teaching that Jesus proclaims in the Sermon on the Mount (Matt. 5:21–48) in the antithetical form, "You have heard. . . . But I say to you. . . ."

Apocalypse: an uncovering or a revelation (e.g., the Apocalypse or Revelation to John). The term "apocalyptic" is applied to a type of literature that is pessimistic about humanity's possibilities and hence discloses God's

465

plan for the last days. Although related to prophecy and eschatology, apocalyptic thought stresses more precisely and forcefully the future intervention of God in the end time. (*See* Eschatology; Revelation.)

Apocrypha: the fourteen books of the Septuagint Bible not found in the Hebrew Bible; usually it is a part of the Catholic Bible but not the Protestant Bible. More generally, the adjectival form *apocryphal* means "hidden or spurious." (*See* Pseudepigrapha.)

Apocryphal New Testament: noncanonical books such as the Gospel of Peter that claim apostolic authorship, but were known in antiquity to be inauthentic.

Apostle: a term meaning "one who is sent," specifically applied to the twelve disciples who were close to Jesus (see Mark 3:14 ff.). Paul also appropriates this designation for himself because of the risen Christ's appearance to him (see 1 Cor. 15:1 ff.).

Apostles' Creed: an ancient Christian creed expressing belief in God the Father, Son, and Spirit, the church, and the resurrection of the dead. Although the name implies that it was composed by the apostles, it does not appear in its present form until centuries later. Nevertheless, its roots go back to an ancient Roman baptismal creed that was already taking shape in the second century. The creed emphasizes the death and resurrection of Jesus, as did much early Christian preaching (1 Cor. 15:3–5).

Apostolic Fathers: a collection of second-century noncanonical writings, such as the letters of Ignatius, that do not claim apostolic authorship. They are apostolic in the sense that they were generally accepted as representing the apostolic faith.

Aramaic: the language of Palestine during the time of Jesus and the early church. A Semitic tongue, it is closely related to Hebrew.

Archaeology: the scientific study of ancient cultures on the basis of their remains, such as fossil relics, artifacts, monuments, pottery, and buildings.

Aristeas, Epistle of: a pre-Christian, Jewish pseudepigraphical writing that presents a legendary account of the translation of the Hebrew Bible into Greek in Alexandria, Egypt.

Ascension: traditionally the visible departure of Jesus into heaven forty days after his resurrection (see Acts 1:9).

Authentic: in biblical criticism the term is applied to writings that are believed to have been written by the person to whom they are traditionally attributed. For example, Romans is without doubt an *authentic* letter of Paul.

Baptism: the act or sacrament of immersion into water by which a person was received into the early Christian church. The Greek term means "to dip" or "immerse."

B.C.:   the abbreviation of "before Christ." (*See* A.D.)

Beatitudes: the nine blessings that stand at the beginning of Jesus' Sermon on the Mount (see Matt. 5:3–12).

Canon: a term originally applied to a reed used for measuring. It was later used of those books or writings that became standard or authoritative for the early Christians. By the close of the fourth century the Christian canon was largely fixed. (*See* Apocrypha; Pseudepigrapha.)

Catholic: universal, affecting humankind as a whole; an adjective used by the early church to refer to whatever was universally shared among the various churches.

Catholic Epistles: James; 1 and 2 Peter; 1, 2, and 3 John; and Jude. These seven letters are supposedly "general" in destination and in character and hence Catholic.

Charisma: "gift of grace." The term came to be used in the early church for the various gifts of the Spirit, such as wisdom, knowledge, faith, healing, and speaking in tongues (see 1 Cor. 12).

Christ: *See* Messiah.

Christology: that aspect of Christian thought concerned specifically with the revelation of God in Jesus the Christ.

Church: the community of believers in Jesus Christ. The term is used of individual congregations and of the entire fellowship of Christians.

Cosmos: the world or universe. A Greek term frequently used in ancient philosophical discussion. In the New Testament it often takes on a negative sense as the world standing in opposition to God (John 1:10; 1 John 2:15–17).

Council of Jamnia: the group of rabbinical scholars who settled in the coastal town of Jamnia shortly before the fall of Jerusalem in A.D. 70 and helped to standardize the Jewish religion. They are usually credited with having fixed the Hebrew canon of the Old Testament, now followed by Protestants as well as Jews.

Covenant: a solemn agreement that binds two parties together. The Old Testament (Covenant) depicts the agreement by which God and the people of Israel were bound together, and the New Testament (Covenant) tells the story of the new agreement effected by God with the new Israel through Jesus the Christ. Ordinarily in biblical usage a covenant is sealed in blood.

Crucifixion: a Roman form of execution in which the victim was nailed or bound to a wooden cross and left to die.

Dead Sea Scrolls: ancient Jewish documents from the period of Christian origins, found near the Dead Sea. (*See* Essenes; Qumran.)

Decalogue or Ten Commandments: the name given to the ten words Moses received, according to tradition, from God on Mt. Sinai (see Exod. 20:1–17 and Deut. 5:6–21).

Diaspora or dispersion: the Jewish community scattered (dispersed) outside the holy land of Palestine. This dispersion originated in the Babylonian exile of 587 B.C.

Didache or "Teaching of the Twelve Apostles": an anonymous second-century Christian manual for church life.

Docetism (derived from the Greek word *dokein* meaning "to seem"): an early Christian heresy according to which Jesus Christ only seemed to suffer and die. A divine being, it was thought, could not suffer.

Epistle: a letter of a formal or didactic nature; the term is traditionally applied to the New Testament letters.

Eschatology: discourse about the last things or the end of the age (Greek, *eschatos,* meaning "last"). Traditionally the term is used of Christian thought concerning all the events and actions associated with both the end of history and the end of human life. (*See* Apocalypse; Parousia.)

Essenes: an ascetic, Jewish religious group existing at the time of the New Testament. They stressed radical obedience to the Jewish law. (*See* Qumran.)

Ethics: a broad term applied to such related matters as moral codes and practices, theories of value, and the imperatives of Christian faith as they pertain to relations of one person to another.

Eucharist: derived from the Greek word meaning "thankfulness" and beginning in the second century used of the sacrament of the Lord's Supper, in which bread and wine are consecrated and distributed to the faithful Christians. (*See* Lord's Supper; Sacrament.)

Exegesis: the critical interpretation of a text. Literally the term means "to lead out" the meaning from the text.

Exile: specifically the removal of defeated Israelites by the Babylonians in 587 B.C.

Exodus: a going out; used specifically of Israel's departure from Egypt under the leadership of Moses about the thirteenth century B.C.

Expiation: "making right," by means of some act or rite, the offense done by one party to another, especially expiation for sin before God. (*See* Propitiation; Sacrifice.)

Form Criticism: the classification of the "forms" in which the tradition, especially the Gospel tradition, circulated before being written down and the attempt to determine the "setting in life" of the church that they reflect. (*See* Pericope; Redaction Criticism.)

Genre: the literary type or form of a document. For example, in modern critical discussion the question of whether the Gospels fit the genre of ancient biography or constitute a distinct and different genre has been widely debated.

Gentile: a non-Jew. The original Greek term tranlated "Gentiles" means "nations."

Gnosticism: a religious movement or attitude widespread about the time of the emergence of the Christian faith. Believers possessed a secret knowledge *(gnōsis)* and sought to escape the ephemeral earthly world for the eternal heavenly world.

Gospel: originally the message of good news that God has revealed himself as gracious in the event of Jesus Christ. (The NRSV translators have generally used "good news" to translate the Greek *euangelion,* formerly translated "gospel".) The term later came to designate also the literary form in which the good news of Jesus' life, death, and resurrection is narrated; for example, the Gospel According to Matthew.

Haggadah: a Hebrew term designating rabbinic traditions, usually in narrative form (stories or legends) that illustrate the moral teaching of the Torah. (*See* Midrash.)

Halakah: a Hebrew term (from the verb meaning "to walk") designating rabbinic tradition regulating conduct. (*See* Midrash; Mishnah.)

Hasmonean: the actual family name for the Maccabees, leaders of the Jewish revolt against Syria. (*See* Maccabees.)

Hellenization: the process or result of the spread of Greek language and culture in the Mediterranean world during and after Alexander the Great (died 323 B.C.).

Hermeneutics: the science dealing with the interpretation and the determination of the meaning of texts. While exegesis is the act of explaining a text against its historical background and in view of its literary character, hermeneutics deals with the principles of interpretation. (*See* Exegesis.)

Historical Criticism: the science, perspective, or method that approaches the Bible with historical questions. Typically, its goal is to understand the historical setting of the writings in the history of Israel or the early church. (*See* Exegesis; Literary Criticism.)

Holy: that which has to do with, or is set apart for, God or the divine power and majesty.

Immanence: the nearness or involvement of God in the world. (*See* Transcendence.)

Incarnation: literally "becoming flesh"; the embodiment of God in Jesus of Nazareth.

Justification: the act or process by which God brings people into proper or right relationship with himself. In Paul the justification or righteousness of God is to be received by faith, not works. (*See* Righteousness.)

Kerygma (literally "proclamation"): the early Christian preaching about Jesus as the Christ intended to elicit the decision of faith.

Kingdom of God or "Rule of God": God's lordship over humankind and the world. The kingdom is the central theme of Jesus' message in the Synoptic Gospels.

Koinē ("common" in Greek):   the everyday Greek speech used through-out the Hellenistic world during the period of early Christianity. The New Testament books are written in *koinē* Greek.

Law: in the New Testament generally the revelation of God through Moses to the people of Israel embodied in the cultic, ritual, and moral com-mandments of the Old Testament. (*See* Gospel; Torah.)

Literary Criticism: the science, perspective, or method that seeks to de-termine the literary character or development of the books of the Bible. It has traditionally been practiced in conjunction with historical criticism, al-though recently it has become more independent as modes of literary crit-icism and theory developed outside biblical scholarship have been applied to the Bible. (*See* Exegesis; Historical Criticism.)

Lord's Supper: the church's continuing reenactment of the last supper of Jesus with his disciples. (*See* Eucharist.)

Maccabees: the name given the priestly family who successfully led a re-volt against Hellenistic Syrian rule beginning in 167 B.C. It is derived from Judas Maccabeus, the Hasmonean brother who first led the revolt. They ruled over Palestine from 142 B.C. to 63 B.C. (*See* Hasmonean.)

Manuscripts: handwritten documents, especially the ancient New Testa-ment documents from which our present text is determined. The earliest complete New Testament manuscripts come from the fourth century, al-though there are sizable fragments of earlier date.

Messiah: from the Hebrew term meaning "anointed one." It was used of the Davidic king, whose restoration was expected in Jesus' day. Its Greek equivalent is *Christos* (Christ), the basic designation of Jesus in the New Testament. He was believed to be the expected Messiah of Israel.

Midrash: the form, activity, or product of biblical interpretation, particu-larly as carried out in rabbinic Judaism. *Midrashim* (pl.) may be legal (ha-lakic) or illustrative and even narrative (haggadic) in character.

Miracle: an extraordinary event, contrary to normal expectations, a man-ifestation of the activity of God.

Mishnah: the authoritative Jewish legal or halakic traditions, ascribed ul-timately to Moses, that developed in rabbinic and Pharisaic Judaism (cf. Mark 10:5–13) and were codified in the early third century. The term is usually applied to the written form. The Mishnah and the learned com-mentary upon it *(Gemara)* constitute the Talmud. (*See* Talmud.)

Myth: the result of efforts to communicate faith in transcendent reality by means of story and symbol. This technical use of the term should be dis-tinguished from the popular meaning of a fantastic or untrue story.

Oral Tradition: any teaching or similar material transmitted from person to person or generation to generation by word of mouth rather than by use of writing; also the process of such transmission.

Parable: a brief story that makes its point by the unusual development or imagery of the narrative. The various details do not function as allegory but are significant for the story itself. Although the parable was already known to the Jewish religious tradition, Jesus made extensive use of it. (*See* Allegory.)

Paraclete: helper, comforter, or mediator. The term is used in the Fourth Gospel of the Holy Spirit as the Christian community's helper after the death of Jesus (see John 14:16; 15:26; 16:7).

Paraenesis: a Greek term meaning moral exhortation. It is frequently applied to those parts of New Testament letters devoted to moral instruction.

Parousia (literally "presence" or "coming"):   the early Christian belief in the appearance or second coming of Christ, a glorious advent in power and judgment at the end of the age. (*See* Eschatology; Son of Man.)

Passion: suffering, particularly the suffering of Jesus during the last week of his life in Jerusalem and especially the suffering leading to his death.

Passover: the annual Jewish celebration of the deliverance from slavery in Egypt under the leadership of Moses. Jesus was crucified at the time of the Passover. (*See* Exodus.)

Pastoral Epistles: 1 and 2 Timothy and Titus. These letters give advice to the church leader or pastor concerning matters of church government and discipline.

Patriarch: the father of a people, especially the three great ancestors of the people of Israel (Abraham, Isaac, and Jacob). The period of Israel's history before the Exodus from Egypt is frequently called the patriarchal period.

Pentecost: the Jewish Feast of Weeks, beginning on the fiftieth day after Passover. According to the Book of Acts it was the occasion of the descent of the Holy Spirit upon the disciples of Jesus, and thus it is looked upon as the beginning of the church.

Pericope: a "cutting around" or section. The term is used of the individual, complete units of tradition about Jesus that circulated separately in the early church and that were ultimately joined together to form the Gospels. (*See* Form Criticism; Redaction Criticism.)

Pharisees: a prominent Jewish religious group at the time of Jesus, who practiced strict observance of both the written and oral law of Judaism. The name probably comes from a Semitic term meaning "separated." (*See* Sadducees.)

Preexistence: the term used to designate the New Testament belief that Jesus of Nazareth in some way existed with God before his earthly advent (see John 1:1–3; 17:24).

Priest: a holy person authorized to perform ritual and cultic acts whereby human beings and God are enabled to commune with another. (*See* Holy; Sacrifice.)

Procurator: an official of the Roman Empire, responsible to the emperor, exercising administrative authority over a province or district.

Prophet: someone who speaks or acts for God. In general, the prophet not only predicted God's action but also pleaded with the people to respond to God's will. Prophets existed in the early church as well as in ancient Israel.

Propitiation: a placating or pacifying of the deity; a sacrifice that induces God to be favorable or beneficent to the sacrificer. (*See* Expiation.)

Pseudepigrapha: literally "false writings," particularly a group of late Jewish writings claiming Old Testament figures as their authors. They reflect Jewish religious thought in the intertestamental period. (*See* Apocrypha.)

Q Source: the hypothetical source, consisting primarily of sayings of Jesus, used by both Matthew and Luke in the writing of their respective Gospels.

Qumran: the site on the northwest shore of the Dead Sea where a Jewish sect lived in strict obedience to the law of its covenant community until approximately A.D. 70. The Dead Sea Scrolls (part of the library of the community) were discovered near this site. (*See* Essenes.)

Rabbi: "master," a Jewish religious leader or teacher (cf. John 1:38) especially trained and qualified to expound and apply the law of Moses.

Redaction Criticism: the separating of tradition from redaction (editorial work) especially in the Gospels. One who edits, revises, or shapes the literary or oral sources at hand is called a redactor. (*See* Form Criticism; Pericope.)

Redemption: literally "to buy" or "take back," particularly the act or process of God's taking back sinful or rebellious humanity by means of the event of Jesus Christ.

Resurrection, a rising from the dead: a central hope in the New Testament based upon the early Christians' belief that Jesus was raised from the dead by God. In general the New Testament view of resurrection of the body or person should be distinguished from the widely held notion of the immortality of the soul.

Revelation (translated from the Greek word *apokalypsis*):   an uncovering, revealing, or laying bare. It refers to the uncovering of the transcendent God in human events, particularly the event of Christ in the Christian tradition. (*See* Apocalypse.)

Righteousness: primarily the quality and action of God; hence human righteousness proceeds from God's initiative in Christ and is based upon a relation with God as revealed in Christ. Righteousness and justification translate the same Greek noun *dikaiosynē* in the New Testament. (*See* Justification.)

Sacrament: a sacred rite, "an outward and visible sign of an inward and spiritual grace," namely, the presence of the transcendent God. The term *sacrament* per se does not occur in the New Testament, but it is commonly used to refer to the acts of baptism and the Lord's Supper, which are reported there. (*See* Baptism; Eucharist.)

Sacrifice: the act of offering something valuable to the deity. By the act of sacrifice, communion with the divine is initiated, reestablished, or continued. (*See* Priest.)

Sadducees: a religious group of the intertestamental period who represented the priestly aristocracy of Jewish life. In distinction from the Pharisees, they held only to the written Mosaic law and did not believe in resurrection.

Salvation: the state of complete liberation from sin, brokenness, and estrangement between humanity and God. In general, the New Testament locates salvation in the future, although its inauguration is already effected in Christ.

Sanctification: the process of being made holy. The term refers to the life of the Christian under the guidance of the Spirit as the effects of Christ's work, especially the love of God and of others, become more and more manifest.

Scribes: a title applied to learned men in postexilic Judaism who studied and copied the law and exercised judgment in matters pertaining to the law (see Ezra 7:6). (*See* Pharisees.)

Second Coming: *See* Parousia.

Semitism: in the New Testament, a stylistic or linguistic feature characteristic of Hebrew or Aramaic, possibly indicating that the writer was influenced by one of these Semitic languages or used a source that was written in one of them.

Septuagint (usually designated LXX, "seventy"):   the Greek translation of the Hebrew Old Testament for diaspora Jews. According to the legend of the Epistle of Aristeas, the translation was accomplished by seventy-two Jewish scholars who worked for seventy-two days; hence the title. The translation originated in the third century before the rise of Christianity. (*See* Aristeas, Epistle of.)

Sin: generally any act that violates the law or will of God. In the New Testament, however, it denotes particularly the broken or estranged relation between the human race and God. (*See* Righteousness.)

Sitz im Leben ("setting in life"):   the term is employed widely by form critics to refer to the community setting and, implicitly, the function of traditions.

Son of God: in Hebraic thought, someone especially selected or anointed by God for a task, such as the king of Israel, a prophet, or the people of Israel. In Hellenistic religious thought the term refers frequently to a male offspring of the gods. In the New Testament Jesus functions as the Son of God primarily in the Hebraic sense.

Son of Man: the title by which Jesus refers to himself in the Gospel narratives. Possibly in Jewish thought the term referred to an apocalyptic figure who was to come at the end of the ages to serve as judge between the righteous and the wicked (cf. Daniel 7:13 RSV; Mark 8:38; John 5:27), although its meaning may be more enigmatic. In the Gospels the use of the title Son of Man is confined almost entirely to Jesus. (*See* Apocalypse; Parousia.)

Soteriology: discourse about salvation. Soteriology refers to the New Testament understanding of the righteousness of God, sin, the work of Christ, the response of faith, and the work of the Spirit in sanctification.

Soul: a spiritual entity, distinct from the body, within each person. This concept of the soul, even the notion of the soul's immortality, plays little role in Hebraic or New Testament thought. Its prominence in Christian thought derives from later Greek influence.

Source Criticism: the work of identifying the written sources that were used in the composition of any given document, such as one of the Gospels.

Spirit: the dynamic power and activity of God directed toward the world, especially active in the history of Israel, the life of Jesus, and the early church; in the Christian tradition usually referred to as the Holy Spirit.

Synoptic Problem: the problem of understanding the relationship between the Synoptic Gospels (Matthew, Mark, and Luke), taking account of their great similarities as well as their distinct differences. The generally accepted solution is that both Matthew and Luke used Mark, the Q source consisting largely of Jesus' sayings, and distinct material to which each had access separately.

Talmud (meaning instruction or study): the authoritative body of Jewish tradition consisting of Mishnah and Gemara (commentary upon it) that developed in the several centuries immediately preceding and following the beginning of the Christian era. It exists in Palestinian (early fifth century) and Babylonian (late fifth century) forms. (*See* Mishnah.)

Targum: an ancient translation of the Hebrew scriptures (Old Testament) into the related Aramaic language that was generally spoken in first-century Palestine.

Theology: discourse on God; the study of or reflection upon the nature of God and the nature of God's relationship to humanity.

Torah: the Hebrew term meaning law or teaching, especially law as divine revelation. (*See* Law.)

Transcendence: in theology, God's distance from the world; alternatively, God's holiness or "otherness" as distinct from the secular or profane. (*See* Immanence.)

Trinity: the Christian doctrine that God exists in three persons: the Father, Jesus Christ as the Son, and the Holy Spirit. The developed doctrine is not found in the New Testament, although Father, Son, and Spirit are spoken of frequently.

Virgin Birth: the miraculous birth of Jesus to Mary, his mother, without the participation of a human father in the conception.

Witness: in the New Testament includes both observation and testimony, especially to the life, death, and resurrection of Jesus. In one sense, martyrdom is an especially appropriate witness to Jesus. The English term *martyr* is based on the Greek word for "a witness."

Word: a technical, literary designation of a complete saying, especially a saying of Jesus. In the Johannine literature Jesus himself is called the Word (John 1:1–18).

Word of God: frequently a designation for the Bible. In the New Testament, however, it is used in close connection with the event of Jesus Christ, especially the preaching about that event. (*See* Kerygma.)

Works, or "works of the law":   in Pauline theology the means of earning righteousness before God instead of acknowledging sin and relying on his grace. (*See* Justification.)

Zealots: a term applied to Jewish revolutionaries who sought to overthrow Roman rule of Palestine by means of violent resistance. Although the term may have come into use only during the Roman War (A.D. 66–70), it is often applied to earlier revolutionary figures.

General Bibliography

I. Tools for New Testament Study

Because relatively few students will likely know Hellenistic Greek, we shall include under I and II such aids as may be employed by the student who uses only English.

Concordances, which cite the occurrences of every significant word in the Bible, are often very helpful when one wishes to determine what a particular word means in the New Testament or in a specific book or author. C. Morrison, *An Analytical Concordance to the Revised Standard Version of the New Testament* (Philadelphia: Westminster, 1979), is particularly valuable in that it indicates the original Greek word upon which the RSV translation is based. There are now concordances for the NRSV, for example, J. R. Kohlenberger III, *The NRSV Concordance Unabridged: Including the Apocryphal/Deuterocanonical Books* (Grand Rapids, MI: Zondervan, 1991).

There are several one-volume Bible dictionaries of quality, for example, *Harper's Bible Dictionary,* edited by P. J. Achtemeier (San Francisco: Harper & Row, 1985) and prepared under the auspices of the Society of Biblical Literature. D. N. Freedman (ed.), *The Anchor Bible Dictionary,* 6 vols. (New York: Doubleday, 1992), is the largest and newest general dictionary. For the meaning of theological terms, see the compact work of X. Leon-Dufour (ed.), *Dictionary of Biblical Theology,* trans. J. P. Cahill (New York: Desclee, 1967). Even those without Hebrew and Greek may be helped by G. Kittel et al. (eds.), *Theological Dictionary of the New Testament,* trans. G. W. Bromiley (Grand Rapids, MI: Eerdmans, 10 vols., 1964–76), all volumes of which are now available in English translation, with the exception of the comprehensive bibliography (vol. 10, part 2 in German). The one-volume abridgment of this work, G. M. Bromiley, *Theological Dictionary of the New Testament: Abridged in One Volume* (Grand Rapids, MI: Eerdmans, 1985), translates all Greek (and Hebrew) words and provides a comprehensive English index so that the reader who knows no Greek can find any entry. H. Balz and G. Schneider (eds.), *Exegetical Dictionary of the New Testament,* 3 vols. (Grand Rapids, MI: Eerdmans, 1990–93), now also provides English transliterations of the Greek, as well as an English index.

There are several good Bible and related atlases: H. G. May (ed.), *The Oxford Bible Atlas,* 3rd ed. rev. J. Day (New York: Oxford University Press, 1984); Y. Aharoni and M. Avi-Yonah, *The Macmillan Bible Atlas,* rev. ed. (New York: Macmillan, 1977); and J. B. Pritchard, *The Harper Concise Atlas of the Bible* (New York: Harper Collins, 1991). Note also F. van der Meer and C. Mohrman, *Atlas of the Early Christian World,* ed. and trans. M. F. Hedlund and H. H. Rowley (New York: Nelson, 1958), which provides detailed maps and information of New Testament and later times. Perhaps the best general guide is J. Murphy-O'Connor, *The Holy Land: An Archaelogical Guide from Earliest Times to 1700*, Rev. ed. (New York: Oxford University Press, 1992).

General treatments of archaeological matters include G. E. Wright, *Biblical Archaeology,* rev. ed. (Philadelphia: Westminster, 1962), and J. Finegan, *The Archaeology of the New Testament: The Life of Jesus and the Beginning of the Early Church* (Princeton, NJ: Princeton University Press, 1969). Finegan has also published a companion volume, *The Archaeology of the New Testament, The Mediterranean World of the Early Christian Apostles* (Boulder, CO: Westview Press, 1981), in which he is remarkably conservative in his historical assessments. More critically skeptical is G. F. Snyder, *Ante Pacem: Archaeological Evidence of Church Life Before Constantine* (Macon, GA: Mercer University Press, 1985), a reliable guide to what can be known with some certainty.

II. Commentaries

Among the tools for New Testament study, none is more important than a reliable commentary on the text. Several good commentary series should be noted. *Black's New Testament Commentaries* (Peabody, MA: Hendrickson) is a serious but nontechnical series, as is *The New Century Bible* (Grand Rapids, MI: Eerdmans). New editions of the Black series are now appearing. A new commentary series, *Interpretation: A Bible Commentary for Teaching and Preaching* (Atlanta: John Knox), will be of interest and use to many readers who value the Bible as scripture and yet wish to understand it critically. Even more recently, *Sacra Pagina* (Minneapolis: Liturgical Press) has begun to appear. It too is solid but not technical. A technical series based on the Greek text, *Hermeneia—A Critical and Historical Commentary on the Bible* (Minneapolis: Fortress), is generally excellent, and because all Greek and other foreign language citations are translated, it can be used by the student who lacks command of Greek. The classic *International Critical Commentary* (Edinburgh: T. & T. Clark) is based uncompromisingly upon the Greek text of the New Testament. A standard for English-language, technical commentaries, it is now beginning to appear in a new series. *The Anchor Bible* (Garden City, NY: Doubleday) is a very ambitious commentary series on both Testaments. The reader or buyer should be aware that inevitably commentaries in a series are not all of the same quality. Among one-volume Bible commentaries, *The New Jerome Biblical Commentary,* edited by R. E. Brown, J. A. Fitzmyer, and R. E. Murphy (Englewood Cliffs, NJ: Prentice Hall, 1990), and *Harper's Bible Commentary,* edited by J. L. Mays, W. A. Meeks, and others (San Francisco: Harper & Row, 1988), stand out. There are editions of modern versions of the Bible that provide brief but useful introductory articles and notes on the text; for example: *The New Jerusalem Bible* (New York: Doubleday, 1990); *The New Oxford Annotated Bible* [NRSV], edited by B. M. Metzger and R. E. Murphy (New York: Oxford University Press, 1991); and *The Oxford Study Bible: Revised English Bible with the Apocrypha,* edited by M. J. Suggs, K. D. Sakenfeld, J. R. Mueller (New York: Oxford, 1992).

III. Text and Canon

A thorough treatment of textual history and criticism is provided by B. M. Metzger, *The Text of the New Testament: Its Transmission, Corruption, and Restoration,* 3rd ed. (New York: Oxford University Press, 1992). A standard, text-critical handbook is K. and B. Aland, *The Text of the New Testament,* trans. E. F. Rhodes, rev. ed. (Grand Rapids, MI: Eerdmans, 1989). For the influence of church doctrine on the text of the New Testament, see B. D. Ehrman, *The Orthodox Corruption of Scripture: The Effect of Early Christological Controversies on the Text of the New Testament* (New York: Oxford University Press, 1993). On the development of the canon of the New Testament, see the Suggestions for Further Reading at the end of Chapter 12.

IV. New Testament Theology and Ethics

R. Bultmann, *Theology of the New Testament,* trans. K. Grobel, 2 vols. (New York: Scribners, 1951–55), has not been displaced as the single most important work, although it virtually ignores the Synoptics and deals principally with John and Paul. There are several other significant general treatments; for example: W. G. Kümmel, *The Theology of the New Testament According to Its Major Witnesses: Jesus—Paul—John,* trans. J. E. Steely (Nashville: Abingdon, 1973); L. Goppelt, *Theology of the New Testament,* 2 vols., trans. J. E. Alsup (Grand Rapids, MI: Eerdmans, 1981, 1982); and J. D. G. Dunn, *Unity and Diversity in the New Testament* (Philadelphia: Fortress, 1977), as well as the same author's *Christology in the Making: A New Testament Inquiry into the Origins of the Doctrine of the Incarnation,* rev. ed. (London: SCM, 1989). The historically important work of C. H. Dodd, *The Apostolic Preaching and Its Developments* (New York: Harper & Row, 1936), is still a valuable introduction to the theological character of the New Testament, especially the Gospels. On Christology specifically, see M. de Jonge, *Christology in Context: The Earliest Christian Response to Jesus* (Philadelphia: Westminster, 1988), as well as Dunn's *Christology in the Making* (see above). D. Juel, *Messianic Exegesis: Christological Interpretation of the Old Testament in Early Christianity* (Philadelphia: Fortress, 1988), argues that the demonstration of Jesus' messiahship lies at the heart of early Christian use of scripture. On that subject see also D. A. Carson and H. G. M. Williamson (eds.), *It Is Written: Scripture Citing Scripture* (Cambridge: Cambridge University Press, 1988).

There are several worthwhile contributions to the discussion of the nature of the field: R. Morgan, *The Nature of New Testament Theology* (London: SCM, 1973), which contains translations of seminal but divergent essays of W. Wrede and A. Schlatter, and H. Boers, *What Is New Testament Theology? The Rise of Criticism and*

the Problem of a Theology of the New Testament (Philadelphia: Fortress, 1979).
H. Räisänan, *Beyond New Testament Theology: A Story and a Programme*
(Philadelphia: Trinity Press International, 1990), advocates a return to the his-
tory-of-religions perspective and goals of Wrede. On the other hand, N. T. Wright,
The New Testament and the People of God (Minneapolis: Fortress, 1992), the
first volume in a projected five-volume work entitled *Christian Origins and the
Question of God,* stands in the tradition of Schlatter. Although she does not in-
tend to write theology, P. Fredriksen, *From Jesus to Christ: The Origins of the
New Testament Images of Jesus* (New Haven: Yale University Press, 1988), engages some of the same issues in a stimulating way.
Studies dealing with ethics in the New Testament include V. P. Furnish, *The Love Commandment in the New Testament* (Nashville: Abingdon, 1972) and J. L. Houlden,
Ethics and the New Testament (New York: Oxford University Press, 1977). More
comprehensive is W. Schrage, *The Ethics of the New Testament,* trans. D. E.
Green (Philadelphia: Fortress, 1988).

V. History of Criticism and Interpretation

The most extensive work on the modern period is W. G. Kümmel, *The New Testament: The History of the Investigation of Its Problems,* trans. S. M. Gilmour and
H. C. Kee (Nashville: Abingdon, 1972). S. Neill and N. T. Wright, *The Interpretation of the New Testament: 1861 1986* (New York: Oxford University Press,
1987), is a revision of the late Bishop Stephen Neill's book, and provides fuller
coverage of British scholarship than does Kümmel. A balanced briefer treatment
is J. K. Riches, *A Century of New Testament Study* (Valley Forge, PA: Trinity Press
International, 1993). William Baird is producing a *History of New Testament Research,* the first volume of which is subtitled *From Deism to Tübingen* (Minneapolis: Fortress, 1992). The history of biblical interpretation in the church is
traced by R. M. Grant with D. Tracy, *A Short History of the Interpretation of the
Bible,* rev. ed. (Philadelphia: Fortress, 1984). The more extensive *Cambridge History of the Bible,* 3 vols., S. L. Greenslade (ed.) (New York: Cambridge University
Press, 1963–70), covers the ground more intensively with articles by appropriate
specialists. The modern history of the hermeneutical issues involved in biblical
interpretation has been subjected to intensive scrutiny by A. C. Thiselton, *The
Two Horizons: New Testament Hermeneutics and Philosophical Description
with Special Reference to Heidegger, Bultmann, Gadamer, and Wittgenstein*
(Grand Rapids, MI: Eerdmans, 1980). Thiselton has extended his study in *New
Horizons in Hermeneutics* (Grand Rapids, MI: Zondervan, 1992). A narrower but
quite useful focus on exegetical perspectives and methods is found in C. M. Tuckett, *Reading the New Testament: Methods of Interpretation* (Philadelphia:
Fortress, 1987).

VI. Other Resources

A number of helpful handbooks contain bibliographic assistance: D. M. Scholer, *A Basic Bibliographic Guide for New Testament Exegesis,* 3rd ed. (Grand Rapids, MI:

Eerdmans, 1995); J. A. Fitzmyer, *An Introductory Bibliography for the Study of Scripture,* rev. ed. (Rome: Biblical Institute Press, 1981); R. P. Martin, *New Testament Books for Pastor and Teacher* (Philadelphia: Westminster, 1984); and F. W. Danker, *Multipurpose Tools for Bible Study,* rev. ed. (Minneapolis: Fortress, 1993). There is now also the ATLA Religion Database on CD-ROM. The journal *New Testament Abstracts,* published at Weston College, Weston, Massachusetts, catalogs and summarizes articles and important books on the New Testament as they appear. Excellent bibliographies accompany the articles on various subfields (e.g., Pauline studies) in E. J. Epp and G. W. MacRae (eds.), *The New Testament and its Modern Interpreters* (Atlanta: Scholars, 1989). J. C. Hurd, Jr., has published *A Bibliography of New Testament Bibliographies* (New York: Seabury, 1966), which will be of value for the student doing a thorough piece of research.

An excellent guide to understanding and applying the historical–critical method is H. Conzelmann and A. Lindemann, *Interpreting the New Testament: An Introduction to the Principles and Methods of New Testament Exegesis,* trans. S. S. Schatzmann (Peabody, MA: Hendrickson, 1988). E. V. McKnight, *Post-Modern Use of the Bible: The Emergence of Reader-Oriented Criticism* (Nashville: Abingdon, 1988), sets that method in the context of late twentieth-century discussions of the nature of reading and understanding that have originated outside biblical studies but are parallel and closely related to certain hermeneutical and theological trends. Conzelmann and Lindemann assume the independence and priority of the historical–critical method over hermeneutical considerations and questions, but it is precisely this priority that, as McKnight shows, has become questionable in recent literary–critical and hermeneutical discussion.

Essays and articles about the New Testament are published in dozens of journals, not all of equal quality or value. Only a few can be mentioned here. The standard scholarly journals in North America are *Journal of Biblical Literature,* the official journal of the Society of Biblical Literature, and *Catholic Biblical Quarterly* of the Catholic Biblical Association (which now includes non-Catholic scholars among its membership). Both journals publish critical reviews of books as well as articles. *Interpretation: A Journal of Bible and Theology* also publishes articles and reviews of general interest. *Biblical Archaeologist,* which contains articles by scholars aimed at the general reader, is published by the American Schools of Oriental Research. *New Testament Studies,* the journal of the international Studiorum Novi Testamenti Societas (Society for New Testament Studies) is published in Cambridge, England. In Germany the standard journal is *Zeitschrift für die Neutestamentliche Wissenschaft,* which often publishes articles in English. These journals are available in college, university, and theological seminary libraries, as well as in large public libraries.

Name and Subject Index

Biblical Index

OLD TESTAMENT

NEW TESTAMENT

THE MEDITERRANEAN WORLD
AT THE TIME OF THE
NEW TESTAMENT

NAMES OF ROMAN PROVINCES THUS: LYCIA

0   100   200   300

SCALE OF MILES

Modern place names are shown in italics, thus: *Cairo*